BOLLINGEN SERIES XCIV

The **Freud/Jung** Letters

The Correspondence between

SIGMUND FREUD *and* C. G. JUNG

Edited by WILLIAM McGUIRE

Translated by RALPH MANHEIM *and* R. F. C. HULL

BOLLINGEN SERIES XCIV ✣ PRINCETON UNIVERSITY PRESS

THIS IS THE NINETY-FOURTH
IN A SERIES OF BOOKS
SPONSORED BY BOLLINGEN FOUNDATION

Translated from the
unpublished letters in German

LCC 76-166373
ISBN 0-691-09890-5
Library of Congress Cataloguing in
Publication data will be found on the last
printed page of this book

PRINTED IN THE
UNITED STATES OF AMERICA
BY PRINCETON UNIVERSITY PRESS,
PRINCETON, NEW JERSEY

TABLE OF CONTENTS

LIST OF ILLUSTRATIONS

Facsimiles

ABBREVIATIONS

Principal Bibliographical References

Abraham, *Sel. Papers* = *Selected Papers of Karl Abraham M.D.* Translated by Douglas Bryan and Alix Strachey. London, 1927.

Alexander and Selesnick = Franz Alexander and Seldon T. Selesnick, "Freud-Bleuler Correspondence," *Archives of General Psychiatry* (New York), XII:1 (Jan. 1965), 1ff.

Bulletin = *Correspondenzblatt der internationalen psychoanalytischen Vereinigung.* Edited by C. G. Jung and F. Riklin. Zürich, 1910–11 (6 nos.); thereafter published as a section in occasional issues of the *Zentralblatt* and *Zeitschrift.*

CW = The Collected Works of C. G. Jung. Edited by Gerhard Adler, Michael Fordham, and Herbert Read; William McGuire, Executive Editor; translated by R. F. C. Hull. New York and Princeton (Bollingen Series XX) and London, 1953– . 19 vols. For list, see appendix 7.

Ellenberger, Henri F. *The Discovery of the Unconscious; The History and Evolution of Dynamic Psychiatry.* New York, 1970.

Freud, Martin. *Sigmund Freud: Man and Father.* London and New York, 1958.

Freud/Abraham Letters = *A Psycho-Analytic Dialogue; The Letters of Sigmund Freud and Karl Abraham 1907–1926.* Edited by Hilda C. Abraham and Ernst L. Freud; translated by Bernard Marsh and Hilda C. Abraham. London and New York, 1965.

Freud, *Letters* = *Letters of Sigmund Freud.* Selected and edited by Ernst L. Freud; translated by Tania and James Stern. London and New York, 1960.

Freud, *The Origins of Psychoanalysis: Letters to Fliess* = *The Origins of Psycho-Analysis: Letters to Wilhelm Fliess, Drafts and Notes: 1897–1902,* by Sigmund Freud, edited by Marie Bonaparte, Anna Freud, Ernst Kris; authorized translation by Eric Mosbacher and James Strachey. New York and London, 1954.

Freud/Pfister Letters = *Psychoanalysis and Faith; The Letters of Sigmund Freud and Oskar Pfister.* Edited by Heinrich Meng and Ernst L. Freud; translated by Eric Mosbacher. London and New York, 1963.

Grinstein = *The Index of Psychoanalytic Writings,* compiled and edited by Alexander Grinstein. Vols. I-IX. New York, 1952–59.

Hale, Nathan G., Jr., *Freud and the Americans: The Beginnings of Psychoanalysis in the United States, 1876–1917.* New York, 1971.

Jahrbuch = *Jahrbuch für psychoanalytische und psychopathologische Forschungen.* See appendix 2.

Jones, Ernest. *Free Associations; Memories of a Psycho-Analyst.* London and New York, 1959.

Jones = Ernest Jones, *Sigmund Freud: Life and Work.* London and New York, 1953, 1955, 1957. 3 vols. (The editions are differently paginated, therefore double page references are given, first to the London edn.)

Jung, "Abstracts" = "Referate über psychologische Arbeiten schweizerischer Autoren (bis Ende 1909)," *Jahrbuch,* II:1 (1910); cf. "Abstracts of the Psychological Works of Swiss Authors (to the end of 1909)," CW 18 (containing only abstracts written by Jung).

Jung, *Letters* = *C. G. Jung: Letters,* selected and edited by Gerhard Adler in collaboration with Aniela Jaffé. 2 vols. Princeton (Bollingen Series XCV) and London, 1973, 1974.

Jung, *Memories* = *Memories, Dreams, Reflections by C. G. Jung,* recorded and edited by Aniela Jaffé; translated by Richard and Clara Winston. New York and London, 1963. (The editions are differently paginated, therefore double page references are given, first to the New York edn.)

Minutes = *Minutes of the Vienna Psychoanalytic Society.* Edited by Herman Nunberg and Ernst Federn; translated by M. Nunberg. New York, 1962–74. (I: 1906–8; II: 1908–10; III: 1910–15, consulted in ms.)

Papers = *Schriften zur angewandten Seelenkunde,* edited by Sigmund Freud. No. 1 (1907)– . Vienna. ("Papers on Applied Psychology.") For list, see appendix 5.

Putnam and Psychoanalysis = *James Jackson Putnam and Psychoanalysis; Letters between Putnam and Sigmund Freud, Ernest Jones, William James, Sandor Ferenczi, and Morton Prince, 1877–1917,* edited by Nathan G. Hale, Jr. Cambridge, Mass., 1971.

Ross, Dorothy, G. *Stanley Hall: The Psychologist as Prophet*. Chicago, 1972.

Schreber, *Memoirs* = Daniel Paul Schreber, *Memoirs of My Nervous Illness*, translated, edited, with introduction, notes, and discussion, by Ida Macalpine and Richard A. Hunter. London, 1955.

SE = The Standard Edition of the Complete Psychological Works of Sigmund Freud. Translated under the general editorship of James Strachey, in collaboration with Anna Freud, assisted by Alix Strachey and Alan Tyson. London and New York, 1953– . 24 vols. For list, see appendix 7.

Short Papers = *Sammlung kleiner Schriften zur Neurosenlehre* [of Sigmund Freud]. Vol. I (1906)– . Vienna. ("Collected Short Papers on the Theory of the Neuroses.")

Zeitschrift = *Internationale Zeitschrift für ärztliche Psychoanalyse*. Vienna, 1913– .

Zentralblatt = *Zentralblatt für Psychoanalyse; Medizinische Monatsschrift für Seelenkunde*. Wiesbaden, 1911–13.

Textual Abbreviations

cs. = conscious(ness)
D. pr., Dem. pr. = dementia praecox
Ψ = psyche, psycho
ΨA = psychoanalysis, psychoanaly-
ΨN = psychoneurosis
ucs. = unconscious

SIGMUND FREUD

Freiberg (Příbor), Moravia   *London*
6 May 1856   23 September 1939

CARL GUSTAV JUNG

Kesswil, Thurgau   *Küsnacht*
26 July 1875   6 June 1961

INTRODUCTION

These letters are the direct evidence of the intensely fruitful and finally tragic encounter of Freud and Jung. The quality of tragedy, however, resides only in the encounter, the drama of the letters themselves, moving forward in almost a classical way toward the foreshadowed catastrophe of conflict and dissension. It can scarcely be said that the career, the life, of either man was tragically altered, but rather that Freud and Jung each derived creative values from the inevitable break.

Unlike their courteous and appreciative references to one another's published work while they were collaborators, or anything that either one wrote about their relationship during the bitter aftermath, the letters bear the most acute witness to the complex interplay of these two unique personalities, so different yet so strongly attracted to one another. The dialogue inevitably tempts analytical and psychoanalytical interpretation, philosophical rumination over its beginnings and its effects and its "meaning," and the weighing up of its aggressions, projections, magnanimities, shafts of wisdom, seminal particles, and whatever else could be put into the balance. A consideration of the correspondence along such lines, however, has been ruled out by the sons of the two principals, who, in concluding an agreement to publish the letters, prudently stipulated that they were to be treated "like historical documents . . . in order to guarantee impartiality."

In the years just before the beginning of this century, Freud was in a state of what he more than once called "splendid isolation."[1] His career had been wracked by frustrations; he had not become a research scientist as he had once hoped to, and he had not become a University professor.[2] His collaboration with Josef Breuer had re-

[1] For the details of this period of Freud's career, see Jones, I, ch. XIV–XVI, and II, ch. I–II; Freud, *The Origins of Psychoanalysis*; Ellenberger, *The Discovery of the Unconscious*, ch. 7; and K. R. Eissler, *Sigmund Freud und die Wiener Universität* (Bern, 1966). (For explanation of abbreviated titles, see pp. ix–xi.)
[2] C. A. Schorske, "Politics and Patricide in Freud's *Interpretation of Dreams*," *American Historical Review*, LXXVIII:2 (Apr. 1973), 330f.

sulted in an important work, the *Studies on Hysteria* (1895; SE II), but afterward the two became estranged. Freud had first used the term "psychoanalysis" in an 1896 publication, and during the latter part of the decade he was elaborating the psychoanalytic technique. Entirely alone, he had embarked in 1897 on the self-analysis of his own unconscious, which led into the writing of *The Interpretation of Dreams* (published in late 1899 but dated 1900; SE IV–V). According to Ernest Jones's account, the book was inadequately reviewed and sold poorly. Nevertheless, it was a turning-point in Freud's life. "He regarded it both as his most significant scientific work, the foundation stone of his whole achievement, and as the work that brought him into the clear personally, giving him the strength to face a troubled life anew."[3]

The year 1902 was marked by three further events of major consequence in Freud's career. Since 1887 he had been carrying on a correspondence and a close friendship with Wilhelm Fliess, an otolaryngologist of Berlin; the letters to Fliess, which have almost miraculously survived,[4] are a principal source of knowledge about the genesis of psychoanalysis. But in 1902 the correspondence and the friendship came to an end. Furthermore, very much through his own exertions, he was appointed to the equivalent of an associate professorship at Vienna University. Finally, in the autumn of that year, Freud inaugurated the "Psychological Wednesday Evenings," at Wilhelm Stekel's suggestion, by inviting four of his acquaintances who were interested in psychoanalysis to meet for discussions in Freud's waiting-room.[5]

Freud's reputation and his contacts were spreading slowly beyond the confines of Vienna. He next wrote *The Psychopathology of Everyday Life* (1901; SE VI) and "Fragment of an Analysis of a Case of Hysteria" (not published until 1905; SE VII); and then, also simultaneously, *Jokes and Their Relation to the Unconscious* (1905; SE VIII) and *Three Essays on the Theory of Sexuality* (1905; SE VII). It was the latter work, Jones has said, "that brought the maximum of odium on Freud's name,"[6] because of Freud's findings concerning the sexual instinct in childhood.

[3] Ibid., 330.
[4] Published in *The Origins of Psychoanalysis*.
[5] Jones, II, p. 8/8. The original four—Wilhelm Stekel, Alfred Adler, Rudolf Reitler, Max Kahane—gradually increased to more than twenty and in April 1908 became the Vienna Psychoanalytic Society. The *Minutes* (see p. x) were recorded, beginning in 1906, by Otto Rank.
[6] Jones, II, p. 321/286.

The first significant focus of interest in psychoanalysis outside Freud's immediate circle was at the Burghölzli Mental Hospital in Zürich (Pl. I). An austere block of buildings on heights overlooking the lake of Zürich, the Burghölzli had been established in 1860 as the cantonal asylum for the insane, and it served also as the psychiatric clinic of Zürich University. Under Auguste Forel, who became director in 1879, it acquired an international reputation for advanced treatment and research, which was carried forward by Eugen Bleuler, Forel's successor in 1898.

On 10 December 1900, Jung arrived at the Burghölzli to take up his first professional post, as an assistant physician. He had completed his medical studies at the University of Basel, his home town, and had received his diploma barely a fortnight before, on 27 November.[7] Despite the hospital's avant-garde reputation, Jung later described his work at the Burghölzli as "a submission to the vow to believe only in what was probable, average, commonplace, barren of meaning, to renounce everything strange and significant, and reduce anything extraordinary to the banal. Henceforth there were only . . . oppressively narrow horizons, and the unending desert of routine."[8] Against this background, Jung's first experience of Freud must have been exciting in double measure. "As early as 1900," he wrote, "I had read Freud's *The Interpretation of Dreams*. I had laid the book aside, at the time, because I did not yet grasp it. . . . In 1903 I once more took [it] up . . . and discovered how it all linked up with my own ideas."[9] In an interview in 1957, Jung said that in 1900 Bleuler had asked him to give a report on *The Interpretation of Dreams* at a staff "report evening."[10]

Before Jung "laid the book aside" in 1900 (or 1901), he had digested enough of Freud's "dream investigations" to cite them for their relevance to his own experimental findings in his doctoral dis-

[7] For Jung's years at the Burghölzli, see *Memories, Dreams, Reflections*, pp. 111–13/113–15, and ch. IV; and Ellenberger, ch. 9. The dating of events in Jung's academic career has been confirmed by Mr. Franz Jung.

[8] *Memories*, p. 111/113.

[9] Ibid., pp. 146f./144f.

[10] R. I. Evans, *Conversations with Carl Jung* (Princeton: Van Nostrand, 1964); also, as a corrected transcript, in CW 18. In Jung's posthumous papers a typescript was discovered, dated 25 Jan. 1901, which constitutes a report not on *Die Traumdeutung* but on *Über den Traum* (= "On Dreams," SE V), a summary of the former which Freud published in *Grenzfragen des Nerven- und Seelenlebens*, ed. L. Löwenfeld and H. Kurella (Wiesbaden, 1901). For Jung's report, see *Spring*, 1973, pp. 171–79, and CW 18.

sertation, published in 1902.[11] Most other publications of Jung's in the years 1902–1905[12] contain citations of Freud's work (though not of his sexual theories).

Jung spent the winter semester of 1902–1903 at the Salpêtrière, in Paris, attending Janet's lectures on theoretical psychopathology. On 14 February 1903, soon after returning to Zürich, he was married to Emma Rauschenbach, and they moved into a flat in the central building of the Burghölzli, upstairs from the flat in which the Bleuler family lived.[13] The resident staff of the hospital in Jung's day also included Karl Abraham, Franz Riklin, Max Eitingon, and Hermann Nunberg, and there were visitors from abroad—notably, A. A. Brill—who came for periods of observation and study.

Freud's first direct contact with the Burghölzli had apparently been a correspondence that he and Bleuler had opened in September 1904, which continued more or less sporadically until at least 1925.[14] In his autobiography Jung says that he himself "first took up the cudgels for Freud at a congress in Munich where a lecturer discussed obsessional neuroses but studiously forbore to mention the name of Freud."[15] In any event, Freud's "Fragment of an Analysis of a Case of Hysteria" had appeared in 1905, and Jung lost no time in drawing on it in his paper "Psychoanalysis and Association Experiments" (CW 2), prepared that year and published the next. Jung

[11] *On the Psychology and Pathology of So-called Occult Phenomena* (CW 1). The M.D. degree was awarded to Jung by Zürich University on 17 July 1902.
[12] "A Case of Hysterical Stupor in a Prisoner in Detention" (1902), "On Simulated Insanity" (1903), "On Hysterical Misreading" (1904), "Cryptomnesia" (1905)—all in CW 1; the first four studies in word association (1904–5) and "The Psychological Diagnosis of Evidence" (1905)—all in CW 2.
[13] Here Freud visited the Jungs for four days in Sept. 1908 and was shown at least one of Jung's classic cases (*Memories*, pp. 125ff./126). In June 1909, when the Jung family removed to their new house at Küsnacht, Jung resigned from the Burghölzli staff.
[14] Alexander and Selesnick, pp. 6, 8. Dr. Manfred Bleuler believes that there were contacts between his father and Freud even earlier, in the 1890's (personal communication). In fact, in 1896, E. Bleuler reviewed *Studien über Hysterie*; cf. Jones, I, p. 278/253. / The letters from Freud to Bleuler in M. Bleuler's possession are at present barred from publication.
[15] *Memories*, p. 148/147. The congress has not been identified, and there may be a confusion here with the Congress of South-West German Neurologists and Psychiatrists at Baden-Baden, 27 May 1906, at which Aschaffenburg attacked Freud's "Fragment of an Analysis of a Case of Hysteria" and Jung took the floor to reply vigorously. Both Aschaffenburg's paper and Jung's reply (CW 4) were published in a Munich periodical—*Münchener medizinische Wochenschrift*, LIII:37 and 47 (Sept. and Nov. 1906). (Cf. 2 J, 6 J.)

The Burghölzli Hospital, Zürich, ca. 1900. Jung's flat was on the next to top floor, to the right of the main doorway; Bleuler's flat was below it

presented a case of obsessional neurosis that he had treated in June 1905 by subjecting the patient first to the association test and then to psychoanalysis—interviews of one and a half to two hours every other day for three weeks. Jung discharged the patient rather inconclusively, but in November she came back and presented herself as cured. In summarizing the case, Jung stated that the association test might be useful "for facilitating and shortening Freud's psychoanalysis."

That paper closed, or climaxed, the volume of *Diagnostic Association Studies*[16] that Jung sent to Freud in April 1906, thus setting in motion their correspondence. The book had the force of a direct message, for in the studies written by both Jung and Bleuler there were citations of Freud's work that amply demonstrated the acceptance psychoanalysis had found at the Burghölzli. The first actual letter was Freud's of 11 April 1906, a warm acknowledgment of the book, which, in his eagerness to read it, Freud had already bought. A reply from Jung was not required by courtesy, and there matters rested for nearly six months. In June Freud gave a lecture that contains his first published comments on Jung, the association experiments, and the theory of complexes.[17] During the summer, Jung completed his monograph on *The Psychology of Dementia Praecox*, for which he had been amassing material since 1903. The book is interlarded with citations and extended discussions of Freud's work, and in the foreword, which Jung dated July 1906, he made the following declarations:

> Even a superficial glance at my work will show how much I am indebted to the brilliant discoveries of Freud. As Freud has not yet received the recognition and appreciation he deserves, but is still opposed even in the most authoritative circles, I hope I may be allowed to define my position towards him. My attention was drawn to Freud by the first book of his I happened to read, *The Interpretation of Dreams*, after which I also studied his other writings. I can assure you that in the beginning I naturally entertained all the objections that are customarily made against Freud in the

---

[16] The studies had already appeared singly in the *Journal für Psychologie und Neurologie* over the previous two years, but there is no evidence that Freud had seen them there.

[17] "Psycho-Analysis and the Establishment of the Facts in Legal Proceedings," SE IX, pp. 104, 106, where Freud refers to Jung's paper on the same subject, "The Psychological Diagnosis of Evidence" (1905). Freud's paper also contained his first reference to Alfred Adler (p. 105).

literature. But, I told myself, Freud could be refuted only by one who has made repeated use of the psychoanalytic method and who really investigates as Freud does; that is, by one who has made a long and patient study of everyday life, hysteria, and dreams from Freud's point of view. He who does not or cannot do this should not pronounce judgment on Freud, else he acts like those notorious men of science who disdained to look through Galileo's telescope. Fairness to Freud, however, does not imply, as many fear, unqualified submission to a dogma; one can very well maintain an independent judgment. If I, for instance, acknowledge the complex mechanisms of dreams and hysteria, this does not mean that I attribute to the infantile sexual trauma the exclusive importance that Freud apparently does. Still less does it mean that I place sexuality so predominantly in the foreground, or that I grant it the psychological universality which Freud, it seems, postulates in view of the admittedly enormous role which sexuality plays in the psyche. As for Freud's therapy, it is at best but one of several possible methods, and perhaps does not always offer in practice what one expects from it in theory. Nevertheless, all these things are the merest trifles compared with the psychological principles whose discovery is Freud's greatest merit; and to them the critics pay far too little attention. He who wishes to be fair to Freud should take to heart the words of Erasmus: "Unumquemque move lapidem, omnia experire, nihil intentatum relinque."[18]

Over the summer, Freud finished assembling the first volume of his *Short Papers on the Theory of the Neuroses*, and he sent a copy to Jung in October 1906. With Jung's letter of reply, the correspondence was under way in earnest—"a most friendly and even intimate exchange of both personal thoughts as well as scientific reflections . . . for nearly seven years."[19] When Jung's *Dementia Praecox* was published in December, he sent one of the first copies to Freud, who had expressed his eagerness to see it. Unfortunately, Freud's comments upon receiving that crucial book were made in a letter that is one of the few missing in this collection.[20]

In his subsequent writings Freud unreservedly acknowledged the services rendered to the spread of psychoanalysis by the Zürich

[18] CW 3, pp. 3f. / "Move every stone, try everything, leave nothing unattempted."—Erasmus, *Adagia*, I.IV.xxx. The tr. here is by Margaret Mann Phillips, to whom acknowledgment is gratefully made. See also 142 J n. 1.
[19] Jones, II, p. 35/30f.
[20] For a list of the missing items, see appendix 1, p. 562.

School, "particularly by Bleuler and Jung." Recounting the history of the psychoanalytic movement in 1914, immediately after the break with Jung, Freud stated, "According to the evidence of a colleague[21] who witnessed developments at the Burghölzli, it appears that psycho-analysis awakened interest there very early. In Jung's work on occult phenomena, published in 1902, there was already an allusion to my book on dream-interpretation. From 1903 or 1904, says my informant, psycho-analysis was in the forefront of interest."[22] After describing his period of isolation and the gradual development in Vienna from 1902 onwards, Freud told how "in 1907 the situation changed all at once and contrary to all expectations. . . . A communication from Bleuler had informed me before this that my works had been studied and made use of in the Burghölzli. In January 1907, the first member of the Zürich clinic came to Vienna—Dr. Eitingon. Other visits followed, which led to an animated exchange of ideas. Finally, on the invitation of C. G. Jung . . . a first meeting took place at Salzburg in the spring of 1908 . . ."[23]

The account of the relationship of Freud and Jung from 1906 forward is, of course, contained in the letters in this volume—the gradual warming of mutual regard, confidence, and affection, the continual interchange of professional information and opinions, the rapidly elaborating business of the psychoanalytical movement, the intimate give-and-take of family news, the often acerb and witty observations on colleagues and adversaries, and at length the emergence of differences, disagreements, misunderstandings, injured feelings, and finally disruption and separation.

*

After Jung's letter of 20 May 1914 resigning from the presidency of the International Association, there is a long silence in the history of these letters.[24] Freud himself did not again engage in a holo-

---

[21] Karl Abraham. See *Freud/Abraham Letters*, 15 Jan. 14, in which Abraham supplied information that Freud had requested.

[22] SE XIV, p. 28.

[23] Ibid., p. 26. Writing 21 years later, Freud gave a more succinct but slightly less exact account: ". . . my isolation gradually came to an end. To begin with, a small circle of pupils gathered round me in Vienna; and then, after 1906, came the news that the psychiatrists at Zürich, E. Bleuler, his assistant C. G. Jung, and others, were taking a lively interest in psycho-analysis. We got into personal touch with one another, and at Easter 1908 the friends of the young science met at Salzburg . . ." ("An Autobiographical Study," SE XX, p. 48).

[24] Jung's letter of 1923 (359 J) is the sole exception.

caust of unwanted papers, as he had done in March 1908, when he took over an adjoining flat and rearranged his study (occurrences which, incidentally, are not mentioned in his letters to Jung). Into the file of Jung's letters to him he also placed some of the programmes of the Congresses and Jung's circular letters to the presidents of the branch societies, as well as several letters from Jung to Ferenczi, which apparently Ferenczi had turned over to Freud.[25] The letters Freud received from Emma Jung were kept separately. There is no evidence that he ever consulted the Jung file again, though he himself must have placed Jung's referral letter of 1923 in it. Freud's correspondence was filed chronologically in cabinets in his study at Berggasse 19. When the time approached for the Freuds to leave Vienna in 1938, Anna Freud and Marie Bonaparte went through Freud's papers and correspondence and burned some items that would have been dangerous if they had fallen into Nazi hands.[26] Then the remaining files of papers and letters—from Jones, Abraham, Eitingon, Pfister, Ferenczi, Lou Andreas-Salomé, Jung, Martha Bernays Freud—were labeled and shipped along with the family's other effects.[27] Professor and Mrs. Freud and Anna boarded the departing train on 4 June 1938 and after a stop in Paris arrived at Dover on 6 June; they had been accorded diplomatic privileges, and none of the luggage was examined there or in London. The files of papers were stored away in the house at 20 Maresfield Gardens, which became the family's permanent home in the autumn of 1938, and where Freud died on 23 September 1939. There the letters rested, surviving another kind of holocaust—the air raids of the Second World War—and afterward, amidst the concerns of the Freud family with the immediacies of life and profession, were seemingly forgotten.

Jung's letters from Freud lay undisturbed for nearly forty years. For a time he kept them in what he called his "cache," a narrow safe set into the wall of an alcove adjoining his large study-library upstairs.[28] The

---

[25] Three of them are published in *Jung: Letters*, ed. Adler, vol. 1.

[26] Private communication from Miss Freud, who added, "Otherwise what we performed were really works of rescue. There was too much accumulated material to take with us to London, and my father was all for throwing away much of it, whereas Princess Bonaparte . . . was all for preservation. Therefore she rescued things from waste-baskets which my father had thrown there." The account given by Jones (III, p. 238/233), of burning everything considered not worth preserving, is not quite exact.

[27] Private communication from Mrs. E. L. Freud.

[28] Private communication from Aniela Jaffé.

"cache," which was locked with a key that Jung carried in his pocket, also contained, among other valuables, the four fragments of a bread-knife that had shattered when he was experimenting with occultism as a student.[29]

In all of his later writings, including his autobiography, Jung never referred to his correspondence with Freud.[30] Nor did Freud ever mention the correspondence in his writings afterward, other than to allude in "The History of the Psycho-Analytic Movement" (1914) to Jung's letter of 11 November 1912 (323 J). The existence of this valuable *Briefwechsel* was not generally known until the publication of volume II of Ernest Jones's *Life and Work of Sigmund Freud* in 1955. Around 1950 Jones had begun work on the biography, the first volume of which (1953) comes up to 1900. By 1952 he had started to prepare the second volume, and in February he wrote to Jung asking if he might see Freud's letters to him. Aniela Jaffé, who was at that time the secretary of the C. G. Jung Institute,[31] had been in analysis with Jung for several years. During an analytical interview in February, Jung asked her if she would read the Freud letters. She agreed, and Jung's secretary, Marie-Jeanne Schmid, brought the bundle of letters from the "cache." As Mrs. Jaffé remembers it, "I was more than excited; but then, after having read all the night, rather disappointed, because I had expected sentences of the deepest wisdom and psychological insight and met with a lot of politics and such, besides the most personal remarks. When I told this to Jung he was pleased, and I suppose his answer to Jones reflects it."[32] Jung replied to Jones:

> They are not particularly important. They chiefly contain remarks about publishers or the organization of the Psychoanalytical Society. And some others are too personal. As a matter of fact I don't care for their publication. On the whole they wouldn't be an important contribution to Freud's biography.[33]

A month later Jung entrusted the bundle of letters to Mrs. Jaffé, and she carried it to the director of the Jung Institute, C. A.

---

[29] Aniela Jaffé, *From the Life and Work of C. G. Jung*, tr. R.F.C. Hull (1971), p. 123. See also *Letters*, ed. Adler, vol. 1, 27 Nov. 34, to J. B. Rhine.
[30] He mentioned the letters in private correspondence late in life.
[31] Established in 1948 in Zürich for training and research in analytical psychology. Courses are given in both English and German.
[32] Private communication.
[33] *Letters*, ed. Adler, vol. 2, 22 Feb. 52, to Jones.

Meier, M.D.,[34] with a covering letter (22 March 1952) in which Jung stated that he was handing over the letters to the Institute for safekeeping, his wish being that the collection be considered a possession that was not for sale. "The letters have a certain historical value, after all," he wrote, "though their contents are unimportant."

Meier replied to Jung, thanking him for the gift on behalf of the Curatorium of the Institute, and he added: "It will interest you to learn that we have been asked by the Sigmund Freud Archives, Inc.,[35] of New York, whether we could prepare photocopies of these letters, and we intend to ask them whether they would be in a position to reciprocate by providing photocopies of your letters to Freud. I'll be glad to keep you informed of this."

The information that Meier received from K. R. Eissler, M.D., the Secretary of the Archives, was abruptly disappointing: "Unfortunately the letters which Professor Jung wrote to Professor Freud have not been preserved. As far as I know, Professor Freud destroyed his whole correspondence before leaving Vienna in 1938, and I assume that Professor Jung's letters were among those documents which were destroyed during those hectic days."[36] Eissler told Meier that he would, with his permission, inquire of the Freud family in London. By the end of the year the Jung letters had not come to light, but the photostats of the Freud letters had been made and sent to New York, with the Jung Institute's proviso that they be kept confidential for one hundred years.

In September 1953, Jung received Eissler at Küsnacht and granted him an interview for the Freud Archives. The transcript of the interview is under standard restriction until the year 2010. Jung also, on the occasion of Eissler's visit, donated various pieces of memorabilia to the Archives.[37] Soon afterward, with the permission of the Jung

[34] Later, professor of psychology at the Federal Polytechnic ("E.T.H."), Zürich.
[35] The Sigmund Freud Archives was incorporated in New York in 1951 as a nonprofit, tax-exempt organization, its goal being the collection of all documents directly or indirectly related to the life and work of Freud; the Archives entered into a formal agreement with the Library of Congress whereby the Library becomes owner of the materials, which, if designated as restricted, are kept confidential for as long as the donor or Archives and the Library consider proper. The Library's Freud collection, which includes the materials donated by the Archives, comprises letters to and from Freud and his family, original manuscripts, official documents, photographs, and interviews with persons who had been in contact with Freud.
[36] Eissler to Meier, 4 June 52. This and other letters written by Dr. Eissler are quoted with his kind permission.
[37] See appendixes 3 and 4 of the present volume.

Institute, the Freud Archives arranged to have Freud's letters transcribed. In November, Jung was again asked if Jones could read the Freud letters, this time by Eissler on Jones's behalf. Jung replied directly to Jones:

> Of course you have my permission to read Freud's letters, copies of which are in the Freud Archives in New York.
>
> Your biographical material [in volume I] is very interesting, although it would have been advisable to consult me for certain facts. For instance you got the story of Freud's fainting attack quite wrong. Also it was by no means the first one; he had such an attack before in 1909 previous to our departure for America in Bremen, and very much under the same psychological circumstances.[38]
>
> Hoping you are going on to continue enjoying old age, I remain, etc.[39]

Jones thus was able to read Freud's letters to Jung, but the other side of the dialogue was assumed to have been lost. On 22 March 1954, however, Eissler wrote again to Meier: "To my very great joy I can tell you that I have just been informed by Miss Anna Freud that the letters from Professor Jung to Professor Freud have been found. I am sure that Miss Freud will have no objection to sending copies, as she had originally agreed to this in case they should be found. I shall probably see her in London this summer and will discuss the matter." Miss Freud has recalled, more recently, that during the war years all the various parcels of correspondence that had been brought from Vienna were safely stored in every possible place in both her house and her brother Ernst's house. It took some time to bring all the material together and catalogue it, and while this work was going on, the Jung letters were securely put away and in due course came to light.[39a]

In the same letter, Eissler broached the question of whether the Jung Institute might be interested in a joint publication of the correspondence. Meier replied that the Institute indeed would.

---

[38] Jones had written of the 1912 fainting attack in volume I (p. 348/317), a copy of which Jung had received from his friend E. A. Bennet, of London, the month before. See *Letters*, ed. Adler, vol 2, 21 Nov. 53, to Bennet, for Jung's version of the event; also *Memories*, p. 157/153. Jones referred briefly to the 1909 attack in volume II (pp. 61/55, 165/146); Jung gives a fuller account in *Memories*, pp. 156/152f.

[39] *Letters*, ed. Adler, vol. 2, 19 Dec. 53.

[39a] Private communication from Anna Freud.

During a visit to New York in November 1954, Meier met Eissler, who gave him the photostats of Jung's letters, and the two talked over the idea of publication. Meier arranged to borrow the uncorrected transcript of the Freud letters, and when he got back to Zürich he read the entire exchange. Surely the first person to read all the letters on both sides, Meier wrote Eissler:

> The first impression is really that of a shattering tragedy. And just for that reason I am completely in favour of publishing the whole thing. It is true that recently Jung thought it should wait until after his death; he didn't want to look at the letters at all, however. I'm therefore of the opinion that he could be persuaded to change his mind. I think not only that the world should learn something from this tragedy, but also that from this publication a great deal of nonsense that is current will finally be laid to rest, which can only be a good thing for clearing the atmosphere. More difficult than consideration for Freud and Jung, it seems to me, is consideration for other colleagues, who turn up frequently in the letters and to some extent are labeled with rather unflattering, spirited expressions. . . . Personally, I think we should give the world a brave piece of scientific objectivity for the common good.[40]

Eissler felt that as much as possible should be published, "with out causing any annoyance or detriment to the individuals mentioned."[41] Transcripts of the entire correspondence should be prepared, he thought, and be read by the persons on whose decision the publication would depend. The work of transcribing the Jung letters went ahead, and the Institute in Zürich, dissatisfied with the New York transcript of the Freud letters, began to make its own transcript of them. Meier hoped that Miss Freud would then examine the authoritative texts and permit their publication.

In 1955, Jones published volume II of his life of Freud, dealing with the "Years of Maturity," 1901–1919. He had had access to some five thousand letters from Freud's correspondence, the most valuable being those between Freud and Abraham, Ferenczi, Jung, and himself. It is not certain at what point he was able to read Jung's letters to Freud; in volume II there are only three direct citations of them, as against some fifty citations of Freud's letters to Jung, in addition to sixteen extended quotations in an appendix (though

[40] Meier to Eissler, 14 Jan. 55, quoted with Dr. Meier's kind permission.
[41] Eissler to Meier, 18 Jan. 55.

Jones refrained from quoting entire letters from this correspondence).[42] Upon the publication of the second volume, with its copious references to himself, Jung made no further comment on Jones's *Freud*, so far as it is known, in his published writings or letters.

During the summer of 1955, the painstaking work of transcribing both sides of the correspondence proceeded at the Jung Institute in Zürich. Then, on 1 October, Meier notified Eissler that he had had a discussion with Professor and Mrs. Jung and that they did not yet agree to the publication of the letters. Jung wanted to see the letters first. Perhaps the letters could be edited by contemporaries of the two correspondents and published in the distant future, for the grandchildren's generation. But for the present nothing was definite until Jung saw the letters.[43]

Eissler replied sympathetically; he also had doubts about an unabridged publication. Many passages, he supposed, might need comments or they would not be understandable to future generations. But would people be willing to devote time to the work without seeing it realized during their lifetime?[44] Meier was wholeheartedly for obtaining commentaries by contemporaries; Mrs. Jaffé stood ready to help on the Zürich side; and Jung had indeed given his approval to the publication, but only after his death. However, Meier expected to discuss this further with Mrs. Jung.[45] There was no doubt that the Institute was truly authorized to publish the correspondence, in view of the statement Jung had made when he turned over the letters.[46] At the end of October, the Institute sent Eissler the Zürich transcripts of both the Jung and the Freud letters, as well as the uncorrected New York transcript of the Freud letters.

Not until March 1956 was a working plan agreed upon among the Freud Archives, Anna Freud, and the Jung Institute: "The transcript . . . should be submitted for evaluation to the following five persons: Dr. Anna Freud, and Drs. Heinz Hartmann, Ernst Kris, Ernest Jones, and Hermann Nunberg. The plan is to obtain and preserve available information from informants who have particular knowledge about events and people who played a prominent role at the time when Professor Freud worked with Professor Jung. Since

[42] Volume III contains five citations of Freud's letters and one of Jung's. Volume II also contains several citations of Jung's letters to Jones, which have now disappeared.

[43] A. Jaffé, on behalf of Meier, to Eissler, 1 Oct. 55.

[44] Eissler to Meier, 4 Oct. 55.

[45] Meier to Eissler, 7 Oct. 55.

[46] Meier to Eissler, 21 Oct. 55. / Mrs. Jung died 27 Nov. 55.

most of this information is probably of a personal nature, it is not intended to publish it. The idea is to have each of the informants provide the manuscript with footnotes, or a longer commentary, as the case may be. These additions to the manuscript would be kept strictly confidential at the Library of Congress for as many years as each of the informants may wish."[47]

In August 1956, Meier notified Eissler that Jung had stipulated that his letters to Freud could be published, at the earliest, twenty years after his death, though Meier hoped that work on the commentaries could proceed anyway.[48] But no commentary or footnotes were ever produced. Kris died in 1957, Jones in 1958, and Nunberg and Hartmann in 1970. The photostats of the original letters and of the Zürich transcripts were deposited in the Library of Congress in 1958, labeled as follows: "Confidential, not to be opened until 20 years after the death of Carl Jung with permission of the Jung Archives, Küsnacht, Zürich."

*

In 1956, Dr. Gerhard Adler put to Jung the idea of publishing a general selection of his entire correspondence. Adler, originally of Berlin and after 1936 in England, was one of Jung's most prominent pupils. As he wrote, some years later, "Originally the idea of such publication had come not from [Jung] himself but from friends who were aware of the unique literary and psychological value of Jung's correspondence. At first Jung had reacted against the whole notion, since he felt that the spontaneity and immediacy of his letters were not for the general public; but in his later years he changed his attitude. . . ."[49] Responding to Adler's proposal, Jung immediately ruled out the inclusion of the Freud/Jung correspondence. In a letter of 24 May 1956 he wrote: "Separate treatment of this correspondence is justified, because it touches in parts upon very personal problems, whereas the planned publication refers to scientific subjects. I consider it inopportune to expose the personal material so long as the waves of animosity are still running so high. At the date suggested by me Freud and I will be 'historical personalities,' and the necessary detachment from events will prevail by then."[50]

In August 1957, Jung confirmed his agreement to the publication of a selection of his letters. In January 1958 he recommended that

[47] Memorandum by Eissler, 20 Mar. 56.
[48] Meier to Eissler, 3 Aug. 56.
[49] Adler, introduction to *Letters*, vol. 1 (1973), p. ix.   [50] Ibid., pp. xi–xii.

the work be entrusted to a committee composed of Mrs. Jaffé, now his secretary, his daughter Marianne Niehus-Jung (an editor of the Swiss edition of the collected works), and Dr. Adler, who was to act as chairman and as editor of the English edition; and at the same time Jung stated that the Freud/Jung correspondence was to be published "only after 1980."[51]

The idea of publication of the Freud/Jung correspondence was broached again in the summer of 1958. It is not clear who succeeded in persuading Jung to change his mind so soon after he had pushed the project into the distant future. The impetus may have originated with the publisher Kurt Wolff, who before World War II had had a distinguished career in Germany and Italy, and had founded the New York firm of Pantheon Books in the early 1940's. Pantheon had been chosen as publisher of Bollingen Series, a programme of the Bollingen Foundation, the keystone of which was the Collected Works of C. G. Jung. Kurt Wolff, who had known Jung for many years, had convinced him in 1956 that his autobiography should be written. This project grew into a collaboration between Jung and Aniela Jaffé; Mrs. Jaffé wrote the greater part of it from interviews with Jung, and he wrote other parts in longhand.[52] Wolff was in Zürich during the summer of 1958 for editorial conferences. And in Europe during the same period were the editor and assistant editor of Bollingen Series, John D. Barrett and Vaun Gillmor, and Sir Herbert Read, a director of Routledge & Kegan Paul, the publishers of Jung's works in England. These three, with Jung, composed the "Editorial Committee," which met once a year to review the progress of the collected works and plan the future programme.

The first document is a letter Jung wrote on 20 July 1958 to Eissler:

As you know, I have stipulated that my correspondence with Freud ought not to be published before 30 years[53] have elapsed

[51] Letters to Bollingen Foundation, 19 Aug. 57, and to John D. Barrett, 29 Jan. 58, in the Foundation archives. / Marianne Niehus-Jung died in March 1965.

[52] *Memories, Dreams, Reflections,* "by C. G. Jung, recorded and edited by Aniela Jaffé," was published simultaneously in New York, London, and Zürich in 1963.

[53] On 12 Aug. 60, Dr. Franz N. Riklin, who had succeeded Meier as director of the Jung Institute, informed Eissler of a further proviso, namely that Jung now wished that no one be permitted to study the correspondence until thirty years after his death. He proposed that a protocol be made by both sides, stipulating

after my death, but lately I have been asked from different sides to permit—inasmuch as I am competent—an earlier publication of the whole correspondence.

Such a change of my will[54] is not a simple matter. First of all I don't know how you feel about such a proposition, and secondly I could not permit an earlier publication without a necessary revision of my letters. My letters were never written with any thought that they might be broadcasted. As a matter of fact, many of them contain unchecked and highly objectionable materials, such as are produced in the course of an analysis, and shed a most one-sided and dubious light on a number of persons who I don't want to offend in any manner whatever. Such material enjoys the protection of the *secretum medici*. These people or their descendants are still alive.

I should be deeply obliged to you, if you would kindly inform me of your feelings in this matter, especially if you would agree with an earlier publication under strict observation of the rule of discretion and the risk of libel.[55]

Dr. Eissler responded:

There are two aspects to the question you asked me regarding the publication of the letters Prof. Freud and you exchanged: the legal aspect and my personal feeling about the whole matter. There can be no doubt that anything which might offend anyone who was under your treatment or a descendant of such persons should not be published. However, permission to publish at least the letters written by Freud does not depend on the Archives, since the Archives never acquired the copyright. This question has to be discussed with the Sigmund Freud Copyrights, Ltd., c/o Mr. Ernst Freud, . . . in London.

Since I consider it an indiscretion to read letters that have not been published, I made it my habit not to read the letters acquired by the Archives unless there is an objective necessity for doing so. Since this did not arise regarding your correspondence with Prof.

---

this limitation, and Eissler referred him to Ernst Freud. Such a document has not been found.

[54] Jung's last will and testament contains no dispositions regarding the correspondence with Freud. He may have used the term "will" here not in its legal meaning, but in the nontechnical sense of intention. (Information from Dr. Hans Karrer and Mr. Franz Jung.)

[55] *Letters*, ed. Adler, vol. 2.

Freud I never took the liberty of reading the letters and cannot express an opinion about whether or not this correspondence should be published at this time. However, I recall the opinion of the late Dr. Kris, the editor of the Freud/Fliess correspondence, who read the letters at the request of the Jung Archives[56] in Zurich. If I recall correctly, his opinion was that it would be worthwhile to publish at present those parts of the correspondence which contain strictly scientific problems such as the questions of narcissism and schizophrenia, which apparently came up quite frequently in your communications with Freud.

This is the only contribution I can make in answer to your letter of July 20th. The most important questions I think have to be straightened out between you and Ernst Freud.[57]

On 23 August, at his home at Küsnacht, Jung met with Barrett, Miss Gillmor, Read, and Wolff. Agreement to publish the Freud/Jung correspondence was reached—in principle. Wolff had read the entire correspondence and prepared a fifty-page summary; this presented the first conspectus of the letters and was testimony to the importance of publishing them.[58]

Shortly afterward, Mrs. Jaffé, Jung's secretary, wrote to John Barrett: "Dr. Jung said that he fully agreed with Dr. Eissler's idea to 'publish at present those parts of the correspondence which contain strictly scientific problems' and asked me to inform Dr. F. Riklin, President of the C. G. Jung Institute, of this fact. (Dr. Jung has given the Freud letters to the Institute as a donation.) Yesterday Dr. Jung told me in a few words about your talk on Saturday, August 23rd, and added that he would very much like to reread or at least peruse the letters in question before giving his definite 'placet.' "[59]

Mrs. Jaffé remembers that Jung did not look at the letters himself—in fact, to her knowledge he never showed any desire at any time to reread any of his correspondence with Freud—but asked another one of his pupils to go through them and to make recommendations. The consequence was the following letter from Jung to Barrett, one week later:

[56] That is, the C. G. Jung Institute.
[57] Letter of 13 Aug. 58 (copy in Bollingen Foundation archives).
[58] Mrs. Helen Wolff kindly gave access to her late husband's summary of the letters and confirmed other details in his diary.
[59] A. Jaffé to J. D. Barrett, 27 Aug. 58, in the Bollingen Foundation archives; quoted by permission of Mrs. Jaffé.

Re: publication of the Freud-correspondence, I want to tell you that I have decided to do nothing further. The letters are too personal and contain too little generally interesting material, so that the great work which ought to be done, to draw something worthwhile from them, would be wasted time.

It was nice to see you again, and I am glad that I am able to spare you a superfluous trouble. Thus the conditions remain as they have been before, namely the publication of the correspondence is postponed *ad calendas graecas*.[60]

The following year, the British writer John Freeman (later, ambassador to the United States) conducted a filmed interview with Jung for the British Broadcasting Corporation. He asked Jung, "When are the letters which you exchanged with Freud going to be published?"

Professor Jung: "Well, not during my lifetime."
Freeman: "You would have no objection to their being published after your lifetime?"
Professor Jung: "Oh, no, none at all."
Freeman: "Because they are probably of great historical importance."
Professor Jung: "I don't think so."
Freeman: "Then why have you not published them so far?"
Professor Jung: "Because they were not important enough. I see no particular importance in them."[61]

Later, the pupil who had read the letters at Jung's request the previous summer happened to write to him quoting his striking remarks about Christianity in the letter of 11 February 1910 (178 J), and Jung replied (9 April 1959):

Best thanks for the quotation from that accursed correspondence. For me it is an unfortunately inexpungeable reminder of the incredible folly that filled the days of my youth. The journey from cloud-cuckoo-land back to reality lasted a long time. In my case Pilgrim's Progress consisted in my having to climb down a thou-

---

[60] Letter of 5 Sept. 58, in the Bollingen Foundation archives.
[61] Transcript to be published in *C. G. Jung Speaking*. An abridged version, not including this passage, is in *Face to Face*, ed. Hugh Burnett (London, 1964), pp. 48–51.

sand ladders until I could reach out my hand to the little clod of earth that I am.[62]

In the fall of 1960, Ernst L. Freud brought out the *Letters of Sigmund Freud*, a volume of selected letters that he had edited. By agreement with the Jung Institute, he included seven of his father's letters to Jung (27, 38, 42, 45, 71, 129, 340, three of them with deletions).

An old friend of Jung's, meanwhile, had been writing a memoir of Jung as he had known him: this was Dr. E. A. Bennet, a psychiatrist and analyst of London, whose book, *C. G. Jung*, was largely based on their conversations and correspondence that had continued up until a short time before Jung's death. In his chapter on Jung's relations with Freud, Bennet writes: "More and more Freud came to rely on Jung and wrote him constantly, often every week. If Jung did not reply, he would get a telegram asking what had gone wrong. Jung has kept these letters, although he never intended to publish them; they are personal, mainly about current events, and in any case of no special importance or general interest."[63] This estimate was based on what Dr. Bennet had been told by Jung, who, furthermore, reviewed the book in manuscript.

Until the time of Jung's death, 6 June 1961, there was no further consideration of the correspondence with Freud and no change in Jung's wish that publication be postponed until long after his death. Editorial work had continued on *Memories, Dreams, Reflections*, and arrangements were made to publish in an appendix parts of three letters from Freud to Jung (139, 255, 260) dealing with occultism. Jung had expressly given his approval, and the permission of Ernst Freud was duly sought and granted.

In August 1961, shortly after Jung's death, there was another meeting in Zürich of Barrett, Miss Gillmor, and Read, this time with Mr. and Mrs. Walther Niehus-Jung, Franz Jung, Aniela Jaffé, Franz Riklin, and Max Rascher, Jung's Swiss publisher. The gathering carried on the tradition of the regular summer meetings to review the progress of the English-language publications of Jung's works. Jung had named Walther Niehus as his literary executor, and his wife Marianne Niehus-Jung had a principal role as an editor of the *Gesammelte Werke* and the selected letters. The main business of

[62] Quoted in a footnote to Jung's 11 Feb. 10 letter to Freud in *Letters*, ed. Adler, vol. 1, p. 19.
[63] *C. G. Jung* (London and New York, 1961), p. 39.

the 1961 meeting was indeed the selected letters, upon which intensive editorial work was now to begin. According to the minutes, "It was tentatively suggested that three volumes be prepared: (1) Freud correspondence, (2) letters concerning religion and theology, and (3) the balance of the scientific letters." This revival of the Freud/Jung correspondence was countermanded as soon as all parties concerned were reminded of Jung's wish that the correspondence remain sealed until 1991. The selected letters were finally arranged chronologically, and Adler stated that "I felt justified in publishing only a very few and quite uncontroversial letters of Jung's to Freud, eight in all," on the pattern of Ernst Freud's choice of seven of Freud's to Jung in the selection he edited.[64]

Earlier on, Freud's correspondence had begun to come out in several different collections. *The Origins of Psychoanalysis*, a volume of letters to Wilhelm Fliess and related papers, was published as early as 1950, and the selection by Ernst Freud, already mentioned, appeared in 1960. Then followed the exchanges of letters with Pfister (1963), Abraham (1965), Lou Andreas-Salomé (1966), and Arnold Zweig (1968).[65]

*

In the spring of 1969, Norman Franklin, chairman of Routledge & Kegan Paul, Jung's publishers in England, called on Ernst Freud at his home in London. Mr. Freud pointed to a storage cabinet in his study and said it contained Jung's letters to his father, which the family were thinking of selling, along with the right to publish his father's letters to Jung. Mr. Franklin wrote to Princeton University Press, as Jung's American publishers, conveying this news. The Princeton University Library, with whose staff the matter was discussed, was not in a position at that time to bid for the letters, which did not fall naturally into the University collections. But at the Press we were troubled at the thought of the letters being scattered or

---

[64] Adler, introduction to *Letters*, vol. I, p. xii. The letters to Freud included in Adler's selection (also in Jaffé's, in the Swiss edition) are 138, 170, 178, 198, 224, 259, and 315, three with deletions. The translation is that of R.F.C. Hull, as in the present volume. The Swiss edition of Jung's *Briefe* appeared in three volumes in 1972–73 and the American-English edition in two volumes in 1973–74.

[65] In February 1965, Eissler wrote Riklin saying that he had heard that the Jung Institute would like to publish the Freud/Jung letters but believed that the Freud family were opposed, whereas he knew that the Sigmund Freud Copyrights had no objection. Riklin responded that the thirty-year embargo had to stand.

perhaps disappearing into some restricted private collection. Furthermore, though we were aware of Jung's embargo on publishing the letters, there was the faint hope that the embargo might somehow be lifted. Accordingly, as executive editor of Jung's works in English, I wrote to Ernst Freud on 23 May: "If your family actually should be entertaining the idea of selling the Jung letters, I would be most grateful if you gave me the opportunity to try to arrange for their purchase in order to place them in the Jung archives in Zürich." At the same time, I wrote the Jung family, through the legal counsel for the estate, Dr. Hans Karrer, asking, "Why shouldn't the Freud and Jung families simply exchange their respective holdings of the original letters?"

On 22 June, Ernst Freud replied, asking whether an offer could be made for the Jung letters which his family could then consider. He added, "It is not correct that there exist any restrictions with regard to the publication of the Freud letters—only Jung found it (unfortunately) necessary to withhold the right for 30 years after his death. And although I have proof that in the last year of his life he was willing to change this condition, the Jung Archives have been unable to free them before this date. Clearly, it would be a pity to publish only my father's letters alone."

Shortly afterward, in Zürich, I took part in meetings with members of the Jung family and their advisers. The consequence of these discussions was a proposal that the Freud letters and Jung letters be exchanged between the C. G. Jung Institute and the Freud family. It was observed that Jung had left conflicting instructions about restrictions on publication—for thirty years, for twenty, for fifty, for one hundred, or until 1980. The family agreed that it would be fortunate if the correspondence could be edited soon, while persons survived who could contribute to an informed annotation. The edited letters would then be put in safekeeping and published only in 1980. I communicated these thoughts to Ernst Freud, who replied on 2 August: "We shall gladly agree to the exchange of the originals. I have taken steps to get the declaration mention [that Jung was willing to change the restrictions] but of course I am not certain how long this may take and whether I will be successful.[66] I share the opinion that an early editing of the letters would be fortunate. . . ." Henceforward, the two parties were in direct communication.

Dr. Karrer wrote to me on 2 December 1969: "My clients have taken a decision of considerable importance. They have come to the

---

[66] This point was never clarified. / (Mrs. E. L. Freud kindly gave permission for publication of parts of her husband's letters.)

conclusion that this question must not be decided on the basis of the late Professor Jung's various and possibly contradictory statements, but in the light of the situation as it presents itself now. Under this angle, they attach overriding importance to the consideration that the publication should take place as long as persons are still available for the editorial work who had known Jung and Freud. Of course, it remains to be seen whether the Freud party shares this view."

The Freud party did share that view. And, on 25 February 1970, Franz Jung flew from Zürich to London with the original Freud letters in his briefcase, and called on Ernst Freud in St. John's Wood. Freud, who had been ill with a heart ailment, dressed and left his bedroom in honour of his guest. As he wrote me on 6 March, "Mr. Jung—whom I liked very much—visited me here, and we didn't only exchange our fathers' letters, but in the easiest and friendliest way agreed on plans for the early publication of the correspondence." Both men were architects, and they readily found a mutual sympathy. Ernst Freud's letter went on: "In order to guarantee impartiality, these letters will be printed like historical documents, that is to say without any comments whatsoever and absolutely complete, unless discretion concerning former patients or colleagues makes omissions unavoidable. The existing typescripts will once more be compared with the originals, necessary notes to explain names, book titles, quotations, etc., will be added." Later, Franz Jung remarked, "It was quite an historic moment. We decided that the letters should be given to publication while there are still people around who knew the personalities of the two men."[67]

Ernst Freud died suddenly on 7 April 1970, but the contractual arrangements for the publication were duly completed, and the news was made public in mid July. Shortly afterward the original Freud letters were purchased from the Freud family by the Library of Congress, through funds provided by an anonymous benefactor, and they are now in the Manuscript Division of the Library. The original Jung letters are in the C. G. Jung Institute at Zürich, and according to the terms of Jung's gift their sale is barred.

*

As explained heretofore, the transcripts of the letters were typewritten in 1955, and photocopies of these transcripts provide the text of the present volume. The transcripts were read against the holo-

---

[67] Article by Henry Raymont, *New York Times*, 15 July 1970, p. 41.

graph letters (or photocopies of them) once more by Anna Freud and her sister Mathilde Hollitscher and by Kurt Niehus-Jung, Professor Jung's son-in-law. On both sides, memoranda were prepared explaining abbreviations and noting handwritten corrections and slips of the pen by both writers.

Both translators—Ralph Manheim for the Freud letters, R.F.C. Hull for the Jung letters—worked from these prepared transcripts. During the course of the translating and editorial work, the transcripts were again checked against the holographs for problematical readings, sometimes with the assistance of other persons familiar with the handwriting.

In the present edition, textual matters have not been presented in exhaustive detail, which would be distracting and tedious for most readers. The German edition of the letters, however, which is being published simultaneously (by S. Fischer Verlag, Frankfurt), will be available to anyone who wants to study Freud's and Jung's original usages especially with respect to the salutations and valedictions of the letters. There are more diverse possibilities for these epistolary formulas in German than in English, and some of them if translated literally would sound stilted and odd. Variety and literality have been sacrificed for the sake of phrases that ring naturally in English. But the chief and most interesting forms and changes of forms have usually been mentioned in the notes. It will be seen that Freud, beginning with a formal expression such as *Sehr geehrter Herr Kollege* (literally, "Very esteemed Mr. Colleague"), came in time to the simple and warm *Lieber Freund*, which he used until the cooling of the relationship caused him to adopt *Lieber Herr Doktor*. Jung began formally with salutations on the order of *Sehr geehrter Herr Professor* and arrived rather slowly at *Lieber Herr Professor*, which he used almost to the end. The valedictions are even more varied; while literality here is, again, also impossible, they have been translated with strict consistency—for example, *Ihr ergebener*, though it allows of various English renderings, is always translated as "Yours sincerely."

The two writers, and particularly Freud, used many abbreviations, as was the custom in that day—it must certainly have expedited letter-writing. In the interests of readability most of the abbreviated words have been spelled out, but certain abbreviations have been retained consistently because they are a characteristic part of the psychoanalytic vocabulary: "ucs." (unconscious), for *Ubw.* (*Unbewusstsein*); "cs." (consciousness), for *Bw.* (*Bewusstsein*); Greek psi-alpha (ΨA) for *Psychoanalyse* (psychoanalysis). (Both letters, psi and alpha, of this Greek abbreviation are consistently capitalized in the present volume, though the writers' usage varied. Freud preferred capitals but often used lower case in adjectival forms. Jung preferred to write Ψ as a capital and a in lower case.) Some other abbreviations—of personal names, journal and book titles, and so on—are retained for flavour. The writers' placement of postscripts and interpolations has been indicated as faithfully as possible. Slips of the pen, cancellations, etc., have been indicated when they are of interest and can be given intelligibly in translation. Confusions of the pronominal forms *Sie/sie* and *Ihr/ihr* (you/they, you/she) have in general been indicated, not only when they caused controversy between the writers but in the fairly frequent cases when they went unnoticed. Underlining has not been reproduced as italic when this device is used differently in German (as for personal names) than in English; underlining for emphasis is, however, usually indicated by italic. Book titles are italicized as they are normally in English.

Dates at the head of the letters, which the writers often gave in European number style, as 3.IV.10 or 3.4.10, have been standardized to the style "3 April 1910" (and, in the notes, "3 Apr. 10"). The printed letterheads have also been somewhat simplified, as explained in the notes.

No letter that was in the two sets at the time they were transcribed in 1955 has been omitted from this edition, and (as indicated in the notes) a few more have since come to light. That the sets are intact is proved by the unbroken sequence of letter or page numbers pencilled by unknown hands on both sets of letters and visible on photocopies made earlier. The loss of some letters, cards, and telegrams (and enclosures, which were apparently not filed with the letters) is sometimes evident from context, and these are mentioned in the notes.[68] It is not necessary to suppose these were suppressed by either recipient, as the surviving letters contain ample material that might have been considered suppressible. What is remarkable is that both sides of this correspondence have survived in nearly complete form.

Within the letters, there are deletions of two kinds: (1) The names of analysands whose cases are discussed are replaced by initials, beginning with "A" for the first case mentioned. As the same initial

---

[68] See appendix 1, p. 562.

is used consistently for an analysand, the references are coherent throughout the correspondence. This discretion, which was requested by both families, is in accordance with medical practice. (2) In Jung's letters, at the request of his family, a few passages have been omitted and replaced by: [. . .]. None of these refers to Freud, but to other personalities whose close relatives may survive.

The system of numbering the letters has, of course, been devised for the present edition. As explained in its annotation, item number 199a F was found (or rather, refound) after the numbers had been established.[69] Thus the total number of items in the exchange is 360: 164 from Freud, 196 from Jung; and, in addition, 7 from Emma Jung. While slightly different totals are given by Ernest Jones (171, Freud; 197, Jung: in vol. II, preface) and by Gerhard Adler (167, Freud; 196, Jung: in vol. 1, introduction), the discrepancies result from later finds and different ways of counting fragments.

As for the annotations, they are documentary and explanatory in the spirit of Ernst Freud's and Franz Jung's agreement, but both families have assented to the inclusion of notes that cite parallel and related publications and events, textual details, and cross-references; passages of editorial comment that bridge discontinuities in the letters (usually because Freud and Jung met and therefore did not write); and illustrations, facsimiles, and documentary appendixes. Occasional gaps in the information are regretted.

8 *November 1973*   W. M.

[69] The postscript of 163 F (see addenda) was also found among a set of photostats in the Library of Congress.

ACKNOWLEDGMENTS

Anna Freud devoted a great many hours to reading the translation, giving advice that only she could give, supplying many pieces of information, and with her sister Mrs. Mathilde Hollitscher, correcting and working over the transcript of the Freud letters. She offered warm encouragement throughout. The late Ernst Freud, a prime mover of the project, Mrs. Lucie Freud, and Mark Paterson, managing director of Sigmund Freud Copyrights, Ltd., were notably helpful.

Mr. Kurt Niehus-Jung, acting for the Jung Estate, carefully corrected and worked over the transcript of the Jung letters and supplied special information and prudent advice. Mr. Franz Jung kindly answered numerous questions and generously assembled much of the illustrative material. Mrs. Lilly Jung was also most helpful. Dr. Hans Karrer, legal counsel for the Jung Estate, was co-operative and encouraging beyond any obligation.

Dr. Kurt R. Eissler, secretary of the Sigmund Freud Archives, Inc., and an authority on the history of the psychoanalytic movement, aided and fostered the work at every stage. The late Dr. Otto Isakower, who had promised his assistance and counsel, contributed good advice before his death.

I am indebted to Aniela Jaffé and Dr. Gerhard Adler for the example of their editions of the selected letters of Jung, for the occasional use of data from their notes, and for their freely given advice and support. Mrs. Jaffé answered countless questions about Jung's life and writings and advised most constructively on textual problems. Jolande Jacobi generously gave valued background information.

Professional persons of long and clear memory, who gave information and confirmation, included Grant Allan, Dr. Roberto Assagioli, Dr. E. A. Bennet, Dr. Grete L. Bibring, Dr. W. Binswanger, Professor Manfred Bleuler, Edmund Brill, Dr. Violet S. de Laszlo, Dr. Helene Deutsch, Dr. Oskar Diethelm, Dr. Muriel Gardiner, Dr. Clara Geroe, Dr. Imre Hermann, Mrs. Ernest Jones, Dr. Maurits

Katan, Mrs. Tina Keller, Dr. Lawrence S. Kubie, Dr. Jeanne Lampl-de Groot, Dr. C. A. Meier, Dr. Henry A. Murray, Emil Oberholzer, Dr. Paul Parin, Professor Jean Piaget, Mrs. Emmy Sachs, and Dr. Jenny Waelder Hall.

Historians and interpreters who responded helpfully included Professor H. L. Ansbacher, Dr. Edward F. Edinger, Professor Henri Ellenberger, Professor Martin Green, Dr. George Gifford, Professor Cyril Greenland, Professor Nathan G. Hale, Jr., Professor Paul Roazen, Professor Dorothy Ross, Professor Carl Schorske, Dr. Hans H. Walser, and Professor Harold S. Wilson.

Among libraries, the work has been most indebted to the Francis A. Countway Library, Boston (especially Richard Wolfe), the Kristine Mann Library, New York (especially Doris A. Albrecht), the Library of Congress (especially Ronald S. Wilkinson and Roy Basler), the New York Academy of Medicine Library, the A. A. Brill Library of the New York Psychoanalytic Institute (especially Phyllis Rubinton), the New York State Psychiatric Institute Library (especially James Montgomery), and Princeton University Library (especially Eleanor V. Weld and Eloise V. Harvey); also to the Boston Psychoanalytic Society Library (Dr. Sanford Gifford), Cornell University Libraries (Barbara Shepherd), the National Library of Medicine, the New York Public Library, the library of Oslo University (H. L. Tveteras), the Riksbibliotek of Norway (Rolf Dahlø), the library of Princeton Theological Seminary, and the library of St. Elizabeths Hospital, Washington.

Among publishers who helped with information, I am grateful to Artemis Verlag, Zürich (Dr. Bruno Mariacher and Dr. Martin Müller), Basic Books, Inc. (its former director, Arthur J. Rosenthal), the Börsenverein des Deutschen Buchhandels (Dr. Adalbert J. Brauer), Franz Deuticke Verlag, Vienna, S. Fischer Verlag, Frankfurt (Ilse Grubrich-Simitis), International Universities Press (Natalie Altman), *Neue Zürcher Zeitung* (J. Heer), Pantheon Books (Iris Bromberg), and Routledge & Kegan Paul, Ltd., London.

In tracing the history of the letters, I have been obliged not only to Mrs. Jaffé, Dr. Eissler, Mr. Jung, Miss Freud, and Dr. Meier, but also to the former president, vice-president, and secretary of Bollingen Foundation, John D. Barrett, Vaun Gillmor, and Mary Curtis Ritter, and to Helen Wolff.

The translators and the editor are indebted to the following for advice on special problems of translation: Professor Ralph Freedman, Dr. James Hillman, Professor Victor Lange, Professor Albert Marckwardt, Professor William Moulton, Dr. Willibald Nagler, Richard Winston, and Professor Theodore Ziolkowski.

The following have answered inquiries and have given information, advice, and other help: Lorna Arnold, M. Baumann (Zürich University), the Bevolkingsregister of Leiden, Angelika Bialas (Institute of the History of Medicine, Zürich), Dr. John B. Blake (National Library of Medicine, Washington), Pastor Wolfram Blocher, Dr. Fred Brown, Joseph Campbell, Dorothy Curzon, Anita De Vivo (American Psychological Association), Professor K. Ernst, Professor Robert Fagles, Joan Ferguson (Librarian, Royal College of Physicians, Edinburgh), Clem L. Fiori, Dr. Eugenie Fischer-Dosuzkov, Dr. jur. Herbert F. Fuerst, Dr. Franz Gall (Archivist, Vienna University), Dr. Samuel A. Guttman, Dr. Molly Harrower, Dr. James B. Hastings, Professor Gilbert Highet, the Institute for Sex Research (Bloomington, Indiana), Uwe Johnson, Mona Karff, Professor George Kennedy, Dr. R. Knab (Director, Rheinau Clinic), William A. Loelsch (Archivist, Clark University), Mary Manheim, Dr. Ian H. Martin, Professor John R. Martin, Dr. Herbert Marwitz, Vladimir Nabokov, Dr. Gene Nameche, Miss C. Nothiger, Elizabeth Oldham, Beate R. von Oppen, Mrs. Emmy Poggensee, Polizeiinspektorat der Stadt Bern, Dr. J. B. Rhine, Professor Robert Rosenblum, Professor Saul Rosenzweig, Dr. Harvey Rothberg, Dr. Ernest Rüegg (Institute of the History of Medicine, Zürich), Professor Paul Schwaber, Peter Stadelmayer, Professor and Mrs. Homer Thompson, Oberpolizeirat Ernst Trybus (Vienna), James D. Van Trump, Professor C. Verdan (Lausanne University), Mrs. L. Veszy-Wagner, Dr. Francis N. Waldrop (National Institute of Mental Health), Professor George Whalley, Rhea White (American Society for Psychical Research), Bart Winer, Dr. H. Winnik, Eunice E. Winters, Professor Vera von Wiren, and Dr. Gerhard Zacharias. Also: Dr. Nicole Belmont, Professor Claude Lévi-Strauss, Ingeborg Meyer-Palmedo, Professor Margaret M. Phillips, and Professor Otto Winkelmann.

Pamela Long has been an ingenious, persistent, and sharp-eyed researcher and a greatly appreciated helper in the editing, correspondence, and organization.

I am deeply grateful to all my colleagues at Princeton University Press for their expertise, co-operation, and patience, and a most heartening spirit of enthusiasm over the publication.

The translators—R.F.C. Hull, the official translator of Jung's works and a sensitive and wise authority on Jungian thought and terminology, and Ralph Manheim, one of the most versatile, ex-

ACKNOWLEDGMENTS

perienced, and graceful of translators—co-ordinated their texts in the most congenial way, though working far apart. Both made significant contributions to the annotation.

Wolfgang Sauerlander was a true coadjutor. He produced a rich fund of information for the notes, particularly on subjects in German literature and history. The index is his work, and he has edited the German edition of the present publication and translated the editorial apparatus for it: thus he has had a double vantage point from which he could survey the notes and translation and make suggestions for reconciling and trueing-up countless details. His long experience as a consultant on translation, editorial disciplinarian, and organizer of learned books has enabled him to make a pervasive and indispensable contribution.

Paula and Mary McGuire have helped inestimably.

W. M.

For permission to quote translations of Nietzsche and Goethe, grateful acknowledgment is made to Penguin Books, and for brief quotations from *Memories, Dreams, Reflections,* by C. G. Jung, edited by Aniela Jaffé, to Pantheon Books, New York, and Routledge & Kegan Paul and William Collins, London.

The **Freud/Jung** Letters

11. 4. 06

Prof. Dr. Freud

IX., Berggasse 19.

Geehrter Herr College

Meinen besten Dank für die Zusendung
Ihrer Diagn. Associationsstudien,
die ich aus Ungeduld bereits in
meinen Besitz gebracht hatte. Ihre
letzte Arbeit, „Psychoanalyse u Asso-
ciationsexperiment" hat mich natürlich am
meisten erfreut, weil Sie aus Erfahrung
sich stützend dafür eingetreten sind,
dass ich nichts anderes als Wahres
aus den bisher unbetretenen
Gebieten unserer Disciplin berichtet
habe. Ich vertraue zuversichtlich darauf,
dass Sie noch oft in die Lage
kommen werden, mich zu bestätigen
u werd. mich auch gerne corrigirt
finden.

Ihr collegial ergebener

Dr Freud

Freud, 11 Apr. 06 (1 F)

1 F

Dear colleague,[2]   11 April 1906, IX. Berggasse 19[1]

Many thanks for sending me your *Diagnostic Association Studies*,[3] which in my impatience I had already acquired. Of course your latest paper, "Psychoanalysis and Association Experiments," pleased me most, because in it you argue on the strength of your own experience that everything I have said about the hitherto unexplored fields of our discipline is true. I am confident that you will often be in a position to back me up, but I shall also gladly accept correction.

Yours sincerely,[4] DR. FREUD

---

[1] The printed letterhead (on a small sheet, 5¼ x 6¾") has been simplified for this edition. For the full heading, see the facsimile of this letter on facing page. "IX." means Vienna's ninth *Bezirk*, or district. Hereafter, "Vienna" is supplied, unless Freud used unheaded paper. At 52 F he began using a different letterhead.

[2] Holograph: *Geehrter Herr College*, a rather formal salutation; Freud used it with occasional variations until 18 F.

[3] *Diagnostische Assoziationsstudien: Beiträge zur experimentellen Psychopathologie*, Vol. I (Leipzig, 1906), containing six studies by Jung and other doctors at the psychiatric clinic of the University of Zürich (i.e., Burghölzli Hospital), edited by Jung, who had directed the research. The studies had first appeared as articles in the *Journal für Psychologie und Neurologie*, 1904–6. Six further studies appeared 1906–9; collected in Vol. II (1909). All were tr. by M. D. Eder, *Studies in Word-Association* (London, 1918). Those by Jung (including "Psychoanalysis and Association Experiments," orig. 1906) are in CW 2. / Freud's first published reference to Jung, an allusion to these association studies, occurred in June 06 in a lecture before a University seminar on jurisprudence: "Tatbestandsdiagnostik und Psychoanalyse," *Archiv für Kriminalanthropologie*, XXVI (1906) = "Psychoanalysis and the Establishment of the Facts in Legal Proceedings," SE IX; cf. p. 104: "[These experiments] only became significant and fruitful when Bleuler in Zürich and his pupils, especially Jung, began to turn their attention to . . . 'association experiments.'"

[4] Holograph: *Ihr collegial ergebener.* (Concerning salutations and complimentary closings in general, see the introduction.)

2 J

Dear Professor Freud,[2] Burghölzli-Zürich, 5 October 1906[1]

Please accept my sincerest thanks for the present you kindly sent me. This collection of your various short papers[3] should be most welcome to anyone who wishes to familiarize himself quickly and thoroughly with your mode of thought. It is to be hoped that your scientific following will continue to increase in the future in spite of the attacks which Aschaffenburg,[4] amid the plaudits of the pundits, has made on your theory—one might almost say on you personally. The distressing thing about these attacks is that in my opinion Aschaffenburg fastens on externals, whereas the merits of your theory are to be found in the psychological realm of which modern psychiatrists and psychologists have somewhat too scanty a grasp. Recently I conducted a lively correspondence[5] with Aschaffenburg about your theory and espoused this standpoint, with which you, Professor, may not be entirely in agreement. What I can appreciate, and what has helped us here in our psychopathological work, are your psychological views, whereas I am still pretty far from understanding the therapy and the genesis of hysteria because our material on hysteria is rather meagre. That is to say your therapy seems to me to depend not merely on the affects released by abreaction but also on certain personal rapports,[5a] and it seems to me that though the genesis of hysteria is predomi-

---

[1] For the printed letterhead (on a sheet 8¼ x 12″), see facsimile. Jung was then living with his wife and two children in a flat in the main building of the Burghölzli, in the eastern part of Zürich. See plate I. / This letter was published in *Letters*, ed. G. Adler, vol. 1.

[2] Holograph: *Hochgeehrter Herr Professor*, an even more formal salutation. In his next letter he changed to the slightly more deferential *Hochverehrter Herr Professor*, which with occasional variations he used until 111 J.

[3] *Sammlung kleiner Schriften zur Neurosenlehre*, Vol. I (Vienna, 1906) = *Collected Short Papers on the Theory of the Neuroses*, in various vols. of SE; most of those comprising Vol. I, and the preface, are in SE III.

[4] Gustav Aschaffenburg (1866–1944), professor of psychiatry and neurology in Heidelberg, later Halle and Cologne; after 1939 in U.S.A., teaching and practicing in Baltimore and Washington. His criticism was made at the Congress of South-West German Neurologists and Psychiatrists, Baden-Baden, 27 May 1906; published as "Die Beziehungen des sexuellen Lebens zur Entstehung von Nerven- und Geisteskrankheiten," *Münchener medizinische Wochenschrift*, LIII:37 (11 Sept. 06). See Jones, II, p. 124/111.

[5] This correspondence is now apparently lost.

[5a] Cf. below, 19 J n. 1.

4

Dr. med. C. G. JUNG
PRIVAT-DOZENT D. PSYCHIATRIE
AN DER UNIVERSITÄT
ZÜRICH

Burghölzli-Zürich, den 5. X. 1906.

Hochgeehrter Herr Professor!

Empfangen Sie meinen ergebensten Dank für Ihre gütige Zusendung. Diese Sammlung Ihrer verschiedenen kleinen Schriften ist Ihnen hochwillkommen mir, der sich rasch und gründlich in Ihre Anschauungsweise einleben will. Hoffentlich wird in Zukunft sich Ihre wissenschaftliche Gemeinde immer fort mehren, trotz der Angriffe, welche Aschaffenburg unter dem Beifall der Autoritäten auf Ihre Lehre, man möchte fast sagen, auf Ihre Person gemacht hat. Das Betrübende an diesem Angriff ist, dass nach meinem Dafürhalten Aschaffenburg sich an Äusserlichkeiten klammert, während das Verdienst Ihrer Lehre auf dem psychologischen Gebiete liegen, welches Psychiater und Psychologe moderner Observanz etwas zu wenig beherrschen. Ich habe vor Kurzem über Ihre Lehre mit Aschaffenburg eine lebhafte Correspondenz geführt und dabei obigen Standpunkt vertreten, mit dem Sie hochverehrter Herr Professor, vielleicht nicht ganz einverstanden sind. Was ich ableiten kann,

und was uns hier psychopathologisch gefördert hat, das
sind Ihre psychologischen Anschauungen, während die
Therapie und die Hysteriogenese bei unserm etwas spärlichen
Hysteriematerial meinem Verständnis nach ziemlich fern
steht; d. h. Ihre Therapie scheint mir nicht bloss auf den
Affecten des Abreagierens, sondern auch auf günstigem persönlichen Rapporten zu beruhen, und die Hysteriogenese scheint
mir zwar eine überwiegend, aber nicht ausschliesslich
sexuale zu sein. Denglichen Standpunkt nehme ich auch
Ihrer Sexualtheorie gegenüber ein. Während Aschaffenburg ausschliesslich auf diesen delicaten theoretischen Fragen
herumreitet, vergisst er die Hauptsache, Ihre Psychologie,
aus welcher die Psychiatrie einmal gewiss unerschöpfliche
Gewinn ziehen wird. Ich hoffe Ihnen bald ein kleines
Buch zusenden zu können, indem ich die Dementia praecox
und ihre Psychologie von Ihrem Standpunkte aus be-
trachte. Ich veröffentliche darin auch deueren Fall,
in dem ich Bleuler auf die Berhandensein Ihrer Principien
aufmerksam machte, damals noch unter lebhaftem
Widerstand einerseits. Wie Sie wissen, ist aber Bleuler jetzt
völlig bekehrt.

                    Mit vorzüglicher Hochachtung
                    Ihr dankbar ergebener
                         C. G. Jung.

Jung, 5 Oct. 06 (2 J, p. 2)

nantly, it is not exclusively, sexual. I take the same view of your sexual theory. Harping exclusively on these delicate theoretical questions, Aschaffenburg forgets the essential thing, your psychology, from which psychiatry will one day be sure to reap inexhaustible rewards. I hope to send you soon a little book[6] of mine, in which I approach dementia praecox and its psychology from your standpoint. In it I have also published the case[7] that first drew Bleuler's[8] attention to the existence of your principles, though at that time with vigorous resistance on his part. But as you know, Bleuler is now completely converted.

With many thanks,

Very truly yours,[9] C. G. JUNG

3 F

Dear colleague, 7 October 1906, Vienna, IX. Berggasse 19

Your letter gave me great pleasure. I am especially gratified to learn that you have converted Bleuler. Your writings have long led me to suspect that your appreciation of my psychology does not extend to all my views on hysteria and the problem of sexuality, but I venture to hope that in the course of the years you will come much closer to me than you now think possible. On the strength of your splendid analysis of a case of obsessional neurosis,[1] you more than anyone must know how consummately the sexual factor hides and, once discovered, how helpful it can be to our understanding and therapy. I continue to hope

[6] "The Psychology of Dementia Praecox"; see below, 9 J n. 1.
[7] Probably the case of B. St., ibid., CW 3, pars. 198ff.
[8] Paul Eugen Bleuler (1857–1939), professor of psychiatry at the University of Zürich, director of the Burghölzli Hospital. In 1898, after 12 years as director of the Rheinau (Cant. Zürich) asylum, succeeded Forel (see 17 J n. 4) at Burghölzli, serving as head until 1927. One of the great pioneers of psychiatry, he revised the entire concept of dementia praecox, renaming it schizophrenia (see below, 272 J n. 7, for his influential book); made major contributions, working under the direct impact of the psychoanalytic method, to the understanding of autism and ambivalence. He may actually have been receptive to Freud's ideas as early as 1901, when he had Jung report to the Burghölzli staff on Freudian dream-interpretation. He was a lifelong advocate of alcoholic abstinence. His *Lehrbuch der Psychiatrie* (1916; tr. A. A. Brill, *Textbook of Psychiatry*, 1924) is still standard.
[9] Holograph: *Mit vorzüglicher Hochachtung / Ihr dankbar ergebener.*

[1] "Psychoanalysis and Association Experiments," CW 2, esp. par. 666.

that this aspect of my investigations will prove to be the most significant.

For reasons of principle, but also because of his personal unpleasantness, I shall not answer Aschaffenburg's attack. It goes without saying that my judgment of it would be rather more severe than yours. I find nothing but inanities in his paper, apart from an enviable ignorance of the matters he is passing judgment on. He is still taking up arms against the hypnotic method that was abandoned ten years ago and he shows no understanding whatever of the simplest symbolism (see his footnote),[2] the importance of which any student of linguistics or folklore could impress on him if he is unwilling to take my word for it. Like so many of our pundits, he is motivated chiefly by an inclination to repress sexuality, that troublesome factor so unwelcome in good society. Here we have two warring worlds and soon it will be obvious to all which is on the decline and which on the ascendant. Even so, I know I have a long struggle ahead of me, and in view of my age (50) I hardly expect to see the end of it. But my followers will, I hope, and I also venture to hope that all those who are able to overcome their own inner resistance to the truth will wish to count themselves among my followers and will cast off the last vestiges of pusillanimity in their thinking. Aschaffenburg is otherwise unknown to me, but this paper gives me a very low opinion of him.

I am eagerly awaiting your forthcoming book on Dem. praecox. I must own that whenever a work such as yours or Bleuler's appears it gives me the great and to me indispensable satisfaction of knowing that the hard work of a lifetime has not been entirely in vain.

Yours very sincerely, DR. FREUD

My "transference" ought completely to fill the gap in the mechanism of cure (your "personal rapport").

4 J

Dear Professor Freud,   Burghölzli-Zürich, 23 October 1906

By the same post I am taking the liberty of sending you another offprint containing some more researches on psychoanalysis.[1] I don't

---

[2] Note 18 in Aschaffenburg's paper.

[1] Apparently "Assoziation, Traum und hysterisches Symptom," *Journal für Psy-*

think you will find that the "sexual" standpoint I have adopted is too reserved. The critics will come down on it accordingly.

As you have noticed, it is possible that my reservations about your far-reaching views are due to lack of experience. But don't you think that a number of borderline phenomena might be considered more appropriately in terms of the other basic drive, *hunger*: for instance, eating, sucking (predominantly hunger), kissing (predominantly sexuality)? Two complexes existing at the same time are always bound to coalesce psychologically, so that one of them invariably contains constellated aspects of the other. Perhaps you mean no more than this; in that case I have misunderstood you and would be entirely of your opinion. Even so, however, one feels alarmed by the positivism of your presentation.

At the risk of boring you, I must abreact my most recent experience. I am currently treating an hysteric with your method. Difficult case, a 20-year-old Russian girl student, ill for 6 years.[2]

First trauma between the 3rd and 4th year. Saw her father spanking her older brother on the bare bottom. Powerful impression. Couldn't help thinking afterwards that she had defecated on her father's hand. From the 4th–7th year convulsive attempts to defecate on her own feet, in the following manner: she sat on the floor with one foot beneath her, pressed her heel against her anus and tried to defecate and at the same time to prevent defecation. Often retained the stool for 2 weeks in this way! Has no idea how she hit upon this peculiar business; says it was completely instinctive, and accompanied by blissfully shuddersome feelings. Later this phenomenon was superseded by vigorous masturbation.

I should be extremely grateful if you would tell me in a few words what you think of this story.

Very truly yours, C. G. JUNG

---

chologie und Neurologie, VIII (1906–7) = "Association, Dream, and Hysterical Symptom," CW 2. / Jung here used the spelling *Psychoanalyse*, but subsequently he tended to use *Psychanalyse*. Cf. 7 J n. 2.

[2] The case is described in "The Freudian Theory of Hysteria," CW 4, pars. 53–58 (orig. a paper at Amsterdam, 1907).

5 F

Dear colleague, 27 October 1906, Vienna, IX. Berggasse 19

Many thanks for the new analysis. You certainly did not show too much reserve, and the "transference," the chief proof that the drive underlying the whole process is sexual in nature, seems to have become very clear to you. As to criticism, let us wait until the critics have acquired some experience of their own before attaching any importance to it.

I have no theoretical objection to according equal importance to the other basic drive, if only it would assert itself unmistakably in the psychoneuroses. What we see of it in hysteria and obsessional neuroses can easily be explained by the anastomoses existing between them, that is, by the impairment of the sexual component of the alimentary drive. But I own that these are knotty questions that still require thorough investigation. For the present I content myself with pointing out what is glaringly evident, that is, the role of sexuality. It is possible that later on we shall find elsewhere, in melancholia or in the psychoses, what we fail to find in hysteria and obsessional neurosis.

I am glad to hear that your Russian girl is a student; uneducated persons are at present too inaccessible for our purposes. The defecation story is nice and suggests numerous analogies. Perhaps you remember my contention in my *Theory of Sexuality*[1] that even infants derive pleasure from the retention of faeces. The third to fourth year is the most significant period for those sexual activities which later belong to the pathogenic ones (*ibid.*). The sight of a brother being spanked arouses a memory trace from the first to second year, or a fantasy transposed into that period. It is not unusual for babies to soil the hands of those who are carrying them. Why should that not have happened in her case? And this awakens a memory of her father's caresses during her infancy. Infantile fixation of the libido on the father —the typical choice of object; anal autoerotism. The position she has chosen can be broken down into its components, for it seems to have still other factors added to it. Which factors? It must be possible, by the symptoms and even by the character, to recognize anal excitation as a motivation. Such people often show typical combinations of character traits. They are extremely neat, stingy and obstinate, traits which

[1] *Three Essays on the Theory of Sexuality* (orig. 1905): II, "Infantile Sexuality," SE VII, p. 186.

are in a manner of speaking the sublimations of anal erotism.[2] Cases like this based on repressed perversion can be analysed very satisfactorily.

You see that you have not bored me in the least. I am delighted with your letters.

Sincerest regards,

Yours, DR. FREUD

6 J

Dear Professor Freud,   Burghölzli-Zürich, 26 November 1906

By the same post you will be getting an offprint, a reply to Aschaffenburg's lecture.[1] I have tailored it a bit to my subjective standpoint, so you may not agree with everything in it. I hope I haven't misrepresented you! In any case I wrote it out of honest conviction. Incidentally, I have also championed your cause at the congress of alienists in Tübingen[2] amid stifling opposition; Geheimrat Hoche[3] in particular distinguished himself by the inanity of his arguments. Happily enough Prof. Gaupp[4] then moved a little closer to our side, at least conceding that the matter was worth looking into.

Recently I have been analysing another obsessional neurosis—a German colleague—naturally with sexual complexes dating back to the 7th year! After the very first sitting the anxiety disappeared, but in the meantime has shown a strong tendency to return, of course only in reaction to traumas. It seems to me that it is of the greatest prognostic importance for therapy whether tic-dispositions and well-established stereotyped habits of thought are present (habitual splitting-off

[2] Freud developed this idea two years later in "Character and Anal Erotism" (orig. 1908), SE IX. See below, 77 F n. 6.

[1] "Die Hysterielehre Freud's: Eine Erwiderung auf die Aschaffenburg'sche Kritik," *Münchener medizinische Wochenschrift*, LIII: 47 (20 Nov. 06) = "Freud's Theory of Hysteria: a Reply to Aschaffenburg," CW 4.
[2] Congress of South-West German Psychiatrists, 3–4 Nov. 1906. See *Zentralblatt für Nervenheilkunde und Psychiatrie*, n.s., XVIII (Mar. 07), p. 185, for report, quoting Jung.
[3] Alfred Erich Hoche (1865–1943), professor of psychiatry at Freiburg; an outspoken adversary of psychoanalysis.
[4] Robert Eugen Gaupp (1870–1953), professor of neurology and psychiatry in Tübingen; editor of the *Zentralblatt für Nervenheilkunde und Psychiatrie*.

9

of everything unpleasant). So far as I have seen, the "habitual hysteric" usually reacts badly to analysis.

It may interest you to know that Dr. Frank,[5] formerly director of the Münsterlingen Asylum, has been using your method of analysis with great success here and has built up a large practice in a very short time. Another expert practitioner is Dr. Bezzola,[6] head physician at the Schloss Hard Sanatorium, Canton Thurgau. They are unanimous in their judgement that your method is a breakthrough in neurological practice. They recently said the same thing in Tübingen. Even so, it gives both of them pleasure (all-too-human) to deviate from you on individual points. So you see your views are making rapid progress in Switzerland. In Germany, on the contrary, it looks as though the present generation will have to die out first. Their prejudices are suffocating.

Very truly yours, JUNG

7 J

Dear Professor Freud,　　　　　Burghölzli-Zürich, 4 December 1906

First of all I must tell you how sincerely grateful I am to you for not taking offence at some of the passages in my "apologia."[1] If I allowed myself certain reservations it was not in order to criticize your theory but a matter of policy, as you will surely have noticed. As you rightly say, I leave our opponents a line of retreat, with the conscious purpose of not making recantation too difficult for them. Even so things will be difficult enough. If one attacked an opponent as he really deserves, it would merely result in a disastrous dissension which could have *only* unfavourable consequences. Even as it is, people find my criticism too harsh. If I confine myself to advocating the bare minimum, this is simply because I can advocate only as much as I myself have unquestionably experienced, and that, in comparison with your experience, is naturally very little. I am only beginning to understand many of your formulations and several of them are still beyond me, which does

---

[5] Ludwig Frank (1863–1935), Zürich neurologist, follower of Auguste Forel (see 17 J n. 4).
[6] Dumeng Bezzola (1868–1936), Swiss psychiatrist, from Cant. Graubünden; leader in the abstinence movement.

---

[1] Freud's letter is missing.

10

not mean by a long shot that I think you are wrong. I have gradually learnt to be cautious even in disbelief.

I have seen *ad nauseam* that the opposition is rooted in affect and I also know that no amount of reason can prevail against it.

If I appear to underestimate the therapeutic results of psychanalysis,[2] I do so only out of diplomatic considerations, with the following reflections in mind:

1. Most uneducated hysterics are unsuitable for psychanalysis. I have had some bad experiences here. Occasionally hypnosis gets better results.

2. The more psychanalysis becomes known, the more will incompetent doctors dabble in it and naturally make a mess of it. This will then be blamed on you and your theory.

3. In practice, the concept of hysteria is still far from clear. Countless cases of mild *hebephrenia* still pass under the diagnosis of "hysteria," and here the results are doubtful to bad, as I know from my own experience. (In a few exceptional cases the results have been provisionally good.) How little clarity reigns in this area is shown by a recent publication from the Heidelberg Clinic,[3] where a case of *unquestionable* catatonia was asserted to be hysteria.

For these reasons I consider it more cautious not to put too much emphasis on therapeutic results; if we do, there may be a rapid accumulation of material showing the therapeutic results in a thoroughly bad light, thus damaging the theory as well.

Personally I am enthusiastic about your therapy and well able to appreciate its signal merits. Altogether, your theory has already brought us the very greatest increase in knowledge and opened up a new era with endless perspectives.

Yours very sincerely, JUNG

8 F

Dear colleague,   6 December 1906, Vienna, IX. Berggasse 19

I am sure you will draw your conclusions from this "acceleration of reaction-time"[1] and guess that your last letter has given me great pleas-

[2] Holograph: *Psychanalyse*, a form in earlier use, preferred by the Zürich group.
[3] Unidentified.

[1] Allusion to Jung's association study "Über das Verhalten der Reaktionszeit beim

ure, which is far from being an auxiliary hypothesis. It did indeed seem to me that you had modified your opinions with the purposive idea of pedagogic effect, and I am very glad to see them as they are, freed from such distortion.

As you know, I suffer all the torments that can afflict an "innovator"; not the least of these is the unavoidable necessity of passing, among my own supporters, as the incorrigibly self-righteous crank or fanatic that in reality I am not. Left alone for so long with my ideas, I have come, understandably enough, to rely more and more on my own decisions. In the last fifteen years I have been increasingly immersed in preoccupations that have become monotonously exclusive. (At present I am devoting ten hours a day to psychotherapy.) This has given me a kind of resistance to being urged to accept opinions that differ from my own. But I have always been aware of my fallibility and I have turned the material over and over in my mind for fear of becoming too settled in my ideas. You yourself once remarked that this flexibility of mine indicated a process of development.[2]

I can subscribe without reservation to your remarks on therapy.[3] I have had the same experience and have been reluctant for the same reasons to say any more in public than that "this method is more fruitful than any other." I should not even claim that every case of hysteria can be cured by it, let alone all the states that go by that name. Attaching no importance to frequency of cure, I have often treated cases verging on the psychotic or delusional (delusions of reference, fear of blushing, etc.), and in so doing learned at least that the same mechanisms go far beyond the limits of hysteria and obsessional neurosis. It is not possible to explain anything to a hostile public; accordingly I have kept certain things that might be said concerning the limits of the therapy and its mechanism to myself, or spoken of them in a way that is intelligible only to the initiate. You are probably aware that our cures are brought about through the fixation of the libido prevailing in the unconscious (transference), and that this transference is most readily obtained in hysteria. Transference provides the impulse necessary for understanding and translating the language of the ucs.; where it is lacking, the patient does not make the effort or does not listen when we submit our translation to him. Essentially, one might say, the

---

Assoziationsexperimente," *Journal für Psychologie und Neurologie*, VI:1 (1905) = "The Reaction-time Ratio in the Association Experiment," CW 2.

[2] Jung, "Psychoanalysis and Association Experiments," CW 2, par. 660.

[3] This paragraph and the next are quoted by Jones, II, p. 485/435f.

cure is effected by love. And actually transference provides the most cogent, indeed, the only unassailable proof that neuroses are determined by the individual's love life.

I am delighted with your promise to trust me for the present in matters where your experience does not yet enable you to make up your own mind—though of course only until it does enable you to do so. Even though I look at myself very critically, I believe I deserve such trust, but I ask it of very few persons.

I hope to learn a good deal from your long-announced work on dementia praecox. I have still formed no definite opinion on the dividing line between dementia praecox and paranoia, still less concerning the more recent terms employed in the field, and must own to a certain incredulity toward Bleuler's communication[4] that the repressive mechanisms can be demonstrated in dementia but not in paranoia. But my experience in this field is meager. In this respect therefore I shall try to believe you.

Yours cordially, DR. FREUD

9 J

Dear Professor Freud,   Burghölzli-Zürich, 29 December 1906

I am sincerely sorry that I of all people must be such a nuisance to you. I understand perfectly that you cannot be anything but dissatisfied with my book[1] since it treats your researches too ruthlessly. I am perfectly well aware of this. The principle uppermost in my mind while writing it was: consideration for the academic German public. If we don't take the trouble to present this seven-headed monster with everything tastefully served up on a silver salver, it won't bite, as we have seen on countless occasions before. It is therefore entirely in the

---

[4] Bleuler, "Freudische Mechanismen in der Symptomatologie von Psychosen," *Psychiatrisch-neurologische Wochenschrift*, VIII (1906–7). Abstracted by Jung in his "Referate über psychologische Arbeiten schweizerischer Autoren (bis Ende 1909)," *Jahrbuch*, II:1 (1910) = "Abstracts of the Psychological Works of Swiss Authors (to the end of 1909)," CW 18. (Cited hereafter as "Abstracts." Only those written by Jung himself are in CW 18.)

---

[1] *Über die Psychologie der Dementia praecox: Ein Versuch* (Halle a. S., 1907; Vorwort dated July 1906) = "The Psychology of Dementia Praecox," CW 3. For tr., see below, 124 J n. 3. Freud's letter acknowledging and commenting on the book is missing. / Jung's foreword's quoted in the introduction, above.

interests of our cause to give heed to all those factors which are likely to whet its appetite. For the time being, unfortunately, these include a certain reserve and the hint of an independent judgment regarding your researches. It was this that determined the general tenor of my book. Specific corrections of your views derive from the fact that we do not see eye to eye on certain points. This may be because I. my material is totally different from yours. I am working under enormously difficult conditions mostly with uneducated insane patients, and on top of that with the uncommonly tricky material of Dementia praecox. II. my upbringing, my milieu, and my scientific premises are in any case utterly different from your own. III. my experience compared with yours is extremely small. IV. both in quantity and quality of psychanalytic talent the balance is distinctly in your favour. V. the lack of personal contact with you, that regrettable defect in my preparatory training, must weigh heavily in the scales. For all these reasons I regard the views in my book as altogether provisional and in effect merely introductory. Hence I am extraordinarily grateful to you for any kind of criticism, even if it does not sound at all sweet, for what I miss is opposition, by which I naturally mean justified opposition. I greatly regret that your interesting letter broke off so abruptly.

You have put your finger on the weak points in my dream analysis.[2] I do in fact know the dream material and the dream thoughts much better than I have said. I know the dreamer intimately: he is myself. The "failure of the rich marriage"[3] refers to something essential that is undoubtedly contained in the dream, though not in the way you think. My wife[4] is rich. For various reasons I was turned down when I first proposed; later I was accepted, and I married. I am happy with my wife in every way (not merely from optimism), though of course

---

[2] See "The Psychology of Dementia Praecox," CW 3, pars. 123–33. The dream is given in par. 123: "I saw horses being hoisted by thick cables to a great height. One of them, a powerful brown horse which was tied up with straps and was hoisted aloft like a package, struck me particularly. Suddenly the cable broke and the horse crashed to the street. I thought it must be dead. But it immediately leapt up again and galloped away. I noticed that the horse was dragging a heavy log with it, and I wondered how it could advance so quickly. It was obviously frightened and might easily have caused an accident. Then a rider came up on a little horse and rode along slowly in front of the frightened horse, which moderated its pace somewhat. I still feared that the horse might run over the rider, when a cab came along and drove in front of the rider at the same pace, thus bringing the frightened horse to a still slower gait. I then thought now all is well, the danger is over."

[3] Apparently in Freud's missing letter.

[4] Emma Jung, née Rauschenbach (1882–1955).

14

this does nothing to prevent such dreams. So there has been no sexual failure, more likely a social one. The rationalistic explanation, "sexual restraint," is, as I have said, merely a convenient screen pushed into the foreground and hiding an illegitimate sexual wish that had better not see the light of day. One determinant of the little rider, who in my analysis at first evokes the idea of my chief, is the wish for a boy (we have two girls).[5] My chief is wholly conditioned by the fact that he has two boys.[6] I have been unable to discover an infantile root anywhere. I also have the feeling that the "package" has not been sufficiently clarified. But I am at a loss for an interpretation. Although the dream has not been analysed completely, I still thought I could use it as an example of dream symbolism. The analysis and use of one's own dreams is a ticklish business at best; one succumbs again and again to the inhibitions emanating from the dream no matter how objective one believes oneself to be.

As for the concept of "indistinctness,"[7] I understand very well how distasteful it must appear from your point of view. It is a concept that does not presume too much, and it is certainly not the last word. But in my opinion its advantages are I. that it links up with Wundt's psychology,[8] and II. that it provides a visual image which makes the vague ideas associated with it accessible to ordinary human understanding. In my view it explains merely the *displaceability* of the dream-image, but not the whence and the whither. Instead of an "indistinct" idea one could equally well say an idea "poor in associations." But I prefer "indistinct." I don't know whether an error of principle is lurking in the background. At present only you can decide. But you should not imagine that I am frenetically set on differentiating myself from you by the greatest possible divergence of opinion. I speak of things as I understand them and as I believe is right. Any differentiation would come far too late anyway, since the leading lights in psychiatry have already given me up for lost. It is enough for them to read in a report that I have championed your standpoint.

[5] Agathe ("Agathli"), born 1904; Gret ("Grethli"), born 1906.

[6] Manfred Bleuler (b. 1903), who became a distinguished psychiatrist and, like his father, was professor in Zürich University and director of the Burghölzli (1942–69); see below, 188 F n. 2; and Richard Bleuler (1905–73), who studied agriculture at the E.T.H., Zürich, and spent most of his life in Morocco as a farmer and agricultural consultant.

[7] See CW 3, pars. 133–35.

[8] Wilhelm Wundt (1832–1920), professor of psychology and physiology at Leipzig; his work in experimental psychology foreshadowed Jung's association studies.

Aschaffenburg's paper has whipped up a storm of protest against you. Faced with these fearsome difficulties there is probably no alternative but the *dosis refracta*[9] and another form of medication.

Very sincerely yours, J U N G

10 F

Dear colleague, 30 December 1906[1]

Perhaps you can make some use of this observation in spite of its sketchiness. I have been called in as a consultant in the case of a woman of 26, who gave birth to her first child 6 weeks ago and whose condition set in about the middle of her pregnancy. According to the family doctor, who is not too familiar with our ideas, the woman's explanation of her severe depression is that she had turned herself into an "imbecile" by the habit formed in childhood of retaining her urine so long that its discharge would provide her with sexual sensations. This she continued to do for some time after her marriage. Then she stopped (her illness probably began at that time). She married for love after an acquaintance of six years and a prolonged struggle with her family. She is very much in love with her husband (he is an actor), but has been totally anaesthetic in sexual intercourse. The patient adds that it has never occurred to her to blame her husband for her lack of satisfaction, that she is convinced it is her fault. Her depression was probably connected with her anxiety about her impending delivery. She had kept insisting that she would not be able to give birth normally, and gloated when a forceps delivery was required: she had been right. She maintains quite seriously that her child is a hopeless "imbecile." She has made repeated attempts at suicide (always taking her precautions) and written her husband mournful letters of farewell. Once she actually left home, but only went as far as her sister's flat, where she played the piano. She has occasionally struck her baby. When asked if she loves the child, she says: Yes, but it's not the right one.

States of manic excitation have been noted. One is struck by megalomaniacal statements in reference to her illness: her condition is unprecedented, the doctors will never be able to help her, and it would

---

[9] = *refracta dosi*, "in repeated and divided doses."

[1] On an unheaded sheet 8¼ x 13¼".

take them years to understand her. She argues very acutely, it is impossible to reason with her. She claims to have only the dimmest memory of her life or even of the things she accuses herself of. She says that her brain is affected by "imbecility," that she cannot think clearly and is incapable of reflection, that only her illness is really clear to her. Though on the whole she gives an impression of dejection, there is an unmistakable affectation in her speech and movements. The family doctor says she behaves like an actress. And she does indeed accompany her speech with a perverse mimicry (eye-movements such as I have seen only in paranoia).

Formerly this would have been called masturbatory insanity, an abominable term. Don't you think it's dementia praecox? Don't you find this revelation of the etiology so carefully kept hidden in hysteria interesting?

This is as much as I have been able to ascertain. It is an initial case, I shall probably see her again in a few weeks. Forgive me for taking up your time.

Yours sincerely, DR. FREUD

11 F

Dear colleague,   1 January 1907

You are quite mistaken in supposing that I was not enthusiastic about your book on dementia praecox. Abandon the idea at once. The very fact that I offered criticism ought to convince you. If my feelings had been different, I should have summoned up enough diplomacy to hide them. For it would have been most unwise to offend you, the ablest helper to have joined me thus far. In reality I regard your essay on D. pr. as the richest and most significant contribution to my labours that has ever come to my attention, and among my students in Vienna, who have the perhaps questionable advantage over you of personal contact with me, I know of only one who might be regarded as your equal in understanding, and of none who is able and willing to do so much for the cause as you. I meant my letter to be longer; I broke it off partly for incidental reasons and partly because my guess, confirmed by you, as to the identity of the dreamer, bade me hold my peace. I merely thought that you might have gone so far as to stress the interpretation log = penis and the "alternative"[1] gallop $<$ horse carcer

[1] Holograph: "Wechsel." See Jung, "New Aspects of Criminal Psychology" (orig.

without giving yourself away. Now I learn that you neglected to make the first point for reasons of diplomatic caution. The only point that struck me as incorrect, that is, likely to suggest an incorrect idea, was your identification of the wish fulfilled in the dream, which, as you know, can be disclosed only on completion of the analysis, but which for reasons of fundamental theory must be different from what you state.

If I may be pardoned an attempt to influence you, I should like to suggest that you pay less attention to the opposition that confronts us both and not to let it affect your writings so much. The "leading lights" of psychiatry really don't amount to much; the future belongs to us and our views, and the younger men—everywhere most likely— side actively with us. I see this in Vienna, where, as you know, I am systematically ignored by my colleagues and periodically annihilated by some hack, but where my lectures[2] nevertheless draw forty attentive listeners, coming from every faculty. Now that you, Bleuler, and to a certain extent Löwenfeld[3] have won me a hearing among the readers of the scientific literature, the movement in favour of our new ideas will continue irresistibly despite all the efforts of the moribund authorities. I believe it would be good policy for us to share the work in accordance with our characters and positions, that you along with your chief should try to mediate, while I go on playing the intransigent dogmatist who expects the public to swallow the bitter pill uncoated. But I beg of you, don't sacrifice anything essential for the sake of paedagogic tact and affability, and don't deviate too far from me when you are really so close to me, for if you do, we may one day be played off against one another. In my secret heart I am convinced that in our special circumstances the utmost frankness is the best diplomacy. My inclination is to treat those colleagues who offer resistance exactly as we treat patients in the same situation.

1908), CW 2, par. 1335, where he cites Freud's use of this term. / Concerning "gallop," etc., see "The Psychology of Dementia Praecox," CW 3, par. 130.

[2] Freud lectured at the University every Thursday and Saturday (Jones, I, p. 375/341).

[3] Leopold Löwenfeld (1847–1923), psychiatrist of Munich, had published Freud's Über den Traum (see below, 246 F n. 5) in 1901 in the series Grenzfragen des Nerven- und Seelenlebens, of which he was co-editor. He included contributions by Freud in two other books, "Freud's Psycho-analytic Procedure" (SE VII) in Die psychischen Zwangserscheinungen (1904) and "My Views on the Part Played by Sexuality in the Aetiology of the Neuroses" (SE VII) in the 4th edn. of Sexualleben und Nervenleiden (1906).

18

A great deal might be said about the "indistinctness" which supposedly makes much of the usual dream-work superfluous; too much for a letter. Perhaps you will be coming to Vienna before you go to America[4] (it's nearer). It would give me the greatest pleasure to spend a few hours discussing these matters with you.

If I have written nothing about a considerable part of your book, it is because I am entirely in agreement; that is, I can only accept your elucidations without discussion. (Still, I believe that my case[5] ought to be diagnosed as authentic paranoia.) But I also learned much that was new. I have been very much concerned for some time with the "problem of choice of neurosis," which, as you say quite correctly, is not clarified by my observations. I was entirely mistaken in my first attempt at an explanation; since then I have been cautious. Yes, I am on the way, but I have not yet reached the goal. In regard to your inclination to resort to toxins[6] in this connection, I should like to observe that you omit a factor to which, I am aware, I attribute far more importance than you do at the present time; as you know, I am referring to + + + sexuality.[7] You thrust it aside in dealing with this question, I make use of it but arrive at no solution; so it is not surprising that neither of us knows anything about it. "Nemo me impune lacessit"[8] rings in my ears from my schooldays. The ancients knew how inexorable a god Eros is.

Best wishes for the New Year. May we continue to work together and allow no misunderstanding to arise between us.

Most sincerely, DR. FREUD

My little observation was all ready for you even before I received your letter.

[4] In his analysis of the dream discussed above, Jung had alluded to his strong desire to visit America; see CW 3, par. 124.
[5] Freud, "Further Remarks on the Neuro-Psychoses of Defence" (orig. 1896), SE III, pp. 174ff.: part III, "Analysis of a Case of Chronic Paranoia"; discussed by Jung in "The Psychology of Dementia Praecox," CW 3, pars. 63ff.
[6] See ibid., par. 75. Also see below, 85 J n. 4.
[7] Three crosses were chalked on the inside of doors in peasant houses to ward off danger.
[8] "No one provokes me with impunity." Apparently not ancient, but coined as the motto of the Order of the Thistle, or Order of St. Andrew, of Scotland (*Elvin's Handbook of Mottoes*, 1860).

12 J

Dear Professor Freud,   Burghölzli-Zürich, 8 January 1907

I am sorry I have been so long in answering your last, exceedingly friendly and detailed letter. Afterwards I was rather embarrassed at having played hide-and-seek with my dream. Bleuler, to whom I showed the interpretation in its first version, found it much too forthright. This gave me a welcome opportunity to hide behind the interpretation again in its second version and in that way to act out the complexes myself. There are special reasons why I did not bring in the interpretation log = penis, the chief of which was that I was not in a position to present my dream impersonally: my wife therefore wrote the whole description (!!).

You may very well be right when you counsel me to practise more "therapy" on our opponents, but I am still young, and now and then one has one's quirks in the matter of recognition and scientific standing. Working in a University Clinic, one has to give a great many considerations their due which in private life one would prefer to ignore. But in this respect you may rest assured: I shall never abandon any portion of your theory that is essential to me, as I am far too committed to it.

I am now firmly resolved to come to Vienna during my spring holiday (April), in order to enjoy the long-desired pleasure of a personal conversation with you. I have an awful lot to abreact.

Concerning the question of "toxins," you have again put your finger on a weak spot. Originally I wanted to leave material causes entirely out of my "psychology." But because I feared misunderstandings owing to the notorious dim-wittedness of the esteemed public, I had at least to mention the "toxin." I was acquainted with your view that sexuality may play a role here. Also, I find it a thoroughly congenial idea that a so-called "inner" endocrine secretion may be the cause of these disturbances, and that perhaps the *sex glands* are the makers of the toxins. But I have no proof of this, so I dropped the conjecture. Moreover it seems to me at present that the latter hypothesis is more applicable to *epilepsy*, where the sexual-religious complex holds a central place.

As to your conception of "paranoia," I can see in it only a difference of nomenclature. With "Dementia" praecox one should on no account think first of imbecility (though that can *also* happen!), but rather of a *complex-delirium* with fixations. Paranoia is built up exactly like Dementia praecox, except that the fixation is restricted to a few associations; with few exceptions, clarity of concepts remains unimpaired. There are, however, numerous fluid transitions to what we call D. pr.[1] D. pr. is a most unfortunate term! From your[2] standpoint my D. pr. case could just as well be described as paranoia, which was in fact done in former times.

The case you kindly wrote to me about is of extraordinary interest as a parallel to my own. Many D. pr. patients have the feeling of being "imbecilic." Megalomania and affectation are practically synonymous. (The latter is usually a female accessory.) Both point to a psychic component that has not developed properly either in the erotic or the social sphere, possibly both. The sexual frigidity in marriage seems to indicate that in spite of her marrying for love there is something the matter with this man, that he was not the right one for her. At least that is what we usually find in our cases where sexual anaesthesia appears in the anamnesis. The lack of love for the children bears this out. As a rule women love the husband in the children; if the husband doesn't suit, then the children don't either. Very often the patients hallucinate that the children have been killed. More often only the daughters are killed, which would indicate that the mother is not sexually satisfied, because the husband is either too old or in some way unsuitable. In D. pr., too, "killing" simply means negating or repressing. In an attack of D. pr. all the complexes that haven't been dealt with are always abreacted, quite in accordance with the pattern in hysteria. Only, everything follows a much stormier and more dangerous course, leaving behind various irreparable disturbances in the mental performance and, in particular, increased difficulty in coping with affects and abreacting them. Later a stronger and more generalized occlusion of emotion supervenes, with characteristic stultification of intelligence. But the emotional disturbance always occupies the foreground and makes the diagnosis certain in spite of all the other intellectual stultifications.

Recently I read with satisfaction that Löwenfeld has resolutely come over to our side, at least so far as the anxiety neuroses are concerned. In Germany his voice will carry further than mine. Perhaps your triumphal entry will begin sooner than we think.

---

[1] "Dementia praecox," introduced by Kraepelin, was the term preferred by the Swiss psychiatrists. It has largely been replaced by the term coined by Bleuler, "schizophrenia."

[2] Holograph: *ihrem*, "their" or "her," slip for *Ihrem*, "your."

21

I still owe you an explanation of the term "habitual hysteric."³ It is yet another makeshift. I have been struck by the fact that there are hysterics who live in perpetual conflict with their complexes, exhibiting violent excitement, fluctuations of mood, and wild changes of symptoms. In my limited experience these cases warrant a favourable prognosis. They have a component within them that resists subjugation by the pathogenic complex. On the other hand there are hysterics who live at peace with their symptoms, having not only *habituated* themselves to the symptom but also exploiting it for all kinds of symptomatic actions and chicaneries, and who batten parasitically on the sympathy of everyone in their environment. These are prognostically bad cases who also struggle against analysis with extreme obstinancy. They are the ones I call "habitual hysterics." Perhaps you will see what I mean from this sketchy description. Of course it is only a very crass and superficial classification, but it has been helpful to me in my work so far. Perhaps you can open my eyes in this respect as well. Countless uneducated hysterics (especially the hospital parasites) come into this category.

With most cordial wishes for the New Year and my warmest thanks!

Yours very sincerely, JUNG

13 F

Dear colleague, 13 January 1907¹

I am taking you at your word. So you are coming to Vienna for Easter² and will inform me of your dates in time for me to make arrangements with my patients. I hope we shall discuss many things and broaden our mutual understanding; I am looking forward to the pleasant prospect opened by your acceptance.

Most sincerely, FREUD

³ See above, 6 J par. 2.

¹ Postcard.
² 31 March.

14 J

Dear Professor Freud,   Burghölzli-Zürich, 20 February 1907

I can get away from Zürich at the beginning of March and would like to come to Vienna for a few days then. As my main purpose is naturally a visit with you, I would like to fix the date of my departure to suit your convenience. Unfortunately it is impossible for me to come later in March or in April. I should be grateful if you would drop me a line.

Yours very sincerely, JUNG

15 F

Dear colleague,   21 February 1907, Vienna, IX. Berggasse 19

I am somewhat disappointed that you cannot come at Easter time, since otherwise I am taken up every day from eight to eight with the occupations known to you. But on Sundays I am free, so I must ask you to arrange your visit to Vienna in such a way as to have a Sunday available for me. If possible, I should also like to introduce you to a small circle of followers on a Wednesday evening.[1]

I further assume that you will be willing to forgo the theatre on the few evenings you will be spending in Vienna, and instead to dine with me and my family and spend the rest of the evening with me. I am looking forward to your acceptance and the announcement of your arrival.

With kind regards, DR. FREUD

[1] In 1902, Freud's followers had begun meeting in Freud's waiting-room on Wednesday evenings—the so-called "Psychological Wednesday Evenings." In 1908 the group became the Vienna Psychoanalytic Society, and in 1910 the meetings were moved to a room in the College of Physicians. See Herman Nunberg's introduction to *Minutes of the Vienna Psychoanalytic Society, I: 1906–1908*, edited by him and Ernst Federn (New York, 1962), p. xviii.

16 J

Dear Professor Freud, Burghölzli-Zürich, 26 February 1907

It is indeed a great pity that it is impossible for me to come at Easter, and I much regret arriving at a time that doesn't suit you. Unfortunately it can't be managed otherwise. I shall be in Vienna next Saturday evening and hope I may call upon you on Sunday morning at 10 o'clock. I am travelling with my wife and one of my pupils, a nephew of Binswanger in Jena.[1] Perhaps I may, if occasion offers, introduce my wife and Herr Binswanger to you. My wife has relieved me of all obligations while I am in Vienna. I shall take leave, before my departure, to let you know at what hotel I am staying, so that you could if necessary send word there.

Most truly yours, DR. JUNG

The Jungs in Vienna

Jung visited Freud on Sunday, 3 March. See Jones, II, p. 36/32 (where the date is given as Sunday, 27 Feb.) and Jung, *Memories, Dreams, Reflections*, pp. 149/146 (also placed in Feb.). According to L. Binswanger's *Sigmund Freud; Reminiscences of a Friendship* (New York, 1957), he also, with the Jungs, was received by the Freud family, and he and Jung attended the Wednesday meeting of 6 March and participated in the discussion (see *Minutes*, I, p. 144, and below, 23 F n. 2). Binswanger remained a second week in Vienna, and Carl and Emma Jung went on to Budapest, where they visited Philip Stein (see below, 33 J n. 1), then to Fiume and by sea to the resort of Abbazia for a holiday, before returning to Zürich. (For this information, from Mrs. Jung's diary, we are indebted to Mr. Franz Jung.)

[1] Ludwig Binswanger (1881–1966), then on the staff of the Burghölzli and a participant in the word-association experiments. Later at Jena; 1911–56, director of Bellevue, a private clinic at Kreuzlingen, on Lake Constance, in northeastern Switzerland. In 1910, became first president of the Swiss Branch Society of the International Psychoanalytic Association. A founder of existential analysis. His uncle, Otto Binswanger (1852–1929), was professor of psychiatry and director of the psychiatric clinic, Jena University, where Nietzsche had been his patient in 1889–90.

17 J

Dear Professor Freud,   Burghölzli-Zürich, 31 March 1907

You will doubtless have drawn your own conclusions from the prolongation of my reaction-time. Up till now I had a strong resistance to writing because until recently the complexes aroused in Vienna were still in an uproar. Only now have things settled down a bit, so that I hope to be able to write you a more or less sensible letter.

The most difficult item, your broadened conception of sexuality, has now been assimilated up to a point and tried out in a number of actual cases. In general I see that you are right. *Autoerotism* as the essence of Dementia praecox strikes me more and more as a momentous deepening of our knowledge—where indeed will it end? Your criteria of the acute stage may be equally cogent, but any attempt at proof encounters great difficulties, chiefly technical: D. pr. allows us only limited insight into the personality. A given case may look quite different according to whether the "withdrawal of libido" takes place in a complex that is accessible to consciousness or in an unconscious one. The connections between infantilism and autoerotism also become increasingly clear. I now have to rely on my own independent thinking more than I did before, since Prof. Bleuler's resistances are more vigorous than ever. In particular he contests the purposivity of dreams, which amounts to denying the masking effect of the complexes, the real core of dream interpretation. Bleuler has insuperable unconscious resistances to analysing his own dreams and associations. In my frequent discussions with him it has become quite clear to me that the expression "libido" and, in general, all the terms (no doubt justified in themselves) that have been carried over into the broadened conception of sexuality are open to misunderstanding, or at least are not of didactic value. They actually evoke emotional inhibitions which make any kind of teaching impossible. Thus I had to launch forth into a long discussion in order to make clear to Bleuler what you mean by "libido." Is it not conceivable, in view of the limited conception of sexuality that prevails nowadays, that the sexual terminology should be reserved only for the most extreme forms of your "libido," and that a less offensive collective term should be established for *all* the libidinal manifestations? Herr Rank[1] is another who simply takes the

---

[1] Otto Rank (1886–1939), born Rosenfeld, changed his name because of conflict with his father. 1906–15, secretary of the Vienna Psychoanalytic Society (the so-called "Wednesday evenings"). His *Der Künstler: Ansätze zu einer Sexual-*

broadened conception of sexuality for granted, in such a way that even I, who have been studying your thought intensively for more than 4 years, have difficulty in understanding this conception. The public Herr Rank writes for won't understand it at all. The libidinal relation of hypersensitive persons to the object needs to be illustrated with countless examples of varying intensity. In this way the public would gradually come to see that your terminology is very largely justified. (Especially "pan-sexuality"!) One also has the uncomfortable feeling that Rank "jurat in verba magistri"[2] and lacks empiricism. In reading him I have more than once had to think of Schelling and Hegel. But your theory is pure empiricism and should be presented empirically too. At any rate this beckons me onward as my foremost task. I am therefore looking round for methods that would develop psychanalysis as exactly as possible, hoping by this means to lay the foundations for a scientific popularization of your teachings. One of my next tasks will be to document the wish-dreams in Dementia praecox with a larger amount of empirical material. Only when this and other such preparatory work has been accomplished can I hope to get closer to the heart of the sexual theory. Certainly dreams, as you have said, are best suited for subjective "confirmation," as I have lately been able to demonstrate with some very fine examples. I am no longer plagued by doubts as to the rightness of your theory. The last shreds were dispelled by my stay in Vienna, which for me was an event of the first importance. Binswanger will already have told you of the tremendous impression you made on me. I shall say no more about it, but I hope my work for your cause will show you the depths of my gratitude and veneration. I hope and even dream that we may welcome you in Zürich next summer or autumn. A visit from you would be seventh heaven for me personally; the few hours I was permitted to spend with you were all too fleeting.

Riklin[3] has promised to send you his piece on fairytales as soon as it is finished, though that will not be for some time yet.

---

psychologie (The Artist: The Beginnings of a Sexual Psychology) was published in early 1907. Ph.D., University of Vienna, 1912. Rank was the first lay psychoanalyst, and one of the five original members of the "Committee"; see below, comment following 321 J. In the early 1920's he dissented from psychoanalysis; after 1935, in the U.S.A.

[2] = "Swears to the words of the master."—Horace, *Epistulae*, I, i, 14.

[3] Franz Riklin (1878–1938), psychiatrist at the Burghölzli 1902–4, during which time he collaborated with Jung on the word-association tests; 1904, they published jointly a study of "The Associations of Normal Subjects" (CW 2). 1905–10, at

Forel[4] has recently been in Zürich, and I took the opportunity of having him interviewed by a friend. It turns out that he hasn't the faintest idea who you are, and his objection to my work is that I *pay too little attention to hypnotism*. There's the rub.

My wife and I thank you, your wife, and all your family most cordially for the kind reception you gave us,

Yours gratefully, J U N G

18 F

Dear colleague,[1]   7 April 1907

I am choosing different paper[2] because I don't wish to feel cramped in speaking to you. Your visit was most delightful and gratifying; I should like to repeat in writing various things that I confided to you by word of mouth, in particular, that you have inspired me with confidence for the future, that I now realize that I am as replaceable as everyone else and that I could hope for no one better than yourself, as I have come to know you, to continue and complete my work. I am sure you will not abandon the work, you have gone into it too deeply and seen for yourself how exciting, how far-reaching, and how beautiful our subject is.

Of course I am thinking of a return visit to Zürich, on which occasion I hope you will demonstrate your famous Dem. praecox case,[3] but I doubt if it will be very soon. At the moment I am also troubled

---

the cantonal hospital, Rheinau (Cant. Zürich). Riklin was married to a cousin of Jung's. He remained with Jung after his dissension from Freud but was not actively concerned with analysis. / The piece on fairytales: *Wunscherfüllung und Symbolik im Märchen* (*Schriften zur angewandten Seelenkunde*, 2; 1908) = *Wishfulfillment and Symbolism in Fairy Tales*, tr. William Alanson White (1915).

[4] Auguste Henri Forel (1848–1931), Swiss neurologist and entomologist, from Canton Vaud; director of the Burghölzli before Bleuler. He was a celebrated specialist in hypnosis and a leader of the abstinence movement; rejected psychoanalysis. He had spoken at the tenth anniversary celebration at Clark University in 1899.

[1] Holograph: *Lieber und sehr geehrter Herr College*. The first time Freud used the salutation "Lieber."

[2] Sheets 8 x 6½" with no letterhead.

[3] See "The Psychology of Dementia Praecox," CW 3, pars. 198ff. (case of B. St.).

by the uncertainty of our relations with your chief. His recent defense of our position in the *Münchener medizinische Wochenschrift*[4] made me think he could be relied on, but now you tell me of a very serious swing in the other direction, which like myself you probably interpret as a reaction to the conviction you took home with you. How the "personal complex" casts its shadow on all purely logical thought!

In regard to Dem. pr. I have a proposal to make to you. Since your departure I have jotted down a few ideas on the subject we discussed. I should like to let you have them unless—for two reasons—you would prefer not to see them. First, because you might hit on them yourself, and second because it may be distasteful to you to accept anything whatsoever. I must say that I regard a kind of intellectual communism, in which neither party takes anxious note of what he has given and what received, as a highly estimable arrangement. Please tell me with Ψanalytic frankness whether you would like to take a look at the stuff, whose value you need not overestimate because of this announcement, or would rather not.

I appreciate your motives in trying to sweeten the sour apple, but I do not think you will be successful.[5] Even if we call the ucs. "psychoid," it will still be the ucs., and even if we do not call the driving force in the broadened conception of sexuality "libido," it will still be libido, and in every inference we draw from it we shall come back to the very thing from which we were trying to divert attention with our nomenclature. We cannot avoid resistances, why not face up to them from the start? In my opinion attack is the best form of defense. Perhaps you are underestimating the intensity of these resistances if you hope to disarm them with small concessions. We are being asked neither more nor less than to abjure our belief in the sexual drive. The only answer is to profess it openly.

I feel sure that Rank will not get very far. His writing is positively autoerotic. He is utterly lacking in pedagogic tact. Besides, as you observe, he has not overcome the influence of his previous intellectual fare and wallows in abstractions that one cannot get one's teeth into. But he is more independent of me than it might appear; he is an able man, very young and, what is especially estimable in one so young, thoroughly honest. It goes without saying that we shall expect far more of your manner of treating the material.

[4] Review of the *Sammlung kleiner Schriften zur Neurosenlehre* 1893–1906, in the *Wochenschrift*, LIV:11 (1907).
[5] This paragraph is quoted by Jones, II, p. 486/436.

Bezzola's paper,[6] which he sent me recently in a very impersonal way and probably out of sheer "piety," does not strike me as honest. The appended remarks are the product of a personal cowardice that gives reason to hope that the man will come to a bad end. It seems downright deceitful to conceal the fact that Ψsynthesis is the same thing as Ψanalysis. After all, if we try by analysis to find the repressed fragments, it is only in order to put them together again. The essential difference—that he makes use not of associations but only of sensations—signifies merely that he works exclusively with cases of traumatic hysteria; in other cases this material is not present. And from what I know of the structure of a neurosis, it is usually quite impossible to solve the therapeutic problem solely by disclosing the traumatic scenes. Consequently he is back where Breuer[7] and I were twelve years ago and has learned nothing since then. He deserves a rap on the knuckles for his "piety," but we have better things to do.

This month you will receive two little publications from me, one of them being the *Gradiva*,[8] which may decide you, soon I hope, to contribute something with a more general appeal to the *Papers*.[9] Thank you very much for Riklin's promise. I hope his work meets our special requirements. I shall get into direct touch with him when sending him my *Gradiva*.

At Easter I was at Kahlbaum's[10] in Görlitz and saw a most instructive case that I should have liked to tell you about if this first letter since your visit had not already grown to inordinate length.

My wife[11] was very pleased with your wife's letter. It is the host, not the guest, who owes thanks for the honour and the pleasure. Un-

[6] "Zur Analyse psychotraumatischer Symptome," *Journal für Psychologie und Neurologie*, VIII (1906–7). Criticized in Jung, "Abstracts."

[7] Josef Breuer (1842–1925), Austrian physiologist and physician; author with Freud of *Studies on Hysteria* (orig. 1895; SE II); they later diverged.

[8] See below, 24 J n. 4; for the other, see 23 F n. 2.

[9] *Schriften zur angewandten Seelenkunde* (*Papers on Applied Psychology*), containing works of various authors edited by Freud. The first two numbers, published by Hugo Heller, were Freud's "Gradiva" study and Riklin's on fairytales (see above, 17 J n. 3); Franz Deuticke took over publication with the third number, Jung's *Der Inhalt der Psychose* (1908). See below, 82 F n. 4. For a list of the *Papers*, see appendix 5.

[10] "Dr. Kahlbaum's Ärztliches Pädagogium für jugendliche Nervenkranke" (medical educational establishment for nervous illness of young people) at Görlitz, eastern Germany, founded by Karl Ludwig Kahlbaum (1828–99), eminent psychiatrist; he coined the term "paranoia." See also addenda.

[11] Martha Freud, née Bernays (1861–1951).

fortunately she cannot answer now, because she is suffering from (benign) iridocyclitis, resulting from an upset stomach.[12]

Looking forward to your answer,

Yours cordially, DR. FREUD

19 J

Dear Professor Freud,   Burghölzli-Zürich, 11 April 1907

Many thanks for your long and exceedingly friendly letter! I only fear that you overestimate me and my powers. With your help I have come to see pretty deeply into things, but I am still far from seeing them *clearly*. Nevertheless I have the feeling of having made considerable inner progress since I got to know you personally; it seems to me that one can never quite understand your science unless one knows you in the flesh. Where so much still remains dark to us outsiders only faith can help; but the best and most effective faith is knowledge of your personality. Hence my visit to Vienna was a genuine confirmation.

An excellent analysis I recently made of a Dementia praec. patient has recalled to my mind many of the things we talked about together. I would like to put one question before you which I am quite particularly racking my brains over. The structure of the case was altogether "hysteriform," so much so that during the analysis I lost all consciousness of talking with a Dem. praec. patient. The rapport (transference) was excellent, so that I got the whole story out of her in *one hour*: nothing but sexual events dating back to the 6th year, all quite typical. The patient accepted the transposition[1] with the greatest affect. Insight into the nature and origin of the illness became quite clear to her during the analysis, so that one might have expected considerable improvement. No sign of it the next day; can still come. Thus far everything would be just as it is in hysteria. But the patient has no "hysterical" associations. She reacts quite superficially, has the shortest reaction-times I have ever seen. This means that the stimulus words don't strike through to her affectivity, as they always do in

---

[12] Holograph: *einer Stomakake.*

[1] Holograph: *Transposition.* In this letter and elsewhere, Jung also used the terms *Rapport* and *Übertragung*, "transference," apparently interchangeably, but eventually he fixed on the latter. Cf. below, 27 F preceding n. 10.

hysteria. You will say: no object-libido, but autoerotism. During the association test the complexes appeared starkly split off so that no affects were aroused. But during the analysis it was just the reverse: fragmentary complexes came pouring out *with no resistance*. In such a situation one might have expected that the stimulus words would also hit the complexes, but they didn't. I have the impression that in Dem. praec. the complex constellates the personality to far fewer associable stimuli than it does in hysteria, with the result that there is much less "working through" of the personality by the complex. In hysteria there is always a synthesis of the complex with the whole personality. But in D. pr. the complexes appear to coalesce only spo-radically, at any rate far less than they do in hysteria, let alone with normals. The complexes are largely isolated from one another. You will say: the complexes become autoerotic and contain all the libido. But how does that come about? We find much the same thing in toxic deliria (alcoholism, etc.): fragmentary complexes mixed with elementary hallucinations due to neural stimuli, an unanalysable *mixtum compositum* I could never make head or tail of (psycho-logically!). In these states dull everyday things come to the surface—bits of complexes, endogenic sensory stimuli, etc., but any meaningful constellation is entirely absent. Would this be analogous to the isola-tion of complexes in Dem. praec.? Naturally the effect of the toxin would have to be thought of as very slight. But why the regression to the autoerotic stage? Autocrotism is certainly something infantile, and yet infantilism is utterly different from D. pr. I have even seen that in the galvanometric investigations[2] the splitting off of affects in Dem. praec. goes so far that strong *physical* stimuli do not exert the slightest influence, whereas psychological stimuli still provoke affects. Thus, even with complete analysis and transference no revolutionizing of the personality occurs as it does in hysteria. As a rule nothing whatever happens, the patients have learnt nothing and forgotten nothing but continue to suffer undisturbed. It is as if their personality had disinte-grated into separate complexes which no longer exert any mutual influence. I should be grateful to have your views on this matter.

You will be interested to hear that I have been asked to report on

[2] In 1907 Jung published "On Psychophysical Relations of the Associative Experi-ment," *Journal of Abnormal Psychology*, I; "Psychophysical Investigations with the Galvanometer and Pneumograph in Normal and Insane Individuals," with Frederick Peterson, *Brain*, XXX; "Further Investigations on the Galvanic Phe-nomenon and Respiration in Normal and Insane Individuals," with Charles Rick-sher, *Journal of Abnormal and Social Psychology*, II; all in CW 2.

"Modern Theories of Hysteria" at this year's International Congress in Amsterdam. My opposite number is Aschaffenburg! I shall naturally confine myself entirely to your theory. I feel in my bones that the discussion will be pretty depressing. A. wrote to me recently; he still hasn't understood anything.

I have just finished Rank's book.[3] There seem to be some very good ideas in it though I haven't understood everything by any means. Later I'll read it through again.

Bleuler has now accepted 70% of the libido theory after I demonstrated it to him with a few cases. His resistance is directed chiefly to the word itself. His negative shilly-shallying seems to have been temporarily occasioned by my visit to Vienna. For a very long time Bleuler was a frosty old bachelor who must have done a lot of repressing in his life; hence his unconscious has become very well-filled and influential. All the same, you have a staunch supporter in him, even though sundry *restrictions mentales* will put in an appearance from time to time. Once Bleuler is on to something he knows is right he will never let it go. He possesses the Swiss national virtues to a fault.

I shall be extremely grateful for your thoughts on D. pr., as indeed for any suggestions on your part.

Of course you are right about "libido," but my faith in the efficacy of sweeteners is deep-rooted—for the present.

Bezzola is a confounded fusspot who has to compensate for a highly disagreeable position in life and thinks he can get rich on the crumbs that fall from the master's table. A hoarder of details with no clear over-all vision, but otherwise a decent fellow still in the grim clutches of the unconscious. I found his paper infuriating.

My wife and I have heard with deep regret of your wife's illness and with all our hearts wish her a speedy recovery.

With best regards and gratefully yours, JUNG

---

20 F

Dear colleague,   Vienna, 14 April 1907

You see, my view of our relationship is shared by the world at large. Shortly before your visit, I was asked to give that report in Amsterdam. I declined in haste for fear that I might talk it over with you and

[3] *Der Künstler.* See above, 17 J n. 1.

let you persuade me to accept. Then we found more important things to talk about and the matter was forgotten. Now I am delighted to hear that you have been chosen. But when I was invited, Aschaffenburg was not to be the other speaker; two were mentioned, Janet[1] and a native. Apparently a duel was planned between Janet and myself, but I detest gladiatorial fights in front of the noble rabble and cannot easily bring myself to put my findings to the vote of an indifferent crowd;[2] but my chief reason is that I am eager to hear nothing of science for a few months and to restore my sorely maltreated organism through all sorts of extra-curricular pleasures. Now you will have to measure yourself with Aschaffenburg. I recommend ruthlessness; our opponents are pachyderms, you must reckon with their thick hides.

And in another connection as well I must welcome you as my successor. I had been meaning to speak to you of the case I saw in Görlitz at Easter. Now I hear that he is being sent to you at the Burghölzli, and that you wish information about him from me. Accordingly, I shall write to his father that I am in direct contact with you and report to you on what I have seen. You will find the boy interesting; he will probably derive little benefit from us and we a great deal from him; and above all, he is the first case we shall both have been able to observe directly. I am curious to know whether you will confirm my contention that it is not Dem. pr. but began with obsession and is continuing as hysteria; I have several times observed this reverse development and I am curious to know what your association experiments will have to say of my diagnosis. He is a highly gifted individual, an Oedipus type, loves his mother, hates his father (the original Oedipus was himself a case of obsessional neurosis—the riddle of the Sphinx), has been ill since his eleventh year when the facts of sexuality were revealed to him; return to infancy even in his dress, his rejection of sex is enormous, "comme une maison," as Charcot[3] used to say. What makes him hard to deal with and prevented me from bringing him to Vienna are his screaming fits when he gets excited. Originally they were merely his infantile means of pressure on his

[1] Pierre Janet (1859–1947), French neurologist and psychologist, one of the first to recognize the unconscious, though he was hostile to psychoanalysis. Jung studied with him at the Salpêtrière (institution for aged and insane women) in Paris, 1902–3.

[2] Quoted in Jones, II, p. 125/112.

[3] Jean-Martin Charcot (1825–93), French neurologist, physician-in-charge at the Salpêtrière; famous for his work on hysteria and hypnosis. Freud studied with him in Paris in 1885–86, translated his lectures into German, and named his eldest son after him.

mother. Now his attacks are as follows: He stands outside a door and screams, roars, raves and spits. In observing the scene, one notices *at the first glance*—though a true psychiatrist mustn't see anything that is not in Kraepelin[4]—that he is running two fingers of his right hand up and down in a groove in the door panel (I saw this myself), in other words he imitates a coitus! When I mentioned this to him after his attack, he denied it; then he told me that the kids in school had imitated it with a finger going like this (into the closed hand). At the same time he counts: two, three, four with long pauses, which indeed makes sense in connection with coitus, and his spitting is obviously an imitation of ejaculation. Meanwhile he hears voices (which also occur in his intervals; this of course presents a doubtful diagnostic picture but does not look like paranoia), his expression is one of extreme bitterness and indignation, in short, he is a spectator at a coitus to which he reacts with rage, and if you bear in mind that he slept with his parents up to the age of ten, you can guess whom he is spying on. Of course he is playing both roles, that of the spectator with his disgust and that of the man with his ejaculation. The best is yet to come. Unfortunately he is also organically infantile, including the formation of his genitals which, as he himself tells one with lofty calm, have not developed since he was eleven. Pride has led him to repress his despair over this and all related affects, and these are the source of his attacks. He would never admit that he attaches the slightest importance to this disgusting performance (of which, it so happens, he is incapable)!

I do not know whether this is his only form of attack, or whether he has modified it since our conversation. When you see him, treat him more or less as you would a colleague, he is frightfully proud and quick to take offense, and in my opinion a good deal more intelligent than Aschaffenburg, for instance.

I must assume a period of infantile sexual activity; I was unable to find out anything about it from his parents. But what a lot parents manage to overlook! Since he has a phimosis (a case for Adler!),[5] it seems hardly possible that he failed to masturbate at an early age.

[4] Emil Kraepelin (1856–1926), German clinical psychiatrist, professor at Munich 1903–22; he evolved the system of psychiatric classification and differentiated dementia praecox (his term) from manic-depressive psychosis. His *Psychiatrie: Ein Lehrbuch für Studierende und Ärzte* (1st edn., 1883) has been authoritative in modern psychiatry.
[5] Alfred Adler (1870–1937), since 1902 a member of the Freudian group in Vienna; he was the first president of the Vienna Psychoanalytic Society, and the

What pleases me most is that you don't reject my remarks on dementia. It is the same thing, you know, though I am accustomed to speak of paranoia, because the paranoiac element in dementia requires after all to be explained. And so I shall use my next free moment— today, Sunday, I don't feel up to it—to put my thoughts into intelligible form. I shall not lose sight of these ideas; if I can make something of them, I will, but I am too far away from the material; I hope you get to it sooner.

Nor, for the same reason, shall I answer your dementia questions today. Besides, I doubt if I could answer them properly at such a distance. I merely have the feeling that you are right in stressing the fact that these patients reveal their complexes without resistance and are inaccessible to transference, i.e., show none of its effects. That is exactly what I should like to translate into theory.

Incidentally, it seems quite possible that a true, correctly diagnosed case of hysteria or obsessional neurosis should take a turn toward dementia or paranoia after a certain time. Such a possibility can easily be demonstrated in theory—something of the sort seems possible in the case of the boy from Görlitz.

My wife is doing well enough and thanks you and your wife for your good wishes. With kind regards,

Yours, DR. FREUD

21 J

Dear Professor Freud,   Burghölzli-Zürich, 17 April 1907

Many thanks for your news! Unfortunately I must tell you at once that we have no room at all in the Clinic at present, which is most regrettable. We are once again in a period of fearful overcrowding. At the same time I would like to remind you that our in-patient department, being a State institution, is not prodigally luxurious and caters

first of Freud's important followers to secede, in 1911, when he founded "Individual Psychology." After 1926, he spent much of his time in the U.S.A. and settled there in 1935. Died May 1937 at Aberdeen, Scotland, during a lecture tour. / In his monograph *Studie über Minderwertigkeit von Organen*, published in Feb. 1907 (given as a paper to the Vienna Society on 7 Nov. 06: see *Minutes*, I, p. 36), Adler had noted that in cases of enuresis one frequently finds phimosis, i.e., constriction of the prepuce. See tr., *Study of Organ Inferiority and its Psychical Compensation* (New York, 1917), p. 72.

only for the general public. The board for foreigners amounts only to 10-12 fr. a day at the maximum. The charge for a private attendant is a little more than 2 fr. a day. Cheap and middling to good, therefore. As I said we are inundated at present, so it is quite impossible for us to take your patient. I hope, however, that this will not set a precedent, for I would dearly like to investigate a case with which you too are thoroughly acquainted. It may be that in a few weeks we shall have enough room again.

I can understand how repugnant it must be for you to get into cock fights, for that is exactly how the public looks at it and satisfies its sublimated blood lust. Since I am not so deeply committed and am not defending my own brain-children, it sometimes tickles me to venture into the arena. The identification with you will later prove to be very flattering; now it is *honor cum onere*.

Your case is most interesting. The attacks look more hysteriform than catatonic. The voices are highly suspicious, indicating a very deep split and a brittleness of the *niveau mental*. I have often had cases that passed with apparent smoothness from hysteria or obsessional neurosis straight into D. pr. But I don't know what to make of them. Were they already D. pr., but unbeknownst to us? We still know far too little, in fact nothing, about the innermost nature of D. pr., so it may well fare with us as it did with the old doctors who assumed that croupous pneumonia occasionally passed over into TB. We only see how at a certain period in the development of various interrelated complexes the rapport with the environment comes to a partial or total stop, the influence of the objective world sinks lower and lower and its place is taken by subjective creations which are hypertoned *vis-à-vis* reality. This state remains stable in principle, fluctuating only in intensity. There are even cases who actually *die* of autoerotism (acute condition, no post-mortem findings). I saw one again only recently. (Symbolic death?) If in such cases there are no grave anatomical anomalies, we must assume "inhibition." But this is accompanied by a positively hellish compulsion to autoerotism (manifested in other cases too), going far beyond all known limits; perhaps a compulsion due to some organic malfunctioning of the brain. Autoerotism is so consummately purposeless—suicide from the start—that everything in us must rebel against it. And it happens nevertheless.

This "nevertheless" reminds me that not long ago an educated young catatonic drank up half the chamber-pot of a fellow sufferer, with obvious relish. He is an early masturbator, and enjoyed premature sexual activity with his sister. Catatonic since puberty. Hallucinates the said sister, who occasionally appears as *Christ* (bisexuality). Then deterioration set in, intense hallucinations, partly unidentifiable, partly concerned with the sister. Mounting excitement, masturbates incessantly, sticks his finger rhythmically into mouth and anus alternately, drinks urine and eats stool. A very pretty autoerotic homecoming, is it not?

The following things have struck me in several cases: feelings of sexual excitement frequently get displaced in (female) D. pr. patients from their original site towards and round the anus. Recently I saw a case where they were localized in the pit of the stomach. Frequent anal masturbation in D. pr.! Does the pit of the stomach also belong to the infantile sexual theory? I have not yet observed displacements towards other parts of the body.

Catalepsy is uncommonly frequent in the acute phases of catatonia. In hysteria I have observed only one case where a cataleptically stiffened arm was a penis symbol. But what is the general stiffness and *flexibilitas cerea* in catatonia? Logically it too should be psychologically determined. It goes together with the severest symptoms of the deepest phase, when the crassest autoerotisms are wont to appear. Catalepsy seems to be more common among women; at any rate it is more common among persons of both sexes who fall ill early, just as, in general, their disintegration apparently goes much deeper and the prognosis is correspondingly worse than with those who fall ill late, and who usually stop short at delusional ideas and hallucinations (Lugaro's hypothesis).[1]

Bleuler is leaning more and more towards autoerotism but in theory only. Here you have your "verité en marche."

Can you lay hands on *The Journal of Abnormal Psychology*? In Vol. I, No. 7 Sollier[2] reports "troubles cénesthésiques" at the onset of D. Pr., associated with alteration of the personality. He claims to have observed the same thing in hysteria at the moment of "personality restitution" (transposition?): storms of affect, throbbing of

---

[1] Ernesto Lugaro (1870–1940), Italian psychiatrist. It has not been possible to identify his "hypothesis," beyond Dr. Assagioli's suggestion (personal communication) that it refers to Lugaro's theory of pseudo-hallucinations.

[2] Paul Sollier, "On Certain Cenesthetic Disturbances, with Particular Reference to Cerebral Cenesthetic Disturbances as Primary Manifestations of a Modification of the Personality," *Journal of Abnormal Psychology*, II:1 (Apr.–May 1907). (Jung's citation is incorrect.) Sollier (1861–1933) was a psychiatrist in Boulogne-sur-Seine.

the blood vessels, fear, explosions, whistlings, acute pains in the head, etc.[†] Have you seen anything like it? Excuse my barrage of questions!

Gratefully yours, JUNG

[†] Rousseau (*Confessions*) similar case.[3]

22 F   A *Few Theoretical Remarks on Paranoia*[1]

The basic situation is roughly this: a person (f.)[2] conceives a desire for intercourse with a man. It is repressed and reappears in the following form: people outside say she has this desire, which she denies. (Or else: the intercourse has taken place during the night against her will. But this is not the primary form.)

What has happened in this type of repression and reappearance typical of paranoia? An idea—the content of a desire—has arisen and persisted, it has even ceased to be ucs. and becomes cs. But this idea which originated within has been projected outward and reappears as perceived reality, against which repression can manifest itself anew as opposition. Belief has been withheld from the wish-affect; with the reappearance of the idea a contrasting, hostile affect is manifested.

The projection requires explanation. What is the condition for the outward projection of an inner affectively cathected process? A glance at the normal situation: Originally our cs. registers only two types of experience. From outside, perceptions (P), which as such are not affectively cathected and have qualities; from within it experiences "sensations," which are manifestations of drives in certain organs. These are only in small degree qualitative, but are capable of strong quantitative cathexis. What shows such quantity is located within, what is qualitative and without affect is localized outside.

Of course this is crudely schematic. All processes of mental representation, thought, etc. are composed of elements from both sides.

What arrives at the P. end meets with immediate belief; what originates within the psyche is subjected to a *reality test* (which consists in reduction to P.) and to the *repressive tendency* which is directed against the unpleasure qualities of the sensations.

---

[3] *Confessions*, Part I, Book VI, 1738.

---

[1] Written and posted between 14 and 20 Apr. 07. On 11 x 8¾" sheets.
[2] Holograph: *f.* inserted before *Person*.

The sexual instinct is originally autoerotic, later on it lends affective cathexis, object-love, to memory-images. A wish fantasy such as that presupposed above is to be regarded as a libidinal object-cathexis, because it must be subjected to repression before it becomes conscious. This can occur in various ways (corresponding to the salient characteristics of the various ΨNeuroses). *If the image-content has been projected upon the P. end, its libidinal cathexis must first have been removed from it. Then it has the character of a perception.*[3]

In paranoia the libido is withdrawn from the object; a reversal of this is *grief*, in which the object is withdrawn from the libido.

The cathexis lost by the image of the object is first replaced by belief. Where the libido has gone is indicated by the *hostility to the object*,[3] found in paranoia. This is an endogenous perception of libido withdrawal. In view of the relation of compensation between object-cathexis and ego-cathexis, it seems likely that the cathexis withdrawn from the object has returned to the ego, i.e., has become autoerotic.

The paranoid ego is consequently hypercathected, egoistic, megalomanic. A counterpart to the process here assumed is provided by anxiety hysteria. Hysteria is very generally characterized by an excess of object-cathexes. It is extreme object-love and even overlays the autoerotic early period with object-fantasies (seduction). It takes as an object anything that bears the remotest relation to a normal object, even places, for which reason hysteria attaches to places (agoraphobia) or to the vicinity of the loved one, as opposed to the instability, the travel urge, of dementia praecox.

In anxiety hysteria the opposite of what we have assumed for paranoia occurs. *Outward stimuli, i.e. P., are treated* like *inner affectively cathected processes*, a mere verbal representation has the effect of an inner experience; proneness to fear. The mere withdrawal of the object-cathexes into the ego—into the autoerotic sphere—occurs as an organic process with transformation of affect (into unpleasure), to wit, in so-called hypochondria. It is only the use of this mechanism for purposes of repression that results in paranoia. Thus hypochondria is related to paranoia as purely somatic anxiety neurosis is to hysteria that goes through the Ψ.[4] Often enough hypochondria approaches paranoia, shifts into it, or mingles with it.

Now it should not be forgotten that in ΨN we are always dealing with unsuccessful defence. That attempted in paranoia seems surest to

---

[3] Holograph: underlined in blue pencil, apparently by Jung.
[4] I.e., hysteria that is psychologically determined.

39

fail, i.e., the libido returns to its object, tries to prevail, and with a reversal to unpleasure clings to the perceptions into which the object has been transformed.

The return-struggle is more clearly evident in paranoia than in the other neuroses. The libidinal cathexis heightens the images that have become perceptions, transforming them into hallucinations. The clinical picture corresponds to this *secondary* defensive struggle against the libidinal fantasy, which now appears from a quarter of the psychic apparatus which ordinarily gives access only to reality.

It should further be considered that as a rule this process is only partial, i.e., affects only one component of the libidinal object-cathexis. All the repressed libido is gradually transformed into belief, the *delusion* is so intense because it has the libido as its source. Delusion is a libido-inspired belief in reality.

Summary. Projection (like conversion, etc.) is a variety of repression, in which an image becomes conscious as perception; the affect pertaining to it is detached and withdrawn into the ego with a reversal into unpleasure. This affect (the libidinal cathexis) then tries, starting from the perceptual end, to force itself once more on the ego.

More readily than other Ψneuroses, paranoia can be explained by normal Ψ processes.

As you see, a formula for the especially successful type of repression in the hallucinatory forms of insanity par excellence (amentia) can be derived from the relations here discussed between libidinal object-cathexes and ego-cathexes. (Cf. the old analysis in *Collected Short Papers*.)[5]

With kind regards, DR. FREUD

Anyone who gives more than he has is a rogue.

23 F

Dear colleague,   21 April 1907

It's splendid of you to ask so many questions even though you know that I can answer only a few of them. I too am coming to regard our exchange of ideas as a necessity, at least on Sundays.

I see that you have come closer to my idea that the regression to auto-

[5] See above, 11 F n. 5; in the *Sammlung kleiner Schriften zur Neurosenlehre*, I (1906).

erotism occurs also in Dem. p. I can do nothing without the direct impact of the material, and I am well aware that one learns more from three detailed analyses than one can ever piece together at one's desk. What I recently sent you from that source is of value only to the extent that it corresponds to what can be inferred from the material of the two other ΨΝ (I am sure you will understand these abbreviations and not take them amiss). On the whole I believe that we must be patient and not expect to answer certain questions until we have learned a good deal more. Still, we are entitled to conjectures, e.g., concerning cases which begin in hysterical or obsessional form. On a theoretical basis, it is easy to understand that at first the one form of defence customary in hysteria (the suppression within the unconscious of the image cathected with libidinal affect) is attempted, and then, if this does not suffice, the far more radical and dangerous method of splitting off the cathexis and retracting it into the ego. On this assumption, the case would start out as hysteria and develop into D. pr.

As you surely see, it would be incorrect to say that hysteria develops into D. pr.; rather, the hysteria is broken off and replaced by D. pr. These phrases of ours become meaningful only when we take account of certain aspects of the process of repression. Other cases can begin directly with the method of defence characteristic of D. pr.; still others do not go beyond hysteria, because somatic compliance permits of an ample discharge. An analogous example in the organic field would be the relationship between locomotor ataxia and general paralysis. As a rule general paralysis occurs only in mild cases of locomotor ataxia; it is well known that the usual tertiary process does not advance if typical syphilitic blindness has developed. To ascertain this at the very beginning of the process requires diagnostic subtlety and depth of experience.

Incidentally, I am very much surprised that in your cases the return to autoerotism is so strikingly successful. In all probability this really is contingent on their youth, and the predisposing moment, the factor our authors call "idiopathic," would be an incomplete transition from autoerotism to object-love in the past. Dementia would correspond roughly to the success and paranoia to the failure of this return, i.e., of the libido from perceptions. With all the intervening gradations. I believe that the return to autoerotism is indeed as catastrophic as you suppose for the integrity of the personality. In the entire process the various libido components and especially bisexuality should be taken into account. I would give a good deal to be able to abandon my shop and join you in studying this undoubtedly most instructive

41

and readily understandable form of ΨN, but unfortunately I have to earn a living and must keep my nose to the grindstone, which now more than ever makes me very tired.

I do not believe that a Ψ determinant is absolutely indispensable in the case of catatonia (I shall have to reread Riklin[1]). The displacement of cathexis must involve considerable modifications in innervation, i.e., physiological effects, as in hysteria. Of course I interpret the displacement of sexual stimulation to the anal region in Dem. pr. and the other perversions as well, in line with my *Theory of Sexuality*, not as displacements of the erogenous zones, but as reinstatements of their old primary power, which, according to my theory, are magnificently evident in Dem. pr. The pit of the stomach belongs to the oral zone or to the upper section of the alimentary tract which includes the stomach, see hysteria. I have not read Sollier's article. What I do know of his work (hysteria, memory) is inept chatter and crude misinterpretation of nature. You must think that I am playing the Pope again, fulminating against heretics. But can I look at these things in two ways?

I must say that what you told me in your next to last letter about the reactions of a Dem. pr. patient—lack of resistance in analysis and fragility of transference—cries out for a diagnosis of autoerotism. That this autoerotism should present an entirely different picture than in a child is self-evident. After all, senile imbecility is also very different from child behaviour, though it represents a regression to the infantile stage. In both cases the ability to progress is absent. We find the same differences between an aphasic and a child learning to speak.

Yesterday my comparison of obsessional neurosis and religion appeared in the first number of the new *Zeitschrift für Religionspsychologie*.[2] I have not yet received any offprints. And I am also still waiting for *Gradiva*.

Perhaps you will be able to take on the boy from Görlitz later. His case ought to be most instructive.

Don't take the burden of representing me too hard. You are so enviably young and independent. Perhaps you will incur the onus but not the odium of our cause, and in later years you will reap the full

---

[1] "Beitrag zur Psychologie der kataleptischen Zustände bei Katatonie," *Psychiatrisch-neurologische Wochenschrift*, VII:32/33 (1906). See Jung, "Abstracts," CW 18.

[2] "Zwangshandlungen und Religionsübung" = "Obsessive Actions and Religious Practices," SE IX. Freud had read part of it at the 6 Mar. meeting of the Wednesday Society, at which Jung and Binswanger were guests (not on 2 Mar., as Jones states, II, p. 36/32; also ed. note, SE IX, p. 116). See *Minutes*, I, p. 142.

reward of your labours. Come to think of it, considering the importance of the cause, the resistance to it is perhaps not so exorbitant.

Write me more news from Burghölzli soon! I feel sure there will be an audible uproar in learned circles when you and Bleuler come out in support of the libido theory.

Yours cordially, DR. FREUD

24 J

Dear Professor Freud,   Burghölzli-Zürich, 13 May 1907

First of all I must beg you to excuse the long pause I have allowed myself. I could not and did not want to write to you until I had seen things a bit more clearly. Above all I wanted to absorb and digest your "Remarks on Paranoia." But first the news! It will soon come to your attention that an assistant of Kraepelin's has slaughtered me with a review of my Dem. pr. book in Gaupp's *Zentralblatt*.[1] You are included too, of course. His helpless flounderings are touching to see! If you don't have the *Zentralblatt* I can send you an offprint for your edification. In spite of everything, he has felt impelled to write a whole article about it. At least they have now started using heavy artillery. But in the end the thing has got me down again, for I see how infinitely difficult it is to communicate your ideas to the public.

Autoerotism has yet another triumph to chalk up. We have recently succeeded in analysing an educated and very intelligent young female catatonic who is blessed with very good introspection. She always walks around stiff and affectless and it is difficult to keep her in a good ward because from time to time she smears herself with excrement. She *spontaneously* admitted to us that since her illness she has become like a child in her thoughts, masses of old infantile memories pop up in which she gets completely submerged. She says the smearing came about simply because it occurred to her (in one of those "absent-minded" states) not to sit on the toilet but to defecate on a piece of paper on the floor. Oddly enough that is what she did as a child. She suffered from constipation and got too tired on the seat, then started

---

[1] Max Isserlin, "Über Jung's 'Psychologie der Dementia praecox' und die Anwendung Freud'scher Forschungsmaximen in der Psychopathologie," *Zentralblatt für Nervenheilkunde und Psychiatrie*, n.s., XVIII (May 1907). Isserlin (1879–1941), Munich neurologist, Kraepelin's assistant; was an adversary of psychoanalysis. Died in England as a refugee.

defecating on a piece of paper. In her illness localized states of excitement occurred, with masturbation. It is significant that sexuality *sensu strictiori* does not have any effect on the psyche whatever, but in the great majority of cases remains *local* and is felt as something alien and oppressive, or at any rate no corresponding repression takes place.

I have mulled over your "Remarks on Paranoia" several times, also together with Bleuler. The derivation of delusional ideas from affects (= libido) is perfectly clear to us. It seems to me, however, that in your explanation of "outward projection" you can mean only the genesis of the idea of persecution. But in D. pr. every single thing is projected outwards. The delusional ideas are as a rule a crazy mixture of wish-fulfilment and the feeling of being injured. The following analogy has always struck me as enlightening: the religious ecstatic who longs for God is one day vouchsafed a vision of God. But the conflict with reality also creates the opposite for him: certainty turns into doubt, God into the devil, and the sublimated sexual joy of the *unio mystica* into sexual anxiety with all its historical spectres. Here we see how the wish directly produces the projection outwards because the wish for reality is present. This same wishing can often be demonstrated with ease in the unconscious of the paranoiac, but usually only the conflict becomes objectivated. Then the feeling of persecution is often compensated by megalomania, though this leads less often to objectivations. In paranoid Dem. pr. the wish-fulfilment is certainly very much more frequent. When you say that the libido withdraws from the object, you mean, I think, that it withdraws from the *real object* for normal reasons of repression (obstacles, unattainability, etc.) and throws itself on a fantasy copy of the real one, with which it then proceeds to play its classic autoerotic game. The projection towards the perception end springs from the original wish for reality, which, if unattainable, creates its own reality by hallucination. But in psychosis everything goes askew because only the conflict is experienced as objectively real. Why this is so is still not quite clear to me; perhaps the conflicting component is reinforced by the normal corrective component. I should be extremely grateful for any correction you can make of my views. My one hope is that it will bring me closer to you.

Bleuler still misses a clear definition of autoerotism and its specifically psychological effects. He has, however, accepted the concept for his Dem. pr. contribution to Aschaffenburg's Handbook.[2] He

[2] See below, 272 J n. 7.

doesn't want to say autoerotism (for reasons we all know), but prefers "autism" or "ipsism." I have already got accustomed to "autoerotism."

Your Görlitz patient now has unquestionably catatonic symptoms on the lowest autoerotic level—he's started smearing himself. So his father wrote me recently. Any psychic treatment, even mere analysis, is completely out of the question, as unfortunately I see every day with our own catatonics.

Maeder is now publishing dream analyses in the latest *Archives de psychologie*.[3]

Your *Gradiva*[4] has just arrived. Heartiest thanks! I shall start reading it at once with great expectations.

At the moment I am treating a 6-year-old girl for excessive masturbation and lying after alleged seduction by her foster-father. Very complicated! Have you had experience with such small children? Except for a colourless and affectless, totally ineffectual representation of the trauma in consciousness, I have not succeeded in obtaining any abreaction with affect, either spontaneous or suggested. At present it looks as if the trauma were a fake. Yet where does the child get all those sexual stories from? The hypnosis is good and deep, but with the utmost innocence the child evades all suggestions for enacting the trauma. One thing is important: at the first sitting she spontaneously hallucinated a "sausage which the woman said would get fatter and fatter." When I asked where she saw the sausage she quickly said: "On the Herr Doktor!" All that could possibly be wished of a transposition! But since then everything sexual has been completely occluded. No sign of D. pr.!

With most respectful regards,

Yours very sincerely, JUNG

---

[3] Alphonse E. Maeder, "Essai d'interprétation de quelques rêves," *Archives de psychologie*, VI (1906). Maeder (1882–1971), Swiss psychotherapist, for a time chairman of the Zürich Psychoanalytic Society; supported Jung after the break; later developed a method of brief analysis and became associated with the Oxford Movement.

[4] *Der Wahn und Die Träume in W. Jensens 'Gradiva' (Schriften zur angewandten Seelenkunde*, 1; Leipzig and Vienna, 1907) = "Delusions and Dreams in Jensen's 'Gradiva,'" SE IX. Jones, II, p. 382/341: "It was Jung who had called [Freud's] attention to the novel, and he told me Freud had written his little book on it expressly to give him pleasure." The present correspondence casts no light on this; however, cf. below, 50 J: Jones may have confused the novel with the "Übermächte" stories.

25 F

Dear colleague, 23 May 1907

Since you have kept me waiting so long for your reaction to the *Gradiva,* I can only assume that you are immersed in D. pr. work, so I shall not make you wait any longer for the information you have asked for.

I see two problems in your letter: a) what the withdrawal of libido from the object means, b) what are the differences between paranoid outward projection and other projections. I shall tell you what I think.

a) I do *not* think that the libido withdraws from the real object to throw itself on the mental representation of the object, with which fantasy it proceeds to play its autoerotic game. By definition, the libido is not autoerotic as long as it has an object, real or imagined. I believe, rather, that the libido departs from the object-image, which is thereby divested of the cathexis that has characterized it as internal and can now be projected outward and, as it were, perceived. Then for a moment it can be perceived calmly as it were and subjected to the usual reality-testing. "People say that I love coitus. That is what they say, but it's not *true!*" Successful repression would accomplish this much; the liberated libido would somehow manifest itself auto-erotically as in childhood. The source of all our misunderstandings, I believe, is that I have not stressed clearly enough the double onset of the process, the breakdown into repression of the libido and return of the libido.

We can now construct three possible cases. 1) Repression by the above-described process is permanently successful, then the case takes the course that seems characteristic of Dem. pr. The projected object-image may appear only briefly in the "delusional idea," the libido turns definitively to autoerotism, the psyche is impoverished in the way you know so well.

2) Or there is a return of libido (failure of the projection), only a part of which is guided into autoerotism; another part goes back to the object which is now to be found at the perception end and is treated as a perception. Then the delusional idea becomes more intense and resistance to it more and more violent, the entire defensive battle is fought all over again as rejection of reality (repression is transformed into rejection). This can go on for some time; in the end the newly arriving libido is diverted to autoerotism or a part of it is

fixated permanently in a delusion directed against the projected object-wish. In varying mixtures this is what happens in paranoid Dem.
praecox, undoubtedly the least pure and most frequent type.

3) Or the repression fails completely, after succeeding for a time
to the point of projecting the object-wish. The newly arriving libido
now seeks out the object which has turned into a perception and develops the most intense delusional ideas, the libido is converted into
belief, and secondary modification of the ego sets in; the result is pure
paranoia, in which autoerotism is not developed; its mechanism, however, can be explained only on the basis of the series extending to total
Dem. pr.

I conceive of these three schemata. How much of this is clinically
demonstrable, that is, can be shown to exist in reality, you will see.
For the present I note that return to autoerotism is most successful in
pure Dem. pr. Your communications are most convincing. In passing
I reiterate my inability to believe, as Bleuler did, that these mechanisms are demonstrable only in Dem. pr. and not in authentic paranoia.

b) What is less clear to me, because I lack impressions of recent
cases, is my own ideas on the problem, i.e., the relation of paranoid
projection to hysterical and amentic projection. The purest hallucinatory realization undoubtedly occurs in the latter, where there is no
repression and where the image of the desired object, over-cathected
with libido, is turned directly into perception via regression. Here, on
the contrary, we find repression of the conflicting ego and of reality.
And there is no reversal of value. Pleasure remains pleasure and is not,
as in paranoia, transformed into unpleasure. This type then has two
distinguishing features—see my old analysis[1]—: No repression of the
wish-object, the libido (hypervalent) stays with the object-representa-
tion. This type sets in suddenly, there is no prolonged struggle and
chronic development as in paranoia (Dem. pr.).

In hysteria an analogous process, hallucination of the wish-repre-
sentation and overpowering of the ego, occurs in a brief episodic attack, brought on by regression from the hypercathected object-image
to perception. This instability is characteristic of hysteria, the repressed becomes the repressive—but only temporarily. However, any
case of hysteria can shift into an acute hallucinatory psychosis of the
character described above.

In paranoia (which remains the theoretical concept; Dem. pr. seems
to be an essentially clinical notion) the image of the wish-object is

---

[1] See above, 11 F n. 5.

never realized directly through augmented libido-cathexis caused by regression. Here repression through projection with *reduced* libido-cathexis comes first, the intensification of the hallucination by the libido returning after repression is secondary. I maintain, though this could only be demonstrated with the help of a well-conceived schema, that regression and projection are different processes and also take different courses. It is also characteristic of paranoia that there is so little regression; the wish-idea is perceived as a word, by audition—i.e. intensified by thought-processes, and not as a visual image. I still fail to understand the undoubtedly secondary visual hallucinations; they look like secondary regression.

The *vicissitudes of the libido*, where it is localized in regard to ego and object, and the *modifications of repression*, what brings them about and in what rhythm—these undoubtedly determine the character of neuropsychoses and psychoses.

———

After these difficult matters something simpler. In your six-year-old girl, you must surely have discovered in the meantime that the attack is a fantasy that has become conscious, something which is regularly disclosed in analysis and which misled me into assuming the existence of generalized traumas in childhood. The therapeutic task consists in demonstrating the sources from which the child derives its sexual knowledge. As a rule children provide little information but confirm what we have guessed when we tell them. Questioning of the families indispensable. When it is successful, the most delightful analyses result.

In regard to Bleuler, I should add: the *Three Essays* do give a clear picture of autoerotism. Psychically negative, if you will.

Another reason why the child fails to talk is that, as your observation shows, she enters immediately and fully into the transference.

My Görlitz patient, like all mistakes, is very instructive. Everything we diagnosed is still present, plus Dem. pr. My *Gymnasium* student of whom I speak in the *Gradiva*,[2] who takes refuge in geometry, showed the loveliest obsessions, the most magnificent fantasies. His genitals, too, have remained infantile; I saw him again some months ago in a state of apathetic dementia.

With kind regards, in anticipation of your reply,

Yours cordially, DR. FREUD

[2] SE IX, p. 36.

48

26 J

Dear Professor Freud,   Burghölzli-Zürich, 24 May 1907

Your *Gradiva* is magnificent. I gulped it at one go. The clear exposition is beguiling, and I think one would have to be struck by the gods with sevenfold blindness not to see things now as they really are. But the hide-bound psychiatrists and psychologists are capable of anything! I shouldn't wonder if all the idiotic commonplaces that have been levelled at you before are trotted out again from the academic side. Often I have to transport myself back to the time before the reformation of my psychological thinking to re-experience the charges that were laid against you. I simply can't understand them any more. My thinking in those days seems to me not only intellectually wrong and defective but, what is worse, morally inferior, since it now looks like an immense dishonesty towards myself. So you may be absolutely right when you seek the cause of our opponents' resistance in affects, especially sexual affects. I am just dying to know what the sexual complex of the public will have to say about your *Gradiva*, which in this respect is wholly innocuous. It would irritate me most of all if they treated it with benevolent patronage. What does Jensen[1] himself say about it? Please tell me sometime what kind of literary reviews you get. One question which you leave open, and which the critics may pick on, is this: why is the complex in Hanold repressed? Why doesn't he let himself be put on the right track by the song of the canary bird and other perceptions?[2]

The part played by the bird is equally diverting. Howsoever, for understandable reasons you have not pursued the meaning of this symbol any further. Do you know Steinthal's writings on the mythology of the bird?[3]

Overwork explains my two lapses into silence these last days. Prof. Bleuler is not well and has gone to a watering-place for 3 weeks.

---

[1] Wilhelm Jensen (1837–1911), North German playwright and novelist. See editorial note to the "Gradiva" study and Freud's postscript, SE IX, pp. 4 and 94.

[2] SE IX, p. 64.

[3] Heymann Steinthal (1823–99), German philologist and philosopher, whose works Jung was to cite in "Wandlungen und Symbole der Libido" (1911–12; see CW 5, index, "Steinthal"). He was editor of *Zeitschrift für Völkerpsychologie und Sprachwissenschaft* (Berlin); see "Die ursprüngliche Form der Sage von Prometheus," ibid., II (1862), 5 and 20f., on bird symbolism. Also see the next letter, n. 8.

49

Meanwhile I have the direction of the Clinic and much else on my shoulders. I have also written another little piece,[4] a "sideline," as you would call it. I had to furnish exact proof of something in connection with disturbances in reproduction, which is as self-evident to you as it is to me; but these pachyderms just can't understand anything unless you write it out as big as your fist on their hides. Even so I shall send it to you later and not let it slip my mind, as did my last paper in English on the galvanometric investigations.[5] That time in Vienna my unconscious was disagreeably upset because it seemed to me you were not paying due attention to our electrical researches. Vengeance was bound to come. Delayed insight!

Lately I've been having unpleasant arguments with Bezzola. I have looked at his work and tested it several times myself. It is the original Breuer-Freud method, with stronger emphasis on hypnosis. He puts a mask on people and gets them to tell him the visual images they see. Many traumatic moments are brought out, which he makes them repeat over and over until these are exhausted. Good results, so far as I have been able to check them. Many of the test-persons fall into auto-hypnosis and experience somnambulistic traumata. But it seems to me that a good deal of it is made up; at least that is what the 6-year-old whom I am now treating does: tells purely made-up stories and circumvents the traumatic moments with the greatest care. So far I have had only failures when using this method on uneducated persons. Frank, using hypnotic suggestion, concentrates attention on the traumatic moment (supposing there is one!) and makes the patient go through it again and again until it is exhausted. The effect of both methods is not altogether comprehensible to me. I conjecture that both of them, at least to some extent, overlook the accompanying transposition. In one case of mine which I treated that way it was quite clear: the woman extolled chiefly my kindness in going so deeply into her affairs. Another one I plagued almost to death in two sittings without obtaining the slightest visual image, and only when I put direct questions about dreams and sexuality did she begin to come alive. The bad thing in all this is that Bezzola, in his benighted blindness, is antagonistic to you and has already started telling lies about me. You discerned his character better than I did—a small [. . .]

---

[4] "Über die Reproduktionsstörungen beim Assoziationsexperiment," *Journal für Psychologie und Neurologie*, IX (1907) = "Disturbances of Reproduction in the Association Experiment," CW 2.

[5] See above, 19 J n. 2; probably the first paper.

soul. Opposition and dissension in one's own camp are the very worst thing.

About your *Gradiva* Bleuler said: yes, it is really marvellous—either all these connections are really there, or one could put them in everywhere. This thorn of doubt still sticks in Bleuler's flesh but it isn't dangerous. At the moment he is engaged on his Dem. praec. book, from which we may expect great things. The continuation of the great "Freud battle" is guaranteed.

Heilbronner[6] in Utrecht has subjected my "Diagnosis of Evidence"[7] to detailed criticism in the latest issue of the *Zeitschrift f. d. gesamte Strafrechtswissenschaft.* I am sending it to you together with Isserlin's criticism.

With best regards,

Ever sincerely yours, J U N G

27 F

Dear colleague,[2]   26 May 1907[1]

Many thanks for your praise of *Gradiva.* You wouldn't believe how few people have managed to say anything of the kind; yours is just about the first friendly word I have heard on this subject (No, I must not be unfair to your cousin (?) Riklin). This time I knew that my work deserved praise; this little book was written on sunny days[3] and I myself derived great pleasure from it. True, it says nothing that is new to us, but I believe it enables us to enjoy our riches. Of course I do not expect it to open the eyes of our hide-bound opponents; I long ago stopped paying attention to those people, and it is because I have so little hope of converting the specialists that, as you have no-

---

[6] Karl Heilbronner, "Die Grundlagen der psychologischen Tatbestandsdiagnostik," in XXVII (1907). Heilbronner (1869–1914), German psychiatrist, then director of the Utrecht University clinic.

[7] "Die psychologische Diagnose des Tatbestandes," *Juristisch-psychiatrische Grenzfragen,* IV (1906) = "The Psychological Diagnosis of Evidence," CW 2.

---

[1] Published in *Letters,* ed. E. L. Freud, no. 124; partially quoted and discussed by Max Schur, *Freud: Living and Dying* (New York, 1972), pp. 249ff.

[2] Holograph: *Lieber Herr College.*

[3] "He had written it in the open air during his summer holiday (1906) . . . at Lavarone, in the Trentino."—Jones, II, pp. 383/341 and 16/15.

ticed, I have taken only a half-hearted interest in your galvanometric experiments, for which you have now punished me. To tell the truth, a statement such as yours means more to me than the approval of a whole medical congress; for one thing it makes the approval of future congresses a certainty.

If you are interested in the reception of *Gradiva,* I shall keep you informed. So far the only review to appear has been in a Viennese daily;[4] it is favourable but shows no more understanding or feeling than, let us say, your dementia praecox patients. Journalists apparently fail to understand how anyone can take a passionate interest in abstract ideas; they think nothing of writing such things as: The mathematicians say that 2×2 is often 4, or: We are assured that 2×2 is not usually 5.

What Jensen himself says?[5] He has been really charming. In his first letter he expressed his pleasure etc. and said that in all essential points my analysis corresponded to the intention of his story. Of course he was not speaking of our theory, the old gentleman seems incapable of entering into any other ideas than his own poetic ones. The agreement, he believes, must probably be laid to poetic intuition and perhaps in part to his early medical studies. In a second letter I was indiscreet and asked him about the subjective element in the work, where the material came from, where his own person entered in, etc. He then informed me that the ancient relief actually exists, that he possesses a reproduction of it from Nanny[6] in Munich, but has never seen the original. It was he himself who conceived the fantasy that the relief represented a woman of Pompeii; it was also he who liked to dream in the noonday heat of Pompeii and had once fallen into an almost visionary state while doing so. Apart from that, he has no idea where the material came from; the beginning suddenly came to him while he was working on another story. He put everything else aside and started to write it down. He never hesitated, it all came to him ready and complete, and he finished the story at one stretch. This suggests that the analysis, if continued, would lead through his childhood to his most intimate erotic experience. In other words, the whole thing is another egocentric fantasy.

4 By Moritz Necker, in *Die Zeit,* 19 May 07 (Jones, II, pp. 384/343).

5 For Jensen's letters, see *Psychoanalytische Bewegung,* I (1929), 207–11.

6 Illegible in Freud's holograph, but in Jensen's letter, which he is paraphrasing, it is Nanny, presumably the art dealer Felix Nanny, Türkenstrasse 92, Munich. The reproduction was probably a copy in plaster. (In the *Psych. Bewegung* transcript, the name appears as Narny.) See plate II.

The "Gradiva" relief. Fragment of a classical work in the Vatican Museum. See 27 F

In conclusion let me express the hope that one of these days you too will come across something that you think likely to interest the general public, and that you will give it to my *Papers* rather than to *Die Zukunft*.[7]

You are right, I have kept silent about the "bird" for reasons well known to you, out of consideration for the publisher and public, or because of your mollifying influence, as you prefer. Someone who is working on the material would be very grateful for the reference of the Steinthal article. Riklin has called my attention to an article in Steinthal's *Zeitschrift* for 1869.[8] Are you referring to the same one?

I am really curious about Bleuler's book on dementia. It will probably show an advance over the *Theory of Sexuality*, but hardly of the kind that is needed. I hope it does not make your study superfluous. I really sweated blood over the two theoretical constructions I sent you recently.[9] I am not used to working in that way, without direct observation. And I am sure you are not taken in by such theorems. If only I were younger or wealthier or more frivolous, any of the three, I would spend a few months at your clinic; together we would certainly work our way through the problem.

I really have no reason to regard Bezzola and Frank as members of our group. If you have rebuffed B. a bit harshly, I should say that he had it coming to him; to judge by his symptomatic actions, we are certainly not being unfair to him. The mechanism of his successful treatments—if they are lasting, which is more than doubtful—is undoubtedly transference, as you presume; you call it transposition. I seem to remember that I myself expressed this suspicion when I first wrote to you about him not so long ago.[10]

Yes, I hope to receive your publications, quite apart from my momentary reaction. All you can expect from me in the near future is the second edition of *Everyday Life* (about the end of June), in which

[7] *Die Zukunft* (Berlin) was a literary and political weekly, founded and edited by Maximilian Harden (1861–1927), in which Jung had published an essay on cryptomnesia (1905; see CW 1).

[8] Hermann Cohen, "Mythologische Vorstellung von Gott und Seele," *Zeitschrift für Völkerpsychologie und Sprachwissenschaft*, VI (1869), especially 121ff., on the soul as a bird. Maeder had cited it in his paper mentioned by Jung, 24 J n. 3. / Subsequently, Abraham used both Cohen's work and that of Steinthal (above, 26 J n. 3) in his *Traum und Mythus* (below, 84 F n. 2), to which Jung expressed his debt in "Wandlungen und Symbole," part II, ch. 3.

[9] Above, 22 F and enclosure to 25 F.

[10] Above, 18 F.

some of your examples are included.[11] Bresler[12] has not sent offprints of the little essay on religion and obsession, passages from which you heard at my house that Wednesday. The publisher neglected to order any! Two short articles have been wrung out of me,[13] but will probably not appear until later.

Thank you very much for the two bombshells from the enemy camp.[14] I am not tempted to keep them for more than a few days, only until I am able to read them without affect. What are they, after all, but emotional drivel? First they write as if we had never published a dream analysis, a case history, or an explanation of parapraxis; then, when the evidence is brought to their attention, they say: But that's no proof, that's arbitrary. Just try to show proof to someone who doesn't want to see it! Nothing can be done with logic, about which one might say what Gottfried von Strassburg, rather irreverently I think, says of the ordeal:

"that Christ in his great virtue
is as wavering as a sleeve in the wind."[15]

But just let five or ten years pass and the analysis of "aliquis,"[16] which today is not regarded as cogent, will have become cogent, though nothing in it will have changed. There is no help for it but to go on working, avoid wasting too much energy in refutation, and let the fruitfulness of our views combat the sterility of those we are opposing. Envy is evident in every line of Isserlin's paper. Some of it is just too absurd, and the whole thing is a display of ignorance.

But all the same, don't worry, everything will work out all right. You will live to see the day, though I may not. As we know, others before us have had to wait for the world to understand what they were

[11] *Zur Psychopathologie des Alltagsleben* (orig. 1901), 2nd edn., Berlin: Karger, 1907 = *The Psychopathology of Everyday Life*, SE VI; Jung's examples at pp. 18, 25, 215.

[12] Johannes Bresler (1866–1936) was founder and co-editor with Freud of the *Zeitschrift für Religionspsychologie*; see above, 23 F n. 2.

[13] See below, "Sexual Enlightenment" (34 F n. 7) and "Hysterical Phantasies" (64 F n. 1).

[14] See above, 24 J n. 1 (Isserlin), and 26 J n. 6 (Heilbronner).

[15] *Tristan* (ca. 1210), III, 469–70. (Tr. partly A. T. Hatto, Penguin, 1960, p. 248.)

[16] ". . . that wonderful example of Freud's in *The Psychopathology of Everyday Life*, where in the verse 'Exoriare aliquis nostris ex ossibus ultor' [*Aeneid* 4.625] Freud was able to trace his friend's forgetting of the word 'aliquis' . . . to the overdue menstrual period of his beloved."—Jung, "The Psychology of Dementia Praecox," par. 117, citing SE VI, pp. 9ff.

saying; I feel certain that you will not be all alone at the Amsterdam Congress. Every time we are ridiculed, I become more convinced than ever that we are in possession of a great idea. In the obituary you will some day write for me,[17] don't forget to bear witness that I was never so much as ruffled by all the opposition.

I hope your chief will recover soon and that your work load will then be reduced. I miss your letters very much when the interruptions are too long.

Yours cordially, DR. FREUD

28 J

Dear Professor Freud,   Burghölzli-Zürich, 30 May 1907

Unfortunately I can send only a short answer today to your very friendly letter as all my time is taken up with the affairs of the Clinic.

Thanks above all for the news about Jensen. It is roughly what one would have expected. Putting it down at his age to his medical studies is splendid and suspiciously arteriosclerotic. In my entourage *Gradiva* is being read with delight. The women understand you by far the best and usually at once. Only the "psychologically" educated have blinkers before their eyes.

I would gladly write something for your *Papers*. The idea is very attractive. Only I don't know *what*. It would have to be something worthwhile. The *Zukunft* article and its like are not good enough; Harden wrung it out of me. I would never have written it of my own accord. At the moment I am particularly keen on experimental studies, but I'm afraid they are hardly suitable for a wider circle of readers. Still, it is not beyond the bounds of possibility that Dementia praecox will send up something good from its inexhaustible depths. The snag is that I am so swamped with the affairs of the Clinic that I can scarcely find the necessary time for my own work. It is impossible for me to immerse myself in the material at present. Any systematic working up of Dementia praecox is equally impossible as it demands unlimited time. I am therefore planning to change my position so as to have more free time to devote myself entirely to scientific work. My plan, which has Bleuler's vigorous support, is to affiliate to the Clinic

---

[17] "Sigmund Freud: Ein Nachruf," *Sonntagsblatt der Basler Nachrichten*, 1 Oct. 1939 = "In Memory of Sigmund Freud," CW 15. But witness was not borne.

a laboratory for psychology, as a more or less independent institute of which I would be appointed director. Then I would be independent, freed from the shackles of the Clinic, and able at last to work as I want. Once in this position, I would try to get the chair for psychiatry separated from the running of the Clinic. The two together are too much and hamper any useful scientific activity. By taking such a step I would of course be abandoning my clinical career, but the damage would not be so great. I would have the material anyway. And I can imagine that I would get sufficient satisfaction from scientific work alone. As I have seen from my recent dreams, this change has its—for you—transparent "metapsychological-sexual" background, holding out the promise of pleasurable feelings galore. Anyone who knows your science has veritably eaten of the tree of paradise and become clairvoyant.

More news soon.

With sincerest regards, JUNG

29 J

Dear Professor Freud, Burghölzli-Zürich, 4 June 1907

The remark in your last letter that we can "enjoy our riches" is admirable. I rejoice every day in *your* riches and live from the crumbs that fall from the rich man's table.

Here is another pretty case of depression in Dem. praec.:

9th year: Patient sees traces of her mother's period; sexual excitement and masturbation.

12th year: Onset of periods. Studies instructive sex books. Has fantasies about genitalia of siblings, especially older brother's. Is admonished by them to be more reserved with her brother as she is a big girl now.

16th year: Symptoms of strong emotivity. Wept all day when fiancé of an older girlfriend was in danger in the Alps. Brother a great Alpinist.

18th year: Violent excitement all day and nervousness during sister's wedding. Heightened sexual urges and accompanying masturbation. Growing feelings of guilt.

20th year: Older brother gets engaged; thunderstruck. Continually compares herself with the bride, who has all the graces, while the patient comes off badly.

21st year: First acquaintance with a man who drops hints of marriage intentions. Finds him attractive because he reminds her of her brother in many ways. Instantly gets increased guilt feelings, it's wrong to think of marrying, etc. Deepening depression, sudden violent urge to suicide. Interned. Very dangerous suicide attempts. Unquestionable D. pr. symptoms.[†] Six months later, sudden swing-over to euphoria at the moment when her sister tells of the brother's wedding presents. From then on euphoric, attends the wedding without a trace of emotion, which seems to her very peculiar because she was dissolved in tears at her sister's wedding 3 years before. After the wedding, abatement of euphoria back to normal. Gets a *distortio pedis*. Doesn't like talking of going home.

I'd like to make an amusing picture-book in this style, to be enjoyed only by those who have eaten of the tree of knowledge. The rest would go away empty-handed.

Case of paranoia (paranoid D. pr.) :

About 10th year: Patient is seduced by an older boy into mutual masturbation.

About 16th year: Falls in love with a flapper (Berty Z.) who has hair cut short like a boy.

About 18th year: Gets to know through this girl a certain Lydia X. with whom he falls head over heels in love.

About 20th year: In London. Loses his job (why?), wanders about the streets in a distracted state for 3 days without eating, hears his name called several times; sees a horse rearing up close by, is terrified: takes this as meaning that he will get a good job. Finally goes home in the evening. On the way to the station an unknown lady comes towards him, obviously she is making advances. But when she comes closer he sees that she is an unknown, respectable lady and not a cocotte. Standing on the station is a young man with a girl—Berty Z. from Zürich; but he is not absolutely certain. At his house door he sees for the first time that it is No. 13. Same night he fires a bullet into his head, not fatally. Recovers.

About 34th year: Job in Zürich. Hears Lydia X. is engaged. Excited state; interned. Megalo- and persecution mania. Is God, monseigneur, doctor, the lot. Lydia X., as well as her sister and mother, are hiding in everyone he sets eyes on. Everything that happens is done by them.

[†] Delusional idea: her brother *cannot* marry because he was going to go bankrupt.

They are around him continually but never show themselves in their true form. "Bring Lydia to me sometime so that I can let my sperm out on her. Then everything will be all right."

Three years ago the delusional picture changed. At a festivity in the Clinic he met a girl with a tremor of the head. She had *hair cut short*. Manifestly fell in love with her. Soon afterwards Lydia does nothing directly herself but only by "pulling a princess around by the hair."[1] This peculiar two-track mechanism now causes everything that goes on in his environment.

No remission since Lydia got married!

I should be most grateful for your theoretical views on this last case. Your previous detailed exposition was, frankly, too difficult for me; I couldn't follow it. My mind is better able to cope with concrete cases.

Next time I will tell you of another, to me theoretically interesting, case which seems to be structured rather differently from these two, but is very characteristic of a large number of D. pr. cases.

At the moment I have a case which despite all my efforts baffles me: I can't make out whether it is D. pr. or hysteria. Altogether, the differences between D. pr. and hysteria are becoming suspiciously blurred since I have started analysing them.

With best regards,

Most sincerely yours, JUNG

30 F

Dear colleague,   6 June 1907, Vienna, IX. Berggasse 19

I am very much surprised to hear that I am the rich man from whose table you glean a few crumbs. This remark must refer to things that are not mentioned elsewhere in your letter. If only I were! Especially your work on Dem. pr. makes me feel quite impoverished. Enclosed[1] you will find the result of the exertions you have asked of me. Since I lack direct contact with the cases, it is most unsatisfactory —I regard this scribbling merely as an occasion to repeat certain

[1] Cf. "The Psychology of Dementia Praecox," CW 3, par. 169, n. 24, where a patient uses this expression.

[1] See below, p. 60.

things which, as you say, I did not express clearly enough the first time.

A picture-book such as the one you are thinking of would be highly instructive. Above all, it would provide a general view of the architectonics of the cases. I have several times attempted something of the sort, but I was always too ambitious. To be sure of making everything absolutely clear, I tried to show all the complications and consequently got stuck every time. But why shouldn't you attempt such a project in earnest? Do you already feel up to a serious struggle for the recognition of our new ideas? If so, the first thing to do would be to start a journal. "for psychopathology and psychoanalysis" you might call it, or more brazenly, just "for psychoanalysis." A publisher can surely be found; the editor can only be yourself, and I hope Bleuler will not decline to join me as a director. So far we have no one else. But such a venture has a force of attraction. There will be no shortage of material, we shall have our work cut out for us selecting, editing, and rejecting contributions. With our own analyses (yours and mine) we can easily fill up more than a volume a year. And if there is truth in the proverb: The more they carp the more they buy—the publishers will do a flourishing business.

Doesn't it tempt you? Think it over!

Now that I have more free time, I am able to fish an idea or two out of the stream that rushes by me each day. I am again taking notes on my analyses. Just now I had a consultation with one of my patients who has made my head spin so that I can think of nothing else. Her main symptom is that she can't hold a cup of tea if anyone is present, clearly exacerbation of the most significant inhibitions. She worked very poorly this morning. "No sooner was I back in the entry hall, she says now, "than I saw it all. Obviously it's innate cowardice! After all, *lâcheté* and *Schale Thee*[2] aren't so far apart." She has a habit of inverting words. She spent her childhood between her mother and her nurse, who stayed with her for many years. The mother's name is *Emma*; turn it around: *Amme*.[3] The devil take our hare-brained critics! Suggestion, etc.!

Yours cordially, DR. FREUD

[2] — Cowardice; cup of tea.
[3] = Wet-nurse.

[ENCLOSURE][4]

So you want my impressions of your two cases. I presume there is no need for me to copy the notes, you must have them at hand.

The first is the simpler: it begins at the age of nine; of course the essential determinants lie farther back, for all hysteria, I believe, relates to the sexuality of the third to fifth year. But this cannot be proved without a prolonged analysis. Your anamnesis provides only the historical material, so to speak; whatever childhood memories have been retained would lead us to prehistory. It seems likely that in Dem. pr. we shall often have to content ourselves with the historical material.

From then on everything is clear; she is dominated by an unrepressed love for her brother, but it springs from unconscious sources. Increasing conflicts, gradual repression, guilt feelings as a reaction. Her behaviour during her brother's engagement is fascinating, comparison with his fiancée. No conversion symptoms, only conflictual moods. When reality is brought home to her by the proposal of the man she associates with her brother, repression sets in and she falls ill. She has probably masturbated all along and it seems likely that this has prevented her condition from taking a hysterical form; a typical case of hysteria would have stopped masturbating long ago and shown substitutive symptoms. Your diagnosis of dementia is in this case quite correct and is confirmed by her delusional idea. After this she seems to have succeeded in disengaging her libido from her brother; substitution by indifference, euphoria, which can be explained theoretically as reinforcement of the ego by withdrawal of the object-cathexis. In other words, a partial case, probably not yet concluded or fully understood.

II The paranoid

He starts out with homosexual experiences. The girl with the short hair brings about the return of his libido to woman.

In London conflictual state; unable to bear the dashing of his hopes, shoots himself because of the desperate situation (symbol: No. 13) after several attempts to procure what he lacks. Tries to do so by hallucination, but fails. Indeed the wish-fulfilment of this process is not hallucinatory, no regression from mental images to perceptions. But his perceptions, or more precisely his memory-images of recent

[4] On both sides of a 16 x 9¾" sheet. The 6 June 07 letter is on the small stationery.

perceptions, are influenced in the direction of wish-fantasies. Wish-fulfilments of this kind are easily distinguished from delusional ideas. But they already have a special character which is peculiar to paranoia and the theoretical explanation of which would be localization. In the conflict between reality and wish-fantasies the latter prove stronger, because they have roots in the ucs. Here there is no repression, but probably an overpowering, i.e., there is a process of psychosis, the ucs. has not been repressed but has overpowered the reality-connected ego. At least temporarily in this case the suicide shows that there was no lasting success; it is a defensive action of the normal ego against the psychosis.

Between this London period and the definitive illness there lies a period of good health, that is, of successful repression. But the libido returns with the news of the engagement, and illness ensues in typical paranoid form with projection. The final outcome, with Lydia being felt as present and active everywhere, means that this object-love has taken full possession of him. But to judge by the form of these manifestations, it is a libido that has re-cathected something repressed. The repression has taken place in the course of recovery and consisted—though this cannot be proved on the basis of the present case—in outward projection, not however in *intense* images as in wish-delirium, but in feeble ones, which can only have been made possible by the detaching of the libido. The returning libido has found its object present as an outward projection. I infer from cases of pure dementia that in the intervening repression the libido has been diverted to auto-erotism; this paranoid case throws no light on the matter. In general paranoia shows only the return of the libido; detachment (repression) becomes visible in your observations of dementia.

The psychological (not the clinical) problem is that of the mechanism of projection into the world of perception, which cannot be identical with simple wish-regression.

What is extremely interesting is the relation between later paranoia (with projection) and an original psychosis of overpowering, and I hope it will soon be possible to study this on the basis of other cases. At first reality is overpowered by an intense wish-fantasy, but in such a way that only memories are falsified whereas wishes are not hallucinated. Then there is a reactive repression of the wish-fantasies. Perhaps it is because of this preliminary stage that when the libido returns later on it finds these wish-fantasies so close to the perception end. In the paranoid process the regression does not really seem to extend to the perceptual system, but only to the preceding one: mem-

61

ory-images. I hope that in further analyses it will be possible to show the deviation from the hysterical-conversion type more clearly.

I can give no more, but I am *very* willing to receive more.

31 J

Dear Professor Freud,   Burghölzli-Zürich, 12 June 1907

In the interval since my last letter I have been under such pressure that I am now pretty flattened. End of last week Claparède,[1] Directeur du Laboratoire de Psychologie expérimentale de Genève, was with me in order to get himself inducted into the technique of the association test. Your teachings have already gained a firm foothold among psychologists in Geneva, though not everything has been digested. The immediate result of Claparède's visit will, however, turn out primarily to my advantage. C. wants to publish a big over-all report on my work in the *Archives de psychologie*.[2] This would be yet another symptom that our cause is making headway. Flournoy[3] is extremely interested in it too. Next week I have to go to Paris and London for 10 days. I shall take this opportunity to call on Janet and interview him about you.

Your annotations on my cases are naturally a great joy to me, for only so can I see how you approach a case, what you think right, and how you abstract more general rules. I entirely agree with you when you say they haven't been sufficiently understood. Undoubtedly they haven't. But with Dem. praec. one learns to be content with little.

As for the first case with the transposition to the brother, I should add: On the morning of the brother's wedding she suddenly got the idea of jumping over a wide drainage ditch, 4 metres deep, hence the *distortio pedis*.

Today I have the following case to report:

[1] Edouard Claparède (1873–1940), Swiss medical psychologist and educator, founder of the Rousseau Institute in Geneva; co-editor with Flournoy of the *Archives de psychologie*.
[2] Never published.
[3] Theodore Flournoy (1854–1920), Swiss psychiatrist; he and Claparède were influenced by William James. Jung drew on Flournoy's work, particularly the Frank Miller case for "Wandlungen und Symbole der Libido" (see appendix to CW 5) and a study of a medium, *Des Indes à la Planète Mars* (1900).

36-year-old woman. Her father was a bad lot, bullied the whole family. Patient therefore attached herself to her mother, who confided all her troubles to her. Thus the two became friends. She had only one friend besides her mother: a woman whose marriage was equally unhappy. Patient had no use for men. At 28, for practical reasons, she married a younger man who was her intellectual inferior. Sexually she had no desires at all and was completely frigid. In time the idolized mother grew old and feeble. Patient declared that she would go mad when her mother died, she could not and *would* not let her mother go. This was the beginning of an ever-deepening depression, neglect of her family, thoughts of suicide, etc. Interned. Now shows symptoms of *abaissement du niveau mental.*[4] Typical catatonic depression.

Your proposal for starting a special journal fits in with my own plans. I would like to suggest the name "Archiv für Psychopathologie," because I'd be glad to have somewhere I could place all the work coming from our laboratory. However, I'd like to give it a good thinking over first, because at the moment it seems to me that, what with a mostly negative public, the chances of success are still very dubious. Also, I must first finish the second volume of my "Diagnostic Association Studies" before entering into new obligations. Meanwhile let the leaven work.

My outpatients' clinic is studded with thorns. Analysing the uneducated is a tough job. I now have someone who for the life of her cannot finish up her coffee without vomiting if there is a crumb of bread in it. "It tickles my throat." If ever she sees a corpse she has to be continually spitting for several days afterwards. This symptom seems to have set in with the death of her mother. Can you advise me?

It is amusing to see how the female outpatients go about diagnosing each other's erotic complexes although they have no insight into their own. With uneducated patients the chief obstacle seems to be the atrociously crude transference.

With kindest regards and best thanks!

Most sincerely yours, JUNG

[4] = "lowering of the mental level" or "low energy-tension"; a term introduced by Janet (*Les Obsessions et la psychasthénie,* 1903) and often employed by Jung in his later writings.

32 F

Dear colleague,   14 June 1907, Vienna, IX. Berggasse 19

Good news that Geneva is taking up the cause. Claparède and Flournoy have always shown a friendly attitude in their journal. I am very glad to learn that they are planning to call attention to your work in a detailed article. I am sure to benefit by it too.

Only today I have received a book by a man who certainly deserves his name, *On the Psychology and Therapy of Neurotic Symptoms* by A. Muthmann.[1] It is subtitled "A Study based on Freud's theory of neuroses." M. was an assistant in Basel. It can't be an accident; the Swiss seem indeed to have more personal courage than free German subjects. The book is good, fine case histories, excellent cures, dignified and modest; I have hopes that the man will become a staunch collaborator. He still lacks perspective, he treats discoveries made in 1893 in the same way as the most recent developments, and he doesn't say one word about the transference.

As for the journal, I am taking you at your word. The need for it will become more and more apparent to you; there should be no lack of readers. We mustn't delay too long, let's say autumn 1908 for the first number.

Of course you have hit the nail on the head with what you say about your ambulatory cases. What with their habits and mode of life, reality is too close to those women to allow them to believe in fantasies. If I had based my theories on the statements of servant girls, they would all be negative. And such behaviour fits in with other sexual peculiarities of that class; well-informed persons assure me that these girls are much less diffident about engaging in coitus than about being seen naked. Fortunately for our therapy, we have previously learned so much from other cases that we can tell these persons their story without having to wait for their contribution. They are willing to confirm what we tell them, but one can learn nothing from them.

Too bad that my case with the teacup is not yet complete, it might throw light on your patient who vomits when there is a bread crumb in the coffee. To judge by certain indications, these symptoms point to the excremental (urine and faeces). The case might be approached through the patient's disgust at her mother's corpse. Disgust with her

---

[1] Arthur Muthmann (1875–19—), *Zur Psychologie und Therapie neurotischer Symptome: eine Studie auf Grund der Neurosenlehre Freuds* (Halle, 1907). German *Muth* = courage.

mother probably goes back to the period of sexual enlightenment. Oh yes, I forgot to say that menstrual blood must be counted as excrement. What makes a brief ambulatory treatment almost impossible is the time factor. No psychic change can be effected in such brief periods, and besides, a woman does not confide in a man she has known for so short a time.

Thank you very much for enriching my knowledge by your communication of Dem. pr. cases. Your last, the 36-year-old woman with mother fixation, can be called ideal. The question: Where does the libido detached from the mother go? can perhaps be answered in further analysis if it takes the same course as some of your other cases: to autoerotism.

It is interesting that this repressed mother-cathexis should have a pathological (compensatory) component from the start. It is excessive because of revulsion from the father; one must presuppose a preliminary state of normal infantile affection for the father. Perhaps theoretically significant.

I am glad to see from your plan to visit Paris and London that your period of overwork is past. I wish you an interesting Paris complex, but I should not like to see it repress your Vienna complex. Our difficulties with the French are probably due chiefly to the national character; it has always been hard to import things into France. Janet has a good mind, but he started out without sexuality and now he can go no further; and in science there is no going back. But you are sure to hear much that is interesting.

With kind regards,

Yours sincerely, DR. FREUD

33 J

Dear Professor Freud,   Burghölzli-Zürich, 28 June 1907

First some "business" news: Dr. Stein[1] of Budapest and another mental specialist, Dr. Ferenczi,[2] want to visit you sometime in Vienna

---

[1] Philip (Fülöp or Philippe) Stein (1867–1918), Hungarian psychiatrist, trained in Vienna. 1906–7, research on the association experiment at the Burghölzli, having met Bleuler at the International Congress for Antialcoholism, Budapest, 1905. Founded the antialcohol movement in Hungary. After 1913 Stein apparently separated from psychoanalysis; was chief neurologist of the Workmen's Hospital in Budapest.

[2] Sándor Ferenczi (1873–1933), born Fraenkel, Hungarian neurologist and psy-

and have asked me to inquire when it would be most convenient to you. Dr. Stein is a very decent fellow with a good intelligence, who has done some experimental work with me. He is still something of a beginner in the art, but has grasped the essentials surprisingly quickly and put them into practice. I think it would be best if you contacted him directly (Dr. Stein, Semmelweisgasse 11, Budapest).

Muthmann was assistant physician at the asylum in Basel. I'm afraid I have never had any personal dealings with him. I ordered his book at once. Bleuler tells me there is an amusing (corrected) passage in it which is very characteristic of Prof. Wolff's[3] virile courage. Muthmann, incidentally, is not a Swiss but may have had his backbone stiffened in Switzerland.

Head physician Bolte[4] in Bremen, who recently stuck up for you, and whose paper will appear in the *Zeitschrift für Psychiatrie*, is so far as I know a Bremener, coming therefore from a *free city*.[5] The milieu obviously makes a big difference.

By the same post I am sending you a paper by a woman student of mine that will perhaps interest you. I think the basic ideas could be developed into a *statistical* complex theory.

I see from your kind gift that your *Psychopathology of Everyday Life* has gone into a second edition—this gives me sincere pleasure. It is good that you have considerably expanded the text—the more examples the better. I hope you will soon be able to manage a new edition of *The Interpretation of Dreams*[6] as well; it sometimes seems to me that your prophecy that you will have won through in 10 years is being fulfilled. There are stirrings on all sides. You too will have received the book by Otto Gross;[7] I certainly don't cotton on to his idea

---

choanalyst, became Freud's close friend and collaborator. Founder of the Hungarian Psychoanalytic Society in 1913 and an original member of the "Committee" (see below, comment following 321 J).

[3] Gustav Wolff (1865–1941), professor of psychiatry in Basel, exponent of neo-vitalism and teleology.

[4] Richard Bolte, "Assoziationsversuche als diagnostisches Hilfsmittel," *Allgemeine Zeitschrift für Psychiatrie*, LXIV (1907), summarized by Jung in his "Abstracts," CW 18.

[5] The German "free cities," in the Middle Ages, were directly under the Emperor's protection. At present only Hamburg and Bremen remain autonomous cities.

[6] *Die Traumdeutung* (orig. 1900) = *The Interpretation of Dreams*, SE IV & V. For the 2nd edn., see below, 112 F n. 8.

[7] Otto Gross (1877–1919) studied medicine at Graz and was assistant in Krae-pelin's clinic at Munich. Jung refers to his *Das Freud'sche Ideogenitätsmoment und seine Bedeutung im manisch-depressiven Irresein Kraepelins* (1907), which

that you are to be merely the mason working on the unfinished edifice of Wernicke's[8] system. Nevertheless this demonstration that *all* the lines are converging upon you is very gratifying. Apart from that there are all sorts of oddities in Gross's book, though at bottom he has an excellent mind. I am eager to hear what you think.

What is the fate of your *Gradiva*? Any new reviews?

It may interest you to know that the D. pr. patient with the transference to her brother has suddenly started having delusions of grandeur: she declares she has personally experienced the content of Forel's *Sexual Question*,[9] claims to be related to all sorts of distinguished people, suspects the doctors of having the most elaborate sexual relationships, wants to marry an assistant physician, says the other one (who is married) has made a patient, a Fräulein Lüders, as well as a Fräulein Skudler, pregnant and must therefore get divorced from his wife. ("Luder" is what we call a woman with an unsavoury sexual reputation!) I don't know any more details yet. The doctor she wants to marry happens to have the same name as she (like the brother!).

My experience on the trip was *pauvre*. I had a talk with Janet and was very disappointed. He has only the most primitive knowledge of Dem. pr. Of the latest happenings, including you, he understands nothing at all. He is stuck in his groove and is, be it said in passing, merely an intellect but not a personality, a hollow *causeur* and a typical mediocre bourgeois. Déjerine's[10] grand *traitement par isolement* at the Salpêtrière is a very bad *blague*. It all struck me as unspeakably childish, not least the lofty haze that befogs all heads in such a clinic. These people are 50 years behind the times. It got on my nerves so

---

dealt with cases at the clinic. / Jung devoted a chapter of *Psychological Types* (orig. 1921; see CW 6, pars. 461ff.) to Gross's typological ideas in *Die zerebrale Sekundärfunktion* (1902) and *Über psychopathische Minderwertigkeiten* (1909). Gross's life ended in hardship, drug addiction, and death by starvation. See Martin Green, *The Von Richthofen Sisters* (New York, 1974); one of the sisters—Frieda, later married to D. H. Lawrence—had a love affair with Gross in Munich in or before 1907. In her memoirs he appears as "Octavio"; see *Frieda Lawrence: The Memoirs and Correspondence*, ed. E. W. Tedlock, Jr. (1964), pp. 94–102. She describes Gross as an abstainer from alcohol and a vegetarian.

[8] Carl Wernicke (1848–1905), professor of psychiatry in Berlin, Breslau, and Halle; discovered the speech centre in the brain and published a valuable book on aphasia (1874).

[9] *Die sexuelle Frage* (1905); tr. C. F. Marshall, *The Sexual Question* (1925).

[10] Joseph Déjerine (1849–1917), Swiss neurologist, director of the Salpêtrière, Paris.

much that I gave up the idea of going to London, where far, far less is to be expected. Instead, I devoted myself to the castles of the Loire. No question of a Paris complex. Unfortunately great demands are still being made on my time. For the summer and autumn I have three applications from people who want to work with me, all very international: one from Switzerland, one from Budapest, and one from Boston. Germany, for the moment, makes a poor showing. Under these circumstances the question of bringing out an Archive is becoming more urgent. I shall therefore look into the matter more closely. Finding a publisher will certainly be difficult. But before taking definite steps in this direction I must finish the second volume of the *Diagnostic Association Studies*. This means a lot more work, as the writings of pupils are far more bothersome than one's own.

Binswanger jr. is now doing psychanalytic work in Jena. I hope he will leave some lasting traces behind him. His uncle wants me to visit him. Unfortunately I can't find the time, profitable though it might be.

With best regards,

Ever sincerely yours, JUNG

34 F

Dear colleague,   1 July 1907, Vienna, IX. Berggasse 19

I was very glad to hear that you are back at work at Burghölzli and am delighted with your impressions of your trip. You can imagine that I should have been very sorry if your Vienna complex had been obliged to share the available cathexis with a Paris complex. Luckily, as you tell me, nothing of the sort happened, you gained the impression that the days of the great Charcot are past and that the new life of psychiatry is with us, between Zürich and Vienna. So we have emerged safe and sound from a first danger.

In your last letter you bring up an unusual number of "business" matters that call for a reply. You are right, the business is doing well. It remains of course to be seen whether it will take ten years and whether I can wait that long. The trend is clearly upwards. Our adversaries' activity can only be sterile; each one lets out a blast and claims to have crushed me (and now you as well); and that is all. There his activity ends. Whereas those who join us are able to report on the results of their work; after which they continue to work and report again. Quite understandably, each one of us works in his own way and perhaps contributes his own specific distortion to the understanding of our still unfinished task.

I hadn't heard of Bolte in Bremen until you mentioned him. What interests me most about Gross's book[1] is that it comes from the clinic of the Super-Pope, or at least was published with his permission. Gross is a highly intelligent man; but to my taste there is much too much theory and too little observation in his book. His analysis is incomplete—undoubtedly through no fault of his; the main point, the steps leading up to theft, unquestionably right, but the motivation inadequate. Have you noticed that he wallows in superlatives? Everybody is a "blazer of trails," a "herald of the new," etc., except me, which is a distinction. This no doubt reflects G.'s abnormal affective life, which you have told me about. He also reminds me a little of the ancient Egyptians, who never modified their pantheon, but superimposed every new god and every new concept on an old one, the result being incredible confusion. Gross makes a synthesis of me and all his old gods: Wernicke, Anton,[2] etc. I am undoubtedly a poor judge of my colleagues; with regard to Wernicke's work in psychology I have always thought that he never had any really new idea, but merely extended to the psyche his anatomist's habit of dividing everything into layers and sections.

About my *Gradiva* there is next to nothing to report. The same journalist[3] who reviewed it favourably in the Vienna *Zeit* has devoted another—far better—article to it in the supplement to the *Allgemeine Zeitung*. He must want something of me. Could it be that the best books are those that get no attention?

The further development of the dementia patient who finds her brother in the doctor is a splendid example of paranoid transference. Fräulein Lüders is of course the patient herself.

I have read your student's paper[4] with great interest and respect for her formulations of the questions of individual psychology. Naturally I find your ideas and your cool-headedness throughout. It is quite true,

---

[1] *Das Freud'sche Ideogenitätsmoment.*

[2] Gabriel Anton (1858–1933), Austrian psychiatrist and neurologist; subsequently, professor in Graz, then in Halle a. S.; renowned as brain surgeon.

[3] Moritz Necker.

[4] Emma Fürst, "Statistische Untersuchungen über Wortassoziationen und über familiäre Übereinstimmung im Reaktionstypus bei Ungebildeten," *Journal für Psychologie und Neurologie*, IX (1907) = "Statistical Investigations on Word-Associations and on Familial Agreement in Reaction-Type among Uneducated Persons," *Studies in Word-Association* (1918). After 1913, Dr. Fürst remained in the Freudian school.

I believe, that attitude toward the examiner is a primary factor in determining the content of the reactions. This would be the best way of effecting "studies in transference." For the fun of it, I examined myself by letting myself react to the stimulus-words she uses in her paper. It worked very well, and I was able to explain the strangest answers. A disturbing mistake was that, while I was copying one word my reaction to it was affected by the following word. For instance, I reacted to *Buch—Buschklepper*, then to *Frosch—Busch*.[5] Then of course it all became clear to me. *Frosch* had co-determined my reaction to *Buch* by reminding me of our friend Busch.[6]

> "For six long weeks the frog was ill,
> But now he's smoking with a will."

Yesterday I had my first good day after several weeks of dyspepsia. Before that I had been reacting exclusively to personal libido-complexes, often in a very obscure and artificial way. The "Klepper" comes from the kleptomania in Gross's book.

So we are agreed about the journal. We can decide on the date later on.

The post will bring you another little thing of mine,[7] a feuilleton wrung from me by a Hamburg colleague. Please judge it accordingly.

I infer from your hints that you will be very busy during these next hot summer months. A respectable number of students have come to you, and the association experiments provide an excellent means of keeping the young people busy. I am eagerly looking forward to becoming a free agent on the 14th of the month; this year has been hard on me, though it has also brought me many good things, first of all your visit and the expectations connected with it. This year I shall really be entitled to spend my time rather empty-headedly, something others indulge in after less work. So don't expect an intelligent word out of me until I have restored myself. All the same, I have a glimmer of an idea for a study on the "epistemological problem of the ucs.,"[8] and I shall take a few books away with me for it.

---

[5] = book—highwayman; frog—bush.
[6] Wilhelm Busch (1832–1908), German humorous poet and illustrator. The verses are from "Die beiden Enten und der Frosch," *Münchener Bilderbogen*, no. 325.
[7] "Zur sexuellen Aufklärung der Kinder," *Soziale Medizin und Hygiene*, II (1907) = "The Sexual Enlightenment of Children" (An Open Letter to Dr. M. Fürst), SE IX. (Not the same as Emma Fürst.)
[8] Never written.

Dr. Stekel,[9] whom you know and whose forte is not ordinarily his critical faculty, has sent me a work on anxiety cases, written at the request of the *Berliner Klinik*[10] (!). I persuaded him to consider these cases of "anxiety hysteria" side by side with "conversion hysteria." I mean to do a theoretical defense of this procedure one of these days[11] and recommend it to you in the meantime. It would enable us to include the phobias.

With kind regards,

Yours, DR. FREUD

35 J

Dear Professor Freud,   Burghölzli-Zürich, 6 July 1907

Would you mind my boring you with some personal experiences? I would like to tell you an instructive story about something that happened to me in Paris. There I met a German-American woman who made a pleasant impression on me—a Mrs. St.,[1] aged about 35. We were together at a party for a few hours and talked about landscapes and other indifferent matters. We were offered black coffee. She declined, saying that she couldn't tolerate a mouthful of black coffee, even a sip made her feel bad the next day. I answered that this was a nervous symptom; it was merely that she couldn't tolerate black coffee at home, but when she found herself "in different circumstances,"[1a] she would surely tolerate it much better. Scarcely had this unfortunate phrase left my mouth than I felt enormously embarrassed, but rapidly discovered that—luckily—it had "slipped by" her. I must remark that I knew absolutely nothing about this lady's history. Soon

---

[9] Wilhelm Stekel (1868–1940), one of the four original members of the Wednesday Evening Society (1902), and earlier in analysis with Freud; considered a brilliant writer and an intuitive psychoanalyst. He was editor (at first with Alfred Adler) of the *Zentralblatt*, which he continued for a year after he separated from Freud in 1911. Later in London, where he took his own life. For the development of his studies of anxiety cases, see below, 61 F n. 5 and 98 J n. 3.

[10] Presumably the *Medizinische Klinik*; Stekel's article could not be traced in it.

[11] Freud did so in his "Analysis of a Phobia in a Five-year-old Boy" (1909), SE X, pp. 115 f.

---

[1] Jung's abbreviation.

[1a] Holograph: *"in andere Umstände kommen,"* which is also the equivalent of our "to be in an interesting condition" = pregnant.

afterwards another lady suggested we should all say a number—such numbers were always significant. Mrs. St. said "3." An acquaintance of hers cried out: "Naturally, you, your husband, and your dog." Mrs. St. retorted: "Oh no, I was thinking all good things come in threes!" From which I concluded that her marriage was barren. Mrs. St. had lapsed into silence but suddenly said to me out of the blue: "In my dreams my father always appears to me so wonderfully transfigured." I found out that her father is a doctor. A few days later she gave me, despite my protests, a magnificent engraving. *Sapienti sat!* My wife, who knows a thing or two, said recently: "I am going to write a psychotherapeutic handbook for gentlemen."

An hysterical patient told me that a verse from a poem by Lermontov[2] was continually going round in her head. The poem is about a prisoner whose sole companion is a bird in a cage. The prisoner is animated only by *one* wish: sometime in his life, as his noblest deed, to give some creature its freedom. He opens the cage and lets his beloved bird fly out. What is the patient's greatest wish? "Once in my life I would like to help someone to perfect freedom through psychanalytical treatment." In her dreams she is condensed with me. She admits that actually her greatest wish is to have a child by me who would fulfil all her unfulfillable wishes. For that purpose I would naturally have to let "the bird out" first. (In Swiss-German we say: "Has your birdie whistled?")

A pretty little chain, isn't it? Do you know Kaulbach's[3] porno-

---

[2] According to Mr. V. Nabokov, there are two mistakes in the reference to the liberated bird: "The poem is not by Lermontov, and it is absurdly paraphrased. Here is the real model, Pushkin's poem of 1822, composed in Kishinev, two years after his expulsion from St. Petersburg (I have retained the iambic structure but not the tetrametric length or the *abab ecec* rhyme scheme):

Ptichka (little bird)

In a strange country I religiously observe
my own land's ancient custom:
I set at liberty a little bird
on the bright holiday of spring.

I have become accessible to consolation;
why should I murmur against God
if even to a single creature
the gift of freedom I could grant!"
(Copyright © 1974 by Vladimir Nabokov.)

[3] A drawing (undated) by Wilhelm von Kaulbach (1805–74), in the Staatliche Graphische Sammlung, Munich, illustrating Goethe's poem "Wer kauft Liebes-

graphic picture: "Who Buys Love-gods?" (Winged phalli looking like cocks, getting up to all sorts of monkey-tricks with the girls.)

Not long ago I asked you about an hysterical patient who can never drink her coffee up. Like me, you conjectured an excremental analogy. It now turns out that up to her 6th (?) year she suffered from an anal prolapse, which sometimes occurred even without evacuation and always had to be pushed back by her mother. Later, itching in the anus, remedied by the patient sitting with bare behind on the stove. She also eases her present hysterical pains by warming her behind, though the pains are localized in the hip and left foreleg. The anal paraesthesias lasted until she was nearly 30. Later she tried to dispel them by getting into her sister's bed and warming herself against her. During the analysis my attention was drawn to the anus story by her telling me that one should just listen to the lower half of her back, there was such a strange "creaking" in the bones. At 20 she had a bad attack of diarrhoea. Her mother wanted to fetch the doctor, but the patient fell into a state of nervous excitement because she didn't want to be examined, fearing the doctor would look at her anus. But what a frightful tussle it was until the whole story was out!

Now for a bit of historical mysticism!

Vienna has produced 3 anthropological-medical reformers: Mesmer, Gall,[4] Freud. Mesmer and Gall felt cramped in Vienna, Freud (in keeping with the times) went unrecognized. Mesmer and Gall then moved to Paris.

Mesmer's views remained confined to Paris until *Lavater*[5] of *Zürich* imported them into Germany, at first *Bremen*. Hypnotism revived in France and was imported into Germany by *Forel* of *Zürich*. Forel's first pupil of many years' standing is *Delbrück*[6] of *Bremen*; he is now director of the asylum there.

Freud first met with clinical recognition in *Zürich*. The first *German* asylum to recognize Freud was *Bremen* (independently of per-

---

götter" (1795). Reproduced in Eduard Fuchs, *Das erotische Element in der Karikatur* (Berlin, 1904), p. 221.

[4] Franz Mesmer (1734–1815), Austrian physician, experimenter with animal magnetism, or so-called mesmerism; Franz Joseph Gall (1758–1828), German physician, founder of phrenology. Both were trained at the University of Vienna and later emigrated to Paris.

[5] Johann Kaspar Lavater (1741–1801), Swiss clergyman, poet, and mystical philosopher; founder of physiognomy.

[6] Anton W. A. Delbrück (1862–1932), German psychiatrist, trained at the Burghölzli, after 1898 director of the asylum at Bremen.

sonal relations with us). Apart from Delbrück the only German assistant at the Burghölzli (so far as I know) is Dr. Abraham[7] of *Bremen*. He came here from Berlin and has no relations with Delbrück.

You will undoubtedly say that thinking in analogies, which your analytical method trains so well, yields poor fruit. But I have enjoyed it.

For the time being Dem. pr. is having an enforced rest. July 14 I must go to Lausanne for 3 weeks on military service.[8] Afterwards my chief will be away for a month. Then once again I shall have the whole Clinic on my shoulders. So the outlook is bad. Binswanger's paper[9] will come out soon, I hope. You will then see that you too have absorbed the secrets of the galvanometer. Your associations are indeed excellent!

With best regards,

Ever sincerely yours, JUNG

Anxiety neurosis and anxiety hysteria
are still wrapped in obscurity for
me—unfortunately—from lack of
experience.

36 F

Dear colleague,   10 July 1907, Vienna, IX. Berggasse 19

I am writing to you—briefly and in haste—in order to catch you before you leave and wish you a period of rest from mental effort. It will do you good.

[7] Karl Abraham (1877–1925); he studied psychiatry in Berlin, joined the staff of the Burghölzli at the end of 1904, and became first assistant to Bleuler. His first contact with Freud occurred in June 1907, when Abraham sent him an offprint; see the next letter, n. 4, and the *Freud/Abraham Letters* (1965), p. 1. In Nov. 1907 he resigned from the Burghölzli and returned to Berlin; he first met Freud in Dec. (see below, 55 F, 57 F), and soon became a close associate. Abraham founded the Berlin Psychoanalytic Society on 27 Aug. 08. One of the original members of the "Committee" (see below, comment following 321 J).

[8] Military service is compulsory in Switzerland. In 1895, Jung had first served with the infantry, and in 1901 he became an officer in the medical corps. From 1908 he was a captain, and from 1914 commander of a unit, until he retired in 1930. Two weeks of service were obligatory each year.

[9] In his paper on the psychogalvanic phenomenon (see below, 61 F n. 1), Binswanger gives a number of citations of Freud's publications.

74

The many charming "trifles"[1] in your last letter remind me that I too am at the end of my year's work. On the fourteenth I am leaving for:

Lavarone in *Val Sugana*[2]
South Tyrol

Hotel du Lac

I should not like to be without news of you all this time—I shall not be coming back until the end of September—your letters have become a necessity for me. So I shall keep you informed of my movements. I hope to be in Sicily when you are reading your paper in Amsterdam. In spite of all the distractions, a part of my thoughts will be with you there. I hope you will gain the recognition you desire and deserve; it means a great deal to me too.

I am already corresponding with Dr. Abraham. I have every reason to be deeply concerned with his work. What is he like? His letter and article[3] have predisposed me very much in his favour. I am expecting to receive your cousin Riklin's manuscript any day. It seems to me that I have come across a nest of especially fine and able men, or am I letting my personal satisfaction becloud my judgment?

Only today I received a letter from a student in Lausanne who wishes to speak about my work at a scientific gathering at Docent Sternberg's[4] house. Things are getting very lively in Switzerland.

My hearty greetings. And don't, during the long holiday, forget

Cordially yours, DR. FREUD

37 J

Dear Professor Freud,   Burghölzli-Zürich, 12 August 1907

Please excuse my long silence. The three weeks of military service left me not a single moment for myself. We were at it from 5 in the morning till 8 in the evening; evenings I was always dog-tired. When I got back home, the chores at the Clinic had piled into mountains and

[1] English in original.
[2] Southeast of Trent; now in Italy.
[3] "Über die Bedeutung sexueller Jugendtraumen für die Symptomatologie der Dementia praecox," *Zentralblatt für Nervenheilkunde und Psychiatrie*, n.s., XVIII (1907) = "On the Significance of Sexual Trauma in Childhood for the Symptomatology of Dementia Praecox," *Clinical Papers* (1955).
[4] Théodore Sternberg, privatdocent of German penal law, University of Lausanne.

on top of that Prof. Bleuler and the 1st assistant[1] went on holiday. So I have more than enough to keep me busy. Just to make the cup brim over, the secretariat of the Amsterdam Congress began clamouring for my manuscript which did not yet exist. I had to throw myself head over heels into working up my lecture. It's a hard nut! The most difficult feat of all is to leach out the wealth of your ideas, boil down the essence, and finally bring off the master-wizard's trick of producing something homogeneous. To me it seems all but impossible to water the product down so as to make it more or less palatable to the ignorant public. Just now I am working on the latest development of your views—the detailed introduction of sexuality into the psychology of hysteria. Often I want to give up in sheer despair. But in the end I always console myself with the thought that none of this will be understood by 99% of the public anyhow, so that in this part of my lecture I can say pretty much what I want. It won't be understood either way. It is only a demonstration, a confirmation, of the fact that in the year 1907 someone officially said something positive about Freud's theory of hysteria at an International Congress. I am becoming more and more convinced that you are right when you attribute the not wanting to understand only to ill will. One makes all sorts of discoveries in this respect. America is on the move. In the last 3 weeks six Americans, one Russian, one Italian, and one Hungarian have been here. No Germans!

As soon as I have finished my lecture, this child of sorrow, I hope to be able to write you again.

Again apologies for the long pause,

Ever sincerely yours, JUNG

38 F

18 August 1907[1]

Dear colleague,   Hotel Wolkenstein in St. Christina, Gröden[2]

My personality was impoverished by the interruption in our correspondence. Fortunately that has now come to an end. Though I

---

[1] Karl Abraham was first assistant physician from 1 Jan. to 11 Nov. 07, under Jung as senior staff physician (*Oberarzt*). (Information courtesy of Dr. Manfred Bleuler.)

[1] Published in *Letters*, ed. E. L. Freud, no. 125, and partially in Schur, *Freud: Living and Dying*, p. 253.

[2] From Lavarone the Freud family went to this resort in the Dolomites; now Italian, called Selva in Gardena.

myself am wandering lazily about the world with my family, I know that you are working again and that your letters will carry me back to what for both of us has become the centre of interest.

Don't despair; I presume it was only a phrase that cropped up in your letter. It doesn't matter whether we are understood by the official figures of the moment. Among the nameless masses hidden behind them there are plenty of individuals who *want* to understand and who at a given moment suddenly step forward; I have had that experience time and time again. Your lecture in Amsterdam will be a milestone in history and after all it is largely for history that we work. What you call the hysterical element in your personality, your need to impress and influence people, the very quality that so eminently equips you to be a teacher and guide, will come into its own even if you make no concessions to the current fashions in opinion. And when you have injected your own personal leaven into the fermenting mass of my ideas in still more generous measure, there will be no further difference between your achievement and mine.

I am not well enough to risk the trip to Sicily we had planned for September, because at this time the scirocco is said to blow without let-up. Consequently I don't know exactly where I shall be in the next few weeks. Until the end of August I shall stay here, hiking in the mountains and picking edelweiss; I shall not be returning to Vienna before the end of September. All in all you had better write to me at my Vienna address for the present, because the post is very unreliable in the mountains in the summertime. I have not made a single entry in my pocket notebook in the last four weeks; my intellectual preoccupations have just faded away. But I shall always be thankful for any reminder from you.

I don't believe that Germany will show any sympathy for our work until some bigwig has solemnly given his stamp of approval. The simplest way might be to arouse the interest of Kaiser Wilhelm—who of course understands everything. Have you any connections in those quarters? I haven't. Perhaps Harden, the editor of *Die Zukunft*, will sniff out the psychiatry of the future in your work.[3] As you see, this place puts me in a jocular mood. I hope your enforced holiday has done you as much good as I am expecting from my intentional rest.

Ever cordially yours, DR. FREUD

[3] See above, 27 F n. 7.

39 J

Dear Professor Freud,   Burghölzli-Zürich, 19 August 1907

As usual you have hit the nail on the head with your accusation that my ambition is the agent provocateur of my fits of despair. But this I must say in my own defence: it is my honest enthusiasm for the truth that impels me to find some way of presenting your teachings that would best bring about a breakthrough. Otherwise my unconditional devotion to the defence and propagation of your ideas, as well as my equally unconditional veneration of your personality, would be bound to appear in an extremely peculiar light—something I would gladly avoid even though the element of self-interest could be denied only by the very obtuse. All the same I have unpleasant presentiments, for it is no small thing to be defending *such* a position before *such* a public. I have now finished my lecture and see that I have taken the general stance which you deem the best: intransigence. If one wants to be honest one can't do anything else. Luckily I have just brought an analysis of hysteria in an uneducated person to a successful conclusion and this has given me heart.

In one of your earlier letters you asked for my views about Dr. Abraham.[1] I admit at once that I am "jealous" of him because he corresponds with you. (Forgive me this candour, however tasteless it may seem!) There are no objections to A. Only, he isn't quite my type. For instance, I once suggested that he collaborate on my writings, but he declined. Now he pricks up his ears whenever Bleuler and I talk about what we are investigating, etc. He then comes up with a publication. Of all our assistants he is the one who always holds a little aloof from the main work and then suddenly steps into the limelight with a publication, as a loner. Not only I but the other assistants too have found this rather unpleasant. He is intelligent but not original, highly adaptable, but totally lacking in psychological empathy, for which reason he is usually very unpopular with the patients. I would ask you to subtract a personal touch of venom from this judgment. Apart from these cavilings A. is an agreeable associate, very industrious and much concerned with all the bureaucratic affairs of the Clinic, which nobody can say of me. A little drop of venom may derive from that source too, for in this respect my chief has long since reached the pinnacle of perfection.

[1] See above, 36 F.

Freud, 27 Aug. 07 (40 F, p. 1)

I would now like to ask you for an explanation: Do you regard sexuality as the mother of all feelings? Isn't sexuality for you merely one component of the personality (albeit the most important), and isn't the sexual complex therefore the most important and most frequent component in the clinical picture of hysteria? Are there not hysterical symptoms which, though co-determined by the sexual complex, are predominantly conditioned by a sublimation or by a nonsexual complex (profession, job, etc.)?

Certainly in my small experience I have seen *only* sexual complexes and shall say so explicitly in Amsterdam.

With kindest regards,

Yours very sincerely, J U N G

40 F

Hotel Annenheim und Seehof am Ossiacher See (Kärnten),[1]
Dear colleague,   Annenheim, 27 August 1907

You will forgive me for addressing you more formally in an open postcard.[2] — Well, your letter was charming and once again showed me more of you than I could have learned from a whole dissertation. At the beginning you found yourself face to face with a serious matter and seemed frightened at the contrast. I should be very sorry if you imagined for one moment that I really doubted you in any way. But then you pulled yourself together and took the only attitude one can take when confronting one's + + +[3] unconscious, to wit, one of humour, and yours turned out delightfully.

I was predisposed in Abraham's favour by the fact that he attacks the sexual problem head on; consequently I was glad to provide him with what material I had. Your picture of his character seems so apt that I am inclined to accept it without further examination. Nothing objectionable, yet something that precludes intimacy. You make him out to be something of an "uninspired plodder,"[4] which is bound to

---

[1] See facsimile. / The family had come to this resort, on a Carinthian lake, for a fortnight (see Jones, II, p. 40/35).

[2] Missing.

[3] See above, 11 F n. 7.

[4] Holograph: "*trockener Schleicher.*" In Goethe, *Faust I*, 521, Faust so describes his pedantic companion Wagner. / Freud had never met Abraham; shortly after

clash with your open, winning nature. It would be interesting to discover the private circumstances at the source of this reserve, the secret wound to his pride, or the thorn of poverty or wretchedness, unhappy childhood, etc. By the way, is he a descendant of his eponym?

As for your question, a ream of this paper would not suffice for an answer. Not that I know so much, but there are so many equally valid possibilities. For the present I do not believe that anyone is justified in saying that sexuality is the mother of all feelings. Along with the poet,[5] we know of two instinctual sources. Sexuality is one of them. A feeling seems to be the inner perception of an instinctual cathexis. Undoubtedly there are feelings that spring from a combination of the two sources. I can make nothing of "personality," any more than I can of Bleuler's "ego" in his study of affectivity.[6] I mean that these are concepts drawn from surface psychology and we in metapsychology are beyond them, although we cannot yet replace them from inside.

I regard (for the present) the role of sexual complexes in hysteria merely as a theoretical necessity and do not infer it from their frequency and intensity. Proof, I believe, is not yet possible. When we see people made ill by their work, etc., that is not conclusive, for the sexual (in the male, homosexual) component can easily be demonstrated in analysis. I know that we somewhere encounter the conflict between ego-cathexis and object-cathexis, but without direct (clinical) observation I cannot even speculate.

I am so out of touch with everything that I don't even know the date of the Amsterdam Congress. But I shall hear from you before that. I shall be here until September 10th.

Most cordially yours, DR. FREUD

---

this, through correspondence and personal acquaintance, his estimate of Abraham became entirely positive.

[5] Schiller, in "Die Weltweisen" ("The Philosophers"), which Freud often cited: "Quite temporarily / While waiting for philosophy / To take the world in hand, / Hunger and love command." (Tr. R.M.)

[6] *Affektivität, Suggestibilität, Paranoia* (Halle, 1906) = "Affectivity, Suggestibility, Paranoia," tr. Charles Ricksher, *New York State Hospital Bulletin* (Utica), Feb. 1912.

41 J

Dear Professor Freud, Burghölzli-Zürich, 29 August 1907

Heartiest thanks for your friendly letter! Last time I got a bit scared because I thought you had taken my long silence amiss. One of my bad qualities is that I can never do two things at once. A letter to you comes into the category of "things."

Dr. Adler, who recently asked me something technical, wrote that you are not feeling too well. You haven't said anything about it to me. I hope it is only a passing indisposition.

May we not hope to welcome you in Switzerland this autumn? For our Clinic it would be a feast and red-letter day, and it would make me extraordinarily happy to see and hear you again. I return from Amsterdam on September 10 and can then give you a report on my apostolic journey.

I fear I have painted Abraham (who is what his name implies) in too dark colours. Of his antecedents I know nothing whatever—which is characteristic. The emotional rapport is missing but I don't feel it's my fault. A. often has mild ideas of persecution about me. His wife[1] comes from Berlin, and suffers from Berlinese autoerotism with all its psychological consequences. That rubs off on A.

Your idea that feeling is the perception of an instinctual cathexis is excellent and seems to me to simplify many things enormously. If you can't make anything of Bleuler's "ego" in his *Affectivity* you can safely lump it together with my conception of the ego-complex.[2] They both amount to nothing and are really only "surface psychology." But in practice we must maintain contact with the surface, for didactic reasons. I am very grateful to you for formulating your view of the role of sexuality; it is much what I expected.

I shall be in Amsterdam from September 1–10. Address: Hôtel de l'Europe, Doelenstraat.

I hope your prophecy will be fulfilled and that someone will be there besides the opposition.

With best regards,

Most sincerely yours, JUNG

[1] Hedwig Marie, née Bürgner (1878–1969).
[2] See Jung, "The Psychology of Dementia Praecox," CW 3, par. 86, n. 9.

42 F

Hotel Annenheim und Seehof am Ossiacher See (Kärnten),
Dear colleague,   Annenheim, 2 September 1907[1]

I know you are now in Amsterdam, just before or after your perilous lecture, engaged in the defence of my cause, and it strikes me as almost cowardly that I should meanwhile be looking for mushrooms in the woods or bathing in this peaceful Carinthian lake instead of fighting for my own cause or at least standing by your side. I take comfort by telling myself that it is better for the cause this way, that you as the other, the second, will be spared at least a part of the opposition that would have been in store for me, that for me to say the same thing over and over would be mere useless repetition, and that you are better fitted for propaganda, for I have always felt that there is something about my personality, my ideas and manner of speaking, that people find strange and repellent, whereas all hearts open to you. If a healthy man like you regards himself as an hysterical type, I can only claim for myself the "obsessional" type, each specimen of which vegetates in a sealed-off world of his own.

Whether you have been or will be lucky or unlucky, I do not know; but now of all times I wish I were with you, taking pleasure in no longer being alone and, if you are in need of encouragement, telling you about my long years of honourable but painful solitude, which began after I cast my first glance into the new world, about the indifference and incomprehension of my closest friends, about the terrifying moments when I myself thought I had gone astray and was wondering how I might still make my misled life useful to my family, about my slowly growing conviction, which fastened itself to the interpretation of dreams as to a rock in a stormy sea, and about the serene certainty which finally took possession of me and bade me wait until a voice from the unknown multitude should answer mine. That voice was yours; for I know now that Bleuler also came to me through you. Thank you for that, and don't let anything shake your confidence, you will witness our triumph and share in it.

I am glad to say that I can no longer claim too much of your sympathy for my ailing state. I made my entry into the climacteric years with a rather stubborn case of dyspepsia (after influenza), but in these

---

[1] Published in *Letters*, ed. E. L. Freud, no. 126, and partially in Schur, *Freud: Living and Dying*, pp. 253f. The second paragraph is quoted in Jones, II, pp. 125f./112.

wonderful weeks of rest it has reduced itself to an occasional gentle reminder.

I made up my mind long ago to visit you in Zürich. But I see it as a Christmas or Easter excursion. Then I shall come straight from my work, stimulated and teeming with problems, not in my present almost somnolent state, with all my cathexes discharged. I too feel the need of chatting with you for a few hours.

With kind regards (and wishes!),

Yours, DR. FREUD

43 J

Hôtel de l'Europe,

Dear Professor Freud,   Amsterdam,[1] 4 September 1907

Just a couple of words in haste by way of abreaction. I spoke this morning but unfortunately couldn't quite finish my lecture as I would have exceeded the time-limit of half an hour, which wasn't allowed.[2] What a gang of cut-throats we have here! Their resistance really is rooted in affect. Aschaffenburg made two slips of the tongue in his lecture ("facts" instead of "no facts"), which shows that unconsciously he is already strongly infected. Hence his furious attack. Typical that in conversation he never tries to learn anything but goes all out to prove to me what a frightful mistake we are making. He won't listen to any of our arguments. I have compiled a pretty dossier of his negative affects. All the rest of them are cowards, each hanging on to the coat-tails of the fatter man in front. The discussion is tomorrow. I shall say as little as possible, for every word sacrificed to this kind of opposition is a waste of time. A ghastly crowd, reeking of vanity, Janet the worst of the lot. I am glad you have never been caught in the bedlam of such a mutual admiration society. I constantly feel the urgent need of a bath. What a morass of nonsense and stupidity! But in spite of everything I have the impression that the ferment is working. However, we still need a few highly intelligent and dynamic men capable of creating the right atmosphere—I mean

---

1 Printed letterhead.

2 For accounts of this episode (and of the entire "Premier Congrés International de Psychiatrie, de Neurologie, de Psychologie, et de l'Assistance des Aliénés," 2–7 Sept.) see Jones, II, pp. 125ff./112ff., and H. F. Ellenberger, *The Discovery of the Unconscious* (1970), pp. 796–98. / For Jung's paper, see below, 82 F n. 3. For Aschaffenburg's, see his abstract in the *Monatsschrift*, XXII (1907), 565f.

in Germany. We in Switzerland are a little too far from the centre. Once again I have seen that if one is to serve the cause one must stick to the most elementary things. What people *don't* know surpasses the imagination, and what they don't *want* to know is simply unbelievable. Aschaffenburg has been treating a case of obsessional neurosis and when she wanted to talk about sexual complexes he forbade her to speak of them—therefore Freudian theory is moonshine! A. announced this in public (with a moral undertone of course), puffing out his chest.

How can one discuss anything with these people?

With best regards,

Ever sincerely yours, JUNG

44 J

Dear Professor Freud,   Burghölzli-Zürich, 11 September 1907

I got back from Amsterdam yesterday evening and am now in a better position to view my experiences at the Congress in the proper perspective. Before I try to describe the subsequent developments I want to thank you heartily for your letter, which came just at the right moment; it did me good to feel that I was fighting not only for an important discovery but for a great and honourable man as well. Whether the facts are recognized slowly or quickly, or are attacked or not, leaves me pretty cold; but pouring unadulterated sewage over everything that isn't approved of is disgusting. *One* thing that has filled me up to the neck at this Congress is a contempt bordering on nausea for the genus *Homo sapiens*.

As I told you, my lecture was, most unfortunately, broken off prematurely and the discussion took place only the following day, although there were no valid reasons for the postponement. The first to take the floor was Bezzola, to "protest" against you, against me, and against the sexual theory of hysteria (moral undertone!). An hour beforehand I had tried in a private conversation to come to a friendly understanding with him—impossible. He begrudges you your books and your income; it's enough to make one die of laughter or burst a blood vessel. Nothing but furious, insensate affect against you and me.

Then Alt[1] of Uchtspringe proclaimed a reign of terror against you,

---

[1] Konrad Alt (1861–1922), director of the sanatorium at Uchtspringe, in Saxony. He wrote the report in the *Monatsschrift*; loc. cit., 43 J n. 1.

he'd never refer any patient of his to a doctor of the Freudian persuasion—unscrupulous, filthy people, etc. Huge applause and congratulation of the speaker by Prof. Ziehen,[2] Berlin. Then came Sachs[3] of Breslau, who only uttered a couple of stupendous asininities that don't bear repeating; again roars of applause. Janet couldn't help letting it drop that he had already heard your name. He knows absolutely nothing about your theory but is convinced that it's all rubbish. Heilbronner of Utrecht found only the association experiments, the "cornerstone of your theory," worth mentioning.[4] Everything I had brought forward as proof was a fake—to say nothing of what Freud may have done. Aschaffenburg was not present at the discussion so I didn't wind up the debate. Before this, Frank of Zürich spoke up for you energetically, as did Gross of Graz, who in the Psychology Section went very thoroughly into the significance of your theory so far as it touches upon the secondary function.[5] It is a pity that G. is such a psychopath; he has a very intelligent head on him and with his *Secondary Function* has influenced the psychologists. I had a long talk with him and saw that he is a keen supporter of your ideas. After the discussion Geheimrat Binswanger, Jena, told me that Aschaffenburg, before his lecture, had said to him that he (B.) *ought to help him in the discussion!* In my last letter, you remember, I told you about A.'s slips of the tongue. The other one, as I discovered afterwards, was "Breuer and *I*" instead of "Breuer and *Freud*." All this fits in very nicely with my diagnosis. His absence the following day was due to a court case that couldn't be postponed. Had he been present I would definitely have given him some more of the truth. The others I found too dumb.

[2] Theodor Ziehen (1862–1950), professor of psychiatry and neurology in Berlin; later in Halle. Remembered especially for works in child psychology and positivist philosophy. He is credited by Jones (II, pp. 127/113) with introducing the term "feeling-toned complex" into psychology in his *Introduction to Physiological Psychology* (1895; orig. 1891); cf. also Ellenberger, p. 692. Jung adopted the term in 1904 (with Riklin, "The Associations of Normal Subjects," CW 2, par. 167) and associated Ziehen with it in a 1905 paper ("The Psychological Diagnosis of Evidence," CW 2, par. 733 n. 13). Freud's first published use of "complex," in connection with the Zürich School, was in 1906: "Psycho-analysis and the Establishment of the Facts in Legal Proceedings," SE IX, p. 104, n. 1.

[3] Heinrich Sachs, professor of psychiatry, Breslau University.

[4] See above, 1 F n. 3. It was Jung who worked with the association experiment, which had never been a concern of Freud's.

[5] The reference is to Gross's hypothesis of two psychological types representing the primary and the secondary function, in his *Die zerebrale Sekundärfunktion*; see above, 33 J n. 7.

Now for a great surprise: among the English contingent there was a young man from London, Dr. Jones[6] (a Celt from Wales!), who knows your writings very well and does psychanalytical work himself. He will probably visit you later. He is very intelligent and could do a lot of good.

Oppenheim[7] and Binswanger maintain a position of benevolent neutrality although both show signs of sexual opposition. In spite of the—at present—overwhelming opposition I still have the comforting certainty that your ideas are infiltrating from all sides, slowly but surely, because they won't let anyone go once he has assimilated them.

Janet is a vain old buffer, though a good observer. But everything he says and does now is sterile. The rest of the proceedings at the Congress were, as usual, futile. Once again I discovered to my satisfaction that without your ideas psychiatry will inevitably go to the dogs, as has already happened with Kraepelin. Anatomy and attempts at classification are still the rule—sidelines that lead nowhere.

I hope your health will soon be fully restored. In the circumstances I naturally dare not insist on my wishes but would be very glad if I might hope to see you again in the Christmas holidays.

Perhaps I may take this opportunity to express a long cherished and constantly repressed wish: I would dearly like to have a photograph of you, not as you used to look but as you did when I first got to know you. I expressed this wish to your wife when we were in Vienna, but it seems to have been forgotten. Would you have the great kindness to grant this wish of mine sometime? I would be ever so grateful because again and again I feel the want of your picture.

With best regards and wishes,

Yours very sincerely, JUNG

[6] Ernest Jones (1879–1958), later one of Freud's staunchest disciples; a co-founder of the American Psychoanalytic Association in 1911 (he had taken a post at the University of Toronto in 1908) and the British Psycho-Analytical Society in 1913; after 1913, he organized the "Committee" (see below, comment following 321 J). Author of *Sigmund Freud: Life and Work* (1953–57), in the preparation of which he had access to the present correspondence, with Professor Jung's permission.

[7] Hermann Oppenheim (1858–1919), Berlin neurologist, founder and director of a well-known private clinic. He was related to Karl Abraham by marriage and helped him with case referrals, but became increasingly opposed to psychoanalysis.

45 F

Dear colleague, Rome, 19 September 1907[1]

On my arrival here I found your letter about the further developments at the Congress. It has not depressed me and I am glad to see that you are not depressed either. On you, I believe, this experience will have an excellent effect, at least of the kind that I like best. As for me, my respect for our cause has increased. I was beginning to think: "What, already gaining recognition after scarcely ten years? There must be something wrong with it." Now I can believe in it again. But you see that your tactics have been unrealistic. Those people don't want to be enlightened. That is why they are incapable right now of understanding the simplest things. If some day they want to understand, you'll see, nothing will be too complicated for them. Until then, there is nothing for it but to go on working and to argue as little as possible. What can we say after all? To this one: you're an idiot!; to that one: you're a scoundrel! And fortunately these are convictions one does not express. Besides, we know that they are poor devils, who on the one hand are afraid of giving offence, because that might jeopardize their careers, and on the other hand are[2] paralysed by fear of their own repressed material. We must wait until they die out or gradually shrink to a minority. All the young fresh blood, after all, is on our side.

Unfortunately I cannot quote from memory the fine verses, from C. F. Meyer's *Hutten*, that end like this:

"And now that bell which rings so merrily
Says: One more Protestant has come to be."[3]

---

[1] Published in *Letters*, ed. E. L. Freud, no. 127. / Freud spent 15–16 Sept. in Florence, where he met Eitingon, and 17–26 Sept. in Rome. See Jones, II, pp. 40ff./35ff., and *Letters*, ed. E. L. Freud, nos. 128–33.

[2] Holograph: *bin* (am) corrected by Freud to *sind*.

[3] Slightly misquoted from *Huttens letzte Tage* (1871), XXIV, poetic cycle by Conrad Ferdinand Meyer (1825–98), Zürich poet. Freud included it in a list of "ten good books" which he among other distinguished people was asked to make by the Vienna bookseller Heinrich Hinterberger for the magazine *Neue Blätter für Literatur und Kunst* the same year (*Letters*, ed. E. L. Freud, no. 135; also SE IX). The preceding couplets that Freud would have liked to quote (tr. R.M.):

"Over the lake an endless sound of bells is carried;
Many, it seems, are being baptized and buried.

"When human blood is born into new veins
The sluggish human spirit new life gains.

But Aschaffenburg, whom you have seen through so brilliantly (see above my slip: "am" instead of "are"), is obviously the chief scoundrel, because he is intelligent and ought to know better. We must remember that. You are quite right in stressing the absolute sterility of our opponents, who can do no better than exhaust themselves with one outburst of abuse or identical repetitions, whereas we are able to forge ahead, and so can all those who join us. The Celt[4] who surprised you is certainly not the only one; before the year is out we shall hear of unexpected supporters, and you will acquire others at your flourishing school.

Now for my *Ceterum censeo*:[5] Let's go ahead with our journal. People will abuse us, buy it and read it. Some day you will remember the years of struggle as the best. But please, don't make too much of me. I am too human to deserve it. Your desire to have a picture of me encourages me to make a similar request that will undoubtedly be easier to meet. In the last fifteen years I have never willingly sat for a photographer, because I am too vain to countenance my physical deterioration. Two years ago I was obliged (by the regulations) to have my picture taken for the Hygiene Exhibition, but I so detest the picture that I won't lift a finger to let you have it. At about the same time my boys took a picture of me; it is much better, not at all artificial. If you like, I shall find a print for you when I get back to Vienna. The best and most flattering of all is probably the medallion that C. F. Schwerdtner made for my fiftieth birthday.[6] Just say the word and I shall have it sent to you.

Here in Rome I am leading a solitary existence, deep in daydreams. I don't intend to return home until the last of the month. My address is *Hotel Milano*. At the beginning of the holidays I put science far away from me, and now I should like to get back to normal and pro-

---

"The bell which just so mournfully has tolled
Said: now a papist's buried, parched and old."

[4] Holograph: *der Celte*; in the E. L. Freud *Letters* version, misread as *der Alte* and translated "the old man."

[5] Cato the Elder (234–149 B.C.) ended all his speeches in the Roman Senate with the phrase "Ceterum censeo Carthaginem esse delendam" (also, I think Carthage must be destroyed).

[6] Freud's group of adherents in Vienna commissioned a medallion for the occasion of his fiftieth birthday, 6 May 1906. It was designed by a well-known Viennese sculptor, Karl Maria Schwerdtner (1874–1916), and had on the obverse a profile portrait of Freud and on the reverse a representation of Oedipus answering the Sphinx, with the lines (in Greek) from Sophocles, "Who divined the famed riddle and was a man most mighty." See plate IV.

Sigmund Freud, 1906: the photograph that he sent to Jung. See 45 F, 48 J

duce something. This incomparable city is the right place for it. Though my main work probably lies behind me, I should like to keep up with you and the younger men as long as I can.

Eitingon,[7] whom I met in Florence, is now here and will probably visit me soon to give me detailed impressions of Amsterdam. He seems to have taken up with some woman again. Such practice is a deterrent from theory. When I have totally overcome my libido (in the common sense), I shall undertake to write a "Love-life of Mankind."[8]

In anticipation of your reply, with kind regards,

Yours very sincerely, DR. FREUD

46 J

Dear Professor Freud,   Burghölzli-Zürich, 25 September 1907

I'm afraid my answer is again a little late; most of the time I have been in bed with acute gastro-enteritis. I'm still pretty run down.

I should be most grateful if you could let me have the picture your sons took of you. May I also ask you to let me know where I can get the medallion? I should like to buy one.

Here we have now founded a Freudian Society of Physicians[1] which will hold its first meeting next Friday. We are counting on about 12 people. The subject for discussion is naturally case material.

[7] Max Eitingon (1881–1943), Russian-born, reared in Leipzig; was working as a voluntary assistant at the Burghölzli when he visited Vienna and attended meetings (23 and 30 Jan. 07) of the Wednesday Society—thus was Freud's first follower to visit him from abroad. (See Freud's letter to him, 24 Jan. 22, in Letters, ed. E. L. Freud.) 1909, inaugural dissertation (Zürich University) on the use of the association experiment with epileptics. Charter member of the Berlin Psychoanalytic Society (1910); 1919, became the sixth member of the "Committee" (see below, comment following 321 J). Founder of the Berlin Psychoanalytic Policlinic (1920) and, after settling in Palestine in 1934, of the Palestine Psychoanalytic Society.

[8] Freud had told the Wednesday Society on 28 Nov. 06 that he was planning "a study of man's love life" (Minutes, I, p. 66). See below, 209 F n. 6 and 288 F n. 1.

[1] Jung reported on German Switzerland in a series of reports on "the present situation of applied psychology in various countries," Zeitschrift für angewandte Psychologie, I (1907/8), 469f., in which he stated: "In autumn 1907 a Society for Freudian Researches (with ca. 20 members) was established, under the chairmanship of Prof. Bleuler." (See CW 18.)

As you know, the plan to start a journal is much to my liking, but I'd rather not rush ahead as I have first to catch up with my other obligations. Only when everything is settled could I turn to such an undertaking. Also, just now I am involved in the question of an international institute for research into the causes of mental illness.[2] The solution of this problem has still to come. In any case I couldn't think of the journal before the second half of 1908. After that the thing will come about pretty much by itself.

I consider Eitingon a totally impotent gasbag—scarcely has this uncharitable judgment left my lips than it occurs to me that I envy him his uninhibited abreaction of the polygamous instinct. I therefore retract "impotent" as too compromising. He will certainly never amount to anything; one day he may become a member of the Duma.[3]

Dr. Gross tells me that he puts a quick stop to the transference by turning people into sexual immoralists. He says the transference to the analyst and its persistent fixation are mere monogamy symbols and as such symptomatic of repression. The truly healthy state for the neurotic is sexual immorality. Hence he associates you with Nietzsche. It seems to me, however, that sexual repression is a very important and indispensable civilizing factor, even if pathogenic for many inferior people. Still, there must always be a few flies in the world's ointment. What else is civilization but the fruit of adversity? I feel Gross is going along too far with the vogue for the sexual short-circuit, which is neither intelligent, nor in good taste, but merely convenient, and therefore anything but a civilizing factor.

With best regards,

Most sincerely yours, JUNG

47 J

Dear Professor Freud,   Burghölzli-Zürich, 1 October 1907[1]

I don't think you can have got my last letter, which I sent to Rome nearly a week ago. The first meeting of our Society was very interest-

[2] Details unavailable.

[3] The Imperial Duma, the Russian elective assembly, had first met the previous year; it was dissolved by the Czar and two successive assemblies, ineffectual in character, were elected in 1907.

[1] Postcard.

Medallion, commissioned by Freud's friends
in honour of his 50th birthday, 1906.
By Karl Maria Schwerdtner. See 45 F, 48 J

IV

ing. There were 12 people present. One of our assistants[2] discussed the sexual symbolism of a catatonic and Riklin gave an analysis of "The Confessions of a Beautiful Soul."[3] Both lectures were followed by a lively and fruitful discussion. Next time Director Bertschinger[4] (a pupil of Forel's, and now an active advocate of your ideas) will talk on "psychosynthesis,"[5] of which he has had only negative experiences.

With best regards,

Most sincerely yours, JUNG

48 J

Dear Professor Freud,   Burghölzli-Zürich, 10 October 1907

Heartiest thanks for the excellent photograph[1] and the splendid medallion.[2] I am delighted with them. I'll send you my picture at once, although such an exchange seems almost absurd.

Yesterday and again today I felt furious with Weygandt,[3] who has published an exceedingly stupid article in Ziehen's *Monatsschrift*. It is one of the worst bits of drivel I have ever read. And mean, too! I know Weygandt personally, he is a super-hysteric, stuffed with complexes from top to bottom, so that he can't get a sensible word out of his gullet; he is even dumber than Aschaffenburg. I would never have believed the German academics could produce so much beastliness.

However, underneath the dismal face of this coin there is a mar-

[2] Hans Wolfgang Maier (1882–1945), pupil of Forel and Aschaffenburg; at the Burghölzli from 1905; from 1927, Bleuler's successor as director.

[3] = "Die Bekenntnisse einer schönen Seele," in Book VI of Goethe's *Wilhelm Meisters Lehrjahre* (1796). Riklin's lecture was not published.

[4] Heinrich Johannes Bertschinger (1870–1935), Swiss psychiatrist, at the Burghölzli under Forel, later director of the Breitenau Sanatorium, Schaffhausen, until his death. Member of the Zürich Psychoanalytic Society.

[5] A theory advanced by Bezzola; cf. his "Des Procédés propres à réorganiser la synthèse mentale dans le traitement des névroses," *Revue de psychiatrie*, XII (1908), his report to the Amsterdam Congress. See below, 151 J n. 3, for a different system of psychosynthesis evolved by Roberto Assagioli; also above, 18 F.

[1] See plate III.

[2] See plate IV.

[3] Wilhelm Weygandt (1870–1939), professor of psychiatry at Würzburg; later at Hamburg. His "Kritische Bemerkungen zur Psychologie der Dementia Praecox," *Monatsschrift für Psychiatrie und Neurologie*, XXII (1907), dealt with Jung's monograph.

vellous reverse side which is giving me much enjoyment: the analysis
of a young woman with Dementia praecox. Every properly analysable
case has something aesthetically beautiful about it, particularly this
one, which is an exact copy of Ibsen's *Lady from the Sea*.[4] The build-
up of the drama and the thickening of the plot are identical with
Ibsen's; unfortunately the dénouement and the solution lead not to
the freeing of libido but to the twilight of autoerotism, where the old
dragon drags all the libido that belongs to him back to himself again.
The Gordian knot is not untied but cut.

The patient loves from afar a rich young man X., apparently without requital. She is coaxed into getting engaged to a decent, good-
natured, but unprepossessing man A. Not long after the engagement
she learns from a friend of X.'s that he was very upset by it. Violent
outburst of passion. Deep depression; consents to the marriage only
after ham-fisted wheedlings by parents. Refuses her husband coitus for
9 months. Husband touchingly patient, mother storms at her, finally
she gives way and once in a while permits totally frigid coitus. Conception. The depression lifts slowly, little by little. Birth of a girl, welcomed with transports of joy and loved with supernatural love. Depression apparently wiped out. Spells of exuberant joy, effusive praise
of her happy marriage. Coitus as frigid as before. Soon after childbed,
fits of rapturous orgasms with compulsive masturbation, accompanied
by visions of her former beloved. The little girl is dressed only in *blue*.
She looks like the husband, but has something special about her—the
eyes; they are not the mother's, nor the husband's, they are "wonderful" brown eyes, the eyes of the beloved. After a second pregnancy she
gives birth to a boy, whom she hates from the start even though she
wanted the pregnancy. Thus far Ibsen. Now comes the classical catastrophe. After 2 years the little girl dies. Patient falls into a frenzy,
blasphemes: "Why should God take my child, why does he take only
the beautiful children and not the cripples? They say he takes children
up to heaven, but it's not true, and even if it were, *nobody knows what
he does with them there!*" (Already a qualification of her love for the
child!) From then on excited, raging, punches husband, threatens to
"hurl the boy against the nearest wall." Suicidal tendencies. Intern-
ment. At times profoundly depressed, at others serene, with transference to me because of my brown eyes and tall figure. The moment the
analysis touched on repressed sexuality during marriage, sudden outburst of wild sexual excitement which quieted down after a few hours.

[4] Published 1888.

The dreams are interesting as they show that her unconscious actually wanted to *kill* not only the boy but also the beloved little girl (because they were her husband's children?); the girl seems to have been merely a symbol for the beloved. It seems to me there is a distinct psychogenic causality in this case.

Particularly interesting from the theoretical point of view is the fact that the successful repression of the disturbing lover after the first birth was the efficient cause of the illness. It was then that the orgasms became autonomous, though they did not permanently hinder the personality in adapting to the marriage.

I would like to ask your sage advice about something else. A lady, cured of obsessional neurosis, is making me the object of her sexual fantasies, which she admits are excessive and a torment to her. She realizes that the role I play in her fantasies is morbid, and therefore wants to cut loose from me and repress them. What's to be done? Should I continue the treatment, which on her own admission gives her voluptuous pleasure, or should I discharge her? All this must be sickeningly familiar to you; what do you do in such cases?

A fortnight ago we had the first meeting of our "Freudian" Society, with 12 participants; lecture by Riklin on "The Confessions of a Beautiful Soul" and by Dr. Maier on a case of catatonia. Second meeting tomorrow:[5] Director Dr. Bertschinger of Schaffhausen will report on his negative experiences with Bezzola's tricks, Dr. Abraham on purposivity in sexual dreams. The whole thing is going very well, great interest all round, lively discussion. I have the joyful feeling of participating in endlessly fruitful work. I have also converted the first theologian to your cause (our chaplain at the Clinic!).[6] That is something of an event. My pupil, Dr. Stein in Budapest, has likewise infected a North German (the first?), the well-known Dr. Juliusburger.[7] J. is one of those people who do not hide their light under a bushel.

You will probably have heard that Abraham has decided to leave.[8]

[5] No less than 20 were present, according to Abraham (*Freud/Abraham Letters*, 13 Oct. 07).

[6] Eduard Blocher (1870–1942), previously a chaplain in the French Foreign Legion. He did not remain active in the psychoanalytic movement. (This information was kindly supplied by his son, Pastor Wolfram Blocher, of Wald, Cant. Zürich.) See also below, 175 J n. 1.

[7] Otto Juliusburger (1867–1952), founding member of the Berlin Society (1908); later withdrew from psychoanalysis. In New York after 1940.

[8] Abraham resigned from the Burghölzli in November and moved to Berlin late that month (*Freud/Abraham Letters*, pp. xv and 13).

Let's hope he will meet with success. I envy Eitingon, who is now regaling us with legends from the holy city; is that story of the Fontana Trevi historically true?[9] The analysis here was unsuccessful.[10]

With best regards and very many thanks,

Most sincerely yours, JUNG

49 J

Dear Professor Freud,   Burghölzli-Zürich, 28 October 1907

I immediately put your good advice[1] about the case of obsessional neurosis into practice with good results. Heartiest thanks.

The Näcke[2] affair is most amusing. In any case N. is hardly worth bothering about. He is a queer bird who flutters like a will o' the wisp over all the backwaters of neurology, psychiatry, and psychology, and who must have popped up with uncanny frequency in your reading. He has just written an exceedingly strange, altogether crack-brained "historical" monograph on cramp in the legs. Ch. 1: Cramp in Ancient Egypt. Ch. 2: Cramp in Assyria, and so on. It doesn't surprise me that he couldn't refrain from sticking his nose into the great Freud debate. I don't know the critique as I haven't got the *Gross Archiv*.[3]

Your last two letters contain references to my laziness in writing. I

---

[9] Miss Anna Freud suggests that the reference is to Freud's having, in accordance with the superstition, tossed a coin into the Fontana di Trevi and vowed to return to Rome (cf. Jones, II p. 22/19f.).
[10] This allusion cannot be explained.

---

[1] Two letters from Freud since 19 Sept. are missing; one evidently commented on the case Jung described in his last. Also see the 3rd par. of this letter.
[2] Paul Näcke (1851–1913), Russian-born German psychiatrist, director of an asylum at Colditz, Saxony. He published prolifically, and is credited with introducing the term "narcissism." He wrote a number of articles on cramp; cf. "Das Vorkommen von Wadenkrämpfen in orientalischen Gebieten in alter und neuer Zeit," *Neurologisches Zentralblatt*, XXVI (1907), 792f. The critique Jung refers to was probably Näcke's article "Über Kontrast-Träume und speziell sexuelle Kontrast-Träume," *Archiv für Kriminalanthropologie und Kriminalistik*, XXIV:1/2 (July 1906), in which he criticizes Freud's dream theory and says, "Unfortunately Jung has let himself be influenced too much by Freud." In the same issue he published adverse reviews of Freud's *Three Essays* and Jung's "The Psychological Diagnosis of Evidence."
[3] *Archiv für Kriminalanthropologie und Kriminalistik* (Leipzig), founded and edited by Hanns Gross (1847–1915), professor of criminology at Graz University. For his son Otto, see above, 33 J n. 7.

certainly owe you an explanation. One reason is my work load, which hardly gives me a breather even in the evenings; the other is to be found in the realm of affect, in what you have termed my "self-preservation complex"—marvellous expression! And indeed you know that this complex has played many a trick on me, not least in my Dem. praec. book. I honestly[4] do try, but the evil spirit that (as you see) bedevils my pen often prevents me from writing. Actually—and I confess this to you with a struggle—I have a boundless admiration for you both as a man and a researcher, and I bear you no conscious grudge. So the self-preservation complex does not come from there; it is rather that my veneration for you has something of the character of a "religious" crush. Though it does not really bother me, I still feel it is disgusting and ridiculous because of its undeniable erotic undertone. This abominable feeling comes from the fact that as a boy I was the victim of a sexual assault by a man I once worshipped. Even in Vienna the remarks of the ladies ("enfin seuls," etc.) sickened me, although the reason for it was not clear to me at the time.

This feeling, which I still have not quite got rid of, hampers me considerably. Another manifestation of it is that I find psychological insight makes relations with colleagues who have a strong transference to me downright disgusting. *I therefore fear your confidence.* I also fear the same reaction from you when I speak of my intimate affairs. Consequently, I skirt round such things as much as possible, for, to my feeling at any rate, every intimate relationship turns out after a while to be sentimental and banal or exhibitionistic, as with my chief, whose confidences are offensive.

I think I owe you this explanation. I would rather not have said it. With kindest regards,

Most sincerely yours, J U N G

50 J

Dear Professor Freud, Burghölzli-Zürich, 2 November 1907

I am suffering all the agonies of a patient in analysis, riddling myself with every conceivable fear about the possible consequences of my confession. There is one consequence I must tell you right now, as it might interest you. You will remember my telling you a short dream I

---

4 Holograph: *redch*, meaningless, crossed out and followed by (*!*) *redlich*(*!*).

had while I was in Vienna. At the time I was unable to solve it. You sought the solution in a rivalry complex. (I dreamt that I saw you walking beside me as a *very, very frail old man.*)[1] Ever since then the dream has been preying on my mind, but to no purpose. The solution came (as usual) only after I had confessed my worries to you. *The dream sets my mind at rest about your + + + dangerousness!*[2] This idea couldn't have occurred to me at the time, obviously not! I hope to goodness the subterranean gods will now desist from their chicaneries and leave me in peace.

I don't know whether I am telling you anything new when I say that the history of Jensen's childhood is now clear to me. A very beautiful solution is to be found in the stories "The Red Umbrella" and "In the Gothic House."[3] Both, particularly the first, are wonderful parallels of *Gradiva*, sometimes down to the finest details. *The problem is one of brother-sister love.* Has Jensen a sister? I refrain from expatiating on the details, it would only spoil the charm of discovery.

Because of my services as an occultist I have been elected an "Honorary Fellow of the American Society for Psychical Research."[4] In this capacity I have been dabbling in spookery again. Here too your discoveries are brilliantly confirmed. What do you think about this whole field of research?

I have the liveliest hopes that you will come to Zürich during the Christmas holidays. May I count on receiving you as a guest in my house?

With best regards,

Yours very sincerely, JUNG

51 J

Dear Professor Freud, Burghölzli-Zürich, 8 November 1907

Heartiest thanks for your letter,[1] which worked wonders for me. You are absolutely right to extol humour as the only decent reaction

---

[1] Cf. a similar dream that Jung relates in *Memories*, p. 163/158.
[2] Holograph: Jung inserted the three crosses after writing *Gefährlichkeit!* (dangerousness!). See above, 11 F n. 7.
[3] Two stories comprising the volume *Übermächte* (Superior Powers; Berlin, 1892).
[4] English in original. The Society, in New York, was then under the direction of James Hervey Hyslop, who probably sponsored Jung.

---

[1] Missing.

to the inevitable. This was also my principle until the repressed material got the better of me, luckily only at odd moments. My old religiosity had secretly found in you a compensating factor which I had to come to terms with eventually, and I was able to do so only by telling you about it. In this way I hoped to prevent it from interfering with my behaviour in general. In any case I am confident that my humour will not desert me in difficult situations. The goal of our common endeavours provides a salutary and considerably heavier counterweight.

It would be nice if you could pick on Christmas—that is, from the 26th on—for your visit to Zürich. No need at all to think you might inconvenience my chief in any way; he will be "affairé" as always, and will treat you to a grand display of dedicated, unassuming scientific interest which always bowls the uninitiated over. My chief is the most notable example of a brilliantly successful pseudo-personality, a problem worthy of the sweat of the noble.[2]

Unfortunately Easter is rather far off—my one cogent reason for preferring Christmas.

As to the *Zeitschrift für Sexualwissenschaft*,[3] a lot depends on the editorship. If the "175-ers"[4] are in charge, that will hardly be a guarantee of its scientific attitude. It is fishy to begin with that you haven't been invited to be a regular contributor. I don't think there is any opening for your ideas there. I believe they will have a smoother passage via psychiatry. The progress of your cause in Switzerland has followed this path, and given the shortness of the time the results have been good. I have now been asked to speak on the significance of your teachings at the Cantonal Medical Society. Right now the 2nd physician of the Préfargier Asylum[5] is here to get himself initiated. Dr. Jones of London has announced his arrival here on November 25 for the same purpose. So everything is going as well as could be wished. If Germany wants to hang back, others will take the lead. Binswanger jr. writes that he will publish from the Jena Clinic an analysis with a preface by his uncle—a point that raises several question marks.[6] But

[2] Holograph: *das Schweisses der Edeln wert*, a quotation from F. G. Klopstock's ode "Der Zürchersee" (1750).

[3] See below, 74 F n. 2.

[4] Colloquial expression for homosexuals, because sec. 175 of the German penal code dealt (and still deals) with homosexuality.

[5] At Marin, Canton Neuchâtel. The identity of the 2nd physician cannot be established.

[6] "Versuch einer Hysterieanalyse"; see below, 167 F n. 2.

in itself it would be all to the good. One thing is certain: the cause will never fall asleep again. The worst thing is being killed by silence, but that stage is over and done with.

With best regards and many thanks,

Most sincerely yours, JUNG

52 F

15 November 1907,
Dear friend and colleague,[1]   Vienna, IX. Berggasse 19

I always find that my day has begun well when the post brings me an invitation to a meeting of the society you have named after me; unfortunately it is usually too late for me to take the express and arrive on time. What you say of your inner developments sounds reassuring; a transference on a religious basis would strike me as most disastrous; it could end only in apostasy, thanks to the universal human tendency to keep making new prints of the clichés we bear within us. I shall do my best to show you that I am unfit to be an object of worship. You probably think that I have already begun. In my last letter I was irritable and sleepy; soon afterward I pulled myself together and said to myself very much what you point out to me in your letter, to wit, that we have every reason for satisfaction. And besides, we must not make the mistake of judging the ferment exclusively by the literary bubbles it sends up. The most significant transformations are not necessarily the result of any explicit publication. One fine day one simply notices that they have taken place.

Despite his uncle's reassuring preface, Binswanger's publication, emanating from one of the citadels of orthodoxy, will create a furore in Germany. In any case what you have done with the boy was a brilliant move. Do you think he has enough toughness and endurance to establish a focus of infection one day?

Yesterday I received a paper by Warda[2] from the volume in honour of Binswanger sr. He means well, as he has already shown in early publications, but he seems without talent, one of those who can't take

---

[1] Holograph: *Lieber Freund und College.* Unless in one of the previous missing letters, this is Freud's first use of this salutation. / With this letter Freud began using a new stationery with "Wien" on the letterhead.

[2] Wolfgang Warda, charter member of the Berlin Branch Society (1910); withdrew 1911. His paper is "Zur Pathologie und Therapie der Zwangsneurose," *Monatsschrift für Psychiatrie und Neurologie,* XXII (1907), supplementary vol.

the slightest step forward by themselves, and so his paper makes a pathetic impression.

Imagine, in spite of the request expressed in my correspondence with him, I have not received an offprint of Näcke's paper,[3] or of Aschaffenburg's[4] either for that matter, though he was polite enough to send me his first attack. I should be far more unconsolable, however, if I were not to see your address to the Amsterdam Congress.

Some time ago, a Dr. Kutner,[5] a former assistant to Wernicke, wrote to me from Breslau that he wished to come to Vienna for a bit of instruction in ΨA. I told him frankly how little I would be able to teach in the course of a short visit. Since then I have had no word from him.

I must own to you that I am not working on anything at the moment; but *it* goes on working inside me without interruption. Riklin's fairy-tale essay ought to be fully corrected by now. *Gradiva* is really getting no attention at all. That tedious bookseller is still keeping me waiting for Jensen's two novellas!

I hope to hear from you soon.

Yours cordially, DR. FREUD

53 F

24 November 1907
Dear friend and colleague,   Vienna, IX. Berggasse 19

I am writing to you today on a personal matter. In the next few days a Dr. A—— will call on you. He is a jurist who intends to study economics in Zürich, a very gifted man who has suffered all his life from a severe disorder. Treatment by Dr. Federn,[1] one of my colleagues, has been brilliantly successful. He will ask your permission to attend the sessions of your society if it is at all possible, because his interest has not ended with his cure. He hopes you will not identify him to anyone as a former patient, and I believe he is looking forward to exchanging a few words with you. His sister, who has hysterical attacks, is a patient of mine; simultaneous analysis of brother and sister provided me with all sorts of valuable confirmations. Their case suggests the two forerunners of *Gradiva*, which you discovered. You

---

[3] See above, 49 J n. 2.   [4] See above, 43 J n. 1.   [5] Not identified.

---

[1] Paul Federn (1871–1950), Viennese internist; one of the earliest adherents of psychoanalysis (1904), and one of the closest to Freud of the Vienna group. After 1938, in New York.

are certainly right. I am not yet sure whether Jensen actually had a sister who died young or whether he never had a sister and transformed a playmate into the sister he had always longed for. The best would be to ask him, but his last letters were so dull that I cannot make up my mind to. The stories are indeed very interesting. In "The Red Umbrella," all the trappings of *Gradiva* are already present, the noonday mood, the flower on the tomb, the butterfly, the forgotten object, and finally the ruin. And also the element of improbability, the same exaggerated agreement between reality and fantasy. The clearing is the same as in his memory, although the location is different, and the new love carries the same umbrella as the old one. With the help of this novella one sees that certain features of *Gradiva* are rudiments of something more significant. Thus the accidental plague of flies in *Gradiva*, described only for the sake of comparison, comes from the bumblebee in "The Red Umbrella," which appears as a messenger from the dead woman and by molesting the hero saves him from death. The writing in this novella is hideously insensitive, but its content is most meaningful. Our love-objects form series, one is a recurrence of another (*the Master of Palmyra*[2]), and each one is a reactivation of an unconscious infantile love, but this love must remain unconscious; as soon as it is aroused to consciousness, it holds the libido fast instead of guiding it onward, and a new love becomes impossible.

The first novella might be translated something like this: I've lost her and I can't forget her. Consequently I can't really love any other woman. The second—"In the Gothic House"—simply expresses this idea: Even if she had lived, I should inevitably have lost her by marrying her to another (which makes it probable that she was his sister), and it is only in the third, our *Gradiva*, that he fully overcomes his grief by saying: I shall find her again. In the old man this can only be an intimation of death and a consolation with the Christian hereafter, represented in diametrically contrary material.

In neither of the two novellas is there any trace of a reference to the girl's "gait," as it figures in *Gradiva*. Here an accidental glimpse of the relief must have reawakened the author's memory of the dead girl. But now what do you think of the following bold construction? His little sister had always been ailing, she had had a horsehoof foot[3] and limped, later she had died of tuberculosis. This pathological element had to be excluded from the embellishing fantasy. But one day the

---

[2] *Der Meister von Palmyra* (1889), play by Adolf von Wilbrandt (1837–1911).
[3] Holograph: *Spitzfuss* = talipes equinus, a deformity in which the sole faces backward and the toe points downward.

grieving author came across the relief and saw that this deformity, the horsehoof foot, could be refashioned into a mark of beauty. *Gradiva* was now complete—a new triumph of wish-fulfilling fantasy.[4]

With kind regards,

Yours, DR. FREUD

54 J

Dear Professor Freud,   Burghölzli-Zürich, 30 November 1907

Last Tuesday I lectured at the Medical Society for nearly an hour and a half on your researches, to great applause.[1] More than 100 doctors were present. No opposition except from two well-known neurologists, who rode the moral hobby-horse.

Yesterday's meeting of our Freudian Society went off very nicely, with much animation. Prof. Bleuler opened the proceedings with some priceless doggerel aimed at your critics. Von Monakow[2] was also present and naturally took the verses as referring to himself, which amused all the old hands enormously. One sees what a difference mass suggestion makes—there were 25 people present—Monakow shrivelled in his seat. This time the opposition got into hot water. May it be a good omen! Dr. A—— was there too. He still exploits his neurosis a bit.

Dr. Jones of London, an extremely gifted and active young man, was with me for the last 5 days, chiefly to talk with me about your researches. Because of his "splendid isolation"[3] in London he has not yet penetrated very deeply into your problems but is convinced of the theoretical necessity of your views. He will be a staunch supporter of our cause, for besides his intellectual gifts he is full of enthusiasm.

Dr. Jones, along with my friends in Budapest, has mooted the idea of a Congress of Freudian followers. It would be held in Innsbruck

[4] See Freud's postscript to the second edn. (1912) of "Jensen's *Gradiva*," SE IX, where he incorporated these ideas.

[1] "Über die Bedeutung der Lehre Freud's für Neurologie und Psychiatrie" (abstract), *Korrespondenz-Blatt für Schweizer Aerzte*, XXXVIII (1908), 218f. = "The Significance of Freud's Teachings for Neurology and Psychiatry," CW 18. Bleuler spoke in support; Max Kesselring (see 293 F n. 7) and Otto Veraguth (see 115 J n. 6) in opposition.

[2] Constantin von Monakow (1853–1930), Swiss neurologist of international repute; originally Russian.

[3] English in original; applied to the British Empire, 1896. Freud had used the phrase for his situation (letter to Fliess, 7 May 1900, *Origins*, p. 318). / Jones (II, pp. 43/38) attended the meeting of the Freudian group on 29 Nov.

or Salzburg next spring, and would be so arranged that the participants would not have to be away from home for more than 3 days, which should be possible in Salzburg. Dr. Jones thinks that at least 2 people would come from England, and there will certainly be several from Switzerland.

My Amsterdam lecture, which I keep forgetting to mention for "complex" reasons, is going to be published in the *Monatsschrift für Psychiatrie und Neurologie*. It still needs a bit of polishing.

This week I'm off to Geneva, the second University town where your ideas will never go to sleep again.

With kindest regards,

Most sincerely yours, J U N G

55 F

8 December 1907,

Dear friend and colleague, Vienna, IX. Berggasse 19

In spite of the trouble you seem to be having with your "complex," you have delighted me with really interesting news. I can offer you nothing comparable in return. The Congress in Salzburg in spring 1908 would make me very proud; but I suppose I should be in the way and that you will not invite me. Dr. A—— has sent (though not to me) an enthusiastic and, I believe, astute account of your performance at the Zürich society. Your Englishman appeals to me because of his nationality; I believe that once the English have become acquainted with our ideas they will never let them go. I have less confidence in the French, but the Geneva people must be thought of as Swiss. Claparède's article on the definition of hysteria[1] amounts to a very intelligent judgment on our efforts; the idea of the building of several storeys comes from Breuer (in the general section of the *Studies*),[2] the building itself, I believe, ought to be described rather differently. Claparède would know more about its plan if he had questioned the patients rather than the good-for-nothing authors. Still, his paper is a step forward; the rejection of "suggestion" was necessary. I hope he will learn, as a result of your visit, to take account of a good many things that he still very noticeably neglects.

[1] "Quelques mots sur la définition de l'hystérie," *Archives de psychologie*, VII (1908). See Jung, "Abstracts."
[2] *Studies on Hysteria*, SE II, pp. 244–45 (Part III, "Theoretical," by Josef Breuer; orig. 1893).

I was very much pleased to find a reference to a review of Jung, "The Freudian Theory of Hysteria" in the table of contents of *Folia Neuro-biologica*, a new journal.[3] I opened to the page given and indeed found—one line. After this traumatic experience I decided not to subscribe to this new "central organ."

Abraham is coming from Berlin to see me next Sunday.

I spent last week planning and writing a lecture that I delivered on the sixth in a small hall at Heller's[4] publishing house; about ninety people were present. It passed off without mishap, which is good enough for me; it must have been heavy fare for all the writers and their wives. *Die Neue Rundschau* acquired the lecture in the foetal stage and will probably publish it. If nothing else, it was an incursion into territory that we have barely touched upon so far, but where I might easily settle down. I see I have forgotten to tell you the title of my lecture! It is: "Creative Writers and Day-dreaming."[5] In it I speak more of fantasies than of poets, but I hope to make up for it another time.

Let me hear from you soon.

Yours cordially, DR. FREUD

56 J

Dear Professor Freud,   Burghölzli-Zürich, 16 December 1907

You deceive yourself mightily if you think we are going to let you off coming to Innsbruck or Salzburg! On the contrary, we hope and expect to meet under your chairmanship. It is proposed that the Congress be held after the Congress of Psychologists in Frankfurt,[1] i.e., after April 20. (Unfortunately I cannot remember the exact date at

---

[3] *Folia neuro-biologica* (Leipzig), I:1 (Oct. 1907), 142: merely a mention of Jung's lecture at the Amsterdam Congress in Sept.; see above, 43 J n. 1, and below, 82 F n. 3. Jung was listed as an editorial consultant of this new "international central organ for the biology of the nervous system" (subtitle). The lecture was reviewed in II:1 (Oct. 1908), 140.

[4] Hugo Heller (1870–1923), one of the earliest members of the Wednesday Society, though not a psychoanalyst; owner of a bookstore where the liberal intellectuals and artists of Vienna used to meet; publisher of *Imago* and the *Internationale Zeitschrift für Psychoanalyse*. See also below, 58 F n. 1.

[5] "Der Dichter und das Phantasieren" = SE IX. The journal was not the *Neue Rundschau*, Germany's chief literary monthly (still being published), but the *Neue Revue* (I:10, Mar. 1908). See also Jones, II, p. 385/344.

---

[1] 3rd Congress for Experimental Psychology, Frankfurt am Main, 22–25 April 08.

the moment.) I hope this time won't be too inconvenient for you. To make attendance easier, it would be best if the meeting were limited to one evening and one day, so that all participants, even those from the most distant places, would not have to be away from their work for more than three days. As soon as you let me know whether this arrangement suits you, I shall submit definite proposals to the prospective participants.

I am presently negotiating the founding of a journal for which I want to ensure a wide distribution. It is to be international, since we must emancipate ourselves as much as possible from the German market. I'll tell you about it as soon as I have definite results in hand.

Claparède will hold himself in reserve for some time yet as he has no material; he is actually a psychologist. His benevolent neutrality is assured.

Please excuse the brevity of this letter. I am very busy.

Most sincerely yours, JUNG

57 F

21 December 1907,
Dear friend and colleague,   Vienna, IX. Berggasse 19

What magnificent plans! You are certainly not lacking in energy. It will be fine for me if the meeting is held after Easter,[1] the sooner the better. If you choose Salzburg rather than Innsbruck—the former is by far the more beautiful and congenial of the two—I can foresee no difficulty on my part, the express from here to Salzburg takes only six hours. But I am still prepared to withdraw if you should decide on second thought that things would go better in my absence—and there is something to be said for that point of view. There is certainly no sense in having me as chairman. That won't do. You or Bleuler must take the lead; nuances, the sharing of roles!

To tell the truth, your plans for the journal please me even more, that is a matter of life or death for our ideas.

From Jensen I have received the following answer to my inquiries. On the one hand, it shows how disinclined he is to help with investigations of this kind; on the other, it suggests that the facts are more complicated than a simple schema can indicate. He left the main question—whether there was anything pathological in the gait of the

[1] 19 April.

104

models for his characters—unanswered. I shall transcribe his letter for you, because it is scarcely legible without a magnifying glass: after an introduction in which he apologizes for a "lapidary" treatment of my questions, he writes:

"No. I had no sister or other female blood relation. However, 'The Red Umbrella' was woven from my memories; my first love for a little girl who was my close childhood friend and died of consumption at the age of eighteen and a young girl with whom I was friendly many years later and who was also snatched away by sudden death. The 'red umbrella' comes from the latter. In my story the two figures merged, so to speak, into one; the mystical element, expressed chiefly in the poems, also had its source in the second girl. The novella 'Youthful Dreams' (from my collection *From Quiet* Times,*[2] Vol. II) rests on the same foundation but is confined to the first girl. 'In the Gothic House' is entirely free invention (!)"

Abraham was with us from Sunday to Wednesday. More congenial than your account of him, but there is something inhibited about him, no dash. At the crucial moment he can't find the right word. He told me a good deal about Bleuler, in whom he is evidently much interested as a Ψ problem.

I wish you a Merry Christmas,

With kind regards, DR. FREUD

* The motivation of this slip is obvious.

58 F

1 January 1908,
Dear friend and colleague,   Vienna, IX. Berggasse 19

I won't write much, for fear that having to answer me will be a burden to you. Just a few points that may be of practical importance.

1. A big Vienna publishing house, Freytag Tempsky (IV. Johann Straussgasse 6) is trying hard to acquire "us" and may take over the *Gradiva* series.[1] They are making great promises. I wanted to inform

---

[2] Holograph: *"Aus stiller Zeit"*: after *Aus* Freud wrote *Schri*, then crossed it out. Apparently he had his *Schriften zur angewandten Seelenkunde* in mind.

---

[1] Heller had published the first two volumes of the *Schriften zur angewandten Seelenkunde,* but Freud was dissatisfied with his slowness and was looking for another publisher; eventually Franz Deuticke took over with the third volume. See below, 68 F.

you of this development. It is not a purely Austrian firm, but German (Leipzig).

2. Dr. A——, who called on me today, told me that Dr. Frank at Burghölzli has been telling a story about a woman patient who became infected with gonorrhea at the age of 47, then learned all sorts of horrors from me, and since then has been incurable. I can't for the life of me remember a patient with such a history; A—— was unable to provide any other distinguishing features. Since it is not at all impossible that the patient or physician has been telling lies, please let me know if you have heard any more and can help me to identify the patient. If so, I shall certainly supply the necessary explanations.

My wife was most pleased at your wife's New Year's greetings from Schaffhausen[2] and asks me to thank her kindly.

Here's to our work in 1908!

In friendship, yours sincerely, DR. FREUD

59 J

Dear Professor Freud,   Burghölzli-Zürich, 2 January 1908

Cordial greetings for the New Year! The past year has brought not a few signs of the rosy dawn, and it is now my heartfelt New Year's wish that the coming year will bring still better things. I needn't repeat how well your crops are coming up; you'll see more of them in Salzburg, I hope. As soon as I can I shall send out a circular, so as to fix the number of participants and the date of the Congress. At the same time I shall write to you and ask you to submit my proposals to your Society.

Two things I have noted with some dismay. First, that my hope of welcoming you in Zürich between Christmas and the New Year has come to nothing. Second, that my description of our colleague Abraham was, after all, too black. For psychanalytical reasons I am always inclined to mind my own business first. In this case, however, the "self-preservation complex" of our colleague towards me has certainly played its part. At any rate he seems to have been more forthcoming with you than with me. This difference may account for our different impressions. It is just as well that A. has told you a good deal about Bleuler, thus making up for my negligence. Bleuler really is a psych-

---

[2] Home of Emma Jung's family, the Rauschenbachs.

analytical curiosity. A. writes that things are going well with him in Berlin; at least his debut, I hear, is encouraging.

My French[1] reviewers have been a disappointment. At first they were full of the best intentions, but when they saw how big and how difficult the task is, they funked it. The only thing we managed to launch into French last year was my own report on the first volume of my *Diagnost. Assoc. Stud.*, which Binet demanded of me.[2] Behind Binet there lurks a Swiss, M. Larguier des Bancels,[3] Privatdocent of Philosophy in Lausanne, who has been infected via Claparède. My galvanic investigations, which actually are of psychological interest only because of the association experiments, are coming out in the *Gazzetta Medica Lombarda*.[4] Also, the *Rivista di Psicologia* has approached me for a report on psychanalysis.[5] So you see the bounty of your knowledge is being poured into numerous channels.

So far no further news about the organization of the journal. Negotiations with America are still up in the air.[6]

I have read your news about Jensen with great interest. Unfortunately nothing can be done with mere recollections of the past when personal confessions are lacking. Regrettable but understandable that he has no inkling of the significance of your inquiries. A particular kind of "esprit" is needed, above all a certain youthfulness.

At the moment I am treating another case of severe hysteria with twilight states. It's going well. She is a 26-year-old student. The case is an uncommonly interesting one. I work almost exclusively with dream analyses, the other sources being too scanty. The transference dreams started very early in the most miraculous way, many of them are of somnambulistic clarity. Naturally everything fits in with your theory. The early sexual history is not yet clear, since from the 13th

---

[1] He means French-Swiss.

[2] Alfred Binet (1857–1911), French experimental psychologist; he and the psychiatrist Theodore Simon devised the Binet-Simon Scale (1905) for testing intelligence. He founded and edited the first French journal of psychology, *L'Année psychologique*, in which Jung's report was published: XIV (1908), 453–55, being a summary in French of the articles in vol. I of the *Assoziationsstudien*. Jung was listed as a collaborating editor of *L'Année psychologique*.

[3] Jean Larguier des Bancels (1876–1961), editorial secretary of *L'Année psychologique*; later professor of psychiatry at Lausanne.

[4] Such a work by Jung could not be located in the *Gazzetta* in late 1907 or 1908.

[5] See below, 99 F n. 3.

[6] According to Jones (II, p. 49/44) negotiations with Morton Prince to amalgamate the journal with the *Journal of Abnormal Psychology*, published at Boston under his editorship, came to nothing. See below, 69 J n. 1.

year everything is shrouded in retrograde amnesic darkness phosphorescently lit up only by the dreams. The twilight states are similar to those in the case I first published ("Occult Phenomena").[7] The patient plays to perfection and with positively thrilling dramatic beauty the personality that is her dream ideal. At first I tried to hand over the analysis to our 1st assistant, Dr. Maier, but this didn't work out because the patient had already set her cap at me although I purposely never visited her. During her twilight states the doctors and nurses cluster round full of wonderment. On the second day of the analytical treatment, immediately before the emergence of the main complex, there occurred a twilight state that lasted for two days. Then no more, except that once, on the day the transference became clear to her, she went to a woman friend and staged a defensive twilight state lasting two and a half hours, for which she blamed herself the next day and showed every sign of remorse. She possesses in rare degree the capacity for arguing about the existence or nonexistence of the symptoms. At present she is expecting a visit from her lover, but is afflicted with a ructus.[8] She is always standing at the window, looking out to see if he is coming. At night she dreams that she is collecting "protozoa" from the window and giving them to some shadowy figure. The ructus appeared for the first time after her 16th year, when she noticed that her mother wanted to marry her off. She refused—disgust—fear of pregnancy—ructus. She now *expects* her beloved *at the window*: she is "expecting" a child from her lover (ructus), and *from the window* she fetches the protozoa, which she at once recognizes as embryological. There are swarms of such things. Cases like this always console me for the widespread neglect of your teachings. We are on to a really good thing and can be glad of it.

On January 16th I shall be giving a public lecture[9] and hope to interest a wide audience in the new research. This just about exhausts my New Year's news. May I ask you to give my best wishes for the New Year to your wife and your whole family?

Ever sincerely yours, JUNG

[7] *Zur Psychologie und Pathologie sogenannter occulter Phänomene* (Leipzig, 1902) = "On the Psychology and Pathology of So-called Occult Phenomena," CW 1. It was Jung's dissertation for his medical degree at the University of Zürich.
[8] Belching, sometimes an accompaniment of pregnancy.
[9] Holograph: *Aulavortrag*, "lecture in the University hall." It was given, however, in the Town Hall. See below, 82 F n. 4.

60 J

Dear Professor Freud,   5 January 1908[1]

I am most interested in your news of an arrangement with a new publisher. If there are prospects of quicker publication, I will gladly offer you a small popular work of about three printed sheets,[2] "The Content of the Psychoses,"[3] for your *Papers*. It is a lecture I am to deliver before the "précieuses ridicules" of our good city.

Yours very sincerely, J U N G

61 F

                                                14 January 1908,
Dear friend and colleague,   Vienna, IX. Berggasse 19

Overwork and illness in the family have been responsible for my delay in answering. I miss out on a good many things when I am unable to communicate with you periodically. If you were here, I am sure we should have the most interesting things to tell each other about what can be learned from our cases—I am working on eleven of them at the moment.

In connection with Abraham you are too hard on yourself. He was very nice, but rather inhibited with me too; he is much freer in his letters. I believe he is prevented from unbending by preoccupations that I understand only too well: the fact of being a Jew and concern over his future. Incidentally, Oppenheim takes an interest in him, and even if he is not our friend, Oppenheim is a very decent fellow.

I received Binswanger's paper today.[1] Of course I had no difficulty in recognizing you as a subject and was delighted with the boy's boldness in disentangling his own muddles.[2]

---

[1] Postcard. Jung started to write XII for the month but struck it out, leaving 5.I.08.
[2] Holograph: *Druckbogen*, which has 16 pages, therefore Jung meant 48. The publication actually came to 26.
[3] See below, 82 F n. 4.

---

[1] "Über das Verhalten des psycho-galvanischen Phänomens beim Assoziationsexperiment," *Journal für Psychologie und Neurologie*, X (1907) = "On the Psychogalvanic Phenomenon in Association Experiments," *Studies in Word-Association* (1918).
[2] The subject of tests I and IV is clearly Jung. Binswanger himself is also a test subject; see pp. 516ff. of the English edn.

All our practical affairs are still in a state of suspense, but I should like to lay hands on your lecture and publish it in a few weeks. I myself have two small articles at the printer's[3] and I am busy writing two more, at least one of which—"Character and Anal Erotism"[4]—(for Bresler?) is almost writing itself.

I hope soon to make the acquaintance of Dr. Stein of Budapest; I was prevented by the above-mentioned domestic matters from receiving his visit last Sunday.

Dr. Stekel (of the Wednesday Society) is soon unleashing a big book about anxiety hysteria,[5] theoretically weak, but rich in skillful analyses and likely to make an impression.

Looking forward to hearing from you, with kind regards,

Yours sincerely, FREUD

62 J *1st Congress for Freudian Psychology*[1]

Dear Sir,

From many quarters the followers of Freud's teachings have expressed a desire for an annual meeting which would afford them an opportunity to discuss their practical experiences and to exchange ideas. Since Freud's followers, though few in numbers at present, are scattered all over Europe, it has been suggested that our first meeting should take place immediately after this year's 3rd Congress for Experimental Psychology in Frankfurt (22–25 April), so as to facilitate the attendance of colleagues from Western Europe. The proposed place of meeting is *Salzburg*.

The provisional programme is as follows:

26 April, evening: Arrival and assembly in Salzburg.
27 April: Meeting. Chairman: Prof. Dr. S. Freud.
28 April: Departure.

[3] Probably "Hysterical Phantasies" (64 F n. 1) and "Creative Writers" (55 F n. 4).

[4] In *Psychiatrisch-neurologische Wochenschrift*, of which Johannes Bresler was editor (see below, 77 F n. 6). For the other article in composition, presumably " 'Civilized' Sexual Morality and Modern Nervous Illness," see below, 77 F n. 6.

[5] See below, 98 J n. 3. Cases from Stekel's book were presented at the Wednesday Meeting on 20 and 27 Nov. 07 and 8 Jan. 08 (*Minutes*, I).

[1] Printed circular, posted ca. 18/20 Jan. 08. / For the programmes of the Congresses, and other invitations, see appendix 4; also below, 354 J.

Lectures, presentation of case material, written questions are *very welcome*. Applications should be sent to the undersigned *before 15 February*.

Should you wish to attend the meeting, you are politely requested to communicate your decision to the undersigned *by 5 February*.[2] The definitive programme will be sent to you later.

Burghölzli-Zürich
January 1908

Very truly yours, Dr. C. G. Jung
Privatdocent in Psychiatry

63 J

Dear Professor Freud,   Burghölzli-Zürich, 22 January 1908

Yesterday you will have received my bundle of impudent invitations, and I hope you will approve. I have moved the date as close as possible to Easter; it couldn't be any closer because of the Frankfurt and Berlin Congresses.[1] Claparède, Jones and his friends are attending the first, Bleuler the second. I'm afraid we shall not be able to expect him in Salzburg, as he jibs at returning via Salzburg from Berlin to Zürich (financial considerations!).

I would now like to turn to you for help in regard to the specific working out of the programme. In the name of all my friends I am asking you to speak at our Congress. Nothing special would be needed by way of preparation. We would all like, just for once, to hear a lecture from you—something quite ordinary—in which you might present one of your cases; we all want to learn from you at this Congress. Perhaps you would be kind enough to tell us something *systematic about your wide experience of hysteria* (this would be of particular interest to me, as my Amsterdam lecture has left me with a frightful *sentiment d'incomplétude!*). I shall try to work up a paper on Dem. praecox, perhaps in collaboration with Riklin, and have encouraged Maeder to talk about sexuality in epilepsy.[2] This will fill up a busy morning. The afternoon might best be spent on peripatetic wisdom.

---

[2] In a copy of this circular in the Sigmund Freud Archives (Library of Congress), to which it was contributed by Professor Jung, *sofort* ("immediately") has been substituted in handwriting.

---

[1] Annual meeting of the German Society for Psychiatry, 24–25 Apr. Bleuler read a paper on dementia praecox; see *Berliner Klinische Wochenschrift*, XLV:22 (1 June 08), 1078f.

[2] Riklin gave a paper on his own, "Some Problems of Myth Interpretation (not in

As I don't know my way about in Salzburg I have no idea what the best place for a meeting would be. Perhaps one of your people in Vienna would be good enough to help me arrange for lodgings. I should be most grateful for any help you can give. I shall know by February 5 about how many people to expect, so the necessary arrangements can be made then. At the beginning of April I shall probably go to the south of France for a fortnight with my relatives, and would like to have everything in order by then.

I have sent you 12 copies of the invitation because I wanted to ask if you would distribute them at the next meeting of your pupils. Let me know if you need more. I hope the Viennese contingent will be a really big one.

I am working incessantly at the organization of our journal. The negotiations are very sticky.

I am looking forward eagerly to Stekel's book. So far I haven't managed to cobble together anything worthwhile as every minute is taken up with the experimental work of my pupils.

Gratefully anticipating an early reply,

Yours sincerely, JUNG

64 F

25 January 1908,

Dear friend and colleague, Vienna, IX. Berggasse 19

I admire your energy and will try to help you with your work. We shall be glad to arrange for accommodation in Salzburg; I am pretty well acquainted with the city and its hotels; we should merely have to know first roughly how many persons are to be provided for, and whether you favour something fashionable or something simple. On Wednesday I shall submit your invitation to my Society; then I shall be able to tell you how many of our members wish to attend.

I also accept the chairmanship (!) since you insist, and will say something or other, what I don't know yet; your saying "nothing

---

the printed programme; it apparently replaced the lecture by Morton Prince, who did not attend; see Jones, II, pp. 44ff./40ff., and appendix 4), and Jung lectured "On Dementia Praecox" (see below, 85 J n. 4). Riklin's was published as "Über einige Probleme der Sagendeutung," *Zentralblatt*, I:10/11 (Aug./Sept. 1911). Maeder (who was then director of the hospital for epileptics at Zürich) did not attend; he wrote his dissertation on the topic suggested by Jung; see below, 132 F n. 1.

special," was a great relief to me. Because a little while ago I thought I had my hands on something really worthwhile, the solution of the choice-of-neurosis problem, in which you too take such an interest, but it slipped through my fingers as it did once before, many years ago. But I shall catch it yet.

I presume there is more than one reason why Bleuler will not be with us. I shall be very glad to see you all and I feel sure that our meeting will not be stiff and hollow. If you people do not know Salzburg, we shall be able to spend a pleasant afternoon in the environs (fortress, Hellbrunn); in the evening we could very well hold a so-called business meeting.

So far I have been unsuccessful in my efforts to find a more effective publisher for the *Papers on Applied Psychology*. But I have not given up; please write me 1) when you can send the manuscript of your "Content of the Psychoses" lecture, and 2) when you would like it to be published. Heller is making every effort to hold me.

In the first issue of the *Zeitschrift für Sexualwissenschaft* you will find a short paper by me with hysteria formulas.[1] Offprints have not yet arrived. If I were in possession of your Amsterdam paper, I should be able, with it as a basis, to produce something more comprehensive about hysteria. As it is, I am losing sight of the whole problem of hysteria; at the moment I am more interested in obsessional neurosis.

This week influenza has been raging in my house and unless I am very much mistaken I am coming down with it myself. My daughter[2] had at the same time an abdominal irritation connected with a stitch abscess, an after-effect of her appendectomy. She is now recovering nicely.

I shall be able to use a few more invitations.

Heartfelt thanks for your efforts. Do please consider the state of my health in judging the present letter,

Yours cordially, FREUD

I am far from begrudging you your trip to southern France before our Congress.

---

[1] "Hysterische Phantasien und ihre Beziehung zur Bisexualität," *Zeitschrift für Sexualwissenschaft*, I:1 (Jan. 1908) = "Hysterical Phantasies and Their Relation to Bisexuality," SE IX. Freud gives a list of hysteria formulas on pp. 163ff.

[2] Mathilde, born 1887; see below, 112 F n. 1.

65 J

Dear Professor Freud,   Burghölzli-Zürich, 25 January 1908

Yesterday evening (at our little Freud gathering) Dr. A—— conveyed to me your greetings and your injunction that I should write to you more often. As you see, I'm doing it! Best thanks for the greetings—but I'm always afraid of boring you with my all-too-frequent letters. In the end you would be forced to complain of my manic busyness. Perhaps you have already done so in another connection, to wit, the pretentious title of the circular. Dr. Jones in London was quite shocked by it.[1] I have therefore sent out a special circular to the few people invited, explicitly stressing the *completely private nature* of the project. Actually this may be superfluous, but I think one can never be careful enough. Dr. Abraham has already announced a lecture on the psychosexual differences between Dem. praecox and hysteria.

I hope you will be pleased with the proposed arrangements. I am on tenterhooks for your opinion. You will now have received my primitive lecture[2] and wondered at the *sentiments* that peek through it—*sentiments d'incomplétude* compensated by sentimental posing. If you can't appeal to people's heads then maybe you can get at their hearts. I am an odd mixture of fear and courage, both of them extreme and off-balance.

I have just received the galleys of my Amsterdam lecture. Publication won't be long now.

Have you read the Berlin discussion in the *Neurologisches Zentralblatt*?[3] You will see that friend Bezzola has discovered the once falsely so-called "Breuer-Freud" method. Isn't that something? Liepmann[4] is slyly making himself a little door through which he will suddenly burst upon the scene as the one who knew all about these vulgar things ages ago. He has struck the right note: "Stale news!" Such will be the inscription over the portal leading to the first circle of the purgatorio of your theory. A pity there are never enough good men around to ap-

[1] Cf. Jones, II, p. 44/39.
[2] "The Content of the Psychoses"; see 82 F n. 4.
[3] *Neurologisches Zentralblatt*, XXVII:2 (16 Jan. 08), 88ff.: Juliusburger read a paper to the Psychiatric Society of Berlin 14 Dec. 07 on psychoanalysis, under which term he included "Bezzola's method." Liepmann joined in the discussion.
[4] Hugo Karl Liepmann (1863–1925), professor of neurology at Berlin University and psychiatrist at its hospital, the Charité (founded 1785).

plaud loudly whenever these weaklings, mixtures of muck and luke-warm water, have to eat humble pie.

I have a sin to confess: I have had your photograph enlarged. It looks marvellous. A few of our circle have acquired copies. So, like it or not, you have stepped into many a quiet study!

With best regards,

Most sincerely yours, JUNG

66 F

27 January 1908,
Vienna, IX. Berggasse 19

Dear friend and colleague,

You are joking about your *sentiments*! Your lecture is charming; too bad I haven't got you here to shake your hand; I'd shake it more than once. Spirit of my spirit, I can say with pride, but at the same time something artistic and soft, lofty and serene, something ingratiating that I could never have produced, for I still have the difficulties of the work in my bones. I shall do my best to have it printed *soon*; the negotiations about the publisher are drawing to an end.

How can you imagine that I would ever complain of your too frequent letters or of your "manic" busyness. I have really missed your letters during the last few weeks, and as for your busyness, I must have a similar bent even though it has never been fully developed, because I approve exceedingly of what you are doing. Splendid of you to be impudent for my sake; I am not lacking in impudence but only in the kind of relations with people that would enable me to show it.

As a companion-piece to Bezzola and Liepmann I offer you Meyer in the issue of *Archiv für Psychiatrie* that appeared today.[1] Remarks on your *Dementia Praecox*. His main objection: everyone has delusions of being injured. Feebleminded arguments of this sort are possible because these gentlemen have learned nothing, they have never developed a psychological insight on the basis of dreams or of everyday life.[2] I believe that if they were analysed it would turn out that they are still waiting for the discovery of the bacillus or protozoon of hys-

[1] Ernst Meyer, "Bemerkungen zu Jung, 'Über die Psychologie der Dementia praecox,'" *Archiv für Psychiatrie und Nervenkrankheiten*, XLIII (1908), 1312ff. Meyer (1871–1931) was professor of psychiatry and neurology in Königsberg University.
[2] From here to end of paragraph, quoted by Jones, II, p. 488/438 (though misdated, and Jones construed "they" to mean Freud's pupils).

teria as for the messiah who must after all come some day to all true believers. When that happens a differential diagnosis from Dem. pr. ought to be a simple matter, since the hysteria parasite will no doubt have only one stiff whiplike appendage, while that of Dem. pr. will regularly show two and also take a different stain. Then we shall be able to leave psychology to the poets!

It seems likely that we shall receive too many rather than too few papers for our Congress. We can't be listening to lectures all day. In my circle I shall plead for restraint and brevity. I also think the deadlines have been set somewhat too early, since the meeting will not be taking place for nine months.[3]

My influenza didn't last long. My daughter's condition is unchanged, subjectively she feels fine.

I hope your whole family is well. I shall write to you briefly after our Wednesday session. With kind regards,

As ever, FREUD

67 F

31 January 1908,
Dear friend and colleague,   Vienna, IX. Berggasse 19

I have received your package. Eight or ten members of my Society wish to go to Salzburg, but a few cancellations are to be expected. I have accepted the applications. I shall have the papers and proposals sent to you directly. I am afraid there may be too many and am trying my best to put on a damper. My eastern contingent will probably be inferior in personal merit to your western contingent.

On February 2nd I am expecting the two colleagues from Budapest, Dr. Stein and Dr. Ferenczy [sic].

A short offprint from the *Zeitschrift für Sexualwissenschaft* is to be sent to you tomorrow.

With kindest regards,

Yours, FREUD

[3] A slip (or joke?) for "nine weeks."

68 F

14 February 1908,[1]

Dear friend and colleague,   Vienna, IX. Berggasse 19

The Content of the Psychoses has gone to the printer's today and will appear as the third number of the *Papers*, published by F. Deuticke, Vienna.

Many thanks,

Yours, FREUD

69 J

Dear Professor Freud,   Burghölzli-Zürich, 15 February 1908

Once more you will be wondering why I haven't written for so long. The reason is that I had to get over a beastly attack of influenza. Today is the first time I have felt more or less normal, so I am taking this opportunity to write to you. Although I attended to my duties at the Clinic, I felt so run down and listless the whole time that I had to let all my private affairs go. Scientific work came to a total stop. I feel an imperative need for a holiday. But the spring holiday is still a long way off; I shall then take a fortnight's leave at the cost of my holiday in the summer. All sorts of psychogenic complications insinuated themselves into my influenza, and this had a bad effect on my convalescence. First of all a complex connected with my family played the very devil with me, then I got disheartened by the negotiations over the journal. Morton Prince[1] made some unacceptable proposals—even with the best will in the world nothing could be done with them. Claparède is still willing, but the prospects for the journal in France are practically nil. Claparède, for instance, pays for his journal out of his own pocket, since there are far too few subscribers to keep it alive. Prince's journal also suffers from a dearth of subscribers. In the end we may have to settle for a German publication, but I can't get around to this until I have finished my *Diagnost. Assoc. Stud.*, besides

---

[1] Imprinted correspondence card.

---

[1] Morton Prince (1854–1929), psychiatrist of Boston, founder and editor of the *Journal of Abnormal Psychology* (1906–29), to which Jung had recently contributed "On Psychophysical Relations of the Associative Experiment," I (1907); in CW 2. See above, 59 J n. 6.

which my working capacity is strained to the limit by my present activities. In addition there are mounting requests from other periodicals, demanding articles from me. I have a horror of mass-produced goods.

Your followers have outdone themselves in their announcements of lectures, our side looks sterile by comparison. However, we now have just about enough to fill out a decent morning from 8–1 o'clock. I am putting the finishing touches to the programme. I think I have told you already that Bleuler is coming after all.

Dr. Brill of New York,[2] who is still here and has now translated my Dem. praec. book into English, is most enthusiastic about the Breuer-Freud *Studies.* He wants me to ask you whether you would agree to a translation. The interest in America is very great at present. So it wouldn't be a bad speculation. The only thing is that he doesn't want to translate the whole book, just the analyses with the epicrises. For understandable reasons he would like to throw out Breuer's theory. I think a very nice book could be put together out of your case histories if you would add your article on psychanalysis[3] (from the *Collected Short Papers*), and if you would perhaps write a short epilogue defining the changes it has undergone and your present viewpoint. The translation of my Dem. praec. book was a difficult job for a beginner and Dr. B. has done very well. I would like to recommend him as a translator. In all probability he will come to Salzburg if he is still in Europe.

Frank, who usually rushes to all Congresses, is for reasons unknown not coming to Salzburg—significantly enough!

I am still not *remis à neuf*, as you will see from my miserable scrawl and the nebulous mood of this letter.

With best regards,

Yours very sincerely, JUNG

[2] Abraham Arden Brill (1874–1948), Austrian-born American psychoanalyst, translator of many works by Freud as well as of Jung's *The Psychology of Dementia Praecox* in collaboration with Frederick W. Peterson (see below, 124 J n. 3). Founded the New York Psychoanalytic Society (1911).
[3] Probably "Die Freud'sche psychoanalytische Methode" (orig. 1904) = "Freud's Psycho-analytic Procedure," SE VII.

70 F

Dear friend,   17 February 1908, Vienna, IX. Berggasse 19

May I, after adequate preparation, cast off the "colleague" in expressing my satisfaction that your influenza has been vanquished and that your silence did not result from any complex. I can sympathize with your complaints, for I myself have not been feeling very *bright*[1] since my illness, and have been beset by all kinds of little difficulties that I would naturally prefer to do without. Especially here in Vienna it is so easy to get the impression that nothing can be done, that nothing can be changed, that one is attempting the impossible, helping Sisyphus to roll his stone,[2] etc. But these moods pass and I still have a long wait until the holidays.

You have no doubt received my little paper with the hysteria formulas. Other trifles are forthcoming; I am determined not to let any more work be wrung from me, such work always turns out far inferior to what one does spontaneously. Take my urgent advice, arm yourself with ill temper against all unreasonable demands. We definitely need a journal of our own. I am sure you will resume your efforts as soon as your temperature is down to normal. To start a German publication would not be at all bad; with your name you should have no difficulty in finding a decent German publisher. Deuticke would certainly be willing, but to be born in Vienna is no advantage for a new undertaking. I can't see why your *Diagn. Asso. Studies* should stand in the way. The papers for the second volume could continue to be published in their old place, and when you come to the third volume[3] you could change over, if that is still your plan.

I shall attend to our accommodations in Salzburg as soon as you let me know how many people are expected. From here there will be from twelve to fourteen; though I hope that not all those who have applied will come, because they are not all fit to exhibit. Here I must often content myself with very little. — If there is still time to do anything about the programme, I must ask you to do what you can to thwart my talkative Viennese; otherwise we shall all drown in the torrent of words. You could impose a time limit and politely reject

[1] English in original.
[2] Holograph: *das Fass* (barrel), struck out and replaced by *den Stein* (stone). The original reference may have been a confusion with the myth of the Danaids, who were condemned to carry water in barrels perforated like sieves.
[3] A third volume was not published.

certain communications as inappropriate. I am thinking, for instance, of a paper on "Psychophysical Parallelism" that Dr. Schwerdtner,[4] one of my contingent, wants to read; it can only be a piece of dilettantism and is sure to take up an enormous amount of time. We needn't worry too much about the man himself, who is new in the circle and rather retiring. I would not like us to make too poor a showing in your eyes, which is a distinct possibility. You may ask why I myself don't do what I can to stop them. I do, but these people are so dreadfully sensitive and naturally they have no *égards* for me; they are much more likely to show consideration for you, the "distinguished foreigner." You know what prestige foreigners enjoy in Vienna.

To pass on to something more pleasant, the prospect of Bleuler's presence rather confuses me. I have mixed feelings towards him and I should like to honour him in some way. Don't you think it would be a good idea to offer him the chairmanship? My Viennese will be much better behaved with him, and by providing the battle cry I play enough of a role. Do support me in suggesting this change in the programme. Frank is certainly right not to come; I suspect him of being a faker.

Since I have not yet had the honour of being translated, what you write is a great temptation. But I shall resist it. I should have to ask Breuer for his consent to this sejunction[4a] and I don't want to. Besides, I know he would be hurt. Moreover, my case histories in the *Studies* are no less antiquated than Breuer's theories and are not worth translating. And, come to think of it, how ca᛫ they put the book together without Breuer's "first case"? It is impossible and would be historically unjust. I should feel differently if Dr. Brill wanted to translate the whole book. If he really wants to introduce something of mine to the English-language public, I can only suggest the *Three Essays* or the *Collected Short Papers*. But he would want neither. *The Interpretation of Dreams* is unfortunately untranslatable and would have to be rewritten in each language, which would be a deserving task for an *Englishman*.[5]

At last I come to science. I have been in contact with a few paranoia cases in my practice and can tell you a secret. (I write paranoia and not Dem. pr. because I regard the former as a good clinical type and

---

[4] Hugo Schwerdtner (1878–1936), physician, member of the Vienna Society. There is no evidence of this paper or any other publication of Schwerdtner's.

[4a] Holograph: *Sejunktion*. The term was Otto Gross's, borrowed from Wernicke, and referred to the isolation of a complex. Cf. Jung, *Psychological Types*, CW 6, par. 467; and above, 33 J nn. 7 & 8.

[5] English in original.

the latter as a poor nosographical term.) I have regularly encountered
a detachment of libido from a homosexual component which until
then had been normally and moderately cathected. The rest, return of
the libido through projection, etc., is not new. What seems important
to me is not that this component is homosexual, but that the detachment is *partial*. Probably it has been preceded by an increase in libido
and the detachment is a kind of repression. Instances of total detachment probably correspond to Dem. pr.; dementia as the end result
corresponds to the success of the pathological process (the detachment of libido) after a fruitless struggle against it, and to the return
to autoerotism. The paranoid form is probably conditioned by restric
tion to the homosexual component. My old analysis (1896) also
showed that the pathological process began with the patient's estrange-
ment from her husband's *sisters*.[6] My one-time friend Fliess[7] developed
a dreadful case of paranoia after throwing off his affection for me,
which was undoubtedly considerable. I owe this idea to him, i.e., to
his behaviour. One must try to learn something from every experience. The breaking down of sublimations in paranoia belongs to the
same context. Altogether I have a good many budding and incomplete
ideas to tell you about. Too bad that we shall not be exactly undisturbed in Salzburg!

Yours cordially, FREUD

71 F

Dear friend,   18 February 1908, Vienna, IX. Berggasse 19[1]

Don't take fright: after this I promise you a long pause. This is
merely a postscript to reiterate my yesterday's suggestion that we offer
Bleuler the chairmanship in Salzburg. You will be doing me a great
favour if you pass on this wish of mine as a personal request. I consider
it quite appropriate and in a way more dignified that he rather than I
should take the chair. It would seem odd if I as an outlawed knight

[6] See above, 11 F n. 5.
[7] Wilhelm Fliess (1858–1928), Berlin otolaryngologist, Freud's closest friend until
1900; see Jones, I, ch. 13, and Freud, *The Origins of Psychoanalysis: Letters to
Wilhelm Fliess, Drafts and Notes, 1887–1902* (New York and London, 1954).
After the friendship was ended, Freud became critical of Fliess's scientific work
because of its highly speculative character.

[1] Published in *Letters*, ed. E. L. Freud, no. 136.

were to preside over the diet that has been called to defend my rights against the imperial authorities. On the other hand, it would be quite honourable for me and would also make a better impression abroad, if he, the oldest and most authoritative of my supporters, should take the lead in the movement in my favour.

Also, my Viennese will behave better under his chairmanship; in short, everything will be fine if he accepts. I do hope that you will agree with me and use your influence with him.

I decided when I started this note not to write about anything else. So my kind regards and thank you for your efforts.

Yours, FREUD

72 J

Dear Professor Freud,   Burghölzli-Zürich, 20 February 1908

I thank you with all my heart for this token of your confidence.[1] The undeserved gift of your friendship is one of the high points in my life which I cannot celebrate with big words. The reference to Fliess—surely not accidental—and your relationship with him impels me to ask you to let me enjoy your friendship not as one between equals but as that of father and son. This distance appears to me fitting and natural. Moreover it alone, so it seems to me, strikes a note that would prevent misunderstandings and enable two hard-headed people to exist alongside one another in an easy and unstrained relationship.

I have read your hysteria formulas with the greatest pleasure. In my opinion they are very successful and will remove many misunderstandings and false views. I regret very much that these theses did not come into my hands earlier, that is, before the Amsterdam lecture. They would have made my work considerably easier; as you will soon see, it bears traces of laborious formulation and polishing, yet fails to do full justice to your ideas. I hope that while reading it you will bear in mind that it was my most fervent wish to present matters in such a way as to strike the line of least resistance among the opposition. If I may say so, you ought not to bury your theses in this second-rate journal with a dubious prognosis,[2] but should furnish them with examples and publish them in a more conspicuous place. This would do a great

[1] See 70 F, salutation.
[2] *Zeitschrift für Sexualwissenschaft.*

122

deal of good and nip in the bud all the schematisms and syllogisms that will predictably attach themselves to my lecture. Your theses afford an extremely lively and realistic insight into your way of thinking and working; subtly coping with the knots and rough edges of the material, your work is true research in the deepest sense of the word. You have thereby shattered the fable that you lay down axioms and have shown that your science is eternally young and alive, which only a handful of people have believed until now; in my case, for instance, only after I had the good fortune to get to know you personally.

I shall take your advice about throwing out Schwerdtner's "Parallelism." I found it just as unwieldy as you did.

My pessimism over the journal was largely the outcome of my influenza mood. Even so we shall probably have no success in America. On the other hand something might yet be arranged with Claparède —and later it might work out with America after all. My friend Jones in London has written very encouragingly. In the end necessity will decide. Still, I am so overburdened at present that I shudder at any new obligations. An exclusively German publication might, I fear, too easily become one-sided—I mean one-sided in the eyes of the opposition. This must be avoided at all costs if we want to remain practical.

I fully appreciate your idea of offering the chairmanship to Bleuler. But if you knew Bleuler you would not insist. Bleuler would feel most uncomfortable in such a position. He shuns anything of that kind like the plague, being a man to whom all forms of outward recognition are an abomination. He is motivated solely by a truly Christian ambition not to stand in the way of others, and has a youthful eagerness to learn such as only an extremely clever and intelligent man possesses at his age. It would be best to dispense with as many formalities as possible at our modest meeting, as is customary at our more republican meetings in Switzerland.

I do not quite see why the cases you published under your own name could not be translated without your having to ask Breuer first; you could always acknowledge Breuer's merits in an introduction. This would come pretty close to a new publication, and surely nobody could contest your personal contribution. If it came to that, Dr. Brill might get into touch with Breuer directly. The *Theory of Sexuality* would not be suitable for translation because it would fall on totally unprepared ground. And you know the English "resistance"!

Your views on paranoia have not lain fallow. I have been able to confirm them many times over. Only the thing is not yet ripe. I have therefore kept silent about it so far. The detachment of libido, its

123

regression to autoerotic forms, is probably well explained by the self-assertion, the psychological self-preservation of the individual. Hysteria keeps to the plane of "preservation of the species," paranoia (Dem. pr.) to the plane of self-preservation, i.e., autoerotism. A patient once told me: "Everything that happens has something so *gripping* about it!" Autoerotism serves as a purposive defence against this. The psychoses (the incurable ones) should probably be regarded as defensive encapsulations that have misfired, or rather, have been carried to extremes. The Fliess case bears this out. Autoerotism, as an overcompensation of conflicts with reality, is largely teleological. This conception has afforded me some valuable insights. The hysteric, besides repressing reality, makes repeated attempts to link up with it again, the paranoiac forgoes even this and is only intent on keeping up his libido[3] defences. Hence the fixation of the complexes. The patients do not, as in hysteria, risk the leap into suitable new situations by linking up with reality, but work for decades at defending themselves against the complex by inner compensations. The paranoiac always seeks inner solutions, the hysteric outer ones, probably, and often quite obviously, because in paranoia the complex becomes an absolutely sovereign and incontrovertible fact, whereas in hysteria it is always a bit of a comedy, with one part of the personality playing the role of a mere spectator. But this wealth of psychic reality could hardly be expressed in a mere 9 theses.

I have just received your short letter[4] with its affective perseveration in regard to Bleuler. I shall do as you wish, but must candidly confess that in this and similar matters he is not likely to listen to me. Nevertheless I shall work on him in the hope that he will at least take over the chair when you are lecturing. But as I said, when you get to know Bleuler you will find him a man who is far above all that. There is nothing, but absolutely nothing, of the Geheimrat about him. He has that magnificent Zürich open-mindedness which I count as one of the highest virtues.

I should be very glad to hear something about paranoia in your next letter, and especially what you think of the views I have expressed.

I hope you will soon have recovered, as thoroughly as I, from the influenza.

With best thanks for the offprint and kind regards,

Yours very sincerely, J U N G

---

[3] Holograph: *Realität* (reality), crossed out and *Libido* substituted.
[4] Freud's letter of 18 Feb. apparently reached Jung at this point.

P.S. By the same post you will
receive an offprint[5] containing
some idiotic printer's errors,
written in an equally idiotic
style and with garbled results.

73 J

[Undated][1]

Best greetings from
Jung & Jünger[2]
(Binswanger)

74 F

Dear friend,   25 February 1908, Vienna, IX. Berggasse 19

What you write about your chief sounds reassuring. I shall admire
the phenomenon as it deserves; it is indeed a rare virtue, of which I
myself do not feel capable.

Your judgment of the hysteria formulas and even more so your
other observations about my work have given me a rarely experienced
satisfaction. I know that what you say is true, that my manner of
working is indeed honest, which is why my knowledge is so fragmentary and why I am usually incapable of handling a presentation of any
length. I have suppressed my habit of conscious speculation as radically
as possible and have absolutely forsworn the temptation to "fill in the
gaps in the universe."[1] But except for you, who believes me?

The appearance of this piece in the new *Zeitschrift für Sexualwissenschaft* can be laid to a bit of skullduggery on the part of the editors. They originally solicited the piece for the *Jahrbuch für sexuelle*

---

[5] Of Jung's article written with Ricksher; see above, 19 J n. 2.

[1] A postcard, showing views of Jena; postmark: Jena 23 Feb. 1908.
[2] German for both "disciple" and "younger."

---

[1] Holograph: "*Stopfen der Lücken im Weltallbau*"; cf. "Stopft er die Lücken des
Weltenbaus," last line of poem LVIII in section "Die Heimkehr," from Heine's
Buch der Lieder. / This passage quoted by Jones, II, p. 488/438f.

Zwischenstufen,[2] and I was not told until several months later that it was to be published in the *Zeitschrift für Sexualwissenschaft* which was just being founded. I asked for a guarantee that this new organ was not to be a chronicle of the W.H. Committee,[3] in which case I preferred to withdraw my contribution, but received no answer. Then suddenly I received proofs with a request that I should not myself correct them but wire my imprimatur. This of course I refused to do. In any case I had the impression that everything was topsy-turvy with Hirschfeld as a result of the Harden lawsuit.[4]

February 27. But it's not so bad. When a second volume of my *Theory of the Neuroses* is published,[5] all these more recent papers will be included. The most important thing about the incident is that it proves once again that we need a journal of our own, my *ceterum censeo!* I don't really understand your fear of one-sidedness. Can it be that your are still dominated by your "conciliation complex" in this matter?

Thank you for your card from Jena, which came today. A few days' change will do you good. I trust that your holiday trip is still to come.

Nothing can be done with the *Studies.* I don't see how we can do without Breuer's first case history.

Your observations on paranoia have struck a chord in me. You really are the only one capable of making an original contribution; except perhaps for O. Gross, but unfortunately his health is poor. I shall write you my fantasies about paranoia soon, they coincide in part with your ideas. Today I am too tired from monotonous hard work and need a Sunday to catch my breath. You are right, the thing is not yet ripe,

---

[2] Magnus Hirschfeld (1868–1935), Berlin sexologist and an original member of the Berlin Psychoanalytic Society (1908; withdrew 1911; see below, 278 F); founder and editor of those periodicals.

[3] = Wissenschaftlich-humanitäres Komitee, founded by Hirschfeld to promote the legalization of homosexuality.

[4] See above, 27 F n. 7. In his attacks in *Die Zukunft* on Count Philipp Eulenburg and his circle (the "camarilla"), who exerted a strong political influence on the German Kaiser, Harden had hinted that these men were homosexuals. Eulenburg brought a civil action for libel against Harden (Oct. 1907), in which Hirschfeld was a witness; Harden was exonerated. Then a criminal action was brought against him, and Hirschfeld withdrew his earlier deposition; Harden was sentenced to four months in prison (3 Jan. 08). For details, see Harry F. Young, *Maximilian Harden: Censor Germaniae* (The Hague, 1959), pp. 82ff., and Hirschfeld, "Sexualpsychologie und Volkspsychologie: Eine epikritische Studie zum Hardenprozess," *Zeitschrift für Sexualwissenschaft,* I:4 (Apr. 1908).

[5] It was issued in 1909.

and I can't work with the shadowy memories now at my disposal. Consequently I wish you would take the whole problem over.

Many thanks for your English offprint, I shall read it Sunday. Let me know when you need my inquiries about accommodation in Salzburg.

With kind regards,

Yours ever, FREUD

75 J

Dear Professor Freud,   Burghölzli-Zürich, 3 March 1908

I don't know how many Viennese are coming to Salzburg. Only four people have sent in applications: Adler, Sadger,[1] Stekel, and Schwerdtner; that makes five including you. Apart from these five I have eighteen definite applications and three indefinite ones. On this basis arrangements might now be made with the hotel. No doubt you will decide where the meeting is to be held. I imagine the hotel could put a room at our disposal, or should we requisition some official building? I am happy to leave these matters entirely in your hands. The draft of the programme is enclosed.[2]

Now for the news from Jena. I got a gorgeous reception from that old fox "Geheimrat" Binswanger. He gave a stag party in my honour with uniforms and other splendours. He used the evening as an occasion for the following pronouncement:

"There are cases of hysteria that do in fact turn out as Freud says. But we must assume that there are various other forms of hysteria for which different formulas will have to be found." I could concur with this view. It shows the influence of the young Binswanger, who as you see is a fine fellow. I also got to know Warda, he's a bit spineless, predominantly intellectual, will therefore never produce anything worthwhile, but will always skulk in the background nodding his head sagely. On the other hand I struck up an acquaintance with a better man, Strohmayer,[3] assistant at Binswanger's private clinic. He does

[1] Isidor Sadger (1867–194?), Viennese psychoanalyst, early member of the Wednesday Society; published prolifically, chiefly on sexual pathology; disappeared during World War II.
[2] See appendix 4.
[3] Wilhelm Strohmayer (1874–1936), privatdocent for psychiatry and neurology,

analyses, has a good understanding and a very clear brain. We can expect good things from him because he is very natural and knows how to give way to the real intentions of his psyche. He also possesses the excellent gift of stubbornness, as he has a lame foot. Such people do not as a rule let themselves be intimidated intellectually. The other assistants are fog without form. I have been contemplating the great hole in German psychiatry with unspeakable glee, as you will readily understand. Naturally not a man jack among them has understood a word of my Dementia praecox book. But that doesn't matter. We are working for the future. Probably Strohmayer will also come to Salzburg.

I am eagerly awaiting your ideas on the paranoia question. With best regards,

Most sincerely yours, JUNG

76 F

Dear friend,   3 March 1908, Vienna, IX. Berggasse 19

Starting from obsessional neurosis I am approaching the choice-of-neurosis problem in the following way: the obsessional neurosis cases are transparent; they hinge on only three (or, if you will, two) basic instincts, the instinct to see and to know and the possessive instinct (sadistic). Hence they can be classified according to predominance of obsessional thinking, i.e., rumination on the one hand, or of obsessional impulses (actions) on the other. It is interesting to note, however, that these are the only non-autoerotic components of the sexual instinct, the only components which from the start are directed towards an object. Hysteria, on the other hand, hinges on erogenous zones, it usually involves direct repression of genital impulses. In line with my idea of tracing the neuroses back to developmental disturbances of the libidinal vicissitudes, hysteria arises through disturbances (fixations and repressions) in the sphere of the erogenous components, while obsessional neurosis arises through disturbances in the sphere of the object components (which should probably be regarded as "anaclitic" instincts); in this context a predisposition to paranoia is created solely by a defect in the other part of the development, in the transi-

Jena University; later in Berlin, where he was a charter member of the Psychoanalytic Society; withdrew 1911.

tion from autoerotism to object-love, whereas defects in the development of genital primacy predispose to hysteria and obsessional neurosis.

Which brings us to paranoia. Here I dimly perceive a distinction between a *reality-testing* and an *unpleasure-testing*, the former coinciding with our "judgment," the latter with our "repression." The main psychological characteristic of paranoia would then be the repressive *projection* mechanism by which it evades the reality-testing, since what comes from outside does not require such a testing. The clinical characteristics of paranoia which you stress, its stability and severity, are adequately explained by this projection. In hysteria and obsessional neurosis there always remains an awareness of reality; this is explained by the fact that contact with the outside world remains unimpaired while the libido-cathected complexes create the upheaval. In paranoia these same complexes approach the personality from the outside world; that is why the patients are so credulous and inaccessible, why they are so utterly overwhelmed by the complexes.

I am too dull-witted to follow these ideas through at present. It should also be considered that paranoia corresponds to an unsuccessful detachment of libido, since the libido returns in the projection with the intensity of cathexis transformed into certainty, very much as in the regression of the dream state it is transformed into palpable reality. Dem. pr. then corresponds to a fully successful return to autoerotism. In all likelihood both are usually partial. Your shoemaker's fiancée[1] proves that even after the most pronounced detachment *one* intensely cathected element of the old libidinal idea still remains.

Your ideas about "defence" are certainly correct, but not only for paranoia. I believe that they apply to all neuroses and psychoses.

With kindest regards,

Yours, FREUD

77 F

Dear friend,   5 March 1908, Vienna, IX. Berggasse 19

As soon as I received your letter, I had my sister-in-law[1] write to the Hotel Bristol in Salzburg (on Makartplatz). From your quarter

[1] See "The Content of the Psychoses," CW 3, par. 358.

[1] Minna Bernays (1865–1941), who lived with the Freud family from 1896 until her death.

eighteen persons are expected, from Vienna there will be ten or twelve, perhaps as many as fifteen. That adds up to lodgings for thirty. Whether we can find a meeting hall in the hotel itself or whether the proprietor will find us one elsewhere, or whether I shall have to make a quick trip to Salzburg to arrange for a hall, will be decided by post in the next few days. I will let you know at once, so that you may start on your April trip free from all business worry. As for the programme, permit me the following remarks. If you must give me the honour of the first lecture, then I think you ought to deliver the last one. That will counterbalance the loss of interest that is otherwise to be feared; in their eagerness to hear you, the intervening speakers will hurry. But in this case, I think, a foreigner, Jones for instance, ought to have second place, followed by a Viennese and then Morton Prince, or both Englishmen[2] right after myself. I hear that Sadger, that congenital fanatic of orthodoxy, who happens by mere accident to believe in psychoanalysis rather than in the law given by God on Sinai-Horeb, has put too much case material into his paper and may withdraw it. — On the list I miss Riklin, whom you had announced, and Abraham who wrote me some weeks ago that he wished to speak on Ψ-sexual differences between hysteria and Dem. pr.[2a] — I have one more suggestion for you. I want to give the floor to a noble spirit who can be present only in the form of a quotation, to wit, Friedrich Schiller, in whose correspondence with Körner (letter of 1 December 1788) our secretary Otto Rank has found a delightful passage in justification of our psychoanalytic technique.[3] It would take Rank only a few minutes to

---

[2] English in original.

[2a] "Die psychosexuellen Differenzen der Hysterie und der Dementia Praecox," *Zentralblatt für Nervenheilkunde und Psychiatrie*, n.s., XIX (July 1908) = "The Psycho-sexual Differences between Hysteria and Dementia Praecox," *Selected Papers* (1927).

[3] The passage, which Rank read at the Wednesday meeting of 4 Mar. 08 (*Minutes*, I, p. 339) and at Salzburg (Jones, II, pp. 46f./42), is as follows: "It would seem to be unfortunate and detrimental to the creative process for the intellect to examine the ideas that press in upon it too closely while they are still as it were in the gateway. Considered in itself, an idea may seem hazardous and unpromising, but perhaps another idea that comes after it will lend it importance; in combination with others that may seem equally inept, it may prove to be a useful component. This the intellect is unable to judge unless it retains the idea long enough to consider it in combination with these others. In a creative mind, it seems to me, the intellect has withdrawn its guard from the gates; ideas rush in pellmell, and only when many are at hand does it survey and examine them. — You critics, or whatever you may call yourselves, are ashamed or afraid of the passing moments of madness which occur in all creative minds, and whose greater or lesser duration

read it and it would close our morning on a suitable note. Rank, who is coming with us, is a pleasant, intelligent youngster. He has qualified in mechanical engineering and is now studying Latin and Greek for admission to the university. He is twenty-three; he must have sent you his monograph on "The Artist"; some of it is not quite clear, but it contains the best explanation of my complicated theories to have reached me thus far. I expect a good deal of him once he has got himself an education.

I believe there is still another matter of importance for our programme. You have not yet told me whether you wish to allow *discussion,* and how it is to be controlled. If the latter precaution is not taken, it is perfectly possible that we shall not get beyond the second lecture in one morning. If we limit each speaker to five minutes, ten speakers will still be able to use up an hour. My Viennese are very voluble. Perhaps we could dispense with discussion altogether in the morning session and make up for it by allotting more time to each lecture. As you know from official congresses, twenty minutes may be time enough to rattle off a few slogans but hardly to expound a point of view. I shall be glad to leave these decisions to your judgment.

I should also like to ask your advice as to what I should say. To present a case as you suggested would take too long and give me a privilege over the other speakers that might be resented. That kind of thing requires an hour or more. Perhaps a more general topic? Some sort of declaration of principles? In any case it will not be easy for me, my head is tired and when that happens it is very stubborn; it does what work *it* pleases; right now, for example, nothing but obsessional neurosis, when I would gladly take up something else. You must have noticed this in my observations on paranoia, which contain nothing really new except in regard to obsessional neurosis. They must have been a big disappointment to you and struck you as a watered-down version of the correspondence we had about paranoia shortly after your visit to Vienna almost a year ago.[4] But my investigations of obsessional neurosis, which go quite deep in places, would hardly be intelligible unless accompanied by case histories.

Well, now about Jena. That fox Binswanger must have a fine flair. Let's hope that more and more people will admit that man has his

---

distinguishes the thinking artist from the dreamer."—*Schillers Briefwechsel mit Körner* (1847), vol. I, pp. 382f. (tr. here R.M.). Freud quoted it in the 2nd edn. (1909) of *Traumdeutung;* see SE IV, pp. 102f.

[4] Beginning with 20 F.

liver on the right side and his heart on the left. Then we shall gladly leave the cases of *situs inversus* to the clinicians employed by the state. Ludwig Binswanger managed that very nicely; nurses are often sadists in disguise, I hope our young friend hasn't come off too badly.[5] I can see how amused you must have been to observe the poverty of present-day psychiatry at first hand. We can really claim to have made things a little more interesting. I was overjoyed to hear that the reception of your "Dem. Pr." taught you that we are working for the future, that our kingdom is not of this world. Let us never forget it!

What would you think of this topic, which just occurred to me: "Transformations in the (conception and) technique of psychoanalysis"?

You will soon receive three articles of mine, only one is spontaneous and worthy of your attention, the others were forced out of me and less valuable.[6] *The Content of the Psychoses* is to be printed on time for you to distribute at the Congress. If you are not coming directly from home, I can bring you the copies from Deuticke.

The evening, I presume, will be devoted exclusively to discussion of the topics provided by our Budapest friends;[7] that ought to make the sparks fly. Don't you want a business meeting too?

With kind regards and sincere thanks for all the trouble you are taking,

Yours, FREUD

78 F

Dear friend,   9 March 1908, Vienna, IX. Berggasse 19[1]

You can confidently put "Hotel Bristol" on the programme. They will definitely provide us with lodging and excellent fare. As for the hall, I am still negotiating.

---

[5] Apparently a reference to Binswanger's marriage; see below, 83 J.

[6] Presumably "Creative Writers" (above, 55 F n. 5); "Die 'Kulturelle' Sexualmoral und die moderne Nervosität," *Sexual-Probleme*, IV:3 (Mar. 1908 = " 'Civilized' Sexual Morality and Modern Nervous Illness," SE IX; and "Charakter und Analerotik," *Psychiatrisch-neurologische Wochenschrift*, IX:52 (Mar. 1908) = "Character and Anal Erotism," SE IX.

[7] See the programme for the Salzburg Congress, appendix 4. For Ferenczi's paper, see "Psychoanalysis and Education," *International Journal of Psycho-Analysis*, XXX (1949).

---

[1] Imprinted correspondence card.

Deuticke has promised to have your monograph[2] ready in time for us to distribute copies at the Congress. Please write and tell him when you need the proofs—in view of your trip to France.

With kind regards,

Yours, FREUD

79 J

Dear Professor Freud,   Burghölzli-Zürich, 11 March 1908

I am sorry I can't get around to answering letters as promptly and fully as you do. I always have a mass of other things to attend to before I can put myself in the right mood to answer your letters. I can never be rushed; if I am, all thoughts instantly go out of my head.

First I must go into the paranoia question. I have the feeling I ought to talk to you personally about it, as I ought to know your material; then your theory would be more intelligible to me. For instance, the Fl.[1] case helped me greatly in understanding your views, since I always knew what you had in mind. Your line of thought on the paranoia question seems to be very different from mine, so I have great difficulty in following you. For you the choice-of-neurosis problem seems to play a crucial role. This is something I daren't touch. At present I am interested only in the way *alleviation of the complex may be obtained.* The following case may serve as an example: A 34-year-old woman declared that the assistant doctor, together with the nurse and an old woman (a patient), had burnt a child (uncertain whether it was the nurse's or the patient's!). Erotic advances to the doctor. The nurse is young and pretty, and the patient likes her *very* much. Pat. is sexually dissatisfied with her marriage and has to support an old mother. So: transference to the doctor, identification with the nurse, assimilation of the old patient as mother. She represses her marriage, also her children, makes a new, unadmitted transference (to the doctor), simultaneously obtaining wish-fulfilment in the role of the pretty nurse. All this in the form of an accusation that could easily pass over into persecution mania. Thus the complex is alleviated by the assertion that it is not in her but is being played out in objective reality by other people. By this means a *very firm dissociation* is achieved. The mechanism is an exaggeration of the normal

---

[2] "The Content of the Psychoses"; see below, 82 F n. 4.

[1] Fliess.

mechanism of *depotentiating reality*, its purpose being to make the dissociation absolute; that is my view. I think it also covers sufficiently well the teleological component of the delusion. In this case I for one could hardly speak of an "unsuccessful detachment" of libido but rather of an "unsuccessful application" of libido, precisely because it gets repressed. There are undoubtedly cases where the libido ought to be detached and then this comes about in a faulty way through the feeling of persecution, but presumably the other mechanism also exists, for one can hardly suppose that the patient would still have to detach libido from her family. This would give a wrong view of the whole case, which in itself is quite a common one. I am eager to hear what you think about it.

Now for Salzburg! I have just received an application from a Dr. Jekels[2] in Silesia, bringing the certainties up to nineteen. Of course the devil had to put a spoke in my wheel with that lecture of colleague Abraham's; I can hear you chuckling. The lecture displeases me because it puts forward what I have fantasied out loud under your stimulation and what I wanted to work up later myself, once it had matured. I agree with your suggestion that we give the second place to Jones and the fourth to Morton Prince, if he comes. (Your description of Sadger delighted me, the cap fits perfectly!) Riklin is not going to lecture. The pious exordium by Rank suits me very well. I've read Rank's book, half understood it, and am distinctly impressed by his intelligence. This man is certainly a good find. The only thing lacking is the empirical "contact with reality." I have seen from his book that in theory he has felt his way into your thinking very deeply, more deeply than I have. But then, he had the privilege of your personal stimulation, which has given him a thousand short cuts to knowledge.

Discussions are usually futile. They had best take place in the evening, when everything frivolous will, let us hope, have blown over and only the serious questions remain. I shall put this right in the programme. We can allot half an hour to each lecture. For you, of course, I am mentally reserving one hour or more, because the only thing that matters to us is to hear you and not Stekel and Sadger and the rest of them. You must have this privilege; it is on your account that we are coming to Salzburg and on your account that we are doing this thing at all. So I regard it as absolutely self-evident that you should

[2] Ludwig Jekels (1867–1954), Vienna-educated Polish psychiatrist, then at a sanatorium at Bistrai near Bielitz (Austrian Silesia, now Poland); became a member of the Vienna Society; later in New York.

speak for a considerably longer time than the others. I beg you for a presentation of *case material*; that is something we can all follow. Personally I would prefer that to your talking about psychanalysis. However, it's not for me to press you, for I don't doubt that your judgment is sounder than mine. May I ask you to tell me your choice soon, and at the same time to return the *draft* of the programme?

I have spoken to Bleuler about the chairmanship; as was to be expected, he waved it away with a smile, saying that such a thing would never even remotely enter his head.

I should be glad if *the copies could be sent to my house*, as I shall have to return home before going to the Congress.

The evening meeting can take the form of a free-and-easy session at which not only various points in the morning's lectures are dealt with but also the questions of the Budapestians. We can settle the "business" matters at the same time.

My negotiations for the journal are beginning to look more cheerful again since my recovery from influenza. I hope there will be only good news to give you in Salzburg.

I marvel at your colossal capacity for work which enables you to produce scientific articles on top of your daily labours. That would be quite beyond me.

I don't rightly know yet what I shall say in Salzburg. In any case no significant novelties will be forthcoming. I feel rather shaky, because here we are still stuck in the rudiments.

No thanks are due to me for the arrangements—the pleasure is mine.

As soon as I have all your data I shall get the programme printed. With best regards,

Most sincerely yours, J U N G

80 F

Dear friend, 13 March 1908, Vienna, IX. Berggasse 19

In view of the business character of this letter, I hope you will forgive me for answering so quickly and in general for writing so often.

Everything is settled with the Hotel Bristol. In complete agreement with your idea of saving the discussion for the end (displacement downward). "Half an hour" might be qualified by "maximum." I hadn't thought of the passage from Schiller's correspondence, which you have received in the meantime, as an introduction but as a final cadence.

Now about my lecture.—I give in, that is the only way in which I can show you my gratitude. But I can't make up my mind to give you a definite title; a report on a case I am now engaged in might at a pinch be compressed into an hour, but the case is not finished, the decisive phase and outcome are still lacking, one mustn't count one's chickens, etc. If it should turn out badly, I want to be free to substitute something else; who knows what may happen in six weeks? So I would like you to announce something vague, "A Piece of Psychoanalysis," or some such thing, whatever you say. That takes care of the business. Now there is nothing to stop you from casting the enclosed programme in the mould of eternity.

Of course I shall have much more to say about paranoia another time. Do you mean Fliess by Fl.? I must break off now because I want to reread your *Dem. Praecox* for tomorrow's final lecture.[1]

Most cordially yours, FREUD

81 J

Grand Hotel Bellevue,

Dear Professor Freud,   Baveno, Italy,[1] 11 April 1908

It seems a very long time since I last wrote to you. All sorts of things have played the devil with me; for instance, a hideous bout of influenza that left me so debilitated that I had to take thermal baths at Baden. Now I'm setting about recovering as thoroughly as possible on Lago Maggiore.

By the same post you will receive an offprint of my Amsterdam report. Please accept it with indulgence. Now I would write much of it very differently.

I shall be here until April 16 when I must return home after an all-too-short holiday. I will write more then. At present I am too dissociated.

I hope you are well. I look forward very much to seeing you again in Salzburg. With best regards,

Most sincerely yours, JUNG

[1] At the University.

[1] Printed letterhead.

82 F

Dear friend,   14 April 1908, Vienna, IX. Berggasse 19

This letter will be waiting for you when you get home. I am sorry to hear that you have been unwell and that you have been obliged to take a short holiday rather than a long one. With your youthful stamina you ought to make short shrift of any illness.

Three of your papers are lying on my desk. The first, the one you did in collaboration with Bleuler,[1] displeases me with its hesitations and concern over the good opinion of E. Meyer;[2] you have forbidden me to speak of the second, your long-awaited Amsterdam report;[3] the third, which is the third number of my *Papers on Applied Psychology*,[4] is a pure delight with its resoluteness and clarity and, as befits such clear thinking, the language is enchantingly warm and beautiful. How boldly you here proclaim the psychic aetiology of psychic disorders, from which you shrank back in the other papers. In this one, to be sure, you were free to express your own opinion, you were speaking only to laymen and ladies; in the others you were hampered by a spirit of compromise and by concern over the prejudices of physicians and the incomprehension of our colleagues!

Oddly enough, I have been reading in your Amsterdam paper that child hysteria does not enter this context,[5] whereas I myself have been toying with the idea of working up my analysis of a hysterical phobia in a five-year-old boy[6] for the Congress. But I doubt if this plan will be carried out.

I am well, but I have worked so hard these last few weeks that I am quite at my wits' end. I shall need half a day of solitude before plung-

---

[1] "Komplexe und Krankheitsursachen bei Dementia Praecox," *Zentralblatt für Nervenheilkunde und Psychiatrie*, n.s., XIX (Mar. 1908) = "Complexes and Aetiology in Dementia Praecox" (omitted from CW, as Jung's contribution is slight).

[2] See above, 66 F n. 1.

[3] "Die Freud'sche Hysterientheorie," *Monatsschrift für Psychiatrie und Neurologie*, XXIII:4 (Mar. 1908) = "The Freudian Theory of Hysteria," CW 4. See above, 43 J.

[4] *Der Inhalt der Psychose (Schriften zur angewandten Seelenkunde*, 3; 26 pp.) = "The Content of the Psychoses," CW 3.

[5] "The Freudian Theory of Hysteria," par. 62: "In any case, hysteria in children and the psychotraumatic neuroses form a group apart."

[6] First reference to the "Little Hans" case; see below, 133 J n. 1. Freud had dealt with the case in "The Sexual Enlightenment of Children" (1907), in SE IX.

ing into the social whirl of our Salzburg gathering. During this period of hard work my insights have become more and more secure; the unanimous opposition of all the psychiatric bureaucrats in this Western world can no longer make the slightest impression on me.

Magnus Hirschfeld was here for a visit a few weeks ago; he looks good-natured and awkward and seems to be an honest sort. He is moving close to us and from now on will take our ideas into account as much as possible. The offprints I sent to Ludwig Binswanger have come back from Jena marked "Moved, address unknown."

I am hoping to find a moment in Salzburg for a private talk with you about paranoia. Be sure to turn up in full vigour.

Yours cordially, FREUD

83 J

Dear Professor Freud,   Burghölzli-Zürich, 18 April 1908

Your last letter upset me. I have read a lot between the lines. I don't doubt that if only I could *talk* with you we could come to a basic understanding. Writing is a poor substitute for speech. Nevertheless I will try to offer some rather incoherent explanations.

1. *Lecture to laymen.* The point was to make the public aware of the psychological connections that are found in psychosis. Hence the strong emphasis on the psychogenic factor. There was no reason to talk about the actual aetiology.

2. *Aetiology of Dem. praec.* The aim here was to set out our conception of the aetiology. From lack of analytical experience Bleuler stresses the organic side, I the other. I think *very many* cases of Dem. praec. are due exclusively to purely psychological conflicts. But besides these there are undoubtedly not a few cases where a physical weakness of some kind precipitates the psychosis. One would have to be a spiritualist to believe in an exclusively psychogenic aetiology here. I never have; for me the "constitution" has always played a fairly significant role. That is why I was actually rather relieved when I saw that you had modified your earlier view of the genesis of hysteria. As you have observed, in discussing the aetiology one gets entangled in the most hopeless difficulties, all of which seem to me to have one point of origin: our totally mistaken conception of the brain's function. Everywhere we are haunted by psyche = *substantia*, playing on the brain

à la piano. The monistic standpoint—psyche = inwardly perceived function—might help to lay this ghost. But I won't go on philosophizing. You yourself will have thought out the logical consequences long ago. The whole question of aetiology is extremely obscure to me. The secret of the constitution will hardly be unveiled from the psychological side alone.

3. *Amsterdam report*. Here I have done bad work, as I am the first to admit. In spite of this I shall be grateful for any criticism. It's nonsense about my forbidding you to speak of it! I can only learn from your criticism. The chief drawback is its brevity. I had to do a lot of cutting. A second and more important drawback is the elementary approach that was forced on me by the ignorance of the public.

Child hysteria must fall outside the formula applicable to adults, for whom puberty plays a large role. A specifically modified formula must be established for child hysteria. All the rest I have written as my conscience dictated. I am really no propagandist; I merely detest all forms of suppression and injustice. I am eager to hear of my errors, and hope to learn from them.

Binswanger has now got married[1] so is no longer in Jena. His address is: Kreuzlingen, Canton Thurgau.

Best thanks for the offprints[2] which arrived during my absence. I haven't read them yet for lack of time. I too hope very much that we can snatch an hour in Salzburg for a talk on some of the things that are still hanging in mid-air.

With best regards,

Most sincerely yours, JUNG

I may be wrong but it seems to me that this letter has an oddly dry tone. It is not meant that way, for a man can also admit his bad mood with a smile. Unfortunately the smile doesn't come through the style —an aesthetic fault that has already driven me to pen a P.S.

[1] In 1907, to Hertha Buchenberger. His new post was at the Bellevue Sanatorium (private); see above, 16 J n. 1.
[2] See above, 77 F n. 6.

84 F

Dear friend,   19 April 1908, Vienna, IX. Berggasse 19[1]

Happy Easter! Hard feelings must not be nursed. If I was cranky and seemed so, there is much more room—in this case—for a somatic than for a psychogenic aetiology. I am so exhausted by work and lack of recreation that I shall surely make the *same* impression on you in Salzburg. What I mean is I am not at all angry with you. My letter is being written under the impression of my second reading of your *Content of the Psychoses*, for which work I feel great affection. It gives me a picture of you from several different angles. It has in it a great deal of what I esteem in you, not only your insight but also your fine artistic feeling and the seeds of greatness. It stands in marked contrast to a manuscript by your Berlin rival (A.), which is to occupy my fourth number,[2] staunch in its support but lacking just that spark (here the ucs. of both writer and receiver smile), and also to your collaboration with Bleuler. In my fatigue I failed to bring out the true constellation; my displeasure was so much more evident than my pleasure, which struck no chord in me, feeling as I did. This, I believe, was the situation, from which I did indeed exclude your Amsterdam report; of course I could equally well have expressed my gratitude to you for putting such zeal into so difficult and dangerous a task. Only the sentence about child hysteria struck me as incorrect. The conditions here are the same, probably because every thrust of growth creates the same conditions as the great thrust of puberty (every increase in libido, I mean). After all, it has never been my habit to reproach you with your partial disagreements, but rather to be pleased with your share of agreement. I know it will take you time to catch up with my experience of the past fifteen years. I am rather annoyed with Bleuler for his willingness to accept a psychology without sexuality, which leaves everything hanging in mid-air. In the sexual processes we have the indispensable "organic foundation" without

---

[1] It cannot be determined whether Freud wrote this letter after receiving Jung's of 18 Apr. or whether it was spontaneous. Letters could reach Vienna from Zürich on the following day (cf. Jung 20 Feb. 07, answered by Freud on 21 Feb.), and there was delivery on Sunday, as the 19th was (cf. Freud 2 Jan. 10: "Today [your letter] has come").

[2] Abraham, *Traum und Mythus* (*Schriften zur angewandten Seelenkunde*, 4, 1909) = "Dreams and Myths," *Clinical Papers* (1955); originally tr. 1913 by William Alanson White. Abraham had sent the ms. to Freud on 4 Apr. 08; see letter of that date, *Freud/Abraham Letters*, pp. 31ff.

which a medical man can only feel ill at ease in the life of the psyche.

I thoroughly dislike the notion that my opinions are correct, but only in regard to a part of the cases.[3] (Substitute point of view for opinions.) That is not possible. It must be one thing or the other. These characteristics are fundamental, they can't vary from one set of cases to another. Or rather: they are so vital that an entirely different name should be given to the cases to which they do not apply. Thus far, you know, no one has seen this other hysteria, Dem. pr., etc. Either a case is our kind or nothing is known about it. I am sure that basically you agree with me.

There. Now I have avowed the full extent of my fanaticism and venture to hope that the injury to your feelings will not survive the interval that separates us from our meeting in Salzburg.

A chat with you there will do me at least a world of good. However, we shall also have to talk about Otto Gross; he urgently needs your medical help; what a pity, such a gifted, resolute man. He is addicted to cocaine and probably in the early phase of toxic cocaine paranoia. I feel great sympathy for his wife: one of the few Teutonic women I have ever liked. — I am planning to arrive Sunday morning so as to indulge in a few hours of solitude. I shall also give myself a day of recreation after the Congress, if it doesn't—rain.[4] I am having great difficulty with my paper, because a real, complete case cannot be narrated but only described; this I know from the experience of my Vienna lectures. And I have no case that is completed and can be viewed as a whole. I have given up the idea of the five-year-old boy because his neurosis, though resolving itself splendidly, hasn't kept the deadline. So it will probably be a potpourri of particular observations and general remarks based on a case of obsessional neurosis.[5] In one point I shall follow your directive implicitly; my talk will be nothing special. I am having plenty of trouble with the contributions of my Viennese companions, I don't want them to contain too many mistakes and hasty judgments. I am certainly unfit to be a chief, the "splendid isolation"[6] of my decisive years has set its stamp on my character.

Keep well, I hope to find you unruffled when we meet in Salzburg.

Yours cordially, FREUD

[3] This paragraph is quoted by Jones, II, p. 488/439.
[4] Salzburg is proverbially rainy.
[5] The "Rat Man" case, as it was later known; see below, editorial comment following 85 J and 150 F n. 1.
[6] English in original.

85 J

Dear Professor Freud,   Burghölzli-Zürich, 24 April 1908

Don't take any notice of my moodiness. If not too much is expected of me personally, I am usually at the top of my form on such occasions. One thing alone bothers me and that is the affair with Gross. His father[1] has written urging me to take him back with me to Zürich. As ill luck would have it, I have some urgent business on the 28th with my architect in Munich.[2] In the meantime of course Gross will give me the slip. Unfortunately Bleuler doesn't enjoy his confidence or he could bring him along. Gross takes not only cocaine but also large quantities of opium.

Apart from this painful intermezzo I am looking forward to seeing you again. I hope we shall have a chance to chat on our walks. Two people have signed off: Morton Prince (Riklin will lecture in his stead), and one *deus minorum gentium*, in whose stead a lady is leaping into the breach—Frau Prof. Erismann,[3] the wife of the famous hygienist formerly at Moscow University. She is a doctor and an enthusiastic adherent of your psychology.

It is the fault of our recent correspondence that my lecture on Dem. praec.[4] has turned into a formulation of my views on D. pr. and

---

[1] Hanns Gross; see above, 49 J n. 3.

[2] Ernst Fiechter, a cousin, was designing the new house in Küsnacht. (Information from Mr. Franz Jung.)

[3] Sophie Erismann, M.D. (1847–1925), wife of Friedrich Erismann (1842–1915), Swiss-born ophthalmologist and hygienist, in St. Petersburg and Moscow 1869–96, then in Zürich. Jones (II, p. 45/40), listing those attending the Salzburg Congress, has her from Vienna: *Bulletin*, no. 1 (July 1910), shows her a member of the Zürich Society. For her stepson Theodor, see below, 312 J n. 4.

[4] According to Jones (II, p. 156/138; cf. 52/47), in Jung's paper on dementia praecox "he ignored the suggestions Freud had made to him on the subject and substituted the hypothetical idea of a 'psychical toxin' that damaged the brain . . ." (Jones cites a letter to him from Jung 21 Jan. 08, now missing.) The paper has not survived, but Jung contributed an abstract to Rank's report on the Salzburg Congress, *Zentralblatt*, I:3 (Dec. 1911), p. 128: "The depotentiation of the association process or *abaissement du niveau mental*, which consequently has a downright dreamlike quality, seems to indicate that a pathogenic agent [Noxe] contributes to dementia praecox which is absent in, say, hysteria. The characteristics of the *abaissement* were assigned to the pathogenic agent, which was construed as virtually organic in effect and likened to a symptom of poisoning (e.g., paranoid states in chronic poisoning)." Jones may have misunderstood Noxe as *Toxin*. However, a toxin theory of schizophrenia did interest Jung throughout his career; for his statements on the theory 1907–58, see CW 3, index.

thus into a theoretical essay despite my original intention to present case material. I had the greatest difficulty in preventing it from becoming simply a peroration addressed to you.

If you manage to get to Salzburg half a day earlier, would you please be kind enough to see the hotel proprietor about the *hall for the meeting*—unless, of course, all this has been settled long ago. So far as can be foreseen I shall arrive in Salzburg on the 9 o'clock train via Munich.

I hope this letter will still reach you in Vienna. Meanwhile with kindest regards,

Most sincerely yours, J U N G

The Salzburg Congress

What was in effect the First International Psychoanalytic Congress took place at Salzburg on Monday, 27 April, the forty-two participants (including Bleuler) having arrived the day before. Nine papers were read, including Jung's on dementia praecox and Freud's on a case history (see appendix 4). The latter—Freud spoke for over four hours—was an early version of "Notes upon a Case of Obsessional Neurosis" (the so-called "Rat Man" case), published in the *Jahrbuch*, I:2 (1909); see 150 F n. 1. At Salzburg the decision was taken to issue a periodical devoted to psychoanalysis—the *Jahrbuch*, which was issued in two semiannual numbers; see below, 133 J n. 1. For details of the Congress see Jones, II, pp. 45ff./40ff. (not always accurate: e.g., Freud could not have arrived from Venice), and Freud's letter to his wife, 29 Apr. 08, in *Letters*, ed. E. L. Freud, no. 138.

86 J

Dear Professor Freud,   Burghölzli-Zürich, 30 April 1908

I am in two minds as to whether I should apply a business or an emotional yardstick to the Salzburg Congress. On balance the results were very good, and this bodes well for the success of our *Jahrbücher*. I have already seen Reinhardt in Munich; he was very hesitant and thought of bringing out the 1st volume of 250–300 pages *as an experiment*, with no payment and stipulating a grandiose title with something about the "subconscious" in it. I shall now turn first to Marhold. Perhaps you could find out from Deuticke what chances we

143

would have there. Reinhardt knows next to nothing of you and equally little of me, which complicates the negotiations considerably. At least Marhold knows how my books are selling.[1]

As to sentiments, I am still under the reverberating impact of your lecture, which seemed to me perfection itself. All the rest was simply padding, sterile twaddle in the darkness of inanity.

With regard to Dem. praec. I now realize (actually I have always realized) what an endless amount of excavation is still needed in order to dig up anything and present it with certainty. Unfortunately there was no physical and psychological opportunity in Salzburg for discussing my particular case. For that I need peace of mind and concentration. Meanwhile I am going ahead patiently with my work; it has become easier, too, for Bleuler made marked progress in Salzburg, so that he is even beginning to doubt that there are organic primary symptoms in Dem. pr., as he had always asserted without qualification earlier. You have shot a big hole in his defences. Only harder work can bring me more clarity. Maybe I have done too little analytical work on Dem. praec. these last nine months, with the result that the impressive material has become too much of an imposition on me. The chief obstacle is my pupils; training them and overseeing their papers consume my time. They get ahead at my expense, while I stand still. This knowledge weighed heavily on me in Salzburg. I beg you to have patience with me, and confidence in what I have done up till now. I always have a little more to do than be just a faithful follower. You have no lack of those anyway. But they do not advance the cause, for by faith alone nothing prospers in the long run.

With kind regards and many thanks,

Most sincerely yours, J U N G

87 F

Dear friend,   3 May 1908, Vienna, IX. Berggasse 19

So you too are pleased with our meeting in Salzburg? It refreshed me a good deal and left me with a pleasant aftertaste. I was glad to find you so flourishing and every suspicion of resentment melted away

---

[1] Carl Marhold, of Halle a. S., had published Jung's pamphlet *Die psychologische Diagnose des Tatbestandes* (1906) and his book *Über die Psychologie der Dementia Praecox* (1907).

when I saw you again and understood you. I know you are in a phase of "negative oscillation" and are now suffering the counter-effects of the great influence you have exerted on your chief all this time. It is not possible to push without being pushed. But I am quite certain that after having moved a few steps away from me you will find your way back, and then go far with me. I can't give you any reason for this certainty; it probably springs from a feeling I have when I look at you. But I am satisfied to feel at one with you and no longer fear that we might be torn apart. You will just have to be patient with some of my idiosyncrasies.

Your complaint that you have rather got out of the habit of analytical work and that your students consume your time is certainly well-founded; but that can be overcome. I am delighted that you think I impressed Bleuler and thereby made your work easier for the future. He is a very strange man!

The *Jahrbuch* is now uppermost in my thoughts. I am offering you two cases, the papers might be entitled "Aphorisms relating to Obsessional Neurosis" and "Little Herbert's Phobia."[1] I am sure we shall be able to publish with Deuticke; I shall tell him to expect some written proposals from you. Still, it seems to me a German publisher would be better.

Jones and Brill have been to see me twice. I have arranged with Brill for the translation of a selection (Selected papers on hysteria).[2] He also called on Breuer and had a very odd reception. Jones is undoubtedly a very interesting and worthy man, but he gives me a feeling of, I was almost going to say racial strangeness. He is a fanatic and doesn't eat enough. "Let me have men about me that are fat," says Caesar, etc. He almost reminds me of the lean and hungry Cassius. He denies all heredity; to his mind even I am a reactionary. How, with your moderation, were you able to get on with him?

I have a great favour to ask of you. It has not escaped me that a rift is in the making between you and Abraham. There are so few of us that we must stick together, and a rift for personal motives is less becoming in us psychoanalysts than in anyone else. I regard him as a man of great worth and I should not like to be obliged to give him up, though there can be no question of his replacing you in my eyes. Accordingly, I have this request to make of you: be helpful if he consults you about the publication of his dementia paper, and accept the

---

[1] = The "Rat Man" case (see below, 150 F n. 1) and "Little Hans" (133 J n. 1).
[2] English in original. For publication, see below, 160 F n. 9.

fact that this time he took the more direct path, whereas you hesitated. Apart from that, you have every advantage over him.[3] In this question the merit will probably lie with the detailed work and not with the pronunciamento. We mustn't quarrel when we are besieging Troy. Do you remember the lines from the *Philoctetes*:

αἱρεῖ τὰ τόξα ταῦτα τὴν Τροίαν μόνα

(These arrows alone will take Troy)?[4] My self-confidence has so increased that I am thinking of taking this line as a motto for a new edition of the *Coll. Papers on the Theory of the Neuroses*.

Jones wants to go to Munich to help the Grosses. The little woman seems to be seriously smitten with him. He should not accede to Gross's insistence that he treat his wife, but try to gain influence over him. It looks as if this were going to end badly.

I shall be seeing Jones and Brill again next Wednesday at the meeting of the Vienna Psychoanalytic Society.[5]

With kind regards,

As ever, FREUD

88 J

Dear Professor Freud,   Burghölzli-Zürich, 4 May 1908

I have now had a *very favourable* offer from Marhold in Halle. He will accept the *Jahrbücher* in the form of two semi-annual volumes. He offers 40 marks per printed sheet (16 large octavo pages). Should a paper be published simultaneously as a pamphlet for its general interest, the payment is 60 marks. For papers from you, Bleuler, and me, 60 marks are offered per printed sheet. Fee for editing each volume: 100 marks. For a scientific publication these conditions are positively dazzling. Bleuler is inclined to accept. He would like to stipulate the

---

[3] Cf. Freud's letter to Abraham the same day: *Freud/Abraham Letters*, pp. 33f.; also in Jones, II, pp. 52f./47.

[4] Sophocles, *Philoctetes*, 113 (Odysseus). Freud did use the motto as he indicated (vol. 2, 1909).

[5] Holograph: *Wiener Vereinigung für Psychoanalyse*. This name for the Wednesday Society was officially adopted at the meeting of 15 Apr. 08, in connection with Magnus Hirschfeld's proposal to draw up a questionnaire "for the purpose of exploring the sex instinct." (See 138 J n. 7.) This would be the Society's first appearance before the public, therefore a name was required. / For the visit by Jones and Brill, see *Minutes*, I, pp. 392ff. (6 May 08).

possible publication of French and English papers as well. Please send word soon whether you agree to go along with Marhold or whether I should approach other publishers for offers.

I am very pleased to see that the market value of our project has risen considerably.

Meanwhile best regards,

Yours sincerely, JUNG

89 F

Dear friend,   4 May 1908, Vienna, IX. Berggasse 19

Deuticke[1] is quite willing to publish the *Jahrbuch*. He will write to you about it, so don't settle with anyone until you have heard from him. He says he feels offended that we didn't think of him first, and calls himself a *German* publisher. I have not discussed conditions with him, since I can leave all that to you. I do not believe 200–300 pages will be enough for our harvest. D. is cautious in business matters but a decent sort.

Very cordially yours, FREUD

90 F

Dear friend,   6 May, 1908, Vienna, IX. Berggasse 19

Enclosed the certificate for Otto Gross. Once you have him, don't let him out before October when I shall be able to take charge of him.

Your news of Marhold's offer sounds splendid. For politeness' sake, wait for Deuticke, but I doubt that he will make a better offer. Two semi-annual volumes strike me as a much better idea than a single annual one. What do you and Bleuler think of

(or $\sqrt{2/1}$)[1]

"Jahrbuch for Psychosexual and Psychoanalytic Researches"

[1] Franz Deuticke (1850–1919) published the *Sammlung kleiner Schriften zur Neurosenlehre* and of the *Schriften zur angewandten Seelenkunde*, having taken over the latter from Hugo Heller.

[1] Holograph: "*J. f. psychosexuelle u. psychoanalytische Forschungen*" with (*oder* $\sqrt{2/1}$) written afterward, above, apparently meaning that the two adjectives could be transposed.

for a title? You are certainly right about the foreign languages; we must keep some vestige—or seed—of your original international project. I implore you, don't be too modest about the number of pages, it would be better to compromise in the matter of payment. Remember, our analyses are long.

Well, this is another success for you. I am fifty-two today; supposing I have another ten working years ahead of me, I shall still be able to make quite a contribution to our work.

Yours with a cordial hand-shake, FREUD

91 J

Dear Professor Freud,   Burghölzli-Zürich, 7 May 1908

Following your wish I will wait until I have heard from Deuticke. Or should I write to him? Otherwise it might go too slowly. Deuticke would be more attractive to me than Marhold, as the firm is sounder. Let's hope D. offers even better conditions.

In the first volume, that is, in the first published part of it, there should unquestionably be a list, i.e., a compilation of brief abstracts of all those works that have to do with our cause, by which I mean chiefly all your books and your numerous articles that are scattered all over the place, as well as those of your pupils.[1] To ensure complete coverage, it would be best if one of your people were to draft the abstracts in chronological order *under your supervision*. I would do the same for the works of the Zürich Clinic in so far as they come into consideration, and would also arrange the whole material in an orderly way. Jones would attend to the English literature, Maeder or Riklin the French. Account must also be taken of the works of our opponents, provided they are original.

I imagine each abstract somewhat as follows: General orientation on the work in question would be given in a few lines. For example: 1896.VIII. "Further Remarks on the Neuro-psychoses of Defence":[2]

---

[1] The abstracts finally published in the *Jahrbuch* were as follows: (I:2, 1909), Abraham on Freud's writings and the Austrian and German literature; (II:1, 1910), Jones on the English and American literature, J. Neiditsch on activity in Russia, Assagioli on activity in Italy, and Jung on the Swiss literature. See appendix 2.

[2] See above, 11 F n. 5.

—Contains [I.] supplementary formulations on the "specific" aetiology of hysteria, especially on the significance of the sexual trauma, II. formulations on the nature and genesis of various types of obsessional ideas, III. *the analysis of a case of chronic paranoia*, considered as a neuro-psychosis of defence.—

Such is my idea of the abstracts. They would have to be drafted by someone who knows how to draw up abstracts and can pick out the essentials impartially. Of all your pupils I consider Abraham the most suitable, since he understands these things. I am sure he would gladly take over at your request. So let him deal with *all* the Viennese works —his own included, of course! You would be doing me a great service if you sounded him out.

You will see from this suggestion that my objective judgment of A. is not in the least impaired. For that very reason I have an undisguised contempt for some of colleague A.'s idiosyncrasies. In spite of his estimable qualities and sundry virtues he is simply not a *gentleman*.[3] In my eyes just about the worst thing that can happen to anyone. I am always ready to subordinate my judgment to someone who knows better, but in this case I find myself in agreement with a large number of people whose opinions I respect. In Salzburg I was able to prevent a scandal only by imploring a certain gentleman, who wanted to shed light on the sources of A.'s lecture, to abandon his plan. This gentleman wasn't a Swiss, nor was he one of my pupils, who (like me) can only gaze in quiet wonderment at such productions but can't help taking note of the facts. Up till now nothing has ever been done from my side that might have led to the rift; on the contrary it is. A. who is pulling in that direction. The latest piece of effrontery (which, be it said, I could not imagine him capable of before) is the news that he will send me his lecture unaltered for publication. Naturally I wouldn't put up with that, for a journal edited by me has to be thoroughly clean and decent and should not publish any plagiarism of your intellectual work or mine.[4]

You can rest assured that so long as A. behaves himself decently everything will remain the same on my side. But if he goes too far, an explosion will be unavoidable. I hope very much that A. will be

[3] English in original.
[4] In the published version of Abraham's lecture (see above, 77 F n. 2a) he acknowledged his debt to Freud, Jung, and Bleuler in a footnote; see *Selected Papers*, p. 65, n. 1. For Abraham's comments on this matter, see *Freud/Abraham Letters*, 11 May 08.

mindful of how far one may go. A break would be a great pity and not in the interests of our cause. He can avoid this eventuality *very easily* by a *little bit* of decency.

I should be most grateful if you could get A., or some other person who might seem to you even more suitable, to start on the abstracts as soon as possible.

Many thanks in advance! With best regards,

Most sincerely yours, J U N G

92 F

Dear friend,   10 May 1908, Vienna, IX. Berggasse 19

Thank you for your birthday wishes;[1] let us as always confront the future with confidence; it looks promising.

These last few days I have been wondering how we might establish closer scientific ties between Zürich and Vienna, so as not to lose sight of each other between now and the next Congress. Do you think it would be a good idea to supply you or your Zürich Society regularly with the proceedings of the Vienna Psychoanalytic Society? Or does a weekly exchange of scientific news between the two of us seem preferable? It wouldn't put too much of a burden on you? *I* always find time for it. I should not like your multifarious other occupations to divert you entirely from your Ψanalytic work on neuroses, which is after all the basis of our whole undertaking.

Once we have the *Jahrbuch*, I presume it will be possible to publish the proceedings of our societies.

We didn't manage to talk enough about A. in Salzburg. An experience of my own[2] gives me a vague idea of how you feel, but this time I think you are much too hard on him. I am sure there was no *animus injuriandi* on his part. I threw out the suggestion, he heard it from you and corresponded with me about it as well. His appropriation of it is perfectly acceptable to me, I only regret that *you* didn't appropriate it. I believe that your reaction to him must be interpreted as a summation of your previous reactions.

As reporter on the Vienna literature I should like to propose little Rank rather than Ab. You know from his "Artist" how well he can

---

[1] Letter or telegram missing.
[2] See below, 94 F n. 2.

formulate my ideas. I am eagerly awaiting the outcome of your negotiations.

Yours cordially, FREUD

93 J

Dear Professor Freud,   14 May 1908[1]

Deuticke offers 50 marks per printed sheet, 60 marks for papers by
you, Bleuler, and me—fee for editing: 200 marks. It's even better than
Marhold! If you agree, we will go to Deuticke. Please give your approval. For the title we, that is Bleuler and I, suggest: "Jahrbücher für
Psychoanalyse und Psychopathologie." The first chiefly for you, the
second for us, i.e., for works from our laboratory.

What do you think about the hiatus in Psycho-analysis?[2] May I
know your reasons?

Only a short letter for now as I have Gross with me. He is taking
up an incredible amount of time. It seems to be a definite obsessional
neurosis. The nocturnal light-obsession has already gone. We are now
down to the infantile identification blockages of a specifically homosexual nature. I am eager to see how it turns out.

Most sincerely yours, JUNG

94 F

Dear friend,   19 May 1908, Vienna, IX. Berggasse 19

Enclosed a letter from Moll[1] which I am passing on to you and
Bleuler with his knowledge. I have already answered, saying that I
approve of his plan but am bound by the decision made in Salzburg
to found a "Journal for ΨA and Ψpathology" and that before telling
him anything definite I must submit the matter to the two of you.
In my opinion Moll's organ cannot take the place of our own journal,

---

[1] On small notepaper, unheaded.
[2] Holograph: *Psycho-analysis.* Jung uses the Greek form apparently for illustration.
Heretofore he has preferred the form *Psychanalyse*, without hiatus.

---

[1] Albert Moll (1862–1939), Berlin sexologist, founder (1909) and editor of the
Zeitschrift für Psychotherapie und medizinische Psychologie, which seems to be
referred to here. See also below, 112 F n. 7, and 131 J n. 1.

151

because we need more space for analyses and association experiments than his more comprehensive programme could allow us. On the other hand, we might perfectly well contribute to his journal and make use of it if it takes on the character of a central organ, publishing meticulous abstracts and short original articles requiring quick publication. Would you prefer, after consulting Bleuler, to answer Moll directly or through me? I imagine you agree with me that starting as we do from very different basic assumptions and working with a technique of our own, we had better remain aloof, i.e. independent, for a while.

Now to Gross! I can imagine how much of your time he must be taking. I originally thought you would only take him on for the withdrawal period and that I would start analytical treatment in the autumn. It is shamefully egotistic of me, but I must admit that it is better for me this way; for I am obliged to sell my time and my supply of energy is not quite what it used to be. But seriously, the difficulty would have been that the dividing line between our respective property rights in creative ideas would inevitably have been effaced; we would never have been able to disentangle them with a clear conscience. Since I treated the philosopher Swoboda[2] I have had a horror of such difficult situations.

I think your diagnosis of Gross is correct. His earliest childhood memory (communicated in Salzburg) is of his father warning a visitor: Watch out, he *bites*! He remembered this in connection with my Rat Man story.

I should prefer to write *Psychoanalyse*[3] without a hyphen. A slight change, I think, would give the title more of a ring:

"Jahr<u>buch</u> für psychoanalytische u. psychopathologische Forschungen."

But these are trifles.

Kind regards to yourself and Bleuler.

Yours ever, FREUD

P.S. My five-year-old patient has definitely been cured of his phobia by ΨA.[4]

---

[2] Hermann Swoboda (1873–1963), psychologist and patient of Freud's; he became involved in a dispute with Fliess (1904–6) over the priority of a published idea, and Freud was drawn in. See Jones, I, pp. 346f./315f., and *Letters*, ed. E. L. Freud, no. 122.

[3] Freud supposed that Jung was concerned about the hyphen rather than the spelling.

[4] See below, 133 J n. 1.

95 J

Dear Professor Freud,   Burghölzli-Zürich, 25 May 1908

I enclose the draft contract from Deuticke. Four hundred pages should be about enough. Please would you forward the enclosed document to Deuticke if you agree with its contents. Binswanger tells me that he wants to publish his manuscript[1] (a very fine case of hysteria) in the *Jahrbücher*, with an introduction by Prof. Binswanger. A welcome broadening of scope.

You must be wondering why I am so slack in writing these days. I have let everything drop and have spent all my available time, day and night, on Gross, pushing on with his analysis. It is a typical obsessional neurosis with many interesting problems. Whenever I got stuck, he analysed me. In this way my own psychic health has benefited. For the time being Gross is *voluntarily* going through with the opium withdrawal. Until the day before yesterday, I had been giving him the full ration so as not to upset the analysis by arousing feelings of privation. Yesterday he voluntarily, and with no feelings of privation, reduced the dose from 6.0 to 3.0[2] per day. Psychically his condition has improved a lot, so that the future looks less sombre. He is an extraordinarily decent fellow with whom you can hit it off at once provided you can get your own complexes out of the way. Today is my first day of rest; I finished the analysis yesterday. So far as I can judge, all that remains now will be gleanings from a very long string of minor obsessions of secondary importance.

The analysis has yielded all sorts of scientifically valuable results which we shall try to formulate soon.

I should be grateful if you would give me a date for the paper you promised for the *Jahrbücher* so that an early beginning may be made. I shall, if at all possible, include the survey of the literature in the first half-year issue.

With best regards,

Most sincerely yours, JUNG

We agree with your proposal: "Jahrb. für psychanalytische u. psychopatholog. Forschung."

[1] "Versuch einer Hysterieanalyse"; see below, 167 F n. 2.
[2] Grams.

96 F

Dear friend,　　　　　　　　　29 May 1908, Vienna, IX. Berggasse 19

Though quite impatient during the long wait for your letter (symptomatic action: made a big tear in it when opening it), I gave myself the right explanation for your silence. And I can't regret it: Gross is such a fine man, with such a good mind, that your work must be regarded as a benefit to society. It would be a fine thing if a friendship and collaboration between the two of you were to grow out of this analysis. I must say I am amazed at how fast you young men work—such a task in only two weeks, it would have taken me longer. But one's judgment of a man is bound to be uncertain as long as he uses drugs to overcome his resistances.

I shall forward your enclosure to Deuticke; I am in complete agreement. If the number of pages in the volume should prove insufficient, I am sure he will have no objection to increasing it. Binswanger's contribution is most desirable. It "will do us no harm in the eyes of the right-minded."[1] I shall submit the "Analysis of a Phobia in a Five-year-old Boy" for the first number. Abraham will report on the Vienna literature with Rank's help; I shall press him to be as succinct as possible, and look through his article myself. I intend to write my piece in Berchtesgaden; it will be in your hands at the beginning of September. 1 January and 1 July strike me as good publication dates for the *Jahrbuch*.

You have not answered me on the subject of Moll. Of course it is not very important, but I should like a reply from you and Bleuler so I can wind up my correspondence with him.

Just as I expected, there has been a great upsurge in our movement since the founding of the *Jahrbuch*. Things have become very lively in my circle as well. I venture to hope that you people will soon force me back into the second rank of warriors, which disposes of one of my two great worries.

Otherwise, I am counting the days till the holidays, when I shall be able to work in peace and also get my corpus back into shape. But I'd better count weeks instead of days. I am hoping that by then certain of my cases will have brought solutions to some very interesting clinical problems. I have a good deal of material, but it is all "patchwork"; syntheses come very hard to me, I can manage them only at my best moments.

---

[1] Source not traced.

Still, I have never had a patient like Gross; with him one ought to be able to see straight to the heart of the matter.

With kind regards and best wishes for your work,

As ever, FREUD

97 J

Dear Professor Freud,   Burghölzli-Zürich, 1 June 1908

Excuse my oversight: I enclose Moll's letter herewith. Bleuler and I are of the opinion that, in view of our own journal, we should make use of this new organ at most within the limits sketched out by you. Moll's name doesn't sound too good to my ears; with his long experience he should really have more understanding of your work.

I am writing this in a great hurry, but shall soon write you a longer letter about Gross.

Once more with apologies,

Yours very sincerely, JUNG

98 J

Dear Professor Freud,   Burghölzli-Zürich, 19 June 1908

At long last I have a quiet moment in which to gather my wits together for a letter. Until now the Gross affair has consumed me in the fullest sense of the word. I have sacrificed days and nights to him. Under analysis he voluntarily gave up *all* medication. The last three weeks we worked only with very early infantile material. Little by little I came to the melancholy realization that although the infantile complexes could all be described and understood, and although the patient had momentary insights into them, they were nevertheless overwhelmingly powerful, being permanently fixated and drawing their affects from inexhaustible depths. With a tremendous effort on both sides to achieve insight and empathy we were able to stop the leak for a moment; the next moment it opened up again. All these moments of profound empathy left not a trace behind them; they quickly became insubstantial, shadowy memories. There is no development, no psychological yesterday for him; the events of early childhood remain eternally new and operative, so that notwithstanding all

155

the time and all the analysis he reacts to today's events like a 6-year-old boy, for whom the wife is always the mother, every friend, everyone who wishes him well or ill always the father, and whose world is a boyish fantasy filled with heaven knows what monstrous possibilities.

I am afraid you will already have read from my words the diagnosis I long refused to believe and which I now see before me with terrifying clarity: Dem. praec.

The diagnosis has been amply confirmed for me by a very careful anamnesis and partial psychanalysis of his wife. His exit from the stage is in keeping with the diagnosis: the day before yesterday Gross, unguarded for a moment, jumped over the garden wall and will doubtless turn up again in Munich ere long, to go towards the evening of his fate.

In spite of everything he is my friend, for at bottom he is a very good and fine man with an unusual mind. He is now living under the delusion that I have cured him and has already written me a letter overflowing with gratitude, like a bird escaped from its cage. In his ecstasy he has no inkling of the revenge which the reality he has never even glimpsed will wreak upon him. He is one of those whom life is *bound* to reject. He will never be able to live with anybody in the long run. His wife sticks it out only because Gross represents for her the fruits of her own neurosis. I now understand her too, but cannot forgive her on that account.

I don't know with what feelings you will receive this news. For me this experience is one of the harshest in my life, for in Gross I discovered many aspects of my own nature, so that he often seemed like my twin brother—but for the Dementia praecox. This is tragic. You can guess what powers I have summoned up in myself in order to cure him. But in spite of the sorrow of it, I would not have missed this experience for anything; for in the end it has given me, with the help of a unique personality, a unique insight into the nethermost depths of Dementia pr.

What is fixated by the disease is not any kind of complex arising in later life but the earliest infantile sexual complex. The ostensibly later "outbreak" of the disease is nothing but a secondary conflict, an "enchevêtrement"[1] resulting from his infantile attitude, and as such soluble but only up to a point. In hysteria there is both Pompeii and Rome, in D. pr. only Pompeii. The devaluation of reality in D. pr. seems to be due to the fact that the flight into the disease takes place

---

[1] = entanglement.

at an early infantile period when the sexual complex is still completely autoerotic; hence the persistent autoerotism.

Meanwhile I still have an unspeakable amount of work to do, as I have to catch up with all the business that has accumulated in the interim.

Are Rank and Abraham getting down to work? I have only leafed through Stekel's book.[2] There has been a lot of talk about it, both + and —. I permit myself no judgment as yet. Can I expect your contribution to the *Jahrbuch* by the autumn?

Bleuler, sad to say, is festooned with complexes from top to bottom; only recently he was again disputing the sexual explanation of rhythm. But he can't be pinned down, talks resistance-language, so that communication ceases of itself, and then compensates with fanatical candour and affability. In the end it gets on one's nerves, for one likes human beings around one and not complex-masks.

Should Gross turn to you later, please don't mention my diagnosis; I hadn't the heart to tell him. His wife knows everything.

With kindest regards,

Most sincerely yours, JUNG

99 F

My dear friend,   21 June 1908,[1] Vienna, IX. Berggasse 19

I have a feeling that I should thank you most vigorously—and so I do—for your treatment of Otto Gross. The task should have fallen to me but my egoism—or perhaps I should say my self-defence mechanism—rebelled against it. From my slip above you can see what a state of fatigue and holiday-hunger I am in—even without O. Gr.—a state that is not without its physical side-effects. By 21 August I hope to have completed quite a few pieces of work; I shall speak of them later.

I would have written to you today, Sunday, in any case, because the day before yesterday I received a telegram from Frieda Gr., who is in

[2] *Nervöse Angstzustände und ihre Behandlung* (1908 = *Conditions of Nervous Anxiety and Their Treatment* (London, 1922). (See also above, 61 F n. 5.) Freud wrote a preface (dated March 1908) for the original edition, but it was omitted after the 2nd edn. (1912); in SE IX.

[1] Freud first wrote 21.8.08, then wrote a 6 over the 8.

Heidelberg, asking for the address of the asylum in Nassau or of any others, since her husband is planning to leave Burghölzli. This made me wonder what had happened, but now you have satisfied my curiosity. I don't quite know what to think of it. His behaviour before the cure was totally paranoid; you must forgive me the old-fashioned term —in paranoia I recognize a psychological-clinical type, whereas Dem. pr. still has no precise meaning for me; it cannot be said that incurability or a bad end is a regular feature of Dem. pr., or distinguishes it from hysteria or obsessional neurosis. But I attributed it [his behaviour] to the medication, especially cocaine, which, as I well know,[2] produces a toxic paranoia. Now I have no reason to doubt your diagnosis, inherently because of your great experience of D. pr., but also because D. pr. is often not a real diagnosis. We seem to be in agreement about the impossibility of influencing his condition and about its ultimate development. But couldn't his condition be another (obsessional) psychoneurosis, with negative transference caused by his hostility to his father, which presents the appearance of absence or impairment of transference? Unfortunately I know too little about the mechanism of Dem. pr. or paranoia as compared with hysteria or obsessional neurosis. I have long wished for a strong impression in this field. The need to make a living and the requirements of therapy stand in the way.

Deeply as I sympathize with Otto Gr., I cannot underestimate the importance of your having been obliged to analyse him. You could never have learned so much from another case; and a further good result, I see, is that your views have once again come much closer to mine. I wasn't worried though. At one time, yes, before our last meeting. But just seeing you in Salzburg, though there was hardly a chance of talking to you, I knew that our views would soon be reconciled, that you had not, as I had feared, been alienated from me by some inner development deriving from the relationship with your father and the beliefs of the Church but merely by the influence of your chief. I must own, I was not entirely pleased with Bleuler, he sometimes made me feel rather creepy, but after a while I felt sure that I would not lose you to *him*. "Complex-mask," incidentally, is a magnificent term; the fact that you have hit upon it indicates that inwardly you have fully prevailed over him.

The differentiation of fixation and repression and the temporal relation between them have often preoccupied me in my cases of

---

[2] See Jones, I, chap. VI: "The Cocaine Episode (1884–1887)"; and Freud, *The Cocaine Papers*, ed. A. K. Donoghue and J. Hillman (Vienna and Zürich, 1963).

delirium; I have not yet got to the bottom of the problem. It seems doubtful to me that the precocity of the infantile fixation creates the predisposition to Dem. pr.; the matter calls for thorough investigation. But after all, have we the right to look for this predisposition and the conditions for the choice of neurosis in such developmental disturbances on the path taken by the libido? In my opinion there is nothing to be gained by speculation; we must wait for especially revealing cases that will show clearly what we can thus far only suspect.—

I recently received the Baroncini article[3] you spoke of. An excellent beginning for Italy. He gives a good account of your work, I should say; and what he says of mine is also remarkably free from misunderstanding. He gives me credit for certain ideas that originated with Breuer, and he stresses the first phase of our theory at the expense of the second, more far-reaching phase, which leads him to pay too little attention to the *Interpretation of Dreams* and the *Theory of Sexuality*. But all the same I was sincerely pleased.

Abraham is at work, seconded by Rank. On the private level, I want to acquaint you with the following programme: On 15 July (if "my constitution holds up"[4] until then) I shall be going to

Berchtesgaden, Dietfeldhof.

There I have the following projects. 1) The second edition of the *Interpretation of Dreams*; 2) "Analysis of a Phobia in a Five-year-old Boy," 3) "The Aphorisms on Obsessional Neurosis," known to you from Salzburg. 2) requires a short complementary essay: "On the Sexual Theories of Children,"[5] in which I shall be able to include a good deal of material useful to analysts. Since I cannot possibly take up the whole *Jahrbuch*, I shall send this paper to Hirschfeld or Marcuse[6] (*Sexual-Probleme*). If it is satisfactory to you, I would put the

[3] Luigi Baroncini, "Il fondamento ed il meccanismo della psico-analisi," *Rivista di psicologia applicata*, IV:3 (May–June 1908). In the next issue, Baroncini (a psychiatrist of Imola) translated an article by Jung, "Le nuove vedute della psicologia criminale" = "New Aspects of Criminal Psychology," CW 2, appendix.
[4] "[One] of those facetious Jewish anecdotes which contain so much profound and often bitter worldly wisdom and which we so greatly enjoy quoting in our talk and letters. . . . An impecunious Jew had stowed himself away without a ticket in the fast train to Karlsbad. He was caught, and each time tickets were inspected he was taken out of the train and treated more and more severely. At one of the stations on his *via dolorosa* he met an acquaintance, who asked him where he was travelling to. 'To Karlsbad,' was his reply, 'if my constitution can stand it.' "—*The Interpretation of Dreams*, SE IV, p. 195.
[5] See below, 118 F n. 1.
[6] Max Marcuse (1877–19—), Berlin sexologist, editor of the journal *Sexual-*

"Phobia" in the first and the "Aphorisms on Obsessional Neurosis" in the second number of the *Jahrbuch*. I shall give priority to the one that is needed first. On 1 September I mean to take a trip, perhaps to England, probably alone, sad to say.

In conclusion a little personal item: I recently came across your birthdate in a medical directory: 26 July, a day we have been celebrating for many years; it's my wife's birthday!

With kind regards,

As ever, FREUD

We'll exchange notes about Stekel another time.

100 J

Dear Professor Freud, Burghölzli-Zürich, 26 June 1908

I thank you with all my heart for your last letter.

There have been further developments in the Gross affair. According to the latest report from Frau Dr. Gross to my chief, Gross is acting really paranoid. He declared for instance that he couldn't remain in his hotel in Zürich because he had noticed that some men on the upper floor were spying on his mental state (!); in his flat in Munich he heard a voice in the street calling "Is the doctor at home?" Then he heard knockings in the walls and on the upper floor. He torments his wife just as before. The wretched woman is probably heading for a breakdown. Despite her admirable points she is one of those people who won't listen to reason but prefer to be hurt. Apparently she wants to tie her[1] whole fate to this symptomatic action.

If I can possibly manage it during the coming year I shall visit you again for a few days. I see no other way of discussing the concept of D. pr. *sive* schizophrenia *sive* paranoia that is weighing on my mind. In my opinion the negative father transference explains nothing, firstly because it is not absolute in Gross's case and secondly because in most other cases of D. pr. we have the exact opposite, as also in hysteria. The only differences, I find, are the infantile fixation, the infantile associations and the absolute but long-drawn-out incura-

---

Probleme (originally called *Mutterschutz*), which had recently published Freud's paper on " 'Civilized' Sexual Morality" (see above, 77 F n. 6).

[1] Holograph: *Ihr*, lit., "your."

160

bility—the permanent exclusion of sizeable chunks of reality. I am now treating a large number of highly educated hysterics and can see the absolute difference between D. pr. and hysteria in these cases, and can only marvel at the profundity of your views. I wish Gross could go back to you, this time as a patient,[2] not that I want to inflict a Gross episode on you too, but simply for the sake of comparison. That would be a gain for science, because with the D. pr. problem 9/10[3] of the psychiatric problems would be solved. (Slip in this peculiar sentence?) Probably because I am angry that you see my efforts to solve the D. pr. problem in a different light.

I am delighted with the July 26 parallel! Best regards,

Yours sincerely, JUNG

101 F

Dear friend,   30 June 1908, Vienna, IX. Berggasse 19

Why, of course! We're not living in different centuries, not even on different continents. Why shouldn't we get together to discuss a matter of such importance to both of us? The only question is when would be the best time and whether I should go to see you or you come to see me.

I shall be in Berchtesgaden from 15 July on. I hope to feel sufficiently rested in a few weeks to put my thoughts in order. Our colleague Ferenczi[1] has announced his visit on 15 August. He wants to do a little mountain climbing in B. and then go to Holland with me some time after 1 September. There we have a first possibility; from 1 to 15 August no obstacle, after the 15th Fer., a very relative obstacle, removable by a few kind words. Then I shall be travelling, this time to Holland and England to visit my aged brother.[2] I could visit you in Zürich in the first days of September, still with Fer., or in the last week of September when I shall be on my way home and alone.

[2] There is no record of Gross's earlier relations with Freud and no evidence that he was Freud's patient. Martin Green agrees (see above, 33 J n. 7).
[3] Holograph: *während* 1/10; Jung struck it out and wrote *wären* 9/10.

[1] Ferenczi had first met Freud on 2 Feb. 08, when he called on him with Philip Stein, who introduced him (above, 67 F; Jones, II, p. 39/34).
[2] Freud's half brother Emanuel (1834–1915), then 74, who lived in Manchester. The two had met unexpectedly at Salzburg (Jones, II, p. 49/44; *Letters*, ed. E. L. Freud, no. 138).

If you come to see me, the advantage is that you too will be free; if I go to see you, the advantage is that you will be able to show me something. Well, compare this program of mine with yours, work out when the two can come together, and make up your mind; the best of all, though probably the most complicated to arrange, would be to take a bit of a trip together. But if it can be managed, everything else is flexible, destination, other companions, etc.

And now a few trifles.

I recently received from R. Vogt[3] in Christiania a few instalments of a *Psykiatriens grundtræk*. Under "Paranoiske tilstande" they cite a good bit of our new mythology, with approval, I hope. Unfortunately I don't understand a single word of Ibsen's language. It seems to be a textbook; if so, the first one to condescend to us comes from Norway! (Offprint from *Nord. mag. f. lægev.* VS 1908)[4]

I have engaged Abraham to review the Viennese and German literature with the exception of the purely *polemical* material. Was I right in understanding you to say that this last should be treated separately?

I am still expecting editorial answers to the questions[5] I asked you in my last letter. I have had news of Gross from Jones, who is with you now, I presume. Unfortunately there is nothing to be said of him. He is addicted and can only do great harm to our cause.

I am overjoyed at the prospect you open up for the coming months and send you my kindest regards.

Yours, FREUD

[3] Ragnar Vogt (1870–1943), then lecturer in psychiatry, University of Christiania (now Oslo), Norway; later, director of the University Psychiatric Clinic. Jung cited his work in "The Psychology of Dementia Praecox," CW 3, par. 12.

[4] "Psykiatriens grundtræk," a series of articles by Vogt published in *Norsk magazin for lægevidenskaben*, 1903–8; the 8th was "Paranoiske og paranoiforme tilstande," V, 5th series (1907). The articles were published in book form, 2 vols., Christiania, 1905, 1909. The paper in question was in the latter vol., and the references in it to Freud were indeed favourable.

[5] Holograph: *Antworten*, "answers," crossed out and *Fragen* substituted.

102 J

Dear Professor Freud, Burghölzli-Zürich, 12 July 1908

Again I have had to keep you waiting a long time for my answer. I am not a free agent and always have to adjust my decisions to the wishes of half a dozen other people. That takes time.

In August[1] my chief has four weeks leave, during which time I shall naturally be chained to the Clinic. In September (1–15) I go on holiday. On the 16th I shall be home again until the 28th, when my military service begins, lasting until the end of October. So if you cared to spend a few days with us between the 16th and the 28th I would be very happy. I should like to spend the miserably short holiday I have in lazy solitude; God knows I need it. This summer term has been gruelling. If I am back in the Clinic at the end of September, I hope my chief will relieve me of most of my duties so that I can devote all my time to you.

Please forgive me for not going further into your work plans in my last letter. I simply took them as settled. Of course I agree with your putting the "Phobia" in the first number and the "Aphorisms on Obsessional Neurosis" in the second. On the other hand I hope you won't mind a mild protest at your lavishing your ideas and articles on Hirschfeld or Marcuse or even Moll. Naturally I won't presume to stop you, since I don't know your reasons. Your ideas are difficult enough for the layman to understand as it is, but they all have a continuity of logical development, and I think it ill advised to scatter them at random on good and stony ground alike. Some fall by the wayside, and the people tread them underfoot; some fall among thorns, and the thorns choke them;[2] whereas I hope the *Jahrbücher* will gather up the scattered seeds and so give a faithful picture of the edifice you have built.

I should be grateful if you could let me have your contribution to the first number by the beginning of the winter. I hope Binswanger's will also be finished by then, as well as the abstracts.

All my available time last week was taken up by Dr. Campbell,[3]

---

[1] Holograph: *Juli*, struck out and *August* substituted.
[2] Cf. Mark 4:5–8.
[3] Charles Macfie Campbell (1876–1943), from Edinburgh; he had just called on Freud (Jones, II, p. 51/46) and was now on his way to take up an appointment as associate in clinical psychiatry at the New York Psychiatric Institute

whom you also know. I took special pains to dispose him in our favour and to send forth another man who could be influential because of his position in New York. Great things cannot be expected of him, but perhaps much good in small things.

Jones is an enigma to me. He is so incomprehensible that it's quite uncanny. Is there more in him than meets the eye, or nothing at all? At any rate he is far from simple; an intellectual liar (no moral judgment intended!) hammered by the vicissitudes of fate and circumstance into many facets. But the result? Too much adulation on one side, too much opportunism on the other?

I gave my patient Frl. B——— the pleasure of writing to you *first* that she is here. I think that, given time, she will cook her own goose.

With best regards,

Yours very sincerely, JUNG

N.B. An emissary from the Tübingen Clinic[4] has arrived.

103 F

Dear friend,   Berchtesgaden, Dietfeldhof,[1] 18 July 1908

I have been here for a few days and am recovering very quickly from all my ailments.

I am delighted at the prospect of seeing you and talking with you for a few days. Of course I accept the dates you suggest and will be with you in Zürich in the latter half of September. I hope to find you rested, for I know how heavy a burden you have taken on and am also well aware that Otto Gross has been a dreadful weight on your shoulders. Were it not for my confidence in your strength and endurance, I should fear to tax you further with whole days of discussion. These thoughts are inspired not by my feeling of friendship for you but by

---

(Ward's Island). Later at the Johns Hopkins University and at Harvard. See also below, 125 F n. 3.

[4] Wolf Stockmayer (1881–1933), assistant to Gaupp at the Tübingen clinic; later practiced as an analytical psychologist in Stuttgart. He remained a personal friend of Jung's. (First mentioned by name in 113 J.)

---

[1] Stationery imprinted "Prof. Dr. Freud" and this address. The family had previously vacationed in Berchtesgaden in 1899 and 1902–4 (Jones, I, p. 369/335f. and II, pp. 16/15, 57f./51f.). Martin Freud gives an account of a summer at Berchtesgaden in *Sigmund Freud: Man and Father* (1958), chap. VIII.

the consideration that I need you, that the cause cannot do without you—less than ever since the founding of the *Jahrbuch*.

Here, in this ideal peace, I shall do whatever is expected of me, probably the two articles for our *periodical*.[2] Let me explain my Marcuse-Hirschfeld policy; then I believe you will relinquish your objection. The paper about little Herbert's phobia must be complemented by an article on children's sexual theories, a subject which, I think, offers the possibility of an important step forward. Now it is certainly not in my interest or in that of the *Jahrbuch* that I should fill it up all by myself; in that we are surely agreed. Consequently I need other outlets. These cannot, as you fear, determine the ultimate fate of my articles; they are mere way stations. As soon as a certain number of short papers have accumulated, they will be gathered into a second volume of the *Collected Papers on the Theory of the Neuroses*. This has already been arranged with the publisher, it will be done in two years at the most, and it is only on this condition that I am letting anyone else have the papers. I hope you find this satisfactory, but please tell me what you think in any case, I don't want to do anything you disapprove of.

These outside connections are also useful in another way: they enable me to place papers by our followers, for which there is no room in the *Jahrbuch*, by substituting them little by little for my own.

I thought you knew more than I about Jones. I saw him as a fanatic who smiles at my faint heartedness and is affectionately indulgent with you over your vacillations. How true this picture is, I don't know. But I tend to think that he lies to the others, not to us. I find the racial mixture in our group most interesting; he is a Celt and consequently not quite accessible to us, the Teuton and the Mediterranean man.

Fräulein B—— is not only homosexual herself, but arouses homosexuality in others.

With kind regards,

Sincerely, FREUD

[2] English in original. / The two articles are the "Little Hans" and the "Rat Man" papers.

104 F

Dear friend,   Berchtesgaden, Dietfeldhof, 5 August 1908

Enclosed Little Hans's Phobia. I worked hard on it, which is not likely to have helped it any. It is ready for the printer except for a few slight changes that can be made in the proof (insertion of reference numbers, checking of quotations, slight stylistic improvements). If it is all right with you, we can save space by using two type sizes. The observations in eight point, the comments and the rest of the trimmings larger.

That's what I've been doing with my holiday so far. How are you?

Very cordially yours, FREUD

P.S. Please acknowledge receipt.

105 J

Dear Professor Freud,   Burghölzli-Zürich, 11 August 1908

I got your manuscript yesterday evening and hasten to thank you for sending it along so quickly. As soon as circumstances permit I shall set about reading it. I am very eager to learn, as I have a great need to see for myself how you treat each individual case. What we lack most is case material. I am never quite satisfied with my own, I always want to know how such cases turn out with other people. I have now read half of Stekel's book. The case material is invaluable. The incompleteness of his analyses is to be regretted, likewise his equally frequent neglect of the conflict, which seems to me far more important than the sexual troubles; these, as we know, can be endured for years so long as no conflict is piled on top of them. Some cases even show quite clearly that the symptoms arise not from sexual defects but from the conflict. (Case of the Jewish sausages!)[1] I have read the book with pleasure because of the case material, otherwise with mixed feelings. Many of the interpretations are, or seem to be, very arbitrary; at any rate they are insufficiently substantiated. I would

---

[1] A woman whose symptom is uncontrollable vomiting is having trouble with her family over her Jewish fiancé; she defiantly eats Jewish sausages.—*Conditions of Nervous Anxiety*, p. 91.

like to see the Fliess things proved.[2] The technique of proof strikes me as thoroughly inadequate, and I don't think Fliess's ideas add anything essential to Stekel's book anyway. They should have been omitted. Even the devil has to compromise a bit. I am anxious to see what the critics will make of it. I have to review it for the *Medizinische Klinik,* Bleuler for the *Münchener med. Wochenschrift.*[3]

All through Stekel's book the theory looks very much as though it were "tacked on," it never really permeates his cases. Stekel's conception of "anxiety hysteria" seems to me a very broad one. It would appear that there is no case of hysteria in which anxiety equivalents do not occur, and in a prominent position at that. I am still not clear what he means.

I am definitely counting on your coming to Zürich in mid-September (around 10–20). I have a mountain of questions. Which would you prefer: to stay with me or in a hotel? I have room enough and you will be undisturbed; my children are away with my wife. Please choose.

With best regards,

Most sincerely yours, JUNG

106 F

Dear friend,   Berchtesgaden, Dietfeldhof, 13 August 1908

Thank you for the speedy acknowledgment; since it is not possible here to register packages to Switzerland, I had no proof of having sent the parcel. No hurry about reading it; I'm afraid it won't be easy in manuscript.

I am very much looking forward to my visit to Zürich-Burghölzli. I gladly accept your invitation to stay with you; in the absence of your little family I trust I won't be in the way. I have various plans in mind, first of all to demolish the resentment that is bound to accumulate in the course of a year between two persons who demand a good deal of each other, to obtain a few personal concessions from you, and to dis-

---

[2] Stekel (ibid., p. 49) stated that the theory of the connection between the genitalia and nose had been irrefutably proved by Fliess, in *Beziehungen zwischen Nase und weiblichen Geschlechtsorganen* (1897).

[3] Jung in *Medizinische Klinik* (Berlin), IV:45 (8 Nov. 08), 1735f. (see CW 18); Bleuler in *Münchener medizinische Wochenschrift*, LV:32 (11 Aug. 08), 1702f.

cuss a few points with you very thoroughly—for this I am not making any preparation. My selfish purpose, which I frankly confess, is to persuade you to continue and complete my work by applying to psychoses what I have begun with neuroses. With your strong and independent character, with your Germanic blood which enables you to command the sympathies of the public more readily than I, you seem better fitted than anyone else I know to carry out this mission. Besides, I'm fond of you; but I have learned to subordinate that factor.

Let me recapitulate your programme. From September 1 to 15 you will be on holiday, which must be respected. From the 15th to 26th you will be in Burghölzli, exposed to my visit. I was planning to arrive toward the end of this period, because I shall be in England beginning September 1st and should like to make full use of my time there. If I have had enough in three weeks, I shall be with you on September 23rd or 24th; after all I can't burden you for more than two or three days. If I come sooner, I shall also leave sooner and treat myself during the last week of September to a bit of southern air, which I should hate to forgo this year. I say nothing about Bleuler, I have abandoned the thought of winning him over because membership in our group is so clearly contrary to his practical interests. You would not have invited me if you did not know that Bleuler has no objection and will not interfere with us.

I subscribe in every detail to your criticism of Stekel's book, but not as a whole. He has an uncritical mind, with him all distinctions merge, journalism has given him an incorrigible tendency to content himself with approximations, his dream analyses are, or seem to be, arbitrary; ever since I proposed "anxiety hysteria" to him, I must keep an anxious guard over all material in which anxiety occurs, for fear that he will lay claim to it as "anxiety hysteria." All that is true, it is as glaring as you say, perhaps even more so. But you have applied a very rigorous standard. The book is addressed to the practising physician, who has no need of what Stekel fails to supply, but can learn from the book a great many things of which he would otherwise have no inkling, and Stekel's picture is after all quite sound. His sloppiness does not mar the general impression; all the essentials are correct, there is no need of completeness when what is desired is quick results; this author's gift for ΨA allows him to make with impunity mistakes that would be more harmful in the work of another, less gifted man. The aura of optimism that hovers over the whole performance—we are always right, all our findings fit together, are useful, and so on—may repel us, but the practitioners won't mind it at all; they welcome illusions. So I hope your criticism won't frighten the public away; from Bleuler, who doesn't really like strong emphasis on the sexual factor, we shall probably have another disguised repudiation.

He could certainly have omitted Fliess's things, but they impressed him. They really are impressive; but not easy to prove. Naturally, since my falling-out with Fliess, I have stopped trying to influence anyone for or against him; and, to tell the truth, it has not made it easier for me to form an opinion of my own. I suppose you know that I had next to no influence on Stekel's book; I have long known that one can't change people. Everyone has something worthwhile in him. We must content ourselves with getting it out of him.

I am gradually recovering from the ravages of this last year's toil, but my night life is still unpleasantly active. One thing and another have turned my thoughts to mythology and I am beginning to suspect that myth and neurosis have a common core.

Moll has asked me for a small contribution to the new *Zentral-blatt*;[1] I have promised him something about hysterical attacks,[2] obviously an application of the insights gained in connection with dream interpretation. Our colleague Ferenczi, who has great personal charm, is now in Berchtesgaden and comes to see us often. He goes mountain-climbing with my boys. Brill in New York seems to be very busy with his translations. — From Gross I haven't had a blessed word.

I have received proof of the second edition of *The Interpretation of Dreams* and of the *Studies*. We shall be making considerable demands on the market this autumn.

I hope to hear from you before our meeting. With kind regards,

As ever, FREUD

107 J

Dear Professor Freud,   Burghölzli-Zürich, 21 August 1908

I am eagerly looking forward to your visit, which you are going to extend by several days. We shall have plenty to talk about—you may be sure of that. I shall be at home again from September 8th to the 28th. Come any time you like during those 20 days. I shall banish all intrusions that might encroach upon our sessions, so we can count on being undisturbed. Prof. Bleuler has nothing against your visit, how

[1] Apparently a slip for Moll's *Zeitschrift*; see above, 94 F n. 1.
[2] See below, 131 J n. 1.

much he has for it no one knows, least of all himself. So there is no
need for further worry. He is extremely well-behaved and obliging at
all times and will put himself out to provide benevolent background.
(The unmistakably venomous tone of these sentences refers to certain
happenings of an internal nature which justify my feelings.)

You are quite right: on the whole I was unfair to Stekel's book. But
only to you. The other side will emerge in my review. Just now I am
treating a case of anxiety hysteria and see how far from simple the
matter is and how many difficulties are glossed over by Stekel's optimism. Apart from that I am fully aware of the value of his book.

Recently I had a visit from Prof. Adolf Meyer[1] of the State Pathological Institute in New York. He is *very* intelligent and clear-headed
and entirely on our side in spite of the toxin problem in Dementia
praecox. In addition he's an anatomist. A while ago I received some
offprints from Sir Victor Horsley[2] and from a third party the news
that he is interested in our work.

My holiday starts tomorrow evening, thank God. I intend to make
the best of it by fleeing into the inaccessible solitude of a little Alpine
cabin on Mount Säntis.

I am very glad you are coming as there are all sorts of things to
clear up.

Please give Ferenczi my very cordial regards. He is highly deserving
of your goodwill.

If you should write again in the near future, please send the letter to
the usual address; everything will be forwarded.

With best regards,

Most sincerely yours, JUNG

108 J

Dear Professor Freud, Burghölzli-Zürich, 9 September 1908

I got back from my holiday yesterday, much too early for my subjective feelings. Still, the holiday brought me a little recuperation so
that I am in a somewhat fresher mood for work. The impetus, however, is slight.

---

[1] Adolf Meyer (1866–1950), originally of Zürich, a pupil of Forel and of J. J.
Honegger, Sr. (see 148 J n. 3); to the United States in 1892. At this time he
was also professor of psychiatry, Cornell University Medical School, New York; after
1910, at Johns Hopkins. He was considered "the dean of American psychiatrists."
[2] Sir Victor Horsley (1857–1916), British physiologist and brain surgeon.

I hope my last letter, written about 18 days ago, reached you safely. I am sending this to Vienna as I don't know your English address. Please let me know fairly soon when you are thinking of coming. I'd like to arrange things in such a way that I have as little as possible to do with the donkey work in the Clinic during your visit. I am looking forward so much to talking with you again in peace, for since I saw you in Vienna very, very many things have changed, much is new and further progress has been made. In this respect Gross as a contrast, no matter how hard to digest, did me a world of good. In spite of his prickliness, talk with him is wonderfully stimulating. I have missed that no end. Only once since then have I had the luck to talk with a really intelligent man, and that was with Prof. Meyer of New York. I think I have already told you about his radical views in my last letter. Bleuler is difficult to bear with in the long run; his infantilisms are intolerable and he ruthlessly acts out his complexes by dint of displacements (naturally!). It's still very hard to talk to him as I am highly suspicious of his goodwill, etc. etc.

I hope you are having good weather in England and *omnium rerum satietatem*.[1]

With best regards,

Most sincerely yours, J U N G

Freud in England and Zürich

While Jung had been vacationing alone in an Alpine retreat south of Appenzell, some 40 miles east of Zürich, Freud left Berchtesgaden on 1 September for England, travelling via the Netherlands. (His only previous visit to England had been in 1875, during the summer when Jung was born; he did not go again until 1938.) Freud spent a week visiting his half-brothers Emanuel and Philipp in Manchester, Blackpool, and elsewhere, and another week alone in London; on 15 September he left with Emanuel for Berlin, where he visited his sister Marie, or Mitzi (married to Moritz Freud). He was in Zürich 18–21 September, staying in Jung's flat at the Burghölzli. At the hospital, Jung showed him the patient B. St. (see below, 110 F n. 2, and *Memories*, p. 128/128). Then Freud went to Italy. (See Jones, II, pp. 57ff./51ff., and *Freud/Abraham Letters*, Freud 29 Sept. o8.)

---

[1] = "abundance of all things." Perhaps a faultily remembered quotation from Cicero, *De senectute*, 20.76: "studiorum omnium satietas vitae facit satietatem," "when you are fed up with your occupations you are fed up with life." (Kindly suggested by Gilbert Highet.)

109 F

Salò, 23 September 1908[1]

With many thanks for the fine days in Zürich.

FREUD

110 F

15 October 1908,
My dear friend and heir,   Vienna, IX. Berggasse 19

The days we spent so auspiciously together in Zürich have left me in high good humour. Please tell your dear wife that one passage in her letter[1] gave me particular pleasure.

I know you are still busy with your military duties and I really ought to leave you in peace, but an observation I made recently leaves me none. Yesterday, one of my patients, the anxiety man, a classic case, now well on his way to being cured, very intelligent, in every way the contrary of Dem. pr., and, incidentally, familiar with all our publications, offered the following idea, which he himself immediately classified as paranoid: I am an officers' corps. Doesn't that sound exactly like the formulas of your woman patient[2] which, as recently as Salzburg, you declared to be fundamentally different from those of a hysteria or obsessional neurosis case? Here is the explanation. He failed to become an officer and feels very badly about it; this is his compensation. The meaning is: first, that he is an officer's body, because his father always told him he was unfit for any other profession, and next that he is as handsome as only an officer can be—he was indeed a handsome young fellow and his good looks were his undoing; having been thoroughly spoiled at home, he expected to succeed in the army thanks to his looks alone, nothing could go wrong, he was sure to be everybody's darling, and at first he apparently was;—secondly, he is a "*Soldatenmensch*"[3]—an officers' catamite. Immediately

----

[.] Picture postcard addressed to *Herrn u. Frau Dr. C. G. Jung.* Salò is on Lake Garda, in northern Italy, and Freud spent 21–28 Sept. there, in company with his sister-in-law Minna Bernays (Jones, II, pp. 58f./52f., and *Letters,* ed. E. L. Freud, no. 142).

----

[1] Missing.

[2] In "The Psychology of Dementia Praecox," a typical formula of the patient B. St. is "I am a Switzerland" (CW 3, par. 253).

[3] = "soldiers' whore."

172

afterward he made the normal statement: The whole officers' corps can kiss my . . .[4] which only requires a projection and change of sign to express the correct paranoid idea of persecution. Obviously the case swarms with the finest hysterical condensation formulas. Here we have preconscious trains of thought in the process of regression as a preparation for their expression in symptoms. In him the "officers' corps," by way of *cor, cordis,* led to cardiac symptoms.

In other words, there is an unconscious paranoia that we make conscious in psychoanalysis. Incidentally, this case provides excellent confirmation of your aperçu that in analysis we guide hysteria patients along the road to Dem. pr.

I also have an opportunity at present to study a true case of Dem. pr. A very intelligent young lady; so far the transference is still enormous.

Your chief and his wife called on us last Friday evening. He is definitely the more bearable of the two. He was as amiable as his stiffness permitted. He came out in defence of infantile sexuality, for which only two years ago he was "without comprehension." Then both of them pounced on me, insisting that I should replace the word "sexuality" with another (on the model of autism); this, they claimed, would put an end to all resistance and misunderstanding. I said I had no faith in such a happy outcome; anyway, they were at a loss to provide this better term.

With kind regards to you and your wife,

Yours, FREUD

111 J

Dear Professor Freud,[1]

Barracks, Yverdon,
Ct. de Vaud, 21 October 1908

My wife was naturally delighted with the surprise package of books. Evidently she has already thanked you in a becoming manner, as I see from your letter. Being on military service I am an even worse correspondent than before, so once again you have forestalled me. Your visit has done me so much good that I am firmly resolved, if circumstances permit, to pay you a short visit in Vienna next spring,

---

[4] Holograph: *kann mich im* . . . .

[1] Holograph: *Lieber Herr Professor.* Jung's first use of the salutation "Lieber." This continued to be his style until the 27 Oct. 13 letter (see below, 357 J). / This letter is written on Jung's Burghölzli stationery.

provided other demands are not made on your time. Many thanks for telling me about that paranoid idea. I have never doubted the possibility that products of this kind are psychogenic in origin since they are often found in normal people as well; only I did not dare to assume that the replacement of reality by such products was also psychogenic.

I have now received Abraham's abstracts.[2] Have you looked at them? My chief writes that he called on you, but no other details.[3]
[...]

I have now regained my zest for work and hope to put my back into it once my military service is over (Oct. 30). Three pupils, though, are lurking in the background like vultures. I shall have to attend particularly to the man from Tübingen.

The latest news of Gross is that his wife doesn't want to part from him because allegedly he is in good shape. Incidentally, have you seen in Harden's Zukunft[4] the sort of thing Gross is writing now? If he keeps it up, the outcome may yet be good. His family have now accepted my diagnosis—a great relief for his wife.

Binet wants me to write an account of your dream theory for L'Année psychologique.[5]

With kindest regards,

Most sincerely yours, JUNG

112 F

Dear friend,   8 November 1908, Vienna, IX. Berggasse 19

I have been paralysed as a correspondent by a mass of work that keeps me gasping, and by a domestic event. My daughter[1] has become engaged to a man of her choice, she is to be married in a few months and the young people are creating quite a commotion. I hope that

---

[2] In Jahrbuch, I:2 (1909). See appendix 2.

[3] See Freud's account of the Bleulers' visit in a letter of 11 Oct. 08 to Abraham: "They were very kind, in so far as his unapproachability and her affectation permit" (Freud/Abraham Letters, p. 54).

[4] Die Zukunft, 10 Oct. 08, published a letter from Gross (then docent for psychopathology at Graz) about a case of his—a girl whose father had committed her to a psychiatric hospital, whereas Gross maintained that she should have been psychoanalysed.

[5] "L'Analyse des rêves"; see below, 152 F n. 2.

---

[1] Mathilde; on 7 Feb. 09 she was married to Robert Hollitscher (1876–1959).

your work is in full swing again; we must make great progress in this working year, both in our thinking and in our activity.

I have started work on a paper. The title—"A General Exposition of the Psychoanalytic Method"²—tells all. It is getting ahead very slowly; at present I can write only on Sundays, and then only a few pages. In any event it is to round out the second volume of the *Collected Papers* which Deuticke is prepared to publish and in which "Dora"³ is to reappear. A Mr. Parker of Columbia University⁴ absolutely insists on having a paper from me; maybe I shall offer him this one, but since, as our translator Brill writes, he is opposed on principle to any mention of sexuality, it seems probable that nothing will come of it. Brill also tells me that you are to contribute an article. He writes that Morton Prince keeps sending out warnings against our "trend."

I won't say much about the most recent wave of abuse. Forel's attacks⁵ are chiefly on you, probably out of ignorance. Professor Mehringer in Graz (slips of the tongue)⁶ is outdoing himself in vicious polemics. Moll's book⁷ is dishonest and incompetent; a discussion of it is scheduled for our next Wednesday. On the credit side I can now announce that the second edition of *The Interpretation of Dreams*,⁸ a copy of which is here on my desk, will reach you in a few days.

Frau C—— did actually come to me a fortnight ago; a very serious case of obsessional neurosis, improvement is bound to be very slow.

---

² Holograph: *Allg. Methodik der Psychoanalyse.* See Jones, II, pp. 258ff./230f., for an account of Freud's work on this project up until 1910, when it "vanished." Freud instead wrote the six "Papers on Technique"; see below, 280 F nn. 2 & 3, and 318 J n. 1.

³ "Fragment of an Analysis of a Case of Hysteria" (orig. 1905; written 1901), SE VII.

⁴ William Belmont Parker (1871–1934), lecturer at Columbia University; literary editor of *World's Work* (New York), an "uplift" magazine, published 1908–9. The first issue announced a contribution by Freud, but none appeared. Brill contributed later. See Hale, *Freud and the Americans*, pp. 231f.

⁵ An article by Forel, "Zum heutigen Stand der Psychotherapie: Ein Vorschlag," *Journal für Psychologie und Neurologie*, XI (1908), had been discussed at the 4 Nov. meeting of the Wednesday Society: "This quite intelligent article also contains a mild attack (on Jung)" (*Minutes*, II, p. 39).

⁶ Rudolf Meringer (1859–1931), author with C. Mayer of *Versprechen und Verlesen, eine psychologisch-linguistische Studie* (Vienna, 1895), quoted extensively in *The Psychopathology of Everyday Life* (orig. 1901), SE VI. Freud misspelled the name.

⁷ Albert Moll, *Das Sexualleben des Kindes* (Leipzig, 1908) = *The Sexual Life of the Child* (New York, 1912). See 11 Nov. meeting in *Minutes*, II, pp. 43ff.

⁸ Revised and enlarged; dated 1909.

The reason for her preference for me was that Thomsen[9] had advised her against me, saying that treatment by me would only make her condition much worse. But that fell in with her need for punishment.

I am very eager to hear from you and Burghölzli, and most of all to learn that your dear wife, who has felt obliged to write a second letter of thanks, is well.

With kindest regards,

Yours, FREUD

113 J

Dear Professor Freud,   Burghölzli-Zürich, 11 November 1908

Magna est vis veritatis tuae et praevalebit![1] What one might call the dismal news in your last letter—Meringer, Morton Prince, Dr. Parker—has bucked me up no end. Nothing is more detestable than to blow the horn of instant public acclaim and settle down on densely populated ground. Hence I am delighted by the vigorous opposition we provoke. Obviously there are plenty more waiting to make fools of themselves. Even Forel still has a chance to do so at the eleventh hour. For some time now I have noticed the gentle zephyrs of prudery blowing across from America, for which Morton Prince seems to have a quite special organ. Everyone is terribly afraid for his practice, everyone is waiting to play a dirty trick on someone else. That is why we hear so little of the people who have worked with me and visited you. In America they are simply pushed to the wall. I have turned down Dr. Parker despite his honeyed letter, three pages long; the project has nothing to commend it. Also I received information about Dr. Parker from Dr. Hoch[2] which doesn't make me at all enthusiastic about him. The man has turned to us merely on Peterson's[3] recommendation, so he has no idea of the real state of affairs.

---

[9] Probably Robert Thomsen (1858–1914), directing psychiatrist of the Hertz private sanatorium, Bonn.

---

[1] = "Great is the power of your truth and it shall prevail." Jung's adaptation of "Magna est veritas, et praevalet."—Vulgate, Appendix, 3 Esdras 4:41 (A.V., Apocrypha, 1 Esdras 4:41).

[2] August Hoch (1868–1919), originally of Basel, to the U.S.A. in 1887. Professor of psychiatry, Cornell University Medical School (New York), 1905–1917; 1910, succeeded Adolf Meyer as director of New York Psychiatric Institute (Ward's Island).

[3] Frederick W. Peterson (1859–1938), then clinical professor of psychiatry, Co-

I am much looking forward to the new edition of *The Interpretation of Dreams*, also to the paper you announce. Why don't you try to place it in Ebbinghaus's journal[4] or, better still, in the *Zeitschrift für Psychiatrie* because of its larger circulation? I have just written a little thing for Binet, some examples of dreams with short analyses. Superficial, of course, but written in such a way that even a Frenchman can understand it, if he wants to. Unfortunately it will only fall into the hands of psychologists, who will make short work of it. The Frenchmen have also lit into our poor Maeder. Binet derives his good opinion of me—so far unshaken—from Larguier des Bancels, Privatdozent in Lausanne and infected via Claparède.

I now have a lot of material for the *Jahrbuch*, only Binswanger's paper is still missing but should reach me by the beginning of December. If at all possible I shall put Maeder's paper[5] on the sexuality of epileptics in the first number; there are some remarkable things in it. If Binswanger's opus is too long it might be split into two parts, don't you think?[6] For the second number I want to contribute some case material on Dem. praecox by way of Maeder,[7] if all goes well. I am now working on the associations in Dem. praec. with Dr. Stockmayer. Besides that I have two youngsters in the laboratory. You see what pests pupils are! *One* good pupil and the pleasure he gives have to be paid for dearly.

My wife and I congratulate you heartily on your daughter's engagement!

Best regards, JUNG

---

lumbia University, New York; poet and art collector. He had recently been at the Burghölzli doing research in collaboration with Jung (see above, 19 J n. 2, "Psychophysical Investigations"); was now working with Brill on the translation of Jung's *Dementia Praecox* (see below, 124 J n. 3). He later became an opponent of psychoanalysis (Brill, *Freud's Contribution to Psychiatry*, New York, 1944, p. 27).

[4] Hermann Ebbinghaus (1850–1909), professor of psychology in Breslau and Halle, with König founded the *Zeitschrift für Psychologie* in 1890.

[5] "Sexuality and Epilepsy"; see below, 132 F n. 1.

[6] It was; see below, 167 F n. 2.

[7] I.e., in Maeder's paper, "Psychologische Untersuchungen an Dementia praecox-Kranken," actually in *Jahrbuch*, II:1.

114 F

Dear friend,   12 November 1908, Vienna, IX. Berggasse 19

I agree with you completely. It is an honour to have plenty of enemies![1] Now that we can live, work, publish and enjoy a certain companionship, life is not at all bad and I should not want it to change too soon. When the day of "recognition" comes, it will be to the present what the gruesome magic of the Inferno is to the holy boredom of the Paradiso. (That is, of course, the other way around.)

I was hesitant about Parker; in the light of Brill's reports, I decided to be very difficult; now that I have received and looked at his first issue, and especially after your remarks, I am declining. The paper is going very slowly; I am in harness from eight to eight. Would you take it for the second half-volume of the *Jahrbuch* if my inner distaste for indiscretion prevents me from writing my other contribution—about the rat man with the obsessional neurosis? (He is getting along splendidly.) I don't like to give anything so specific to other journals; it can only be intelligible to our more immediate circle, because it presupposes a knowledge of the *Studies* and of heaven knows what else. I would welcome your frank editorial opinion. But bear in mind that the paper is to be published in any case in the second volume of the *Collected Papers*.[2]

Since you ask me, I see no objection to breaking up Binswanger's analysis. The boy should have finished it by now. The bit of nimbus provided by the preface will be very good for the *Jahrbuch*.

I hear from Abraham that he has survived his first battle in Berlin.[3] He is on dangerous ground in that advance outpost.

My anxiety man who, as you no doubt remember, was an officers' corps, is now in the midst of the most beautiful solutions which he himself discovers; he really deserves a doctor's degree as much as the

---

[1] Holograph: *Viel Feind, viel Ehr!*—popular saying, originally slogan of the German general Georg von Frundsberg (1473–1528). / This paragraph was published in Jones, II, pp. 49f./44f.

[2] "A General Exposition of the Psychoanalytic Method" (see above, 112 F n. 2) was not completed.

[3] Abraham had spoken 9 Nov. to the Berlin Society for Psychiatry and Nervous Diseases on intermarriage between relatives and neurosis (= "Die Stellung der Verwandtenehe in der Psychologie der Neurosen," *Jahrbuch*, I:1, 1909), and was attacked by Ziehen, Braatz, and others. See his letter of 10 Nov. 08 in *Freud/Abraham Letters*, p. 55; also Jones, II, p. 128/114.

malade imaginaire. He says he hopes to conclude his recovery with a literary work that will serve our purposes.

Moll's book on the sex life of the child is both meagre and—dishonest. What a mean, malicious soul, and what a narrow mind he must have. Even your chief has now accepted infantile sexuality. True, he wants to call it something different, for fear of offending the squeamish, perhaps sexity, on the model of autism.

I am delighted with your good humour. You will be able to cope with both pupils and enemies, I have no doubt whatever.

The Interpretation of Dreams is already out, but I have no copies yet. In a few days it should bring you greetings from

Yours cordially, FREUD

P.S. We hope your dear wife is very well.

115 J

Dear Professor Freud,   Burghölzli-Zürich, 27 November 1908

Having dropped all my duties today because my wife is about to be confined, I at last have time to write to you. I have long been meaning to ask you whether you intend to write an editorial preface yourself or in collaboration with Bleuler. A preface is the normal thing, one must after all blow one's own trumpet. I should be glad if you would let me know soon so that I can tell Bleuler of your intentions. I think of it roughly as follows: you would lead off from the standpoint of psychoanalysis and Bleuler would follow up from the standpoint of psychotherapy. The preface would be signed by both you and Bleuler. The material for the first number is complete except for Binswanger's paper. 1) Your paper; 2) Abraham: "Intermarriage"; 3) Maeder: "Sexuality and Epilepsy"; 4) Binswanger; 5) me: "The Significance of the Father in the Destiny of the Individual."[1] I am relegating the abstracts to the second number, as I want to make the first more interesting for purposes of publicity. The abstracts wouldn't help much, despite their usefulness. I reckon the first number will run to about 250 pages, which together with the second would make about 500 pages in all. That's a really imposing volume. For the second number

[1] See below, 133 J n. 1.

179

I have some Dem. pr. case histories. (Actually paranoia is a better term, but one can't make oneself understood with it here.) [2]

By now you will have received Brill's paper. [3] From the point of view of loyalty it is good, but he has omitted what I recommended as interesting and printed what I objected to $\left(\frac{\text{Pennsylvania}}{\text{Parsifal}}\right)$. As a first attempt I could have wished for something better. Still, for thoughtful people the father sublimation is significant, and anything better would be lost on flatheads anyway. I have had some offprints and a letter from Morton Prince. The dawn is not yet. My friend Peterson has delivered a lecture on the "Seat of Consciousness" (it's in the *corpus striatum,* if you want to know) which was enough to turn the stomach of even the most hardened listener. [4] A new flank attack has appeared in Löwenfeld's *Grenzfragen:* [5] Veraguth [6] has had Waldstein's abysmally insignificant book *The Subconscious Self* [7] translated by his wife, just to show who was the first to know about the "subconscious." It is full of trivial stuff, even allowing for the fact that it was published in 1897. In the preface Veraguth speaks of the growing exclusivity of the Freudian school, by which he means that we have stopped inviting him to our evenings since he never once responded to our initial invitations. Monakow is making himself conspicuous too. He has founded a society of neurologists with Dubois, [8] to which every last hillbilly in our fair land has been invited, even the experimental psychologist from Zürich; [9] the only thing he understood on the entire programme was the dinner. I was solemnly passed over

[2] See above, 12 J n. 1, and below, 122 F n. 2.

[3] See below, 116 F nn. 5 & 6.

[4] At the New York Neurological Society, 6 Oct. 08; published in the *Journal of Abnormal Psychology,* III (1908–9). / The *corpus striatum* is a mass of grey matter at the base of either half of the cerebrum.

[5] *Grenzfragen des Nerven- und Seelenlebens* (Wiesbaden: Bergmann), ed. L. Löwenfeld and H. Kurella.

[6] Otto Veraguth (1870–1944), neurologist, professor of physical therapeutics, Zürich University.

[7] Louis Waldstein (1853–1915), *The Subconscious Self and Its Relation to Education and Health* (New York, 1897); tr. Gertrud Veraguth, *Das unbewusste Ich und sein Verhältnis zur Gesundheit und Erziehung* (Wiesbaden, 1908); reviewed by Jung, *Basler Nachrichten,* 9 Dec. 09 (in CW 18). Veraguth's preface was included in the 1926 New York edition.

[8] Paul-Charles Dubois (1848–1918), professor of neuropathology at Bern; he treated neurosis by persuasion and other rational means. Regarding the Society of Neurologists, see below, 164 J end.

[9] Unidentified.

and so, I am delighted to say, was Frank; all his beatings about the bush are no help to him, he is stuck with the reputation of being a Freud follower. Anyway the hullabaloo has not harmed my practice; on the contrary, I am inundated.

How is Frau C—— doing? Is Frl. D—— with you? She never came to me. Oddly enough her brother visited me once on some pious pretext.

We have had a charming letter from Muthmann's wife. They are really good sorts.

We have received *The Interpretation of Dreams* with the greatest pleasure. The book by Ruths which you mention has in fact appeared · "On Musical Phantoms" is the subtitle.[10] The man is a bit dotty and terribly pompous. *Parturiunt montes, nascetur ridiculus mus*[11] should be his motto.

With many kind regards,

Most sincerely yours, JUNG

116 F

Dear friend, 29 November 1908, Vienna, IX. Berggasse 19

No, the dawn is not yet. We must carefully tend our little lamp, for the night will be long. To all the items which you have read and to which you have called my attention I add a publication by Steyerthal in Hoche's series, *What Is Hysteria?*[1] It is worth reading. The

---

[10] Freud put the following addendum in the 1st edn. of *Die Traumdeutung* (1900): "While I was correcting the last proofs in September 1899 I learned of a little publication *Inductive Untersuchungen über die Fundamentalgesetze der psychischen Phänomene*, by Dr. Ch. Ruths, 1898, which announced a larger work on the analysis of dreams. From the hints given by the author I venture to anticipate that his findings correspond in many details with mine." The subtitle of that work, or correctly the title of its Vol. I, was *Experimentaluntersuchungen über Musikphantome* (Darmstadt, 1898); the author was Christoph Ruths (1851–1924). Freud carried the addendum over to the 3rd edn. of *Die Traumdeutung*, but thereafter it was dropped. A further volume by Ruths on the analysis of dreams could not be traced.

[11] "The mountains labour and bring forth a mouse" (Horace, *De arte poetica*, 1.139).

---

[1] Armin Steyerthal, *Was ist Hysterie? Eine Nosologische Studie* (Sammlung zwangloser Abhandlungen aus dem Gebiet der Nerven- und Geisteskrankheiten, ed. Alfred Erich Hoche, VIII:5; Halle, 1908). Discussed in the Wednesday meeting of 9 Dec. 08 (*Minutes*, II, p. 79).

happy author is from Mecklenburg, if he has a shirt a famous problem is solved.[2] Without knowing the personal circumstances, I interpreted the Waldstein-Veraguth opus in the same way as you; the news about the seat of consciousness left me shaken. But I am quite used to irresponsible statements by my followers. Not long ago one of my Wednesday people screwed up his courage and read a paper on the nature of the perversions;[3] it sounded as if I had never said a word about them in the *Three Essays*, and friend Stekel backed him up. The essence of the perversions, he says, is unknown and will long remain so.[4] I can see that those who proclaim errors do mankind a great service; they incite men to look for the truth, whereas those who tell the truth are the greatest malefactors of all, because they drive others into opposition to the truth. Originality can also be an aim in life.

I want to defend Brill's paper against your criticism.[5] I thought it was pretty good; of course, I don't know how much of what you recommended to him he omitted. Penns-Parcival[6] looks good to me. I have ventured to translate it from the paranoiac. Then it reads: Am

[2] Cf. the proverb "Wenn er ein Hemd hat, so ist der Rock nicht weit" = "If he's got a shirt, the jacket is not far away." Mecklenburg was a notoriously poor state.

[3] Fritz Wittels, "Sexual Perversity," *Minutes*, II, pp. 53ff. (18 Nov. 08). Freud's remarks, very much as here, on p. 60. / Wittels (1880–1950), Viennese psychoanalyst, nephew of Isidor Sadger; he left the Vienna Society in 1910, became allied with Stekel, and later wrote a somewhat critical biography: *Sigmund Freud, His Personality, His Teachings, and His School* (tr. E. and C. Paul, 1924); but in 1925, he was readmitted to the Society and subsequently published an entirely favourable book, *Freud and His Time* (tr. L. Brink, New York, 1931). After 1928, in New York.

[4] The rest of this paragraph is quoted by Jones, II, p. 489/439. Jung paraphrased it in "New Paths in Psychology" (orig. 1912), CW 7, rev. edn., par. 411 end. See also 291 J n. 5.

[5] Brill, "Psychological Factors in Dementia Praecox (An Analysis)," *Journal of Abnormal Psychology*, III:3 (Oct.-Nov., 1908). Brill gives a more readable account of the case in *Freud's Contribution to Psychiatry* (1944), pp. 93ff., quoting Freud's and Jung's letters to him regarding the analysis. Freud discussed the article at the meeting of 9 Dec. 08 (*Minutes*, II, pp. 78f.).

[6] Penns = abbr. of Pennsylvania. The patient in Zürich (Brill treated the case while at the Burghölzli) had received a letter from his former sweetheart, who was a servant with a family in Pittsburgh named Thaw. "Pennsylvania, Thaw" played a part in his hallucinatory delirium. In Brill's analysis, the patient converts "Pa" (abbr. of Pennsylvania) into "Parsifal" and "Thaw" into "Thor." During his psychotic episode the patient knelt in prayer and constantly repeated, "Am I Parsifal the most guileless fool?" (In Wagner's music-drama, Parsifal is called *reiner Thor*, "guileless fool.")

I still in love with **,[7] who is (in) Penns (with) Thaw? Have I still a right to identify myself with her? It looks like an abandonment of heterosexuality for homosexuality, which draws him to his father. It is true that he has not interpreted the significance of the father correctly. He is the chief character in the drama. With the help of his illness he achieves a belated obedience, so as to be a son after his father's heart. Osiris and Isis are again his parents. Deification, but also the wish that his father had died (like Banker O.)[8] and left him an inheritance. I was very glad to hear that you have tackled the father complex. I have high hopes for the volume. It is only a month till the publication date.

In the meantime, I venture to hope, fate has made you a father again, and perhaps the star you spoke of on our long walk has risen for you. The transfer of one's hopes to one's children is certainly an excellent way of appeasing one's unresolved complexes, though for you it is too soon. Let me hear from you; until then I assume that the valiant mother is well; to her husband she must indeed be more precious than all her children, just as the method must be valued more highly than the results obtained by it.

I have neither heard nor seen anything of Fräulein D———. Frau C—— will probably be a hard nut to crack. Of course it is easy to see what ails her, but the other part of the problem, to make her understand and accept it, will no doubt be difficult. An example: Ever since her carriage almost ran a child over when she was out for a drive (or she inferred from a scream that this had happened) she has been very unhappy when riding in a carriage, every few minutes she wants to turn back to make sure that nothing has happened; she would like to give it up altogether. In crowds she is afraid of shoving someone. All that is very simple: in her fantasy she is a man who *drives back and forth* and begets (kills)[9] a child; the *pushing* means that she herself would push violently. She is a man because she needs a man but doesn't want to look for one and identifies herself with a man instead. Her illness began when she found out that her husband had been rendered impotent by epididymitis. And so it goes. It's so clear it makes your hair stand on end. Nevertheless the therapy is bringing

---

[7] As holograph.

[8] According to Brill's article, a wealthy banker of Basel, the accounts of whose death had interested the patient, formerly a bank clerk. Apparently Daniel Osiris, a Franco-Greek philanthropist who died in Feb. 1907. He bought the chateau of Malmaison, near Paris, and gave it to the French State.

[9] Holograph: (*umbringt*), underlined with dots.

183

meagre results. She pins herself up at night to make her genitals inaccessible; you can imagine how accessible she is intellectually.

I know Ruths' book on musical phantoms: it is not the announced book on dreams.

I am willing to write the preface if *you* think it necessary. I myself have no desire to do so. It seems to me that this *Jahrbuch*, which really does offer something new and finds its justification in its table of contents, is not bound by the same requirements as still another journal of psychiatry and nervous disorders, which must artificially present a programme in the first number. But as you wish. Or we could put the programmatic article at the end of the first volume. The reason for my reluctance may simply be that I am overworked and therefore not feeling too energetic.

I am quite ready to believe that the agitation against you does you no harm. From all this hostility we may infer that we have made much more of an impression than we thought. Moral: Go on slaving.

With kind regards and congratulations on the blessed event,

Yours, FREUD

117 J

Dear Professor Freud,   Burghölzli-Zürich, 3 December 1908

Heartiest thanks for your congratulatory telegram![1] You can imagine our joy. The birth went off normally, mother and child[2] are doing well. Too bad we aren't peasants any more, otherwise I could say: Now that I have a son I can depart in peace. A great deal more could be said on this complex-theme.

As for Brill, my opposition does not mean that I consider Penns.-Parsifal impossible. In theory I agree with it, but in practice I think it inopportune to present such—for the layman—inconclusive parallels in a beginner's work. For this reason I advised Brill not to include it. What he omitted was important. The day before the outbreak of delirium the patient visited the wife of a good friend of his, a man who had been in an asylum for quite a long time. (It seems that the wife was not altogether indifferent!) While with her he read a letter which she had recently received from his friend and which made a

---

[1] Missing.
[2] Franz Karl Jung.

184

deep impression on him. Whereupon he went to an inn and had a lively discussion on the Catholic religion with a stranger, and then something else happened that reminded me of Parsifal's love-magic[3] (?) or something of the sort; unfortunately the details escape me at the moment. It all fitted together very nicely and I advised Brill not to omit it. I know my tetchiness by this time but am always glad when you point it out to me. A pretty good accommodation has now been reached with Abraham, for instance.

I shall make haste to get that book you mentioned on hysteria from Hoche's series. One has to see from time to time whether the ravens are still flying round the mountain.[4] My paper on the father complex is no great shakes but is, I think, a decent job. I hope you will like it. In any event its staunchness to the cause leaves nothing to be desired. Now that I am inwardly detaching myself more and more from my previous mode of existence, I am beginning to feel how much the Clinic and its milieu have cramped my intellectual freedom. I have become considerably more mobile and therefore more of a stimulus to my pupils. The result is that the Dem. praec. analysis is making progress. We have now got another very pretty case in the bag. With men homosexuality seems to play a tremendous role.

Naturally I have given up the idea of a preface to the *Jahrb.*; there is no need for it. Bleuler is not insisting either. Thank heavens the contents will do the job for us, if I may allow myself a touch of immodest self-satisfaction.

With many kind regards,

Most sincerely yours, JUNG

[3] Holograph: *Minnezauber*, as in Wagner's music-drama, but Jung was apparently uncertain that he had used the correct word and put a question mark.

[4] Allusion to a German legend: Emperor Frederick Barbarossa (d. 1190) is asleep inside Kyffhäuser Mountain in Thuringia. There he will remain until it is time for him to come forth and restore the old glory of the empire. Every hundred years he sends out a dwarf to see whether the ravens are still flying round the mountain, if they are, the emperor must wait another hundred years. The legend was recorded by the Brothers Grimm (*Deutsche Sagen*, I, 1816, no. 23) and popularized through a poem by Friedrich Rückert, "Barbarossa," written soon after.

118 F

Dear friend,   11 December 1908, Vienna, IX. Berggasse 19

By the same post you will receive an offprint of the "Sexual Theories of Children."[1] I can account for my delayed reaction—not a usual failing of mine—by overwork and indisposition. No need to look for an explanation on your side. The note of freedom in your letters since it is settled that you are to be your own master comes as an answer to my heartfelt wishes. You will see what a blessing it is to have no master over you. The conjunction—social liberation, birth of a son, paper on the father complex—suggests to me that you are at a crossroads in your life and have taken the right direction. My own fatherhood will not be a burden to you, there is little I can do for you, and I am accustomed to giving what I have.

I must say, your regret at being unable to play the ideal hero-father ("My father begot me and died")[2] struck me as very premature. The child will find you indispensable as a father for many many years, first in a positive, then in a negative sense! We are very glad that mother and child are doing so well. Is your wife nursing the baby herself? (Feminine curiosity.)

Deuticke tells me that he has already received the manuscript of the *Jahrbuch*. At the same time he has sent the second volume of my *Collected Papers on the Theory of the Neuroses* to the printer's; nothing in it will be new to you (except for two pages on hysterical attacks, which will also appear in Moll's journal).[3] Business is worrying along in every respect, but my spirits do not always hold up. I have endured a good deal and need a bit of a let-up now and then.

I am so obsessed by the idea of a nuclear complex[4] in neuroses such as is at the heart of the case of Little Herbert that I cannot make any headway. A recent observation tempted me to trace the poisoning complex, when it is present, back to the infant's interpretation of its mother's morning sickness. I also have some dim notions on the theory

---

[1] "Über infantile Sexualtheorien," *Sexual-Probleme*, IV:12 (Dec. 1908) = "On the Sexual Theories of Children," SE IX.

[2] Allusion to the hero of Wagner's music drama *Siegfried*; see Act II, scene iii.

[3] See below, 131 J n. 1.

[4] Holograph: *Kerncomplex*. The first occurrence (in this correspondence) of this term, in place of which Freud began using "Oedipus complex" in 1910. See "A Special Type of Choice of Object Made by Men," SE XI, p. 171, n. 11; also "Sexual Theories of Children," SE IX, p. 214, n. 1.

of projection in paranoia; I must have them worked out in time for your anticipated visit next spring.

The other day I received a paper from Frank[5] in which he carries his tail several inches lower and even gives it a friendly wag now and then. But it is obvious that anyone who makes use of hypnotism will not discover sexuality. It is used up, so to speak, in the hypnotic process.

With kind regards,

Yours ever, FREUD

119 J

Dear Professor Freud,   Burghölzli-Zürich, 15 December 1908

I enclose two drafts for the title-page of the *Jahrbuch*. Please let me know which version seems to you more suitable. In support of his suggestion Bleuler argues that he can make only quite modest contributions and can therefore not put his name on the same line as yours. My objection to this is that I am *most unwilling* to let myself be pushed so conspicuously to the forefront, for I know it would be to our detriment. I am too young, and success is the hardest to forgive. Hence I fear that certain contributors who are happy to be published under *your* aegis would not appreciate my appearing to head the project. So I hope you will opt for the version that bears some semblance to my suggestion. Naturally it went against the grain to put Bleuler's name before yours; I did so only because Bleuler has the advantage of being Professor publicus ordinarius.[1] There's not much to choose between his third version and his second, though the third is a little better.

Many thanks for the offprint. It is very good to have all the theories together at last. Yesterday I came across a new theory (in a case of hysteria)—the incubation theory: one must warm the body in order to get it with child. I think this is done occasionally.

I thank you very much for your last letter, which I hope to be able to answer in detail soon.

In haste with best regards!

Most sincerely yours, JUNG

[5] Ludwig Frank, "Zur Psychanalyse" (Festschrift for Forel's 60th Birthday), *Journal für Psychologie und Neurologie*, XIII (1908). See Jung's lengthy critique in his "Abstracts."

[1] = full professor.

120 F

Dear friend,   17 December 1908, Vienna, IX. Berggasse 19

I approve your arguments and support your suggestion. I object to Bleuler's attitude on the ground that his modesty defeats its purpose, i.e., it can only hurt us both. It is easy to see that if his name comes first this reflects not an order of rank but an alphabetical order, as is customary in such publications. For the same reason it would be an order of rank and highly objectionable if my name were to come first.

I should also like to suggest a slight change in your draft. It has to do with titles and is designed to conceal my nakedness.

Directed by

Prof. Dr. E. Bleuler	and Prof. Dr. Sigm. Freud
Director of the Psychiatric Clinic	of Vienna
in Zürich	

My "professor"[1] is only a title and cannot be put in anywhere else. I hope I have convinced you of the importance of this change.

Well, however the two of you work it out, my heartfelt wishes for the birth of Jung's *Jahrbuch*, as everyone will call it.

Very cordially yours, in haste, FREUD

121 J

Dear Professor Freud,   Burghölzli-Zürich, 21 December 1908

Many thanks for your decision. I am sure it will be best that way. Meanwhile you will have seen that the typesetter is busily at work. I shall not put the abstracts in this number but in the second, as the number of pages is already far more than I expected: ca. 320, which means more than 600 pages for the whole year, an amount I hadn't really counted on.

Everything is fine here. My wife is, of course, nursing the child herself, a pleasure for both of them. I feel that the conjunction of the

---

[1] Freud was granted the right to use the title of professor in 1902, but this did not confer academic standing in the University. (See Jones, I, pp. 372ff./339ff.) Bleuler, on the other hand, was a full professor holding a chair in psychiatry.

birth of a son with the rationalization of the father complex is an extremely important turning-point in my life, not least because I am now extricating myself from the social father-relationship as well. It doesn't grieve me. Bleuler has delusions of homosexual persecution in his dreams and is beginning to boast of his intensified heterosexual fantasies. The tie on his side seems to be the stronger.

Dr. Stockmayer of Tübingen is analysing D. pr. patients; there is ample opportunity for discussion and I am compelled to formulate my views. What makes the deepest impression in D. pr. is unquestionably the autoerotism. It should be noted, however, that this is characteristic only when it appears in the attempt at compensation. So far as I can see at present, it is only the unsuccessful attempt that yields the impressive picture. One form of autoerotism is found in hysteria as well; actually every repressed complex is autoerotic. From this autoerotism, which deprives the object of a certain amount of libido cathexis, comes, or so it seems to me, the hysterical hypercathexis of the object, i.e., the increase of object-libido, due to the failure of compensation. In hysteria it often succeeds only too well, in the ways we all know. Dem. pr. begins in much the same way, but the autoerotism appears as a specific factor only in the attempted compensation, which is always a failure and usually "crazy." Recently we had a very fine case, classic in its simplicity: a 40-year-old woman, rather anaemic, had to be interned because she solicited every man she met in the street, demanding coitus.

The libido for her husband had been decreasing for years, then (in wretched circumstances) came an exhausting pregnancy and a difficult childbirth; all trace of libido disappeared. But in direct proportion to its disappearance the conviction grew upon the patient that her husband had changed and no longer loved her. She considered his libido a fake, he was carrying on with other women and wasn't giving her the right kind of love. She therefore forced him, by every means in her power, to have coitus with her up to four times a night, also during the day, and it was observed that she was very passionate up to the moment of ejaculation but then went quite limp. No sooner was the coitus finished than she wanted it again. She seemed insatiable. Finally she demanded coitus of her brother-in-law in the presence of her husband. She also tried to get into bed with the brother-in-law while he was sleeping with his wife; even demanded coitus of her own brother; went around the streets begging for it. But she never once got coitus in this way (hysteria!!), and was herself astonished when a man once followed her. She said she knew very well that her brother

189

and brother-in-law would never dream of having coitus with her; she only wanted to point out to them that they *had to help her* because something had gone wrong.

In this case we can see perfectly the hollowness of the compensation. It seems to me, therefore, that the difference between the two illnesses is to be found without exception in the attempt at compensation. In hysteria it is successful within the known limits and to that extent is genuine; in D. pr. it is unsuccessful and is always false. We get the impression of autoerotism only from the attempt at compensation. What do you think about the failure of libido production? When people are tired, they get autoerotic, suffer from anxiety, have hallucinations, etc. Let them sleep or eat, and the spectre of anxiety is gone. For instance, senile melancholias and anxiety states are the negative counterparts of sexuality, obviously the result of *underproduction* of libido. I once saw a typical obsessional neurosis that had lasted for years pass over into senile anxiety melancholia. In many young D. pr. cases what you see at first is a marked anxiety that often turns later into persecution mania. Exhausting physical illnesses favour the outbreak of acute catatonia and suchlike. May I hear your views sometime?

With kind regards and best wishes for Christmas and the New Year,

Yours very sincerely, JUNG

122 F

Dear friend,   26 December 1908, Vienna, IX. Berggasse 19

I have just finished correcting the first proofs of the "Phobia" and the first sixteen pages of the reprint of "Dora." Ferenczi, who always gives me a good deal of pleasure, has come from Budapest and brought me an excellent paper on transference;[1] and your letter with paranoia[2] solutions is in front of me: things are going ahead and we shall not have worked in vain.

(Incidentally, Abraham has told me about your recent difference with him.[3] I gave him a good piece of my mind, because he is entirely

[1] "Introjection and Transference"; see below, 168 J n. 1.

[2] In the previous letter, Jung's terminology is "dementia praecox."

[3] Abraham took it amiss that Jung had postponed publishing Abraham's abstracts

in the wrong. It's too bad, but everybody requires some measure of indulgence.)

What you write about paranoia tallies exactly with certain of the hypotheses we, Ferenczi and I, worked out in Berchtesgaden, but didn't wish to disturb your work with. Our first theorem was: What paranoiacs tell us is false; i.e., the opposite is true. (Here there are two antitheses: man and woman, love and hate.) The second theorem: What we regard as the manifestations of their disorder (everything that strikes the eye, the outbursts, the upheaval, and their hallucinations as well) is their attempt to cure themselves—you call it an attempt at compensation. Which amounts to the same thing. The patients seem to know of the excellent formula you thought up in the course of our walks, because they try to cure themselves by becoming—hysterical.

On the other hand, I would not say that we see autoerotism only in attempted compensation. We *see* it, rather, in the clear-cut culmination in dementia; we must expect to find it behind the conflicts and strivings for compensation. In true paranoia the relapse into autoerotism has been a total failure, the libido may return entirely to the object, but distorted and transformed, because once detachment has taken place it cannot be wholly made good. So here is my conclusion: In every case: Repression by detachment of libido.

a) Successful, autoerotism—simple Dem. pr.
b) Unsuccessful, full recovery of libido cathexis, but after projec tion and transformation—typical paranoia.
c) Partial failure—attempted compensation—false hysteria—conflict culminating in partial autoerotism—forms intermediate between Dem. pr. and paranoia.

May I suggest that you should not use the term autoerotism as inclusively as H. Ellis,[4] that it should not include hysterical utilizations of libido, but only truly autoerotic states, in which all relations with objects have been abandoned. Provided we differentiate between fantasy and reality, we should be able to avoid this extension of the concept.

When not absolutely necessary, I should not yet like to operate with the notion of underproduction in Dem. I suspect that this factor may

---

in the first number of the *Jahrbuch* in order to publish a paper of his own. See A.'s letter of 18 Dec. o8 and Freud's reply, 26 Dec. o8, in *Freud/Abraham Letters*.
[4] Havelock Ellis (1859–1939), English scientist, author of *Studies in the Psychology of Sex*. The reference is to "Autoerotism: A Study of the Spontaneous Manifestations of the Sexual Impulse" (orig. 1899), in Vol. I of that work.

enter into the melancholia-mania syndrome. But we can also do without it.

Here's to 1909.

Yours cordially, FREUD

123 F

Dear friend,   30 December 1908, Vienna, IX. Berggasse 19

First a resounding prosit for the year 1909, which looks so promising for you and for our cause. Special good wishes to your little son, who is now embarking on psychic labours that we still have no conception of. Many thanks for your thoughtful Christmas present, which by association has recalled to my mind the splendid days in Burghölzli.[1] I have it all to myself—an unusual occurrence—the rest of the family has rejected it with indignation. I like it much better than the sample I tasted at your house. I am amazed to hear that you knew nothing about Abraham.[2] I gather, then, that he has not written to you that he is withdrawing the "other" abstracts and reiterating his request for the publication of his review of my work in the first number? His letter to me sounded as if he had *already written* to you. But I can only rejoice that he has thought better of it; since he is so completely wrong, you will find it easier to forgive him now than last time. Just pretend to know nothing. Take my word for it that I gave him a good dressing down. Too bad, too bad.

Now finally I come to the news that I have been invited by Clark University, Worcester, Mass., Pres. Stanley Hall,[3] to deliver four to six lectures in the first week of July. They expect my lectures to give a mighty impetus to the development of psychotherapy over there. The occasion: the twentieth (!) anniversary of the founding of the university. I have declined without even consulting you or anyone else, the crucial reason being that I should have had to stop work 2[4] weeks

---

[1] Miss Anna Freud has recollected that the present was a cheese.

[2] Apparently a letter or other communication from Jung is missing.

[3] G. Stanley Hall (1844–1924), professor of psychology and pedagogics at Clark University as well as president. At first sympathetic to psychoanalysis, and a charter member (1911) of the American Psychoanalytic Association, he later drew closer to Adler's school. See Dorothy Ross, G. *Stanley Hall: The Psychologist as Prophet* (Chicago, 1972).

[4] Holograph unclear: possibly 3.

sooner than usual, which would mean a loss of several thousand kronen. Naturally the Americans pay only $400 for travel expenses. I am not wealthy enough to spend five times that much to give the Americans an impetus. (That's boasting; two-and-a-half to three times as much!) Janet, whose example they invoke,[5] is probably richer or more ambitious or has no practice to lose. But I am sorry to have it fall through on this account, because it would have been fun. I don't really believe that Clark University, a small but serious institution, can postpone its festivities for three weeks.

Ferenczi has brought me a *very* good paper on transference which he wrote for the second number but which in his interest I should like to publish *sooner*, since it comes very close to the corresponding section of my "General Exposition of the Psychoanalytic Method." If it is not accepted elsewhere—I have already been turned down once— we shall have to foist it upon you after all.

Sincerely yours, FREUD

May we remain close together in 1909!

124 J

Dear Professor Freud, Burghölzli-Zürich, 7 January 1909

This is a real triumph and I congratulate you most heartily! Too bad it comes at such an inconvenient time. Perhaps you could arrange to go after the anniversary; even then your lectures would still be of interest to the Americans. Little by little your truth is percolating through to the public. If at all possible, you ought to speak in America if only because of the echo it would arouse in Europe, where things are beginning to stir too.

You will have received Strohmayer's paper[1] by now. I am very pleased that the seed has taken in Jena. It won't be long before *pro et contra* writings appear from other quarters as well. Juliusburger, for instance, has informed me of a forthcoming publication on Dem.

---

[5] Janet accepted invitations to lecture at the International Exposition at St. Louis, Missouri, in 1904, and at Harvard in 1906. See Ellenberger, p. 344.

---

[1] "Über die ursächlichen Beziehungen der Sexualität zu Angst- und Zwangszuständen," *Journal für Psychologie und Neurologie*, XII (1908–9).

praec.[2] In America Jones[2a] seems to be busily at work, also Brill. My Dem. praec. book is soon coming out in English.[3] My Tübingen man[4] is hard at it, I'm glad to say, and will assuredly become a keen supporter at one more German clinic.

Yesterday a patient died of catatonia in the following manner: a few months ago, after decades of apathy, she suddenly got into an anxiety state in which she felt she was going to be killed. ("Let me go to my uncle so I can plant a garden with him"—her marriage was childless.) The anxiety mounted to the point of terrified derangement with tremendous excitation, then quieted down a bit, fever rose to 40° [C.], then symptoms of acute bulbar paralysis, followed by death. Postmortem findings: body: negative; brain: slight oedema of the pia[5] in the parietal region, apparently atrophied convolutions, hyperanaemia of the pia. Otherwise nothing. We are having the brain examined by Dr. Merzbacher[6] in Tübingen. The snag is that we know next to nothing of "psychophysics" despite all the shouting of the anatomists.

This business with Abraham is really depressing. I am far from bearing him any grudge, as his intentions were not put into effect. Even so, it will become very unpleasant for me later, because in these circumstances I dare not ask him for further abstracts. I would like to live at peace with him, but a little goodwill is needed on his side also.

About America I would like to remark that Janet's travel expenses were amply compensated by his subsequent American clientèle. Recently Kraepelin gave one consultation in California for the modest tip of 50,000 marks. I think this side of things should also be taken into account.

I have written to Dr. Brodmann[7] for Ferenczi. Perhaps his paper can be placed there; we could also try the *Allgemeine Zeitschrift für*

---

[2] Perhaps "Zur Psychotherapie und Psychoanalyse," *Berliner klinische Wochenschrift*, 8 Feb. 09, pp. 248–50 (cf. Jones, II, p. 32, n. 4/29, n. 10).

[2a] From Oct. 1908, associate in psychiatry at the University of Toronto.

[3] *The Psychology of Dementia Praecox*, tr. A. A. Brill and F. W. Peterson (Nervous and Mental Disease Monograph Series, 3; New York, 1909). Brill revised the tr. alone (ibid., 1936). For original, see above, 9 J n. 1.

[4] Stockmayer. [5] = pia mater, soft membrane covering the brain.

[6] Ludwig Merzbacher (1875–1942), German psychiatrist; after 1910, in Buenos Aires.

[7] Korbinian Brodmann (1868–1918), editor of the *Journal für Psychologie und Neurologie*. See 6 Jan. 09 letter to Ferenczi in Jung, *Letters*, ed. G. Adler, vol. 1.

Psychiatrie. They generally like new things. The work of one of my pupils[8] was gladly accepted.

Here Docent (for experimental psychology) Wreschner,[9] [. . .], has announced lectures on your theory at the Teachers' Association. Pastor Pfister,[10] a clever man and a friend of mine, has started a big propaganda campaign for your ideas. Wreschner wants to forestall that. But I have goaded Pfister into ensuring that W. does not get up to the dirty tricks I heartily suspect him of. [. . .]

Not long ago a young lady said to me in conversation: "One has to believe you, you look at people so *convincingly.*"[11] The accent on *con-* was so surprising that I had to burst out laughing.

With kind regards, J U N G

125 F

Dear friend,   17 January 1909, Vienna, IX. Berggasse 19

At last a Sunday when I am able to chat with you. During the week there is too much work.

I am really pleased with Strohmayer. His paper was accompanied by a very modest letter, which I answered most amiably. I told him he was one of ours despite his protests, that we did not demand thoughtless parroting of our views, and that all my followers had reserved judgment until convinced by their own work. Strohmayer agrees with us on so many points that I could easily delude myself into thinking that he is holding back only in order to create more of an impression. But of course that would be a delusion.

Your courageous friend Pfister has sent me a paper[1] for which I

---

[8] Probably Richard Bolte; see above, 33 J n. 4.

[9] Arthur Wreschner (1866–1931+), German experimental psychologist and physician, after 1906 at Zürich University and the E.T.H. Jung cited his work on the association experiment; see CW 2, index, s.v. Wreschner.

[10] Oskar Pfister (1873–1956), Protestant pastor of Zürich, founding member of the Swiss Psychoanalytic Society (1910); remained with Freud after 1914. Co-founder (with Emil Oberholzer) of the new Swiss Society for Psychoanalysis (1919). See his correspondence with Freud, *Psychoanalysis and Faith* (1963).

[11] Holograph: *überzeugungsvoll.* When normally stressed on third syllable = "convincing"; when stressed on first syllable = "over-full of procreative power."

---

[1] "Wahnvorstellung und Schülerselbstmord," *Schweizer Blätter für Schulgesund-*

shall thank him at length. It's really too nice of him—a Protestant clergyman—though rather upsetting to me to see ΨA enlisted in the fight against "sin."

I was nauseated by Peterson's paper on the seat of consciousness. There is a good deal to be said about America. Jones and Brill write often, Jones's observations are shrewd and pessimistic, Brill sees everything through rose-coloured spectacles. I am inclined to agree with Jones. I also think that once they discover the sexual core of our psychological theories they will drop us. Their[2] prudery and their material dependence on the public are too great. That is why I have no desire to risk the trip there in July. I can't expect anything of consultations. Kraepelin had an easier time of it. Anyway I have heard nothing more from Clark University. But I have had a very nice letter from Campbell,[3] who asks for contributions, etc.

I am glad to say there is better news from Abraham. He absolutely denies that he took my reprimand amiss; he has been ill, which accounts for his long silence. True, he does not explain why he told me he had made his complaint when in reality he hadn't, but at least this enables you to treat the whole incident as *non arrivé*. It was very kind of you, I should say, to give his paper first place in the *Jahrbuch* after Little Hans.

Many thanks for your efforts toward placing Ferenczi's article. I finished correcting the proofs of Little Hans only fifteen minutes ago. The second volume of my *Collected Papers on the Theory of the Neuroses* will also appear in February. Deuticke is just too friendly, butter wouldn't melt in his mouth, a good sign. Karger[4] in Berlin has offered to publish a *third* edition of the *Everyday Life*.

We are certainly getting ahead; if I am Moses, then you are Joshua

---

heitspflege, 1909, no. 1. Freud's letter of acknowledgment, 18 Jan. 09, began their correspondence of nearly 30 years.

[2] The slip of the pen mentioned by Jung in the next letter—that Freud wrote *Ihre*, "your," instead of *ihre*, "their"—is problematical. In the holograph, Freud put a full stop after *uns fallen lassen*, "will drop us," so that the next word *Ihrer* begins with a capital and can mean either "their" or "your"; but the full stop is obscured by the ascender of the word below. The second *ihre* is clearly lower case, "their." See facsimile.

[3] Charles Macfie Campbell (see above, 102 J n. 3), at this time in New York, was an editor (1905–15) of the *Review of Neurology and Psychiatry* (Edinburgh), which occasionally published papers about psychoanalysis. / The name in the holograph (see facsimile) could also be read as "Pampleca," but that name could not be traced.

[4] S. Karger (d. 1935), Berlin publisher.

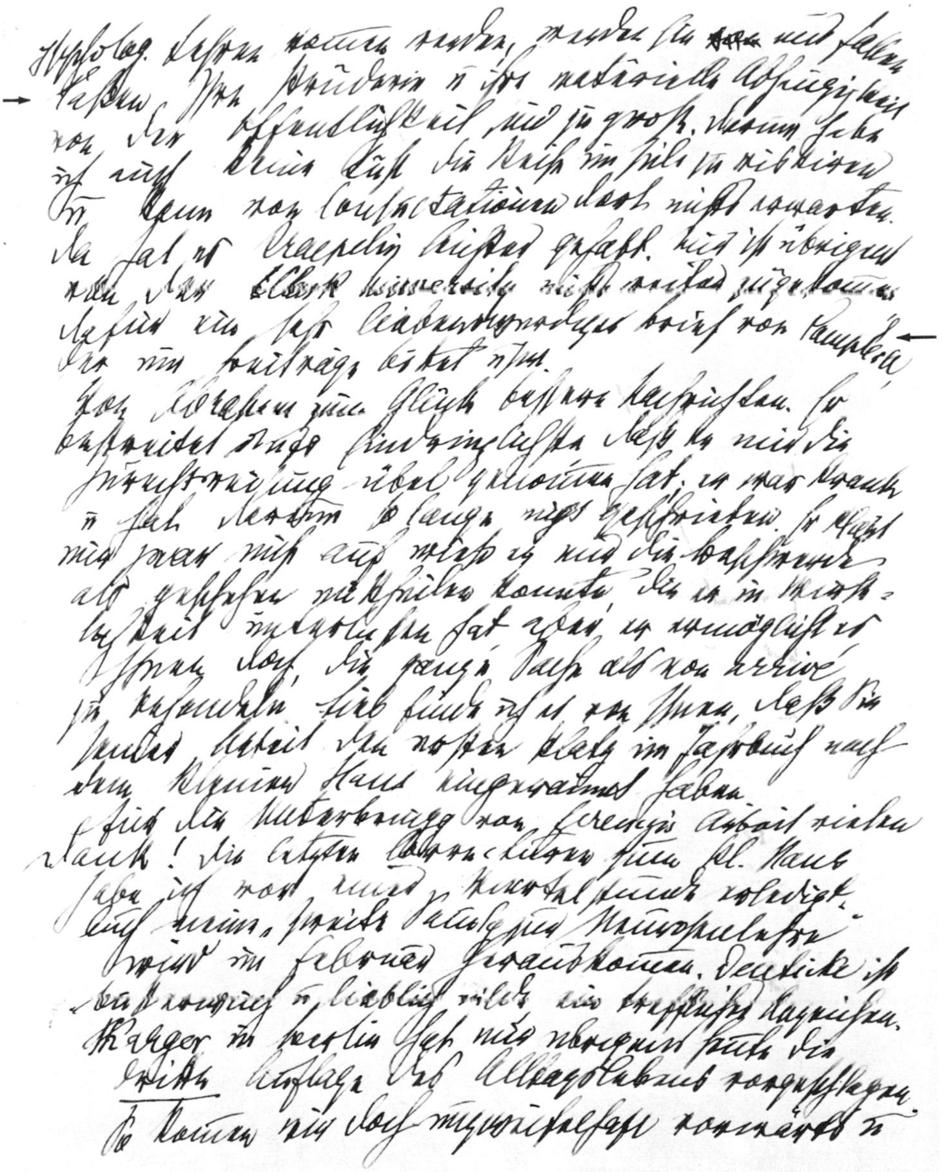

Freud, 17 Jan. 09 (125 F, p. 2)

and will take possession of the promised land of psychiatry, which I shall only be able to glimpse from afar.

Frau C—— is extremely interesting and her case is becoming fairly clear. I hope we shall soon be able to spend a few hours talking about her.

Franz Karl is thriving, I trust. You will receive an announcement of my daughter's marriage, which is to take place on February 7.

Don't keep me waiting as long for an answer as I once kept you.

Cordially yours, FREUD

126 J

Dear Professor Freud,   Burghölzli-Zürich, 19 January 1909

As you wished, I am hastening to answer your letter at once. I am delighted with your good news. All goes well with us too, except for the last two days which were taken up with enforced inactivity and influenza. Today my head is more endurable.

I am glad you appreciate my efforts to be as indulgent as I can with Abraham. I should be extremely grateful if you could cure him in time. Since getting to know more about the practice of a nerve specialist this year, I understand Abraham's touchiness very well. What a bitter brew it is! Whenever I find myself stuck with some hopeless resistance, I have to think not so much of you (for I know how quick you are to find a way out) as of my other analytical fellow sufferers, who are obliged to make a living out of their patients' resistances and have as little wisdom to fall back on as I have.

Pfister is a splendid fellow, a neurotic himself of course, though not a severe one. Nothing scares him, a redoubtable champion of our cause with a powerful intelligence. He will make something of it. What? I don't know yet. Oddly enough, I find this mixture of medicine and theology to my liking. His present aim is naturally sublimation, permissible enough in a man of his intelligence. You will shortly receive another longish paper[1] from him. He is feverishly busy. Another very good man, recruited by the young Binswanger, is Dr. Häberlin,[2] formerly director of a teachers' college, now privatdocent of phi-

[1] "Psychanalytische Seelsorge"; see below, 129 F n. 3 and 160 F n. 6.
[2] Paul Häberlin (1878–1960), of Basel, later distinguished as a philosopher and pedagogue. He was born in Kesswil, Jung's birthplace. See Ellenberger, pp. 683ff.

losophy[3] in Basel. He has founded a school for problem children there, where he teaches "analytically." He divides psychology into "pre-Freudian" and "post-Freudian"! Which tells a lot.

Our little circle is thriving. Last time there were 26 participants. Monakow again made *acte de présence* but is as dumb as ever. There's a revolution going on among our pedagogues. I have been asked to give a special course of lectures introducing your psychology. Meanwhile Bleuler, with an air of innocence, has quietly handed the teaching post for mental hygiene over to Riklin without even consulting me. This is the second time a teaching post has slipped through my fingers, not without Bleuler's passive connivance. Teaching posts, you see, are important things with us because we have no honorary professorships. My academic prospects are therefore very bad, though at present this doesn't worry me too much. Other successes are a consolation.

The Americans are a horse of a different colour. First I must point out with diabolical glee your slip of the pen: you wrote "your prudishness" instead of "their prudishness."[4] We have noticed this prudishness, which used to be worse than it is now; now I can stomach it. I don't water down the sexuality any more.

You are probably right about the trip to America. Peterson has broken with me—ostentatiously and for no reason. I share Jones's pessimism absolutely. So far these people simply haven't a notion of what we're at. One of these days they will creep into a corner, prim and abashed. Nevertheless it will rub off on some of them and is doing so already, despite their audible silence (Meyer and Hoch!). In any case the American medical material isn't up to much. (Please don't think of the fox and the grapes.)

Now for a few observations:

First the so-called "baby pains," the little syncopes with slight eclampsia during and after feeding. The convulsion is usually very mild, a rolling of the eyes upwards and twitchings of the facial muscles around the mouth, occasionally also a jerking of the arm or leg. It gives the impression of a "sucking orgasm" (rhythmic action—orgasm), perhaps also "satiation orgasm" (?). The convulsion of the facial muscles often produces a kind of laughing, even at a time when babies can't laugh yet. The first active mimetic attempts are: staring at a

---

[3] Jung wrote *Psychiatrie*, struck it out, put an exclamation point, and wrote *Philosophie*.

[4] See previous letter, n. 2.

198

shiny object, opening the mouth, clicking the tongue, mimetic convulsion = laughing or crying. In the course of normal development
this much of the infantile reflex-convulsion is retained. Children who
later get eclamptic attacks when teething, or with intestinal worms,
have retained rather more of this mechanism, most of all *epileptics*
(abdominal aura). I think these things deserve closer investigation.

Contributions by my 4-year-old Agathli: the evening before Fränzli's
birth I asked her what she would say if the stork brought her a little
brother? "Then I shall kill it," she said quick as lightning with an embarrassed, sly expression, and would not let herself be pinned down to
this theme. The baby was born during the night. Early next morning
I carried her to my wife's bedside; she was tense and gazed in alarm at
the rather wan-looking mother, without showing any joy; found nothing to say about the situation. The same morning, when Mama was
alone, the little one suddenly ran to her, flung her arms round her neck
and asked anxiously: "But, Mama, you don't have to die, do you?"
This was the first adequate affect. Her pleasure over the baby was
rather "put on." Up till now the problems had always been: Why is
Granny so old? What happens to old people anyway? "They must die
and will go to heaven." — "Then they become children again," added
the little one. So somebody has to die in order to make a child. After
the birth A. went to stay for several weeks with her grandmother,
where she was fed exclusively on the stork theory. On her return home
she was again rather suspicious and shy with Mama. Lots of questions:
"Shall I become a woman like you?" "Shall I then still talk with you?"
"Do you still love me too, not just Fränzli?" Strong identification with
the nurse, weaves fantasies about her, *starts making rhymes and telling
herself stories.* Often unexpectedly fractious with Mama, pesters her
with questions. For instance, Mama says: "Come, we'll go into the
garden." A. asks: "Is that true? You're quite sure it's true? You're
not lying? I don't believe it," etc. Scenes of this kind were repeated a
number of times, all the more striking because they were about quite
irrelevant things. But once she heard us talking about the earthquake
in Messina[5] and all the people who had been killed. She literally hurled
herself on this theme, had to be told the story over and over again; every
bit of wood, every stone in the road, could have tumbled down in an
earthquake. Mama had to assure her hourly that there were certainly
no earthquakes in Zürich, I had to assure her too, but she came back
again and again to her fears. Recently my wife hurried into my room

---

[5] On 28 Dec. 08; 75,000 deaths.

looking for books; A. wasn't leaving her a moment's peace, my wife had to show her all the pictures of earthquakes and volcanoes. A. would pore over the geological pictures of volcanoes for hours on end. Finally, on my advice, my wife enlightened A., who showed not the least surprise on hearing the solution. (Children grow in the mother like flowers on plants.) Next day I was in bed with influenza.[6] A. came in with a shy, rather startled look on her face, wouldn't approach the bed but asked: "Have you a plant in your tummy too?" Ran off merry and carefree when this possibility was ruled out. Next day a fantasy: "My brother [a fantasy hero] is also in Italy and has a house made of glass and cloth and it doesn't fall down." During the last two days no trace of fear. She merely asks our female guests either whether they have a child or whether they had been in Messina, though with no sign of anxiety. The 3-year-old Grethli ridicules the stork theory, saying that the stork brought not only her little brother but the nurse as well.[7]

What an enchantment such a child is! Only recently A. praised the beauty of her little brother to her grandmother: "Und luog au, was es für es herzigs Buobefüdili hät" (And look what a pretty little boy's bottom he has). "Füdili" = double diminutive of "Füdli" = posterior, the latter a vulgar word which sounds decent to children only as a double diminutive. "Füdli," a simple diminutive, must come from a no longer existing "Fud" ("pfui" / "furzen" [fart]?), meaning posterior. A very coarse word "Futz" has been preserved for female genitalia. "Füdili" is used by children in the sense of "cloaca"; A. naturally means the genitals.

With best regards,

Most sincerely yours, JUNG

127 F

Dear friend,   22 January 1909, Vienna, IX. Berggasse 19

This is not an answer to your letter, which gave me great pleasure when it arrived this morning; no, it is my hurried—hence the dry, businesslike tone—reaction to a communication from Deuticke that I received at the same time.

Deuticke telephoned me yesterday, he has his doubts about one or

---

[6] Holograph begins a new page with date 20 Jan. 09.
[7] Cf. Jung, "Psychic Conflicts in a Child," CW 17 (see below, 209 F n. 2).

two passages in your draft,[1] and now I am reminded of them by his question marks in the ms. His first objection is that your *"ferner"*[2] seems to create an opposition, or at least a dividing line between my school and the Zürich Clinic; the second refers to your announcement that papers from outside sources are reviewed but not accepted for publication. Undoubtedly you will be more concerned by the second objection; I am more interested in the first. I think you might as well make both changes. To tell the truth, I would rather you did not identify any particular school with me, because if you do I shall soon be obliged to confess that my pseudo-students or non-students are closer to me than my students *sensu strictiori*. Also, I should not like to be held more directly responsible for the *work* of Stekel, Adler, Sadger, etc. than for my *influence* on you, Binswanger, Abraham, Maeder, etc.

If you accept my observations, I trust I can leave the wording to you.

My meddling in editorial affairs has been quite involuntary. D. thought he could save time by communicating with me rather than with the man in charge, something I hope he will stop doing. He has let me look at the next few signatures of our *Jahrbuch*. They made me feel very proud; I think you have avenged yourself brilliantly for Amsterdam. Here we have something fit to be seen! I only hope we can sustain this level.

I am happy in the thought that I shall have time on Sunday to answer your letter. Until then,

With kindest regards, FREUD

128 J

Dear Professor Freud,   Burghölzli-Zürich, 24 January 1909

Your meddling in my editorial activities is of course quite accept able to me as I still don't[1] feel too firm in the saddle. In particular, I can't cope properly with the advertising style. Enclosed is the new

[1] Jung's editorial preface to the first number of the *Jahrbuch*; see below, 130 F n. 2.
[2] = "also," "as well as."

[1] Jung forgot to write the negative, then inserted: *nicht* (!) (*zu dumm!*) = "not (!) (too stupid!)." Cf. below, 130 F par. 1.

version of the preface which I hope will be more to your liking. I have taken your wishes fully into account, also Deuticke's.

May I ask a favour of you? Recently I was consulted about a young man (apparently a severe case of hysteria with fugues) who is at present in Vienna. His family are middling well-to-do. I would like to hand him over to one of your pupils. For various reasons he doesn't want to go to Stekel (he has been to him once already), so I'd rather send him to someone else. Whom could you recommend? May I take this opportunity to ask you the addresses of Sadger, Adler and Federn?

My Agathli dreamt she was riding in *Noah's Ark*, the bottom could be opened and then something fell out.[2] Thus the daughter confirms the interpretation given by her mother, as you may remember from last autumn.

With best regards,

Most sincerely yours, DR. JUNG

129 F

Dear friend,   25 January 1909, Vienna, IX. Berggasse 19

I know, once a psychoanalyst has his first successes behind him, he is in for a hard, bitter time during which he will curse ΨA and its originator. But then things arrange themselves and he arrives at a *modus vivendi*. Such are the realities! *C'est la guerre*. Perhaps my article on Methodology[1] (which I am having trouble finishing) will help you all to cope with the most obvious problems, but probably not very much. However, it is only in struggling with difficulties that we learn, and I am not too displeased that Bleuler has deprived you of a teaching post. You will be a teacher in any event, sooner or later you are sure to have all the teaching you want, but one must be driven into ΨA-tical experience. It's good to have no alternative. "Only those who have no alternative do their best," as (more or less) C. F. Meyer has the man on Ufenau say.[2] I often appease my conscious mind by

---

[2] Cf. "Psychic Conflicts in a Child," CW 17, par. 32.

---

[1] Published partially in *Letters*, ed. E. L. Freud, no. 145.

[2] Cf. "Das Grösste tut nur, wer nicht anders kann!"—Meyer, *Huttens letzte Tage*, XXXII. Ufenau is an island in Lake Zürich where Ulrich von Hutten, the subject of the poem, spent his last days and died (1523).

saying to myself: Just give up wanting to cure; learn and make money, those are the most plausible conscious aims.

I have had another letter from Pfister, very intelligent and full of substance. Think of it, me and the *Protestantische Monatshefte*![3] But it's all right with me. In some respects a psychoanalyst who is also a clergyman works under better conditions, and besides, I presume, he will not be concerned with money. Actually all teachers ought to be familiar with our subject, if only for the sake of the healthy children. For this reason I give a joyful prosit to your course for teachers!

I laughingly acknowledge my slip in writing. Good resolutions are of no avail against these little tricks of the daemon, one just has to put up with them.

Your Agathli is really charming. But surely you recognize the main features of Little Hans's story. Mightn't everything in it be typical? I am setting high hopes in a neurotic nuclear complex which gives rise to the two chief resistances: fear of the father and disbelief towards grownups, both fully transferable to the analyst. I am convinced that we shall discover still more and that our technique will benefit by it.

Recently I glimpsed an explanation for the case of fetishism. So far it concerns only clothing and shoes. But it is probably universal. Here again repression, or rather idealization of the substitute for the repressed material. If I see any more cases, I shall tell you about them.

With kind regards to you and your now complete family,

Yours, FREUD

130 F

Dear friend,   26 January 1909, Vienna, IX. Berggasse 19

So kind of you to send me the text after all and so repay me in full for my latest *gaffe*. From now on I shall use t.s. (too stupid)[1] as a standing formula for such incidents.

To remedy your dissatisfaction with your own product, I have, with the help of "condensation and displacement," made a change in your sentences which I present to you as my last illegitimate step in this

---

[3] In which (XIII, Jan. 1909) Pfister's paper "Psychanalytische Seelsorge und experimentelle Moralpädagogik" was published.

---

[1] Holograph: Z.d. (*zu dumm*). Cf. above, 128 J n. 1.

matter. I should also like you to insert "of the psychology created . . . and its application and relevance to the (theory of the) nervous and mental disorders" or something of the kind. Of course you must suit *yourself* and then send it straight to the printer's.[2]

Dr. Adler, II. Czerningasse 7
Dr. Federn, I. Wollzeile 28
Dr. Sadger, IX. Lichtensteinstrasse 15

Adler is very busy, Federn is the most congenial and competent to deal with human problems, Sadger is the ablest practitioner; he is most in need of encouragement.

With your next kiss please give Agathli an extra one from her absent great uncle. I was very much impressed by the strand of heredity.

Sincerely, FREUD

131 J

Dear Professor Freud, Burghölzli-Zürich, 21 February 1909

Your offprint[1] arrived today and I read it at once with avidity. I too have my misgivings about the *arc de cercle*.[2] I am fond of telling my students about an *arc de cercle* group of hysterical symptoms. They

---

[2] Jung's editorial preface in the *Jahrbuch*, I:1:

"In the spring of 1908 a private meeting was held in Salzburg of all those who are interested in the development of the psychology created by Sigmund Freud and in its application to nervous and mental diseases. At this meeting it was recognized that the working out of the problems in question was already beginning to go beyond the bounds of purely medical interest, and the need was expressed for a periodical which would gather together studies in this field that hitherto have been scattered at random. Such was the impetus that gave rise to our *Jahrbuch*. Its task is to be the progressive publication of all scientific papers that are concerned in a positive way with the deeper understanding and solution of our problems. The *Jahrbuch* will thus provide not only an insight into the steady progress of work in this domain with a great future, but also an orientation on the current state and scope of questions of the utmost importance for all the humane sciences.

"Zürich, January 1909 Dr. C. G. Jung"

---

[1] "Allgemeines über den hysterischen Anfall," *Zeitschrift für Psychotherapie und medizinische Psychologie*, I:1 (Jan. 1909) = "Some General Remarks on Hysterical Attacks," SE IX.

[2] Ibid., p. 230 (3). / *Arc de cercle* = "A pathological posture characterized by pronounced bending of the body . . . sometimes observed as a symptom of hysteria."—L. E. Hinsie and J. Shatzky, *Psychiatric Dictionary* (1953).

include, in an ascending series: pain at the back of the head, in the nape of the neck, in the back ("spinal irritation"), pseudomeningitis hysterica, stiffness of throat and back, clonic spasms of arms and legs, and finally the genuine *arc de cercle*. The spastic component goes with the display of libidinal excitement; the pain component pertains more to the pregnancy complex. Both components are combined in the sticking out of the belly. I think *arc de cercle* is direct provocation with infantile defence—you can observe it in dancing and other erotic situations. *Arc de cercle* can just as well be a bending back of the upper part of the body in disgust or a sticking out of the genitalia for sexual display. Probably both. Concerning epileptic convulsions I'd like to remind you of my modest hypothesis about primitive sucking convulsions (–orgasms).

Alas, once again it can't be done: I cannot see how we, that is my wife and I, can come to Vienna for Easter.[3] That's just when I want to betake myself to northern Italy for a fortnight to get a bit of rest. We can't go earlier because of the weather, nor later because of the beginning of term and the house moving.[4] Of course you must not neglect your practice in any way on my account. I should like, as last time, to enjoy your company in the evening and make the best of a Sunday with you. For the present, would the middle or end[5] of March suit you better?

My wife and I were very pleased to hear that your daughter will visit us (t.s.)[6] with her husband on their honeymoon. They must come by all means. We are trying to arrange our trip to Vienna so as to welcome our guests in Zürich either before or afterwards.

Your judgment on Morton Prince is right. No firm foundation to build on. Of Muthmann I have the same impression as you: too verveless, too downed, probably, by the demands of life, but able and decent.

With best regards,

Most sincerely yours, JUNG

[3] A letter from Freud inviting the Jungs to Vienna and mentioning the subjects of the next two paragraphs is apparently missing. / Easter in 1909 was 11 April.
[4] To the new house that the Jungs were building in Küsnacht.
[5] Holograph: *Anfang*, "beginning," scored out and replaced by *Ende*.
[6] Holograph: *uns* inserted afterward, with: (*z.d.*). See above, 130 F n. 1.

132 F

Dear friend,   24 February 1909, Vienna, IX. Berggasse 19

Middle or end of March is all the same to me. Suit your own convenience. Splendid that you are bringing your wife. Or am I wrong in extending the "we" from the one trip to the other? During your visit I shall not be able to abandon my practice entirely, but I shall keep it within limits. I shall not be as busy as I was at this time two years ago, provided there is no change between now and then.

I am looking forward in high good spirits to your second visit: since the last one things have changed for the better. My people (I am referring mainly to my family) are also very eager to see you and are busily discussing whether you like this or that to eat. You have also built up an excellent reputation as a guest.

My children are expected here on Sunday and ought to pass through Zürich on Saturday. Whether they can stop, I do not know, but if they do, you can be sure of their visit. Possibly they will arrive soon after this letter; or perhaps homesickness will spur them to haste or perhaps they have stayed too long in Lyons.

I read your remarks on hysterical-epileptic convulsions with interest. I didn't react because I know nothing about this side of it. Maeder's idea of starting to attack epilepsy on the basis of hysteria rather[1] than the other way round strikes me as very promising. He is altogether an excellent man.

What leisure I have been able to spare from my correspondence with you in the last few weeks I have used for correspondence with Pfister and the Americans. The former seems a splendid fellow. From Jones and about him I have received very strange news and I am in very much the same situation as you when he was with Kraepelin.[2] Brill, our translator, is certainly a thoroughly honest soul. We shall have plenty to talk about.

Ferenczi's presence will make us all very happy. He will probably come over on Sunday; on the other days we shall be able to talk alone, which is a good thing too.

Your answers to my family inquiries were very indirect. I hope all is well. With kind regards,

Yours, FREUD

---

[1] Presumably a reference to Maeder, "Sexualität und Epilepsie," *Jahrbuch*, I:1 (1909). It was then in press.

[2] Jones studied with Kraepelin in Munich in Nov. 1907 and again in mid 1908. See his memoir *Free Associations* (1959), pp. 163f. and 170-74.

JAHRBUCH

FÜR

PSYCHOANALYTISCHE UND PSYCHO-
PATHOLOGISCHE FORSCHUNGEN.

HERAUSGEGEBEN VON

PROF. DR. E. BLEULER UND PROF. DR. S. FREUD
IN ZÜRICH, IN WIEN.

REDIGIERT VON

DR. C. G. JUNG,
PRIVATDOZENTEN DER PSYCHIATRIE IN ZÜRICH.

I. BAND.

I. HÄLFTE.

LEIPZIG UND WIEN.
FRANZ DEUTICKE.
1909.

The *Jahrbuch*: title-page of first issue. See 133 J

133 J

Dear Professor Freud,   Burghölzli-Zürich, 7 March 1909

Your telegram[1] today has thrown me into a fluster. I hope you haven't put a bad construction on my longish silence. I have been waiting a fortnight for this Sunday in order to write to you in peace. All this time I have been under a terrific strain day and night. I had a mass of correspondence to cope with every evening I happened to be free. All the other evenings were taken up with invitations, concerts, 3 lectures, etc. Also my house-building is giving me a great deal to do. I didn't want to write to you until I could definitely say when I am coming. The fixing of this date is particularly difficult for me, *still* chained by the neck, as I have also to consider the wishes of my colleagues. The last and worst straw is that a complex is playing Old Harry with me: a woman patient, whom years ago I pulled out of a very sticky neurosis with unstinting effort, has violated my confidence and my friendship in the most mortifying way imaginable. She has kicked up a vile scandal solely because I denied myself the pleasure of giving her a child. I have always acted the gentleman towards her, but before the bar of my rather too sensitive conscience I nevertheless don't feel clean, and that is what hurts the most because my intentions were always honourable. But you know how it is—the devil can use even the best of things for the fabrication of filth. Meanwhile I have learnt an unspeakable amount of marital wisdom, for until now I had a totally inadequate idea of my polygamous components despite all self-analysis. Now I know where and how the devil can be laid by the heels. These painful yet extremely salutary insights have churned me up hellishly inside, but for that very reason, I hope, have secured me moral qualities which will be of the greatest advantage to me in later life. The relationship with my wife has gained enormously in assurance and depth. Fate, which evidently loves crazy games, has just at this time deposited on my doorstep a well-known American (friend of Roosevelt and Taft, proprietor of several big newspapers, etc.) as a patient. Naturally he has the same conflicts I have just overcome, so

---

[1] Missing. Presumably it announced the publication of Vol. I, part 1, of the *Jahrbuch für psychoanalytische und psychopathologische Forschungen* (see title-page facsimile). The first paper was Freud's "Analyse der Phobie eines fünfjährigen Knaben" = "Analysis of a Phobia in a Five-year-old Boy," SE X; the fourth, Jung's "Die Bedeutung des Vaters für das Schicksal des Einzelnen" = "The Significance of the Father in the Destiny of the Individual," CW 4. For the complete contents, see appendix 2. / Also see addenda.

I could be of great help to him, which is gratifying in more respects than one. It was like balm on my aching wound. This case has interested me so passionately in the last fortnight that I have forgotten my other duties. The high degree of assurance and composure that distinguishes you is not yet mine, generally speaking. Countless things that are commonplaces for you are still brand new experiences for me, which I have to relive in myself until they tear me to pieces. This urge for identification (at the age of eleven I went through a so-called traumatic neurosis)[2] has abated considerably of late, though it still bothers me from time to time. But I think I have now entered the stage of convalescence, thanks to the buffetings fate has given me.

Your joy over the *Jahrbuch* is my joy too. Now the bed is dug for the stream.

My Agathli continues merrily with her discoveries. New and delightful attempts at explanation have resulted.[3] The act of birth is now fully understood, as the little one announced in an amusing game. She stuck her doll between her legs under her skirt so that only the head was showing, and cried: "Look, a baby is coming!" Then, pulling it out slowly: "And now it's all out." Only the role of the father is still obscure and a subject for dreams. I'll tell you about it in Vienna.

I shall leave here on March 18th and hope to be in Vienna on the 19th. I can probably turn up at your place that evening.

I still can't figure out the news about Jones. In any case he is a canny fellow. I don't understand him too well. I had a good and sensible letter from him recently. He displays great affection not only for me but also for my family. To be sure, he is very nervous about the emphasis placed on sexuality in our propaganda, a point that plays a big role in our relations with Brill. By nature he is not a prophet, nor a herald of the truth, but a compromiser with occasional bendings of conscience that can put off his friends. Whether he is any worse than that I don't know but hardly think so, though the interior of Africa is better known to me than his sexuality.

My small son is flourishing, my wife is in good shape as you will see in Vienna. We greatly regretted that your daughter evidently had no time to visit us. But we understand.

Pfister is without doubt a very fine acquisition, from the theoretical side, although Häberlin is a still better one. He is a dazzlingly brainy fellow with an all-round education. For the next semester he has an-

---

[2] See *Memories*, pp. 30ff./42ff. ("My twelfth year was indeed a fateful one . . .")

[3] Cf. "Psychic Conflicts in a Child," CW 17, par. 40.

nounced a *privatissimum* at Basel University: "Readings from Freud's *Interpretation of Dreams.*" We have discovered a new friend in Pastor Adolf Keller,[4] of Geneva, who is busily at work in psychanalysis.

Have you seen Schultz's report on psychanalysis in the *Zeitschrift für angewandte Psychologie?*[5] Verily the dawn is not yet.

I am looking forward eagerly to the Vienna trip and not least to recuperating from all my batterings.

With kindest regards,

Most sincerely yours, J U N G

Please don't chide me
for my negligence.

134 F

Dear friend,   9 March 1909, Vienna, IX. Berggasse 19

Many thanks for[1] your telegram and letter, which (the telegram in itself did the trick) put an end to my anxiety. I evidently still have a traumatic hyperaesthesia toward dwindling correspondence. I remember its genesis well (Fliess) and should not like to repeat such an experience unawares. In the end—though I could imagine that certain obstacles must have accumulated in your overcrowded existence and though I had rejected the idea of illness as too neurotic—in the end I just had to hear from you so as to be able to inform you of a matter which now occupies my thoughts and about which I have written to others.

This I shall dispose of first, then I shall have a free mind with which to answer your very interesting letter. You recall that last December I received an invitation from Clark University in Worcester, Mass., which I had to decline because the festivities during which my lectures were to be delivered were scheduled for the second week in July

---

[4] Adolf Keller (1872–1963), then pastor of a German-speaking congregation in Geneva; to the St. Peter church, Zürich, later the same year. After 1914 he continued an interest in Jung's school of psychology, but his chief concern was the ecumenical movement. Later in the U.S.A.

[5] J. H. Schultz, "Psychoanalyse: Die Breuer-Freudschen Lehren, ihre Entwicklung und Aufnahme," *Zeitschrift für angewandte Psychologie*, II (1909). Johannes Heinrich Schultz (1884–1970), neurologist and psychiatrist in Berlin-Charlottenburg, is known for his *Das autogene Training* (1932).

---

[1] Holograph: *und* for *für*. / The telegram is missing.

and I would have lost too much money by the transaction. At the time you yourself regretted that I was unable to manage it. Well, a week ago a second invitation came from Stanley Hall, the president of Clark University, who at the same time informed me that the festivities had been postponed to the week of September 6. Also the travel allowance has been increased not inconsiderably from $400 to $750. This time I have accepted, for at the end of August I shall be free and rested. On October 1 I hope to be back in Vienna. I must admit that this has thrilled me more than anything else that has happened in the last few years—except perhaps for the appearance of the *Jahrbuch*—and that I have been thinking of nothing else. Practical considerations have joined forces with imagination and youthful enthusiasm to upset the composure on which you have complimented me. In 1886, when I started my practice,[2] I was thinking only of a two-month trial period in Vienna; if it did not prove satisfactory, I was planning to go to America and found an existence that I would subsequently have asked my fiancée in Hamburg to share. You see, we both of us had nothing, or more precisely, I had a large and impoverished family and she a small inheritance of roughly 3000 fl. from her Uncle Jacob,[3] who had been a professor of classical philology in Bonn. But unfortunately things went so well in Vienna that I decided to stay on, and we were married in the autumn of the same year. And now, twenty-three years later, I am to go to America after all, not, to be sure, to make money, but in response to an honourable call! We shall have a good deal to say about this trip and its various consequences for our cause.

I too have had news of the woman patient through whom you became acquainted with the neurotic gratitude of the spurned. When Muthmann came to see me, he spoke of a lady who had introduced herself to him as your mistress, thinking he would be duly impressed by your having retained so much freedom. But we both presumed that the situation was quite different and that the only possible explanation was a neurosis in his informant. To be slandered and scorched by the love with which we operate—such are the perils of our trade, which we are certainly not going to abandon on their account.

Navigare necesse est, vivere non necesse.[4] And another thing: "In

---

[2] On Easter Sunday, 25 April.

[3] Jakob Bernays (1824–1881). Cf. Jones, I, p. 112/101, where details about him are not in accord with the facts that Freud gives here.

[4] "It is necessary to sail, not necessary to survive."—Plutarch, *Pompey*, 50. Pompey addressed these words to cowardly sailors. The epigram is the motto of the Hanseatic cities Hamburg and Bremen.

league with the Devil and yet you fear fire?"[5] Your grandfather[6] said something like that. I bring up this quotation because you definitely lapse into the theological style in relating this experience. The same thing happened to me in a letter to Pfister[7]—I borrowed every conceivable metaphor from the flame-fire-pyre etc. complex. I couldn't help myself, respect for theology had nailed me to this quotation (!): "One way or the other, the Jew will be burned."[8] I was still so unaccustomed to being on good terms with Protestant theologians.

Häberlin's course is really a sign of the times. Perhaps our fifteen years of trials will soon be over. The *Jahrbuch* is still an inexhaustible source of joy to me. If I didn't know that I'd be able to talk it over with you in ten days, I should have a good deal to write on the subject.

I hope Agathli is original and hadn't heard the story of Little Hans? If so, the agreement between the two symptomatic actions and the unresolved residue is striking.

I don't think any ill of Jones cither, though I shall show you Brill's letter, which makes a strong impression when compared with his. He writes about his harem, he lives with his wife and several sisters (his).

Good. I shall expect you and your dear wife for dinner on Friday the 19th. Amuse yourself as you see fit during the day, in the evenings and on Sunday we shall exchange our experiences of these last months. I have no need to tell you how much such meetings with you mean to me both professionally and personally. Unfortunately I can return only a small part of your hospitality, but I hope you have no other social commitments here.

Very cordially yours, FREUD

135 J

Dear Professor Freud, Burghölzli-Zürich, 11 March 1909

I must answer you at once. Your kind words have relieved and comforted me. You may rest assured, not only now but for the future,

[5] Holograph: *"Bist mit dem Teufel du und du Und willst dich vor der Flamme scheuen?"*—*Faust I*, 2585–6.

[6] For the legend that Jung's grandfather, also named Carl Gustav Jung, was Goethe's natural son, see *Memories*, p. 35 n./47 n. ("No proof of this item of family tradition has been found . . .") and p. 234/222.

[7] Letter of 9 Feb. 09, last par., in *Freud/Pfister Letters*, p. 17.

[8] Holograph: *Macht* [for *Tut*] *nichts, der Jude wird verbrannt.*"—Lessing, *Nathan the Wise*, IV, 2.

that nothing Fliess-like is going to happen. I have experienced so much of that sort of thing; it has taught me to do the contrary at all times. Except for moments of infatuation my affection is lasting and reliable. It's just that for the past fortnight the devil has been tormenting me in the shape of neurotic ingratitude. But I shall not be unfaithful to ΨA[1] on that account. On the contrary, I am learning from it how to do better in the future. You mustn't take on about my "theological" style, I just felt that way. Now and then, I admit, the devil does strike a chill into my—on the whole—blameless heart. The story hawked round by Muthmann is Chinese to me. I've never really had a mistress and am the most innocent of spouses. Hence my terrific moral reaction! I simply cannot imagine who it might have been. I don't think it is the same lady. Such stories give me the horrors.

I must congratulate you heartily on your American triumphs. I believe you will get an American practice in the end. My American has been behaving quite well so far. I am all agog for more news.

What you say about Jones is astonishing, but it fits in with certain expressions of his that have struck me.

My Agathli's achievements are guaranteed original: she has never heard of Little Hans. We simply listen and meddle as little as possible. A great outcry this morning: Mama must come—I want to go into your room—what is Papa doing?—But Mama won't have her in the room—"Then you must give me some sweets." Later, when we had got up, Agathli hops in, jumps into my bed, lies flat on her stomach, flails and kicks out with her legs like a horse—"Is that what Papa does? That's what Papa does, isn't it?"[2] At the end of next week I shall be in Vienna and will show you my material. My colleagues are encouraging me to write the thing up for the *Jahrbuch*. But I want your opinion first, for after Little Hans I no longer have much self-confidence. All the same, some things seem to have turned out very prettily. I have spoken about[2a] it twice at our meetings with great success—before "Little Hans" was known.

I have made a nice discovery in Hoffmann's "The Devil's Elixir"[3] (a good deal of my "theology" evidently comes from there). I am

[1] Holograph: Ψ (without A).
[2] Cf. "Psychic Conflicts in a Child," CW 17, par. 47.
[2a] Holograph begins a new page with date 12 Mar. 09.
[3] *Die Elixiere des Teufels* (1815–16), a novel by E.T.A. Hoffmann (1776–1822), about a sinister brother-figure. It is cited by Jung in several places, the earliest being the 1917 revision of "New Paths in Psychology" (see below, 290 F n. 1),

thinking of writing something on it for your *Papers*. A whole tangle of neurotic problems, but all palpably real. Altogether, I have endless plans for work next year, and I look forward so much to the new era of outer (and inner) independence that is so important for me.

Meanwhile you will have received my card.[4] The Grand Hotel is rather too grand for me, besides which it is too far away from Berggasse.

If you are going to America in September, I earnestly hope that you will put in a week with us here as a way-station. You will have all the holiday peace and quiet that could be wished for, and we'll then be living *procul negotiis*[5] in the country. We are boldly taking it for granted that you will come. After all, the road to America runs through Zürich too. (This piece of impudence was only half intentional, otherwise I would have deleted the sentence.)

With kindest regards, also from my wife,

Most sincerely yours, JUNG

136 J

Dear Professor Freud, Burghölzli-Zürich, 17 March 1909

Fate seems to have conspired against my trip to Vienna. I have just received a telegram from the wife of a patient summoning me urgently to Berlin. The case is unfortunately such that I cannot refuse, as it is someone to whom I have obligations also as a friend. I don't know yet what it's all about, but it seems to be something serious. The trip is postponed, not abandoned! As soon as I can, i.e., as soon as the matter is more or less settled, I shall come. If worst comes to worst I'll give up a bit of Italy. Naturally, my wife is not amused by this turn of events either. We both give vent to our exasperated regrets and meanwhile wave to you sorrowfully from afar.

Most sincerely yours, JUNG

under the title "On the Psychology of the Unconscious," CW 7, par. 51. He apparently did not publish an earlier study of Hoffmann's tale.
4 Missing.
5 = "far from business worries" (Horace, Epode II).

137 J

Dear Professor Freud,   Burghölzli-Zürich, 21 March 1909

I really think that all obstacles are at last out of the way now. Next Thursday (March 25th) I shall, irrevocably, be in Vienna towards evening. My trip to Berlin passed off in no time, without incidents, and was of course less necessary than expected, which is the way the world wags. At least I have the good still to look forward to. I have re-booked our room at the Hotel Regina.

Recently I got a letter from a neurologist in Munich, Dr. Seif,[1] asking if he could work with me for a few weeks. Something seems to be stirring after all. My man from Tübingen has made good progress. He is a fine and honest chap who will do his work under the cover of secrecy. Otherwise no great news; the holiday lull has descended and I have little time to think of useful work as my house-building and private patients give me plenty to do. I'm waiting for the summer, when I shall plunge into work with rapture. The shackles of the institute hang heavier on me every day.

Lately I visited Häberlin. He is a far-sighted fellow with an unforeseeable future. I don't know how well his creative drive will hold up. I only hope the cares of this world don't get him down; his financial situation is not exactly brilliant. A doughty character with plenty of fight in him. He was born in the same village as I, he the son of a schoolteacher, I of a parson. Now we meet again in this field. He tops Pfister by a head in psychological acuity and biological knowledge, and has studied theology as well as philosophy and natural science. Nor does he lack a certain mystical streak, on which account I set special store by him, since it guarantees a deepening of thought beyond the ordinary and a grasp of far-reaching syntheses.

Don't know yet what the critics are saying about the *Jahrbuch*.

Joyfully looking forward,

Most sincerely yours, JUNG

---

[1] Leonhard Seif (1866–1949), founded a Freudian group in Munich 1911. 1913, separated from psychoanalysis; 1920, met Adler and thereafter became a leading figure in the Society for Individual Psychology. Adler broke with him in the 1930's after Seif's group compromised with the Nazis.

The Jungs Again in Vienna

Carl and Emma Jung were in Vienna from Thursday, 25 March to Tuesday, 30 March (Jones, II, p. 57/51). Beyond what the next two letters tell us, nothing more is known of this visit.

According to family records (as communicated by Mr. Franz Jung), Jung terminated his work at the Burghölzli at the end of March. The visit to Vienna therefore must have been a celebratory holiday, and also Jung's bicycle tour in Italy in mid April. After resigning from the Burghölzli, Jung continued to lecture as privatdocent in the University until April 1914 (see below, 358 J n. 2).

138 J

Dear Professor Freud,   Burghölzli-Zürich, 2 April 1909[1]

Worry and patients and all the other chores of daily life have beset me again and quite got me down for the first 2 days. Now I am slowly coming to the surface and beginning to bask in the memory of the days in Vienna. I hope you received my offprints in good time for Wednesday evening.[2]

12 April.[2a]

After a 10-day interruption I have at last succeeded in continuing my letter. From this interlude it appears that the above complaint was premature, because, as usual, worse was to follow. Today I have put the last bad day behind me. All during the Easter holidays, when other people were out walking, I've been able to snatch only one day's breath of air. On the 15th I'll wrench myself free without fail and start my bicycle tour. Since Vienna all scientific work has been out of the question. But in my practice I have accomplished much. At the moment a madly interesting case is stretching me on the rack. Some of the symptoms come suspiciously close to the organic borderline (brain tumour?), yet they all hover over a dimly divined psychogenic depth, so that in analysing them all one's misgivings are forgotten. First-rate spiritualistic phenomena occur in this case, though so far only once

[1] Published in *Letters*, ed. G. Adler, vol. 1.
[2] There is no clue as to what offprints these were. They are not mentioned in the *Minutes* for the 31 Mar. meeting.
[2a] Easter Monday.

in my presence. Altogether it makes a very peculiar impression. The patient is a man-slaying Sara, Raguel's daughter.[3]

The case I told you about—evil eye, paranoiac impression—was cleared up as follows. She was abandoned by her last lover, who is altogether pathological (Dem. praec.?); abandoned also by an earlier lover—this one even spent a year in an asylum. Now the infantile pattern: hardly knew her father and mother, loving instead her brother, 8 years older than she and at 22 a catatonic. Thus the psychological stereotype holds good. You said the patient was merely *imitating* Dem. praec.; now the model has been found.

When I left Vienna I was afflicted with some *sentiments d'incomplétude* because of the last evening I spent with you. It seemed to me that my spookery[4] struck you as altogether too stupid and perhaps unpleasant because of the Fliess analogy.[5] (Insanity!) Just recently, however, the impression I had of the last-named patient smote me with renewed force. What I told my wife about it also made the deepest impression on her. I had the feeling that under it all there must be some quite special complex, a universal one having to do with the prospective tendencies in man. If there is a "psychanalysis" there must also be a "psychosynthesis" which creates future events according to the same laws. (I see I am writing rather as if I had a flight of ideas.) The leap towards psychosynthesis proceeds via the person of

---

[3] Tobit (Apoc.) 3:7ff. Also cf. Jung, "Significance of the Father," CW 4, pars. 742ff.

[4] While Freud and Jung were discussing precognition and parapsychology in the former's study, and after Freud had rejected the subject as "nonsensical," there was a loud report in the bookcase. Jung predicted that another would follow in a moment, and that indeed happened. Jung gave this account in *Memories*, pp. 155f./152f.; Jones mentions the incident in III, 411/383f. It is debatable whether another experience related by Jung occurred during the same visit: According to Jung, Freud told him that they must make an unshakable bulwark of the sexual theory, "against the black tide of mud of occultism." See *Memories*, p. 150/147f., where Jung states that the conversation took place in Vienna "some three years later" than their first meeting, Feb. 1907. However, there is no other evidence that Jung visited Freud in Vienna after 1909. Cf. 187 F n. 1.

[5] For Fliess, see above, 70 F n. 7. The "Fliess analogy" is unclear. Jones (I, p. 320/290) refers to the "mystical features" of Fliess's work, and on the other hand to Fliess's having called Freud "only a 'thought-reader' " (p. 345/314); cf. *Origins*, letter 143. Aside from what Freud could have told him in conversation, Jung could have known of his disagreement with Fliess through the latter's *In Eigener Sache; Gegen Otto Weininger und Hermann Swoboda* (Berlin, 1906) and A. R. Pfenning's *Wilhelm Fliess und seine Nachentdecker: Otto Weininger und H. Swoboda* (Berlin, 1906); see also Ernst Kris, introduction to *The Origins of Psychoanalysis: Letters to Fliess* (1954), pp. 41f.

my patient, whose unconscious is right now preparing, apparently with nothing to stop it, a new stereotype into which everything from outside, as it were, fits in conformity with the complex. (Hence the idea of the objective effect of the prospective tendency!)

That last evening with you has, most happily, freed me inwardly from the oppressive sense of your paternal authority. My unconscious celebrated this impression with a great dream which has preoccupied me for some days and which I have just finished analysing. I hope I am now rid of all unnecessary encumbrances. Your cause must and will prosper, so my pregnancy fantasies tell me, which luckily you caught in the end. As soon as I get back from Italy I shall begin some positive work, first of all for the *Jahrbuch*.

I hope you had a good Easter holiday and feel the better for it.

N. Ossipow,[6] head physician of the psychiatric University Clinic in Moscow, has published a fine report on our affairs. They seem to be working along our lines.

I have heard that Abraham with some others has issued a "psychanalytical questionnaire."[7] Let's hope it's a canard!

With kindest regards,

Yours gratefully, JUNG

[6] Nikolai Evgrafovich Osipov (1877–1934), or Ossipow, co-founder of the Russian Psychoanalytic Society in 1911 (Jones, II, p. 97/86) and translator of Freud (Grinstein 10432, 10575). The report mentioned here probably was "Recent Works of the Freudian School" (in Russian; Moscow, 1909). Subsequently he reported on "practically all of Freud's writings" (M. Wulff, *Zentralblatt*, I:7/8, Apr./May, 1911). After the Revolution, director of the Bechterew Institute, Leningrad (C. P. Oberndorf, A *History of Psychoanalysis in America*, 1953, p. 192); after 1921, lecturer on psychoanalysis at Charles University, Prague.

[7] The questionnaire was published by Magnus Hirschfeld in an article, "Zur Methodik der Sexualwissenschaft," *Zeitschrift für Sexualwissenschaft*, I:12 (Dec. 1908); it contains 127 questions in a dozen pages. For help in making it up, Hirschfeld thanks Abraham, Stein, Iwan Bloch, Otto Juliusburger, van Römer, and others. An English tr. of an earlier version, discussed in the Vienna Society the previous April (see above, 87 F n. 5), is in *Minutes*, I, pp. 379–88.

139 F

Dear friend,   16 April 1909,[1] Vienna, IX. Berggasse 19

I hope this letter doesn't reach you for a while. I'm sure you see what I mean. I simply prefer to write now while the feelings aroused by your last letter are still fresh.

I wrote your wife a card from Venice, where I went on an Easter trip in the vain hope of getting a foretaste of spring and a little rest. I thought you were already bicycling in northern Italy.

It is strange that on the very same evening when I formally adopted you as eldest son and anointed you—*in partibus infidelium*[2]—as my successor and crown prince, you should have divested me of my paternal dignity, which divesting seems to have given you as much pleasure as I, on the contrary, derived from the investiture of your person. Now I am afraid of falling back into the father role with you if I tell you how I feel about the poltergeist business. But I must, because my attitude is not what you might otherwise think. I don't deny that your stories and your experiment made a deep impression on me. I decided to continue my observations after you left, and here are the results. In my first room there is constant creaking where the two heavy Egyptian steles rest on the oaken boards of the bookshelves. That is too easy to explain. In the second, where we heard it, there is seldom any creaking. At first I was inclined to accept this as proof, if the sound that was so frequent while you were here were not heard again after your departure—but since then I have heard it repeatedly, not, however, in connection with my thoughts and never when I am thinking about you or this particular problem of yours. (And not at the present moment, I add by way of a challenge.) But this observation was soon discredited by another consideration. My credulity, or at least my willingness to believe, vanished with the magic of your personal presence; once again, for some inward reasons that I can't put my finger on, it strikes me as quite unlikely that such phenomena should exist; I confront the despiritualized furniture as the poet confronted undeified Nature after the gods of Greece had passed away.[3] Accordingly, I put my fatherly horned-rimmed spectacles on again

---

[1] Published in Jung, *Memories*, Appendix I (without pars. 1–2), and in Schur, *Freud: Living and Dying*, pp. 230ff. (without par. 1), where it is discussed at length. Both versions contain discrepancies based on misreadings of the holograph. See also K. R. Eissler, *Talent and Genius* (New York, 1971), p. 145.

[2] = "in the lands of the unbelievers."

[3] Schiller, in his poem "Die Götter Griechenlands."

and warn my dear son to keep a cool head, for it is better not to understand something than make such great sacrifices to understanding. I also shake my wise head over psychosynthesis and think: Yes, that's how the young people are, the only places they really enjoy visiting are those they can visit without us, to which we with our short breath and weary legs cannot follow them.

Then, invoking the privilege of my years, I become garrulous and speak of one more thing between heaven and earth that we cannot understand.[4] Some years ago I discovered within me the conviction that I would die between the ages of 61 and 62, which then struck me as a long time away. (Today it is only eight years off.) Then I went to Greece with my brother[5] and it was really uncanny how often the number 61 or 60 in connection with 1 or 2 kept cropping up in all sorts of numbered objects, especially those connected with transportation. This I conscientiously noted. It depressed me, but I had hopes of breathing easy when we got to the hotel in Athens and were assigned rooms on the first floor. Here, I was sure, there could be no No. 61. I was right, but I was given 31 (which with fatalistic licence could be regarded as half of 61 or 62), and this younger, more agile number proved to be an even more persisent persecutor than the first. From the time of our trip home until very recently, 31, often with a 2 in its vicinity, clung to me faithfully. Since my mind also includes areas that are merely eager for knowledge and not at all superstitious, I have since attempted an analysis of this belief, and here it is. It made its appearance in 1899. At that time two events occurred. First I wrote *The Interpretation of Dreams* (which appeared postdated 1900), second, I received a new telephone number, which I still have today: 14362. It is easy to find a factor common to these two events. In 1899 when I wrote *The Interpretation of Dreams* I was 43 years old. Thus it was plausible to suppose that the other figures signified the end of my life, hence 61 or 62. Suddenly method entered into my madness.[6] The superstitious notion that I would die between the ages of 61 and 62 proves to coincide with the conviction that with *The Interpretation of Dreams* I had completed my life work, that there was nothing more for me to do and that I might just as well lie down and die. You will admit that after this substitution it no longer sounds so absurd. Moreover, the hidden influence of W. Fliess was at work; the superstition erupted in the year of his attack on me.

[4] Cf. *Hamlet*, I, 5.
[5] Alexander, in Sept. 1904. See Jones, II, pp. 26f./23f.
[6] Cf. *Hamlet*, II, 2.

You will see in this another confirmation of the specifically Jewish nature of my mysticism. Otherwise I incline to explain such obsessions as this with the number 61 by two factors, first heightened, unconsciously motivated attention of the sort that sees Helen in every woman,[7] and second by the undeniable "compliance of chance," which plays the same part in the formation of delusions as somatic compliance in that of hysterical symptoms, and linguistic compliance in the generation of puns.

Consequently, I shall receive further news of your investigations of the spook complex with the interest one accords to a charming delusion in which one does not oneself participate.

With kind regards to you, your wife and children,

Yours, FREUD

140 J

Dear Professor Freud,   Burghölzli-Zürich, 12 May 1909

I must again make amends for a sin of omission. Once more you haven't heard from me for a long time. Well, I got back safe and sound from Italy and found your letter awaiting me. I am entirely of your opinion that one must be careful not to be carried away by impressions or indulge in expectations and plans that go too far. The trouble is that one is so eager to discover something. However, I have not gone over to any system yet and shall also guard against putting my trust in those spooks.

Pfister was here the day before yesterday and relayed your greetings. He says your daughter[1] has recently been operated on. I hope there won't be anything serious, i.e., complications. P. of course was full of you and of his warm reception in your family. I hope you got a good impression of him. He is, all told, a very acceptable theologian with admirable traits of character. He also told me that Moll was with you at the same time. What was *that* black spirit doing in your house? Amazing that the fellow was not ashamed after all his pestering.

---

[7] See *Faust I*, 2603–4, where Mephistopheles tells Faust: "A dose like that within your guts, my boy, / And every other wench is Helen of Troy" (tr. P. Wayne, Penguin edn.).

---

[1] Mathilde.

220

Quite spineless, obviously. I am dying to hear of the warm reception you gave *him*.

The "psychoanalytical questionnaire" is a horrid fact which I have now seen with my own eyes. A perfectly idiotic concoction that does Hirschfeld no credit. I find the desecration of the word "psychoanalytic" unforgiveable. It is most regrettable, to say the least, that Abraham and Stein have subscribed to this sorry rigmarole. I feel like protesting at this infamous bamboozlement of the public. In Zürich everyone is sedately shocked.

I am still at Burghölzli as my house has naturally not been finished on time. We move on May 25th. From then on my address is Küsnach bei Zürich.

I have two assistants again: Dr. Décsi[2] from Budapest (for 5 months) and Dr. Gibson[3] from Edinburgh (for 6 weeks), the former highly intelligent, the latter less so, but well recommended. The one, sent by Stein, is a neurologist, excellent training; the other, sent by Dr. Mott[4] in London, is a psychiatrist but of the English breed: knows how to catch pike and salmon, sails and rows very well, but has only a few barbaric notions of the psyche. Prognosis therefore *dubia*; nevertheless a straw in the wind. Stockmayer has returned to his household gods and has sent me a detailed report on the Tübingen clinic. Gaupp says that if things go on like this they will lead to the conception of an individual psychosis, and if he were 20 years old he would probably go along, but, etc. . . . Psychanalysis is said to have got off rather more lightly than before in the new edition of Kraepelin's *Lehrbuch*.[5] Forel is supposed to have remarked a while ago that

[2] Imre Décsi (1881–1944), born Deutsch, Hungarian neurologist and popular writer on psychiatry; head of the neurological ward, Budapest Workmen's Hospital. He did not remain in the psychoanalytical movement. Murdered by the Nazis.

[3] George Herbert Rae Gibson (1881–1932), Scottish physician; at this time a psychiatrist, later an administrator. He lectured to the Royal Medical Society of Edinburgh on 14 Jan. 10 on "The Association Method as an Aid in Psychotherapy." See below, 151 J.

[4] Frederick Walker Mott (1853–1926), English psychiatrist and neurologist.

[5] 8th edn. (1909), vol. I, pp. 498ff.: "Obviously, on the one hand, this penetrating method is apt to provide the physician with deep insights into the mental life of the patient. On the other hand, however, the few extensive reports so far published show that the physician exerts an uncommonly strong influence, wholly determined by his own preconceptions, and that to achieve the desired result requires an interpretative art commanded by very few. The method therefore, at least with its present aims, is not likely to become common property." A similar evaluation is on pp. 612ff.

221

it is a good thing I am quitting Burghölzli so that Bleuler can be rid of my baneful influence. Despite which he has sent Stein in Budapest a case of obsessional neurosis for psychanalysis. Devil only knows what to make of that.

At the moment my time is still taken up with my house-building and my private patients, so my scientific work has not yet got into its stride. Instead I am delivering a thumping course of lectures on psychotherapy and besides that a *privatissimum* on Freudian psychology for ca. 10 *parsons*[6] and 2 pedagogues, beginning Monday next. In addition I have 4 voluntary workers in my outpatients' clinic. At times it's almost too much of a whirl.

Prof. Foerster,[7] the well-known "pedagogue," has recently attacked you and has more up his sleeve. He is a dangerous know-all and a malevolent wiseacre. I hope Pfister will slap him down.

All well here. With kindest regards,

Most sincerely yours, JUNG

141 F

Dear friend, 16 May 1909, Vienna, IX. Berggasse 19

Once more I am writing to Burghölzli. You know how much pleasure your letters give me, but I am far from wishing to burden you with the obligation of a formal correspondence at times when you have other things to do and nothing to say to me. Still, I hope you will not be surprised to hear from me as often as my own need prompts me to write.

We have all grown very fond of Pfister. He is really an acceptable priest, and he has even helped me by exerting a moderating influence on my father complex. We were like old friends in no time; he is a little fulsome in his enthusiasm, but there is nothing false or exaggerated in his warmth. Whether he will be able to preserve his residue of faith for long strikes me as doubtful; he is only at the beginning

[6] Holograph: underlined three times.
[7] Friedrich Wilhelm Foerster (1869–1966), German educator, pacifist, and philosopher, exiled from Germany for *lèse majesté*, in Switzerland 1897–1913, at Zürich University; later in New York, where he died in poverty. His attack mentioned here is "Neurose und Sexualethik," *Hochland* (Munich), VI:3 (Dec. 1908), an attack on Freud's paper in *Sexual-Probleme*; see above, 77 F n. 6. Also see below, 160 F n. 6 and 170 J n. 4.

of a far-reaching development, and the bad company he keeps is bound to have its effect. Moll's visit provided a contrast staged by fate. To put it bluntly, he is a brute; he is not really a physician but has the intellectual and moral constitution of a pettifogging lawyer. I was amazed to discover that he regards himself as a kind of patron of our movement. I let him have it; I attacked the passage in his notorious book[1] where he says that we compose our case histories to support our theories rather than the other way round, and had the pleasure of listening to his oily excuses: his statement was not meant as an insult, every observer is influenced by his preconceived ideas, etc. Then he complained that I was too sensitive, that I must learn to accept justified criticism; when I asked him if he had read "Little Hans," he wound himself up into several spirals, became more and more venomous, and finally, to my great joy, jumped up and prepared to take flight. At the door he grinned and made an unsuccessful attempt to retrieve himself by asking me when I was coming to Berlin. I could imagine how eager he must be to return my hospitality, but all the same I wasn't fully satisfied as I saw him go. He had stunk up the room like the devil himself, and partly for lack of practice and partly because he was my guest I hadn't lambasted him enough. Now of course we can expect all sorts of dirty tricks from him. And then I called Pfister into the room.

My daughter's abscess has finally cleared up and she is feeling better than before the incident. She is coming to see us today for the first time. I am glad the trouble has been taken care of now, rather than later, on some serious occasion like childbirth.

Foerster has delivered a lecture here but made no mention of me in it. Kurt Redlich,[2] who[3]

---

[1] The Sexual Life of the Child; see above, 112 F n. 7, and Freud/Abraham Letters, pp. 73f.

[2] Probably Kurt Redlich, Edler von Vezeg (1887–1939+), originally of Brno; later a Viennese industrialist and patron of Hugo Heller's publishing and artistic activities. Jones (II, p. 46/41) lists a "von Redlich" at the Salzburg Congress (1908).

[3] The rest of the letter is missing.

142 J

Im Feld,[1] Seestrasse, Küsnach bei Zürich
Dear Professor Freud,   2 June 1909

Frl. E—— has just put in an appearance. Many thanks for your kind attention, also for the reminder about Adler, for whom I enclose a letter. Would you be good enough to send it on to him? Because of the total disarray of my belongings, I have for the moment mislaid his address. This last miserable week should now be followed by festive days,[2] for it really was a bad week, only my wife has kept her head above water. Luckily this entry into my *tusculum* by the lake was a climax *a minori ad majus*. I only wish you could, by your timely presence, shower the appropriate blessings on this abode. I am just beginning to guide my thoughts back into rectilinear channels, until now I haven't been able to concentrate on a thing. Although we began the move last Tuesday, only four rooms are really finished today. In the dining room, for instance, not even the floor is ready.

But enough of this! Your last letter sounded rather annoyed,[3] no doubt because of the affect I poured out over the unfortunate questionnaire. Still, I don't think I stand on too bad a footing with Abraham. I asked him to go on with the abstracts and he consented most willingly. I think the *modus vivendi* has been found. I have very good news of Seif in Munich; he is working hard on psychanalysis and is full of enthusiasm. Have you seen Marcinowski's paper?[4] I

---

[1] Jung's new house was in a rural part of Küsnach called Im Feld, on the Lake of Zürich about half a mile from the village itself. Küsnach (later spelling: Küsnacht) is about seven miles southeast of the center of Zürich. Jung did not use the street address (Seestrasse 1003) in his letters until a year later (196 J). Subsequently the houses were renumbered, and Jung's became no. 228, as it is still. Over its doorway Jung had the following inscription carved when the house was built: "Vocatus atque non vocatus deus aderit" (Invoked or not invoked, the god will be present).—From Erasmus' adages, a 1563 edn. of which Jung had acquired when 19 (E. A. Bennet, *C. G. Jung*, 1961, p. 146); originally from the Delphic oracle (see Thucydides 1.118.3, on the Lacedaemonians' war against Athens). / Through 186 J, Jung used the Zürich/Burghölzli stationery; he crossed out the printed address and wrote the new address in longhand.

[2] Holograph: *Auf die letzte saure Woche sollten nun eigentlich frohe Feste folgen.* Jung is echoing the line "Saure Wochen! Frohe Feste!" from Goethe's poem "Der Schatzgräber."

[3] Evidently the missing part of 141 F.

[4] Jaroslaw (or Johannes) Marcinowski (1868–1935), practicing then at a sanatorium in Holstein. His paper probably was "Zur Frage der infantilen Sexualität,"

know it[4a] merely from hearsay, but shall write to him, then he can make contact if he cares to. So you liked Pfister—that pleases me *very much*. He is extraordinarily keen and has drummed up a brilliant audience for the *privatissimum*; we even have a university professor in our midst (Prof. Schweizer,[5] Germanist). I lead off with associations, which is how I myself came to understand your teachings. I think that is the best way for me.

For the coming *Jahrbuch* Stekel will submit case material on dreams; I think I have already told you what else is in the offing. May I express hopes for your paper,[6] or do you want to reserve it for the winter half-volume? You are probably feeling very tired now after your winter exertions and will scarcely have time and desire for further work? I am very interested to hear how you think of organizing your lectures in America. Will you hold them in reserve for the next *Jahrbuch* but one? Excuse my insatiable appetite, but I really would like to present the latest résumé from your pen to the public. They are panting for it and it's urgently needed anyway. A man from the Moscow Clinic is with me now for instruction (tiring enough with the help of a female interpreter) on, of all things, the latest development, namely "resistance analysis" (I think that is what you too call it). This Dr. Asatiani[7] (such is his name) complains about the lack of therapeutic results. Aside from the imperfection of his art, I think the trouble lies with the Russian material, where the individual is as ill-differentiated as a fish in a shoal. The problems of the masses are the first things that need solving there. This week, together with Décsi, I am starting experiments (with the galvanometer) on the "attitude" in Dementia praecox, and with Stockmayer I am collaborating on "paraphrenic" associations. Only when these general foundations have been laid can I launch into the bigger problems of

---

Berliner klinische Wochenschrift, 1909. He was not, as Jones states (II, p. 79/72), an original member of the Berlin Psychoanalytic Society (1910); see *Bulletin*, no. 7 (Sept. 1910), p. 1, and below, 204 J n. 2.

[4a] Holograph: *Sie*, "you," corrected to *sie*, "it," after which Jung put: (*!*).

[5] Eduard Schweizer (1874–1943), professor of Indo-European philology and Sanskrit in Zürich, after 1932 in Berlin. Attended Society meetings 1910–11.

[6] The "General Exposition"; see above, 112 F n. 2.

[7] Mikhail Mikhaylovich Asatiani (1882–1938), of Georgian origin, then interning at the Moscow University psychiatric clinic. From 1921, head of the department of psychiatry, Tbilisi (Tiflis) University, and founder of the Asatiani Psychiatric Research Institute. Wrote on psychoanalysis 1910–13, but later followed Pavlov.

the metamorphosis of libido in Dem. pr. The problem of the choice of neurosis is crucial here, I see that already.

Out here my practice is picking up again—something I hadn't expected.

With kindest regards,

Most sincerely yours, JUNG

143 F

Dear friend,   3 June 1909, Vienna, IX. Berggasse 19

Hurrah for your new house! I would say it louder and longer if I didn't know how you Swiss disliked emotional effusions. This year my trip to America deprives me of the pleasure, but I hope before too long to admire your house and enjoy the company of its inhabitants.

Of course I understood your silence and even now I would leave you more time if another letter—which I enclose—had not reached me at the same time as yours. Weird! What is she? A busybody, a chatterbox, or a paranoiac? If you know anything about the writer or have some opinion in the matter, would you kindly send me a short wire, but otherwise you must *not* go to any trouble. If I don't hear from you, I shall assume that you know nothing. I've forwarded your letter to Adler. Now, thanks to the above-mentioned coincidence, you will receive an immediate answer to your questions and suggestions. My irritation over your criticism of the questionnaire didn't really amount to much. I just happened to be in a "mellow" mood, as though I had got the better of all my own complexes. *Pfister* has just received his first compliment from Spielmeier;[1] I suppose he's not terribly excited about it. I have heard very good things about Marcinowski from a private source. I myself think we ought to recruit him and have written to Abraham to that effect. Seif amazes me. He hasn't been to see you yet; where did he learn these things? Your Russian (and I must tell you again how I admire your patience, or rather your resignation) probably has some utopian dream of a world-saving therapy and feels that the work isn't getting on fast enough. The Russians, I believe, are especially deficient in the art of pains-

---

[1] Walter Spielmeyer (1879–1935), pathologist and psychiatrist in Freiburg, later Munich. Freud refers to an attack on Pfister, not located. Spielmeyer had criticized Freud's "Fragment of an Analysis" in 1906 (*Zentralblatt für Nervenheilkunde und Psychiatrie*, XXIX, 15 Apr. 06).

taking work. By the way, do you know the story about the "glass rear end"?[2] A practising physician should never forget it. I shall be able to tell you very shortly where it is to be found.

Something else: yesterday I received a book by Otto Gross: *On Psychopathic Inferiorities*.[3] I haven't studied it yet, but obviously it's another outstanding work, full of bold syntheses and overflowing with ideas. And again two different ways of indicating emphasis (bold type and letter spacing), which makes an exquisitely paranoid impression. Too bad, the man has a good mind! To tell the truth, I don't know if I shall be able to understand the book. A good deal of it is too high-flown for me, and on the whole I believe he has taken a step backward from me to his earlier phases (Anton, Wernicke). Is it neurotic regression in him[4] or is it *my own* obtuseness?

I shall be glad to postpone my paper on method until next year, first because I want Ferenczi to appear ahead of it,[5] and second because I can't promise to finish it in the four weeks of the July holiday. Our readers won't catch up with us so soon. On the other hand, I suddenly feel like writing about the Salzburg rat man, and if you like I can give you the piece for the second number. It will *not* be long, because in print I shall have to be much more discreet than in a lecture. But here is a case that will enable me to throw full light on certain aspects of the truly complicated phenomenon of obsessional neurosis. I am no longer tired, I shall have a full schedule in June, but shall only be working half-time during the first two weeks of July and am confident of being able to complete the article before the summer holiday.

I have recently taken stock and seen that I now have eight irons in the fire, some of which will be glowing for a long time. Is Agathli to appear in the January number? I have corresponded with Binsw about the second part of his piece and have only now come to understand his analysis fully. It is ingenious and very well done—as far as it goes.[6]

Your way of leading off with the association experiment strikes me as excellent. Another way might be on the basis of everyday life.

I should like very much to talk with you about America and have

---

[2] See addenda.

[3] *Über psychopathische Minderwertigkeiten*. See above, 33 J n. 7.

[4] Holograph: *in ihm* inserted afterward.

[5] "Introjection and Transference," which Ferenczi had withdrawn from Brodmann (see above, 124 J, and Freud to Ferenczi, 18 Jan. 09, in *Letters*, ed. E. L. Freud; below, 168 J n. 1).

[6] See below, 167 F n. 2.

your suggestions. Jones threatens me, not entirely without ulterior motive, with the absence of all leading psychiatrists. I expect nothing of the moguls. But I wonder if it might not be a good idea to concentrate on psychology since Stanley Hall is a psychologist, and perhaps to devote my 3–4 lectures entirely to dreams, from which excursions in various directions would be possible. Of course these questions have little practical interest in view of my inability to lecture in English.

With very special regards to you, your wife and children in your new house.

Yours, FREUD

144 J

Im Feld, Küsnach bei Zürich,

Dear Professor Freud,   4 June 1909

In accordance with your wish I sent you a telegram[1] this morning, framing it as clearly as I could. At the moment I didn't know what more to say. Spielrein[2] is the person I wrote you about. She was published in abbreviated form in my Amsterdam lecture of blessed memory.[3] She was, so to speak, my test case, for which reason I remembered her with special gratitude and affection. Since I knew from experience that she would immediately relapse if I withdrew my support, I prolonged the relationship over the years and in the end found myself morally obliged, as it were, to devote a large measure of friendship to her, until I saw that an unintended wheel had started turning, whereupon I finally broke with her. She was, of course, systematically planning my seduction, which I considered inopportune. Now she is seeking revenge. Lately she has been spreading a rumour that I shall soon get a divorce from my wife and marry a certain girl

---

[1] Missing.

[2] Sabina (or Sabine) Spielrein (1886?–1934+), of Russian origin. 1905–11, studied medicine at the University of Zürich; M.D. 1911. Later in 1911 she became a member of the Vienna Society. From 1912, in Berlin. In 1921–23, Dr. Spielrein (then called Spielrein-Scheftel) practiced in Geneva; Jean Piaget underwent his didactic analysis with her. In 1923, she returned to the Soviet Union and taught at the North Caucasus University, Rostov on the Don, and was listed in the *International Journal* as a member of the Russian Society until 1933, after which year the psychoanalytic movement was officially abolished in the Soviet Union. Grinstein lists 30 publications in French and German, beginning with articles in the *Jahrbuch* in 1911 and 1912; the last article listed was in 1934.

[3] Cf. "The Freudian Theory of Hysteria," CW 4.

student, which has thrown not a few of my colleagues into a flutter. What she is now planning is unknown to me. Nothing good, I suspect, unless perhaps you are imposed upon to act as a go-between. I need hardly say that I have made a clean break. Like Gross, she is a case of fight-the-father, which in the name of all that's wonderful I was trying to cure *gratissime* (!) with untold tons of patience, even abusing our friendship for that purpose. On top of that, naturally, an amiable complex had to throw an outsize monkey-wrench into the works. As I have indicated before, my first visit to Vienna had a *very* long unconscious aftermath, first the compulsive infatuation in Abbazia,[4] then the Jewess popped up in another form, in the shape of my patient. Now of course the whole bag of tricks lies there quite clearly before my eyes. During the whole business Gross's notions[5] flitted about a bit too much in my head. Incidentally, Gross hasn't sent me his book. I shall try to buy it. Could you give me the name of the publisher? Gross and Spielrein are bitter experiences. To none of my patients have I extended so much friendship and from none have I reaped so much sorrow.

Heartiest thanks for your blessings on my house! I take them as the best omen.

I am very glad to know that you too have "mellow" moods. I fancied you in permanent possession of the highest esoteric wisdom, which I as your *famulus* would have to emulate. Not all my goals are unattainable, thank heavens.

If you don't want to keep your American lectures entirely on the elementary didactic level, I fully agree that dreams offer the most suitable material. I have no great hopes of American psychiatry, some of the psychologists are better, but only a few. Anyway your success is guaranteed in advance, for the kudos lies in the appointment itself, and those who appointed you won't go back on it if only for reasons of self-interest. What if you do lecture in German? There's nothing they can do about it. I expect double dealing only from Münsterberg.[6]

What you say of the Russians hits the nail on the head. Little patience and depth, all quibblings and vapourings, a good-for-nothing lot. The Poles are a notch better, but still too wishy-washy.

[4] Holograph: *in Abbazia*, could equally mean "with Abbazia" (Adriatic resort, now Opatija, Yugoslavia).
[5] See above, 46 J.
[6] Hugo Münsterberg (1863–1916), psychologist, originally German; after 1892, at Harvard.

My Agathli will appear in the August number; I haven't written it up yet for lack of time. I'll get to work on it next week.

I once heard the story of the "glass rear end" but have entirely forgotten the point. However, I have inscribed your classic apophthegm "just give up wanting to cure"[7] in block letters on my heart, for the above reasons. I have learnt my lesson for keeps.

The Polish lady[8] you sent me called it off after the first session, but turned up today and allegedly will be heard from again tomorrow. She seems to use her illness as an occasion to travel. She was also with Kocher[9] in Bern to get her pelvis X-rayed.

With kindest regards, JUNG

145 F

Dear friend,　　　　　　　　7 June 1909, Vienna, IX. Berggasse 19

Since I know you take a personal interest in the Sp. matter I am informing you of developments. Of course there is no need for you to answer this.

I understood your telegram correctly, your explanation confirmed my guess. Well, after receiving your wire I wrote Fräulein Sp. a letter in which I affected ignorance, pretending to think her suggestion was that of an over-zealous enthusiast. I said that since the matter on which she wished to see me was of interest chiefly to myself, I could not take the responsibility of encouraging her to take such a trip and failed to see why she should put herself out in this way. It therefore seemed preferable that she should first acquaint me with the nature of her business. I have not yet received an answer.

Such experiences, though painful, are necessary and hard to avoid. Without them we cannot really know life and what we are dealing with. I myself have never been taken in quite so badly, but I have come very close to it a number of times and had *a narrow escape*.[1] I believe that only grim necessities weighing on my work, and the fact that I was ten years older than yourself when I came to ΨA, have

---

[7] See above, 129 F.
[8] Presumably Frl. E——.
[9] Theodor Emil Kocher (1841–1917), Swiss surgeon, specialist in thyroid research; Nobel Prize for medicine, 1909.

---

[1] English in original.

saved me from similar experiences. But no lasting harm is done. They help us to develop the thick skin we need and to dominate "counter-transference," which is after all a permanent problem for us; they teach us to displace our own affects to best advantage. They are a *"blessing in disguise."*[2]

The way these women manage to charm us with every conceivable psychic perfection until they have attained their purpose is one of nature's greatest spectacles. Once that has been done or the contrary has become a certainty, the constellation changes amazingly.

Now for some general news:

Gross, *Über psychopathische Minderwertigkeiten*, Vienna, Braumüller, 1909. I received the book from his old man, who, in response to my letter of thanks and appreciation, asked me to write to Otto, telling him how much I had liked the book and that I should like to discuss certain parts of it with him. Then, after meeting with him, I was to write the father my opinion. This I firmly declined to do, citing the results of your examination. I have too much respect for Otto Gross.

Today I received a charming letter from Marcinowski, in which he declares himself to be our staunch supporter and comrade in struggle. He tells me that three further papers are being published in various places. He is trying to make contact with our group and is asking for addresses. His is: Sanatorium Haus *Sielbeck a. Uklei*, Holstein. I believe he is a worthwhile acquisition, an able man. I haven't received his paper yet.

I haven't seen anything either about the *Jahrbuch* as a whole. Our Ferenczi has written a review for a Vienna paper.[3] The first blast against Little Hans has finally appeared in today's *Neurologisches Zentralblatt*. The reviewer is Braatz;[4] he provides such a beautiful example of affective imbecility that one is tempted to forgive him for everything. Right next to it there is a review of Fräulein Chalewsky's[5] little paper by Kurt Mendel[6] in person—unforgivably

---

[2] English in original.

[3] Not traced; perhaps not published.

[4] Emil Braatz (1865?–1934), Berlin psychiatrist, in *Neurologisches Zentralblatt*, XXVIII (7 June 09), 585. Braatz also criticized Jung's Amsterdam lecture in the review. For his attack on Abraham in Nov. 08, see 114 F.

[5] Fanny Chalewsky, "Heilung eines hysterischen Bellens durch Psychoanalyse," *Zentralblatt für Nervenheilkunde und Psychiatrie*, n.s., XX (1909). Chalewsky, from Rostov on the Don (Russia), had earned her M.D. at Zürich in 1907.

[6] Kurt Mendel (1874–19—), Berlin psychiatrist, editor of the *Neurologisches Zentralblatt*. See Jung, "On the Criticism of Psychoanalysis," CW 4 (orig. *Jahr-*

impudent. Today I also chanced to receive the new *Lehrbuch der Nervenkrankheiten* (Curschmann).[7] Aschaffenburg does the neuroses. There is none of his usual acrimony, but of course it is dismal, empty, etc.

An eventful day, as you can see. The story about the "glass rear end" appeared in the *Zukunft*,[8] I don't remember when. The context of your letter shows you haven't forgotten the meaning.

With a confident hand-shake and kind regards,

Sincerely yours, FREUD

146 J

Im Feld, Küsnach bei Zürich,

Dear Professor Freud, 12 June 1909

Many thanks for your letter. I had to tell myself that if a friend or colleague of mine had been in the same difficult situation I would have written in the same vein. I had to tell myself this because my father-complex kept on insinuating that you would not take it as you did but would give me a dressing-down more or less disguised in the mantle of brotherly love. For actually it is too stupid that I of all people, your "son and heir," should squander your heritage so heedlessly, as though I had known nothing of all these things. What you say about intellectual overvaluation is right on every point, and to cap it I still have the absurd idea of some kind of moral obligation. All that is too stupid, but useful (last word in bold type and letter-spaced).

Not a word from Adler. From Frl. E——, who has started coming for treatment again, I heard that he is moving away from you and going off on his own, in the opposite direction to you, even.[1] Is there any truth in it?

---

buch, II:2, 1910): in a discussion of professional antagonism to psychoanalysis he reprinted entirely a review by Mendel satirically attacking the Freudian standpoint, in his *Zentralblatt*, XXIX:6 (1910).

[7] Hans Curschmann (1875–1950), with F. Kramer, *Lehrbuch der Nervenkrankheiten* (1909).

[8] See 143 F n. 2.

---

[1] At the Vienna Society's meeting of 2 June 09, Adler's paper on "The Oneness of the Neuroses" was severely criticized by Freud and others, and "the latent discords with Adler became manifest for the first time" (*Minutes*, II, p. 274, n. 5).

I had a letter today from Marcinowski (in answer to my request for a contribution to the *Jahrbuch*). I don't really know, but I have mixed feelings about this letter (enclosed).

Isn't it splendid about America?[2] I have already booked a cabin on the G. *Washington*—unfortunately only a very expensive one was left. I shall sail with you from Bremen. Now I am in for it—what am I to say? What *can* one say of all this in 3 lectures? I'd be grateful for advice.

Curschmann's *Lehrbuch* has just arrived. Aschaffenburg's bit on hysteria is a beggarly scribble. A couple of pages on hysteria! So that's all these people can say about *the* illness compared with which all other nervous ailments are rarities. Foerster has published a book on sexual ethics[3] where you are conjured up as a ghoulish caricature, a "theoretician with no sound sense of reality." Really, it's high time you compiled an alphabetical collection of your *epitheta ornantia*.[4]

Seif was with me for about 3 weeks in Zürich and derived much profit from it, hence his ability. He is coming again in the summer holidays.

Today my children have moved into the new house. Everything is going well, including my practice, which makes me very happy. Frl. E—— is a gorgeous case. Did she tell you about her experiences with doctors? She seems to be dangerous. (Here I tweak myself severely by the ear.)

With many kind regards,

Yours, JUNG

[2] Jung evidently had sent Freud the news of his invitation to Clark University, but the telegram or letter is missing. On 13 June, Freud wrote Pfister, "You too must have been impressed by the great news that Jung is coming with me to Worcester" (*Freud/Pfister Letters*, p. 25). In *Memories*, Jung says that he and Freud were invited "simultaneously and independently" (p. 120/121). It has not, however, been possible to document Hall's invitation to Jung. Ross, in G. *Stanley Hall: The Psychologist as Prophet*, indicates that Hall's papers contain "no firm evidence of when Jung was invited" (p. 387, n. 13)

[3] *Sexualethik und Sexualpädagogik* (Munich, 1907).

[4] Decorative epithets, as in Homer.

147 F

Dear friend,   18 June 1909, Vienna, IX. Berggasse 19

Your being invited to America is the best thing that has happened to us since Salzburg; it gives me enormous pleasure for the most selfish reasons, though also, to be sure, because it shows what prestige you have already gained at your age. Such a beginning will take you far, and a certain amount of favour on the part of men and fate is a very good thing for one who aspires to perform great deeds.

Of course your joy is now beginning to be clouded by the same concerns as mine, culminating in the question: What am I to say to those people? On this score I have a saving idea, which I shall not keep secret from you. Here it is: we can think about it on shipboard, on our long walks round the deck. Otherwise I can only refer you to the astute observation with which you yourself recently allayed *my* misgivings: that the invitation is the main thing, that the audience is now at our mercy, under obligation to applaud whatever we bring them.

A most gratifying detail is that you too are sailing on the G. *Washington*. We shall both be very nice to Ferenczi.

About Marcinowski I can set your mind at rest. He is a good, sincere man, his letters to me (which I may also enclose) are not lacking in warmth. If parts of his letter to you sound wooden, I think it is because the letter was dictated; his other communications give off a fine metallic ring. Perhaps he is a bit of a loner, which is explained by his difficult beginnings. In the matter he raises I don't disagree with him; long analyses like that of Little Hans or of Binswanger's Irma[1] can easily become boring and lead the reader to resist their impact by not reading them. Essentially, after all, the *Jahrbuch* is not only by us but also *for* us, for our mutual edification. Short papers dispersed meander-like among all manner of publications in many different places can really exert a good deal of influence on outsiders. I am sure M. will not decline to contribute to the *Jahrbuch* when he has something new or more general to say.

Fräulein Spielrein has admitted in her second letter that her business has to do with you; apart from that, she has not disclosed her intentions. My reply was ever so wise and penetrating; I made it appear as though the most tenuous of clues had enabled me Sher-

---

[1] The subject of "Versuch einer Hysterieanalyse"; see below, 167 F n. 2.

lock Holmes-like to guess the situation (which of course was none too difficult after your communications) and suggested a more appropriate procedure, something endopsychic, as it were. Whether it will be effective, I don't know. But now I must entreat you, don't go too far in the direction of contrition and reaction. Remember Lassalle's fine sentence about the chemist whose test tube had cracked: "With a slight frown over the resistance of matter, he gets on with his work."[2] In view of the kind of matter we work with, it will never be possible to avoid little laboratory explosions. Maybe we didn't slant the test tube enough, or we heated it too quickly. In this way we learn what part of the danger lies in the matter and what part in our way of handling it.

I shall be working full-time for another week, then up to July 15th only half-time, during which period I shall complete the "Obsessional Neurosis."[3] Just remind me now and then not to let it get too unwieldy. My wife is still in Hamburg with Sophie,[4] detained by Grandmother's[5] illness, but is expected back next week. My second son[6] is taking his final examinations quite painlessly.

What brings Fräulein E—— to the subject of Adler? He has never heard of her. Yes, I believe there is truth in the story. He is a theorist, astute and original, but not attuned to psychology; he passes it by and concentrates on the biological aspect. A decent sort, though; he won't desert in the immediate future, but neither will he participate as we should like him to. We must hold him as long as possible.

I am enclosing the letter from M. You can have the other documents mentioned (Fräulein Sp. and Dr. M.) whenever you like; I just didn't want to bother you with these things unless you asked.

With kind regards to you and the lady of the new house.

Cordially yours, FREUD

[2] Ferdinand Lassalle (1825–1864), German Socialist. The quotation is from his plea in his own defense ("Science and the Worker") before the Criminal Court, Berlin, 16 Jan. 1863: Reden und Schriften, ed. E. Bernstein, Vol. II (Berlin, 1893), pp. 110f. Freud used the quotation, as a "remarkably fine" example of an analogy which "I am never tired of admiring and the effect of which I have not grown out of," in Jokes and Their Relation to the Unconscious (1905), SE VIII, p. 82. / This passage of Freud's letter is quoted by Jones, II, p. 492/442f.
[3] The "Rat Man" case; see below, 150 F n. 1.
[4] Freud's second daughter (1893–1920), later married to Max Halberstadt (see below, 329 F n. 7).
[5] Emmeline Bernays, née Philipp (1830–1910).
[6] Oliver Freud (1891–1969).

148 J

Im Feld, Küsnach bei Zürich,

Dear Professor Freud,   21 June 1909

I have good news to report of my Spielrein affair. I took too black a view of things. After breaking with her I was almost certain of her revenge and was deeply disappointed only by the banality of the form it took. The day before yesterday she turned up at my house and had a *very decent* talk with me, during which it transpired that the rumour buzzing about me does not emanate from her at all. My ideas of reference, understandable enough in the circumstances, attributed the rumour to her, but I wish to retract this forthwith. Furthermore, she has freed herself from the transference in the best and nicest way and has suffered no relapse (apart from a paroxysm of weeping after the separation). Her intention to come to you was not aimed at any intrigue but only at paving the way for a talk with me. Now, after your second letter, she has come to me in person. Although not succumbing to helpless remorse, I nevertheless deplore the sins I have committed, for I am largely to blame for the high-flying hopes of my former patient. So, in accordance with my original principle of taking everyone seriously to the uttermost limit, I discussed with her the problem of the child,[1] imagining that I was talking theoretically, but naturally Eros was lurking in the background. Thus I imputed all the other wishes and hopes entirely to my patient without seeing the same thing in myself. When the situation had become so tense that the continued perseveration of the relationship could be rounded out only by sexual acts, I defended myself in a manner that cannot be justified morally. Caught in my delusion that I was the victim of the sexual wiles of my patient, I wrote to her mother that I was not the gratifier of her daughter's sexual desires but merely her doctor, and that she should free me from her. In view of the fact that the patient had shortly before been my friend and enjoyed my full confidence, my action was a piece of knavery which I very reluctantly confess to you as my father. I would now like to ask you a great favour: would you please write a note to Frl. Spielrein, telling her that I have fully informed you of the matter, and especially of the letter to her parents, which is what I regret most. I would like to give my patient at least this satisfaction: that you and she know of my "perfect honesty."[2] I ask your pardon

---

[1] See above, 133 J par. 1; also 35 J par. 2.
[2] English in original.

many times, for it was my stupidity that drew you into this imbroglio. But now I am extremely glad that I was not mistaken, after all, about the character of my patient, otherwise I should have been left with a gnawing doubt as to the soundness of my judgment, and this would have been a considerable hindrance to me in my work.

I am looking forward very much to America. I have booked a passage on the G. *Washington*, a very expensive cabin, however. You have set my mind at rest about Marcinowski, I need no further documents.

You will have received a letter from the *studiosus* Honegger[3] which will surely amuse you. The young man is very intelligent and subtle-minded; wants to take up psychiatry, once consulted me because of loss of reality-sense lasting a few days. (Psychasthenia = libido introversion = Dem. praec.) Indirectly, I am nudging him towards analysis so that he can analyse himself *consciously*; in that way he may perhaps forestall the automatic self-disintegration of Dem. pr.

Your letter has just arrived—many thanks! Reality has already consoled me. All the same I am grateful for your sympathetic interest.

I look forward to your paper for the *Jahrbuch*. Adler has been kind enough to hold out hopes of something.[4]

Frl. E—— is carrying on bravely; it's interesting. She knows an unnamed female patient of Adler's.

Best regards,

Gratefully yours, J U N G

[3] Johann Jakob Honegger, Jr. (1885–1911), psychiatrist of Zürich, worked at Burghölzli and at Territet. His father, also a psychiatrist, was Adolf Meyer's teacher. The present correspondence is a principal source of information about Honegger; the other chief source is Hans H. Walser, "J. J. Honegger (1885–1911) —ein Beitrag zur Geschichte der Psychoanalyse," *Schweizer Archiv für Neurologie*, CXII (1973), 107ff. = "An Early Psychoanalytic Tragedy: J. J. Honegger and the Beginnings of Training Analysis," *Spring* 1974 (Zürich). / When Freud says in a letter to Pfister, "Honegger has fathomed me well," he apparently means this letter from Honegger (*Freud/Pfister Letters*, 12 July 09); see also 177 F, below. The Honegger letter has not been recovered.

[4] "Über neurotische Dispositionen," *Jahrbuch*, I:2 (1909).

149 F

Dear friend,   30 June 1909, Vienna, IX. Berggasse 19

It is high time I wrote you again. Yours would have reconciled me to greater misdeeds on your part; perhaps I am already too biased in your favour. Immediately after receiving your letter I wrote Fräulein Sp. a few amiable lines, giving her satisfaction, and today received an answer from her. Amazingly awkward—is she a foreigner by any chance?—or very inhibited, hard to read and hard to understand. All I can gather from it is that the matter means a great deal to her and that she is very much in earnest. Don't find fault with yourself for drawing me into it; it was not your doing but hers. And the matter has ended in a manner satisfactory to all. You have been oscillating, as I see, between the extremes of Bleuler and Gross. When I think that I owe your ultimate conversion and profound conviction to the same experience with Gross, I cannot possibly be angry and can only marvel at the profound coherence of all things in this world.

Now to myself. My energy is pretty well exhausted, except for one undertaking. In a fortnight I shall be going to Munich and from there to Ammerwald (address follows). This one undertaking is my paper about the Rat Man. I am finding it very difficult; it is almost beyond my powers of presentation; the paper will probably be intelligible to no one outside our immediate circle. How bungled our reproductions are, how wretchedly we dissect the great art works of psychic nature! Unfortunately this paper in turn is becoming too bulky. It just pours out of me, and even so it's inadequate, incomplete and therefore untrue. A wretched business. I am determined to finish it before leaving and to do nothing more before setting sail for our America. I'm too tired this year.

Oh yes, I mustn't forget to announce the arrival of Dr. Karpas[1] and to recommend him to you, he's a *good boy*,[2] a student of Brill. He wants to go to Zürich in mid-July and stay a few months. He has attended a number of our Wednesdays[3] with interest. An outsider has given me a short but very significant piece about dreams to sub-

[1] Morris J. Karpas (1879–1918), a charter member of the New York Psychoanalytic Society.
[2] English in original.
[3] 7 Apr.–2 June 1909 (*Minutes*, II).

mit to you for the *Jahrbuch*. If you have no space left, keep it for the next number.

I am too deep in my rats.

With kind regards to you and yours,

Sincerely yours, FREUD

150 F

Dear friend, 7 July 1909, Vienna, IX. Berggasse 19

I am enclosing the manuscript of the Rat Man[1] and H. Silberer's short piece on the observation of dream-work,[2] both for your editorial consideration. Mine was hard going and hasn't turned out to my satisfaction. I feel like prefacing it with Busch's fine verses about the painter Klecksel's childhood drawing:

> "It gives us an uncommon view
> Of what our inner natures do."[3]

But that's enough. You'll read it.

It's high time for this season to end. My psychic unpleasure in working has become really acute, I can't wait for the all-too-short holiday. On the evening of the 14th we shall be going via Munich to Ammerwald, Post Reutte, Tyrol. Of course letters to my Vienna address will always reach me. In the meantime a consultation trip may come through, to—Salonica. But I have asked for so much money for the five days that the need for me will probably vanish. It's not even a case for ΨA.

Marcinowski tells me that Simon[4] in London has sent him a case to analyse. Upon our return M. wants to meet in Hamburg, where I

[1] "Bemerkungen über einen Fall von Zwangsneurose," *Jahrbuch*, I:2 (1909) = "Notes upon a Case of Obsessional Neurosis," SE X.
[2] Herbert Silberer (1882–1922), Viennese psychoanalyst, writer on alchemical symbolism. He committed suicide. The reference is to his "Bericht über eine Methode, gewisse symbolische Halluzionations-Erscheinungen hervorzurufen und zu beobachten," *Jahrbuch*, I:2 (1909). / More than 40 years later, Jung wrote: "Silberer has the merit of being the first to discover the secret threads that lead from alchemy to the psychology of the unconscious" (CW 14, par. 792).
[3] Holograph: *So blickt man klar, wie selten nur / Ins innre Walten der Natur.* From Wilhelm Busch's "Maler Klecksel" (1884).
[4] Not identified.

shall have to stay for a while in any case because of my aged mother-in-law. I am purposely not thinking very much about America and our trip. I want every pleasant experience to come as a surprise, I am determined not to spoil my enjoyment by hypercathected anticipation and to take all disappointments lightly. Do likewise, don't let the thought of your lectures weigh too heavily on you. Have you any idea who else has been invited?

Recently a Mr. McCormick[5] identified himself as a patient of yours and asked for an appointment with me. I gave him one but he didn't show up.

My second son has his final examination behind him and has gone off on his first trip alone. The eldest[6] has got his face chopped up in a student duel and been very brave about the whole thing. Little by little the young people are becoming independent and all of a sudden I have become *the old man*.[7]

With kind regards to you and your wife,

Sincerely yours, FREUD

P.S. The manuscripts will be sent in two days under separate cover.

151 J

Im Feld, Küsnach bei Zürich,

Dear Professor Freud, 10 July/13 July 1909[1]

I owe you an answer to two letters. First of all I want to thank you very much for your kind help in the Spielrein matter, which has now settled itself so satisfactorily. Once again I took too black a view. Frl. S. is a Russian, hence her awkwardness.

Meanwhile the manuscripts have arrived; I am reading them with great interest. Who is Silberer? I understand perfectly your impressions of your own paper. This is something that also holds me back

---

[5] Harold Fowler McCormick (1872–1941), Chicago industrialist and philanthropist; subsequently, a generous patron of analytical psychology.

[6] Jean Martin Freud (1889–1967), later in London. See his memoir *Sigmund Freud: Man and Father* (1958).

[7] English in original.

---

[1] Jung dated the letter 10.VII and above that wrote 13.VII, apparently when, after an interruption, he continued the letter with the second paragraph.

from presenting my cases. We just cannot do things as beautifully and as truly as Nature does. I am about to finish the analysis of Agathli and shall then start immediately on the American lectures. I really don't know what to say. I shall start nibbling away at some corner just to see what happens. I have a vague idea of speaking first on the family constellation, second on the diagnostic significance of associations, and third on the educational questions raised by psychanalysis. Naturally I am not a little bothered by the fact that you will be present and know all this far better than I do. I shall go through with it all the same. Once the essentials are down on paper it won't worry me in the least, and I shall be able to give my whole attention to the impressions of the voyage. The one snag is that my former patient McCormick has booked a passage on the same boat together with his wife.[2] He wanted to call on you in Vienna, where he was caught with a passing relapse, but was intercepted by his wife, who started making his resistances clear to him, which exhausted him so much that he evidently gave up the visit. A few days later he left for Karlsbad. He is an interesting man, but it was without my knowledge that he staged the journey to Vienna.

Again I have a great deal to do, 6 patients, 2 forensic reports, and now come the *Jahrbuch* and the American lectures. The birds of passage are also moving in, i.e., the people who visit one. Among them is a very pleasant and perhaps valuable acquaintance, our first Italian, a Dr. Assagioli[3] from the psychiatric clinic in Florence. Prof. Tanzi[4] assigned him our work for a dissertation. The young man is *very* intelligent, seems to be extremely knowledgeable and is an enthusiastic follower, who is entering the new territory with the proper *brio*. He wants to visit you next spring. My Englishman has left; he is to lecture in Edinburgh at the Medical Association on the novelties that go

[2] Edith Rockefeller McCormick (1872–1932), patron of analytical psychology and of musicians and writers; in particular, see Richard Ellmann, *James Joyce* (1959), pp. 135, 180–83.

[3] Roberto Assagioli (1888–), whose doctoral dissertation, "La Psicosintesi," was accepted at the University of Florence in 1910 and published partially in a journal he founded, *Psiche: Rivista di Studi Psicologici*, I:2 (1912). Later withdrew from the psychoanalytical movement and evolved his own system, now fostered by the Psychosynthesis Research Foundation (Florence and New York), which he heads. Cf. his *Psychosynthesis: A Manual of Principles and Techniques* (New York, 1965).

[4] Eugenio Tanzi (1856–1934), psychiatrist of Reggio d'Emilia and Florence; author with Ernesto Lugaro of a textbook on mental hygiene.

forth from you.[5] His understanding wasn't too good. A most stupid person from Coimbra has been with me, also a professor of psychology.[6]

All's well with my family.

With kindest regards,

Most sincerely yours, JUNG

152 F

Dear friend,   19 July 1909, Ammerwald[1]

I haven't thanked you yet for the surprising gift of your article on the interpretation of dreams,[2] which I took with me in my briefcase. Here I am not planning to do a thing, not even to think of America; I am too tired. Yesterday, after dragging my weary bones to a mountain slope, where nature achieves such a magnificent effect with the simplest props, white rock, red fields of Alpine roses, a patch of snow, a waterfall, and lots of green, I hardly knew myself. You could have diagnosed Dem. pr. Unfortunately the house, which is otherwise splendid, is situated in a wooded gully and there is no view, something I miss very much. The first overcast days were quite a trial. Now the weather is perfect, but we are not planning to stay beyond August 1st.

Otherwise I have little to report that would bear comparison with your interesting news. Silberer is an unknown young man, probably a better-class degenerate; his father is a well-known figure in Vienna, a member of the city council and an "operator." But his piece is good and throws light on an aspect of dream work. A few days ago I received a bittersweet letter from Morton Prince thanking me for something I had sent him; I must be aware (he says) that he does not agree with me on all points, the problem of neuroses admits of many sorts (!) of solution, he favours different ones; he regrets that he has already booked[3] passage to Genoa (or Geneva?), so that he will miss me on

[5] See above, 140 J n. 3.
[6] Not identified.

---

[1] For an account of the family's summer at this resort on the Austro-Bavarian frontier, see Martin Freud, *Sigmund Freud: Man and Father*, chs. XVIII–XIX.
[2] "L'Analyse des rêves," *L'Année psychologique*, XV (1909) = "The Analysis of Dreams," CW 4. Jung had first mentioned it in 111 J (21 Oct. 08).
[3] Holograph: *gebookt*.

both continents, etc. I shall be just as glad not to see him. — I have just written to a colleague in Prussia, a Dr. Hundertmark[4]—isn't that a beautiful name, even if it is rather too rich in associations?—in answer to his request for a list of books that might help him to eat his way into the promised land of ΨA. I wonder if his stomach will bear up. Against McCormick we will both defend you; I can be very ghoulish when I want to be. Your lectures will be quite new to me, the material is known to me only from a very superficial reading of your "Diagnostic Association Studies" and I will listen very attentively. Then, when my turn comes, I shall comfort myself with the thought that at least you and Ferenczi will be listening.

Here on the northwestern frontier of the Empire I am much nearer to you than in Vienna. Kind regards to you and your charming wife and also to the little heroine Agathli.

Sincerely yours, FREUD

153 J

Im Feld, Küsnach bei Zürich,
Dear Professor Freud,   5 August 1909

I have just spent a week in Munich, where I enticed away a follower of Kraepelin and gorged myself on art. Now I am sitting at home before a mountain of work. I know you are having a pleasant holiday rest and won't want to be disturbed, so I will plague you with only one small question: I have a pupil, a Polish Jewess, Frl. Dr. Gincburg,[1] who is really clever and has a very nice way with her in analysing children. She assisted me most efficiently at the outpatients' clinic all through the summer term. Now she is looking for work of the same kind. I remembered that you often find yourself in the position of having to recommend a suitable person for children. Might something be arranged with Frl. G.? I'm afraid I know of nothing for her. She wouldn't be too demanding.

I hope to have finished my American lectures by August 11th. Then I shall go on a 5-day excursion with my sail-boat. I leave here on the

---

[4] Not identified.

---

[1] Mira Gincburg (1887–1949), from Lodz, was medically trained in Zürich, practiced in Schaffhausen; early member of Zürich Society. She married Emil Oberholzer (see below, 319 F n. 2), and both emigrated to New York in 1938. She was one of the first psychoanalysts to treat children.

18th, stay one day in Basel with old friends, visit Häberlin (whose course of lectures I hear is turning out very well).

Agathli is still guessing:[2] she dreamt of a row of men urinating, among them Papa. To greet me on my return from Munich she stuck a stick between her legs. Asked Mama if her (A.'s) genitals should not be "planed off." She had seen the carpenter planing drawers that didn't fit. I remember a Dem. praec. delusion of the genitals being dressed and "stretched" for Pastor X. Altogether, Dem. praec. is one colossal titivation of the genitals.

With kind regards and *auf Wiedersehen,*

Yours sincerely, JUNG

154 F

Dear friend,   Ammerwald, 9 August 1909

I am writing this in the hope of catching you before you start on your complicated trip, so as to acquaint you with the final arrangements. I am leaving Munich at 4:25 on the 19th and arriving in Bremen at 5:35 on the morning of the 20th. Ferenczi is to arrive the same morning, we must still arrange when to meet. Of course we shall leave our addresses at the office of the North German Lloyd so as to find you the moment you arrive. You might also drop me a card there, indicating your time of arrival.

In Munich you were very close to us, theoretically at least. Two and one-half hours by train to Oberammergau and then again as long by carriage. But you were definitely right not to stop over, since we shall soon have so many days together.

I shall think of Fräulein Gincburg as soon as I get back to work. Last semester I was in urgent need of such an assistant. At the moment of course I have nothing.* I have had a thorough rest, interrupted only by an occasional call from the workaday world. At Eitingon's suggestion a Russian in Geneva has written asking me for permission to translate *Everyday Life*;[2] yesterday received a telegram

* My table in the woods is wobbly.[1]

[2] Cf. "Psychic Conflicts in a Child," CW 17, pars. 65–66.

[1] Irregular writing above.

[2] A Russian translation by "Medem" appeared in 1910, according to Grinstein.

from Bazhenov[3] in Moscow, announcing that a certain lady, seriously ill, is coming to me for analysis. I have heard from various sources that Oppenheim[4] is preaching a crusade against us; Jones writes from Geneva that he has met a number of supporters we hadn't known of at the Congress there.[5] He invites both of us to Toronto; he is arriving in New York on September 4th and will go to Worcester with us, etc.

Agathli is very interesting; one must be endlessly tolerant; they are entitled to more understanding. The carpenter reminds me very much of Little Hans's plumber. In the course of an interesting excursion into archaeology I have conceived some ideas about the nature of symbolism, but they are not yet clear enough. I have not yet made any preparations for America, I am incapable of such things.

I too give you a joyful *Auf Wiedersehen* and send your wife and children my kind regards.

Sincerely yours, FREUD

The Clark Conference

Freud met Jung and Ferenczi on 20 August at Bremen (see below, 329 F par. 2), and the following day, the three sailed on the North German Lloyd ship *George Washington*. During the voyage, they analysed one another's dreams, and Jung has recounted one of his own dreams (*Memories*, pp. 158ff.), which foreshadowed his concept of the collective unconscious.

They arrived in New York on Sunday evening, 29 August, and were joined by Brill and later by Jones. The week was given to sightseeing and entertainment, and on Saturday evening, 4 September, the party departed by steamer for an overnight voyage to Fall River, Massachusetts, then by train via Boston to Worcester, the site of Clark University.

Freud and Jung were guests in Stanley Hall's home. Freud gave five lectures, at 11 o'clock each morning, Tuesday through Saturday; Jung gave three during the week; both spoke in German. The participants in the

---

[3] Nikolay Nikolayevich Bazhenov (1857–1923), or Bagenov, then chief of the Preobrazhenskoye Psychiatric Hospital, Moscow. Later, a leader in reform of psychiatric institutions.

[4] Oppenheim had recently published a paper, "Zur Psychopathologie der Angstzustände," *Berliner klinische Wochenschrift*, XLVI (12 July 09), in which he supported an attack on psychoanalysis by Dubois and called for a "war" against it. See Jones, II, p. 128/114.

[5] Sixth International Congress of Psychology, 2-7 Aug., under the chairmanship of Claparède.

conference included William Stern, of Munich (see below, 208 F n. 3), and Leo Burgerstein, of Vienna; from the United States, William James, Adolf Meyer, Franz Boas, E. B. Titchener, and in particular James Jackson Putnam (see below, 166 F n. 4). At the closing ceremony, on Saturday, 11 September, honorary doctorates of law were conferred on Freud (in psychology) and on Jung (in education and social hygiene). See plate V.

During the following two days, Freud, Jung, and Ferenczi travelled extensively: west to Niagara Falls and back east to Keene, New York, in the Adirondack Mountains near Lake Placid, where they spent four days at the Putnam family camp.[1] During the weekend, they returned to New York, whence they embarked on Tuesday morning, the 21st, aboard the *Kaiser Wilhelm der Grosse*. They arrived in Bremen on 29 September; Jung went home to Küsnacht, and Freud stopped in Hamburg and Berlin (for his visit to a medium with Ferenczi, see below, 158 F n. 8) before arriving home in Vienna on the morning of Saturday, 2 October.

(The full story of the American episode is to be found in Jones, II, pp. 59ff./53ff.; in Jung's *Memories*, pp. 120/121, 156/152, 158, and in particular his letters to his wife from America (ibid., Appendix II), as well as his reminiscences written to V. Payne, 23 July 1949, in *Letters*, ed. G. Adler, vol. 1; and in Ross, G. *Stanley Hall: The Psychologist as Prophet*, pp. 383–94, which draws upon Hall's papers, interviews, and contemporary newspapers. See also Freud, "On the History of the Psychoanalytic Movement," SE XIV, pp. 30–31, and Hale, *Freud and the Americans*, ch. I.)

Freud's lectures, entitled *Über Psychoanalyse* and dedicated to Hall, were published by Deuticke in 1910, and in the same year, translated by H. W. Chase as "The Origin and Development of Psychoanalysis," in the *American Journal of Psychology*, XXI:2, 3, and (reprint) in *Lectures and Addresses Delivered before the Departments of Psychology and Pedagogy in Celebration of the Twentieth Anniversary of the Opening of Clark University* (Worcester), Part I. Now entitled "Five Lectures on Psychoanalysis," in SE XI.

Jung's lectures, entitled "The Association Method," appeared in the same American publications in the translation of A. A. Brill. Only the third lecture was published in German: "Über Konflikte der kindlichen Seele," *Jahrbuch*, II (1910) = "Psychic Conflicts in a Child," CW 17. The first two lectures are in CW 2.

---

[1] For a vivid account of the camp and the psychoanalysts' visit, as recalled by members of the Putnam family circle, see George E. Gifford, Jr., "Freud and the Porcupine," *Harvard Medical Alumni Bulletin*, 46:4 (Mar.–Apr. 1972); cf. below, 177 F n. 3.

At Clark University, September 1909. Front row: Freud, Hall, Jung; back row: Brill, Jones, Ferenczi

Most of the participants in the Clark Conference. Front row:
Franz Boas, E. B. Titchener, William James, William Stern, Leo
Burgerstein, Hall, Freud, Jung, Adolf Meyer, H. S. Jennings.
Ferenczi, Jones, and Brill are standing behind Freud

V

155 J

Dear Professor Freud,   Küsnach bei Zürich, 1 October 1909

Here I stand on your doorstep with a letter of welcome to greet you in Vienna on resumption of work. For my part I have got down to it in real earnest. I feel in top form and have become much more reasonable than you might suppose. My wife is bearing up splendidly under the psychoanalysis[1] and everything is going à merveille. On the journey back to Switzerland I never stopped analysing dreams and discovered some priceless jokes. A pity there's no time for this now. How are you? and the stomach? Well, I hope.

I have leafed through Stransky's opus[2] and find it really stupid. A long letter from Forel awaited me, inviting me to participate in an organization of psychotherapists. I do not find the prospect alluring. What to do? I should be glad of your views soon as I haven't yet answered Forel.[3]

No galleys yet of the *Jahrbuch.*

It is amazing how our work is spreading among the primary-school teachers here. A young teacher was with me today, asking for advice; for months he has been treating his severely hysterical wife with good results and extraordinary understanding; he is also treating one of his pupils who suffers from a phobia. The scalpel is being cold-bloodedly wrested out of the doctors' hands. What do you say to this? The young man also tells me that in Zürich people have started calling me names, particularly colleagues. Understandable, because now their reputation is at stake. One must let the forest fire rage, there's no stopping it now. In Zürich a Dr. *Bircher*[4] (please note the name!) has

---

[1] Here Jung began regularly using the spelling *Psychoanalyse* instead of *Psychanalyse.*

[2] Erwin Stransky (1877–1962), Vienna neurologist. The work mentioned was probably *Über die Dementia Praecox* (Wiesbaden, 1909).

[3] But see Jung to Forel, 12 Oct. 09, in *Letters*, ed. G. Adler, vol. 1: "I sympathize with your project for the coalition of all psychotherapists, but, given the present irreconcilability of opposites, I doubt very much whether we of the Freudian school would be welcome guests." Forel, with Oskar Vogt, Ludwig Frank, and others, had founded the International Society for Medical Psychology and Psychotherapy at Salzburg 19–25 Sept. 09. The first president was Professor Fulgence Raymond, of the Salpetrière, Paris. (Forel, *Out of My Life and Work*, tr. B. Miall, 1937, p. 271.)

[4] M. O. Bircher-Benner (1867–1939), Zürich physician who specialized in dietetics and physiotherapy at a clinic founded in 1897. He popularized a healthful dish called *Birchermüsli*, a mixture of cereal, fruit, and milk.

set up as a psychoanalyst. Formerly he believed in uric acid and apple-sauce and porridge. Naturally he hasn't a clue. He is very much to be warned against, especially as he is much in vogue and assiduously avoids personal relations with me.

All's well with my family, and I hope with yours too. Most cordial regards,

Yours, JUNG

156 F

Dear friend,   4 October 1909, Vienna, IX. Berggasse 19

First many thanks for your letter. Then a few addenda to the wonders of our trip. The day after we separated an incredible number of people looked amazingly like you; wherever I went in Hamburg, your light hat with the dark band kept turning up. And the same in Berlin. Our friend Ferenczi made a strange admission to me, but only after our return. He took the key to his room at the Manhattan Hotel[1] along with him! This means, of course, that he has taken possession of the *(Frauen)zimmer*[2] so as to keep everyone away until his return. With this as a basis we could do a nice bit of analysis. He too has developed the transposition of fantasies we spoke about. Many of the ideas that he communicated to you and me really relate to his woman-complex. (My wretched fountain-pen is on strike today!)[3]

I arrived here Saturday morning and found all well, except for—my old mother[4] and my two elder daughters. Mathilde is probably in for another operation. She is very brave and sensible, our son-in-law less so. So I am suddenly thrust back into life with all its surprises.

Other events have quickly followed. Hoche seems to have done a good deed by calling off his lecture, because my Vienna brood had banded together in indignation or fear and were hatching out all sorts of plans for a counter-offensive. My foreseeable anger over such poor tactics does not seem to have deterred them in the least. Saturday and Sunday were still relatively peaceful, today the turmoil has begun, and very soon I shall be busy eight or nine hours a day. How I am going to work on my many, absolutely necessary scientific projects, God only

---

[1] In New York City, at 42nd Street and Madison Avenue; no longer standing.
[2] *Zimmer* = room; *Frauenzimmer* = woman (contemptuously).
[3] It was skipping.
[4] Amalie Freud née Nathansohn (1835–1930).

knows. Luckily I managed to restore poor Konrad's[5] digestion by going easy on it in Hamburg and Berlin.

In regard to my stay in Berlin I must also report that Abraham was extremely pleasant and affectionate and not at all paranoid; I was almost ashamed in front of Ferenczi at having turned against him recently. He even put up with my praise of you, from which I could not refrain. He is working on hostile ground and is carrying on very bravely. At the end he took the train with me as far as Frankenberg, an hour and a half's journey. What he tells me about the ignorance of the Berlin moguls, Oppenheim, for instance, is a great comfort. After difficult beginnings his practice is looking up, and this has undoubtedly had a good effect on him.

On my arrival I found a letter from Pfister, which affected me as his letters always do.[6] At first I believe everything, I tend to be credulous about good news—everything looks wonderful. Then after a while I relapse into my usual wretched state. All the same, I do hope he gives Foerster a good dressing down.[7]

I also found Forel's circular waiting for me. I have written explaining that our absence on such and such dates had prevented us from answering on time. I am glad to say that we have avoided the worst, because the meeting has now taken place in our absence. If Forel asks us to join later on, I too should prefer to decline, but I shall first reply that I must consult with you and Bleuler.

I am sure you will approve of what I did yesterday (Sunday). I corrected the Rat Man. I still didn't like it. Let me know as soon as you have seen it if you get a different impression. I am annoyed that you and Adler, and others no doubt as well, should still have no proofs. Our one answer to the periodically recurring abuse must be: a new volume of our *Jahrbuch*.

They must really be cursing you in Switzerland. On my return I found no less than five letters from your country—which is so important to us despite its small size—either announcing the arrival of patients or asking for information and advice. On the first day I wrote no less than 11 letters to foreign parties. In the end this will get to be monotonous and *a nuisance*.[8] But as you say, you can't stop a forest

---

[5] In Carl Spitteler's novel *Imago* (1906), the hero referred to his body as "Konrad" "because he was on such good terms with it." Jung also adopted the usage. See Jones, II, pp. 92/83, 437/391 (though Jones took the term to mean the bowels rather than the entire body); also below, 196 J n. 3 and 212 F.

[6] For Freud's reply, see *Freud/Pfister Letters*, p. 29.

[7] See below, 170 J n. 4.

[8] English in original.

fire. It serves the medical men right. We'll make a note of Dr. Bircher. Fortunately we have no need to copyright psychoanalysis, it is a little too hard to imitate.

Today I changed my dollars into local currency. Now I hope that all the petty unpleasantness will soon go out of our memories of America and that only our surprisingly grand and beautiful impressions will remain. My wife and children thank you kindly for your companionship during the trip, thanks to which I never felt that I was among strangers.

Good luck in your new year's work!

Yours, FREUD

157 J

Dear Professor Freud,   Küsnach bei Zürich, 14 October 1909

Occasionally a spasm of homesickness for you comes over me, but only occasionally; otherwise I am back into my stride. The analysis on the voyage home has done me a lot of good. I have much zest and little opportunity for scientific work, by which I do not mean instructing students. In this respect I am doing far too much at present. What would you think if I planned to organize things in such a way as to exploit the situation financially a bit? I find it quite as necessary to guard myself against so-called normal people as against neurotics (the differences between them are remarkably small). I hold myself justified in this depravity, for these people will draw a fat profit later on while I merely lose time and energy for work.

How goes it with your daughter, or rather, your two daughters? You say you found both your elder daughters ill.

Have you seen the new article by Friedländer?[1] And Siemerling's, I think in the *Archiv*,[2] on the *Jahrbuch*? Imagine, Friedländer was with me yesterday, sweet as sugar and wagging his tail. He would like to be answered *à tout prix*, you were absolutely right. Unless the fellow has taken it into his head to convert me, I simply don't know

---

[1] Adolf Albrecht Friedländer (1870–1949), psychiatrist then at the Hohe Mark Sanatorium, near Frankfurt a. M.; an aggressive critic of psychoanalysis. See also Jones, II, pp. 131f./117. Friedländer's article has not been traced.

[2] *Archiv für Psychiatrie und Nervenkrankheiten*, XLV:3 (July 09), 1251; edited by the German psychiatrist Ernst Siemerling (1857–1931). He wrote a brief unfriendly notice of the *Jahrbuch* and the 2nd edn. of *Studien über Hysterie*.

what his real purpose was in coming. He told me he would be delighted to have more contacts with us so as to learn something from our work. (A damned sight too many patients seem to be demanding psychoanalytical treatment, don't you think?) He must have a mighty big bee in his bonnet that leaves him no peace. From all this I gather that our opponents are inconsolable because of our inviolate silence. He tried to work up my enthusiasm for a public appearance, so naturally I put on an unenthusiastic air. I distrust the fellow, especially as I cannot believe that he has any real scientific interests. He must be pursuing a quite different purpose which is still opaque to me. He wants to come again tomorrow, to sit in at a conference with my students. I almost hope these people will remain our opponents for a long time to come.

I am reading with pleasure Inman's book on symbols.[3] In Reibmayr (*Entwicklungsgeschichte des Genies und Talentes*)[4] I found valuable *statistics* on the sterility of American women. Your Rat Man has filled me with delight, it is written with awesome intelligence and full of the most subtle reality. Most people, though, will be too dumb to understand it in depth. Splendid ingenuities! I regret from the bottom of my heart that I didn't write it. (In the revised proofs there are a number of misprints which presumably won't escape your eye.) As I have frequently observed with my students, it is not so much a matter of resistances due to complexes as of simple intellectual incapacity to understand the logical sequence of psychological facts and the connections between them. Where an intelligent person sees striking connections they see nothing, they are incapable of following logical trains of thought and stand there glumly, ears drooping. It will be just the same with the Rat Man, you'll see, although every sentence is made to measure and fits reality to a T. Sometimes I regret every word I have wasted on these lunkheads. When I have gone through the proofs (they aren't all here yet) I may have a couple of theoretical questions. Have you read the Stekel proofs[5] and gone to work benevolently with the blue pencil? I have only part of them.

I am obsessed by the thought of one day writing a comprehensive account of this whole field, after years of fact-finding and preparation, of course. The net should be cast wide. Archaeology or rather mythol-

---

[3] Thomas Inman, *Ancient Pagan and Modern Christian Symbolism Exposed and Explained* (New York, 2nd edn., 1874).

[4] Albert Reibmayr, *Entwicklingsgeschichte des Talentes und Genies* (Munich, 1908).

[5] "Beiträge zur Traumdeutung," *Jahrbuch*, I:2 (1909).

ogy has got me in its grip, it's a mine of marvellous material. Won't you cast a beam of light in that direction, at least a kind of spectrum analysis *par distance?*

Today I received a letter from Forel in which he writes that the Society is already constituted, with 49 members. If I "wish to join" I should apply to him. Should I? I'm none too keen, we know what's going on there. But maybe you'll see tactical reasons.

Dr. Maeder has got *dis*engaged to Fräulein Dr. Chalewsky.[6] He is to be congratulated. Such marriages, as we know, never work out.

Riklin has achieved a son.[7]

This winter I have to give 6 lectures on mental disturbances in childhood[8] and am working on them right now. After that the American lectures. I haven't got my warlike address[9] down on paper yet.

No crush of patients this autumn. So far I have only 2 thin ones— a pleasant change. Otherwise my time is all taken up.

In my family all is well, thanks to lots of dream analysis and humour. The devil seems to have been beaten at his own game.

With many kind regards,

Yours sincerely, JUNG

New synonym for penis:
"the Great Elector."[10]

158 F

Dear friend,   17 October 1909, Vienna, IX. Berggasse 19

I am glad to find a number of things in your letter that call for an immediate answer. This is Sunday and I am entitled to rest from a hard week's work. Actually I have a great deal to tell you and discuss with you. Let's start with the business matters.

---

[6] See above, 145 F n. 5.

[7] Franz Riklin, M.D., died 1969. He trained at the Burghölzli and became one of the leading exponents of Jungian psychology, serving as the president of the C. G. Jung Institute, Zürich, and co-editor of the Gesammelte Werke—the Swiss edition of Jung's works.

[8] See below, 175 J n. 1.

[9] Presumably for the Swiss psychiatrists' meeting in Nov.; see below, 164 J.

[10] Holograph: *Der grosse Kurfürst.* The epithet by which Friedrich Wilhelm (1620–88), Elector of Brandenburg, is known to history. In the compound word, *Kur* = "election"; otherwise, "cure."

I hope and trust Friedländer hasn't got anything out of you. He is an unsavoury individual, even in his private affairs; he left his country because of some crooked business, he owes his clinic to his marriage to a woman he has since then divorced, and is now operating it for his former father-in-law, etc. All he wanted of us, it seems to me, was a kind of rehabilitation through our hostility. Now he is inconsolable because we have shown by our silence that we regarded him as unfit to duel with, so to speak. Either he has some specially beastly plan in visiting you, or he is stupid as well; can he think that we don't notice the contrast between the sweets he is dispensing and his public statements? In private the fellow deserves to be treated with all possible rudeness, in our literature we must simply ignore him; he is plain riffraff.

What shall we do about Forel? In his brief answer to me he says among other things that I have failed to answer his main question, whether or not I wish to join. I decided to wait for your letter and propose to you that we reply—either you or I can do the actual writing—to the effect that we feel no great need to cooperate as long as certain of his colleagues permit themselves every kind of insolence towards us and others seem silently to agree with them; that, having been absent, we do not know what decisions his Society has made and what obligations membership entails, and finally, that if he wishes to enlighten us on this, we shall see — Still, I know that Forel is a different type from our other opponents; I shall be glad to give in if you favour a milder approach.

Siemerling is just plain incompetent and, to judge by what I hear from Abraham, the same is true of Oppenheim. The best policy, I think, is to ignore them politely.

A few days ago I received from the first Congress of Polish Neurologists a telegram of homage signed, "after violent debate," by seven illegible and unpronounceable Poles. The only one of them known to me is Dr. Jekels; Frau Dr. Karpinska,[1] I hear, has studied with you. I have never heard of the five others; I note the names for your information:

Luniewski — Sycianko — Kempinski — Chodzko — Rychlinski.[2]

---

[1] Luise von Karpinska (1871–1936), psychologist of Zakopane, Poland, attended the 15 Dec. 09 meeting of the Wednesday Society (Minutes, II, p. 353). Published a long article on the psychological basis of Freudianism in the Zeitschrift, II (1914). Later, professor at Lodz University.

[2] Witold Luniewski (1881–1932+), psychiatrist at the Hospital for Mental Diseases, near Warsaw. Details of the others were unavailable. On 12 Oct. Jung

253

A Dr. F—— of Strassburg has asked me to react in writing to his neurosis; I declined in no uncertain terms. You will agree, I trust, that the man is a disgusting snob. — We have been annoyed with *Sexual-Probleme*[3] for some time because of the tone and content of Birnbaum's reviews.[4] I recently wrote to Dr. Marcuse saying that without questioning his right to publish what criticism he chose, I should like my name taken off the list of "regular contributors." Now Dr. Marcuse writes me an imploring letter in which he chooses to call Birnbaum "objective" but declares his willingness to drop this objective critic and replace him by someone of my choosing. Isn't it strange that only "opponents" are regarded as "objective"? Do you think we ought to secure this position for our camp? And if so, have you anyone in mind?

But enough of this small change. Your idea of getting some profit out of your students strikes me as quite justified. Couldn't you announce a course of lectures—call it "An Introduction to the Technique of ΨA"—and let your "guests" enroll at a reasonable fee?[5] It can do no harm to clarify your relations.

You are the first critic of the Rat Man. Because I myself was dissatisfied with it I was waiting anxiously for your opinion. I am overjoyed at your praise. Of course you will notice the obvious shortcomings. It seemed to me that since the emergence of the *Jahrbuch* I could change my mode of presentation. ΨA now has an audience and I am justified in writing for this audience. It is no longer necessary to restate our most elementary assumptions and refute the most primitive objections in every single paper. It is just as absurd for people to expect to understand our papers without the prerequisite training as to pick up a treatise on integral calculus without having gone beyond elementary arithmetic. — Last week the newspapers carried the Rat Man's announcement of his engagement to the "lady"; he is facing

---

also received a telegram from the same seven Poles: "Polish Freudians send from the Congress now in session expressions of highest esteem." (Photostat in the Library of Congress, included in the photostats of Freud letters which the Sigmund Freud Archives obtained from Zürich in the early 1950's; i.e., Jung apparently had placed it in his Freud file.)

[3] See above, 99 F n. 6.

[4] Karl Birnbaum (1878–1950), Berlin psychiatrist and criminologist. In 1908–9 he published reviews of works by Abraham, Jung ("Die Freud'sche Hysterietheorie," IV, 1908), and Strohmayer in *Sexual-Probleme*. After 1939, in Philadelphia, Pennsylvania.

[5] In an unpublished letter to Ferenczi, 4 Nov. 09, Jung wrote: "I am now asking 100 frs. for a 3-week course."

life with courage and ability. The one point that still gives him trouble (father-complex and transference) has shown up clearly in my conversations with this intelligent and grateful man.

I am glad you share my belief that we must conquer the whole field of mythology. Thus far we have only two pioneers: Abraham and Rank. We need men for more far-reaching campaigns. Such men are so rare. We must also take hold of biography. I have had an inspiration since my return. The riddle of Leonardo da Vinci's character has suddenly become clear to me. That would be a first step in the realm of biography. But the material concerning L. is so sparse that I despair of demonstrating my conviction intelligibly to others. I have ordered an Italian work[6] on his youth and am now waiting eagerly for it. In the meantime I will reveal the secret to you. Do you remember my remarks in the "Sexual Theories of Children" (2nd *Short Papers*)[7] to the effect that children's first primitive researches in this sphere were bound to fail and that this first failure could have a paralysing effect on them? Read the passage over; at the time I did not take it as seriously as I do now. Well, the great Leonardo was such a man; at an early age he converted his sexuality into an urge for knowledge and from then on the inability to finish anything he undertook became a pattern to which he had to conform in all his ventures: he was sexually inactive or homosexual. Not so long ago I came across his image and likeness (without his genius) in a neurotic.

Eitingon is now in Vienna and lets me analyse him in the course of evening walks. In collaboration with Ferenczi I am working on a project[8] that you will hear about when it begins to take shape.

My Viennese welcomed me with a social evening that proved very pleasant.[9] Stekel told a funny story about a "beastly non-paying patient" (himself) in whom he observed a strange phobia brought on by

[6] N. Smiraglia Scognamiglio, *Ricerche e Documenti sulla Giovinezza di Leonardo da Vinci* (1452–1482) (Naples, 1900); cited in SE XI, passim.

[7] See above, 118 F n. 1; the paper had been reprinted in the *Sammlung kleiner Schriften zur Neurosenlehre*, II (Feb. 1909). The passage mentioned is on p. 219; also quoted in "Leonardo," SE XI, p. 79.

[8] Probably the following, Miss Anna Freud believes: After their return from the U.S.A., Freud and Ferenczi were in Berlin together on about 1 Oct. and visited a woman medium whom the latter knew. Her performance provoked an interest in "thought transference," and Freud wrote Ferenczi 6 Oct., "I am afraid you have begun to discover something big." (See Jones, III, 411f./384f.) See also below, 254 J n. 6 and 293 F n. 6.

[9] Apparently on 12 Oct. 1909, at the Hotel Residenz, with 27 present. See *Minutes*, II, p. 275.

my trip to America; Adler made some apt observations about ΨA and *Weltanschauung* to which others contributed by prearrangement. Over the coffee I served up our analysis of America. I had read Stekel's proofs before leaving; now he is not letting me make any cuts.

Many thanks for your "family news," in the extended sense as well. My daughter, who was twenty-three yesterday,[10] is having trouble again with postoperative inflammation; but at least she is cheerful and generally in good health. The developments are uncertain. As for the second, her stay in Karlsbad has not helped her. Both grandmothers[11] are shaky. All in all nothing very serious.

My week's work leaves me numb. I would invent the seventh day if the Lord hadn't done so long ago. Forgive this long letter; writing it has enabled me to take stock of myself. Except on Sunday afternoon I cannot possibly work for Worcester. Once this unpleasant task is over I want to start working methodically for the *Jahrbuch* again. Nothing much can be expected of me on weekday evenings. Quite against my will I must live like an American: no time for the libido.

Your good news of your family has given me great pleasure.

With kind regards,

Sincerely yours, FREUD

159 J

Dear Professor Freud,   Küsnach bei Zürich, 8 November 1909

You will, no doubt, have arrived at a fair explanation of my long silence. It's just that one has so much to do, and I expect this is the case on your side as well. Many thanks for the long letter. Meanwhile, some more news has cropped up. But back to the past first.

Friedländer: I treated him in the "grand" or haughty manner and received him in the circle of my 4 foreigners.[1] They started talking in English, and it turned out afterwards that he doesn't understand a word. Yet he acted so sagely that I never noticed it. Otherwise I was

---

[10] Mathilde was actually twenty-two on 16 Oct. 09.
[11] For Emmeline Bernays, see above, 147 F n. 5. For Freud's mother, 156 F n. 4.

---

[1] These included Hoch as well as Trigant Burrow (1875–1950), of Baltimore, whose practice of psychoanalysis later veered from both the Freudian and Jungian schools. His selected letters, *A Search for Man's Sanity* (New York, 1958), pp. 23–35, dwell on his year in Zürich and his analysis with Jung.

polite, keeping my distance. Pfister also suffered a visitation from him, likewise Foerster.

Forel's Society: Dr. Seif of Munich has been with me, working busily at ΨA. He is a member of the new Society and has divulged that Frank has spoken out strongly in our favour. S. pressed me to join along with you. Exactly what the Society wants to do or is supposed to do S. doesn't know either, but he thinks that in the end everything will be grist to our mill. Maybe join after all?

Dr. F—— got his deserts from you. He is, or seems to be, an obsessional neurotic; he was with me for about 3 weeks (also with Dubois,[2] etc. etc.) but proved quite unapproachable because of the most incredible and laughable resistances. He therefore took to his heels after confessing that he habitually reached his climax *only* with *dirty* prostitutes. He could not forgive me this confession.

Bleuler recently told me that he intended to take up matters of principle with us, i.e., to say how far he is able or willing to follow, and how far not. Naturally I am dying to know what sort of obliquities will come out. He is struggling to communicate, and this in itself is not bad. But . . . ? I think we might take the edge off his paper (which to my knowledge doesn't exist yet) if it is published in the *Jahrbuch*.[3] In any case it won't be too awful. Polemics inside our camp are bound to start sooner or later. To take an example: Stekel's method of presentation will be hard to stomach in the long run, even though he is usually right. We should, however, emphasize the distinction between real psychoanalysis and Stekel's brand. I have to fight like mad with my students until I have dinned it into them[4] that ΨA is a scientific method and not just guesswork. My English speech therapist,[5] for instance, thinks on the strength of Stekel's letters that dream interpretation is something quite simple, a kind of translation with the aid of the *clef de songes*. Now the poor chap is sadly disappointed after seeing how toilsome the work is. Most people reading Stekel have little appreciation of what we have achieved,

[2] See above, 115 J n. 8.
[3] Subsequently referred to sometimes as Bleuler's "apologia." See below, 226 F n. 1.
[4] Jung wrote *Ihnen* (you) instead of *ihnen* (them).
[5] Holograph: *Mein englischer Stottererlehrer.* Unidentifiable, as is the reference to Stekel's letters. However, Stekel's *Conditions of Nervous Anxiety and Their Treatment* presents several cases of stammering that were cured. Ernest Jones, who had a "very extensive clinical experience" of stammering, wrote Putnam, "I fully accept all that Stekel says of it, that it is an Angsthysterie, always of sexual origin . . ." (13 Jan. 10, in *Putnam and Psychoanalysis*, pp. 213ff.).

not to mention other things. Also, St. is definitely tending towards stock interpretations, as I can often see here with my students. Instead of bothering to analyse, they say: "This is . . ." As if the common-or-garden resistances were not enough, I now have to drive Stekel out of their heads as well. But I don't want to drop him entirely; as usual, his paper for the *Jahrbuch* contains things that are astonishingly right. He is valuable because of his findings, but deleterious for the public.

One of the reasons why I didn't write for so long is that I was immersed every evening in the history of symbols, i.e., in mythology and archaeology. I have been reading Herodotus and have made some wonderful finds (e.g., Book 2, cult at Papremis).[6] Now I am reading the 4 volumes of old Creuzer,[7] where there is a huge mass of material. All my delight in archaeology (buried for years) has sprung into life again. Rich lodes open up for the phylogenetic basis of the theory of neurosis. Later I want to use some of it for the *Jahrbuch*. It's a crying shame that already with Herodotus prudery puts forth its quaint blossoms; on his own admission he covers up a lot of things "for reasons of decency." Where did the Greeks learn that from so early? I have discovered a capital book in Knight's *Two Essays on the Worship of Priapus*,[8] much better than Inman, who is rather unreliable. If I come to Vienna in the spring, I hope to bring you various ancient novelties.

As a basis for the analysis of the American way of life I am now treating a young American (doctor). Here again the mother-complex looms large (cf. the *Mother-Mary cult*).[9] In America the mother is decidedly the dominant member of the family. American culture really is a bottomless abyss; the men have become a flock of sheep and the women play the ravening wolves—within the family circle, of course. I ask myself whether such conditions have ever existed in the world before. I really don't think they have.

With kind regards,

Yours, JUNG

[6] Cf. *Symbols of Transformation*, CW 5, par. 390. (Also in 1911/12 edn.)
[7] Ibid., pars. 354f. The work is Friedrich Creuzer, *Symbolik und Mythologie der alten Völker* (Leipzig and Darmstadt, 1810–23).
[8] English in original. The book is Richard Payne Knight, *A Discourse on the Worship of Priapus, and Its Connection with the Mystic Theologie of the Ancients* (London, 1865).
[9] English in original.

160 F

Dear friend,   11 November 1909, Vienna, IX. Berggasse 19

It probably isn't nice of you to keep me waiting 25 days (from October 14 to November 8; I checked because I suspected one of Fliess's 23-day periods, but wrong again) for an answer—as though the promptness and length of my last letter had frightened you away. I don't wish to importune you in the event that you yourself don't feel the need of corresponding at shorter intervals. But I can't help responding to my own rhythm, and the only compromise-action I am capable of is not to post the letter I am now writing until Sunday. For I am obliged to reserve Sunday for my American lectures, the first of which is already on the high seas.

As for Forel, I too think we should join. Please tell him so for both of us. Then he may let us know what the purpose of his Society is.

Your idea about Bleuler is excellent. We must persuade him to contribute his discussion of principles to the *Jahrbuch* (third half-volume); if you think it advisable, I shall ask him myself, just let me know when. That will oblige him to show special moderation, and besides, it is the only solution compatible with his position as director. There can be no objection to discussion in our own camp; still, it must be constructive. You are quite right, a discussion with Stekel will also be inevitable. He is a slovenly, uncritical fellow who undermines all discipline; I feel the same as you do about him. Unfortunately, he has the best nose of any of us for the secrets of the unconscious. Because he is a perfect swine, whereas we are really decent people who submit only reluctantly to the evidence. I have often contradicted his interpretations and later realized that he was right. Therefore we must keep him and distrust him and learn from him. I don't think it will be possible to avoid including critical reviews in the *Jahrbuch*, beginning with the second volume. All publications that we want to single out from the bibliographical abstracts ought to get special reviews. For the present there are not many. But Stekel is planning a dictionary of dream symbols,[1] he is a fast worker and it will no doubt be on the market soon. A review of it will give us an opportunity to tell him publicly what we think of him. I suggest that you and I share the work on this critical section, you will rap the Viennese on the knuckles and I the Zürich people

[1] Became *The Language of Dreams*; see below, 240 F n. 3.

when they start producing versions of their own. These reviews must be the expression of our very personal convictions; this is an attempt at literary dictatorship, but our people are unreliable and need discipline. I must own that I sometimes get so angry at my Viennese that I wish you/they* had a single backside so I could thrash them all with one stick.

I was delighted to learn that you are going into mythology. A little less loneliness. I can't wait to hear of your discoveries. I ordered Knight in July but haven't received it yet. I hope you will soon come to agree with me that in all likelihood mythology centers on the same nuclear complex as the neuroses. But we are only wretched dilettantes. We are in urgent need of able helpers.

> "Although it was the Devil who taught her,
> He cannot do it by himself."[3]

But recently chance brought me a young *Gymnasium* teacher who is studying mythology. His ideas are similar to ours, but backed up by solid erudition. His name—another Oppenheim;[4] decidedly intelligent, but so far I have a feeling that new ideas throw him off. At our first meeting I learned from him that Oedipus is thought to have originally been a phallic demon like the Idaean Dactyls (!); his name means simply erection. Also that the hearth is a symbol of the womb because the ancients looked on flame as a phallus. The Vestal Virgins were like nuns, the brides of this hearth phallus, etc. I tried to explain to him the apotropaic significance of the erect penis, but soon realized how radically our thinking already differs from that of other mortals.

Since then, a noble spirit, Leonardo da Vinci, has been posing for me—I have been doing a little ΨA of him. Whether it will turn out

---

*This makes up for a similar slip in your letter ("until I have dinned it into you/them that ΨA is a scientific method," etc.)! You'll agree it's amusing.[2]

[2] Freud wrote *Ihnen* (you) instead of *ihnen* (they). He wrote this note between lines across the page immediately after the word in question.

[3] Holograph: *Der Teufel hat sie's zwar gelehrt, / allein der Teufel kann's nicht machen.*—Goethe, *Faust I*, 2376–77.

[4] David Ernst Oppenheim (1881–?1943), classics teacher in a Vienna *Gymnasium*, who was associated with the psychoanalytic movement in 1910–11, then adhered to Adler's school. Died in a concentration camp during the second World War. For Freud's collaboration with him, see below, 246 F n. 4.

to be a brief note or a number of the *Papers*, I don't know yet. In any event I am setting it aside for the moment. Hasn't anyone sent you anything that we can use for the next number of the *Papers*? Now, after Sadger's (no. 6),[5] I am without material, I must admit I was expecting more cooperation.

Foerster's attack in *Die Evangelische Freiheit*[6] is very interesting, half idiotic, half clairvoyant (toward the end). In one point he is right. The line quoted from the *Oedipus* really is 944 and not 995.[7] On the other hand he blames the denunciation of K. F. Meyer, for which Sadger was apparently responsible, on me.[8] But the Oedipus has made quite an impression; and that is a good thing. The Vienna newspapers have been carrying little squibs by some of our outstanding thinkers, to the effect that Hamlet presents no problem: He can't make himself believe that a murder has been committed, because no one can believe a ghost. So he is right in not taking vengeance. The only sensible thing to do would have been to call in a Copenhagen detective agency. You see that a good deal of nonsense can accumulate in three weeks.

A nice contrite letter from Jones: the English translation[9] hasn't reached me yet, it seems to be lost. Eitingon is the only one I can

---

[5] *Aus dem Liebesleben Nicolaus Lenaus* (*Schriften zur angewandten Seelenkunde*, 6; 1909).

[6] "Psychoanalyse und Seelsorge," *Evangelische Freiheit*, n.s., IX (Sept., Oct. 1909), 335–46, 374–88. Foerster aimed his attack partly at Pfister's articles "Psychanalytische Seelsorge und experimentelle Moralpädagogik" (see above, 129 F n. 3) and "Ein Fall von psychanalytischer Seelsorge und Seelenheilung," *Evangelische Freiheit*, n.s., IX:3–5 (Mar.–May 1909).

[7] Foerster actually wrote (p. 342) that the cited words of Jocasta are in verse 954, not in 995 as Freud cited; his reference was to *Traumdeutung*, 1906, an error for 1909. (The 2nd edn., dated 1909, actually appeared before 23 Nov. 08, when Abraham wrote Freud to thank him for a copy.) Freud made a slip in writing 944 for 954; the passage is at vv. 954–956 in J. J. C. Donner's translation of *Oedipus Rex* (6th edn., Leipzig, 1868) and is marked with a pencil in Freud's copy, as Miss Anna Freud has confirmed. Freud corrected the citation to "955ff." in the 3rd edn. (1911). The passage is in lines 982–84 in the L. Campbell tr. cited in SE IV, p. 264, and in the Loeb edn. (which reads: "How oft it chances that in dreams a man / Has wed his mother! He who least regards / Such brainsick phantasies lives most at ease").

[8] Sadger, *Konrad Ferdinand Meyer: eine pathographisch-psychologische Studie* (Grenzfragen des Nerven- und Seelenlebens, 59; Wiesbaden, 1908). Sadger discussed the influence of Meyer's mother and sister in his sexual life.

[9] Apparently Brill's translation of *Selected Papers on Hysteria* (New York, 1909); for comments on Brill as a translator, see Jones, II, pp. 50f./45.

261

talk to here; we take walks in the evening and I analyse him just in passing. He is leaving tomorrow.

With kind regards to you and your family,

Yours, FREUD

161 J

Dear Professor Freud, Küsnach bei Zürich, 12 November 1909

The bearer of this letter is Dr. Décsi[1] of Budapest, newly arrived from Zürich, where he has patiently been doing tedious work for about 6 months. He is gifted with a keen understanding of the things of ΨA and now he naturally wants to meet the Master who gives us these things. Dr. Décsi comes equipped not only with a good professional training but also with an excellent knowledge of literature, which would seem to make him a worthy acquisition.

I hope you received my letter safely; it evidently crossed with your card.[2]

With kind regards,

Most sincerely yours, JUNG

162 J

Küsnach bei Zürich, 15 November 1909

Pater, peccavi[1]—it is indeed a scandal to have kept you waiting 25 days for an answer. From the last paragraph of your letter it is clear why the intervals need to be shorter: you seem to be very isolated in Vienna. Eitingon's company cannot be counted among the highest joys. His vapid intellectualism has something exasperating about it. If I appear to be such a sterile and lazy correspondent it is because I am positively wallowing in people and social life here. I spend much of my time with young Honegger—he is so intelligent and subtle-minded. Hardly a day goes by without an exchange of ideas. Thus I

---

[1] See above, 140 J n. 2. Décsi was a guest of the Vienna Society on 17 Nov. 09 (*Minutes*, II, p. 325).
[2] Missing.

---

[1] Luke 15:21.

fill up my gaps and do not sense the passing of 25 days. Well, it is scandalous and shall not happen again.

I will arrange matters with Forel at once, and for you too. Bleuler, I hear, has already joined. He is chewing the cud of countless resistances. His main grudge against us is that he is incapable of doing any ΨA. He also seems to think that we back up Stekel in every particular. (I am very glad that we are in agreement on St. A dictionary of dream symbols! Good Lord, that's all we needed! Too bad he's usually right.)

Now to better things—mythology. For me there is no longer any doubt what the oldest and most natural myths are trying to say. They speak quite "naturally" of the nuclear complex of neurosis. A particularly fine example is to be found in Herodotus: at Papremis, during the festival in honour of the mother of Ares (Typhon), there was a great mock-battle between two opposing crowds armed with wooden clubs. Many wounded. This was a repetition of a legendary event: Ares, brought up abroad, returns home to his mother in order to *sleep* with her.[2] Her attendants, not recognizing him, refuse him admission. He goes into the town, fetches help, overpowers the attendants and sleeps with his mother. These flagellation scenes are repeated in the Isis cult, in the cult of Cybele, where there is also self-castration, of Atargatis (in Hierapolis), and of Hecate: whipping of youths in Sparta. The dying and resurgent god (Orphic mysteries, Thammuz, Osiris [Dionysus],[3] Adonis, etc.) is everywhere phallic. At the Dionysus festival in Egypt the women pulled the phallus up and down on a string: "the dying and resurgent god." I am painfully aware of my utter dilettantism and continually fear I am dishing you out banalities. Otherwise I might be able to say more of these things. It was a great comfort to me to learn that the Greeks themselves had long since ceased to understand their own myths and interpreted the life out of them just as our philologists do. One of the most lamentable seems to me to be Jeremias[4] (this time *lucus a lucendo*),[5] who reduces everything to astronomy when the opposite is staring you

---

[2] Cf. *Symbols of Transformation*, CW 5, par. 390. Also in 1911/12 edn.

[3] Jung's brackets, after which and before *Adonis* he wrote *Adon*, probably a false start on *Adonis*.

[4] Alfred Jeremias, *Das Alte Testament im Lichte des alten Orients* (Leipzig, 1906).

[5] Paraphrase of Quintilian's example of ludicrous etymology, *lucus a non lucendo* (*De institutione oratoria*, I, 6, 34): "a wood is called a wood (*lucus*) because it does not shine (*non lucet*)."

in the face. Now I am laboriously ploughing through the components of the Artemis myth; it has been fearfully distorted by syncretism. Although the philologists moan about it, Greek syncretism, by creating a hopeless mishmash of theogony and theology, can nevertheless do us a service: it permits reductions and the recognition of similarities, as in dream analysis. If A is put in place of C, then one may conjecture a connection from C to A. One of the greatest difficulties is the dating of myths, so important for the genesis of the cults. It also seems to me extremely difficult to estimate what was folkloristic and widely disseminated and what merely a poetic variant, doubtless very interesting to the philologist but quite unimportant to the ethnologist.

I was most interested in your news about Oedipus. Of the *dactyls* I know nothing, but have heard of St. Cosmas[6] that people kiss his great *toe* and offer up wax phalli *ex voto*. Can you give me sources for the Oedipus myth and the Dactyls? A counterpart of the nunlike Vestal Virgins would be the self-castrated priests of Cybele. What is the origin of the New Testament saying: "There be eunuchs which have made themselves eunuchs for the kingdom of heaven's sake"?[7] Wasn't self-castration practically unheard of among the Jews? But in neighbouring Edessa[8] self-castration of the Atargatis priests was the rule. In that same place, incidentally, there were 180 ft. high "spires" or minarets in phallic form. Why is the phallus usually represented as winged? (Joke: "The mere thought lifts it.") Do you know those early mediaeval lead medallions in Paris, on one side the Christian cross, on the other a penis or vulva? And the penis-cross of Sant'Agata de'Goti?[9] (Inaccurate illustration in Inman.) There seem to be indications of early mediaeval phallus worship.

I have recommended Frl. Dr. L. von Karpinska to Dr. Jekels. Frl. Gincburg[10] couldn't be traced.

With many kind regards,

Yours, JUNG

[6] 3rd cent., a patron saint of physicians, invoked in some parts of Italy for sexual troubles or needs.

[7] Matthew 19:12.

[8] Modern Urfa, in southeast Turkey.

[9] Holograph: *Sta. Agnata di Goti.* / There is a drawing of the cross in Inman, *Ancient Pagan and Modern Christian Symbolism*, pl. XI, 4; it "was found at St. Agati di Goti, near Naples" (p. 15).

[10] See 153 J n. 1. The significance of the allusions in this paragraph is unknown, beyond the fact that all three were Polish.

163 F

Dear friend,   21 November 1909, Vienna, IX. Berggasse 19

At last you have realized how Vienna fare must taste to me now that I have been spoiled by my six weeks' absence. Then I need say no more about it.

Stanley Hall wrote me recently: "I am a very unworthy exponent of your views and of course have too little clinical experience to be an authority in that field; but it seems to me that, whereas hitherto many, if not most pathologists have leaned upon the stock psychologists like Wundt, your own interpretations reverse the situation and make us normal psychologists look to this work in the abnormal or borderline field for our chief light."[1] We are still very far from that in Germany. But coming from the old man such serious, thoughtful compliments are very nice.

Out of sheer gratitude I have already sent him three of the lectures and am working desperately on the last. I am making a few changes and additions, and also putting in a few defensive, or rather, aggressive, remarks. Deuticke wants to publish them in German, but I don't know if Hall would like that, and it troubles me that there is nothing new in them.

I am delighted with your mythological studies. Much of what you write is quite new to me, e.g., the mother-lust, the idea that priests emasculated themselves to punish themselves for it. These things cry out for understanding, and as long as the specialists won't help us, we shall have to do it ourselves.

E.g., the castration complex in myth. Since castration was of course unheard of among the Jews, I can't see the point of the New Testament passage. There is a monograph on the Dactyls by Kaibel: *Die idaeischen Daktylen*[2] (the Cretan Mt. Ida). I shall read it as soon as I have time to breathe. In private I have always thought of Adonis as the penis; the woman's joy when the god she had thought dead rises again is too transparent! And isn't it odd that none of the mythologists, neither the prigs nor the lunatics, has seen the need for an interpretation on different levels! We really ought to shake them into

---

[1] English in original.

[2] Georg Kaibel (1849–1901), "Daktyloi Idaioi," *Nachrichten von der Königl. Gesellschaft der Wissenschaften zu Göttingen, Phil.-hist. Klasse*, 1901 (pub. 1902), 488–518. Dactyls were finger-sized beings that were in attendance on Rhea when she gave birth to Zeus on Mount Ida.

consciousness. Oedipus, I believe I have told you, means swollen foot, i.e., erected penis. Quite by accident I recently hit on what I hope is the ultimate secret of foot fetishism. In the foot it has become permissible to worship the long-lost and ardently longed-for woman's penis of the primordial age of infancy. Evidently some people search as passionately for this precious object as the pious English do for the ten lost tribes of Israel. I have still not received the Knight book. I do wish I could show you my analysis of Leonardo da Vinci, I am desperately sorry not to have you here. It would be too long in a letter and I haven't the time. I am coming to attach more and more importance to the infantile theories of sexuality. My treatment of them, incidentally, is deplorably incomplete. How I underestimated the —[3] theory for example!

In my practice I come across little that is new, little that was not already known to me. For the profound problems of choice of neurosis I must wait for the rare cases in which an analysis is really completed. That is why I let myself be lured into amusing myself with side-issues[4] and why most of my time is lost in rehashing the old material and working on papers such as those I am doing for Hall, etc. And yet slow progress is the best safeguard against error. A book on dream symbols doesn't strike me as impossible, but I am sure we shall object to the way Stekel goes about it. He will work haphazardly, taking whatever he can lay hands on without regard for the context, and without taking myth or language or linguistic development into account.

One might quote:

> "Woe unto those who lend the light
> Of heaven to the eternally blind[5]
> etc."

In my university lectures, which I am now reorganizing as a seminar, I have arranged for a critical discussion of your "Father Destiny"[6] paper next Saturday. So far I have had two of the case histories from

---

[3] Illegible in holograph.

[4] Holograph: *So entsteht die Neigung zu den Allotriis.* Freud, who viewed such indulgence with misgivings, had described his coca studies (1884–87) as *Allotria* (see Jones, I, p. 92/83f.).

[5] From Schiller, "Das Lied von der Glocke." The "etc." stands for: "For him it does not shine, it only burns / Turning towns and countries into ashes."

[6] "The Significance of the Father in the Destiny of the Individual," CW 4 (orig., *Jahrbuch*, I:1).

266

the *Studies*[7] brought up to the level of our present knowledge (quinze ans après).[8] I will tell you how it turns out.

In my practice I am chiefly concerned with the problems of repressed sadism in my patients; I regard it as the most frequent cause of the failure of therapy. Revenge against the doctor combined with self-punishment. In general sadism is becoming more and more important to me, which does not prevent its theoretical relation to love from becoming more and more obscure.

Something to remember: the evil eye is an excellent proof of the contention that envy and hostility always lurk behind love. The apotropaea are entirely in our possession, they are always consolations through sexuality; as onanism is in childhood. It has also been explained to me why a chimney sweep is regarded as a good omen: *chimney-sweeping*[9] is an action symbolic of coitus, something Breuer certainly never dreamed of. All watch charms—pig, ladder, shoe, chimney-sweep, etc.—are sexual consolations.

With kind regards to yourself and family,

FREUD[10]

164 J

Dear Professor Freud,   Küsnach bei Zürich, 22 November 1909

You have no doubt received the postcard[1] with the various names. It is from the meeting of Swiss psychiatrists in Zürich. It was an *historic moment*! The meeting was absolutely packed. Three lectures on ΨA were on the programme—Bleuler: Freudian Symptoms in Dem. praec.; Frank: Psychoanalytical Treatment of Depressive States; Maeder: On Paranoids. The whole interest centred on these. The Tübingen, Strassburg, and Heidelberg clinics were officially represented by assistants. Dr. Seif of Munich was present, as well as an

---

[7] *Studies on Hysteria*, SE II. Four case histories are Freud's and one Breuer's.
[8] Cf. the novel by Alexandre Dumas père, *Vingt ans après* (1845).
[9] English in original. On the continent, it is considered lucky to see a chimney-sweep. Breuer's patient Anna O. used the expression "chimney-sweeping" (in English) for her analytical talk; see *Studies on Hysteria*, SE II, p. 30. The passage is quoted by Jones, II, p. 494/445.
[10] For a postscript to this letter, see addenda.

---

[1] Missing.

assistant of Pick's[2] in Prague, two directors of sanatoria from Würt-temberg, one from the Bergstrasse,[3] etc. The opposition was headed by a medical friend of Foerster's, who only emitted a miserable squeak. Forel was on our side, although he fought against infantile sexuality, but mildly. Your (that is, our) cause is *winning all along the line,* so that we had the last word, in fact we're on top of the world. I was even invited by German colleagues to give a holiday course on ΨA. This is something I shall have to think about.

So—that was the first prank.[4] Monakow & Co. lay on the floor, totally isolated. Now for once they can savour the joys of being in the minority. One circumstance came to my aid, and I exploited it. Forel first attacked Monakow because of the rival founding of the neurologists' society. I resolutely took Forel's part, thereby winning him over so that his subsequent opposition was very mild. This political coup made a deep impression, so deep that the opposition no longer dared to show its face. The whole discussion, which was very lively, centred exclusively on ΨA.

The psychiatrists' society is ours. The rival neurologists' society is a defensive and offensive alliance between Monakow and Dubois. The (unwritten) programme of the two societies will be: Freud and Antifreud.

Now it's Germany's turn.

With many kind regards,

Yours, JUNG

165 J

Küsnach bei Zürich, 30 November 1909

Dear Professor Freud,   2 December 1909

I have to be continually thanking you—this time for the new edition of *Psychopathology.*[1] Your editions follow one another with enviable speed. So quickly that the opposition will have their work

---

[2] Arnold Pick (1851–1924), professor of psychiatry in the German University of Prague.

[3] The western slope of the Odenwald between Darmstadt and Heidelberg. The sanatorium could not be identified.

[4] Holograph: *Dieses war der erste Streich*: quoted from Wilhelm Busch's *Max und Moritz,* a favourite of both Freud and Jung.

---

[1] 3rd German edn. (1910) of *The Psychopathology of Everyday Life,* SE VI.

cut out to keep pace. We can also rejoice over the new issue of the *Jahrbuch*. The prospects are excellent.

I feel more and more that a thorough understanding of the psyche (if possible at all) will only come through history or with its help. Just as an understanding of anatomy and ontogenesis is possible only on the basis of phylogenesis and comparative anatomy. For this reason antiquity now appears to me in a new and significant light. What we now find in the individual psyche—in compressed, stunted, or one-sidedly differentiated form—may be seen spread out in all its fullness in times past. Happy the man who can read these signs! The trouble is that our philology has been as hopelessly inept as our psychology. Each has failed the other.

I have now found out what the Idaean Dactyls are:[2] they are the *Kabiri* or *Kuretes*. You probably know of the old Kabiric elements in Greek mythology. The Dactyls were a legendary folk inhabiting the Phrygian Ida, discoverers of iron mines and inventors of the blacksmith's art, akin to the Kabiri, but they were also gods, almost always a plurality, very unindividual (Herakles and the Dioscuri descend from them or are related to them). Originally they were *"Toby jug" gods* ("kanobos"),[3] always depicted as pygmies and wearing hoods, i.e., as *Invisibles* (cf. our dwarfs, goblins, pixies, Tom Thumbs, etc.). An extremely important, profoundly archaic streak in Hellenic mythology! They are direct animators of inert matter (*lares* and *penates* in Italy). Not primarily phallic, but elemental. Only the great, that is the *epic*, gods seem to be phallic.

Did Kaibel's monograph on the Idaean Dactyls appear in book form or in a journal?

For technical reasons I am very interested to hear that you are reorganizing your lectures as a seminar. I consider this form of instruction the best of all, although it limits the size of the audience. I teach incessantly, about 12 hours a week, nothing but ΨA, of course.

The alcohol statistics[4] have been noted with pleasure. I myself am doing pretty well as a non-abstainer.

[2] See *Symbols of Transformation*, CW 5, par. 183.
[3] Jung's "kanobos"; apparently a confusion with the Greek for Canopus, in Lower Egypt, source of the term "canopic jar," a human-headed vessel which contained the viscera of the deceased and was placed in an ancient Egyptian tomb. Jung's *Kruggötter* is suitably rendered by " 'Toby jug' gods," a phrase which suggests the grotesque character of the Dactylic figures. (Prof. and Mrs. Homer Thompson kindly supplied this information.)
[4] See postscript to 163 F, in addenda.

I often wish I had you near me. So many things to ask you. For instance I should like to pump you sometime for a definition of libido. So far I haven't come up with anything satisfactory.

I am very much interested in the psychology of incurables. I have one such poor devil who despite goodwill is making hardly any headway. The main trouble seems to be a supine slipping back to the infantile attitude, due to external difficulties. The fellow has insights but no prospects in life because he is deaf.

In my American seminar I've been gratified to find that my ideas on the theory of Dem. praec. are already clear enough to hold out hopes of further progress. Unfortunately my time is so taken up with people and things that I find it difficult to concentrate. This morning (Dec. 2) I received your card from Budapest.[5]

With kind regards,

Most sincerely yours, J U N G

166 F

Dear friend,   2 December 1909, Vienna, IX. Berggasse 19

That revenge has anything to do with my failure to answer your victory letter before now is something which I should naturally deny and you affirm—in accordance with the customary ΨA sharing of roles. But you will admit that work, fatigue and America add up to an excellent rationalization. The truth is that I am rather low in health and spirits, but I am hoping for an improvement, for I was able at the end of the month to reduce my work schedule by two hours and the fourth of the Worcester lectures was sent off the day before yesterday. Since you have already promised to treat me better, my complaints can no longer be construed as blackmail.

A little change was provided by my consultation in Budapest, which gave me an opportunity to see Ferenczi and share in his work. I was delighted to see how well he is finding his way in a difficult case. The bit of money was most helpful to the complex over which, for reasons that go back to my childhood, I have the least control, and, not least, I was glad to be able to correct an opinion that had me worried. Ferenczi introduced me to his lady friend and I no longer have to feel sorry for him. She is splendid, a woman who has only recently

---

[5] Missing.

stepped down from the summit of feminine beauty, clear intelligence and the most appealing warmth. I needn't tell you that she is thoroughly versed in our lore and a staunch supporter.[1]

Yesterday I tried my Leonardo da Vinci paper on the Society.[2] I was dissatisfied with it, but now I can hope for a little peace from my obsession. My Viennese exasperate me more and more, or am I getting "cranky"? I found the *Jahrbuch* waiting for me on my return from Budapest and I was as delighted as my present mood permits. ("It is not as it was of yore"[3]—you know the line and have promised to send the complete text.) I have not yet been able to read it, I only got back yesterday, Wednesday morning, but I think we have shown the gentlemen that we know what we are doing, and even though my name will not appear so often in later volumes, I shall still have this proof that I have not lived in vain. It will give me pleasure to think, as each half-volume appears, that it is your work and achievement.

Today I received a letter from Putnam[4] bearing witness to sincere interest and good intentions; of course with puritanical reservations about the sublimation that he had actually been hoping for. When really one should just be glad to be alive!

Your "Father Destiny" paper gave us a pleasant evening last Saturday. The speaker was a special variety of enthusiast, a cavalry lieutenant and Ph.D.[5] He also discussed the Association Experiments and gave the following example of unusual reactions: If you call out "horse" to me and I answer "library," you will be surprised. He had failed to notice that his real intention in giving this sample had been to introduce himself to the audience, who were all strangers to

[1] Gizella Palós (1863–1949), née Altshol, whom Ferenczi married in 1919.
[2] See *Minutes*, II, pp. 338ff.
[3] Holograph: "*Doch ist es nicht wie ehedem.*" Apparently from the poem Freud acknowledges in 171 F (at n. 7); cf. "It is not now as it hath been of yore"— Wordsworth, "Ode on Intimations of Immortality" (1807), stanza 1.
[4] See *James Jackson Putnam and Psychoanalysis*, ed. N. G. Hale, Jr. (Cambridge, Mass., 1971), pp. 86f., for Putnam's letter, dated 17 Nov. 09. Putnam (1846–1918), professor of neurology at Harvard, had gone to Worcester with William James to hear Freud's Clark University lectures. He was founder and first president of the American Psychoanalytic Association in 1911. See also comment following 154 F.
[5] Stefan von Maday (1879–1959), Hungarian psychotherapist, then of Innsbruck University, who is identified as "First Licut. Dr." upon his admission to the Wednesday Society on 4 May 10 (see *Minutes*, II, pp. 507f.). For his resignation as an Adlerian, see 273 F n. 1. Subsequently he was president of the Society for Individual Psychology in Budapest and a specialist in child and animal psychology.

him. It made a great impression when I pointed this out. A good illustration of the fact that in this experiment everything depends on an attitude of transference. We have not yet concluded the discussion. So far what struck us as most significant in your paper was its recognition of the type of disorder characterized by a belated attempt of the individuality to liberate itself. Some paladins eager to defend the cause of the neglected mothers have already come forward. It will interest you to know that we have become worthy of the Dürerbund.[6] In their Christmas catalogue my books, especially those in the *Applied Psychology Papers,*[7] are reviewed at length and warmly recommended, though to be sure in so turgid and unintelligible a style that my little Sophie exclaimed: it's good you know what you want, you'd never find out from reading that. All the same, Heller says recognition by the Dürerbund betokens significant progress in the good opinion of the German people.

So Germany is coming along! Aren't we (justifiably) childish to get so much pleasure out of every least bit of recognition, when in reality it matters so little and our ultimate conquest of the world still lies so far ahead?

With kind regards to you and your wife,

Sincerely yours, FREUD

167 F

Dear friend,   12 December 1909, Vienna, IX. Berggasse 19

Your letters delight me because they suggest a frenzy of satisfying work. That is as it should be. In my own case there is a little less joy and excitement, but no lack of interest. It is rare that two days pass without some new indication—if only a trifling one—that our ideas are spreading. An Italian, a Dr. Modena[1] of Ancona, already known

---

[6] A society founded 1903 by Ferdinand Avenarius (1856–1923) for the promotion of aesthetic culture on rather conservative lines. It issued an annual report reviewing the literary production of the year. This passage of the letter is quoted by Jones, II, p. 495/445f.

[7] The *Schriften zur angewandten Seelenkunde,* of which six numbers had appeared by this time.

---

[1] Gustavo Modena, psychiatrist of Ancona; see his "Psicopatologia ed etiologia dei fenomeni psiconeurotici; Contributo alla dottrina di S. Freud," *Rivista sperimentale di Freniatria,* XXXIV-XXXV (1908–9). According to Jones, II, p. 85,

to me from a very good paper, has just asked permission to translate one of my books into his language.

About Kaibel—I have given instructions and shall soon be able to provide you with information.

The new volume of the *Jahrbuch* is sure to make an impression. In the next one the Swiss must have more to say; you have been much too modest and retiring. The absence of abstracts on the Zürich literature has already been deplored. When questioned by the author, I did not withhold my praise of Binswanger's excellent and effective analysis.[2] But at the same time, in an access of crankiness, I expressed my objection to his utterly superfluous mention of Ziehen[3] and in general accused him of being a little too diplomatic. He has answered me very amiably. What I did not write was the general impression his piece made on me: it was as though a member of polite society had taken up with bohemians and was writing to inform his social equals that his new friends were interesting, halfway decent people, and that it might perhaps be safe to associate with them. In his concluding words of thanks to the Geheimrat there was something that irritated me. Was it because I felt that this praise was due to me, who had expressed the same sort of interest in neuroses without the flowery phrases? In short, I gave vent to a bit of my irritation and it seems to have done no harm.

Our colleague Brecher[4] (in Meran) has thought up a good joke. He thought the analysis required a subtitle, which he modeled on the title of your paper:

"The Significance of the Uncle in the Destiny of the Individual"

How is Bleuler doing? The "incurables" would be an excellent topic for a long evening discussion. They present all sorts of unsuspected

---

Modena began translating the *Three Essays on the Theory of Sexuality*, but the only Italian translation listed by Grinstein is that of M. Levi-Bianchini, 1921.

[2] "Versuch einer Hysterieanalyse," *Jahrbuch*, I:1–2 (1909), 174–356 (continued from the 1st to the 2nd half-vol.). The paper had no introduction by his uncle Prof. Otto Binswanger but was subheaded "Aus der psychiatrischen Klinik in Jena (Geh. Rat Prof. O. Binswanger)" and closed with a quotation from his *Die Hysterie* (1904) and an expression of thanks to him.

[3] For letters between Binswanger and Freud discussing the paper and, in particular, the mention of Ziehen, see Binswanger, *Sigmund Freud: Reminiscences of a Friendship*, pp. 11–21.

[4] Guido Brecher (1877–19—), a member of the Vienna Society but practising in Bad Gastein and later at Merano (then Austrian, now Italian). Jones appreciatively mentions Brecher's wit (II, pp. 49/44). Brecher did not remain with psychoanalysis.

resistances, which provide a deep insight into character formation. It is as true as ever that we learn more from the bad cases than from the "nice" ones.

I have finished my American lectures and can now start revising the *Theory of Sexuality*, though I do not wish to obscure its historical character by making too many changes.

Ferenczi has told me about a good case of paranoia; once again the homosexual factor is evident.

Cordially yours, FREUD

168 J

Dear Professor Freud,   Küsnach bei Zürich, 14 December 1909

Your letter came yesterday evening and I am replying at once. Your impressions of Binswanger's paper tally with my own, though I haven't dared to say so out loud. I too was annoyed with B. for pushing the business end so blatantly to the fore; his obeisances in various directions obviously amount to just that. Oh well, he has a sanatorium round his neck, so I suppose we must stretch a point. Besides, there is a colossal and apparently still unresolved father complex rumbling in his depths.

May I expect something from you for the January issue of the *Jahrbuch*? Contributions are coming from Maeder, Abraham, Sadger, Pfister, Riklin and me. So space is already tight. Pfister or Riklin could be held in reserve if necessary.

So far as I have heard, Ferenczi's paper[1] is greatly appreciated here. He wrote me a very nice letter, so understanding and friendly that I probably sent him a very clumsy answer.[2] Such letters should really be answered with a blank page,[2a] but that too would look unfriendly.

I have made some glosses on your Obsessional Neurosis. The notion that obsessional ideas are, by their very nature, *regressive substitutes for action* sounds very convincing to me. The formula for D. pr. ideas would be: regressive substitutes for *reality*. Both formulae, it seems to me, describe the main tendency very aptly. With reference to p. 415,[3]

---

[1] "Introjektion und Übertragung," *Jahrbuch*, I:2 (1909) = "Introjection and Transference," *First Contributions to Psycho-Analysis*, tr. Ernest Jones (1952).
[2] See Jung to Ferenczi, 6 Dec. 09, in *Letters*, ed. G. Adler, vol. 1.
[2a] Holograph: *Gedankenstrich*, lit., a dash, a device Jung liked to use in his letters.
[3] SE X, p. 240.

the sadistic component of libido, I must remark that I don't like the idea of sadism being constitutional. I think of it rather as a reactive phenomenon, since for me the constitutional basis of the neuroses is the imbalance between libido and resistance (self-assertion). If, at the start, the libido displayed too strong an attraction or need for love, hate would soon appear by way of compensation, and would subtract a good deal of the work of gratification from the masochistic libido (which by nature is much more nearly akin to masochism than to sadism). I think this is the basis for the immense self-assertion that appears later on in obsessional neurosis: the patient is always afraid of losing his ego, must take revenge for every act of love, and gives up the sexually destructive obsessional system only with the greatest reluctance. Obsessional neurosis never gets lost in actions and adventures as in the case of hysteria, where ego-loss is a temporary necessity. Obviously the self-assertion in obsessional neurosis is far exceeded in D. pr.

P. 411,[4] *omnipotence of his thoughts.* This expression is certainly very significant in this particular case. But I have misgivings about attributing any general validity to it. It seems to me much too specific. Of course it is idiotic of me to find fault with your clinical terminology, to which you have as much right as the next man. But, like Herakles of old, you are a human hero and demi-god, wherefore your dicta unfortunately carry with them a sempiternal value. All the weaker ones who come after you must of necessity adopt your nomenclature, originally intended to fit a specific case. Thus "omnipotence" will later be included in the symptomatology of obsessional neurosis. But this seems to me only an expression of self-assertion sadistically coloured by reactive hypercathexis and to be on a par with all the other symptoms of self-overvaluation, which always has such a hurtful effect on everyone in the vicinity. Here, it seems to me, we also have the reason for the obsessional neurotic's boundless belief in the rightness of his conclusions; they are taken as universally valid regardless of all reason and logical probability: he is and must remain right. From this rightness of his ideas, which brooks no exception, it is only a step to superstition, which in turn is only a special instance of self-hypercathexis, or rather weakness in adaptation (the two always go together). All superstition springs from this soil; it has been the weak man's weapon of attack and defence from time immemorial. It is not uncommon for the enfeebled to go in for witchcraft, especially old women who have long since lost their natural witchery.

[4] Ibid., p. 233.

The question of the original sexual constitution seems to me particularly difficult. Would it not be simplest, for the time being, to start with sensitivity[5] as the general foundation of neurosis, and to regard all other abnormal conditions as reactive phenomena?

I have just finished my American lectures and have sent them to Brill to translate. Congratulations on the Italian translation!

With kindest regards,

Yours, JUNG

169 F

Dear friend, 19 December 1909, Vienna, IX. Berggasse 19

If you feel the same way about Binswanger's paper, I shall stop accusing myself of "crankiness"; I must have been right. But he doesn't seem aware of it, his answer was perfectly amiable and essentially evasive—when not illegible. He means to come to Vienna in January.

Ferenczi is definitely flourishing. The trip did him a world of good. I would venture to call him a trustworthy, superior, absolutely authentic man.

This time I should like to contribute very little or nothing to the *Jahrbuch*. Perhaps a very short piece[1] in the style of the "Anal Erotism." There was too much of me in the first volume. This time I hope the Swiss will take the center of the stage and I also hope the abstracts will do them justice. I know that many readers are waiting eagerly for these abstracts to guide them in their choice of reading matter. Our colonists in foreign fields, such as Pfister, should also speak up. I long for mythologists, linguists, and historians of religions; if they won't come to our help, we shall have to do all that ourselves.

Apropos of mythology: have you observed that the sexual theories of children are indispensable for the understanding of myth? I have finally received Knight, but not yet laid hands on Kaibel.

In the seminar yesterday a few impetuous young analysts submitted some papers which after due purification seem to show that the diction and symbolism of a literary work reveal the influence of uncon-

---

[5] Holograph: *Empfindsamkeit*.

[1] Freud may have been thinking of "A Special Type" (see below, 288 F n. 1), but he actually contributed " 'Antithetical Meaning' " to *Jahrbuch*, II:1 (see below, 185 F n. 1).

276

scious infantile complexes in the poet. Such studies can lead to very interesting developments if pursued tactfully and critically. Unfortunately these elements of moderation are seldom found in combination with the analytic faculty.

Your notion that after my retirement from the ranks my errors may come to be worshiped as relics amused me a good deal, but I don't believe it. I believe on the contrary that the younger men will demolish everything in my heritage that is not absolutely solid as fast as they can. Developments in ΨA are often the exact opposite of what you would expect to find in other fields. Since you are likely to play a prominent part in this work of liquidation, I shall try to place certain of my endangered ideas in your safekeeping.[2]

First, your difficulty regarding "my" libido. In the first sentence of the *Theory of Sexuality* there is a clear definition in which I see nothing to change: The analagon to hunger, for which, in the sexual context, the German language has no word except the ambiguous "*Lust.*"[3]

And now as to the gains from my obsessional neurosis paper, which, to be sure I would have preferred to pocket in the course of a prolonged face-to-face discussion, amid creakings of the wall and furniture if you will: I am very glad that you accept my formula for obsession: "regressive substitute for action." I would be glad to do the same for yours in regard to Dem. pr.: regressive substitute for reality. But I am troubled by the fact that reality is not, like action, a Ψ factor; or do you mean "recognition of reality"?

In defense of sadism I should like to observe that its nature as an original component of instinct can hardly be questioned, since the biological function argues in its favour. Reactive phenomena are not at all of the same nature as sadism; on the contrary they are purely passive. We have already agreed that the mechanism underlying the onset of neurosis is the opposite of instinct, that the ego is the repressive, the libido the repressed factor. This view is first stated in my old article on anxiety neurosis.[4] But, oddly enough, it is very hard for us with our human minds to fix our attention equally on these two instinctual camps and to carry over the opposition between ego and libido into our observation, so as to embrace them both without bias. Thus far, it is true, I have concentrated on the repressed material, because it is new and unknown; I have been a Cato championing the

[2] This paragraph is quoted by Jones, II, p. 495/446.
[3] = "desire."
[4] "On the Grounds for Detaching a Particular Syndrome from Neurasthenia under the Description 'Anxiety Neurosis'" (orig. 1895), SE III.

causa victa. I hope I have not forgotten that there is also a *victrix.*[5] Adler's psychology takes account only of the repressive factor; consequently he describes "sensitivity,"[6] this attitude of the ego in opposition to the libido, as the fundamental condition of neurosis. And now I find you taking the same line and using almost the same word: i.e., by concentrating on the ego, which I have not adequately studied, you run the risk of neglecting the libido, to which I have done full justice.

Obsessional neurosis offers the main opportunity of doing this, because it is characterized mainly by an enormous damming up of reaction-formations in the ego, behind which it screens itself off very much as Dem. pr. does with its autoerotism and projection. But it is through these dams that a break-through is attempted. Still more of what you tell me about obsessional neurosis is seen from the standpoint of the ego, and valuable as it is, one must judge it in the light of this limitation.

What you say about the omnipotence of the affects can probably be attributed to a lack of clarity on my part. It is not *I* who proclaimed the omnipotence of the affects to be a symptom of obsessional neurosis, but the patient, who believes in this omnipotence—in which belief he is not alone.

I also have something to ask of you in connection with the Congress.[7] If you drop the spring date, I request most urgently that it should not be held in the middle of September but in the first or last days of that month. For selfish reasons. I want very much to take—without interruption—the trip to my beloved Mediterranean world that I sacrificed to our American undertaking this autumn. To judge by Putnam's letters[8] things are doing well over there.

Now I shall abandon the illusion of having you here for a visit and get back to a letter-writing frame of mind by concluding with kind regards to the lovely lakeside house and its inhabitants.

Yours, FREUD

[5] Cf. "Victrix causa deis placuit, sed victa Catoni" (the victor found favour with the gods, the vanquished with Cato).—Lucan, *Pharsalia* (A.D. 62), I, 128.
[6] Holograph: *Empfindlichkeit.*
[7] First reference to the projected Nuremberg Congress, March 1910.
[8] For his letters of 17 Nov. and 3 Dec. 09, see *Putnam and Psychoanalysis*, pp. 86–89. In the latter, Putnam sent Freud "a few photographs of the Adirondacks, as a reminder of your three days' stay." See below, 171 F.

170 J

Dear Professor Freud,   Küsnach bei Zürich, 25 December 1909[1]

My attempt at criticism, though it looked like an attack, was actually a defence, which is why I apparently had to tilt at the "*omnipotence* of thoughts." Of course the term is dead right as well as elegantly concise and trenchant, for that's how it is, especially in D. pr. where new fundamentals are constantly being uncovered by it. All this has shaken me very much, in particular my faith in my own capacities. But most of all I was struck by your remark that you longed for archaeologists, philologists, etc. By this, I told myself, you probably meant that I was unfit for such work. However, it is in precisely these fields that I now have a passionate interest, as before only in Dem. pr. And I have the most marvellous visions, glimpses of far-ranging interconnections which I am at present incapable of grasping, for the subject really is too big and I hate impotent bungling. Who then is to do this work? Surely it must be someone who knows the psyche and has the passion for it. D. pr. will not be the loser. Honegger, who has already introduced himself to you, is now working with me with *great* understanding, and I shall entrust to him everything I know so that something good may come of it. It has become quite clear to me that we shall not solve the ultimate secrets of neurosis and psychosis without mythology and the history of civilization, for *embryology* goes hand in hand with *comparative anatomy*, and without the latter the former is but a freak of nature whose depths remain uncomprehended. It is a hard lot to have to work alongside the father creator. Hence my attacks on "clinical terminology."

31 Dec. The Christmas holidays have eaten up all my time, so I am only now in a position to continue my letter. I am turning over and over in my mind the problem of antiquity. It's a hard nut! Without doubt there's a lot of infantile sexuality in it, but that is not all. Rather it seems to me that antiquity was ravaged by the struggle with *incest*, with which sexual *repression* begins (or is it the other way round?). We must look up the history of family law. The history of civilization, taken by itself, is too skimpy, at least what there is of it today. For instance, Burckhardt's *History of Greek Civilization*[2] remains wholly on the surface. A particularly significant topic is Greek

---

[1] Published in *Letters*, ed. G. Adler, vol. 1.
[2] Jakob Burckhardt (1818–97), Swiss historian; his *History* was published posthumously (1898–1902).

demonology, which I hope to penetrate into a little via Rohde
(*Psyche*).[3] I'd like to tell you many things about Dionysos were it not
too much for a letter. Nietzsche seems to have intuited a great deal of
it. I have an idea that the Dionysian frenzy was a backwash of sexuality, a backwash whose historical significance has been insufficiently
appreciated, essential elements of which overflowed into Christianity
but in another compromise formation. I don't know whether I am
writing you banalities or hieroglyphics. An unpleasant feeling. How
much I'd prefer to talk it over with you personally!

Will it suit you to hold the Nuremberg meeting on Easter *Tuesday*?
As soon as I know, I will work up the idea in a circular and send it
to you.

I note that my difficulties regarding the question of libido and also
of sadism are obviously due to the fact that I have not yet adjusted
my attitude sufficiently to yours. I still haven't understood properly
what you wrote me. The best thing is to postpone it until we can *talk*
in peace. I would really have to question you on every sentence in
your letter.

Dr. Seif of Munich has been here for 3 days, and I have put him
through his ΨA paces, which he needed very much. He is a good acquisition.

Meanwhile Dr. Bircher-Benner has been decent enough to call on
me and I hope to find a place for Honegger with him later. So please
lift the boycott.

Prof. Hoch, the most important of my Americans, has now gone
through his own ΨA with me and become a stalwart adherent. As he
holds one of the most important psychiatric positions in the U.S.A.
(Meyer's successor), his support is particularly valuable. Another
foundation stone laid.

So far I have had no news from Meyer in Königsberg. I'm puzzled.

As regards Nuremberg I must add that I am naturally counting very
much on your taking first place as speaker. That, as in Salzburg, is
what we all hope.

I have heard many appreciative opinions of the new *Jahrbuch*. No
doubt the critics will set up another wail.

Pfister's rejoinder[4] to Foerster presents difficulties because it is too
long. I have advised him to cut it drastically.

---

[3] Erwin Rohde (1845–98), *Psyche, Seelenkult und Unsterblichkeitsglaube der
Griechen* (1890–94; tr., *Psyche*, 1925).
[4] "Die Psychoanalyse als wissenschaftliches Prinzip und seelsorgerliche Methode,"

Tomorrow I must prepare a lecture for the students here on "symbolism," which fills me with horror. God knows what I shall patch together. I have been reading Ferrero,[5] but what he writes about is not our kind of symbolism. Let's hope a good spirit will stand by me.

With many kind regards and wishes,

As ever, JUNG

171 F

Dear friend,   2 January 1910, Vienna, IX. Berggasse 19

My New Year's greetings have been postponed by my waiting for your letter; I didn't want our correspondence to get out of kilter again. Today it has come belatedly and I give you my greetings loudly and officially. They are also addressed to the beautiful house which I hope to see this year. Because this summer we are planning to go somewhere with woods and a lake and a certain altitude in French Switzerland, where some of the mountain resorts are warmer than Austria, and of course we shall make a long stopover in Zürich on the way. That is our plan at least. May the powers of fate not frustrate it!

Your letter gave me special pleasure in these lovely quiet holidays. It is gratifying in every way. You feel the need of discussing certain fundamental problems with me; that is wonderful. And you promise[1] me your visit for next spring. Will the Congress interfere with that? No, of course not. My wife thought you would come to Vienna first and then take me with you to Nuremberg, or come back to Vienna with me from there; I don't know what you have in mind, but I think it could be combined with the Congress; my minimum expectation is that after the Congress we spend a day strictly alone in Nuremberg or somewhere else, and share our problems and budding projects. I should very much like you to accept the Easter date, but I have the following objection to Tuesday: it would mean travelling on Easter

---

Evangelische Freiheit n.s., X:2–4 (1910). See *Freud/Pfister Letters*, pp. 31–33, for Freud's comments (10, 19, and 24 Jan. 10) on Pfister's paper.

[5] Guglielmo Ferrero (1874–1942), author of *I simboli in rapporto alla storia e filosofia del diritto* (1893). Jung used a quotation from its French tr., *Les Lois psychologiques du symbolisme* (1895), as the motto prefacing "Wandlungen und Symbole der Libido," in *Jahrbuch*, III:1 (1911); cf. CW 5.

---

[1] Holograph: *zugesagt*, implying this was *viva voce*, perhaps during the U.S.A. trip.

Monday, which would not suit some of us. One must really knock off for three days in order to be rested for one day's work, and also to have some time for personal relationships.

But there is more to be said about the Congress and if you don't mind I shall dive right in. The situation has changed since the first Congress. At that time we chiefly had to show each other how much there was to say and how much work there was to be done; the natural consequence was the founding of the *Jahrbuch*. Since then the *Jahrbuch* has taken over this function. It follows that this Congress can be devoted to other tasks such as organization and the discussion of certain matters of fundamental importance. Perhaps only a few, specially chosen lectures (in the meantime the printing press has been invented so to speak for our benefit, we are no longer dependent on the oral tradition), but more attention to practical questions concerning the present and immediate future. What do you think?

My own feeling about the Congress: my first thought, of course, is that I have nothing to say. My second, by way of rectification: that I am willing to do anything you consider necessary. The least you have a right to expect is that I create no difficulties for you.

Since Easter comes so early this year, we ought really to start moving.

Your displeasure at my longing for an army of philosophical collaborators[2] is music to my ears. I am delighted that you yourself take this interest so seriously, that you yourself wish to be this army; I could have dreamed of nothing better but simply did not suspect that mythology and archaeology had taken such a powerful hold on you. But I must have hoped as much, for since October something has diverted me from working in those fields, though I have never for a moment doubted their importance for our purposes. I have an excellent opinion of Honegger, who probably offers the best prospects. But may I confide a source of misgiving? I don't think it would be a good idea to plunge directly into the general problem of ancient mythology; it strikes me as preferable to approach it in a series of detailed studies. Perhaps you have had the same idea. What I have valued in the specialists was simply the sheer knowledge that is so hard for us to acquire. But that after all is not an impossible task. I have reread your detailed remarks with close attention; I know the other fellow has an easier time of it if one does not interfere with him.

In exchange for your news of our friends and acquaintances I have the following to report: Dr. Osipov, assistant at the psychiatric clinic

---

[2] I.e., people from the "faculty of philosophy."

in Moscow, has written to me; his credentials are two thick offprints, in one of which the tangle of Cyrillic signs is interrupted every two lines by the name Freud (also Freudy and Freuda) in European print, while the other makes the same use of the name Jung. The man has two other, original works at the printer's and is planning to compete for the Moscow Academy prize which is being offered specifically for work in ΨA; the jury is meeting in March. Then in May he is coming to Vienna, whence I shall direct him on to Zürich. Here is his complete address, so you can notify him of the Congress:

Dr. N. Osipov,
Assistant at the Psychiatric Clinic
Dyevushcheye Polye, Moscow[3]
   (means Virgins' Field, so I'm told)

Modena in Ancona, who has offered to do the translation, has lapsed into silence (like your man in Königsberg, these things seem to go in waves), but yesterday I received a letter from Assagioli in Florence, in perfect German incidentally. The other day I had a letter from Jones, more contrite than necessary. "I'll be good from now on," he says. His resistance seems to have broken down for good. Putnam is doing several friendly articles, which he will send when finished. He has sent me a few photographs from the Adirondacks, they don't amount to much; the most interesting is of the log cabin that sheltered the three of us. If you don't get one, I can let you have mine.[3a]

I have definitely decided not to take up too much space for myself in the *Jahrbuch* this time. I may ask you to accept a tiny paper, "A Special Type of Choice of Object Mode by Men," or a *short* piece of case-material by Rank: "A Dream that Analyses Itself"—*or both*.[4] In no event do I want to crowd out your Swiss and I should like to incite you to stem the interminable flow of Sadger's rubbish on the biography of *un*important men. I know the piece;[5] like all Sadger's papers, it must to the barber's, as Hamlet says.[6]

Of my own flashes of inspiration—I am quite well again and correspondingly unproductive—I can confide only one. It has occurred to me that the ultimate basis of man's need for religion is *infantile*

---

[3] Holograph: *Dewitschje Pole, Moskau*
[3a] The photographs have not been recovered.
[4] English in original.
[5] Presumably "Ein Fall von multipler Perversion mit hysterischen Absenzen," *Jahrbuch* II:1 (1910): anonymous case of a Danish nobleman. Sadger had read part of the paper at the Vienna Society on 3 and 10 Nov. 09 and the rest on 5 Jan. 10 (*Bulletin*, no. 2, p. 2).
[6] *Hamlet*, II, ii, 507.

helplessness, which is so much greater in man than in animals. After infancy he cannot conceive of a world without parents and makes for himself a just God and a kindly nature, the two worst anthropomorphic falsifications he could have imagined. But all that is very banal. Derived, incidentally, from the instinct of self-preservation, not the sexual instinct, which adds its spice later on.

I did not understand your remark about my lifting of the boycott against Bircher. I hardly know who he is. Or have I forgotten something?

I found the poem[7] you sent me quite unintelligible; I can guess neither who the poet is nor what he is driving at. The former you probably did not expect of me; perhaps I may attribute the latter failure to a deficiency in the poem.

Oh yes; if you tell me the context of:

"It is most lovely, most pleasant,"[8]

I shall finally let you know where Kaibel's monograph on the Idaean Dactyls was published. We have both failed to keep our promises.

This is my prelude to the chat which I am so looking forward to, but which is evidently not to take place for quite some time. I assure you that I shall be briefer in later phases of this new year. Kind regards to you and your wife. On this occasion I cannot repress the hope that the year 1910 holds something as pleasant as our American trip in store for our relationship.

Yours cordially, FREUD

172 J

Dear Professor Freud,   [Postmark: Unterwasser, 8 Jan. 1910][1]

We have spent 6 days in this beautiful spot in marvellous winter sunshine. I shall answer your letter with all its news in detail shortly after I get back to Zürich.

Best regards, C. G. JUNG — EMMA JUNG

---

[7] Evidently the poem from which Freud quoted a line in 166 F.

[8] Holograph: *"Es ist ganz schön, ganz angenehm"*—from an unidentified song by Dominik Müller; see below, 173 J n. 1.

---

[1] Picture postcard, showing a local Alpine scene. Unterwasser is a secluded mountain resort in Canton St. Gallen, east of Zürich.

173 J

Dear Professor Freud, Küsnach bei Zürich, 10 January 1910

Many thanks for your heartening letter. Mythology certainly has me in its grip. I bring to it a good deal of archaeological interest from my early days. I don't want to say too much now but would rather wait for it to ripen. I have no idea what will come out. But I quite agree with you that this whole field must first be divided up for monograph treatment, which shouldn't be too difficult as there is any amount of typical material that crops up now here, now there in variant form. So that's no problem. The main *impedimentum* is lack of knowledge, which I am trying to remedy by diligent reading. I am most grateful to you for your promise about Kaibel's monograph. The reason why I can't supply Dominik Müller's song[1] in return is the sad fact that it is not included in the anthology, as I ascertained long ago. I have now written to the editor of the periodical where it was published.

It is with the greatest joy that I hear you will be coming to Switzerland in the summer. *When* will it be? My wife is looking forward to the company as eagerly as I. Your suggestion that I come to Vienna before or after Nuremberg has fallen upon equally fertile ground. Whether it will be before or after I don't yet know, because my military service is giving me a lot of bother this year—I must count on 7 weeks or more. I shall know my sentence in a few days and will then give you a definite date.

An answer plus an invitation has come from Königsberg. I don't know whether it can be combined with Nuremberg.

The enclosed is for you to correct.[2] I'd be grateful if you could lecture on case material in Nuremberg, and I'd also be very glad if you could worm some lectures out of your pupils. I will do the same with my people. I'll try to organize something too, but am very unsure of myself as I'm oppressed by the feeling that I am just starting to learn. I caught this *sentiment d'incomplétude* from my coy new love, mythology. This "cour d'amour" will set me many a test of courage.

Dr. Osipov has been taken note of. I know the gentleman from offprints and personal news. Assagioli will contribute to the *Jahrbuch*

---

[1] Pseudonym of Paul Schmitz (1871–1953), poet who wrote in the Basel dialect. His work often appeared in *Samstag*, a humorous Basel weekly.

[2] Unidentified; perhaps the text of the invitation to the Nuremberg Congress.

(abstracts). From Jones I too had a frightfully long letter which I am putting off answering because of the agony.

Dr. *Bircher*-Benner is the man who I already told you does psychoanalysis after *his* fashion; I warned against him then. Now I only wanted to tone the warning down a bit since he has been decent enough to make contact with us.

Another new American, Dr. Young,³ has turned up. Putnam's highly personal article has just appeared in the *Journal of Abnormal Psychology*!⁴

Many kind greetings,

Most sincerely yours, J U N G

174 F

Dear friend,   13 January 1910, Vienna, IX. Berggasse 19

I am answering you without delay in the interest of the Congress.

First a few words about the last post from America, which is very rich and might give one a feeling of triumph. Apart from Putnam's article, which you have already mentioned, I have received letters from St. Hall, Jones, Brill, and Putnam himself. Hall reports on the congress of psychologists at Harvard,¹ which devoted a whole afternoon to ΨA, in the course of which he and Putnam gave the malignant Boris Sidis² a thorough trouncing. You have probably received the same news; if not, it will give me pleasure to send you the letters. The old man, who is really a splendid fellow, writes that in April he is devoting a special number of the *American Journal of Psychology* to us; it is to contain your lectures, Ferenczi's paper on dream-work in

³ G. Alexander Young (1876–1957), of Omaha, Nebraska; born in England. He was a charter member of the American Psychoanalytic Association (see below, 257 J n. 1).
⁴ "Personal Impressions of Sigmund Freud and His Work, with Special Reference to His Recent Lectures at Clark University," part 1, *Journal of Abnormal Psychology*, IV (Dec. 1909–Jan. 1910). Part 2 was in the Feb.–Mar. 1910 issue.

¹ Eighteenth annual meeting of the American Psychological Association, Cambridge, Massachusetts, 29–31 Dec. 09. Putnam read a paper on "Freud's and Bergson's Theories of the Unconscious," Jones on "Freud's Theory of Dreams" (see below, n. 3). See *Psychological Bulletin*, VII:2 (15 Feb. 10), 37ff. Jones (II, pp. 129f./115) mistakenly places the meeting in Baltimore.
² Boris Sidis (1876–1923), emigrated from Russia, pupil of William James at Harvard; later, director of his own sanatorium at Portsmouth, New Hampshire.

translation, the shorter paper by Jones, and perhaps also my five lectures.[3] Putnam seems to be *truly ours*.[4] Jones is so sincerely contrite in his letters that I vote for taking him back into our favour. He is doing good work. His article "ΨA in Psychotherapy"[5] is just what the people over there need. Brill tells me that Peterson is keeping him busy and that he has made $660 in one month. My prophecy come true! Our trip to America seems to have done some good, which compensates me for leaving a part of my health there.

I am glad you are able to find distraction and recreation in the midst of the working year and do not propose to live as foolishly as I have done. You must hold out longer and lead our cause to victory. I hope we shall have a day alone together before or after the Congress. If you can't spare the time, it needn't be in Vienna. We have a lot to talk about.

And now I have a suggestion: a good subject for your talk would be our trip to America and the situation of psychoanalysis over there.[6] That will impress and encourage our people. I have been contemplating a paper on the prospects for ΨAtical therapy; I could weave in a discussion of technique. If you insist on case-material, I shall probably have to fall back on my little piece on the love life of men, which may be too specialized and besides our people here are familiar with it. At the moment I have nothing else. All the same, I do think our ΨAtical flag ought to be raised over the territory of normal love life, which is after all very close to us; maybe I'll contribute the few pages to the *Jahrbuch*. Rank's "Dream" is not yet really presentable.

I have asked the members of the Vienna ΨA Society for papers but requested advance notice so as to be able to eliminate certain propositions. A piece on faulty interpretive technique and the danger of succumbing to certain temptations would be in order one of these days.

Please send me thirty copies of the invitation.

Binswanger is due here on Saturday. In his own interest I am not going to spare him a few ΨAtical truths. His letters are full of attacks

[3] For Jung's and Freud's lectures in the *Journal*, XXI:2 (Apr. 1910), see above, editorial comment following 154 F. The other papers were Ferenczi's "On the Psychological Analysis of Dreams" and Jones's "Freud's Theory of Dreams."
[4] English in original.
[5] "Psychoanalysis in Psychiatry," *Journal of Abnormal Psychology*, IV (1909); it had been read before the American Therapeutic Society, New Haven, Connecticut, 6 May 09.
[6] See below, editorial comment following 183 J.

on Stekel, from whom he could still learn a good deal. All in all, some people are beginning to count me among the reverendi on a number of points, and those who feel the need of attacking me have a way of substituting the name of Stekel or someone else. When I see that happening, I overcome my inner resistance and profess my solidarity with the attacked parties.

I should like to bring up an idea of mine that has not yet fully ripened: couldn't our supporters affiliate with a larger group working for a practical ideal? An International Fraternity for Ethics and Culture is being organized in pursuit of such ideals. The guiding spirit is a Bern apothecary by the name of Knapp,[7] who has been to see me. Mightn't it be a good idea for us to join as a group? I want no dealings with the anti-alcohol organization. I have asked Knapp to get in touch with you. Forel is a leading light in the Fraternity.

I feel confident that the three months between now and the Congress will bring us many gratifying developments.

Kindest regards, FREUD

175 J

Dear Professor Freud,   Küsnach bei Zürich, 30 January 1910

At last I can settle down to write to you at leisure. These last days have been a nightmare. I had two public lectures this week. One of them was part of a series of 6 lectures on mental disturbances in childhood,[1] the other was to students, or rather to several scientific societies of students. The subject was "symbolism."[2] I have worked at it and have tried to put the "symbolic" on a psychogenetic foundation, i.e., to show that in the individual fantasy the *primum movens*, the individual conflict, material or form (whichever you prefer), is mythic, or

---

[7] Alfred Knapp; his organization was the Internationaler Orden für Ethik und Kultur. *Zentralblatt*, I:3 (Dec. 1910) carried an appeal from Knapp for contributions and members.

[1] Pastor Blocher (see above, 48 J n. 6) noted in his diary that he attended Jung's first lectures on mental disturbances in childhood—imbecility, moral insanity, epilepsy, and hysteria—on 12 Jan., 19 Jan., 26 Jan., and 2 Feb. 1910. The remaining two must have been given on 9 Feb. and 16 Feb. The lectures were never published.

[2] As subsequently transpires, the lecture was an early draft of "Wandlungen und Symbole der Libido," 1911/12. See below, 193 J par. 3.

mythologically typical. The supporting material is rather thin. The thing might have been better and more illuminating, but I don't think it was too bad. Sometime I'd like to show it to you for advice. I wouldn't mind taking it into the *Jahrbuch* as I suspect that Honegger's paper on Dementia praecox is moving in the same direction. The man does excellent work such as none of my pupils has produced before. He has also done a lot for me personally: I have had to hand over some of my dreams to him. During the time when I didn't write to you I was plagued by complexes, and I detest wailing letters. This time it was not I who was duped by the devil but my wife, who lent an ear to the evil spirit and staged a number of jealous scenes, groundlessly. At first my objectivity got out of joint (rule 1 of psychoanalysis: principles of Freudian psychology apply to everyone except the analyser) but afterwards snapped back again, whereupon my wife also straightened herself out brilliantly. Analysis of one's spouse is one of the more difficult things unless mutual freedom is assured. The prerequisite for a good marriage, it seems to me, is the license to be unfaithful. I in my turn have learnt a great deal. The main point always comes last: my wife is pregnant again, by design and after mature reflection. In spite of tempestuous complexes my enthusiasm for work is riding high. The new *Jahrbuch* is practically finished and should go to the printer early in February. It is solid and many-sided.

On Jan. 25th, in the person of Prof. Hoch, who has been working with me for more than a quarter of a year, I sent a valuable apostle into the diaspora. He has taken Meyer's place on Ward's Island.[3] He is a fine and extremely decent man of whom I have grown very fond. I also treated him for periodic depressions, successfully, I hope.

I would gladly send you the invitations for Nuremberg at once but they still haven't come back from the printer. They should go off this week. I shall lodge a complaint tomorrow.

I'd be very grateful if you would let me know to what extent you are thinking of contributing to the *Jahrbuch* for July 1910 and whether one of your Viennese will send something. I hope to have got Bleuler's article by then. (He has been in hospital for perityphlitis.)[4] There will be a contribution from me, probably from Riklin too. Whether Honegger will have finished by then is questionable.

The news from America is extraordinary. Jones is working really well. Brill richly deserves his success. I have just had a letter from him

---

[3] The New York State Psychiatric Institute, on Ward's Island, in the East River (New York City).
[4] Old name for appendicitis.

telling me how brilliantly Morton Prince interprets dreams. Another one who should be heading for extinction.

I hope you will have received the *poem* safely.

Thanks for the information on Kaibel.[5] Due to pressure of other work my mythological studies have had to take a back place for the time being.

I'm afraid I still haven't heard from the army authorities when I have to go on my military exercises, so I can't say yet whether I shall be free before or after Nuremberg.

Your suggestion that I should talk about America at Nuremberg is beginning to simmer. I think I shall do so in the form of a report on the development of the movement in general.

Many kind greetings,

Yours, JUNG

176 J

Dear Professor Freud,   [Postmark: Zürich 31 January 10][1]

By the same post I am sending you the invitations for Nuremberg. I shall not send any others to Vienna but would ask you to take care of the Viennese invitations for me. In the next few days I'll send you a list of the people I have invited, with the request that you add to it if warranted.

Kind regards, JUNG

177 F

Dear friend,   2 February 1910, Vienna, IX. Berggasse 19

Although experience has taught me to harden myself against the anticipation of your letters, the one that came yesterday gave me great pleasure and even consoled me with its varied contents. Living so far apart, we are bound to have experience of all sorts that we cannot share. You are living on the high seas, while I often can't help

---

[5] Apparently sent separately, as was the poem.

[1] A commemorative postcard imprinted "1909 Inauguration du Monument commemoratif de la Fondation de l'Union Postale Universelle," with a picture perhaps of the monument.

thinking of our little Dalmatian islands where a ship puts in every second Monday.

Ferenczi was a balm to me last Sunday; at last a chance to talk about the things closest to my heart; there is another man I am really sure of. Binswanger had taken up my two previous Sundays, he is a good sort, correct and even intelligent, but he lacks the bit of afflatus I need to lift me up, and his wife, or rather their relationship, is not an unmingled pleasure.

I should have thought it quite impossible to analyse one's own wife. Little Hans's father has proved to me that it can be done. In such analysis, however, it seems just too difficult to observe the technical rule whose importance I have lately begun to suspect: "surmount counter-transference."

I trust you will bring Honegger to Nuremberg with you, he has made a splendid impression on me too by an attempt to analyse me.[1] Perhaps he will bring us Stekel's sensitivity in the interpretation of the unconscious without Stekel's brutality and uncritical approach.

Your deepened view of symbolism has all my sympathy. Perhaps you remember how dissatisfied I was when in agreement with Bleuler all you had to say of symbolism was that it was a kind of "unclear thinking." True, what you write about it now is only a hint, but in a direction where I too am searching, namely, *archaic regression*, which I hope to master through mythology and the *development of language*. It would be wonderful if you could do a piece on the subject for the *Jahrbuch*.

I have no intention whatever of contributing my paper on general method to the *Jahrbuch*; it can only benefit from being set aside for a while. Either I shall submit nothing or one or two trifles such as those I sent you yesterday, or perhaps something I am not yet aware of will occur to me before you pronounce your *rien ne va plus*. I shall inform my Viennese of your appeal. Usually I want to restrain them. Adler is the only one who can be accepted without censorship, though not without criticism. Sadger's writing is insufferable, he would only mess up our nice book; Stekel read us a paper on obsessions, it was absolutely frivolous and faulty in method; he was thoroughly heckled, as Binswanger will confirm.[1a]

The invitations arrived today. Thank you very much for the poem, the third stanza fulfills all my expectations, it is still on my desk, it

[1] Presumably in Honegger's letter to Freud; see above, 148 J at n. 3.
[1a] Binswanger was a guest at the 19 Jan. meeting of the Society, when Stekel gave

obsesses me. In addition to this fiendish writer's cramp, I have brought back from America the appendix pains I had at the Camp:[2] so far my sense of humour has borne up fairly well under the test. By the way, has Bleuler been operated on?

For the Congress I now have the following: You on the development of ΨA (but mainly America, the rest is familiar to most of our people), me on the prospects for psychoanalysis, a happy combination since you represent the lady's future and I her past. Ferenczi means to speak on organization and propaganda and will get in touch with you about it; Adler promises a paper on psychosexual hermaphroditism, which will probably be rich in substance. Perhaps there will be more. I have purposely let it be known that in view of the abundance of material the management must reserve the right to effect a selection and that no one must feel offended. Won't mythology and pedagogy be represented on the programme? Hoch is certainly a good replacement for Meyer, who is rather tricky. I am now awaiting word from America as to when I can release the German version of the lectures.

The idea of a trip to Switzerland this summer is very popular with my family. Perhaps I have already written that we want a place with moderate altitude in French Switzerland, but we shall certainly stop for a day or two in Zürich. This and the Congress are my great expectations for the year. Since I must always have an object to love, the *porcupine*[3] has been replaced by a charming Japanese dwarf tree, with which I have been sharing my study since Christmas. My Indian summer of eroticism that we spoke of on our trip has withered lamentably under the pressure of work. I am resigned to being old and no longer even think continually of growing old.

I read Löwenfeld's well-meaning but feeble article in proof.[4] Even so he is a good and upright man.

---

a paper on "The Psychology of Doubt" (*Minutes*, II, pp. 394f.), probably = "Der Zweifel," *Zeitschrift für Psychotherapie und medizinische Psychologie*, IV (1912).
[2] Freud had had a mild attack of appendicitis while staying at Putnam's camp in the Adirondacks. See Jones, II, p. 65/59.
[3] English in original. / See the article by Gifford (cited above, comment following 154 F, n. 1) for Freud's interest in seeing a wild porcupine for the first time at the Putnam camp and receiving a small brass figure of a porcupine as a parting gift from his hosts. Miss Anna Freud has recalled that her father kept the brass porcupine on his desk, using the quills to hold letters waiting to be answered. Cf. also Jones's account, II, pp. 65f./59.
[4] "Über die hypermnestischen Leistungen in der Hypnose in bezug auf Kindheitserinnungen," *Zeitschrift für Psychotherapie und medizinische Psychologie*, II:1 (1910).

I shall gladly go over the list. Here they will certainly be asking me whether and on what conditions "guests" are desirable.

Kind regards to you and your growing family,

Sincerely yours, FREUD

178 J

Dear Professor Freud,   Küsnach-Zürich, 11 February 1910[1]

I am a lazy correspondent. But this time I have (as always) excellent excuses. Preparing the *Jahrbuch* has taken me an incredible amount of time, as I had to work mightily with the blue pencil. The bulk of the manuscripts goes off today. It will be an impressive affair.

Enclosed is the list of addresses. Please let me know if I have forgotten anyone from abroad. You will see that I am setting about it on a rather large scale—I hope with your subsequent approval. Our cause is forging ahead. Only today I heard from a doctor in Munich that the medical students there are taking a massive interest in the new psychology, some of them poking fun at the gentlemen at the Clinic because they understand nothing about it.

Meanwhile I too have received an invitation from the apothecary Knapp in Bern to join the I.F.[2] I have asked for time to think about it and have promised to submit the invitation to the Nuremberg Congress. Knapp wanted to have me also for lectures. The prospect appals me. I am so thoroughly convinced that I would have to read myself the longest ethical lectures that I cannot muster a grain of courage to promote ethics in public, let alone from the psychoanalytical standpoint! At present I am sitting so precariously on the fence between the Dionysian and the Apollinian that I wonder whether it might not be worthwhile to reintroduce a few of the older cultural stupidities such as the monasteries. That is, I really don't know which is the lesser evil. Do you think this Fraternity could have any practical use? Isn't it one of Forel's coalitions against stupidity and evil, and must we not love evil if we are to break away from the obsession with virtue that makes us sick and forbids us the joys of life? If a coalition is to have any ethical significance it should never be an artificial one but must be nourished by the deep instincts of

---

[1] Published in *Letters*, ed. G. Adler, vol. 1.
[2] Holograph: *I.O.* = Knapp's Internationaler Orden für Ethik und Kultur.

the race. Somewhat like Christian Science, Islam, Buddhism. Religion can be replaced only by religion. Is there perchance a new saviour in the I.F.? What sort of new myth does it hand out for us to live by? Only the wise are ethical from sheer intellectual presumption, the rest of us need the eternal truth of myth.

You will see from this string of associations that the problem does not leave me simply apathetic and cold. The ethical problem of sexual freedom really is enormous and worth the sweat of all noble souls.[3] But 2000 years of Christianity can only be replaced by something equivalent. An ethical fraternity, with its mythical Nothing, not in-fused by any archaic-infantile driving force, is a pure vacuum and can never evoke in man the slightest trace of that age-old animal power which drives the migrating bird across the sea and without which no irresistible mass movement can come into being. I imagine a far finer and more comprehensive task for ΨA than alliance with an ethical fraternity. I think we must give it time to infiltrate into people from many centres, to revivify among intellectuals a feeling for symbol and myth, ever so gently to transform Christ back into the soothsaying god of the vine, which he was, and in this way absorb those ecstatic in-stinctual forces of Christianity for the *one* purpose of making the cult and the sacred myth what they once were—a drunken feast of joy where man regained the ethos and holiness of an animal. That was the beauty and purpose of classical religion, which from God knows what temporary biological needs has turned into a Misery Institute. Yet what infinite rapture and wantonness lie dormant in our religion, waiting to be led back to their true destination! A genuine and proper ethical development cannot abandon Christianity but must grow up within it, must bring to fruition its hymn of love, the agony and ecstasy over the dying and resurgent god,[4] the mystic power of the wine, the awe-some anthropophagy of the Last Supper—only *this* ethical develop-ment can serve the vital forces of religion. But a syndicate of interests dies out after 10 years.[5]

ΨA makes me "proud and discontent,"[6] I don't want to attach it to Forel, that hair-shirted John of the Locusts, but would like to affiliate it with everything that was ever dynamic and alive. One can only let this kind of thing grow. To be practical: I shall submit this crucial

---

[3] See above, 51 J n. 2.
[4] A reference to Dionysus-Zagreus; cf. *Symbols of Transformation*, CW 5, par. 527. (Also in 1911/12 edn.)
[5] For a 1959 comment, see *Letters*, ed. G. Adler, vol. 1, p. 19, n. 8.
[6] Holograph: *stolz und unzufrieden.*—Goethe, *Faust I*, 2178.

question for ΨA to the Nuremberg Congress. I have abreacted enough for today—my heart was bursting with it. Please don't mind all this storming.

With many kind regards,

Most sincerely yours, JUNG

179 F

Dear friend,   13 February 1910, Vienna, IX. Berggasse 19

Yes, in you the tempest rages; it comes to me as distant thunder. And though I ought to treat you diplomatically and humour your obvious distate for writing with an artificial delay in answering, I am unable to restrain my own precipitate reactions. I can only offer the excuse of practical necessity.

Please tell Knapp that we do not wish to submit the question of the Fraternity to our Congress just yet, that there are too few of us, that we ourselves are not yet organized, which is true. But you mustn't regard me as the founder of a religion. My intentions are not so far-reaching. Considerations of a purely practical, or if you will diplomatic nature led me to make this attempt (which at heart I have already abandoned). I suspect that Knapp is a good man, that ΨA would bring him liberation, and I thought: if we join the Fraternity while it is *in statu nascendi*, we shall be able to draw the moralists to ΨA rather than let the Ψ-analysts be turned into moralists. Perhaps the idea was too diplomatic. Glad to abandon it. I was attracted by the practical, aggressive and protective aspect of the programme, the undertaking to combat the authority of State and Church directly where they commit palpable injustice,[1] and so to arm ourselves against the great future adversaries of ΨA with the help of larger numbers and methods other than those of scientific work. I am not thinking of a substitute for religion; this need must be sublimated. I did not expect the Fraternity to become a religious organization any more than I would expect a volunteer fire department to do so!

I am returning the list without comment. Most of the outsiders will not come, we shall keep warm among ourselves. The only omission I can think of is O. Gross, but I don't know his address. I have added Eitingon's. As to the programme and the organizational proposals, we ought to agree in advance.

[1] Quoted by Jones, II, pp. 74f./67f.

The quick publication of the new *Jahrbuch* before they had time to pour abuse on the last one will confuse our adversaries. The proofs of the German edition of the Worcester lectures have arrived. It seems to me now that I was rather aggressive in places. The second edition of the *Theory of Sexuality* will probably reach you in a week. Nothing is changed. I work every day to the point of exhaustion and then I write a few lines on the *Leonardo*. Riklin gave me pleasure by sending me a study on the "Beautiful Soul,"[2] but the presentation is so dull and colourless that I hesitate to include it in the *Papers*. Deuticke has shown me a new article by Friedländer in Bresler's journal,[3] as stupid and impudent as the others.

I send you my kind regards. I am looking forward to the best of news of you and your family.

Sincerely yours, FREUD

180 J

Dear Professor Freud,   Küsnach Zürich, 20 February 1910

As a matter of fact I did think you had something practical in mind with your proposal about the I. F. I have discussed it with various people here, they are all very skeptical about the popularity of the organization. Nevertheless I think it would do no harm to lay the matter before the Nuremberg Congress. Perhaps certain people who join privately will produce the necessary ferment. Have you any objection? My last letter was naturally another of those rampages of fantasy I indulge in from time to time. This time unfortunately it hit you, which was probably the intention. All sorts of things are cooking in me, mythology in particular, that is to say mythology should gain by it, for what is cooking is the nuptial complex as is evidently fit and proper at my time of life. My dreams revel in symbols that speak volumes, for instance my wife had her right arm chopped off (I had injured my thumb the day before, thus lending a helping hand to self-castration). Luckily the Walpurgis Nights of my unconscious do not affect my capacity for work although my mythology is temporarily at a standstill, partly because of the *Jahrbuch* and partly because of the crush of patients, which thank heavens

---

[2] See above, 47 J n. 3.

[3] "Hysterie und moderne Psychoanalyse," *Psychiatrisch-neurologische Wochenschrift*, XI:48/50 (1910). For tr., see below, 237 J n. 2.

has begun to fall off this week. Otherwise I am in good shape and still have resistances to writing you at the right time, my conscious motivation being that I must select a particularly undisturbed moment which of course never comes until one takes it. The reason for the resistance is my father-complex, my inability to come up to expectations (one's own work is garbage, says the devil). This time Binswanger is partly to blame. I distrust him somewhat, he praises certain people to the skies (e.g., Veraguth)[1] and is too hard on others, and this made me jumpy. In general I must concur with your verdict. I never got along with him as well as with Honegger for instance, who is honest to the core, considerably more honest than I, I'd say.

As regards Nuremberg I have been in touch with Dr. Warda, who has suggested the Grand Hotel as meeting-place and living quarters. I see no objection. Quarters will be reserved only for those who have applied[1a] (22 so far). Please would you inform the Viennese gentlemen, of whom only Jekels and Stekel have submitted applications. Marcinowski announces a lecture: sejunctive processes as the basis of psychoneurosis; Abraham on fetishism.[2] No more announcements of lectures yet. I will put together a report on America, dealing more with the inside than the outside.

Has Dr. G—— been with you? I hear you are taking him for analysis. The walking counterpart of his complex, the boy's nanny, often comes to see me here and is doing well. Fräulein E——, whom you will remember, is also in top form. A case of obsessional neurosis has deserted me at the climax of homosexual resistance. This brings me to my real question: the sequence and course of resistances. There must obviously be much that is typical. I'd like to sound you out on this point: the resistances must surely follow a more or less typical course depending on sex, age, and situation. I hope to find short-cuts and direct routes such as you in all probability have found already. So I'd like to profit by your experience. It seems to me that homosexuality is one of the richest sources of resistance in men, with women it is perversions or variations of sexuality *sensu proprio* (variations of coitus,

[1] Earlier, Veraguth had done research with the galvanometer as a measure of psychic stimuli. Jung added a corrigendum, giving primary credit to Veraguth for such work, in his and Peterson's "Psychophysical Investigations" (see above, 19 J n. 2). See CW 2, par. 1043.

[1a] Holograph begins a new page with date 22 Feb. 10.

[2] Marcinowski, "Sejunktive Prozesse als Grundlage der Psychoneurosen," abstracted by himself, *Jahrbuch*, II:2 (1910); Abraham, "Bemerkungen zur Analyse eines Falles von Fuss- und Korsettfetischismus," *Jahrbuch*, III:2 (1911) = "Remarks on the Psycho-analysis of a Case of Foot and Corset Fetishism," *Sel. Papers*.

etc.). The homosexual resistances in men are simply astounding and open up mind-boggling possibilities. Removal of the moral stigma from homosexuality as a method of contraception is a cause to be promoted with the utmost energy. Here we have a new hobby-horse to ride through the history of culture—contraceptive methods in ethnology: monasteries, self-castration (castration rites among the Australian aborigines). Homosexuality would be a tremendous advantage since many inferior men, who quite reasonably would like to remain on the homosexual level, are now forced into marriage. It would also be excellently suited to large agglomerations of males (businesses, universities, etc.). Because of our shortsightedness we fail to recognize the biological services rendered by homosexual seducers. Actually they should be credited with something of the sanctity of monks.

I still don't know when I have to go on military service and so am not master of my future.

Kind regards,

Yours sincerely, JUNG

Thanks for the excellent critique of "The Content of the Psychoses." The man seems to be gifted.[3]

181 J

Dear Professor Freud,   Küsnach/Zürich, 2 March 1910

I was very perturbed by your letter[1]—all sorts of misunderstandings seem to be in the air. How could you have been so mistaken in me? I don't follow. I can't say any more about it now, because writing is a bad business and all too often one misses the right note.

Many thanks for all your news. The first thing about your conception of the ucs. is that it is in striking agreement with what I said in my January lecture on symbolism. I explained there that "logical" thinking is thinking *in words*, which like discourse is directed outwards. "Analogical" or fantasy thinking is emotionally toned, pictorial and wordless, not discourse but an inner-directed rumination on materials belonging to the past. Logical thinking is "verbal thinking."

[3] Unidentified. / Postscript written at the top of the first page.

---

[1] Missing.

Analogical thinking is archaic, unconscious, not put into words and hardly formulable in words.

Now for the Nuremberg questions! Naturally I am very grateful for your suggestions and quite agree with them, except for the question of time. Five lectures have been announced so far + the two pro-posals by Ferenczi and Stekel.[2] These 5 lectures, which I hope will be augmented by the one I want from you, will barely suffice to fill out 2 mornings. I therefore propose either to schedule the first session for the *afternoon* of March 30th or to conclude the meeting officially on the afternoon of March 31st, or else hold the discussion (Stekel) in the morning and keep the afternoon free for informal conversation. Somewhat as follows: 30 Mar., morning, 8.30–1, lectures; evening at 5, Ferenczi. 31 Mar., morning, rest of lectures + Stekel; afternoon unoffi-cial. Do you agree with this arrangement?

I welcome your suggestion that Löwenfeld[3] be asked to report on the use of hypnosis and shall write to him at once. He has not yet applied for Nuremberg. Nor do I know the article you speak of. I'd be grateful for information where to find it. It is very questionable whether Bleuler can come. He wants the operation now and this will probably stop him. I have asked Honegger for a lecture on D. pr. I am thinking of getting down to work on mine, but would ask you to tell me what you think I should say in my report on America. It would be nice to feel myself in agreement with you. The *group research on symbols* is an excellent idea. I have long been thinking along those lines. It would be of great importance for the technique of ΨA, not to mention the theory. I think I can trust Warda not to let us down. To make sure I can fix it up with the hotel personally. I shall come to the Congress whatever happens. The military will allow for that, never fear.

Recently I received a letter from Isserlin in Munich asking whether he might attend our meeting. He disagreed with us, but, etc. . . . As you know, the man is a member of the blackest Munich clique

[2] Stekel proposed that a collective study of symbolism be instituted, and Ferenczi that an international association be formed, for which he presented a draft of statutes; see appendix 4. (Cf. "On the Organization of the Psycho-Analytic Move-ment" [first pub. 1927], *Final Contributions to the Problems and Methods of Psycho-Analysis*, ed. Michael Balint, 1955.) For abstracts, see Rank's report on the Congress, *Jahrbuch*, II:2 (1910); also Jones, II, pp. 75ff./68ff.

[3] Holograph begins a new page with date 3 Mar. 10. / Löwenfeld gave a lecture "Über Hypnotherapie," not published but abstracted by Rank in the *Jahrbuch*, II:2 (1910).

and slanders us for all he is worth. I beg you to let me know *by return* whether we should allow such vermin to come to N. Myself, I'd rather not have the bastard around, he might spoil one's appetite. But our *splendid isolation*[4] must come to an end one day.

I think it well that you have declined Vogt's invitation.[5] Such requests are a bit too naïve and totally "arriéré." (I enclose his letter.)

So far I have ca. 30 applicants for N. (Frank wants to come too). In addition some 20 will come unannounced, as at Salzburg, so we can count on about 50 in all.

Much looking forward to seeing you again. Many kind regards,

Your not in the least vacillating, J U N G

182 F

Dear friend,   6 March 1910, Vienna, IX. Berggasse 19

Believe me, there are no further misunderstandings between us, nor do I regard you as "vacillating." I am neither so forgetful nor so touchy, and I know how closely we are united by personal sympathy and by pulling on the same cart. I am merely irritated now and then— I may say that much, I trust—that you have not yet disposed of the resistances arising from your father-complex, and consequently limit our correspondence so much more than you would otherwise. Just rest easy, dear son Alexander, I will leave you more to conquer than I myself have managed, all psychiatry and the approval of the civilized world, which regards me as a savage! That ought to lighten your heart.

As to my suggestion in regard to Isserlin, you have no doubt complied with it in modified form. I too believe that our isolation must come to an end some day, and then we shall not have to hold separate congresses. But I think that day is still far off and that we can do with other guests than Isserlin. As you see, J. G. Borkmann,[1] who may not live to see the day, has been musing in his study for several years.

---

[4] English in original. / Concerning Isserlin's request, see Alexander and Selesnick, p. 4 (letter of Freud to Bleuler, 16 Oct. 10).
[5] Oskar Vogt (1870–1959), German psychiatrist and brain pathologist, early associate of Forel, director of the Kaiser Wilhelm Institute for Brain Research. As president of the forthcoming Congress for Medical Psychology and Psychotherapy, in Brussels 7–8 Aug., he had evidently invited Freud to give a report.

---

[1] A reference to the hero of Ibsen's play *John Gabriel Borkman* (1876). As Bernard Shaw wrote, Borkman's "conception of his own power grows hyperbolical

I see your report on America just as you intended, as part of a review on the internal and external destinies of ΨA up to now, designed to encourage our people. My paper can be entitled: The Future Prospects for ΨA Therapy. You didn't expect another contribution, did you? I am very sorry to hear of Bleuler's operation. I am doing well in that respect; I may get by with a cure in Karlsbad. Löwenfeld's article is to be found in Moll's *Zeitschrift*, Vol. II, No. 1; it is feeble like everything he writes, but he is a good, honest fellow.

The second edition of the *Theory of Sexuality*, unchanged except for a few notes, will be on its way to you tomorrow. May I ask you not to start out with the heretical papers like Adler's[2] (and maybe Marcinowski's), they would depress the atmosphere.

Otherwise I am all Leonardo. I am worried about the immediate future of my daughter who must undergo another operation. I am eagerly awaiting news of your timetable, so as to know whether we shall have any time together in addition to the few hours at the Congress.

Kindest regards, FREUD

From Emma Jung

Dear Professor Freud,[1]   Küsnacht, 8 March 1910

I am writing to you in the name of my husband, who suddenly left for Chicago today, where his former patient, McCormick, is seriously ill. According to the reports it could be paralysis or mania; but thinks it possible that the trouble is psychogenic and therefore followed the call. He urgently requests you not to worry about Nuremberg as he will *quite certainly* be there. He will arrive either on March 29th, 9.34 p.m. or on the 30th, 5 a.m., and in any case will arrive in time for the beginning of the Congress. His boat, *Kronprinzessin Cäcilie*, picks him up tomorrow in Cherbourg and arrives in New York on the 15th. On the 22nd he leaves again on the same steamer, will be in Cherbourg on the 28th and in Nuremberg via Paris-Cologne on the 29th.

Then I have to ask you what kind of title you want to give your Nu-

---

and Napoleonic in his solitude and impotence" (*Dramatic Opinions*, 1907). (For Borkman's first initial, Freud wrote D and changed it to J.)

2 "Über psychischen Hermaphroditismus," abstracted by Pfister in the *Jahrbuch*, II:2 (1910); pub. as "Der psychische Hermaphroditismus im Leben und in der Neurose," *Fortschritte der Medizin*, XXVII (1910).

---

1 Holograph: *Sehr geehrter Herr Professor!*

remberg lecture and whether it is all right with you to be the first speaker on the morning of the 30th. I should be very grateful to you if you would tell me this as soon as possible on a postcard, so that the programmes can then be printed and sent off.

Just at the moment of departure a letter arrived from Vogt in Berlin inquiring about the paper on the neurosis theory for Brussels.[2] I am asking him to be patient as the letter came too late, and would you in the meantime please give my husband your opinion of it. His military service may make the whole thing impossible.

Is it of interest to you that Isserlin asked if he might attend the Congress in Nuremberg as a "silent listener" (an objective one, of course!), and that this was refused for very convincing reasons?

With kind regards to you and all your family,

EMMA JUNG

Letters should be addressed to Oelrichs & Co., Broadway 5, New York.[3]

183 J

Grand Hotel Terminus, Rue St. Lazare
Dear Professor Freud, Paris,[1] le 9 Mars 1910

Now don't get cross with me for my pranks! You will already have heard from my wife that I am on my way to America. *I have arranged everything so as to be back in time for Nuremberg.* Everything else is so arranged that it will function automatically, i.e., with the help of my wife and the assistance of Honegger, to whom I have entrusted my patients.

I had a severe conflict of duties to overcome before I could make up my mind to travel. But the journey *had* to be made, and it can be because I shall be back in Cherbourg on the afternoon of March 28th, having spent 6–7 days in America, enough for a trip to Chicago and a few other things besides. It will also be good for my mental health.

Löwenfeld has consented to do the report. I have also prodded Honegger into a lecture on paranoid delusions.[2] So we shall have a fine programme.

---

[2] After Freud declined (above, 181 J n. 5) Vogt extended the invitation to Jung, who evidently also refused it. See below, 283 F n. 4.
[3] Agents for the North German Lloyd steamship line.

---

[1] Printed letterhead.
[2] "Über paranoide Wahnbildung," abstracted by himself in the *Jahrbuch*, II:2 (1910).

On this American trip I shall repeat what we said last time. This time I shall have a good friend over there in the person of Prof. Hoch. If circumstances are favourable I shall pay a quick visit to Putnam. Can scarcely make it to Worcester.

My New York address is: Messrs. Oelrichs and Co.

Broadway 5, N. Y. City.

I send you a hearty farewell and please forgive me all my misdemeanours.

Most sincerely yours, JUNG

From Emma Jung

Dear Professor Freud,[1] Küsnacht, 16 March 1910

Here at last you have the programme for Nuremberg, from which you will see that your lecture comes first after all. My husband had never said anything about his speaking on the 1st day, and as the title is only "Report on America" it will not upset the plan. I also think he will be glad not to have to speak first, as he may be arriving in Nuremberg at 5 in the morning and will probably be rather tired.

Many thanks for your kind letter[2] and offer of help which I shall gladly accept if anything more difficult happens. I can set your mind at rest by telling you that a young friend and pupil of my husband's, Dr. Honegger, is deputizing with the patients and looking after the Nuremberg business with me, otherwise I would be rather nervous about everything turning out all right.

Today I am expecting news of my husband's safe arrival in New York; I do hope it comes soon. Incidentally, America no longer has the same attraction for him as before, and this has taken a stone from my heart. It is just enough to satisfy the desire for travel and adventure, but no more than that.

I was very sorry to hear that Frau Hollitscher has had to undergo another operation; I hope she will soon recover and that it will be a lasting success this time. Please give her my warmest greetings and wishes.

I send greetings to you and all your dear ones,

EMMA JUNG

Dr. Honegger sends best regards.

[1] Holograph: *Verehrter Herr Professor!*
[2] Missing.

The Nuremberg Congress

The Second International Psychoanalytic Congress was held at Nuremberg on 30–31 March 1910. Freud's anxiety over Jung's prior absence in America is evident in what he wrote Pfister 17 Mar. 10: "I still have not got over your not coming to Nuremberg. Bleuler is not coming either, and Jung is in America, so that I am trembling about his return. What will happen if my Zurichers desert me?" After the Congress, however, Freud wrote Ferenczi (3 Apr.): "There is no doubt that it was a great success" (Jones, II, p. 77/70).

Freud opened the proceedings with his paper "The Future Prospects of Psycho-analytic Therapy" (see below, 217 J n. 5). Jung's "Report on America," given the next day, survives only as a brief abstract, "Bericht über Amerika," *Jahrbuch*, II:2 (1910); in CW 18. For the other speakers, mentioned in the preceding letters, see the programme, appendix 4.

The chief accomplishment of the meeting was the founding of the International Psychoanalytic Association (Internationale Psychoanalytische Vereinigung), of which Jung was elected president and Riklin secretary; its headquarters were at the place of residence of its president, i.e., then Zürich. Jung and Riklin were also made editors of a new official publication, the *Correspondenzblatt* (*Bulletin*) of the Association, to be issued every month. A second new periodical was also established, the monthly *Zentralblatt für Psychoanalyse: Medizinische Monatsschrift für Seelenkunde*, directed by Freud, edited by Adler and Stekel, and published by J. F. Bergmann, Wiesbaden. The existing local psychoanalytic societies were to become branch societies of the International Association. For the Statutes of the Association, adopted at Nuremberg, see appendix 3.

After the Congress, Freud and Jung made an excursion to Rothenburg, a walled town west of Nuremberg, admired for its picturesque Gothic architecture.

184 J

Dear Professor Freud,   Küsnach-Zürich, 6 April 1910

This time I'm settling down quickly to a letter so as not to give the devil a chance to conduct his well-known time-extending experiments. I have reluctantly let Honegger go to his sanatorium in Territet;[1] now my libido is thrashing around for a suitable object. Riklin will in some measure replace the temporary loss. Nuremberg did him a lot of good

---

[1] East of Montreux, on Lake Geneva.

and he is coming much closer to me than before. All the same I won't let go of Honegger, and will do everything in my power to carry out this plan.[2]

Nothing new to report yet about the International Psychoanalytic Association. The notice for the *Jahrbuch* has gone off to Deuticke. Proofs have begun to arrive so we can hope for early publication. As soon as term begins our local group will put itself in order.

As a perseveration from America I am still reading the interesting book by Maurice Low, *The American People, A Study in National Psychology*.[3] He holds the climate largely responsible for the frequency of neurosis in America.[4] There must be something in it, for it is really too weird that the Indians were unable to populate that fertile country more densely. Low thinks the colossal differences of temperature between summer and winter are to blame. Perhaps a harshly continental climate really is ill-suited to a race sprung from the sea. "Something is wrong,"[5] as Low says.

When I have fulfilled this duty (the reading of this book) I shall return to the overflowing delights of mythology, which I always reserve as dessert for the evening.

I found wife, children, and house in good shape, and work aplenty.

I forgot to ask whether Deuticke has inquired about the separate publication of my child analysis.[6] What do you think? I'd welcome it myself, but shall take account of business interests and your advice.

Kind regards, JUNG

185 F

Dear friend,   12 April 1910, Vienna, IX. Berggasse 19

Why should I object to your publishing your child analysis separately? If I didn't do so with Little Hans and the Rat Man, it was for fear of cutting down on the sales of the *Jahrbuch*. The period in which that might be so must be over by now. Actually Deuticke never

---

[2] See below, 200 J n. 5.

[3] By A. Maurice Low (Boston and New York, vol. I, 1909).

[4] See p. 60 on "the correspondence between climatic severity . . . and insanity."

[5] English in original.

[6] "Psychic Conflicts in a Child," the third of Jung's Clark lectures, soon to be published in the *Jahrbuch*; see below, 209 F n. 2. Deuticke reprinted the *Jahrbuch* text as a pamphlet.

asked me. The proofs of my contribution[1] and of the *Leonardo* have not yet come. I presume Deuticke has written to you about converting the *Jahrbuch* into a bi-monthly; at the same time no doubt you have been told about the conflicting plan for an Adler-Stekel *Zentralblatt*. Perhaps you are considering your decision at this very moment.

I was sorry to hear that you have let Honegger go off. I hope it will not be for long and that your self-confidence will soon catch up with your new position; that will obviate a number of delicate situations. In less than a year, I believe, the world will show you who you are, and a wise man prepares for all eventualities. At last Wednesday's meeting of our Society[2] I ceded the presidency to Adler. They all behaved very affectionately, so I promised to stay on as chairman of the scientific sessions. They are very much shaken, and for the present I am satisfied with the outcome of my statesmanship. Fair competition between Vienna and Zürich can only benefit the cause. The Viennese have no manners, but they know a good deal and can still do good work for the movement.

This evening I am expecting Prof. Modena of Ancona, a swarthy Judaeo-Italian. My week has been taken from me by an obligation, a contribution[3] to a special number of a medical journal in honour of Königstein (60th birthday). I produced, or rather aborted, something about psychogenic disturbances of vision—poor, like everything I do to order. I have returned rather depressed from our lovely Diet of Nuremberg. Analysis [of my depression] leads far afield to the distress which the state of my daughter's health causes me—I have been trying in vain to replace her. You will discern the note of resignation in *Leonardo*.

Jones writes excellent letters. Couldn't you prod him into setting up groups in Boston and New York? Isserlin seems almost to be having lucid moments, if he speaks and thinks as he writes.[4] I send you kind regards. I shall always be glad to hear from you.

Sincerely yours, FREUD

[1] " 'Über den Gegensinn der Unworte,' " *Jahrbuch*, II:1 (1910) = " 'The Antithetical Meaning of Primal Words,' " SE XI.

[2] See *Minutes*, II, pp. 463ff., for a spirited discussion headed "An Epilogue to the Congress"; it continued at the next meeting, on 14 April.

[3] "The Psycho-analytic View of Psychogenic Disturbance of Vision," SE XI; originally a contribution to a Festschrift in honour of Leopold Königstein (1850–1924), professor of ophthalmology in Vienna and an old friend of Freud.

[4] Max Isserlin, "Die psychoanalytische Methods Freuds," *Zeitschrift für die gesamte Neurologie und Psychiatrie*, I (1910).

186 J

Dear Professor Freud,   Küsnach/Zürich, 17 April 1910

I too have now read Isserlin's article and can only see that the fellow has stooped even lower than before. At the back of it all is still the same twisted mind, but he has now done a bit of reading and is worried by the criticism of his associates and by our success. As late as last autumn, in the holiday course in Munich, he compared the Freudian school with Titania's obsessed lover who woke up one day with an ass's head on him—something his own demon has obviously whispered in his ear. We won't have to wait long for his conversion. His unconscious at least knows this much, that Puck has already "miracled"[1] the ass's head on to Ziehen and Oppenheim. And then all the equivocations! *Your* discovery of repression is nothing, but *his* conception of it suddenly amounts to something. The psychoanalytic method is not worth a button, yet he uses it to clear up the complexes of his patients. When all's said and done, the whole of Herr Isserlin lives and breathes only because of what you and I have discovered, yet he reviles us, not as impudently and loudly as before, but in private and therefore all the more dirtily, and still he can't help trying to cadge an invitation to Nuremberg. What's more he has put into my mouth a piece of nonsense I never said. But it hardly seems worth sending a correction to the *Zeitschrift*?

Friedländer has been puking again—in the *Umschau*,[2] where he

---

[1] Holograph: "*angewundert*," a word from Schreber's "basic language" in his *Memoirs* (see next letter, n. 5, and 197 F n. 2). Because Jung writes it in quotation marks without explanation, it may be inferred that he and Freud had discussed Schreber's book and its striking language while together in Nuremberg and Rothenburg. In a note that he added to *Symbols of Transformation* (1952), the revision of "Wandlungen und Symbole der Libido," Jung stated: "The [Schreber] case was written up at the time by Freud in a very unsatisfactory way after I had drawn his attention to the book" (CW 5, par. 458, n. 65). Jung mentioned the Schreber case first in "The Psychology of Dementia Praecox" (written 1906; see CW 3, index); also in "Wandlungen und Symbole," part I (cf. CW 5, pars. 39 n. 41 and 62 n. 4), in the same issue of the *Jahrbuch* (III:1) as Freud's paper (see below, 225 F n. 1). / Schreberisms occur frequently in the correspondence hereafter.

[2] "Hamlet—ein sexuelles Problem?" *Die Umschau*, XIX:15 (9 Apr. 10), attacking Jones's psychoanalytic interpretation as reported by a scientific writer, Wilhelm Gallenkamp, "Hamlet—ein sexuelles Problem," ibid., XIX:11 (12 Mar. 10), dealing with Jones, "The Oedipus Complex as an Explanation of Hamlet's Mystery: A Study in Motive," *American Journal of Psychology*, XXI:1 (Jan.

fulminates against one Herr Gallencamp, who is dealing with Jones's "Hamlet." Our "treatment" seems to have put the screws on Fr., he is at his wits' end. He is also moaning that Abraham refuses to be impressed either by Ziehen or by Oppenheim. All sorts of things are cooking. Old Uncle Binswanger[3] was with Oppenheim in Meran, where they howled together about you. Some of the after-wails reached my ears via Kreuzlingen. In Munich too there are wild goings-on at the clinic, with violent discussions rending the air. The ferment is evidently at work with no assistance from us. The gentlemen no longer sleep soundly o' nights. Incidentally, the snub I sent Isserlin has put Kraepelin's nose out of joint; he has again accused us, on the occasion of a consultation in Switzerland, of being mystics and spiritualists. (Bleuler is a mystic too!!) In Burghölzli my policies are regarded with displeasure, as my successor Maier gently indicated to me. The limping along in both directions is getting worse, I'm afraid, they have no one who understands the least thing about ΨA. Honegger, who was there as a voluntary worker, came down so heavily on my side that he immediately lost contact with the clinic.

We haven't held our constituent assembly yet, as I am waiting for Bleuler's return (after his successful operation). I have already written to New York. I am glad to hear that everything went off well in Vienna. Stekel and Adler have asked me to collaborate. I certainly don't want to increase my work load unnecessarily, but wouldn't refuse although I shan't be able to contribute much as my own work and my students eat up all my time. Also, as I recently discovered, I have a decided resistance to publication. I "abort" with increasing reluctance. At present I am pursuing my mythological dreams with almost auto-erotic pleasure, dropping only meagre hints to my friends. I also notice that my whole desire for publication is concentrated on the *Jahrbuch*, which seems to soak up all my libido. Probably it must be so. I often feel I am wandering alone through a strange country, seeing wonderful things that no one has seen before and no one needs to see. It was like that when the psychology of Dementia praecox dawned upon me. Only, I don't yet know what will come of it. I must just let myself be carried along, trusting to God that in the end I shall make a landfall somewhere.

1910); tr., *Das Problem des Hamlet und der Oedipus-Komplex* (*Schriften zur angewandten Seelenkunde*, 10; 1911). Friedländer interlarded slurs against Jones and Abraham with dubious praise for Freud.
[3] Otto Binswanger, uncle of Ludwig Binswanger, who was then at Kreuzlingen.

Still no improvement in your daughter's health? Such a confounded twist of fortune—I too would find it hard to bear.

With kind regards and wishes,

Yours sincerely, JUNG

Apropos of Deuticke: I stand firmly by the bi-annual publication of the *Jahrbuch*.[4]

187 F

Dear friend,   22 April 1910,[1] Vienna, IX. Berggasse 19

If Isserlin's article had appealed to me in any other way than by giving me a good laugh at his intimations of respectful commiseration, I should really deserve to be put down as a fool. No, I disagree with nothing in your criticism and adjure you to persist in your silence until those gentlemen approach us in a *very different way*.

Friedländer's resemblance to our companion in the car going to Rothenburg is becoming more and more striking. He thinks he can take us in as he did poor Löwenfeld. No, my friend, not a bit of it!

I can warmly recommend the *Hamburger Ärzte-Correspondenz* for April 3rd.[2] In it you will find a magnificent mixture of $\bar{a}\bar{a}$[2a] arrogance and ignorance, Hamburg respectability and German love of authority. Still, it has certain new features that give it special spice. They say, for instance, that we cannot be called to account because we do not show ourselves at congresses; also that we have made a colossal blunder with our presumptuous attempt to apply insights derived from hysteria to obsessional states (!!) and to Dem. pr., which is caused by modifications in the cerebral cortex (!). Incidentally, you are not even mentioned in connection with Dem. pr., and in general the criticism is leveled at the "Freudians," perhaps because with them one can still

---

[4] Postscript written at top of first page, next to date, sideways.

[1] Jones states (II, p. 158/140) that Jung and his wife visited Freud in Vienna on 19 April, but the contents of this letter do not support the likelihood of such a visit, which is not otherwise documented.

[2] On 29 Mar. 10 "there was a violent explosion of contumely at a meeting of the Medical Society of Hamburg," led by Weygandt (Jones, II, p. 130/116, citing the *Hamburger Ärzte–Correspondenzblatt*, 4 Apr. 10).

[2a] Pharmaceutical abbreviation = *ana*, meaning "in equal parts."

reason, which, thank the Lord, they have given up attempting with me.

On the other hand it was with pure distaste that I read Frank's cowardly and abject book[3] on psychoanalysis, in which he naturally accuses me of exaggerating the importance of sexuality and then proceeds to go me one better. *La sexualité c'est l'homme*—says Frank.

Enough of that, today the *American Journal of Psychology* arrived,[4] and the German edition of my lectures will come to you very shortly. Once again Jones is excellent. I am overjoyed to hear that mythology is again giving you the "fairytale forest feeling" that comes of a sound conception. Autoerotic enjoyment is sure to be followed by exhibition —a development that I am eagerly awaiting. I am also delighted about your libidinal attachment to the *Jahrbuch*. I mean to write something for it myself soon: a first Contribution to the Psychology of Love: Surely no one can expect you actually to work on the *Zentralblatt*, provided you merely enter into some sort of connection with it so as to avoid any appearance of competition. The Viennese are now busily at work, the emancipation is bearing good fruit so far. I am trying to persuade Deuticke to take over the *Zentralblatt*, though he would rather enlarge the *Jahrbuch*. He probably will. I personally should prefer it that way; the work would be shared, the restless spirits here would be kept busy and taught responsibility.

I am now reading the proofs of the *Leonardo*; I am very curious to know your impression of it. It will see the light of day in May. Apart from that, I am deep in our psychological problems, but I have nothing that seems ripe for communication. These playful occupations are my reaction against an excess of ΨA activity; thirteen patients, nine hours a day. Dr. G—— is probably the most amusing, very interesting theoretically, because he is not really entitled to a neurosis. Luckily Frau C—— is with her mother, who is very ill; otherwise it would be too much.

I feel that I am moving into a quiet period of immersion in my work, during which all the blows being struck in Berlin and elsewhere will glance off from my indifference. My daughter seems to be somewhat better; she came to see us yesterday for the first time in three months.

I still have no proof of my contribution to the *Jahrbuch*.

[3] Probably Ludwig Frank, *Die Psychoanalyse, ihre Bedeutung für die Auffassung und Behandlung psychoneurotischer Zustände* (Munich, 1910).
[4] See above, 174 F n. 3.

Havelock Ellis has sent me the sixth volume of his studies: *Sex in Relation to Society*. Unfortunately my receptivity is consumed by my nine analyses. But I shall set it aside for the holidays along with the wonderful Schreber,[5] who ought to have been made a professor of psychiatry and director of a mental hospital.

Don't worry, Burghölzli will limp after us as it has always done. Bleuler can't retreat, and since he can no longer hold you back he can only be useful and invaluable as a "middle link." Have I already written to you that Dr. Modena has been here? He is looking for a publisher for the *Theory of Sexuality*. (Ah yes, now I remember speaking of him in my last letter.)

It remains for me to acknowledge receipt of the equivalent of 50 marks. With kind regards to your dear wife and the children (Anna!).[6]

Sincerely yours, FREUD

188 F

Dear friend,   26 April 1910, Vienna, IX. Berggasse 19

Your telegraphed request[1] for advice has caused me a certain perplexity. But gathering my wits, I come to the comforting conclusion that it makes no difference at all whether or not Bleuler joins, the result will be the same in either case. We shall not be deterred from going ahead with our organization and from keeping on with psychoanalysis. Once this is settled, we can tell ourselves that his joining would nevertheless be most welcome to us, and cajole him a little by pointing out that by declining he would make a bad impression on our adversaries and harm the cause in a way which he certainly does not intend. If he merely refuses to assume the leadership of the Zürich group, this would have its counterpart in my withdrawal from the leadership in Vienna, and could be presented in this guise. Then it

---

[5] Daniel Paul Schreber, *Denkwürdigkeiten eines Nervenkranken* (Leipzig, 1903); tr. I. Macalpine and R. A. Hunter, *Memoirs of My Nervous Illness* (London, 1955). The *Memoirs* were the basis of Freud's "Psycho-analytic Notes on . . . a Case of Paranoia"; see below, 225 F n. 1. / Schreber (1842–1911), between spells of mental illness, had a distinguished career as a judge.

[6] The case name for Agathli in "Psychic Conflicts in a Child"; see below, 209 F n. 2.

---

[1] Missing.

would not be difficult for you to foist the dignity on someone else, maybe Pfister (?), since you and Riklin, in accordance with our agreement, I believe, are disqualified by the central positions you now hold. I feel sure we can persuade him to join as a rank-and-file member, like myself here in Vienna. His motives are not clear to me. Is it only a demonstration against your elevation? Is he opposed to your policy of keeping away from congresses and polemics? Or is his refusal entirely the product of his unconscious, originating in the impression that you infringed on his rights by citing his Freddy[2] en passant? I hope you won't leave me entirely in the dark on the subject.

The last article sent by Strohmayer[3] (from Moll's *Zeitschrift*) was accompanied by a letter that I must answer today. It is really vicious and shows that the man could do with treatment. He has evidently made nothing of his own dreams and has never been able to provoke affects in his patients, but it doesn't occur to him that the fault may lie more with him than with ΨA. Apart from you and me, perhaps only Ferenczi takes self-analysis seriously.

Kind regards. I am hoping that the approaching difficulties will soon give us the opportunity for a cheery conversation.

Sincerely yours, FREUD

189 J

Grand Hotel Victoria and National,

Dear Professor Freud,　　　　　　　　　　Basel,[1] 30 April 1910

At last I can report to you after the uproar last week. In a private talk beforehand, Bleuler, very huffy and irritable, gave me a flat refusal and expressly declared that he would not join the Society—he would dissociate himself from it altogether. Reasons: its aim was too

---

[2] "Fredi" was the family nickname of Bleuler's son Manfred (see above, 9 J n. 6), and apparently Jung had used that or "Freddy" for the newborn baby (i.e., Franz) in the original version of "Über Konflikte der kindlichen Seele." Professor Manfred Bleuler has stated in a private communication that "it is certain that Freud meant by Freddy myself, as my father certainly had no other Fredi." In the published paper, the name appears as "Fritzchen"; in Brill's translation in the *American Journal* just received (187 F par. 5), "Freddy" (see also "Psychic Conflicts in a Child," par. 20).
[3] Wilhelm Strohmayer, "Zur Analyse und Prognose psychoneurotischer Symptome," *Zeitschrift für Psychotherapie und medizinische Psychologie*, II:2 (1910).

---

[1] Printed letterhead.

biased, it took too narrow a view of the problems, it was too exclusive, you had slighted Frank in Nuremberg and thereby ostracized him, one didn't want to sit down with everybody (a dig at Stekel). He simply would not join, that was the long and short of it. I told him what the consequences would be, but it was no good. Yesterday we had our constituent assembly, which Frank also attended. The same opposition was shown with the same hollow resistances; another "reason" they gave was that they didn't want to commit themselves to a confession of faith, etc. In the course of the discussion it became clear that Frank is the grey eminence who has been working on Bleuler. I let the discussion go on until both Bleuler and Frank were properly cornered and were forced to admit that they just didn't want to join. I had so arranged matters that the local group had already constituted itself with 12 members before the meeting took place, which faced them with a *fait accompli*. The overwhelming majority are on our side. Taking your Nuremberg tactics as a model, I postponed the final decision until the next meeting in the hope that Bleuler's resistances will have melted by then. As the evening wore on he became noticeably milder and I almost venture to hope he will come along with us. In any case Frank can go by the board and I would gladly speed his departure with a joyful kick, [. . .]. We shall manage with or without Bleuler, but with him would be better. Most of the others stuck by me splendidly and did their best to unhorse Bleuler. After the meeting he again favoured us *privatim* with a dream, naturally in order to dispute the interpretation. All 10 of those present were shaking with laughter and fully agreed with my interpretation. The key to the mystery is that Bleuler understands far too little of ΨA, so little that he has not assimilated even the elements of dream interpretation. No wonder he yields so willingly to Frank's subversive influence.

As a matter of fact his whole opposition is a revenge for my resignation from the abstinence societies. (Hence his charge of exclusiveness, narrowness, and bias.)

When Kraepelin was here he went on at poor Bleuler for my having excluded Isserlin from Nuremberg. That, I am glad to say, has made a big impression in Munich. Those gents are getting jumpy.

I heard from Putnam that he is planning to organize something in Boston. Let's hope something will come of it soon.

Otherwise all's well. Nuremberg has produced happy results for us all.

Kind regards, JUNG

190 F

Dear friend,   2 May 1910, Vienna, IX. Berggasse 19

Your idea of tracing Bleuler's objections back to the abstinence societies is both clever and plausible. Towards them such an attitude is perfectly reasonable, towards our International it is an absurdity. We can't very well inscribe such things as providing freezing schoolchildren with warm clothing on our banners side by side with the furtherance of ΨA. One would be reminded of certain hotel signs: Hotel England and Red Cock.[1] But it's amusing how such an incident brings out the latent resistances in our so-called supporters. In this we are at a great advantage though; when a man stands firm as a rock, all the tottering, wavering souls end by clinging to him for support. Which is just what will happen now, and undoubtedly Bleuler, after setting too high a price on himself, will find out how unpleasant it is to fall between two stools.

Frank is just as ambivalent as his "psychanalysis." He simply has a bad conscience towards me. You may not have been far away when he had someone bring him in (or wasn't it you yourself?) and I said: I have heard a good deal ((all very ambivalent)) about you, and he left without a word. A propos of Isserlin, let's share the credit.

From Jones, who is getting nicer and abler by the day, I received today copies of a correspondence with A. Meyer and Warren[2] about the censoring of an article. I am enclosing it. It is extremely interesting from a cultural point of view, it would be good material for your "America." — From Löwenfeld two of our nasty mongrel's accomplishments, also very funny.[3] Of course I shouldn't be letting them out of my hands, but I am counting on you to send them right back, so I can promptly cheer the rightful owner's heart with them.

On the scientific side, just an oddity. I have two patients with nuclear complexes involving their witnessing acts of infidelity on the

---

[1] Quoted by Jones, II, p. 80/73.

[2] Howard Crosby Warren (1867–1934), professor of psychology at Princeton University, was an editor of the *Psychological Bulletin* (Baltimore). The 15 Apr. 10 (VII:4) issue, dealing especially with psychopathology, was "prepared under the editorial care" of Adolf Meyer and featured a paper by Jones, "Freud's Psychology," seemingly an uncensored presentation of that subject. The correspondence referred to has not been recovered.

[3] Unidentified, but apparently publications by Friedländer. See below, 191 J first par.

part of their mothers (the one historical, the other perhaps a mere fantasy). They both tell me about it the same day and preface their story with dreams about *wood*.[3a] In one a building supported by wooden posts collapses, in the other the woman is represented *directly* by old wood, i.e., antique furniture. Now I am aware that boards mean a woman, also cupboards, but I never heard of any close connection between wood and the mother complex. It occurs to me though that wood in Spanish is *madera* = matter (hence the Portuguese name of the island of Madeira) and undoubtedly *mater* lies at the root of *materia* (matter). Force and matter would then be father and mother. One more of our dear parents' disguises.

Things are quite lively in Vienna: I am being treated very tenderly. The two editors have agreed to discuss each number of the *Zentralblatt* with me in advance, and I am to have full veto power. The matter of a publisher is not yet settled. Deuticke is reluctant, he wants to wait for the outcome of our negotiations with Bergmann. If nothing comes of them, I'm pretty sure he will be willing, ΨA has been selling well and that mellows him. The *Jahrbuch* is disgracefully late, he puts the blame on the printers. Too bad. A new volume always encourages our friends and annoys our enemies; one would come in very handy right now.

Our summer plans are taking shape. The poor health of our grandmother[4] in Hamburg (aged 80) makes it necessary to reduce the distance between her and us, so we have decided in favour of a beach resort in Holland within a day's journey of Hamburg. We are now corresponding with someone in Nortwyige[5] (or something of the sort) near Leyden through my Dutch patient's nurse. If the project materializes, we should welcome visitors—a fantasy, of course, but no harm in mentioning it.

My daughter's health is definitely a little better; I don't dare expect any more. One becomes so anxious and resigned in old age!

A sign of the times: I have received a letter to the effect that Geheimrat Ostwald[6] would be pleased to have an article from my pen for the *Annalen der Naturphilosophie*. If I were more ambitious, I

[3a] Freud was to discuss the symbolism of wood in a lecture to the Vienna Society 1 Mar. 11 (*Minutes*, III).

[4] Emmeline Bernays; see above, 147 F n. 5.

[5] Noordwijk, resort on the coast north of The Hague.

[6] Wilhelm Ostwald (1853–1932), German philosopher and professor of chemistry; Nobel Prize for chemistry, 1909.

would already have consented and would know what to write. But I am far from having made up my mind.

I hope you are safely back in your own house, to whose inhabitants I send my kind regards.

Yours ever, FREUD

191 J

Dear Professor Freud,   Küsnach-Zürich, 5 May 1910[1]

Enclosed are the choice documents of modern times: Germany and America! The contortions of the latter are priceless. The so-called freedom of research in the land of the free has indeed been well guarded—the very word "sexual" is taboo. There's nothing more to be said about that liar and clown Friedländer except that it was a thousand pities Löwenfeld mentioned him at all. He won't do him the same honour a second time, I hope.

This evening I shall have a talk about the Society with Dr. Maier, my successor with Bleuler. The latest proposition is: out of gratitude for their[2] friendliness and helpfulness towards us, we should hold our meetings jointly with them, i.e., present them everything on a silver salver, at no risk to themselves and with no demands upon their backbone. Their naïveté is so staggering that I was dumbfounded. These good people are imitating the neurotic evasions of alcoholics which they themselves pillory so relentlessly. The general wail about coercion is thoroughly understandable if one has ever been present while Bleuler was interrogating an alcoholic. The decision is to be next week. After that no quarter will be given. Let Bleuler and Frank go ahead and found a Society together. It will doubtless produce marvellous results for ΨA.

I still have not heard from America whether they are reacting to my missives or not.

Deuticke really is a bore. Never yet has the printing been so abominably slack. I shall write to him today.

The wood symbol is extraordinarily interesting. The "old furniture" struck a familiar note, but I knew nothing of the wood. I have two

[1] This letter and 193 J are not on the Burghölzli stationery but on blank paper.
[2] Holograph: *Sie*, "you," slip for *sie*, "they."

fine number dreams from a patient.[3] Do you ever get any? Is it worth reporting in the *Jahrbuch*? ("Holland"[4] has been taken note of.)

Best regards, JUNG

192 F

Dear friend,   17 May 1910, Vienna, IX. Berggasse 19

I don't know whether you are troubled as much by my failure to write as I am in the opposite case, but after this bit of malice I will confide without further ado that on the day when you last wrote I was taken with a nasty case of influenza, which took away my voice and has left me feeling wretched. I needed all my energy to keep on with my patients and none was left to write a letter with. Over the two days of Whitsun[1] I was in Karlsbad with my wife and daughter. I have just come home this morning and hasten to write to you.

It is now definite that we shall arrive in Noortwiyk near Leyden on 1 August. Nothing has yet been arranged for the preceding period. I may spend two weeks in Karlsbad alone.

This morning I found a long letter from Jones in Washington waiting for me. He reports on the exciting events at the American Psychopathological Association[2] on 2 May. By and large they were favourable to us. Since he must have written you the same thing, I won't dwell on it. As usual, Putnam seems to have done very well and Jones himself is making up for last year's ambiguities with indefatigable zeal, great skill and, I was going to say, humility. Which is most gratifying. The founding of an American branch society strikes him as difficult for the time being, or at best possible only in a formal sense. But such organizational worries are your department. I believe we too should content ourselves with a formal organization (dues and *Bulletin*!).

[3] Cf. Jung, "Ein Beitrag zur Kenntnis des Zahlentraumes," *Zentralblatt*, I:12 (Aug. 1911) = "On the Significance of Number Dreams," CW 3.
[4] For the Freuds' summer holidays.

[1] Whitsun = 15 May.
[2] Following the annual meeting of the American Neurological Association, in Washington, D.C., the American Psychopathological Association was founded (2 May), under the presidency of Morton Prince; honorary members: Claparède, Forel, Freud, Janet, Jung. See Jones, II, p. 84/76.

317

In Vienna they are busily at work; which shows that I was perfectly right. Bergmann wanted me to be the director of the ΨA *Zentralblatt*; the contract is already signed, the conditions are most favourable. I shall start with my Nuremberg paper. First number in October.

I hope Deuticke doesn't keep me waiting much longer with *Leonardo*. As soon as I feel up to it, I shall send you two little things for the *Jahrbuch*. A first Contribution to the Psychology of Love and an excellent analysis of Egmont's dream by Dr. Alfred Robitsek.[3]

Naturally I am very eager to hear how your difficulties are resolved. My guess is that in the end they will join.

You know why I am not writing more. My kindest regards to you and yours.

Yours, FREUD

193 J

Dear Professor Freud,   Küsnach-Zürich, 24 May 1910

Now I have had to get in arrears myself to keep the parallelism going. When you failed to answer me for so long it occurred to me to ask you what was wrong. But I consoled myself with the thought that you must have had good reasons for not writing. I hope your influenza is better and is no longer impeding your strenuous work. I also hope you have good news of your daughter. Here all is well internally, but war rages on the frontier—war with Bleuler, who has refused to join our Society. That is why everything has been held up so idiotically. Also, as a result of our Pyrrhic victory, we have no suitable person in Zürich for a president. In the interim I must act as chairman together with Riklin. To mitigate somewhat the wartime conditions of the transition period, I have promised to hold a public meeting as soon as occasion offers, at which "dissenters" can be present. But my pent-up wrath is so great that I shall take revenge in one way or another. I'm only waiting for an opportunity. As soon as we are strong enough, the whole obstreperous gang can be kicked out. At any rate I'll have 10–12 people on my side, all quite "young" with the exception of Pfister, Binswanger, and Maeder. I wanted Pfister for president, but

[3] Alfred Robitsek (1871–1937), Ph.D., of Vienna; for his paper (on the dream in Goethe's tragedy *Egmont*, Act V) see below, 209 F n. 6.

Binswanger with his jealousy opposed it on "objective" grounds. I shall therefore wait until Maeder is in Zürich and make him president.[1] We shall draw up our definitive list of members next Friday.

Frau Prof. Erismann has stopped coming to our meetings since Nuremberg.(??)[2]

On Whitmonday I spoke on "symbolism" at the Meeting of Swiss Psychiatrists in Herisau,[2a] mythological stuff that aroused great applause. Our adversaries have given up the fight, except in the hick papers; officially not one of them has anything to say. Only Bleuler has taken it into his head to carp at the notion of verbal and non-verbal thinking, without advancing anything positive. I shall have the lecture copied, just as it is, and send it to you for an opinion with all its present imperfections.

I am immersed in Pfister's paper on Zinzendorff[3] and am most enthusiastic. Splendid material. The presentation is thoroughly scientific and I am terribly keen to have it for the *Jahrbuch*. I hope you will find it too long and too scientific for your *Papers*—that is my secret egotistic wish. Some of the material, it goes without saying, is truly universal and of the greatest mythological interest.

I have a great desire to attend the Congress in Baden-Baden next Sunday, where Hoche is speaking on "An Epidemic of Insanity among Doctors."[4] I am eager to hear this historic outpouring for myself. How delightful to be publicly sneered at as insane! I scarcely think the epidemic is raging anywhere except among us.

Deuticke continues to be a bore, the proofs of 3 or 4 of the last papers for the *Jahrbuch* still haven't arrived. I have prodded him but he merely emits excuses.

I have got into a tight corner again and am no longer master of my own time. I need help badly, no doubt of that. Honegger's fiancée is doing valuable work as my secretary. I judged her much too un-

---

[1] Maeder was then on the staff of the Bellevue Sanatorium, Kreuzlingen.

[2] See above, 85 J n. 3.

[2a] See also above, 175 J n. 2 (perhaps the same lecture) and below, 199a F. / Herisau is in Canton Appenzell.

[3] *Die Frömmigkeit des Grafen Ludwig von Zinzendorf*; see below, 212 F n. 7. Zinzendorf, German religious reformer (1700–1760), was leader of the "Moravian Brethren" sect, many of whom he helped to settle in the United States. Pfister related his religious fanaticism to perverse eroticism.

[4] At the Congress of South-West German Psychiatrists, 28 May. Cf. Jung, "New Paths in Psychology" (orig. 1912), CW 7, 2nd edn., par. 411, and Jones, II, p. 131/116. For Hoche's paper, see below, 201 F n. 1.

favourably, she is an excellent worker. Honegger[5] wins all hearts. I think he won't lack for success.

Many kind regards,

Yours very sincerely, J U N G

194 F

Dear friend, 26 May 1910, Vienna, IX. Berggasse 19

I was delighted to hear that I shall soon have an opportunity to read another fine piece by you. I won't be quite so busy in June and reading it will be pure joy, especially as I am counting on your formulations to clarify certain vague ideas of my own.

The difficulties in Zürich are of course a product of all-too-human jealousy, hence indirect confirmation of your merit, which had hitherto been hidden from view. Your dream, which Jekels has communicated to me, seems to contain a reference to the days when Bleuler lived downstairs and you upstairs and to the occasion when I—on your recommendation—neglected to stop by to see him. Our main tactic must be not to let Bleuler and his following notice that their secession troubles us in any way. Then they will come to us one by one. For tactical reasons we must therefore found the International Association and issue a bulletin as soon as possible. Zürich will not be able to cut much of a figure at first, but don't let that trouble you; don't make concessions with a view to concealing your internal conflicts from our adversaries. ΨAtic candour! There will be an opportunity for revenge, which tastes very good cold. For the present you will be paying the price for the help you once received from Bleuler; it could not have been had for nothing any more than the help I received from Breuer.

Too bad that you couldn't put through Pfister as chairman! How do you account for Binswanger's stupid objection? And what has become of Pfister's parsons and schoolteachers who were supposed to join? Perhaps we should look to our therapy for an analogy to our present situation. After an important step forward there is always a pause. The movement is now going through such a phase. And it is quite possible that we forged ahead too fast, perhaps we should have waited for things to ripen a bit. Be that as it may, I should say that no harm has

---

[5] In Territet, till the end of June.

been done and that we can now afford to wait for the others to fall in line.

Here in Vienna it has definitely helped. The style has improved and enthusiasm is great. Stekel is in seventh heaven; journalism has at last given him an opportunity for self-sublimation. My influence on the new *Zentralblatt* will be unlimited. A little subscription to cover the costs of moving into our offices has quickly brought in about 1000 Kronen.

In connection with Pfister's paper you have conjured up an internal conflict between the editor of the *Papers* and the editor of the *Jahrbuch*. The *Papers* deserve special consideration, because no one but the editor seems to care anything about them; I even had to decide to publish my Leonardo in the *Papers*, to avoid a suspension of more than six months. The *Jahrbuch* on the other hand is like the rich man in the Book of Kings,[1] who wants to take away the poor man's one little lamb. In view of all this I am not exactly eager to forgo Pfister's smutty count. Only if for one reason or another it does not fit in, shall I remember that it's more or less a question of whether to put a coin into one's right or left trousers pocket. The author has promised me the manuscript for three weeks from today, and I promise to make up my mind very soon thereafter.[2]

Because of my temporary indisposition my trifle on "Love Life" has not progressed beyond the first sentence; but I hope to recover my strength in the next few days and to send you this piece along with Dr. Robitsek's Egmont's Dream in time for the next *Jahrbuch*.

I have complained to Deuticke myself, but Heller assures me that the printers really are creating great difficulties. Yesterday Deuticke accepted from Dr. Hitschmann a compendium[3] of my work in ΨA—a kind of manual for elementary schools(?).

Your idea of attending Hoche's lecture is delightful—I envy you your sense of humour. But are you sure that he has us in mind? If so, it will be splendid publicity. If not, you will be dreadfully bored.

[1] II Samuel 12:1–4. In the Roman Catholic canon (but not the Hebrew or Protestant) the books of Samuel are called I and II Kings, followed by III and IV Kings.
[2] Freud had written Pfister on 6 Mar. 10 that he was "quite prepared" to accept his study of Zinzendorf, and on 17 Mar. he accepted it definitely. (*Freud/Pfister Letters*, pp. 34–35.)
[3] *Freuds Neurosenlehre; nach ihrem gegenwärtigen Stande zusammenfassend dargestellt* (1911). Eduard Hitschmann (1871–1957), originally an internist, joined the Wednesday Society in 1905. He remained a psychoanalyst; after 1940 in Boston. / Jung reviewed his book in *Jahrbuch*, III:1 (1911); see CW 18.

Still another sign of the times: Geheimrat Ostwald and the *Wiener Neue Presse* have asked me for articles. I put the former off, the latter I turned down because I must be especially careful in Vienna.

My daughter is much better. I count 50 days until the holidays. From 14 July to 1 August we shall very probably be in Bistrai near Bielitz, staying with our colleague Jekels.[4]

I am glad things are looking up with Honegger.

With many thanks for your news and an avowal of ardent desire for more,

With kind regards,

Yours, FREUD

195 F

Dear friend,   30 May 1910, Vienna, IX. Berggasse 19

On the 28th something amusing happened.[1] I must tell you about it. I was in a good humour because Deuticke had told me he was planning to bring out a *third* edition of *The Interpretation of Dreams* next autumn (after one year!) and that the first volume of the *Papers on the Theory of the Neuroses* was soon to be reprinted. At that point a Hofrat Schottländer of Frankfurt phoned to ask me when he might see me for a talk. I asked him to come at nine for coffee. At nine o'clock a card was brought in. On it I read: Hofrat *Fried*länder, Hohe Mark bei Frankfurt am Main. I stood there dumbfounded and had the little man shown in. He denied having misstated his name and pointed out that it is very easy to misunderstand over the phone, but he showed rather too little emotion, he didn't seem surprised or indignant enough. I was certain that he had said Schott, but what could I do? So there was our great enemy. I quickly pulled myself together and hit on an excellent tactic. I'll come to that. But first about the man. He had hardly sat down when he began denouncing. First Ferenczi for having said in his paper on introjection[2] that all our methods of therapy—electricity, massage, water, etc.—owed their effect purely to suggestion, i.e. transference, when in reality their success in rheumatism etc. was unquestionable. I picked up the *Jahrbuch* and

---

[4] See addenda.

[1] Cf. Jones, II, p. 132/117.
[2] "Introjection and Transference"; see above, 168 J n. 1.

showed the demon that F. had spoken exclusively of the treatment of psychoneuroses. Beelzebub pulled in his horns, emitted his well-known stench, and went on denouncing. First someone not unknown to you whom he had called on in Zürich; he even remarked (how right he was!) on this person's restraint in not throwing him out. And then our friend Pfister. He asked me to restrain him, he was not a critical mind, he had discredited himself by an attempt at an analysis. Then he came to Stekel and Sadger, who, he said, had been practising medicine for at most two years. Especially Stekel, who claimed the figure 1 meant the penis. I held a sheltering hand over all my dear ones and asked my visitor, who was born in Vienna, if he had ever heard what the "eleven" meant in Vienna (the two legs). Of course he didn't know. He went back to Pfister's attempted analysis and identified me completely with all my followers, which was not at all in keeping with his original plan of poisoning me with sweets and inciting me against the younger men.

The conversation began to amuse[3] me more and more. As I've told you, I developed an excellent technique. Slipping into the father role he was determined to force on me (Pfister was perfectly right), I affected hearty good humour and took advantage of the atmosphere and situation to make the most insulting remarks, which produced exactly the desired effect. He whined and whimpered, but he was helpless against my Ψ-analytic frankness. I told him that he knew nothing of the analytic technique, which accounted for his negative results, that his methods were those of 1895 and that he hadn't learned a thing since that date because he was too well off to bother, what a shame it was that there was no one in his vicinity who might teach him something, that his conversion would make an enormous impression in Germany, that he was essentially a brute, a retarded guttersnipe (this in more polite language, to be sure),[4] that his friendliness and obsequiousness were pure pretense, that I myself has passed the word around not to answer him, because obviously he was itching for attention, etc.

I was having a fiendishly good time, I couldn't get enough. I kept him there until one in the morning. I've forgotten the choicest details, anyway they would take too long to tell. Just one point, which is of general interest. Out of sheer hypocrisy he launched into a self-analysis; it turned out that he has an immense amnesia on the subject of his childhood up to the age of 7–8. Then conscious memory of child-

---

[3] Holograph: *analysiren*, "analyse"; a slip for *amüsiren*.
[4] Holograph: (*das doch verblümt*), with ΨA written just under *verblümt*.

hood misbehaviour set in. From the earlier period he remembers only one thing. When he was four, he was in love with an eighteen-year-old girl, *Pauline,* and was very unhappy when she got married. An hour later he claimed that I had first up with personal attacks—in my analysis of *Lina* H. I denied the existence of this Lina and it turned out that he ment Dora. Now comes the analysis! "Why did you remember her mistakenly as Lina?" — He: "But I've told you about *Karoline,* the girl I was in love with at the age of four." — "No, my dear colleague, we're not on the phone now. I am prepared to swear that you called the girl *Pauline* and not *Karoline.*" He had to admit it! Consequently I do not believe I heard wrong on the phone; he made the slip (or rather, lied) because he was afraid I wouldn't see him if he presented himself as Friedländer.

One of my present patients, a Russian,[5] was with him for a week a year ago. I brought the conversation round to this young man and was told something which the patient, who is quite trustworthy, has already half exposed as a lie. When his mother comes to see me, I am hoping to have the same luck with the other half. Final judgment on my visitor: professional liar and hypocrite, wolf in sheep's clothing, braggart and faker, ignorant brute, juvenile delinquent who made a habit of swindling his father. It is such people who mould the opinion of the general public about our ΨA. He admitted to me that he can't even "go along" with my *Everyday Life,* that he sees no explanation for cases of forgetfulness and slips in speech. His main argument is that with the unconscious one can *prove anything.* The successful cures he speaks of prove that he works with the technique we discarded (1895) but has never understood it. He is obviously colour-blind as it were toward the perception of his own unconscious, and this with excellent complexive motivation: otherwise he would drown in filth.

To think we have to trouble our heads over such riffraff!

It gives me great satisfaction to reflect that we after all are different. With kind regards,

Yours, FREUD

Hoche seems indeed to have us in mind if Karlchen Schottländer hasn't been lying again.

---

[5] Probably the patient known as the "Wolf-Man," who in his memoirs tells of spending a short time in a sanatorium near Frankfurt in late 1908. See *The Wolf-Man, by the Wolf-Man,* ed. Muriel Gardiner (New York, 1971), p. 71; also below, 306 F n. 2.

Dr. med. C. G. Jung. LL. D. !
Privatdocent der Psychiatrie

1003 Seestrasse
Küsnach-Zürich

2. VI. 10.

Lieber Herr Professor!

Sie haben mich mit Ihren Neuigkeiten sehr überrascht. Die Geschichte mit dem „Schottländer" ist famos; natürlich hat der schmutzige Kerl ge- logen. Hoffentlich haben Sie den Kerl so recht zu- grünnig und von Herzen geröstet, geschunden und gepfählt, dass er sich einmal nachdrücklich der Wirkung der Ufdx vergewissern konnte. Ihr Abschlussurteil unterschreibe ich aus vollem Herzen. So sind eben diese Leute beschaffen. Da ich ihm den Druck vom Gesichte ablesen konnte, hätte ich ihn gewiss am liebsten am Kragen genommen. Ich hoffe zu Gott, dass Sie ihm alle Wahrheiten so deutlich gesagt haben, dass sein Hühner- gehirn es auch Alles richtig aufsaugen konnte. Jetzt wollen wir sehen, was sein nächster Coup sein wird. Ich möchte am liebsten seinen Hausbuben- complex noch mit einer Tracht Schweizerprügel „befetten".

Hoch hat thatsächlich uns sich Jürs verrückt erklärt. Stockmayer war dort und

196 J

1003 Seestrasse, Küsnach-Zürich,
2 June 1910[1]

Dear Professor Freud,

I was amazed by your news. The adventure with "Schottländer" is marvellous; of course the slimy bastard was lying. I hope you roasted, flayed, and impaled the fellow with such genial ferocity that he got a lasting taste for once of the effectiveness of ΨA. I subscribe to your final judgment with all my heart. Such is the nature of these beasts. Since I could read the filth in him from his face I would have gone for his throat. I hope to God you told him all the truths so plainly that even his hen's brain could absorb them. Now we shall see what his next coup will be. Had I been in your shoes I would have softened up his guttersnipe complex with a sound Swiss thrashing.

Hoche did indeed declare us ripe for the madhouse. Stockmayer was there and has told me about it. The lecture fell into the well-known pattern: charges of mysticism, sectarianism, arcane jargon, epidemic of hysteria, *dangerousness*, etc. Isolated clapping. Nobody protested. Stockmayer was quite alone and hadn't the gumption. Even Gaupp and Hoche's faithful henchmen Bumke[2] and Spielmeyer found the tone not quite to their liking. But not one of the 125 people present raised a murmur. This report turned my stomach. I don't know what to say except Foul! Foul!! Foul!!![3]

We have now constituted a branch society here with ca. 15 members. The president hasn't been elected yet for lack of suitable candidates. Only 2 of the younger assistants from Burghölzli have joined. Bleuler and Maier are hanging back. Frank too, mercifully. The Zürich foundation was a difficult birth. One more such victory——

I enclose Honegger's last letter from Territet. With intent to delay his return, I have written him that in my view he could very well work on his dissertation there under his own steam. I would like to make him my assistant publicly only when he has earned his doctor's degree or finished his dissertation. But I have promised to ask for your grandfatherly opinion first, so that no injustice be done him because of my private opinion. For I do have my opinions in the matter of work discipline. He reads too little and "works" too much by flashes of genius. In Territet he would have all the time he needs for working

---

[1] For Jung's new letter paper, see facsimile. The LL.D. was the honorary degree from Clark University.

[2] Oswald Bumke (1879–1950), professor of psychiatry in Freiburg.

[3] Holograph: *Pfui Teufel Pfui Teufel!*

and especially for reading, a particularly big lacuna in his case. His continual dependence on stimulation seems to me a cloak for lack of self-reliance. I don't like that sort of thing; altogether I am very much against such shiftlessness. One really cannot let work depend entirely on the "rabbit," as Spitteler says.[4] Maybe I am judging too harshly, seeing that I myself often have great trouble in pinning my stubborn Konrad[5] to the writing-table. All the same, my greatest joy is in work and I am happy when I have enough time for it.

My mythology swirls about inside me, and now and then various significant bits and pieces are thrown up. At the moment the unconscious "interest-draughts"[6] centre entirely on the inexhaustible depths of Christian symbolism, whose counterpart seems to have been found in the Mithraic mysteries. (Julian the Apostate, for instance, reintroduced them as being the equivalent of Christianity.) The "nuclear complex" seems to be the profound disturbance—caused by the incest prohibition—between libidinal gratification and propagation. The astral myth can be solved in accordance with the rules of dream interpretation: Just as the sun mounts higher and higher after the winter, so will you attain to fruitfulness in spite of the incest barrier (and its odious effects on your libido). This idea is expressed very clearly in the Song of Tishtriya (*Zendavesta*).[7] Twice the white horse (Tishtriya = Sothis) tries to drive the demonic black horse Apaosha from the rain-lake. Finally he succeeds with the help of Ahura-Mazda. You will soon get the material where all this is described.

Many kind regards,

Most sincerely yours, JUNG

[4] "And feeling small and humble he wrote to a lady friend in another city: 'Honestly, without being in the least considerate: Is it impossible to get along with me?' The answer was: 'Your question makes me laugh, it is as easy as child's play, just as with a rabbit. Only, one must deeply care for you, as it should be, and from time to time tell you so.'"—Carl Spitteler, *Imago* (Gesammelte Werke, Zürich, 1945, vol. IV), p. 322. (Tr. W. S.)

[5] See above, 156 F n. 5.

[6] Neologism of the schizophrenic patient in "The Psychology of Dementia Praecox," CW 3, par. 234.

[7] See *Symbols of Transformation*, CW 5, par. 395. (Also in 1911/12 edn.)

197 F

Dear friend,   9 June 1910, Vienna, IX. Berggasse 19

I have noticed your new writing paper and congratulate you on it. In the last few days I have sent you several silent parcels;[1] but I should have liked to answer your letter of 2 June, to which I am now reacting, more promptly if it had been possible. I take a keen interest in young Honegger and am glad to speak of him, since you asked me for my "grandfatherly" opinion.

Grandfathers are seldom harsh and I doubt if I have even been so as a father. It is unreasonable of you, I think, to expect his working methods to be as independent of the human libido as yours: we agree that he belongs to a later generation, that he has had little experience of love thus far, and is in general of softer stuff than you. We would not want him to be a copy of yourself. He will be far more useful to you as he is. He possesses a fine receptivity, psychological flair, and a good sense of the "basic language."[2] He seems to be exceedingly devoted to you, and his personal value is further enhanced by the present situation, in which you must stand up to our opponents in the Zürich camp. Why then don't you take him as he is and train him on the basis of his own nature, rather than try to mould him to an ideal that is alien to him?

Our opponents are suffering keenly from our treatment of them; they do not merit our indignation. Keep silent and go on working—that's all we have to do.

What Schottländer is telling people about his experience with me must be very interesting. I make no bones about denying it all unheard. Incidentally, speaking of one of my patients who spent some time with him, he told me things that my questioning of the very decent young man and his mother proved to be the crude lies I had supposed. I wanted to send him this supplement to his self-analysis in a letter, but his old school-friends in the Vienna circle pleaded with me not to.

---

[1] Evidently containing manuscripts for the next issue (II:2) of the *Jahrbuch*. See below, 209 F n. 6 and 210 J.

[2] Holograph: "*Grundsprache*." Schreber's name for his own fantastic terminology; in his words, "the language spoken by God Himself . . . ; a somewhat antiquated but nevertheless powerful German, characterized particularly by a wealth of euphemisms . . ." (*Memoirs*, pp. 49f.).

> "Lovely lady, let him go;
> He's unworthy of your wrath."[3]

Eagerly awaiting your mythology, I send you my kindest regards.

Yours, FREUD

The *Jahrbuch* is being dreadfully delayed.

198 J

1003 Seestrasse, Küsnach-Zürich,

Dear Professor Freud,   17 June 1910[1]

I answered Adler today. His first letter went to Riklin, who filed it. Unfortunately his letter of 1 June was unanswered because I first had to wait for the founding of the Zürich group in order to give Adler positive news.[2] As I hold the view that the International Association has been founded since Nuremberg, I cannot imagine why the Viennese group has not been able to consolidate itself. Perhaps I have misunderstood something? We were of the opinion here that a group already existed in Vienna just as in Berlin and now also in Zürich. Please forgive me for the delay in answering. The break with Bleuler has not left me unscathed. Once again I underestimated my father complex. Besides that I am working like mad. I just keep alive in a breathless rush. It's high time I got some help. Unfortunately Honeg-

---

[3] From Leporello's aria in Mozart's *Don Giovanni*, I, iv (in the German standard version, near end of aria).

---

[1] Published in *Letters*, ed. G. Adler, vol. 1.

[2] At the Vienna Society's meeting of 14 April, "Adler cannot yet report anything definite about the planned journal [*Zentralblatt*], since Jung's reply to the announcement of our plan as well as to Deuticke's proposal to have the *Jahrbuch* appear monthly, has not yet been received" (*Minutes*, II, p. 475). Jung, 17 April (186 J), mentions hearing from Stekel and Adler, asking him to collaborate. At the 1 June meeting, Adler reported that, "since no communication about the 'International Association' has been received up to now, the decision has been made to inquire in Zürich whether the date of the founding of this Association can be made public" (ibid., p. 553). Thus Adler's letter of 1 June. Again, at the 15 June meeting, Adler reported that "no notice concerning the foundation of the International Association has been received up to the present, and therefore [he] proposes to carry through the independent foundation of the [Vienna] Society. . . . If the Society is going to send a third letter to Jung, the secretary should be delegated to do this" (ibid., pp. 573f.).

ger is coming only at the end of next week. Till then I'll have to let the correspondence pile up unanswered. I have at last succeeded in getting the Juristic-Psychiatric Society, of which I was president,[2a] off my neck. Etc., etc. . . .

The founding of our group was a painful affair. We have about 15 members,[3] several of them foreigners. As yet we haven't got down to debating the statutes because of the difficulties at the Burghölzli. But we have elected Binswanger president and my cousin Dr. Ewald Jung[4] secretary—he is coming along very nicely. Now the hair in the soup: I proposed holding *occasional* public meetings and then inviting Burghölzli, etc. Binswanger declared he would accept the vote for president only if all meetings were held in common with non-members. I put it to the vote and my proposal fell through. So now we have a Society with a few regular members and an audience of non-members who do nothing but have all the privileges. I don't like it a bit. But what can I do? I suggested asking your fatherly advice beforehand but this was turned down. So we in Zürich limp along making a poor show. You won't be happy about it. Neither shall I.

Leonardo[5] is wonderful. Pfister tells me he has seen the vulture[6] in the picture. I saw one too, but in a different place: the beak precisely in the pubic region. One would like to say with Kant: play of chance, which equals the subtlest lucubrations of reason. I have read *Leonardo* straight through and shall soon come back to it again. The transition to mythology grows out of this essay from inner necessity, actually it is the first essay of yours with whose inner development I felt perfectly in tune from the start. I would like to dwell longer on these impressions and brood quietly on the thoughts which want to unroll in long succession. But the present rush that has already gone on for several weeks leaves me no peace.

2a Since 1907.

3 Actually 19, according to the *Bulletin*, no. 1 (July 1910); these included Assagioli in Florence, Burrow of Baltimore (then studying in Zürich), Seif in Munich, and Stockmayer in Tübingen.

4 Psychiatrist, then at the Brunner sanatorium in Küsnacht, later in Winterthur and Bern (d. 1943).

5 *Eine Kindheitserinnerung des Leonardo da Vinci* (*Schriften zur angewandten Seelenkunde*, 7; Leipzig and Vienna, 1910) = "Leonardo da Vinci and a Memory of His Childhood," SE XI.

6 Pfister discovered the outline of a vulture in the drapery of Mary, in Leonardo's *St. Anne with Virgin and Christ Child*; see his "Kryptolalie, Kryptographie und unbewusstes Vexierbild bei Normalen," *Jahrbuch*, V:1 (1913). Freud mentioned this in a footnote to the 2nd edn. (1919); SE XI, p. 116 n.

Again many thanks for your friendly advice about Honegger. Your advice has been anticipated by events. I had already told Honegger that things simply couldn't go on as they were. You can hardly imagine the uproar in my office and the German-French-English caterwaulings my bloodsuckers have set up. So I beg your forgiveness once more for the delay. Be patient with me—when Honegger is here I shall be able to breathe more freely and cope with my outer obligations a bit more decently.

I think I have already told you that I received the manuscripts safely, with best thanks.

Many kind regards and again a plea for forgiveness,

Most sincerely, JUNG

199 F

Dear friend, 19 June 1910, Vienna, IX. Berggasse 19

I am really sorry to hear of all your overwork and irritation and thank you very much for your friendly explanations. You mustn't suppose that I ever "lose patience" with you; I don't believe these words can apply to our relationship in any way. In all the difficulties that confront us in our work we must stand firmly together, and now and then you must listen to me, your older friend, even when you are disinclined to. You see, if you had taken my advice right away in regard to Honegger a good many difficulties would have been avoided. It was to be foreseen that in your position and with your practice you would need an assistant. You might have been more generous about it, less concerned with the expense, especially as you had no need to worry after the rich yield of your trip to America.

Naturally I was very much dismayed not to see you take a firm stand in your first official functions. You know how jealous they all are—here and elsewhere—over your privileged position with me (it is the same with Ferenczi; I mean, his closeness to me is equally begrudged), and I think I am justified in feeling that what people say against you as a result is being said against me.

In any case I must enlighten you about matters in Vienna. The Vienna Society was set up long ago, but not officially, and if it is to submit its statutes to the public authorities, it must include those of the parent organization. Also they were waiting to be asked to pay dues and for the publication of the *Bulletin* according to decisions arrived at in Nuremberg. And I cannot make out from your letter whether Riklin has answered Adler's first letter. You say: "He filed it." Adler is hypersensitive and deeply embittered because I consistently reject his theories. So it looked as if a secession were going to be attempted in Vienna, as though he would call on other members to take a step that implied calling the authority of the chairman into question. This I luckily managed to avoid. If you yourself agree to the *modus vivendi* suggested by Adler, then the entire difference is formal and meaningless.

The goings-on in Zürich strike me as stupid. I am amazed that you could not summon up the authority to forestall a decision which is quite untenable. Two things are involved: to pay 10 francs in dues and put one's name on the list. Why on earth should certain people enjoy all the privileges without meeting these obligations? It will discourage the others from meeting them. I fail to understand Binswanger. Is he really so obstinate or obtuse? Would you like me to ask him in writing what his intentions are? It seems to me I might risk it. Because really the present state of affairs in Zürich is untenable.

In your place I should never have given in. If you activate the *Bulletin* now—and you should as soon as possible—all you can do is fill it with reports on the Nuremberg Congress, the new Vienna organizations, and the programmes of our meetings, and for the present hold off with the membership list,[1] lest the Philistines rejoice at our internal division. Once the *Bulletin* is in existence, the logic of the obligation to support it will dawn even on your Swiss blockheads. Make it clear to them that as non-members they cannot attend the next congress or participate in our forthcoming decisions!!

If you do, I'd be curious about the *audiatur et altera pars*.[2] I simply can't imagine what they would say. Could you have given the impression that you were indifferent to them as individuals? That is something to be avoided at all costs; in these matters as in therapy everything depends on personal transference.

Now to something more agreeable. I was overjoyed at your interest in *Leonardo* and at your saying that you were coming closer to my way of thinking. I read your essay[3] with pleasure the day it arrived; I have

---

[1] However, the first issue of the *Bulletin* (July 1910) did publish the lists of members of the three branches then organized, Vienna, Munich, and Zürich.

[2] = "Let the other party be heard too." Medieval legal maxim, derived from the oath of the Athenian judges; cf. Seneca, *Medea*, II, 2, 199.

[3] The Herisau lecture (see above, 193 J), eventually a part of "Wandlungen und Symbole der Libido."

331

been thinking about it and will write you more soon. I couldn't reread it today because Ferenczi and Brill have been with me all day—a happy occasion. Friends are after all the most precarious acquisitions. Don't be surprised if you recognize certain of your own statements in a paper of mine that I am hoping to revise in the first weeks of the holidays, and don't accuse me of plagiarism, though there may be some temptation to. The title will be: The Two Principles of Mental Action and Education.[4] It is intended for the *Jahrbuch*. I conceived and wrote it two days before the arrival of your "Symbolism"; it is of course a formulation of ideas that were long present in my mind.

I identified your vulture only today, undoubtedly under the influence of your letter; but it isn't as "neat and beyond doubt" as Pfister's. I presume Pfister has already told you that I am not inclined to let you have Count Zinzendorf for the *Jahrbuch*. Don't take it amiss; it fits in very well with the *Papers* and will attract more attention there. There is really no reason to hide it from the wider public as the author wished.

I am suffering from a recurrence of the intestinal trouble I picked up in America and am undergoing treatment. They tell me it is plain colitis and that there is nothing wrong with my appendix. But it is not improving very much; I am on a strict diet that is not compatible with travelling and threatens to interfere with my plans for September. I still count twenty-five days until my well-earned holidays. I have a great deal to do in the meantime but I feel cheerful and energetic.

With kindest regards to you and your family, whom you haven't mentioned for quite some time.

Yours ever, FREUD

199a F

[Undated][1]

p. 2 "Are symbolical" — Vague, not really correct when formulated in such general terms.

---

[4] See below, 246 F n. 3.

---

[1] Written and posted ca. 22 June 10. / These notes were discovered (after the entire correspondence had been numbered, edited, and set in type) in two states: (a) A photocopy of a typewritten transcript, headed in unknown handwriting (English): "Undated fragment, between 19-6-10 and 5-7-10." It was in a set of photocopied transcripts originally in the possession of the Sigmund Freud Copyrights, Ltd. (b) A photocopy of an undated holograph, among miscellaneous

p. 8 The customary symbolism of our ceremonial (bridal wreath, ring, flag, in religious terms: Last Supper) has here been wholly overlooked.

p. 14 True only of superficial perceptions. When we are taking it easy, ucs. purposive images usually take over. But this does not affect the essence of your statement.

p. 23 The opposites are actually fantastic-real, not symbolic-real.

p. 24 "The first cause" — the only untenable point I have so far encountered. It smacks of Ψ caprice and, in respect of the dream, looks like a revival of the medical dream theory.

p. 25 The dream does this only *apparently*, in its *form*. In content it is perfectly logical and consistent. But the forces, the drives, at work in it are archaic.

p. 26 The doubt also extends to the conclusion drawn in the foregoing sentence on this page.

p. 38 The symbolism in the dream from Scherner![2] I didn't go deeply enough into symbolism in my dream-book. Stekel is now filling in this gap in his papers.[3]

p. 39 This would be more apt if the ancients, who lived in mythology, had not also had dreams. I regard the underlined sentence as clever, but misleading.

---

fragments in the Sigmund Freud Archives at the Library of Congress. The original holograph has not come to light. / Since Jung's Herisau lecture (see above, 193 J par. 3) has not been recovered, it is not possible to correlate Freud's criticisms with that or with the work for which the lecture was an early draft, "Wandlungen und Symbole der Libido." Jung's reply, 200 J, contributes somewhat toward such correlation, but it is evident that his early drafts were much revised and dispersed in the published work.

2 K. A. Scherner, whose *Das Leben des Traumes* (Berlin, 1861) is frequently cited in *The Interpretation of Dreams*; see SE V, Bibliography A. The only dream from Scherner there reported is about two rows of boys, symbolizing teeth, who attack each other; see SE IV, p. 227. There is no reference to Scherner in Jung's published work.

3 Cf. Stekel, *Die Sprache des Traumes* (Wiesbaden, 1911).

p. 46 The sentence is splendid, but somehow the subject, "fantasies," does not fit the content. Fantasies, day-dreams, as you know, are usually highly personal.

p. 65 This sentence, "Sexuality destroys itself,"[4] provokes a vigorous shaking of the head.[5] Such profundity is perhaps not clear enough for mythological thinking. Would it not be more natural to consider all these representations of self-sacrifice, which in the case of Mithras[6] derive with special clarity from the killing of the animal ego by the human ego, as the *mythological projection of repression,* in which the sublimated part of the human being (the conscious ego) sacrifices (regretfully) its vigorous drives? Basically, a part of the castration complex. Snake, horse,[7] etc., are cumulations for the sake of clarity, which, however, conceal the strict meaning.

p. 66 The myth, originally psychological, is overlaid by adaptation to the calendar and so projected into the realm of natural phenomena, just as, e.g. in agoraphobia, fantasy is projected into space via a verbal language bridge; here however, via analogies of content. Typical.

p. 68 Here you yourself accept the mythological projection of repression in the place of your earlier interpretation that sensuality destroys itself.

As usual, I have mentioned only objections and made no comment on the many things I liked very much. I don't know whether this will make me popular with you. But I'm sure you didn't send it just for applause.

[4] Transcript: *"Die Sexualität geht an sich selber zugrunde."* Not found in Jung's published work.
[5] Transcript: *Schütteln des Kopfes.* From Carl Arnold Kortum (1745–1824), *Die Jobsiade* (1784, 1799), a mock-heroic epic. In I, 19, whenever the hero as a theological candidate gives a wrong answer, the examining board of clergy shake their heads. Wilhelm Busch illustrated an edition (1874).
[6] God-hero of the ancient Iranian religion called Mithraism, which the Roman legions adopted widely and which was the chief rival of Christianity in the 2nd century A.D. In the myth of the cult, Mithras sacrifices the divine bull. Jung drew heavily on Mithraic mythology in "Wandlungen und Symbole"; see CW 5, index.
[7] The snake and horse occur in Miss Miller's fantasy of Chiwantopel; see below, n. 8, and 200 J n. 5.

Despite all its beauty, I think, the essay lacks ultimate clarity. The dream is not pertinently characterized. This indeed is a serious objection. The whole thing should not really be titled "Symbolism," but "Symbolism and Mythology," since more light is thrown on the latter than on the former. I wonder if it wasn't actually a Mithras image that Miss Miller[8] had in mind. Yet the analogy is not overwhelming. On the Mithras stones I have seen, a crab pinches the bull's testicles.[9] And the myth has certainly undergone many modifications. — Nevertheless everything essential in your essay is right. But there is a gap between the two forms of thinking on the one hand, and the contrast between fantasy and reality on the other.

I thank you very much.

Yours, FREUD

200 J

1003 Seestrasse, Küsnach-Zürich,

Dear Professor Freud, 26 June 1910

Today being a Sunday I am using it to go over your critique in peace. I am most grateful to you and quite agree with what you say. I should have warned you beforehand that I am presenting myself in my shirt-sleeves. The piece is only a very rough sketch. The Mithras problem in particular is dealt with in a most inadequate way, in addition to which the copyist left out a key passage on self-sacrifice. It is bound to make a highly unsatisfactory impression as the discussion of the incest problem is also missing. I would be very grateful if I might lay the second part before you sometime in completely revised form. With regard to the sentence, "Sexuality destroys itself," I would remark that this is an extremely paradoxical formulation which I do not regard as in any way valid or viable. But there is something in it that I must hang on to because, at least for the present, I don't feel

---

[8] This is the first reference to the "Miller fantasies," Jung's analysis of which is the basis of "Wandlungen und Symbole der Libido." Frank Miller, an American woman patient of Theodore Flournoy (see above, 31 J), recorded her fantasies, published as "Quelques Faits d'imagination créatrice subconsciente," with Flournoy's introduction, in *Archives de psychologie* (Geneva), V (1906). The English original was published, with a foreword by James H. Hyslop (see above, 50 J n. 4), in the *Journal of the American Society for Psychical Research* (New York), I:6 (June 1907). (Tr. from French in CW 5, appendix.)

[9] See 200 J n. 7.

satisfied with your admittedly much simpler suggestion (the sublimated part sacrifices its regret), and for the following reason: There
must be something very typical in the fact that the symbol of fe-
cundity, the useful and generally accepted (not censored) *alter ego* of
Mithras (the bull), is slain by another sexual symbol. The self-sacrifice is voluntary and involuntary at once (the same conflict as in the
death of Christ). There is an evil necessity in it. This dualism is altogether in keeping with the thoroughly dualistic thinking of Iranian
theology. What it boils down to is a *conflict at the heart of sexuality
itself.* The only possible reason for this conflict seems to be the *incest
prohibition* which struck at the root of primitive sexuality. You could
also say: the incest prohibition blocks the nearest and most convenient outlet for the libido and makes it altogether bad. Somehow
the libido has to free itself from this repression since it must reach
its propagative goal (fight between Tishtriya and Apaosha, who guards
the rain-lake).[1] In this well-known neurotic struggle the astral myth
came to the aid of the old Iranians: just as the sun or the fruitfulness
of Nature languishes in the grip of winter and yet finally triumphs, so
will you wrench yourself free and blossom with fruitfulness. Up to
that point I consider the interpretation as simple as could be wished:
Tishtriya = active libido, Apaosha = resistant (incestuous) libido.
The figure of Mithras brings a new development: Tishtriya and Apaosha now symbolize the dual aspect of Mithras as man's active and
resistant libido (bull and serpent), just as horse and serpent = brother
and sister of Chiwantopel.[2] This conflict must have been deadly serious (self-castration of the priests in the worship of Dea Syria, etc.).
Hence the imperative need for the prototype of a hero who *understands how to accomplish of his own free will* what the repression is
after—namely, temporary or permanent renunciation of fruitfulness
(the social background is questionable: overpopulation?) in order to
realize the ethical ideal of the subjugation of instinct. The sufferings
of humanity must have been immense during the various attempts at
"domestication." Hence the comforting and truly dithryambic outcome of the self-sacrifice: and *yet* we shall be fruitful again. In the
Christ myth everything goes awry in the end: here no garlic sprouts
from the bull's nostrils, no grain from his tail.[3] The Christian identi-

---

[1] See above, 196 J end.

[2] In one of Miss Miller's fantasies, "Chiwantopel" is the name of an Aztec war-
rior; he and his horse die from a serpent's bite. See CW 5, pp. 459f.

[3] In the Mithraic myth, the plants and animals beneficial to man sprang from the
body of the sacrificed bull.

fies with the self-conqueror, eats his way right into his dead body, propagates himself only furtively and on sufferance, without inner conviction. That is why Julian the Apostate attempted, meritoriously and with the utmost energy, to oppose the Christian mystery with that of Mithras (because of its favourable outcome).

Certainly the Mithras myth has undergone an adaptation to the calendar: the *crab* that pinches the bull's testicles[4] is the *scorpion* of the autumnal equinox, depriving the bull of its fruitfulness. The *bird* depicted on some of the monuments is the raven,[5] messenger of the gods, which brings Mithras the command for self-sacrifice; the daimonion that stands warningly at man's side in his attempts at self subjugation, in other words the *force compelling him towards culture.*

I may say that my paradoxical dictum about sexuality destroying itself had some pretty gruesome archaic parallels which must have made a profound impression on man and of which our inner change of feeling on begetting a male child is but a pale reflection. When the parents were no longer of any use they were killed and eaten by their young, or their dead bodies thrown into the bush. The advent of the next generation is the beginning of the end. The thought of mortality, which with increasing domestication naturally acquired the character of fear, is already pushing to the fore in the Mithraic sacrifice but is still counterbalanced by the joyfulness of the outcome. On higher and later levels of culture, when pessimism was making itself felt even in philosophy, this thought needed a special mystery of its own which Christ initiated: the mystery of immortality gained by the total suppression of instinct (through identification with the dead man).

Although I can't be sure that I have expressed myself clearly, it does seem to me that we have here a series of tangible connections, roughly sketched though they may be.

Coming now to the letter from Adler, I gave it to Riklin with the request that he answer it, and took the matter as settled. R. forgot the letter, as he recently informed me. This is, of course, very stupid and distressing, but excusable inasmuch as R. has an extraordinarily heavy work load to carry. From now on I shall let Honegger take care of these things. You are right, I should have taken H. at once. But he had already made commitments in Territet when you pointed out

---

[4] See preceding letter, at n. 9. For Jung's use of this in the published work, see CW 5, par. 665, n. 66; also in 1911/12 edn.
[5] See CW 5, par. 369, n. 85; also in 1911/12 edn.

that I should take him on as assistant.[6] I am always open to good advice.

Things are gradually—but painfully—righting themselves in our Society. Actually I could do nothing to oppose the decision. My authority doesn't extend that far. Except for Riklin all the rest wanted Bleuler and about 9 other persons to be present, on the ground that exceptional conditions had to be created for the transition period. At the same time the hope was expressed that these persons would soon think better of it and join. I have not given up my plans and shall make my proposals in due course, if they haven't joined by then. As for my authority, the chairman was always Bleuler; wherever there are resistances he plays them off against me. Binswanger has always had the knack of saying something unpleasant to me and is everybody's friend. Pfister was also in favour of conciliation. The situation really was such that I *had* to give in.

The *Bulletin* is supposed to be printed this week; my share of the work was completed a week ago. When this thing is finally wound up, the Association will at last be on a firm footing.

With many kind regards,

Most sincerely yours, JUNG

201 F

Dear friend,   5 July 1910, Vienna, IX. Berggasse 19

I am at the end of my working year but also of my strength (still nine days to go). I was indisposed a good deal of last week, which is why I haven't answered your letter—a good letter full of important ideas. Today I see that my criticism was quite premature; still, I believe that such far-reaching interpretations cannot be stated so succinctly but must be accompanied by ample proof, which, I am sure, you will now add. Of course I shall be very glad to see the opus

[6] Among recently discovered letters from Honegger to his close friend Walter Gut (1885–1961; in 1911, a member of the Zürich Society; later professor of theology and 1952–54 rector of Zürich University), one of 17 June 10 states: "May I ask you to help my fiancée find suitable quarters for the firm of Jung-Honegger? The intermediate stage in Küsnacht is now to be skipped after all. . . . We'll need three rooms, unfurnished, with telephone. . . ." It is not known why this plan to open a private practice together in the city of Zürich did not materialize. See Walser's article on Honegger, above, 148 J n. 3.

again in its modified form. The main difficulty in such work of interpretation cannot have escaped you; to wit, that one cannot interpret
the whole façade as in the case of allegory, but must confine oneself
to the content, tracking down the genesis of its elements so as not
to be misled by later overlayings, duplications, condensations, etc.
In other words, we must proceed very much as we do with dreams.

Though you have not asked me to, it seemed to me that I might, on
my own responsibility, ask Binswanger to throw some light on the
extraordinarily schizophrenic behaviour of the Zürich people. I have
seen Hoche's paper[1] but not read it yet; I ordered three copies, so as
to pass the others on; my impression after a brief glance is that this is
the greatest recognition that I have received up to now. Here it is
certified in writing that we are 15 years in advance of our opponents.

I have had little time for scientific work in these stupid last weeks,
though plans for three theoretical articles[2] have been stirring in my
mind. Brill has now introduced ΨA in Cuba; today I received one of
his articles from Havana, in Spanish translation.[3] The translator is a
Dr. Fernandez. It's most annoying about the *Jahrbuch*; I have finished
the paper for the *Zentralblatt* (my Nuremberg lecture). — All this
sounds like Busch's famous alphabet:[3a]

> "The ass is stupid, hence his name.
> The elephant is not to blame."

or

> "The onion is the Hebrew's fare;
> The zebra lives both here and there."[4]

In this stylistic frame of mind, I ought really to stop writing. It's
no wonder, I'm very tired and shall be working nine hours a day up
to the last moment.

[1] "Eine psychische Epidemie unter Ärzten," *Medizinische Klinik*, VI (1910),
1007f.
[2] Miss Anna Freud suggests that these theoretical articles ultimately took form as
the "Papers on Metapsychology" published in the *Zeitschrift*, III (1915); in SE
XIV.
[3] Presumably "Las psico-neurosis concebidas por Freud," *Crónica médico-quir-
úrgica de la Habana*, 1910; tr. from "Freud's Conception of the Psychoneuroses,"
Medical Record, LXXVI (1909).
[3a] Holograph: *Abc*. Freud first wrote *Einma* (beginning of *Einmaleins*, the multi-
plication table) and crossed it out.
[4] Holograph: *Der Esel ist ein dummes Thier / Der Elephant kann nichts dafür. /
Die Zwiebel ist der Juden Speis', / Das Zebra trifft man stellenweis.*—Wilhelm
Busch, "Naturgeschichtliches Alphabet," *Münchener Bilderbogen*, nos. 405–6.

It isn't settled yet where we shall spend the first fortnight, since there will not be room for us in Noordwijk until 1 August. I shall probably go to The Hague with two of my sons and take little trips about Holland with them from there. The women and small fry will find something else to do; my eldest son is going to the mountains. My daughter is surprisingly well, she is now in the South Tyrol with her husband, Levico and Lavarone, places we know well and love.

Of course I was thinking of Switzerland for this second half of July, but we are too much in need of rest, and if I go to see you, you know we shall spend hours on end in discussion. I can assimilate no more, I am *full to the brim*,[5] and to counteract that I must take it easy.

I am becoming more and more convinced of the cultural value[6] of ΨA, and I long for the lucid mind that will draw from it the justified inferences for philosophy and sociology. I am under the impression— but perhaps this is only a projection of my present listless state— that we have come to a standstill for the moment and are waiting for some new impetus. But I am not impatient.[7]

Please stick to my Vienna address pending more definite information. With kind regards,

Yours ever, FREUD[8]

202 F

Dear friend,   10 July 1910, Vienna, IX. Berggasse 19

Hotel *Wittebrug Den Haag* is my address from 19 July to the end of the month. I shall be going there with my two younger sons.

As editor of the *Jahrbuch* you will be receiving two papers emanating from the Vienna circle. A well-conceived piece by Silberer, whose acquaintance I have now made, and a dream analysis by Rank, which, I think, deserves to be accepted. I believe you should intersperse the literary-psychological material that comes to you through me with straight clinical papers; otherwise we shall be accused of moving too far away from medicine. The *Jahrbuch* is being dreadfully delayed. Tomorrow I shall go and complain to Deuticke.

[5] English in original.
[6] Holograph: *Welt*, "world," error for *Wert*, "value."
[7] Quoted by Jones, II, p. 498/448f.
[8] In the blank space at the end of this letter, upside down, Jung jotted: "A. Dieterich. Eine Mithrasliturgie. Teubner"; see below, 210 J n. 1.

Your next word from me ought to be postcards from Holland. Kind regards to you, your wife, and the children from

Yours ever, FREUD

203 J

1003 Seestrasse, Küsnach-Zürich,
Dear Professor Freud,   24 July 1910

This last week I have been working like mad again. But now thank heavens the holidays have come for me too. This evening I am going sailing on Lake Constance. I have had my boat sent on ahead. Meanwhile Honegger will deputize for me in Zürich. My military service is scheduled for August 14–29. I hope to write to you from Lake Constance once I have got my wits together. The *Jahrbuch* should be out soon. What a torment it has been!

I hope you are enjoying your holidays *procul negotiis*. Kindest regards,

Most sincerely yours, JUNG

My address remains *Küsnach*.

204 J

Hotel Bodan, Romanshorn,[1] 6 August 1910
Dear Professor Freud,   Address is Küsnach-Zürich

I have been gadding about again like mad. For a fortnight I have pottered around Lake Constance and its inlets with my sail-boat, a marvellous change and relaxation. At the same time the basic principles of the ΨA way of life have been observed pretty strictly. For my morning devotions I religiously analysed dreams. Last week Riklin was with me, seconding my ΨA exertions. I am almost entirely destitute of news, thank goodness! From Abraham I have heard that Marcinowski has energetically protested against belonging to the I. ΨA. A. It seems to give people the horrors. And Muthmann has shied off too.[2] From Budapest one goes on hearing nothing.

---

[1] Printed letterhead.
[2] In the *Bulletin*, no. 1 (July 1910), Marcinowski's name was erroneously included in the list of members of the newly founded Berlin Branch Society; in the

Hasn't Ferenczi found anybody? In Zürich the work was doing splendidly when I left, Bleuler badly. At the last meeting I pleaded vigorously for a clean sweep at the beginning of the winter term; this abortion ought not to be kept alive. Since I can no longer get along with Bleuler at all after having abjured his faith in abstinence, I have instructed Binswanger to maintain the necessary nerve-contact[3] and sound all those conches that might allure Bleuler. He is a regular crank who [. . .] can never be relied on. One never knows where one is with him.

Today I dropped in on Binswanger from the lake.[4] His misfortune is that he is rather too isolated in his sanatorium, consequently his homosexual component is not organized properly. His "shoe-heel" case,[5] of which you have heard already, got a bit of a mauling at the last ΨA meeting, firstly because the transference problem was conspicuously absent and secondly because he regarded the localization in the heel as hysterical *conversion*, which caused some merriment.

I have no news of the *Jahrbuch*. I trust you will approve if the Nuremberg Congress proceedings are published at some length in the second half. There is a whiff of uncertainty in the air as to how far the new Viennese organ wants to extend its coverage.

With kind regards and best wishes for your holiday,

Most sincerely yours, JUNG

205 F

Noordwijk, 10 August 1910
Dear friend,   Pension Noordzee

Thus far I have respected your holiday, but yesterday you broke the peace, so now I feel free to write. I am sitting here by the most beautiful beach, watching a fabulous sunset, but I miss various things, and I can't think of anything much to do on a flat beach. Besides, I have no little corner to be alone in and collect my thoughts. On the 29th of the month I am supposed—nothing has

next *Bulletin* a correction appeared. (He did join the Berlin Society in 1912; see *Zeitschrift*, I, p. 112.) Muthmann's name was absent.

[3] Holograph: *Nervenanhang*. Schreberism.

[4] Kreuzlingen, site of Bellevue Sanatorium, is on the lake a mile southeast of Constance and about 11 mi. northwest of Romanshorn. (Jung's birthplace, Kesswil, is on the same lakeshore.)

[5] "Analyse einer hysterischen Phobie," *Jahrbuch*, III:1 (1911).

been settled yet—to board ship at Antwerp for Genoa with Ferenczi; we are planning to spend September in Sicily. Tomorrow the geographically most distant of our friends is expected here in Noordwijk, where a relative of his owns a villa: Jones from Toronto. He has risen a good deal in my affections this past year.

From the outside world I have received all sorts of news, which combine with what you tell me to give me the impression that we are going through a critical period, a negative fluctuation, in the history of ΨA. My suspicion is confirmed by the behaviour of men with instinct and flair like Marcinowski and Strohmayer (who, Stekel writes, does not wish to be named on the title-page of the *Zentralblatt*). Maybe I am to blame, but it is easy to find explanations after the event, and the outcome could not have been foreseen. All the same, when I look at the situation objectively, I believe I went ahead too fast. I overestimated the public's understanding of the significance of ΨA, I shouldn't have been in such a hurry about founding the I. A. My impatience to see you in the right place and my chafing under the pressure of my own responsibility also had something to do with it. To tell the truth, we should have done nothing at all. As it is, the first months of your reign, my dear son and successor, have not turned out brilliantly. Sometimes I have the impression that you yourself have not taken your functions seriously enough and have not yet begun to act in a manner appropriate to your new dignity. Probably all this comes from the impatience of old age. Now we must merely keep still for a while, let the unpleasant events take their course, and meanwhile go on with our work. I have high hopes for the new organ; I hope you will show no hostility towards it, but commit yourself and your closest associates to its support. One who wishes to rule must carefully cultivate the art of winning people; I thought you had great talents in that direction. As to reporting on the Congress, it strikes me as advisable that both journals should do so, the *Zentralblatt* in succinct form; its function after all is to inform readers of everything that goes on in ΨA, a function which the *Jahrbuch* has expressly rejected. Incidentally, I have only today received word from Deuticke that a copy of the volume published a week ago is on its way to me. We mustn't let our publisher friend put us off like this again. August instead of February is too much.

My mood and the atmosphere have prevented me from doing any work here. And I am not capable of enjoying the rest. A number of things, e.g., the paper on the two principles of Ψ functioning, are already tormenting me like a blocked bowel movement. (There is good reason for the metaphor too.) I discovered while still in Vienna that I have no need to plagiarize you, since I can refer back to certain paragraphs in the Ψ part of *The Interpretation of Dreams*. I have received some philosophical articles here that I shall read when I am feeling more intelligent. In regard to symbolism, a hunch I have already mentioned to you has become a subjective certainty with me, to wit, its infantile, hence genetic origin. I must answer a silly letter of Löwenfeld's—he thinks I am offended by it. Quite mistakenly, I esteem him personally and don't expect him to understand anything. He wrote to me at length about the horror which my *Leonardo* aroused even in persons "favourably disposed." But on this score I feel quite easy in my mind, for I myself am very pleased with *Leonardo*, and I know that it has made an excellent impression on the few who are capable of judging it: you, Ferenczi, Abraham, and Pfister. — I have had no news or replies from America: in my most recent letter[1] I had asked Putnam to put himself at the head of an American group. Jones will report to me on what they've been up to in Brussels.

As you see, nothing but petty worries and concerns. As for you, the captain will now be replacing the Augustus[2] *in partibus infidelium* for a while; I am a little put out with him, for obviously he is depriving me of your visit in Holland, and I should have liked to talk with you. Have I already written to you that the first volume of the *Papers on the Theory of the Neuroses* is appearing in a new edition and that Deuticke wants me to write a preface? *Do you think I ought to, and if so would you like to read it?* It would deal of course with the recent developments in psychoanalysis and with the opposing trends, but doesn't strike me as indispensable.

With cordial wishes for a restful end to your vacation,

Yours ever, FREUD

206 J

1003 Seestrasse, Küsnach-Zürich,

Dear Professor Freud,   11 August 1910

I realize now that my debut as regent has turned out less than brilliantly because of the resistances I contracted in Nuremberg to Adler

---

[1] Of 16 June 1910; see *Putnam and Psychoanalysis*, pp. 100f.

[2] Captain: Jung's military rank. Augustus: title of Octavian, the adopted son of Julius Caesar.

and Stekel. I shall try to do better next time. So far as the Vienna organ is concerned, I have encouraged everyone in my vicinity to collaborate and shall myself contribute to the first number—nothing much as my hands are pretty empty. It was only to be expected that *Leonardo* would meet with opposition since the intellectual freedom of this work far exceeds that of its predecessors. In the meantime, I have been reading about Leonardo so as to deepen my impression of your work and get down to the bed-rock—you are right on every point. If we can rely on the facts, it can only have been as you say. What the rabble say about it is neither here nor there; the thing is beautifully done and leads to exalted spheres of knowledge. Only simpletons will stumble over the difficulties of detail. It is a grim pleasure to be God knows how many decades ahead of these duffers.

I try to be as amiable with people as I can. But to get any results I would have to be on duty day and night. Hardly is my back turned than they start getting paranoid. This is not my fault, it's the fault of the progress of your ΨA. It is inevitable that a ray of light should break forth from occasional remarks, revealing the rapid advances in knowledge which till now we have enjoyed in silence. Each of these sparks is a threat and an insult in itself. I am well aware of that and am doing my best to keep quiet, but "out of the abundance of the heart the mouth speaketh,"[1] though rarely. I heartily agree that we went ahead too fast. Even among the "favourably disposed" there are far too many who haven't the faintest idea of what ΨA is really about and especially of its historical significance. My ear is now cocked at our adversaries; they are saying some very remarkable things which ought to open our eyes in several ways. All these mutterings about sectarianism, mysticism, arcane jargon, initiation, etc. mean something. Even the deep-rooted outrage, the moral indignation can only be aimed at something gripping, that has all the trappings of a religion. Our ideal should also be μηδεὶς ἀμαθηματικός εἰσίτω.[2] Might this become a phase, however unexpected, in the development of ΨA? The keen interest of our theologians is suspicious. And finally, ΨA thrives only in a very tight enclave of like minds. Seclusion is like a warm rain. One should therefore barricade this territory against the ambitions of the public for a long time to come. So I am not in the

[1] Matthew 12:34.

[2] "Let no one enter here who is ignorant of mathematics"—paraphrase of the legendary inscription over Plato's door, the traditional word being "geometry." Traced to the 6th century A.D. (See P. Friedländer, *Plato* 1, tr. H. Meyerhoff, 1958, p. 92 and n. 12.)

least worried by this period of depression; it is a guarantee of unsullied enjoyment, like a beautiful valley high in the mountains not yet discovered by Thos. Cook & Co. Moreover ΨA is too great a truth to be publicly acknowledged as yet. Generously adulterated extracts and thin dilutions of it should first be handed around. Also the necessary proof has not yet been furnished that it wasn't you who discovered ΨA but Plato, Thomas Aquinas and Kant, with Kuno Fischer[3] and Wundt thrown in.[4] Then Hoche will be called to a chair of ΨA in Berlin and Aschaffenburg to one in Munich. Thereupon the Golden Age will dawn. After the first 1000 years ΨA will be discovered anew in Paris, whereupon England will take up the opposition for another 500 years and in the end will have understood nothing.

After this apocalyptic vision I turn back to the present. I have now been home for 3 days. On the 14th I go on military service until the end of the month. In September my wife will be confined. At the beginning of October (1–14) I am bicycling to Italy (Verona?). If only you were nearer in September I would visit you for a couple of days. But Sicily is too far. Furthermore, I have secret obligations to my unconscious ("inconscient supérieur") as regards Rome and the south, which make a quick run through the country altogether impossible. Rome in particular is not yet permitted to me,[5] but it draws nearer and I even look forward to it at odd moments.

I have sent a letter to Jones poste restante in Brussels. Please would you ask him if he has collected it? I'm expecting an answer.

I wish you likewise a good and productive holiday,

Most sincerely yours, JUNG

207 J

Dear Professor Freud,   Küsnach-Zürich, 13 August 1910[1]

To yesterday's letter I must add that I wrote to Putnam some time ago.[2] No answer. Neither from Prof. Hoch in New York. Concerning

---

[3] Kuno Fischer (1824–1907), professor at Heidelberg, historian of philosophy and literary critic.

[4] See 9 J n. 8.

[5] For Jung's unconscious taboo on visiting Rome, see *Memories*, pp. 287f./268f.

---

[1] Postcard.

[2] About the International Association and the founding of an American branch. See *Putnam and Psychoanalysis*, ed. Hale, p. 103, Putnam to Freud late July 1910.

the preface to the 3rd edition[3] I am much in favour of your writing one. I'll read it with pleasure—and "quickly."

Kind regards,

Yours sincerely, JUNG

208 F

Hotel-Pension Noordzee, Noordwijk aan Zee,[1]

Dear friend,   14 August 1910

Your letter has shamed me and restored my good humour. You are probably right in saying that we can't really expect to control the course of events by deliberate effort, but must observe with interest how they are shaped by the dark powers. We have let ourselves in for something bigger than ourselves. That calls for modesty.

I hear from Ferenczi that the *Jahrbuch* makes a very good impression; I haven't managed to get a copy yet. You haven't answered my question—whether I should do a preface for the new edition of the *Collected Papers*. I don't much feel like it. Jones[2] was here for two and a half days, he made an excellent personal impression; he seems much more secure. He represented only one of his stories as a personal experience, and then my boys told me it was an old anecdote. He had already left when I received your request to ask him about your letter.

The details of our September trip are still uncertain because we have thus far been unable to obtain passage on the ship leaving Antwerp on the 29th. In any event I have made a note of the fact that you will be home in September and will write to you often. How wonderful it would be to see the company from the *Washington* (with the exception of Stern[3]) reunited on the Palatine!

[3] Jung confused the third edition of *Die Traumdeutung*, which Freud had mentioned earlier (above, 195 F), with the second edition of the *Sammlung kleiner Schriften zur Neurosenlehre*, vol. I, for which Deuticke wanted a new preface (above, 205 F end). In fact Freud did not write a preface to the latter.

---

[1] Printed letterhead.

[2] Jones had attended the Congress for Medical Psychology and Psychotherapy at Brussels, 7–8 Aug. For his reactions see his letter to Putnam, 14 Aug. 10, in *Putnam and Psychoanalysis*, pp. 224f.

[3] William Stern (1871–1938), professor of applied psychology at Breslau, who was also invited to the Clark University conference, where he lectured on the psychology of evidence and on educational psychology. Jung had praised Stern's work on the psychology of evidence in his (1905) "Die psychologische Diagnose des

Our warmest congratulations to your dear wife. Little Franz's development must already be a source of pleasure to you.

It is glorious here and I am still very stupid and lazy. I am reading Motley's *Rise of the Dutch Republic*[4] in order to discover how something incredibly small can become great through obstinacy and unswerving determination.

Yours cordially, FREUD

209 F

Dear friend,   Noordwijk, 18 August 1910

At the beginning of the summer I resolved not to flood you with my letters, but the fates have decreed otherwise and now I must write to you again. I have received the *Jahrbuch* and of course I must express my thanks and appreciation. At last I see you in full control as editor and feel your firm hand. Your remarks about Wittels[1] are supremely wise—a programme that seems to well from deep layers of my soul. We understand each other. I have reread with pleasure the charming story of the children (cf. Worcester, Anna and Sophie[2]) but regretted that the scientist did not entirely overcome the father; it is a delicate relief when it might have been a vigorous statue, and because of its subtlety the lesson will be lost on most readers. In the children's fear that their father intends to drown them, one glimpses the symbolism of water-dreams (disguised childbirth). The analogies with Little Hans are developed only here and there; you forget that the reader is by definition a simpleton and deserves to have his nose rubbed in these things. Your reviews and abstracts show a freedom and humour that I would like to see in the *Zentralblatt*. If I could rely on similar attitudes in the *Zentralblatt*, I would be glad to re-

Tatbestandes" = "The Psychological Diagnosis of Evidence," CW 2, pars. 728, 759–61. / 1916–33, Stern was at Hamburg, and after 1934, at Duke University, Durham, North Carolina.

[4] Title in English; the work of John Lothrop Motley (1856).

[1] "Randbemerkungen zu dem Buch von Fr. Wittels: *Die sexuelle Not*," *Jahrbuch*, II:1 (1910). A review ("marginal notes") of Wittels' book, published 1909, Vienna and Leipzig. In CW 18. Jung speaks well of Wittels' work but devotes most of his article to philosophical considerations of psychoanalysis.

[2] "Über Konflikte der kindlichen Seele," *Jahrbuch*, II:1 = "Psychic Conflicts in a Child," CW 17. The third of the three lectures Jung gave at Clark University, and the only one published in German.

move the muzzle those who write its criticism are obliged to wear. So far I have not read much of the rest. Abraham is as usual marvellously clear and correct, much to be admired.[3] I had already seen Pfister in proof.[4] I am saving the ponderous Swiss for later.

Many thanks, and good luck for the next volume! To avoid any misunderstanding, I want to make it clear at this point that when I send you a paper for the *Jahrbuch* I never mean to anticipate your decision. If you think Rosenstein's[5] little paper is better suited to the *Zentralblatt*—my own opinion—and don't care for Silberer's article, you must not feel bound by my recommendation. I have never given anyone final acceptance in your name. You yourself will probably regard the Egmont analysis and Rank's dream as worthwhile acquisitions. From me, apart from the Love Life, you may expect the general article we have discussed: the Two Principles of Ψ Functioning.[6]

The plans for my trip with Ferenczi have changed somewhat. Because of unfavourable dates and the impossibility of obtaining comfortable accommodations, I have given up the sea voyage from Antwerp. We shall probably travel overland, that gives us more time for Sicily. We shall also rest for a day in the Eternal City.

I am expecting F. here in a week or ten days.

If my personal health is of interest to you, I am very well and still quite incapable of mental work, unable to form an idea. With me physical well-being and intellectual activity never go hand in hand.

Debruine[7] has invited me to visit him in Leiden next Tuesday. I

[3] "Über hysterische Traumzustände," *Jahrbuch*, II:1 = "Hysterical Dream-states," *Selected Papers* (London, 1927).

[4] "Analytische Untersuchungen über die Psychologie des Hasses und der Versöhnung," *Jahrbuch*, II:1.

[5] Gaston Rosenstein, later Roffenstein (1882–1927), member of the Vienna Society from 1911, frequent contributor to the Zentralblatt, 1911–13. According to F. Wittels (*Freud and His Time*, 1931, p. 132), he was run over by an automobile and died.

[6] All these papers except Freud's "Two Principles" appeared in *Jahrbuch* II:2, and apparently are the manuscripts that Freud sent Jung in "several silent parcels" (above, 197 F and 198 J). These were: Rosenstein, "Die Theorien der Organminderwertigkeit und der Bisexualität in ihren Beziehungen zur Neurosenlehre"; Silberer, "Phantasie und Mythos"; Robitsek, "Die Analyse von Egmonts Traum"; Rank, "Ein Traum der sich selbst deutet"; and Freud, "Über einen besonderen Typus der Objektwahl beim Manne" (see below, 288 F n. 1). For Freud's "Two Principles," see below, 246 F n. 3.

[7] Jan Rudolf de Bruine Groeneveldt (1872–1942), Dutch physician. He is said to have arranged the place in Leiden where Freud had an analytic consultation with the composer Gustav Mahler, during this month. (Information from Dr. M.

am to meet one van Emden,[8] a very intelligent colleague who wants to go in for ΨA.

With kind regards and many good wishes for your family.

As ever, FREUD

210 J

1003 Seestrasse, Küsnach-Zürich,
31 August 1910

Motto for ΨA:

ἐξάφες ὅ ἔχεις καὶ τότε λήψει.

"Give what thou hast, then shalt thou receive."
(Mystic injunction from a Magic Papyrus, Paris, the so-called Mithras Liturgy.)[1]

Dear Professor Freud,

It gave me enormous pleasure to hear that the *Jahrbuch* and especially my marginal notes on Wittels have earned your approval. I knew of course that I could not quite disown the father when writing about my Agathli, but I don't think this personal note will worry the initiates. The analogies with Little Hans should have been developed if only it had been possible to keep these explanations short. I had the feeling that I would have had to say very many things I wanted to avoid. The thicker a work is the less it is read. Finally, one must after all leave something to the reader's imagination. I wonder very much what the critics will make of this feminine counterpart to Little Hans ("Poor little boy, poor little girl").[1a]

I hope to publish all the papers you have so kindly rounded up for me in the next *Jahrbuch*. Bleuler has just announced a com-

---

Katan.) See also Jones, II, pp. 88f./80, and Alma Mahler Werfel, *And the Bridge Is Love* (New York, 1958), p. 53.

[8] Jan E. G. van Emden (1868–1950), of The Hague. He and his wife became good personal friends of the Freud family. Translated Freud's Clark lectures into Dutch: *Over Psychoanalyse* (Leiden, 1912). In 1919, president of the Dutch Psychoanalytic Society.

---

[1] See Albrecht Dieterich, *Eine Mithrasliturgie* (Leipzig, 1905); the 2nd edn., 1910, is cited frequently in *Symbols of Transformation*, CW 5, and in the 1911–12 version (first citation in Part I, ch. iv = CW 5, par. 102, n. 51). / See facsimile.

[1a] Quoted from Mendel's article cited above, 145 F n. 5.

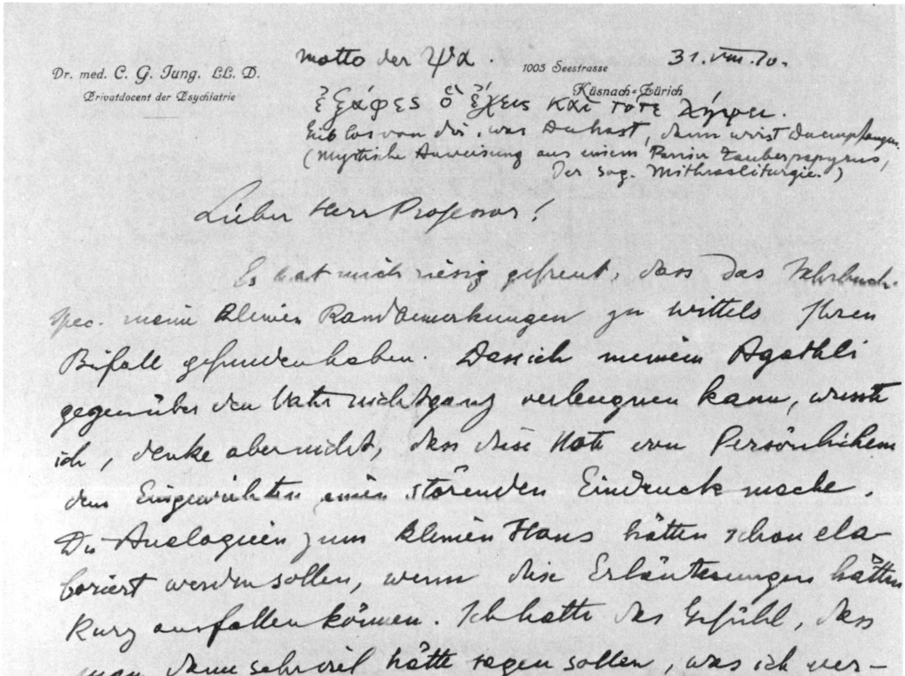
Dr. med. C. G. Jung. LL. D.
Privatdocent der Psychiatrie

Motto der ΨA. 1003 Seestrasse Küsnach-Zürich 31.VIII.10.

ἄφες ὃ ἔχεις καὶ τότε λήψει.
Gib los von Dir, was Du hast, dann wirst Du empfangen.
(Mystische Anweisung aus einem Pariser Zauberpapyrus, der sog. Mithrasliturgie.)

Lieber Herr Professor!

Es hat mich riesig gefreut, dass das Jahrbuch, spec. meine kleinen Randbemerkungen zu Wittels Ihren Beifall gefunden haben. Dass ich meinem Agathli gegenüber den Vater nicht ganz verleugnen kann, wusste ich, denke aber nicht, dass diese Note von Persönlichem den Eingeweihten einen störenden Eindruck mache. Die Analogieen zum kleinen Hans hätten schon elaboriert werden sollen, wenn die Erläuterungen hätten kurz ausfallen können. Ich hatte das Gefühl, dass man dann sehr viel hätte sagen sollen, was ich vermeiden wollte. Je dicker eine Arbeit, desto weniger liest man sie. Schliesslich muss Einiges auch der Phantasie des Lesers überlassen bleiben. Es nimmt mich sehr wunder, was die Kritik draussen mit diesem weiblichen Gegenstück zum kleinen Hans anfangen wird. („Armer Bubi, armes Mäderl")

Ich hoffe, alle die Arbeiten, die Sie mir gütigst besorgt haben, im nächsten Jahrbuch publicieren zu können. Soeben kündigt mir Bleuler einen umfangreichen Beitrag an, eine Apologie Ihrer Psychologie, die er gerne auch in Sonderauflage gedruckt haben möchte, um ihr weite Verbreitung zu sichern.

300

Jung, 31 Aug. 10 (210 J, p. 1)

pendious contribution, an apologia for your psychology, which he would like to have printed in a separate edition as well, to ensure wide distribution. I haven't seen the manuscript yet.[2]

On Friday evening I am off to London for a consultation (via Paris-Calais). I could return via the Hook of Holland or Vlissingen and take this opportunity to see you if you are still in Holland by then.[3] The cholera in Italy[4] has probably upset your arrangements as well. I want to be back in Zürich by Tuesday evening, so I could not stay long. If you abandon the sea voyage to Italy it would surely be on your way to stop off in Zurich. For us it would naturally be a great pleasure. My wife's confinement is not expected until the end of September, it now turns out. Whether I can return via Holland is rather uncertain, as it depends on how things go in England. Perhaps you would write me in London about your travel plans (Hotel Russell, Russell Square, W.C.).

I was very happy to hear that your health is good. Mine is equally satisfactory. Because of my overextended preliminary studies I may not be able to finish the Mithras problem in time for the *Jahrbuch*. I don't want to rush it. In that case it can come after the New Year. The second half of the current *Jahrbuch* goes to press on October 15th.

Kind regards,

Most sincerely yours, J U N G

211 J

1003 Seestrasse, Küsnach-Zürich,

Dear Professor Freud,   8 September 1910

Many thanks for your cards.[1] Too bad everything got muddled up. I crossed by the Hook of Holland after all.

I really cannot remember whether I have already told you that Sister Moltzer[2] is reproaching herself for having painted too black a

---

[2] See above, 159 J n. 3, and below, 226 F n. 1.

[3] The letter did not reach Freud in time, as he left on 31 August, with Ferenczi, on a trip to Paris, Rome, and Sicily. See *Freud/Abraham Letters*, 30 Aug. 10 ("I am off early tomorrow").

[4] This epidemic provides the background of Thomas Mann's novella, *Death in Venice* (1911).

---

[1] Missing.

[2] Mary or Maria Moltzer (1874–1944), daughter of a Netherlands distiller, became a nurse as a protest against alcoholic abuse. Had psychoanalytic training with

351

picture of Frl. Boeddinghaus.[3] Between the two ladies there is naturally a loving jealousy over me. Since I don't know just how much Frl. Boeddinghaus, who is really quite nice and appealing, has been blackened by Sister Moltzer's description, I don't know how to rehabilitate her. I can only say that she is still pretty much taken up with herself but now has a post with an American lady in Zürich, and is doing well by all accounts.

I was in England for one day only and saw Dr. Hart,[4] who now holds a *lectureship of psychiatry*.[5]

I enclose a letter from Binswanger which will show you how matters stand here. Were I on my own and responsible only for myself, I would put Bleuler in his place and do what has to be done. But it is being intimated to me from all sides that Bleuler's loss would be dangerous. Naturally I don't want to harm the cause and am therefore prepared for any compromise. It is up to us to decide whether we shall tolerate the present situation. In any event I shall try to keep the joint sessions to a minimum. I really don't see why we should scatter our good seed *gratis* and reap nothing but opposition.

Recently I heard that Bleuler is sending people who want further psychiatric training to Kraepelin. He has worked himself into a regular delirium of fear over Kraepelin since developing a resistance to me. Now he crawls on his belly before the German mogul. I think I told you in my last letter that Bleuler has earmarked 90 printed pages of the *Jahrbuch* for his apologia pro Freud. I am eager to read it and shall if necessary append a few editorial remarks (only with your imprimatur, of course).

So you see, the present situation is disagreeable and confused, and there are prospects of an even longer Babylonian captivity.

I wish you a very good holiday and send regards to Ferenczi,

Most sincerely yours, JUNG

Jung and after 1913 continued as an analytical psychologist. Co-translator of Jung's *The Theory of Psychoanalysis* (CW 4, p. 83 and par. 458).

[3] Martha Böddinghaus, of Munich; attended the Weimar Congress, 1911. Later, under her married name, she published articles on Jungian psychology. She married Hermann Sigg (d. 1925), a Swiss businessman of Küsnacht who was often Jung's companion on cycling and mountain-climbing trips. It was Sigg who took Jung along on a business trip to Algeria and Tunisia in 1920 (see *Memories*, ch. IX, i). (Information from Mr. Franz Jung.)

[4] Bernard Hart (1879–1966), English psychiatrist; championed psychoanalysis as early as 1909; charter member of the British Psycho-Analytical Society, 1913.

[5] English in original. It was at the University College Hospital Medical School.

212 F

Dear friend,   Rome, 24 September 1910

I am writing to you on a dark, cold, dismally rainy morning that reminds me of our November. This evening we are planning to leave the Eternal City for home. In the meantime you have no doubt become a father; I hope to find the best news of you waiting for me at home.

The trip has been very rich and has supplied several wish-fulfilments that my inner economy has long been in need of. Sicily is the most beautiful part of Italy and has preserved unique fragments of the Greek past, infantile reminiscences that make it possible to infer the nuclear complex. The first week on the island was delightful, the second, because of the continuous scirocco, a hard trial for poor Konrad. Now at last we feel that we have come through it all: the scirocco and the threat of cholera and malaria. September is not the right time of year to enjoy the beauty here. My travelling companion is a dear fellow, but dreamy in a disturbing kind of way, and his attitude towards me is infantile. He never stops admiring me, which I don't like, and is probably sharply critical of me in his unconscious when I am taking it easy. He has been too passive and receptive, letting everything be done for him like a woman, and I really haven't got enough homosexuality in me to accept him as one. These trips arouse a great longing for a real woman. A number of scientific notions I brought with me have combined to form a paper on paranoia,[1] which still lacks an end, but takes quite a step forward in explaining the mechanism of the choice of neurosis. I don't know if I shall be able to finish it before the end of October.

Monday, 26 Sept. 10

Now I am at home and rather tired from the trip and the change of scene. Still, I want to answer your letter and not delay my congratulations on the birth of your third daughter[2] and my kind regards to your wife.

I suggest patience with Bleuler. You know how contrary such an attitude is to my temperament, but . . . his name on the *Jahrbuch*

---

[1] I.e., on the Schreber case; see below, n. 3.
[2] Marianne (d. 1965); married Walther Niehus. She was co-editor of Jung's Gesammelte Werke and a member of the Editorial Committee for Jung's *Letters*.

and his historic role oblige us to practise self-denial. We must pay the price, as it were, for your historical development. I think he will withdraw little by little, I too am very curious about his apologia, we shall talk it over together when we have read it. Of course we shall draw the logical conclusion and not invite him to the Congress. In the meantime we must go on working.

Binswanger's letter is enclosed. Fräulein M. is going too far in the way of overcompensation—I myself have ventured to observe that the other young lady's letters seem rather muddled. Once I get through my backlog, I shall write to you again, also about scientific projects. Among the printed matter I found waiting on my arrival, my attention was caught by a characteristic review by the fleetingly improvised[3] Professor and Hofrat Schottländer in the *Zeitschrift für Psychologie und Physiologie der Sinnesorgane*;[3a] some other hack has devoted a tender article to *Leonardo* in the Berlin *Sturm*,[4] entitled "Genius Spat Upon." Otherwise good, serious things showing that the world is taking an interest in us, an article by Putnam[5] which you too must have, a number of *The Lancet*, in which for variety's sake your "complexes" are attributed to me,[6] etc.

Pfister[7] is finished and will be published soon, likewise Hitschmann.[8]

[3] Holograph: *flüchtig hingemacht*, a Schreberism; this translation is based on Macalpine and Hunter's "fleeting-improvised-men" rather than on Strachey's "cursorily improvised men" (SE XII, p. 21). Schreber's explanation: "human shapes set down for a short time by divine miracles only to be dissolved again" (*Memoirs*, p. 43). Cf. Macalpine and Hunter's note: "not complete beings, but improvised, with an anal implication" (p. 357)—i.e., as if defecated.

[3a] LVII (1910), 142–51, reviewing *Jahrbuch* I entire.

[4] R. K. Neumann-Lankwitz, "Das bespuckte Genie," *Sturm*, 28 July 1910, p. 174. *Sturm*, founded the same year and edited by Herwarth Walden (1878–?1941), was one of the first Expressionist magazines.

[5] See below, 214 F n. 2.

[6] Unsigned, "The Antics of Sportsmen: A Psychological Note," *The Lancet* (London), 10 Sept. 1910, pp. 837f.: "Professor Freud of Vienna has clearly pointed out the value of what he terms 'complexes' . . . the forgotten remnants of mental states which, coming perhaps by accident into play, influence action. . . . The complicated proceedings of the fast [cricket] bowler with a long run and a high delivery are examples of Freud's 'complex' . . . , the result of earlier voluntary acts which have become reflex."

[7] *Die Frömmigkeit des Grafen Ludwig von Zinzendorf* (*Schriften zur angewandten Seelenkunde*, no. 8; 1910). Pfister dedicated it to Jung "with gratitude and high regard." Also see above, 193 J n. 6.

[8] See above, 194 F n. 3.

Häberlin's book is here before me,[9] another volume of *Anthropophyteia*,[10] in which we are now taking a more active interest, a new edition of Havelock Ellis (*Modesty-Autoerotism*),[11] as usual with a charming inscription. When am I going to read and answer all this? I am allowing myself a holiday until October 1st; then I shall start in.

I send you my kind regards and an expression of my certainty that nothing can befall our cause as long as the understanding between you and me remains unclouded.

Yours ever, FREUD

213 J

1003 Seestrasse, Küsnach-Zürich,
29 September 1910

Dear Professor Freud,

So you are back safe and sound from the cholera country! Nevertheless I wish I could have been with you. I understand very well what you say about your travelling companion. I find that sort of thing exasperating, and still have an aftertaste of it from our American trip.

Your advice concerning the way to treat our Uncle "Euler"[1] is opportune and reinforces my natural bent for philanthropy. I shall have the galleys of his manuscript sent to you; I was unable to read it because it was sent direct to Deuticke at the last moment.

Silberer's paper on mythology[2] is good, except that his "functional category" for the investigation of myths has not blossomed into a thorough-going working hypothesis. I think you will recommend it for separate publication.

I am working like a horse and am at present immersed in Iranian archaeology. I think my conjecture that the Miller fantasies[3] really add up to a redemption mystery can be proved to the hilt. Only the

[9] Probably *Wissenschaft und Philosophie, ihr Wesen und ihr Verhältnis*, vol. I (Basel, 1910).
[10] A periodical, published annually 1904–14 at Leipzig, under the editorship of Friedrich S. Krauss; it dealt principally with anthropological material of a sexual character. See Freud's letter to Krauss, 26 June 1910, in SE XI.
[11] *The Evolution of Modesty: The Phenomena of Sexual Periodicity; Auto-Erotism*, vol. I (orig. 1899) of *Studies in the Psychology of Sex*.

[1] Bleuler. (*Eule* is German for "owl.")
[2] See above, 209 F n. 6. Concerning "functional category," cf. below, 231 F n. 9, "functional phenomenon."
[3] See above, 199a F n. 8.

other day a so-called Dem. praec. patient, whom I have almost set on her feet again, came out with a really grand, hitherto anxiously guarded, moon-fantasy which is a redemption mystery composed entirely of liturgical imagery. A thing of marvellous beauty but very difficult, built on incest with her brother. In the case of another patient I could spot fragments of a Peter-Antichrist legend; origin obscure. The interesting thing in the first case is that prior knowledge is entirely lacking; the fantasy originated in early childhood (about the 7th year). She is now 18½ years old, Jewish.[4] — As I said, I wallow in wonders.

I was touched and overjoyed to learn how much you appreciate the greatness of Schreber's mind and the liberating ἱεροὶ λόγοι of the basic language. I am still very intrigued by the fate of those unfortunate corps brothers who were miracled up to the skies and are described as "those suspended under Cassiopeia."[5] The Manichaeans (Schreber's godfathers?) hit on the idea that a number of demons or "archons" were crucified on, or affixed to, the vault of heaven and were the *fathers of human beings*.

I use the winged word "Why don't you say it (*scil.* aloud)?"[6] every day in analysis, where it proves its efficacy. The book is a worthy one; it deserves the place of honour in every psychiatric library if only for the sake of "little Flechsig."[7]

I have had a disgruntled letter from Jones. Everybody seems to have it in for him. He says the directors have stopped the *Asylum Bulletin*[8] because of his ΨA writings.

"Schottländer" has announced an article in the *Journal of Abnormal Psychology*: "Hysteria and Modern Psychoanalysis."[9] There you will reap the rewards of your ΨA endeavours with him. Won't you admit now that my kicking-out technique is therapeutically unsurpassable in such cases?

With many kind regards,

Yours very sincerely, JUNG

[4] The case is in "Schizophrenia" (1958), CW 3, pars. 571f.

[5] Schreber, *Memoirs* (tr. Macalpine/Hunter), p. 71.

[6] Ibid., p. 70, n. 26, and p. 121.

[7] Ibid., p. 135; cf. p. 109: "superior Flechsig" and "middle Flechsig." (Paul Emil Flechsig (1847–1929), professor of psychiatry at Leipzig, was Schreber's physician.)

[8] The *Bulletin of the Ontario Hospitals for the Insane* did not "cease publication" (Jones, II, p. 123/109), but Jones was removed as a co-editor because of objection to an article of his, according to Cyril Greenland, "Ernest Jones in Toronto," *Canadian Psychiatric Association Journal*, VI:3 (June 1961).

[9] See below, 237 J n. 2.

214 F

Dear friend, 1 October 1910, Vienna, IX. Berggasse 19

I am delighted at the cheerful tone of your letters and infer from it that mother and child are doing very well, though you have neglected to say so *aloud*. Pleased with everything you say, only in regard to Schottländer you do me an injustice. I kept him that time just to tease and punish him, and I only wish you could have been there to see him squirm. Incidentally, his article had already been sent off to America at the time, he mentioned it if I am not mistaken.

In the meantime I have written a long letter[1] to Uncle Bleuler—I presume you have no other in mind—not humble and pleading, more on the severe side, but nevertheless inspired by the consideration that he may feel offended at my not having got in touch with him directly. I tried to explain how unjust it is of him to punish us for rejecting Isserlin's inquisitorial presence and to let our opponents, his honoured colleagues, get away with statements like those of Ziehen and Hoche; I expressed my regret that he should renounce his influence on the development of the movement but assured him that we would survive none the less. I pointed out most emphatically that the gulf between him and his German colleagues is in any event unbridgeable, so sprinkling a little pepper on his anal crogenous zone. I expect no good to come of it, but I believe my step was justified and will not create any trouble for you.

I was frankly enthusiastic over Putnam's article in the *Boston Medical Journal* of 21 July 1910.[2] I thanked him at once and asked his permission to translate it for the *Zentralblatt*. Since he is not likely to refuse, I have already done the translation. It will be an excellent apologia for ΨA and a good indirect answer to the last or next lot of abuse. The old man has indeed worked his way brilliantly into the field, he understands almost everything. Strangely enough, he makes

---

[1] Dated 28 Sept. 10; quoted extensively in Franz Alexander and Sheldon T. Selesnick, "Freud-Bleuler Correspondence," *Archives of General Psychiatry*, XII:1 (Jan., 1965), 2–3.

[2] "On the Etiology and Treatment of the Psychoneuroses" (read before the Canadian Medical Association, Toronto, 1 June 10), *Boston Medical and Surgical Journal*, no. 163 (21 July 10); tr. Freud, "Über Ätiologie und Behandlung der Psychoneurosen," *Zentralblatt*, I:4 (Jan. 1911). See discussion of the paper in Putnam to Freud 4 Aug. 10, Freud to Putnam 29 Sept. 10, in *Putnam and Psychoanalysis*, pp. 104, 109f.

a reservation to my disadvantage in speaking of what is precisely my very own contribution: repression and the role of sexuality.

This work interrupted my study of Schreber, which I shall now resume. I didn't even read half the book in Sicily, but I have fathomed the secret. The case is easily reduced to its nuclear complex. His wife falls in love with the doctor and keeps his picture on her writing-desk for years. He too, of course, but in the woman's case there are disappointments, attempts to have children are unsuccessful; a conflict develops; he ought to hate Flechsig as his rival, but loves him, thanks to his predisposition and the transference from his first illness. The infantile situation is now complete, and soon his father emerges behind Flechsig. Fortunately for psychiatry this father was also—a doctor. One more confirmation of what we found in so many paranoid cases when I was in Zürich; that paranoiacs are unable to prevent the re-cathexis of their homosexual leaning. Which brings the case into line with our theory.

During my trip I was able to amplify this theory a little, and now I mean to test my progress against Schreber's case history and various other publications on paranoia. Still, measured by my original design, the whole thing is so incomplete that I do not know when I shall be able to publish it or how long it will be. In any case the outcome will be a study on Schreber and people will think I designed my theory with the book in mind.

I share your enthusiasm for Schreber; it is a kind of revelation. I plan to introduce "basic language" as a serious technical term— meaning the original wording of a delusional idea which the patient's consciousness (as in the case of the Rat Man) experiences only in distorted form. After another reading I may be able to resolve all the intriguing fantasies; I didn't quite succeed the first time. Since the man is still alive, I was thinking of asking him for certain information (e.g., when he got married) and for permission to work on his story. But perhaps that would be risky. What do you think? —

I see that you go about working in the same way as I do; rather than take the obvious path that leads straight ahead, you keep your eye peeled for one that strikes your fancy. This is the best way, I think; afterwards one is amazed at the logical sequence in all these digressions.[3] Consequently I wish you luck with your immersion in mythology. To judge by a remark he makes in his paper Putnam is also using this method of taking projected material back into the psyche.

[3] Quoted by Jones, II, p. 498/449.

Today I resumed my practice and saw my first batch of nuts again. I must now transmute the nervous energy gained during my holiday into money to fill my depleted purse. It always takes a week or two before they all turn up, and for a while there is enough resilience and alertness left for scientific work. Later on one is content with sheer survival.

With kind regards and special good wishes to the happy mother.

Yours, FREUD

215 J

1003 Seestrasse, Küsnach-Zürich,

Dear Professor Freud,   20 October 1910

It is now 4 days since my return[1] and I feel it is time to resume our correspondence. The days in Italy were glorious, and fruitful in several respects. I found some very lovely things in the Museo Civico in Verona: you remember the Mithraic sacrifice with the snake biting the bull's fore-foot? The circle is now closed: I found a Priapus stele with a snake biting the god's penis. Priapus is pointing his finger at it with a smile.[2] Stockmayer has taken a photograph of it. And various other things of lesser interest.

Since term is starting up again, I am working under high pressure at my mythological studies; in term time there is too much distraction. What I sent you will be completely reworked on the basis of further studies which reached into the most impenetrable obscurities of philosophy.

On my return I found a card from you[3] with a note about not receiving the *Bulletin*.[4] I was a little alarmed until I cleared up the

[1] The bicycle tour that Jung mentioned in 206 J, near end. It is apparently the trip that Jung describes in *Memories*, pp. 306f./284f., where it is dated 1911, though there is no evidence in these letters that such a trip was taken that year. Jung tells of making the trip with a friend, evidently W. Stockmayer; on the way home they spent the night at Arona, on the lower part of Lake Maggiore. Jung had a vivid dream which left him with a feeling of humiliation, and when he awoke he thought of the paper he was then working on, "Wandlungen und Symbole der Libido." "I had such intense inferiority feelings . . . that I immediately took the train home in order to get back to work."
[2] See *Symbols of Transformation*, CW 5, pl. LXI b. In the original (1911/12) edn., this was one of six illustrations given.
[3] Missing.
[4] No. 2, Sept. 1910.

mystery. Nevertheless, despite all my urging it has gone much too slowly, for which the printer is partly to blame. I'd be grateful for editorial hints. I have had nothing from Putnam, but would very much like to announce his article in the *Bulletin*. Perhaps your secretary[5] would send me a short notice dictated by you together with the bibliographical data?[6] Thanks.

Yesterday a German *cand. med.* (by name of Weinmann[7]), pupil of Kraepelin's, showed up with the intention of studying ΨA with me later—*rara avis*! He told me a very good joke that perfectly explains Hoche's nerve-contacts. H. is tormented by a (minuscule) *Freudian* soul:[8] in his clinical seminars he is taking an *exclusive interest in the problem of jokes and the problem of dreams*, as his fellow student, the Heidelberg pathological anatomist Ernst,[9] relates. I think we are more justified than ever in taking Hoche's views about us seriously, in basic language.

All goes well with my family, and I hope all is well with yours.

Kind regards, JUNG

216 F

Dear friend,   23 October 1910, Vienna, IX. Berggasse 19

After my own wallowing in nature and antiquity, I can hardly begrudge you your trip, but I am very glad you are within reach again. I have all sorts of things to tell you.

First you will be interested to hear about Bleuler. The nerve-contact I have made with him led to a copious correspondence[1] and I am just now answering one of his letters. It is difficult with him, his argu-

---

[5] Otto Rank.
[6] The notice appeared; see next letter, n. 7.
[7] This M.D. candidate could not be identified.
[8] Allusion to the "little men" (souls) who tormented Schreber by "nerve-contact."
[9] Paul Ernst (1859–1937), originally of Zürich; distinguished for bacteriological and biochemical researches.

---

[1] Alexander and Selesnick (p. 4) publish passages from a letter of Freud to Bleuler, 16 Oct. 10, in which he tries to clarify the "Isserlin affair which—in itself unimportant—became a kind of test case for the sectarianism" of the movement; and Freud quotes Jung's 3 Mar. 10 letter to him (181 J, wherein Isserlin's request to attend the Nuremberg meeting is first mentioned): "But our splendid isolation must come to an end one day." Bleuler's reply, 19 Oct. 10, trying to explain his hesitancy to join the International Association, is also quoted at length.

Zentralblatt

für

Psychoanalyse.

Medizinische Monatsschrift für Seelenkunde.

Herausgeber:

Professor Dr. **Sigm. Freud.**

Schriftleitung:

Dr. **Alfred Adler,** Wien. — Dr. **Wilhelm Stekel,** Wien.

Unter Mitwirkung von:

Dr. **Karl Abraham,** Berlin; Dr. **A. A. Brill,** New-York; Dr. **S. Ferenczi,** Budapest; Dr. **E. Hitschmann,** Wien; Dr. **E. Jones,** Toronto; Dr. **Otto Juliusburger,** Steglitz; Dozent **C. G. Jung,** Zürich; Dr. **F. S. Krauss,** Wien; Professor **August di Lutzenberger,** Neapel; Prof. **Gustav Modena,** Ancona; Dr. **Alfons Mäder,** Kreuzlingen; Dozent **N. Ossipow,** Moskau; Dr. **Oskar Pfister,** Zürich; **Otto Rank,** Wien; Dr. **Franz Ricklin,** Zürich; Dr. **J. Sadger,** Wien; Dr. **A. Stegmann,** Dresden; Dr. **M. Wulff,** Odessa; Dr. **Erich Wulffen,** Dresden.

I. Jahrgang Heft 1/2.

Wiesbaden.

Verlag von J. F. Bergmann.

1910.

Jährlich erscheinen 12 Hefte im Gesamt-Umfang von 36 bis 40 Druckbogen zum Jahrespreise von 15 Mark.

The *Zentralblatt*: cover of first issue. See 216 F

ments are so vague that I can't pin him down; and if I were to point out his secret motives it would only antagonize him. He does nothing but skirmish with indirect statements. He has expressed a desire for an interview. Since he adds that he cannot get away before Easter when the next Congress is presumably to be held, I offered to go to Zürich during the Christmas holidays if he holds out some hope of an understanding. My position is that he is no more indispensable than anyone else, but that his loss would be regrettable and would widen the gulf between us and the others. Consequently it is worth a sacrifice to hold him, of what I don't know yet, certainly not of the Association which we have been at so much pains to found and which is destined to do great things. There is an enormous disproportion between his objections to our procedure and the conclusions he draws from them. And he fills in the gap with imponderables and unintelligibles. But he seems to court my good opinion, he believes in the cause and doesn't want to break with us. My awareness that we are indebted to him for your beginnings inclines me in his favour. I can only suggest that we wait and see what comes of our correspondence and possible meeting.

He makes a great point of our treatment of Isserlin, who was first invited and then rebuffed. He tells me you speak of it as a bad joke at his expense. Since you yourself were certainly not the perpetrator of this joke, the incident provides one more argument for the necessity of a unified leadership.

I have not received the proofs of Bleuler's apologia for ΨA. He himself has asked me to read it to suggest changes, but I am quite content not to be involved, because one thing we must not do under any circumstances is to provide nourishment for the myth that we gag deviating opinions among our own members.

I believe that you and I must come to an agreement on a policy concerning attacks on us. I see now that we cannot just go on ignoring them. That would suit me, but there is no need for the whole group to take this attitude. I have been very much amused by the blows you mete out in the *Bulletin*,[2] but I wonder if we oughtn't to go about it more systematically, and if so, in which of our organs.

The *Zentralblatt* appeared today.[3] I should like very much to bring

[2] In no. 2, pp. 3ff., Jung deals sarcastically with Hoche's Baden-Baden paper (see above, 201 F n. 1) and quotes other adverse criticism.

[3] *Zentralblatt für Psychoanalyse; Medizinische Monatsschrift für Seelenkunde*, directed by Sigmund Freud, edited by Alfred Adler and Wilhelm Stekel (Wiesbaden: J. F. Bergmann). For the front cover of the first issue, see facsimile. Each

the three organs into harmony with each other. Consequently I am proud that you ask me for editorial "hints." I have quite a few to offer.

In my opinion the reports of meetings in the *Bulletin* should be very brief, merely indicating the subjects of the papers, and more detailed in the *Zentralblatt*, because in the former they do not come to the attention of the public.

I do not regard the *Bulletin* as the proper place for a critique of Bleuler's "Negativism," because scientific statements are the business of the other two organs. His paper deserves to be reviewed by you. If you do not wish to publish your review[4] in the journal whose director he is (though there would be no harm in it), the *Zentralblatt* is open to you at all times, as is only natural. Your paper[5] incidentally is being published in the next issue. As president of the International Association you are entitled to an influence on this journal. Don't neglect to exert it. And I hope the memory of the events preceding your election will impel you to recognize the special rights of the Viennese.

If one day there are not enough personal, business, and bibliographical items to fill the *Bulletin*, why not run a "manifesto" to "Your People"[6] defining and justifying the attitude you propose to take toward enemies, or prescribing such an attitude to the other members.

You will receive Putnam's paper directly from him. Rank will send you the notice[7] you have asked for.

Your scientific news interested me very much and I am looking forward eagerly to the reborn paper. I myself am much too tired today (from migraine) to report on my varied activities. I shall do so another time.

With kind regards to you and your family,

Yours ever, FREUD

Jahrgang (vol.), beginning in Oct., contained 12 numbers, during the first year sometimes issued double. For Adler's resignation, see below, 262 F n. 1.

[4] Jung's critique of Bleuler's "Zur Theorie des schizophrenen Negativismus" (*Psychiatrisch-neurologische Wochenschrift*, XII, 1910–11); see below, 252 J n. 6.

[5] "Psychology of Rumour"; see below, 223 F n. 1.

[6] Allusion to the manifesto "To My People" by Frederick William III, king of Prussia, in 1813, during the war of liberation against Napoleon.

[7] In the *Bulletin*, no. 3 (Dec. 1910), p. 8.

217 J

1003 Seestrasse, Küsnach-Zürich,

Dear Professor Freud,   29 October 1910

Yesterday there was a meeting of our Society at which the case of Bleuler was discussed. We decided to "wait and see." But nothing was decided about the gaggle of assistants that Bleuler trails behind him and with whom he professes his solidarity. A second important point was the criticism meted out to the *Bulletin*. Afterwards I took counsel with myself and have decided to suggest to you that we dispose of this abortion. We would never have begotten such a thing had we known that the Vienna people were bringing out a journal anyway and in addition were publishing the minutes of their meetings separately. With its limited funds the *Bulletin* can only make a very fatuous appearance and is pretty pointless because everything it contains might just as well be published in the *Zentralblatt*. The membership dues could then be considerably reduced. The *Bulletin* can never become a journalistic masterpiece in my hands, for I am not a journalist but am only carrying out my research work or what I regard as such. For the above proposition I have the unanimous support of the Zürich section, but not *for* the *Bulletin*. Before speaking of it publicly I would like to have your advice.

Further, in Zürich we have the rule that *only holders of academic degrees* can be accepted as members. Students at most as guests and for limited periods only. I say this because I fear that Ferenczi is starting something with that stage director.[1] But I would like our Society to be rigorously restricted to men with academic credentials, otherwise it will be a League of Monists.[2] When I have your approval I will lay the matter before the Association. (Circulars are sufficient for communications of this kind, no *Bulletin* is needed.)

I also very much doubt whether I should continue to publish abstracts (i.e., complete lists of publications) in the *Jahrbuch*. I would prefer to stand aside and leave it to the *Zentralblatt* since it has tacitly taken over the abstracts. What do you think?

I very much hope that if you come to Zürich you will stay with me.

---

[1] Holograph: *Theaterregisseur*. Presumably Dr. S. Hevesi, chief stage director of the National Theatre, Budapest, who had lectured on "Psychoanalytic Observations in the Theatre" 14 Oct. in a psychoanalytic seminar under Ferenczi's direction at Budapest. See *Bulletin*, no. 3 (Dec. 1910), p. 3.

[2] The Monistenbund was founded 1906 in Jena under the auspices of Ernst Haeckel (1834–1919), German biologist and philosopher, for the propagation of materialist monism. The Bund (League) had unrestricted membership.

I would be delighted to see you again, and am already planning to take the trip myself if you don't come here. For, on top of everything else, Bleuler is a coward. Recently in Berlin he failed dismally to stand up to Oppenheim's attacks.[3] Once again, of course, he has only half disgraced himself, for I hear that in his yet-to-be-published apologia he has ranged himself bravely on our side. I have not received the manuscript, but Binswanger has. Sometimes it makes my gorge rise to think that I have to dirty my hands with all these machinations and cleaning up of messes. I am not a politician, I believe in the right of self-defence and, for the rest, leave our opponents to devour each other. If you had heard *how* I talked to Bleuler you would be convinced that any sporting person, even if he were my deadly enemy, would have listened.

I am in entire agreement when you emphasize the need for discussion (in order to avoid "polemics"). Bleuler's criticisms will have to be answered. Presumably that will be done by you. I'm thinking of rapping Morton Prince over the knuckles.[4] It goes without saying that I shall first submit the manuscript to you for an opinion. Then I'll go after Janet. I shall deal with Bleuler's "Negativism" in the *Jahrbuch*.

Many thanks for sending me your article in the *Zentralblatt*.[5] But surely the journal brings out offprints as well? I don't quite understand what influence I could exert. To do so, I would have to have personal rapport with the editors, which is totally out of the question in Adler's case. Any such influence can only be exerted through you. The most I can do is criticize—Stekel for his own sweet self and his theoretical superficiality, and Adler for the total absence of psychology. It would be most inopportune to say it aloud. And it's not worthwhile picking on trivia (such as Schwedenborg instead of Swedenborg).[6] The only way to teach these people is to do it better oneself.

With kind regards,

Most sincerely yours, JUNG

[3] Abraham in a letter to Freud 18 Oct. 10 gives an account of the behaviour of Oppenheim, Bleuler, and others at the 4th annual meeting of the Society of German Neurologists, 6–8 Oct., in Berlin; see *Freud/Abraham Letters*, pp. 93f., and below, 253 F n. 2.

[4] Prince, "The Mechanism and Interpretation of Dreams," *Journal of Abnormal Psychology*, V (1910–11). For Jung's critique, see below, 235 J n. 1.

[5] "Die zukünftigen Chancen der psychoanalytischen Therapie," *Zentralblatt*, I.1/2 (Oct./Nov. 1910). = "The Future Prospects of Psycho-analytic Therapy," SE XI.

[6] Reviewing Karl Abel's "Über den Gegensinn der Urworte," Stekel had used the spelling Schwedenborg (*Zentralblatt*, I:1/2, 65, n. 1).

218 F

Dear friend,   31 October 1910, Vienna, IX. Berggasse 19

I hope the niggling tone of my last letter hasn't had a lasting effect and that such features are not present in the final image.

Your letter received today, just in time for the present phase of my "negotiations" with Bleuler. Tired[1] of his interminable evasions and zigzaggings, I have presented him with a kind of ultimatum.[2] I have asked him to state explicitly what parts of our statutes[3] were repellent to him; assuring him that as far as possible we would take his wishes into account (at the next Congress)—and reveal his ideas on the subject of controversy with outsiders, in which case I would be willing (and hoped to influence you in this direction) to give him a decisive say on our foreign policy. But, I concluded, this was contingent on his joining the Society, which I could not renounce and would not sacrifice to him. This letter was posted three days ago.

This correspondence (my part of which I cannot submit to you) has been exhausting, because on the one hand I agree with you completely, while on the other considerations of a selfish and sentimental nature, with which you are acquainted, have inclined me to moderation and, for instance, deterred me from asking him the question which you suggest and which I would very much have liked to ask, the famous question: Why didn't you say so aloud? (i.e., in Berlin.) At the end of my letters nature always asserted itself and I started to fume. I am no great diplomat and I cannot bring myself to believe that I have got anywhere with him. If he doesn't accept, of course I can't go to Zürich. In this case I should like to take you at your word and expect you in Vienna. If I go to Zürich, of course I shall stay with you. I was counting on your invitation.

And now to politics and the right of self-defence! You speak after my own heart. If I had been alone, my tactics would have been to wait for our adversaries to destroy each other. But now we have become a little band, we have assumed responsibilities towards our supporters, we have a cause to defend before the public. And so we must do violence to our own nature, show that we are capable of adapting ourselves to reality, and do what has to be done as intelligently as possible. For the President of the International Association and his

[1] Holograph: missing word, construed as *müde*, "tired."
[2] Freud to Bleuler, 27 Oct. 10, quoted partially by Alexander and Selesnick, p. 4.
[3] For the text of the Statutes, see appendix 3.

mentor (!) the right of self-defence is no longer appropriate; it is time for the witches "Politics" and "Diplomacy" and the changeling "Compromise" to take a hand. But we can make it up to ourselves with humour when we talk about these "farts" together one day. Of course there must be limits. Cases can easily arise in which the diplomatic approach would be unwise and we must give our nature free rein. Then I am prepared to sally forth arm in arm with you and challenge the century.[4] I have become neither timid nor dishonest, I am merely trying to be impersonal.

You are a master of the art of winning people; I should be glad if in the interest of ΨA you were to make more use of it. I also believe that you have not overcome your dislike of our Viennese colleagues, and that you extend it to the *Zentralblatt*. You are unquestionably right in your characterization of Stekel and Adler; for the latter you have even found the brilliant formula I have always been looking for. I can confide in you, as Montezuma did in his companion in misery,[5] that I am not lying on a bed of roses myself. But it does not befit a superior man like you to bear a grudge against them. Take it with humour as I do except on days when weakness gets the better of me. My guess is that the insides of other great movements would have been no more appetizing if one could have looked into them. There are never more than one or two individuals who find the straight road and don't trip over their own legs.

Now let us patiently consider the most important affairs of state, one by one.

a) *Zentralblatt*.

This time you have received the presidential copy from me; the next time it will come directly from the publisher. Each of us three (director and editors) is to receive three copies in accordance with a decision that has already been made. So you have nothing to thank me for. I am grieved to hear that you have not received the offprint, because my second daughter[6] (the one who looks like your wife), now my secretary, has spent the last few days sending out the last three papers ("Disturbances of Vision," "Antithetical Meaning," "Future Prospects") and must have sent yours too. I'll shoot off a second arrow tomorrow and hope it strikes home.

How you are to exert an influence on the *Zentralblatt*? By direct

---

[4] Echoing the lines "Arm in arm with you, / So I challenge the century," in Schiller, *Don Carlos* (1787), I, 9.
[5] See addenda.
[6] Sophie.

statements as President. If this doesn't appeal to you, I offer my services as a go-between. As director, to whom the contents of each number are submitted, I can put through all your demands and block anything that doesn't suit you. As time goes on, my supervision will become stricter; I was absent while the first number was being put together.

b) The *Bulletin*. Since you ask me for advice, I cry out: Stop! The *Bulletin* is provided for in Point 9 of our statutes. If the President oversteps one point, there will be no lack of imitators to do the same for the other points. If it is to be abolished, this can only be done by decision of the next Congress. Beware of the law!

The standards by which you judge it strike me as too high. It can never be compared to the *Zentralblatt*, it is intended neither as a literary nor as a journalistic masterpiece, but is merely supposed to convey the President's communications to the members, and certain items of personal news. Above all, it is not supposed to say anything whatever to the public, whereas the two journals are addressed to the general public. It will surely be possible after a certain amount of trial and error to determine what material is suitable for the *Bulletin* and what is not, and then it will prove to be an indispensable organ. For one thing, it ought to make circular letters, etc. superfluous; they will be issued only on very special occasions. Whether it is to have two, four or six pages is immaterial. As many as are needed. If it carries the programmes of the meetings (even without outlines of contents) it will not be rendered superfluous by the more detailed accounts in the *Zentralblatt*, which are intended to catch the eye of friend and foe. There is no need to reduce the dues, nor would there be any advantage in it. Finally, as a "political" reason for keeping the *Bulletin*, I wish to cite the fact that our opponents are lurking in wait, only too eager to trumpet the abandonment of an undertaking provided for in the statutes as an unmistakable sign of "inevitable collapse."[7]

c) *Restriction of membership to holders of academic degrees.* Here the statutes leave us free, although their spirit does not tend towards such exclusiveness. Consequently, the Zürich Society can accept such a provision without making it obligatory for the other Societies. In Vienna it is impossible, if only because we should then have to exclude our secretary of many years (Rank). It would also be a pity to exclude several new and very hopeful student members. Finally,

---

[7] Willy Hellpach (see below, 230 J n. 7) had written of "the inevitable collapse of the Freudian movement" in an article in *Der Tag* (25 June 10) quoted in *Bulletin*, no. 2 (Sept. 1910), p. 4.

such a "regressive" measure is not really appropriate in the era of *University Extension*.[8] As to any similarities to the League of Monists, that can be avoided by policy and purpose. In Vienna we have only the tacit rule that "active" patients are not to be admitted. The restriction you plan would never be accepted in Vienna and is also displeasing to me personally.

d) *The Lists of Publications.*

This is the least important point. The *Zentralblatt* is obligated by its name to record everything that appears on the subject of ΨA. The *Jahrbuch* is free to do as it pleases. The possibility of group reviews is certainly not curtailed by the existence of the *Zentralblatt*. The professed principle of taking notice only of positive publications in itself relieves the *Jahrbuch* of any need for completeness.

———

And now at last, after all this rubbish, I can speak to you of science. I am now in a somewhat more productive phase, which is reflected in minor productions. I have contributed a highly educational article on "Wild Psychoanalysis"[9] to the next number of the *Zentralblatt*, another, not much more significant, on the understanding of the concepts neurotic, psychogenic, and hysterical, is intended for a later number.[10] I should feel more secure if you were to read it first. But don't expect it too soon, the laws of my periodicity have not yet been laid bare. More interesting are my forthcoming contributions to the *Jahrbuch*. An article: "In what sense may one speak of unconscious feelings?"[11] and the beginning of the studies on paranoia.[12] First an analysis of our dear and ingenious friend Schreber. Because one can guess a good deal in reading the book. (I don't remember if I have already written to you about it.) First the father complex: Obviously Flechsig–father–God–sun form a series. The "middle" Flechsig points to a brother who like the father was already "blessed," that is, dead, at the time of the illness. The forecourts of heaven or "anterior realms

[8] English in original.
[9] See below, 229 J n. 1.
[10] Never published.
[11] Miss Anna Freud believes this ultimately became one of the "Papers on Metapsychology," "Das Unbewusste," *Zeitschrift*, III (1915) = "The Unconscious," SE XIV.
[12] Freud published one further study on paranoia: "Mitteilung eines der psychoanalytischen Theorie widersprechenden Falles von Paranoia," *Zeitschrift*, III:6 (1915) = "A Case of Paranoia Running Counter to the Psychoanalytic Theory of the Disease," SE XIV. On later references to paranoia, see editor's note to the Schreber study, SE XII, p. 5.

of God" (breasts!) are the women of the family, the "posterior realms of God" (buttocks!) are the father and his sublimation, God. There is no mention of any "soul-murder" in *Manfred*,[13] but there is of—incest with a sister. The castration complex is only too evident. Don't forget that Schreber's father was—a doctor. As such, he performed miracles, he miracled. In other words, the delightful characterization of God—that he knows how to deal only with corpses and has no idea of living people—and the absurd miracles that are performed on him[14] are a bitter satire on his father's medical art. In other words, the same use of absurdity as in dreams. The enormous significance of homosexuality for paranoia is confirmed by the central emasculation fantasy, etc. etc. — I am still waiting for Stegmann[15] to send me news of our Paul Daniel.

(In other words, his father bellowed too)[16]

With kindest regards,

Yours, FREUD

219 J

1003 Seestrasse, Küsnach-Zürich,
Dear Professor Freud,   7 November 1910

All your words shall be treasured in a "faithful and upright heart."[1] At present I am frightfully busy. First with patients, secondly with scientific work, thirdly with Honegger, whose worries oppress me. The moment has come, we are in the thick of the mess we spoke of in Nuremberg: the question of his fiancée. The situation has become sickly and unendurable. I have the impression that he hangs on, and thereby hangs himself, but gets stuck in the attempt.[2] It is all very

---

[13] Schreber refers to Lord Byron's dramatic poem *Manfred*. See SE XII, p. 44.
[14] I.e., Schreber.
[15] Arnold Georg Stegmann, psychiatrist of Dresden (Schreber's home); had used Freud's method as early as 1904 (Jones, II, pp. 33f./30) and became a charter member of the Berlin Branch Society (1910). Jones states that he died in 1912, but in a 1926 letter (Jones, III, p. 477/447) Freud says that he fell in the war. For his wife, see 286 F n. 3. / For references to the information on Schreber that Stegmann supplied to Freud, see SE XII, index, s.v. Stegmann.
[16] Schreber tells of his attacks of bellowing at night, which he calls the "bellowing-miracle"; see *Memoirs*, pp. 165 and 247.

---

[1] Holograph: "*getreuen und aufrichtigen Herzen*"—unidentified.
[2] Holograph: *Mir scheint, er hängt ab, und sich auf, bleibt aber beim Versuche*

dismal and depressing. As a result I have not had the least help from Honegger. I have to pull the whole cart by myself. My cousin Ewald Jung, on the contrary, is delightful. He has established himself in Winterthur and has a ΨAtic practice.

Your card[3] has just arrived. Bleuler's answer is just what I expected. He is going to hold a big soirée to which Riklin and I are invited. This may well be a bad sign. He stresses our "personal relationship" only in order to repudiate the official one more easily. Bleuler's virtues are distorted by his vices and nothing comes from the heart. I take a very pessimistic view of things. The younger elements in our Society are pressing for separation from Burghölzli but Binswanger is hanging on grimly.

As for my relations with the Vienna people, I admit that not everything is as it should be. The less than cordial reception in Nuremberg (I don't mean the election of the pope, but the purely personal aspect) has chilled me somewhat. I have never sought the presidency and therefore object to being looked at askance or envied because of it. I think I shall take myself at my own word and come to Vienna. I shall then pay Adler and Stekel a visit, especially in connection with the *Zentralblatt*.

My remarks about the *Bulletin* were greatly influenced by ill-humour over all the obstacles. I am grateful for your hints. Accordingly, we shall confine ourselves in the *Bulletin* to mere announcements and carry no more abstracts.

I have been able to finish this boring letter only a paragraph at a time. There have been too many interruptions. Honegger seems to have got himself disengaged at last, thus probably saving his skin. Tomorrow I shall be with Bleuler.[4] Afterwards I will write to you.

Kind regards, JUNG

---

stehen. This is difficult to construe in German. Apparently Honegger was ambivalent about breaking his engagement.

[3] Missing.

[4] This letter was begun on Mon., 7 Nov., but this sentence and the first of the next letter suggest that it was completed on Thurs., 10 Nov.

220 J

Dear Professor Freud,   13 November 1910

The discussion with Bleuler took place last Friday evening. The first thing he wanted was that I should analyse a dream he had been keeping for me for 5 days. Naturally the analysis had to be staged before the public (to make the exhibition more effective). I humoured him by not mincing any words. He dreamt he was *suckling his child himself*. Here we have the obvious answer. His wife is still feeding it. So now he's becoming a woman. He still can't decide (consciously) to stop producing children. At last he holds *me*, his child, to his breast again. He is dying to be analysed and torments himself with delusional ideas: I haven't the time, reject his love, etc. He does not feel in the least homosexual. Consequently, from love of me, he is turning himself into a woman and wants to behave exactly like a woman, to go along with our Society only *passively*, to be scientifically *fecundated* since he cannot express himself *creatively*, is afraid of being violated. So, for the time being, he won't join chiefly because of homosexual resistance. He did ask me, though, whether I would advise him to encourage you to come to Zürich. The whole apparatus that is being set in motion to win him over gives him enormous pleasure, so he would be frightfully offended if the negotiations were broken off. You may already have heard from him. Riklin and I were very sweet with him. Sometime this week I'll invite him to my place for further softening up. I now have the impression he will join after all, if we are prepared to pay a very high price.

I hope you have received the proofs of Bleuler's paper from Deuticke by now. Fine how he polishes off our opponents. But unfortunately a good deal of it is vague and tortuous, all from lack of personal experience. For instance he still has astonishing difficulties with dream analysis.

All in all, Bleuler has been surprisingly agreeable and obliging. He has not given one reason for his unwillingness to join. The "tone" gets on his nerves, he "just can't," "not yet" at least. He has *no conscious reason*; the dream tells us what the real reason is. It is not, as he says, that *Stekel* is in the Society; *I am the one who is holding him back*. He throws Isserlin in my face, obviously as a screen for his homosexual resistance. He identifies with Isserlin. Scorned love! In the light of this analysis I shall have quite a few things to straighten out.

Meanwhile with kindest regards, JUNG

221 F

Dear friend,   25 November 1910, Vienna, IX. Berggasse 19

Bleuler's letter[1] enclosed. He starts by confirming the failure of all attempts at a rational solution, but seems to be assuring us of something else, to wit, that he does not want to forsake us and the cause. We can only rejoice at the prospect of holding him. But you must have studied him enough at your last meetings to be able to decide what is to be done. Would this be possible: purge the Zürich Society, throw the others out mercilessly, create a special place for him as an elder statesman, and invite him to the scientific sessions, though not to all of them. But we should have to get along without him at the Congress. Then he would soon feel isolated in Burghölzli and advise the others to join the Society. Would that be feasible?

As for my trip, I am now being punished for my disingenuousness. Naturally I wanted to reap my private profit from the diplomatic undertaking, to spend a day with you and get to know your house and your children. Now he insists on my staying with him. If I do that, I won't see your family at all; my time is very much restricted by the costliness of my working day and my compelling need to earn money every day for all sorts of necessities and obligations. But I don't dare to decline to stay at his house;[2] that would probably cancel out the entire effect of the trip; his whole performance looks to me like revenge for the situation when I was staying *with* you, *above* him, and neglected to call on him. That was really a mistake, I shouldn't have given in to you. Now it serves me right.

If I take up his first suggestion and meet him somewhere half-way, I won't see any more of you. Besides, a whole day alone with him would be very trying; he probably won't hit on the idea of taking you along with him. If he did, I should prefer Munich to Innsbruck, which holds hideous memories[3] for me. Maybe consideration for Kraepelin will keep him away from Munich.

In short, I am still quite undecided. Please return Bleuler's letter immediately so I can give him a provisional answer, and also tell me what you think, so I can definitely make up my mind.

My work on Schreber would get ahead nicely if only I had time for

---

[1] Not included in Alexander's and Selesnick's article.
[2] Holograph: *an sein Haus* inserted afterward.
[3] "Can only refer to his discussions with Fliess at Innsbruck in the Easter of 1899."—Jones, II, p. 80/73.

it. Sunday afternoon is really all I have, and it comes only once a week. My spirits are dampened by the irritations with Adler and Stekel, with whom it is very hard to get along. You know Stekel, he is having a manic period, he is destroying all my finer feelings and driving me to despair; I have had just about enough of defending him against everybody. Recently a strong opposition to him has developed in the Society. Adler is a very decent and highly intelligent man, but he is paranoid; in the *Zentralblatt*[4] he puts so much stress on his almost unintelligible theories that the readers must be utterly confused. He is always claiming priority, putting new names on everything, complaining that he is disappearing under my shadow, and forcing me into the unwelcome role of the aging despot who prevents young men from getting ahead. They are also rude to me personally, and I'd gladly get rid of them both. But it won't be possible. I wouldn't mind throwing the *Zentralblatt* after them, then we could enlarge the *Jahrbuch* to handle the rush of material. But they don't want a break and they can't change. And on top of it all, this absurd Viennese local pride and jealousy of you and Zürich! ΨA has really made no change in these people. The rest of them in Vienna are quite all right, though not exactly brilliant.

I hope my tale of woe is a comfort to you in your local difficulties.

By the way, the *Zentralblatt* seems to be meeting with a good deal of interest, it really was needed.

Concerning our friend Friedländer, I have finally learned that during his military service he was demoted for cheating at cards. That is why he left Vienna. Morton Prince is now publishing an article by him, which seems to be a really vile denunciation of psychoanalysis for the benefit of American prudishness. If this should prove to be true, I shall have the reviewer in the *Zentralblatt*[5] express surprise that *"he of all people* should include denunciation among the instruments of scientific controversy." At last he would have succeeded in making us take notice of him.

My kind regards to you, your wife and children. Here things are back to normal again after our grandmother's death (in Hamburg).[6]

Yours ever, FREUD

[4] Adler, "Die psychische Behandlung der Trigeminusneuralgie," *Zentralblatt*, I:1/2 (Oct./Nov., 1910).

[5] The review was not published.

[6] Emmeline Bernays, on 27 Oct. 10.

222 J

1003 Seestrasse, Küsnach-Zürich,

Dear Professor Freud,   29 November 1910

I had a faint suspicion that your present attitude to the divergent tendencies of Stekel and Adler is not exactly a simple one. There is in any case a noticeable analogy between Adler and Bleuler: the same mania to make the terminology as different as possible and to squeeze the flexible and fruitful psychological approach into the crude schematism of a physiological and biological straitjacket. Bleuler is another one who fights against shrivelling in your shadow. Last Sunday, at the Meeting of Swiss Psychiatrists in Bern,[1] he spoke about *ambivalence*, i.e., pairs of opposites. It was dreadfully superficial and schematic. It looks as though biology were taking all the spirit out of psychology.

Now for Bleuler's letter! Another masterpiece of tortuosity and "diplomatic vagueness." It is quite evident that his ratiocinative faculties have gone bankrupt. He was unable to advance a *single* reason when talking with me. There is no doubt at all that it is not you or the statutes or Stekel or anything else that is the cause of his negativism but simply and solely *myself*, ostensibly because of the Isserlin affair. But this is merely a pretext. *The real and only reason is my defection from the abstinence crowd.* After I had broken down his cover-resistances through the last dream-analysis, the following dreams came out at the party, accompanied by venomous asides (he told them to me in front of the company, all unsuspecting—as if to prove how little he understands dream-analysis!): He was the guest of the German Kaiser, who looked like a fat grocer, sodden with drink. In a second dream he was summoned to Berlin *in order to analyse the Kaiser*. But he didn't get round to that, for the *Kaiser locked him in the cellar*. Bleuler would like more than anything to pick a quarrel with me about the reasons for my defection. He won't do that for the sake of discretion, instead he refuses to join *our* crowd. However, it still seems to me that he will come along once the smoke from the first shots has cleared away.

Regretfully I must share your view that, if you came to Zürich, you

---

[1] Winter Meeting of Swiss Psychiatrists, 26–27 Nov. Also, Binswanger read part of his paper on a hysterical phobia (see above, 204 J n. 5) and Riklin spoke on the "omnipotence of thoughts." See *Bulletin*, no. 3 (Dec. 1910), p. 5, and Riklin's report, *Zentralblatt*, I:5/6 (Feb./Mar. 1911), 266ff., with excerpts from the discussion led by Jung.

would have to grit your teeth and lodge with him. Bleuler is extremely touchy, loudly proclaiming that it doesn't matter a hang to him. This would be so miserable for us that I must counsel you to get together with Bleuler in Munich. You can't possibly spend a whole day alone with him; he is thoroughly exhausting because he is quite inhuman. Furthermore, the situation being so uncertain, you would accomplish just as much or as little in Zürich as in Munich. I would therefore not stake too much on this card but rest content with a meeting in Munich; after 2–3 hours Bleuler's arguments have long since petered out and he turns nasty, i.e., then comes the barrage of "Why"'s. So it would be best to spend 4–5 hours with him one evening,[2] let us say from 6 or 7 until the departure of the night train for Zürich. The evening Bleuler departs I shall arrive in Munich and hope very much to spend the next day with you. There is no need whatever for you to sacrifice any more time. I now have sufficient contact with Bleuler to hold him to our cause. The gaggle of assistants can be lopped off. Once more I recommend my plan "chaleureusement." It should meet all the requirements.

It is a good thing we know this about Friedländer. The man really is a damned swine. If ever he comes again I really shall kick him out. Thank God I guessed what kind of skunk had crawled in under my roof and treated him as I did. I am now more than ever convinced that these hogs have every reason to oppose us. I shall not consort with them in the future either. This technique pays off.

With us everything is going ahead nicely. In Bern the *whole interest* centred on ΨA. In that Society it has made a lasting abode for itself.

Have you read Bleuler's apologia?

With many kind regards,

Most sincerely yours, JUNG

We hope you will pay us a fleeting visit in the spring.

223 F

Dear friend,   3 December 1910, Vienna, IX. Berggasse 19

If it can be done, splendid. I've written to Bleuler suggesting that we meet in Munich on a Sunday. I hinted *gently* that I was pressed

2 Holograph: *Abend,* struck out and replaced by *Nachmittag.*

for time and would be quite satisfied if we could get together for a few hours. Now let's hope that he creates no difficulties and suspects nothing. And you will be coming later in the day—a secret, I presume. I find the intrigue delightful. If he insists on coming Monday rather than Sunday, it will cost me a day's work; I shall sacrifice it to him un-willingly, but to you willingly if you can come. If you do, I hope you will be nicer to me than my so-called oldest supporters here, who are finally beginning to get under my skin.

It is getting really bad with Adler. You see a resemblance to Bleuler; in me he awakens the memory of Fliess, but an octave lower. The same paranoia. In the second issue of the *Zentralblatt*, which will also contain your charming bit of school gossip,[1] you will find a review by him of your so-called Little Anna.[2] Read it carefully; otherwise it's hard to see what he is driving at. His presentation suffers from para-noid vagueness. But here one can see clearly how he tries to force the wonderful diversity of psychology into the narrow bed of a single aggressive "masculine" ego-current—as if the child rejected her fem-ininity and had no other thought than to be "on top" and play the man. To make his point he is obliged to misinterpret certain elements completely, such as the planing off of the genital organ, and to dis-regard others, such as her fear that her father will also get a child. The crux of the matter—and that is what really alarms me—is that he minimizes the sexual drive and our opponents will soon be able to speak of an experienced psychoanalyst whose conclusions are radically different from ours. Naturally in my attitude toward him I am torn between my conviction that all this is lopsided and harmful and my fear of being regarded as an intolerant old man who holds the young men down, and this makes me feel most uncomfortable.

Today I received from Putnam the second of his lectures on behalf of our ΨA.[3] An absolutely genuine and straightforward man, a pre-cious acquisition for the cause. He hasn't forgotten to mention you most particularly. Jones has also sent me a transcript of the discussion[4]

---

[1] "Ein Beitrag zur Psychologie des Gerüchtes," *Zentralblatt*, I:3 (1910) = "A Contribution to the Psychology of Rumour," CW 4. (The first *Zentralblatt* issue had been double: 1 & 2.)

[2] "Über Konflikte der kindlichen Seele," rev. in *Zentralblatt*, I:3 (Dec. 1910).

[3] "Personal Experience with Freud's Psychoanalytic Method," *Journal of Nervous and Mental Disease*, XXXVII:11 (Nov. 1910); read before the American Neuro-logical Association, Washington, May 1910.

[4] Presumably the discussion published in ibid., I:10 (Oct. 1910), though perhaps Jones's own transcript.

about it. All the flat, sterile, insipid objections we are accustomed to are to be heard unchanged on the other side of the Great Water; they seem admirably suited to the American prudishness we know so well. In our studies of America, have we ever looked into the source of the energies they develop in practical life? I believe it is the early dissolution of family ties, which prevents all the erotic components from coming to life and banishes the Graces from the land. Do you know *Der Amerikamüde* by our Kürnberger?[5] It is terribly true, you must read it. Everything is in it except for your discovery of the Negro complex.[6] That is missing, I think, which falsifies the picture.

I am all Schreber and will make a point of bringing the manuscript to Munich for you. I am not pleased with it, but it is for others to judge. All the same, a few points come out very clearly. I shall have to leave other parts of my speculation on paranoia for a later paper. I can never start writing before ten o'clock at night, and seldom in the right mood. Today I had to call off my lecture because of hoarseness brought on by influenza; tomorrow I shall stay home, and in this constellation, since I have no fever, I hope to write a few pages.

Our movement seems indeed to be spreading vigorously. Not long ago I received a first letter from France (!) from a Dr. Morichau-Beauchant,[7] professor of medicine at Poitiers, who reads psychoanalysis, works at it, and is convinced: "Cette lettre vous montrera que vous avez aussi des disciples en France qui suivent passionnément vos

---

[5] Ferdinand Kürnberger, Viennese journalist, published the book in 1855—a novel inspired partly by Nikolaus Lenau's experiences in the U.S.A. The title (based on Heine's "europamüde") means "The Man Weary of America."

[6] Jung's theory of an American "Negro complex," based on impressions during his 1909 and 1910 visits, was advanced in his "Report on America" at the Nuremberg Congress, Mar. 1910 (see above, editorial comment following 183 J); see also Rank's briefer abstract in *Zentralblatt*, I:3 (Dec. 1910), p. 130: "Lecturer sees in the psychological peculiarity of Americans features that point to energetic sexual repression. The reasons for repression are to be sought chiefly in living together with the Negro, which has a suggestive effect on the laboriously subjugated instincts of the white races. Hence strongly developed defensive measures are necessary, which manifest themselves in the peculiar aspects of American culture." Jung aired the theory in a lengthy interview in the *New York Times*, 22 Sept. 12 (in *C. G. Jung Speaking*, in press) and a lecture to the Zürich Society on 22 Nov. 12 (see below, 323 J n. 3), but published it only in 1927, in an essay, "Die Erdbedingtheit der Psyche," in *Mensch und Erde*, ed. Count Hermann Keyserling; see "Mind and Earth," CW 10, pars. 95ff.

[7] Pierre-Ernest-René Morichau-Beauchant (1873–1930+), "the first Frenchman to adhere publicly to psycho-analysis" (Freud, "History of the Psycho-Analytic Movement," SE XIV, p. 32); later on the editorial board of the *Zentralblatt*.

travaux." *The Interpretation of Dreams* has found readers in Paris and Madrid, as is proved by letters, from persons with German names, I must admit. Of course the negative aspect of my fame is even more pronounced; sometimes it annoys me that no one abuses you—after all you too have some responsibility in the matter. But let's hope the next generation is destined to something better than the role of a "cultural manure."

I hope to hear soon that all are well in your house, which is escaping me once again. I am looking forward to our meeting.

With kind regards,

Yours ever, FREUD

224 J

1003 Seestrasse, Küsnach-Zürich,

Dear Professor Freud, 13 December 1910[1]

I have postponed my answer so as to give you time to come to terms with Bleuler. I take it that you have now reached agreement. Any day between Christmas and New Year will suit me. Only not New Year's Day. I would like if possible a few days' rest in the mountains at Sylvester.[2]

I am greatly looking forward to Munich, where the Schreber will play a not unimportant role. I hope my hands won't be empty either, though unfortunately I cannot bring my manuscript[3] along with me. For one thing it has still to be copied out, and for another it is only the first half. The earlier lecture I sent you[4] has been vastly expanded. Moreover the second half, the so-called drama of Chiwantopel,[5] has proved to be so rich in archaeological material that I haven't yet been able to put everything in order. I have still a lot more reading to do, so that I can publish the second half only in the summer issue.[6] It seems to me, however, that this time I have hit the mark, or nearly so, as the material is falling into a surprising pattern. Too much shouldn't be revealed yet. But be prepared for some strange things the like of which you have never yet heard from me. I have thoroughly revised

---

[1] Published in *Letters*, ed. G. Adler, vol. 1.

[2] On the Continent, New Year's Eve = Sylvester.

[3] "Wandlungen und Symbole der Libido," part I.

[4] The Herisau lecture; see above, 193 J and 199a F.

[5] See above, 200 J n. 2.

[6] Part II did not appear in the summer issue, III:2, but in IV:1 (1912).

and documented the introductory section on the two kinds of thinking. I think it is now presentable and expresses what I want to say, though not in a masterly fashion. For me it has become something of a chore. Besides, the problem really is a difficult one. I shall take shelter behind a motto from Guglielmo Ferrero[7] in defense of the scholar who exposes himself to criticism. My conscience is clear, I have done honest work and drawn nothing out of a hat. There is little to report about our work in Zürich although all sorts of things are being produced. I would only like to ask you if you have an objection in principle to the occasional appearance in the *Jahrbuch* of *experimental studies* having to do with the psychophysiology of complexes. Dr. Beauchant is, I believe, an acquaintance of Dr. Assagioli. I cannot complain about my martyrdom. Not only do people abuse me, but this winter I haven't even brought off my course of lectures—for want of an audience.

With kind regards,

Yours sincerely, JUNG

225 F

Dear friend,   18 December 1910, Vienna, IX. Berggasse 19

You must be curious to know what arrangements Bleuler has made for our meeting. Answer: none at all; I haven't had a word from him so far. I expect him to write at the very last minute and to create more difficulties after that. He is amazing. But I assume that you and I will meet in Munich in any event. We can exchange wires if necessary.

Your mysterious remarks about your paper make me very curious. You are right, one must reveal no more. My Schreber is finished,[1] a short supplement or rather preface formulating the two principles, is being put in final shape today. I'll give you the whole thing to read when I see you. The piece is formally imperfect, fleetingly improvised,[2]

---

[7] See above, 170 J n. 5.

[1] "Psychoanalytische Bemerkungen über einen autobiographisch beschriebenen Fall von Paranoia (Dementia paranoides)," *Jahrbuch*, III:1 (1911) = "Psychoanalytic Notes on an Autobiographical Account of a Case of Paranoia (Dementia paranoides)," SE XII.

[2] Schreberism; see above, 212 F n. 3.

I had neither time nor strength to do more. Still, there are a few good things in it, and it contains the boldest thrust at $+ + +$ psychiatry since your *Dem. Pr.* I am unable to judge its objective worth as was possible with earlier papers, because in working on it I have had to fight off complexes within myself (Fliess). In the title of the *Jahrbuch* we have expressly accorded ourselves the right to include such papers as your *Diagnostic Assoziation Studies.* The new half-volume has been promised me for this week. I must read the apologia before I meet him (Bl).

Yesterday the English translation of the *Theory of Sexuality* arrived, with a splendid short preface by Putnam.[3] The old Puritan's understanding and conduct are really amazing.

Dr. Bjerre[4] of Stockholm (I have already mentioned him to you) has announced his visit for early in January. He wants to introduce psychoanalysis in Sweden.

Dr. G—— is now here with me. He is in great difficulties, both as to money (secret!!) and as to ΨA. He is meeting with resistance now, so maybe he will be pliable.

I have only received two copies of the *Zentralblatt*, so I hope the third has come to you.

I shall write to you as soon as I know anything about the Procrastinator of Burghölzli. I long for a few free days and free words.

Very cordially yours, FREUD

[3] *Three Contributions to the Sexual Theory,* tr. A. A. Brill, intro. J. J. Putnam (Journal of Nervous and Mental Disease Monographs, 7; New York, 1910). After the *Selected Papers on Hysteria* (see above, 160 F n. 9) it was Freud's first work to be translated into English.
[4] Poul Carl Bjerre (1876–1964), Swedish psychotherapist; for his visit and lectures, see below, 231 F. It was Bjerre who introduced Lou Andreas-Salomé (below, 291 J n. 3) to psychoanalysis and brought her to the Weimar Congress (1911); see Rudolph Binion, *Frau Lou* (Princeton, 1968), pp. 400ff. He later withdrew from psychoanalysis. During the mid 1930's he worked with Jung in the General Medical Society for Psychotherapy (see *Letters*, ed. G. Adler, vol. 1, index).

226 F

Dear friend,   19 December 1910, Vienna, IX. Berggasse 19

Today everything has come at once: a letter from Bleuler, his answer to a telegram of mine, and the *Jahrbuch* with the Apologia.[1] I hasten to acquaint you with the state of affairs.

Bleuler writes that he will arrive in Munich on Sunday morning at 6 (my son says 6:55) and asks where we should meet and when I intend to leave. The latter question succeeded in embarrassing me. I wired as follows: Accept with thanks, inquire length your stay Munich. The answer has just come: Regret have only two days in all. My wise women think this means he will be leaving Monday mid-day (1:50) since he would hardly want to spend two nights on the train. If he did, he would have to leave at 11 Monday night at the latest. I shall stay on in Munich and wait for you. If you leave Zürich Monday afternoon, you will arrive in the evening; at the worst you will have to keep out of sight for a few hours. I shall stay at the Park Hotel, to which of course I shall direct him.

I have only been able to leaf through the Apologia, it arrived an hour ago. But it is amazing how he works off his misbehaviour in his private dealings, which enables him to stand up very well in his public activity. I believe the piece will be enormously helpful. His questionable ideas seem to have taken refuge in the last section. But it's distinguished and very good.

Auf Wiedersehen. I shall thank you in person for this volume.

Yours, FREUD

227 J

Dear Professor Freud,   1003 Seestrasse, Küsnach-Zürich,
                                20 December 1910

A few words in haste! The *earliest* I can be in Munich is *Monday the 26th at 5 in the evening*. The family holidays and the family itself won't let me go earlier. They attach a great deal of importance to these things here. I shall be satisfied if I may spend at least one evening with you. After New Year it will be impossible.

[1] "Die Psychoanalyse Freuds: Verteidigung und kritische Bemerkungen," *Jahrbuch*, II:2 (1910).

I have now read Adler's review of my "Psychic Conflicts in a Child." Suspicious, very suspicious indeed is the remark that my view is entirely dependent on the Freudian theory of libido, as though that were a fault or a limitation. Were that so, the high point of your researches would be juggled out of existence before ever attaining the incalculable heuristic significance that is destined for it. It is, as I see more and more clearly, the real key to mythology, quite apart from the neurosis problem.

It seems to me that the question, "How does one turn a girl into a man?" stands something directly on its head instead of on its feet. The question should surely be, "How do I become a woman?" The planing off of the genitals is arbitrarily and, above all, *falsely* interpreted, without regard for the material.

Equally arbitrary is the conjecture that the material is "consistently slanted," since the mother was just as much involved in its collection and arrangement as the father.

I should prefer to speak of Dr. G—— by word of mouth.

Looking forward, with kind regards,

Most sincerely yours, J U N G

228 F

Dear friend,   22 December 1910, Vienna, IX. Berggasse 19

Just a few words in haste. I am assuming that you will not leave Tuesday morning if you arrive Monday evening. — I think it would be more dignified not to conceal from Bleuler that I am expecting you. He will be leaving Monday noon before your arrival or in the evening after it. In the latter—unlikely—event, the three of us could spend a few hours together. In any case I have booked rooms at the Park Hotel.

I am very glad that you see Adler as I do. The only reason the affair upsets me so much is that it has opened up the wounds of the Fliess affair. It was the same feeling that disturbed the peace I otherwise enjoyed during my work on paranoia; this time I am not sure to what extent I have been able to exclude my own complexes, and shall be glad to accept criticism.

Don't be dismayed if you do not find me in the best of health; it will do me good to see you.

A thousand apologies to the children for taking their papa away at Christmas time.

Very cordially yours, FREUD

229 J

1003 Seestrasse, Küsnach-Zürich,

Dear Professor Freud, 23 December 1910

I am sending this letter to Vienna in the hope that it will still catch you.

Whatever happens I shall arrive in Munich on Monday the 26th at 5.15 in the evening and go straight to the Park Hotel, where I too am staying.

Your "wild" ΨA[1] was a delight.

My impressions of Adler in my last letter may have been a bit exaggerated; you may think I was judging blindly in an outburst of affect. It does seem to me, though, that he is trying to replace the libido, this veritable Proteus and πολύτροπος,[2] by rigid instinctual forms, and crushing the spirit and the life out of our theory. I am afraid that in the person of Adler ΨA has acquired its first really "scientific" representative.

I lectured[3] at the ΨA Society on my forthcoming opus. The theologians were deeply impressed, especially Pfister. The spiritual trend in ΨA now taking shape in Zürich seems to me much more promising than the Bleuler-Adler attempts to squeeze everything into biology (biophysics).

Kindest regards, JUNG

Please leave me a note at the hotel saying when you wish to see me and how I have to conduct myself so as not to bump into Bleuler.

---

[1] "Über 'wilde' Psychoanalyse," Zentralblatt, I:3 (1910) — " 'Wild' Psychoanalysis," SE XI.

[2] polytropos, lit., "much-changing," epithet of Ulysses in Odyssey, I, 1, translations of which are extremely varied—"skilled in all ways of contending," "ingenious," etc.

[3] On 16 Dec.; see Bulletin, no. 4 (Feb. 1911), p. 3.

The Munich Meetings

Freud reported on the meetings in Munich in other letters—to Ferenczi, 29 Dec. 10, quoted at length by Jones, II, p. 158/140 ("I came to a complete understanding with [Bleuler] and achieved a good personal relationship. . . . After he left Jung came. . . . I am more than ever convinced that he is the man of the future"), and to Abraham, 20 Jan. 11, *Freud/ Abraham Letters*, p. 98 ("With Bleuler things went well. . . . We parted as friends").

At the meeting of the Vienna Society on 4 January, Freud announced that Bleuler, "who published in the latest *Jahrbuch* his magnificent *apologia* for psychoanalysis, has joined the Psychoanalytic Society in that area and may perhaps soon appear officially as its leader" (*Minutes*, III).

230 J

Dear Professor Freud,

1003 Seestrasse, Küsnach-Zürich,
18 January 1911

Now that I have partly disposed of the mass of work that always threatens to engulf me after the holidays, I can think of writing to you again. The event that will interest you most is this: Bleuler has now joined the Society. I bow to your arts! Binswanger will probably cede the presidency to him. I shall confer with Binswanger on this matter. Last Sunday I invited Bleuler over to my place; he was most amiable, everything went off smoothly, we spent the whole evening talking with a physicist about something far removed from our usual concerns—the electrical theory of light. The assistant physician at the Clinic, Dr. Maier, has not yet made up his mind to join, though he actually gave a lecture at our last meeting.[1]

My paper is now in the process of being copied out. It grows and grows. After seeing a performance of *Faust* yesterday,[1a] including bits of Part II, I feel more confident of its value. As the whole thing sprang into life before my eyes, all kinds of thoughts came to me, and I felt sure that my respected great-grandfather[2] would have given my work his placet, the more willingly as he would have noted with a smile

[1] On 13 Jan. Maier spoke as a guest, presenting a case of paranoid dementia (*Bulletin*, no. 4, Feb. 1911, p. 3).
[1a] At the Pfauentheater; the famous actor Alexander Moissi played Faust. (See below, 255 F n. 2).
[2] See above, 134 F n. 6. In *Memories*, p. 234/222, Jung discusses his "curious reactions" to *Faust*.

that the great-grandchild has continued and even extended the ancestral line of thought. But it is a risky business for an egg to try to be cleverer than the hen. Still, what is in the egg must eventually summon the courage to creep out. So you see what fantasies I must resort to in order to protect myself against your criticism.

They say here that your son Martin has broken his foot skiing.[3] Is that true?

I still owe you thanks for the two offprints. I am sorry I haven't been able to send you mine yet.[4] As I said, I am in arrears with everything. My wife will send you the two photoes for your patient, whose address I mislaid. The photographer's address is: C. Ruf, Bahnhofstr. 40, Zürich. He has been notified (as we arranged in Munich). The photoes are 12 francs each. The one to Mr. Bernays[5] in New York was sent ages ago.

I have read Putnam's article with pleasure and astonishment. It is really amazing how a man of his age has been able to work his way into the material, and how valiantly he champions our cause. If only we had an equally valiant "boxer"[6] in Germany who is not afraid to pick a quarrel with the age.

The chorus of vilification in Germany seems to have died down for the moment, probably to draw breath. You may have seen Hellpach's latest article in the *Neue Rundschau*.[7] Everyone here is staggered by the incredible megalomania of this miserable pen-pusher.

I am eager for news of events in Vienna—Adler. Binswanger tells me that Adler was all ears for Häberlin, who still feels at odds with us. His article[8] (listed in the last *Bulletin*) does not mention the name "Freud"; evidently he has discovered everything by himself.

My family is well, and so am I. I am exercising my libido in various ways and testing out the modicum of stupidity that I must allow myself.

---

[3] On the Wiener Schneeberg (6808 ft.) (not, as Jones states, II, pp. 93f./84, in the Salzkammergut).

[4] The offprints are not identifiable.

[5] Eli Bernays (1860–1923), brother of Freud's wife, who married Freud's sister Anna (1858–1955) and settled in New York, 1893.

[6] Holograph: "*Boxer*."

[7] Willy Hellpach (1877–1955), professor of psychology and psychiatry in Karlsruhe and Heidelberg, later active in German politics. The article here mentioned is "Die Psychoanalyse," *Die Neue Rundschau*, Dec. 1910. For Jung's review of an earlier work of his, *Grundlinien einer Psychologie der Hysterie* (1904), see CW 18. See also above, 218 F n. 7.

[8] Paul Häberlin, "Über zärtliche und strenge Erziehung," *Zeitschrift für Jugenderziehung*, I:1 (1910).

I hope Munich has done you good. My beautiful vase arrived safely. After your departure you let me in for some diabolical expenses. Your example was contagious. I bought myself a small oil painting and three marvellous drawings, getting myself in the red for a round 1000 francs.[9] As you see, it cost me a pretty penny to salve my conscience for your beautiful gift. Where objets d'art are concerned I easily go *non compos mentis*. Afterwards I crept home with my tail between my legs. Consequently, I shall have to go hard at it to earn money.

I still owe you a mountain of thanks for Munich!

Most sincerely yours, J U N G

231 F

Dear friend,   22 January 1911, Vienna, IX. Berggasse 19

I didn't want to resume our correspondence after the refreshing hours in Munich until I could report that my son was beyond danger of complications and that his temperature was normal, as is now the case. He broke his leg on a skiing trip. He lay motionless in the snow for five hours before help came, and some of his appendages would certainly have frozen if a friend had not[1] watched over him. This happened at an altitude of some 7800 feet and it was another two and a half days before he could be brought down to a hospital. Well, I suppose such accidents are determined by the same causes as those of nonΨanalysts' sons.

Dr. Bjerre[2] of Stockholm called the same day. He is rather dry and laconic, but I could soon see that he is a thorough and serious thinker. I advised him to join the Berlin group.[3] He had already delivered a lecture in Helsingförs[4] and was planning one in Stockholm immediately after his return.[5] In H. the audience was interested chiefly in

---

[9] At the time, = about \$193 or 40 pounds sterling. (*Enc. Britannica*, 1911, "Money.")

---

[1] Holograph: *nicht* (not) omitted.
[2] See above, 225 F n.4.
[3] He did; see *Bulletin*, no. 6 (Aug. 1911), p. 1.
[4] Former (Swedish) name of Helsinki; 1809–1917, Finland was a Grand Duchy under the Russian Czar.
[5] Bjerre lectured on Freud's method on 17 Jan. 11 at the Society of Swedish Physicians in Stockholm; see also below, 234 F n. 1.

"abreaction"—because they are an oppressed people, as he shrewdly observed.

Perhaps I should be pleased with the outcome of my interview with Bleuler, but don't forget all the preparations that were made for it in Zürich. Now I shall "moisten" him with letters from time to time to keep him from relapsing.

I have also been having trouble with my health. The benefit of the Munich intermezzo was soon destroyed by work, excitement, visits, etc. I haven't even been able to revise the short paper on the two principles.[6] Today I feel normal again for the first time in this new year and am determined to finish it before the end of the month. Naturally the accident has exacerbated my money-making complex. It has had the effect of a negative first prize in the lottery.

Many thanks to your dear wife for attending to the photography and for sending the two pictures. Now I owe you 36 francs; how improvident of you to have sent me those 40 marks through the Schaffhausen Bank. Now I in turn must set my bank in motion. I still owe you another mark in addition.

. Adler is still being consistent with himself and will soon have carried his ideas to their logical conclusion. Recently he expressed the opinion that the motivation even of coitus was not exclusively sexual, but also included the individual's desire to *seem* masculine to himself. It's a nice little case of paranoia. So far it hasn't occurred to him that with such a theory there can be no explanation for the real sufferings of neurotics, their feelings of unhappiness and conflict. On one occasion[7] (since Munich) he defended a part of his system at the Society and was attacked from various quarters, not by me. Now that I understand him fully, I have become master of my affects. I shall treat him gently and temporize, though without hope of success. — I am enclosing an article by Stekel, which my veto has eliminated from the *Zentralblatt*. Be careful about showing it around; it is too compromising.

[6] Freud had presented it to the Vienna Society on 26 Oct. (*Minutes*, III.) See below, 246 F n. 3.

[7] In the Vienna Society on 6 Nov., Hitschmann had moved that Adler's theories be thoroughly discussed with particular attention to their divergence from Freud's doctrine "so that there may be achieved, if possible, a fusion of the two views or at least a clarification of the difference between them." Freud moved that the discussion be limited to the "masculine protest." Adler began his presentation on 4 Jan. with a paper on "Some Problems of Psychoanalysis" (see below, 316 F n. 1), and Federn was the first to speak in rebuttal. (*Minutes*, III.)

As I say, I have not been able to do anything for science these last few weeks, but oddly enough I have done better analytical work than ever, in a few cases. I have arrived at a few really striking insights, which will be lost for reasons of discretion, but I think they will have reinforced my own conviction.

Yesterday I received a little essay on the cult of Mithras by Kluge (*Der alte Orient*, Vol. 12, No. 3).[8] I don't know why you are so afraid of my criticism in matters of mythology. I shall be very happy when you plant the flag of libido and repression in that field and return as a victorious conqueror to our medical motherland. Endopsychic perception—Silberer's functional phenomenon[9]—is clearly destined to solve many more riddles.

If you speak to your little great-grandfather in the near future, tell him I have long taken an interest in his Mignon[10] and that he is quite a master of concealment.

With kind regards to you and your dear ones,

Yours ever, FREUD

[8] Theodor Kluge, *Der Mithrakult: seine Anfänge, Entwicklungsgeschichte und seine Denkmäler* (Der alte Orient, XII, 3; Leipzig, 1911).

[9] A concept introduced by Silberer in two papers—"Bericht" (see above, 150 F n. 2) and "Phantasie und Mythos" (209 F n. 6)—and further developed in his lecture, "Magic and Other Topics," 18 Jan. at the Vienna Society (*Minutes*, III, and *Bulletin*, no. 4, Feb. 1911, p. 2). See below, 251 F; and also Jung, *Symbols of Transformation*, CW 5, par. 302.

[10] In Goethe's *Wilhelm Meisters Lehrjahre* (1796) Mignon is a nymphlike Italian girl of rather ambiguous sexuality. Concerning Freud's interest in her, Philipp Sarasin writes in a paper, "Goethes Mignon," *Imago*, XV (1929), that Freud encouraged him to suppose that Goethe's siblings died of tuberculosis accompanied by convulsions, and the recollection of such attacks may have influenced Goethe's description of a seizure suffered by Mignon (pp. 375, 389–90). (K. R. Eissler has kindly supplied this reference. In his monumental *Goethe: A Psychoanalytic Study 1775–1786*, Detroit, 1963, II, pp. 759ff., he proposes a different interpretation of Mignon's attack.) On the motif of concealment, see also Freud's Address on the Award of the Goethe Prize, Frankfurt, 28 Aug. 30: ". . . Goethe was not only, as a poet, a great self-revealer, but also, in spite of the abundance of autobiographical records, a careful concealer" (SE XXI, p. 212).

232 J

1003 Seestrasse, Küsnach-Zürich,
Dear Professor Freud,   31 January 1911[1]

Many thanks for all the news in your last letter. — As I am laid low with influenza, this will be only a soulless typed letter.[2] Stekel's aphorisms are atrocious. A blessing they were suppressed — The real reason for my writing to you in haste and so disjointedly, and sending the letter by a third hand, is to introduce a friend from my student days at Basel University, a surgeon. He is an amiable fellow with a laudable if limited interest in psychoanalysis. He won't make a nuisance of himself in any way, only wants to take a modest seat in the Vienna Society and learn a thing or two. The name is Dr. Achilles Müller.[3]

I had no idea of the mishap that has befallen your son. In the circumstances it is a miracle that he got off so lightly. These accidents are terribly dangerous. — My wife and I send heartfelt wishes for speedy recovery.

Best regards and wishes for your own health,

Most sincerely yours, JUNG

233 F

Dear friend,   9 February 1911, Vienna, IX. Berggasse 19

Putnam (who has cabled an order for 400 offprints of the German translation of his paper published in the Zentralblatt[1]) writes to me that he is prepared to come to Europe with his wife and children to

[1] Typewritten and signed. / Jones (II, p. 159/140) cites a letter from Freud to Ferenczi of 8 Feb. 11 to support the statement "In 1911 . . . Jung was paying another visit to America, which made Freud express his regret that the 'Crown Prince' should be so long out of his country." But these letters do not support the likelihood of such an absence.

[2] According to Mr. Franz Jung, his father's sister Gertrud (1884–1935), who had been a nurse at the Burghölzli 1906–8, moved to Küsnacht around 1909 to live with her mother (Emilie, née Preiswerk, 1848–1923) and worked as C. G. Jung's secretary until about 1925.

[3] Müller (1877–1964) had a distinguished career as a surgeon and urologist in Basel. Minutes, III, report him a guest at several meetings from 22 Feb. on.

[1] See above, 214 F n. 2.

attend our Congress in Lugano,[2] if we can arrange matters so that he can sail from Genoa on 28 September.

I think we should agree and set the dates of the Congress accordingly but will wait to hear from you before answering him.

I have been quite well again since the gas tube was changed in my study,[3] and glad as I would be to see you before September, I don't believe I shall have to summon you to Vienna in accordance with our agreement. I really was poisoned. My son is at home and is making attempts at walking.

The third edition of *The Interpretation of Dreams* is now a certainty. Are there any points you would like me to consider for the addenda?

So far the debates with Adler at the Society have been going very favourably,[4] revealing the enemy's weak points.

With kind regards to you and your dear wife and all the little ones,

Yours ever, FREUD

234 F

Dear friend,   12 February 1911, Vienna, IX. Berggasse 19

I don't want to let this Sunday pass without writing to you. The weekdays are too frantic. I didn't receive your "soulless" letter until the 10th and hope you have thrown off your influenza by now. It was indeed strange not to see your handwriting over your name. I have asked the new Achilles to call on Tuesday and will be glad to take him with me to the Society as my guest. My son is at home, learning to walk. My condition really did begin to mend once the smell of gas was removed.

I am occupied at the moment with the Swede Bjerre, a serious fellow and undoubtedly a man to be reckoned with. He has sent me an abstract of his Stockholm lecture for the *Zentralblatt*, and also part of a *successful* analysis of a case of paranoia, which he had already

[2] The Third International Psychoanalytic Congress, which Jung originally wanted to hold at Lugano, took place at Weimar.

[3] See below, 236 F.

[4] At the Vienna Society meeting on 1 Feb. 11 Adler read another heterodox paper, on "The Masculine Protest as the Nuclear Problem of Neurosis"; the meeting of 8 Feb. was devoted to debate on Adler's position, which was to continue on 22 Feb. See Jones, II, pp. 148f./131f.; also below, 238 F n. 5 and 316 F n. 2.

told me about in Vienna.[1] Now I am to read the paper, give him my opinion, and forward everything to you for the *Jahrbuch*. Don't you think we should make room for it there? I doubt if it will be finished in time for the first number, which would mean carrying the paranoia campaign over into the following one. It seems to be a case of hysterical paranoia, something which, I tend to think, actually exists, identical in form to real paranoia, but reducible because it is based on *identification* with a genuine paranoiac. Have you ever had firm evidence of the occurrence of this type? I'll write you more about it when I have read the paper.

For some weeks now I have been pregnant with a larger synthesis,[2] and hope to be delivered of it this summer; for that I need a room where I can be alone and a forest nearby. However, our summer plans are still quite indefinite. For us the summer is one of those insoluble problems.

Recently a woman patient told me a dream which brilliantly refutes the theory. It is short. She dreams someone is knocking at her door and wakes up; no one has knocked. No associations. What is the solution? An ingenious chess problem.[3]

My kindest regards to you, the little ones and their mother.

Yours, FREUD

What has become of Pfister? Haven't heard from him in a long time.

235 J

1003 Seestrasse, Küsnach-Zürich,
Dear Professor Freud, 14 February 1911

First of all I am very glad to hear you are well again. Couldn't anyone smell the gas? From a very discreet source a little of your son's "complex" story has come to my ears. Is Martin his mother's favourite? I am sure you know the rest as well as I do.

I am thinking of having all Adler's publications reviewed *in extenso* and discussed in Zürich. Putnam is a real brick. Even before your

[1] The abstract was in the *Zentralblatt*, I:7/8 (May/June 1911). For the paper on paranoia, see below, 263 J n. 3.
[2] Apparently the work that became *Totem and Taboo*, which Freud began writing in the summer. See below, 268 F n. 2, 270 F, 293 F n. 2.
[3] The "chess problem" is solved in "A Case of Paranoia Running Counter to the Psychoanalytic Theory of the Disease," SE XIV, p. 270.

letter arrived I had written him that in agreement with you I would advance the date of the Congress so that he might leave Genoa on September 28th. He will meet you in Zürich at my place; you could then give the seminar instead of me, for Putnam personally, of course. He will be here for 2–3 weeks, working. An amazing man, a natural aristocrat.

Yes, I do have some wishes in regard to the third edition of your *Interpretation of Dreams*: I have criticized Morton Prince's "Mechanism and Interpretation of Dreams" very sharply and in detail,[1] and have also drilled my seminar students in the most rigorous Freudian usage. Now, I have noticed that my students (and I myself) take exception to the following passages: p. 92 (2nd edn.) "The dreams of young children . . . quite uninteresting compared with the dreams of adults."[2] This sentence is objectionable in terms of *Freudian* dream interpretation; likewise p. 94: "though we think highly of the happiness of childhood,"[3] etc., objectionable in terms of the *Freudian* sexual theory. The children's dreams on pp. 92 and 93 seem to me insufficiently interpreted; the interpretation uncovers only a superficial layer of the dream, but not the whole, which in both cases is clearly a sexual problem whose instinctual energy alone explains the dynamism of the dreams. But you may have reasons (didactic?) for not revealing the deeper layer of interpretation, just as in the preceding dreams (your own). I also miss a specific reference to the fact that the essential (personal) meaning of the dream (e.g., Irma,[4] uncle,[5] monograph,[6] etc.) has *not* been given. I insist on my students learning to understand dreams in terms of the dynamics of libido; consequently we sorely miss the personally painful element in your own dreams. Perhaps this could be remedied by your supporting the Irma dream with a typical analysis of a patient's dream,[7] where the ultimate real motives are *ruthlessly* disclosed, so that the reader will realize (right from the start) that the dream does not disintegrate into a series of individual determinants, but is

[1] Jung's critical review of Prince's article (see above, 217 J n. 4) was in *Jahrbuch*, III:1 (1911) = CW 4.
[2] SE IV, p. 127, where footnotes indicate Freud's revisions for the 1911 edn., apparently arising from Jung's suggestions.
[3] Ibid., p. 130.
[4] Ibid., pp. 106ff.
[5] Ibid., pp. 136ff.
[6] Ibid., pp. 169ff.
[7] Not added in the 1911 edn.

a structure built around a central motif of an exceedingly painful nature. In my seminars we always concentrate for weeks on *The Interpretation of Dreams*, and I have always found that inadequate interpretation of the main dream-examples leads to misunderstandings and, in general, makes it difficult for the student to follow the argument since he cannot conceive the nature of the conflicts that are the regular sources of dreams. (For instance, in the monograph dream the crucial topic of the conversation with Dr. Königstein,[8] which is absolutely essential if the dream is to be understood properly, is missing.) Naturally one cannot strip oneself naked, but perhaps a model would serve the purpose. I also wish there could be a supplementary bibliography[9] of the literature concerned with your work.

I hope you won't be angry with me for my bold criticism and wishes.

There's a tremendous lot of work to do before I can get the *Jahrbuch* together. This time I wanted to write something for it myself.

Many kind regards,

Yours sincerely, JUNG

236 F

Dear friend,   17 February 1911, Vienna, IX. Berggasse 19

I see you don't believe me; you seem to think I have my cycles and that suddenly, at certain intervals, I feel the need of looking at the world through rose-coloured spectacles. I see I must give you further details. In the daytime there was no smell of gas because when the cock was closed none escaped. But in the evening from ten to one, when I was working under the desk lamp, the gas escaped from the loose joint between the metal pipe and the rubber tube connected with the lamp. On inspection, a flame shot out of this leak. I smelled nothing because I sat swathed in cigar smoke while the gas gradually mixed with the atmosphere. The result was strange headaches which set in, or increased, in the evening when I was working, and by day annoying lapses of memory, which obliged me to keep asking myself: Who said that? when did that happen? etc. I am still very proud of

---

[8] SE IV, p. 171. The conversation was not added.
[9] The bibliography was added; see SE IV, pp. xiii, xxi. It is absorbed in Bibliography A, SE V.

the fact that I did not attribute all this to neurosis, but I admit that I diagnosed it as arteriosclerosis, to which I resigned myself. Well, now the whole thing has cleared up. The headaches gradually stopped within three days after the tube was changed.[1]

As for my son's secret motives, I was aware of the social or, if you prefer, homosexual ones, and definitely expected the accident. He had told me nothing about this projected skiing trip. I knew that a few days before he had been in a fight in the barracks yard and was expecting to be called before a court of honour. As for the erotic or heterosexual motives, I heard of them only later, probably from the same source as yourself. His little adventure will probably set him back a year; I only hope that he comes off with two legs of approximately the same length. But something seems to be wrong with your combinations. He is not his mother's favourite son; on the contrary, she treats him almost unjustly, compensating at his expense for her overindulgence towards her brother, whom he resembles a good deal, whereas, strangely enough, I compensate in my treatment of him for my unfriendliness towards the same person (now in New York).[1a]

I too think it most advisable that you people in Zürich should take a position on Adler's work. The two discussion evenings here have hurt him a good deal. You must also have heard from Putnam that he has postponed his departure until 1 October. That leaves us free. The prospect you hold out for the Zürich seminar is most attractive; but the two of us—and that makes two against one—would be more interested in having *you* perform.

Many thanks for your remarks about *The Interpretation of Dreams*. In principle I shall take account of them *all*, but everything you say cannot be reflected in changes in the third edition. The supplementary bibliography you wish had already been prepared by Rank. The sentence on p. 92 about the dreams of small children will be set right by the addition of "seem."[2] It is undeniable that the children's dreams on p. 94 are interpreted only superficially, without reference to their sexual motivation, but you yourself provide the explanation when you stress my expository or pedagogic purpose. It is not possible to presuppose a knowledge of the *Theory of Sexuality* in a reader of *The*

[1] This paragraph was published in Schur, *Freud: Living and Dying*, p. 260.
[1a] Eli Bernays; see above, 230 J n. 5.
[2] Holograph: *scheinen*. The word added was actually *häufig*, "frequently"; see SE IV, p. 127.

Interpretation of Dreams, or to inculcate this knowledge while providing an elementary introduction to our conception of dreams. That is why I cannot alter the 1899 text in the light of my findings of 1905. You have very acutely noticed that my incomplete elucidation of my own dreams leaves a gap in the over-all explanation of dreams, but here again you have put your finger on the motivation—which was unavoidable. I simply cannot expose any more of my nakedness to the reader. Of each dream, consequently, I explain only as much as is needed to bring out a specific point; one throws light on the dissembling, the second on the infantile material, the third on wish-fulfilment. In none do I bring out all the elements that can be expected of a dream, because they are my personal dreams. And as for the *corpora vilia*[3] in whose dreams we may *ruthlessly* disclose everything, these can only be neurotics, that is patients; and it was not possible to communicate their[4] dreams, because I could not presuppose the secrets of neurosis, which were precisely what the interpretation of dreams was intended to disclose. (In the dream about the monograph, the crucial conversation with Königstein dealt with the very topic we touched on in Munich. Cf. the Egyptian statue allegedly costing 10,000 kronen. When I was a young man my father chided me for spending money on books, which at the time were my higher passion. As you see, all this is not for the common people.)

So even if the critic and the seminar are perfectly right, the author cannot do anything about it. The book proves the principles of dream interpretation by its own nature, so to speak, through its own deficiencies. But the author intends to remedy this mischief in another way. In the preface that has already been written, I state that this book will not be re-issued, but will be replaced by a new and impersonal one,[5] for which I shall collect material in the next three or four years with Rank's help. In this book I shall deal with dreams, presupposing or perhaps setting forth my findings concerning the theory of the neuroses, while Rank will follow out the literary and mythological implications. Though the project was conceived some

---

[3] = "vile bodies." Cf. Philippians 3:21 (AV): ". . . we shall change our vile body, that it may be fashioned like unto his glorious body . . ." The Latin phrase is of course as in the Vulgate. Concerning Freud's *Gymnasium* years and early reading of the Bible, see Jones, I, pp. 22f./19f.

[4] Holograph: *Ihrer,* "your."

[5] The preface to the third edition (SE IV, p. xxvii) does not state this; *The Interpretation of Dreams* reached its eighth German edn. in Freud's lifetime. See also below, 255 F par. 1.

395

time ago, your criticism will help me to explain its purpose, and if you have no objection I shall use it, pretty much in your own words, in the preface.

The last number of the *Zentralblatt* is a dreadful mess; it is Adler's doing—he and Stekel take turns as editor—and very interesting from a psychoanalytical point of view. I complained to Adler, and of course, instead of elucidating the secret motives behind his aberrations, he gave me nothing but lame excuses. You can work out a more detailed interpretation for yourself. Obviously Silberer cannot have said *that* in his lecture on magic.[6] The cuckoo's egg comes from the abstracts, intended for the next issue, of Adler's paper.

The Society for Psychical Research[7] has asked me to present my candidacy as a corresponding member, which means, I presume, that I have been elected. The first sign of interest in *dear old England*.[8] The *list of members*[8] is most impressive.

With kind regards to you and yours, big and little,

Yours ever, FREUD

237 J

1003 Seestrasse, Küsnach-Zürich,
Dear Professor Freud, 28 February 1911

Last Sunday, the day I could best have written to you, was clouded by a mighty hangover from the carnival. It was a propitiatory offering to the chthonic gods not to disturb my work.

Many thanks for the information about *The Interpretation of Dreams*. Pp. 128/129 (bottom) there is a passage where you make children's dreams an exception to the rule.[1] Just how significant

---

[6] Rank's report on the activities of the Vienna Society to the end of 1910 (*Zentralblatt*, I:4, Jan. 1911, 184f.) was followed on the next page by a stray piece of copy (unsigned) headed "15th Meeting, 18 Jan. 11, Herbert Silberer, 'Magisches und Anderes,'" with an abstract that obviously belonged to Adler's lecture on 4 Jan. 11 (see above, 231 F n. 7); in the next issue (I:5/6, 271) both papers were listed and abstracted correctly.

[7] English in original. According to Jones (II, p. 99/88) he was made an honorary member, but the Society *Proceedings*, XXV (1911), 479, list Freud as a corresponding member. Other members include A. J. Balfour, Madame Curie, Henri Bergson, Nicholas Murray Butler, Stanley Hall, Pierre Janet, etc.

[8] English in original (both).

---

[1] SE IV, p. 190.

children's dreams can be has been admirably documented by my Grethchen: she dreamt that her "little friend Hans had pulled his felt hat right down over his head (so that the head was hidden) and she had to swallow it." Or she dreams of a wolf "that sits in the tunnel." She is now 5 years old. The knowledge of foreskin and glans is remarkable. "Consequently" she was violently *sick* (at the age of 4) when her godfather was here with his fiancée. Grethe was terribly jealous.

I am very busy in my thoughts with the incest problem and have found splendid fantasies among my patients. Something should come of it.

I was very much interested in your announcement of a new dream-book, especially in the parallelism of our points of view. For me dream analysis is still one of the most difficult of our problems, and the most rewarding.

Now for the news! I need hardly say anything about the *Journal of Abnormal Psychology*. You will already have discovered our friend Schottländer in it.[2] The Jones-Prince controversy is good.[3] I shall provide the bass part in the *Jahrbuch*: I too have taken Prince by the ear and shown him that one does not do dream analysis *like that*. I hope you will approve of this independent sortie. I have made a thorough job of it—nothing but criticism. I am all for speaking out as soon as people start doing "positive" work, or rather, tinkering in our field. I won't be too gentle with Prince, especially after reading his incredibly arrogant reply to Jones.

One of my young pupils here, Dr. Lenz,[4] is a voluntary worker with Geheimrat Kraus[5] at the Second Medical Clinic of the Charité in Berlin. He has been successfully importing ΨA. He writes: "Kraus is very enthusiastic at present and wants ΨA to be fostered and vigorously promoted at his clinic." Considering Kraus's standing, he is an acquisition not to be underestimated. He seems to want to make my acquaintance. I am thinking of striking while the iron is hot, and

[2] Friedländer, "Hysteria and Modern Psycho-analysis," *Journal of Abnormal Psychology*, V (Feb.–Mar., 1911). See above, 179 F n. 3.

[3] The same issue of the *Journal* contained Jones's "Remarks on Prince's Article: 'The Mechanism and Interpretation of Dreams,'" and Prince's "Reply to Dr. Jones."

[4] Emil Lenz (1886–1933), M.D. Zürich 1910, joined the Berlin Society in July 1911, returned to Zürich in Mar. 1912. Later, privatdocent in experimental pharmacology at Bern.

[5] Friedrich Kraus (1858–1936), professor of medicine at Berlin University; director of the medical clinic at the Charité.

for this purpose shall betake myself to Berlin (in 2–3 weeks). It wouldn't be a bad thing if we made a breach there.

At our last ΨA meeting Pfister got a bit of a mauling because his "cryptography"[6] made an unsatisfactory impression. Some basic objections had not been considered. The phenomenon itself was not in doubt, but its determinants were not brought out with sufficient clarity. I would like you to look the paper through before it goes to press.

Rank's contribution[7] came too late, unfortunately. Silberer's too, the last of all,[8] will probably have to stand back and wait till the summer as the current *Jahrbuch* is bulky enough as it is.

I hope all is well with you. Everything fine with us.

Kind regards,

Most sincerely yours, JUNG

238 F

Dear friend,   1 March 1911, Vienna, IX. Berggasse 19

I have good reasons for answering your letter—that arrived today—in two instalments, separated by a Wednesday evening.[1] Thank you again for your answer to my questions about *The Interpretation of Dreams*. As I have told you, I agree with you on almost every point but cannot modify the text accordingly and propose to meet your objections in a different way. I shall send you the preface when I have made the insertion[2] based on your letter.

I see with at least partial satisfaction that *The Interpretation of Dreams* is becoming obsolete and must be replaced by something better, though for a whole decade I had thought it unassailable. Which means that we have made a good bit of progress.

I won't see Prince's journal until this evening. I *fully agree* with your strong criticism of him and the conclusion you draw. He has no talent at all and is something of a schemer. I myself have devoted

---

[6] See below, 287 J n. 2.
[7] "Ein Beitrag zum Narcissismus," *Jahrbuch*, III:1 (1911)—included after all.
[8] "Über die Symbolbildung," *Jahrbuch*, III:2.

---

[1] I.e., the regular meeting of the Vienna Society on this evening; see below, text at n. 5.
[2] See SE IV, pp. xxviif.; probably Freud's reference to the expansion of future editions.

a few hard words to him in the third edition,[3] in connection with the objection he raises to a point I make about the forgetting of dreams.

I had already heard that Kraus was interested in ΨA, but I didn't think he would take an active part. Though he was in Vienna before he went to Berlin, I have never seen him here. I only hope that his friendliness to us has a solid personal basis, e.g., a wholesome hostility to Ziehen. It would be splendid if you put in an appearance there. It would give you as president an opportunity to inspect one of our local groups for the first time. The Berliners (i.e., Abraham) are holding up very well.

I congratulate you on the enlargement of your empire, thanks to the founding of the New York group.[4] I trust that from now on no year will pass without some new addition to it. On the strength of this likelihood I am considering a plan for creating closer ties between the *Zentralblatt* and the International Association by providing all dues-paying members with a subscription, discontinuing the *Bulletin*, and giving the President a section of the *Zentralblatt* for his communications. I have written to Bergmann on the subject and when I hear from him—his answer is overdue—I shall write to you more. The change could be voted by the Congress and go into effect beginning with the second year of the *Zentralblatt*.

3 March 1911

Since reading the *Journal of Abnormal Psychology*, I am even more heartily in favour of your lambasting Morton Prince. He really is an arrogant ass, who would be conspicuous even in our menagerie. Jones's criticism is moderate and polite—indeed he has earned our heartfelt gratitude by his conduct and his work since Worcester. The choice you made at the time has been brilliantly justified.

Today I received an answer from Bergmann to my plan for the *Zentralblatt*; he thinks we should wait and says so in a way that is half a refusal. But I have not abandoned the idea and should welcome your opinion.

Since the day before yesterday I have been chairman of the Vienna

[3] SE V, p. 521.
[4] A. A. Brill founded the New York Psychoanalytic Society on 12 Feb. 11, with 21 members. See Jones, II, p. 98/97; *Zentralblatt*, II:4 (1911–12), p. 233, President's report; and Hale, *Freud and the Americans*, pp. 317, 527, where the founding membership is given as 15, with details of 12 members.

group.[5] It had become impossible to go on with Adler; he was quite aware of it himself and admitted that his chairmanship was incompatible with his new theories. Stekel, who now sees eye to eye with him, followed suit. I have decided, after this unsuccessful attempt, to take the reins back into my own hands and I mean to keep a tight hold on them. Even so, considerable damage may already have been done. The deputy chairman is Hitschmann, who as you know is quite orthodox. There was strong opposition to Adler among the older members, whereas the younger and newer men showed considerable sympathy for him. I now feel that I must avenge the offended goddess Libido, and I mean to be more careful from now on that heresy does not occupy too much space in the *Zentralblatt*. I see now that Adler's seeming decisiveness concealed a good deal of confusion. I would never have expected a Ψanalyst to be so taken in by the ego. In reality the ego is like the clown in the circus, who is always putting in his oar to make the audience think that whatever happens is his doing.

In the next few days I am expecting our most exotic supporter, Lt.-Colonel Sutherland[6] from Saugor in India, who means to spend two days here on his way to London. England seems definitely to be stirring.

With kind regards to you and your family,

Sincerely, FREUD

239 J

1003 Seestrasse, Küsnach-Zürich,

Dear Professor Freud, 8 March 1911

I really do hope you didn't take my remarks about the third edition of *The Interpretation of Dreams* as disparaging criticism. I am con-

---

[5] At a committee meeting following the regular meeting of 22 Feb., at which the Adler debate continued (see above, 233 F n. 4), Adler had resigned as chairman "because of the incompatability of his scientific attitude with his position in the Society," and Stekel declared himself in agreement with him to the extent of resigning as vice-chairman. A resolution was unanimously passed, thanking them for their services and expressing the hope that they would remain in the Society. Both continued to attend the meetings, but no remarks by Adler were reported until 24 May. (*Minutes*, III; cf. Jones, II, p. 149/132f.)

[6] W. D. Sutherland (1866–1920), medical officer from a cavalry school at Sagar (or Saugor), in the former Central Provinces (now Madhya Pradesh). He joined the American Psychoanalytic Association and in 1913 transferred to the London Psycho-Analytical Society as a founding member.

vinced that the book is far from becoming obsolete. We haven't even made a start with the renovations, at least I haven't. "Let him who made him bring near his sword," as is said in Job.[1] Even so, ten fruitful years have passed since 1900, and have assuredly brought many a problem nearer to you.

Your plan for the *Zentralblatt* is admirable. It would put an end to the schism with the *Bulletin*, condemned as it is to eke out a beggarly existence alongside the *Zentralblatt*. The greater part of the membership dues could be used for subscriptions to the latter. This could be arranged without further ado once I have sounded out the local groups. But first I would like to have your approval. There will be difficulties with America since not everybody there reads German. We would have to make subscription optional, and reduce the dues for those who do not take the *Zentralblatt*. Please tell me what you think about this.

Dr. Haslebacher[2] is urging me to move the Congress to Locarno (where he spends the summer). Technically, accommodation could easily be arranged there, but Locarno is half an hour's journey from the Gotthard line,[3] so that arrivals and departures would not be all that simple.

I suggest the Congress be held on Sept. 24th and 25th.

Congratulations on your elevation to the chairmanship! I was quite flabbergasted by the latest turn of events. Perhaps you will give me some more details about this rebellion in your next letter. Adler is becoming a menace. It is utterly irresponsible of Stekel to ally himself with Adler merely because they have the same complexes. What will become of the *Zentralblatt* if the wind blows from that quarter? Will you replace the editors?

I have been invited to lecture on ΨA at the first Congrès International de Pédologie[4] (August in Brussels). I shall go with a guarantee of safe-conduct, like Luther to the Diet of Worms, but with no illusions of convincing anybody. I am merely curious to see what they are up to. I haven't seen any foreigners for years, and I haven't been to a Congress since Amsterdam. After four years it's about time I saw whether the ravens are still flying round the mountain.

Prince's reply to Jones is singularly arrogant and I shall add a post-

[1] Job 40:19 (here tr. RSV), referring to Behemoth.
[2] Johannes Adolf Haslebacher, physician from Bern; a member of the Zürich Society, practicing in Bad Ragaz.
[3] Railway route from northern Switzerland to Italy, to which Locarno is connected by a spur.
[4] So in holograph; actually, de Pédagogie. See below, 269 J n. 2.

script to my review. Our people in America seem to be at each other's throats. I have to admire Jones's courage. You too will have been stupefied by that swine Schottländer in the same issue.[5] I am sorry for our poor young friends who will be caught in the deluge of hypocrisy let loose by this article. Let's hope Putnam wades in with a few upper-cuts. My everlasting regret is that I didn't give Schottländer a good hiding and throw him down the stairs. What a brute!

Apart from that, all the numbers of the *Journal of Abnormal Psychology* look very gratifying. Nothing but ΨA, one might say. Will the *Neurologisches Zentralblatt* take a leaf out of their book?

Deuticke is still sitting like a broody hen on the manuscripts for the *Jahrbuch*. Have you still received no proofs? I sent him an urgent card today. Silberer's and Rank's papers have at last arrived, but I doubt if I can take them because of the swelling bulk of the *Jahrbuch*.

Would you please read the galleys of Pfister's paper and make changes where you see fit? It is very audacious. The second part, which I am holding back for lack of space, is a bit risky. I'll send it to you later on for an opinion.

I hope everything goes well with you personally and also in the family. All is well here. Kind regards,

Yours very sincerely, JUNG

Bleuler doesn't want to take over the presidency now. Instead, he is thwarting my "softening up" attempts with "unconscious meanness."

240 F

Dear friend,   14 March 1911,[1] Vienna, IX. Berggasse 19

I am not yet fully employed, which makes me carefree, troubled only by the money complex. I don't like to count on the gratitude of my respected fellow men, but prefer to make lots of money myself.

The 24th and 25th of September are fine for me. Lugano is unquestionably nicer than the like-sounding Locarno.

I shall be glad to read Pfister if you instruct Deuticke to send me the proofs and if Pfister himself doesn't mind. Deuticke, to whom I gave *The Interpretation of Dreams* today, has promised me the first

[5] See above, 237 J n. 2.

---

[1] Actually written 13 Mar.? Cf. opening of 241 F.

galleys of my paper[2] for tomorrow; apart from that, he complained about the printers.

Here is the present situation with the *Zentralblatt*. Bergmann's first reaction was a gentle refusal, he'd have to think it over, and so on. This in itself is nothing. It is now high time for you, as president of the Association, to put the request to him; in support of it you can cite the present membership figure and an estimate of future membership. As for America, we had better think it over. If we forgo the American subscribers, there won't be much in it for Bergmann. I don't see why Americans interested in ΨA can't be expected to read German. But they will be more likely to fall in with our plans if their representatives at the Congress (Putnam) have accepted in their name. I doubt if the matter can definitely be settled before the second year of the *Zentralblatt* begins and the next annual subscription to the Association falls due—both of which coincide with the date of the Congress. By then you could arrive at an agreement with Bergmann; you would only have to include a clause making the contract contingent on the consent of the Congress—which will thus have an important business matter to decide on. I also wrote to Bleuler a fortnight ago on matters connected with the *Zentralblatt*, in order to maintain our nerve-contact. So far no answer. We must be patient. Men like him are never more disagreeable than after they have made a concession. One step forward, half a step backward; compulsive character.

The palace revolution in Vienna has had little effect on the *Zentralblatt*. Naturally I am only waiting for an occasion to throw them both out, but they know it and are being very cautious and conciliatory, so there is nothing I can do for the present. Of course I am watching them more closely, but they put up with it. In my heart I am through with them. None of these Viennese will ever amount to anything; the only one with a future is little Rank, who is both intelligent and decent.

The repercussions of Adler's rebellion will be visited on us in the literature. It was high time for me to step in, because he dissimulates a good deal that would soon have come to light. In one discussion he used the following argument: If you ask where repression comes from, the answer will be: from culture. But if you ask where culture comes from, the answer will be: from repression. So you see, it is only a play on words. But I paid him back for his pettifoggery; where, I asked

[2] See below, 246 F n. 3.

him, is the paradox in expecting the individual to repeat the work of repression which his ancestors accomplished before him and which, as it happens, results in culture? — On another occasion I chided him for saying in a paper that had already been set up in print that a hostile attitude towards the father had formed as early as the *asexual* period of childhood. He denied it, but I showed it to him in print; he had written presexual, but doesn't *pre*sexual mean *a*sexual?

Stekel's new book[3] is as usual rich in content;—the pig finds truffles, but otherwise it's a mess, no attempt at coherence, full of hollow commonplaces and new lopsided generalizations, all incredibly sloppy. *Cacatum non est pictum.*[4] He represents the uncorrected perverse unconscious, Adler the paranoiac ego; the two of them together might add up to one human being as seen by ΨA. Adler's ego behaves as the ego always behaves, like the clown in the circus who keeps grimacing to assure the audience that he has planned everything that is going on. The poor fool!

My kind regards. I am glad things are going well with you and your family. I'll write to you soon about summer plans.

Yours ever, FREUD

241 F

Dear friend,   14 March 1911, Vienna, IX. Berggasse 19

Supplementary items for which I had no room yesterday (letter purposely predated).

a) First proofs from Deuticke today.

b) Bleuler's answer today. His usual procrastination disguised as modesty. I have already answered him, offering him, as a continuation of his Apologia, the job of reviewing the "better" (!) articles of our opponents for the *Zentralblatt*.

c) First sign of life from Australia. The secretary of the Neuropsychiatric Section of the "Australasian Medical Congress," Sydney 1911, a Dr. Davidson[1] (the name at least sounds familiar) introduces him-

---

[3] *Die Sprache des Traumes* (Wiesbaden, 1911).

[4] = "Excreted is not painted" or "An excrement is not a painting." The source could not be traced.

---

[1] Andrew Davidson (1869–1938), Scottish-born psychiatrist of Sydney, secretary of the Section of Psychological Medicine and Neurology, Australasian Medical Congress; in his subsequent career he did not follow psychoanalysis.

self as a subscriber to the *Jahrbuch* and supporter of ΨA. He asks me, "since my teachings are still completely unknown in Australia," for an introductory article to be published in the Transactions of the Congress.[2] — The most recent exotic specimen was Sutherland from Saugor (India), who called on me ten days ago. He had translated a part of *The Interpretation of Dreams*; a magnificent Scotsman. Behind him there is another who has been Ψanalysing the Hindus and believes that in India as elsewhere the libido is at the bottom of all mental "states": a Dr. Barkley (?) Hill,[3] son of the famous London syphilologist. This younger man is also going to publish soon.

d) What about your trip to Berlin? It interests me even more than the one to the Brussels Congress.

e) Can you do anything with this formula: the symbol is an ucs. substitute for a cs. concept; symbol formation is the initial stage of concept formation, just as repression is the forerunner of judgment?

Most cordial regards,

Yours, FREUD

242 F

Dear friend,   16 March 1911, Vienna, IX. Berggasse 19

You must be bewildered at the way I am bombarding you with my letters. But this one is an *official communication*, which I as chairman in Vienna am addressing to you as president of the International Association. Its content does not reflect my own views.

At yesterday's meeting I was instructed to convey the following to you:

"In view of the importance of the Congress, it seems desirable that as many members as possible should be enabled to attend. The choice of Lugano[1] would mean an inordinately long trip and excessive expenditure for the Viennese and would probably prevent many of them from attending, especially since the date (24/25 September) falls in

---

[2] See below, 255 F n. 1.

[3] Owen A. R. Berkeley-Hill (1879–1944), medical officer in Bengal, later in Bombay. He joined the American Psychoanalytic Association and in 1913 transferred to the London Psycho-Analytical Society as a founding member. His father was Dr. Matthew Berkeley-Hill, of the University College of Physicians, London.

---

[1] In southernmost Switzerland, on the "Gotthard line," about fourteen hours by rail from Vienna.

the medical working year. The Viennese group would therefore favour a more centrally located meeting place, on the assumption that a few miles one way or the other would make no difference to our American guests. They further request that in case Lugano or another Swiss city should nevertheless be chosen, you apply to the Swiss Railways for reduced fares; they believe a reduction will be obtainable for the Austrian part of the trip. Finally, they propose that one of the next congresses be held in Vienna itself."

So much for my message. In submitting these wishes to you, I am only doing my duty in total disregard of my own complexes and preferences.

Most cordially yours, FREUD

243 J

1003 Seestrasse, Küsnach-Zürich,
Dear Professor Freud,   19 March 1911

I have three letters to thank you for, and am answering your points in chronological order.

I will gladly take the question of the *Zentralblatt* in hand. Only, I would first like to make sure of the American project. I am having a lively correspondence with Jones[1] about the organization of the American "branch."[2] No further news from New York. The group cannot be recognized until the list of members has come in together with the "contribution."[3] The size of our European membership wouldn't make much of an impression on Bergmann. I have heard rumours of a group being founded in Munich.

The news about Adler is very interesting. In Zürich, too, several members have noticed that patients use Adler's writings as a source of resistance, also certain remarks of Bleuler's about "certain" followers of Freud. Adler's question about repression and culture is a typical examiner's question, calculated only to trap people and not to promote a truth.

Stekel's new book hasn't arrived yet, I had no idea that he had

---

[1] The correspondence between Jung and Jones, though Jones often cited it in his *Freud: Life and Works*, II (1955), disappeared after the publication of that volume. (Information from the Institute of Psycho-Analysis, London.)
[2] English in original. / See 257 J n. 1.
[3] English in original.

written one. I am revolving in my mind whether it might not eventually become necessary to be openly critical in our own camp. Stekel's crass "pig-and-truffle tactics" make me sick. They are thoroughly misleading; one really shouldn't fly in the face of all good taste.

As I have had no further news from Berlin I take a less optimistic view of the situation. Kraus is indeed Ziehen's deadly enemy—so far so good. If the news proves favourable I would naturally go there without delay.

From Tübingen I have heard that Privatdozent Busch[4] wants to honour me with his presence in Zürich. He seems to have been infected via Stockmayer.

So far as your summer plans are concerned, I am making bold to take you, most emphatically, at your earlier word that you and your wife will be our *guests*. I pray nothing will shake this fact. To that end I have already postponed my military service.

Only now that I have the galleys can I enjoy your Schreber. It is not only uproariously funny but brilliantly written as well. If I were an altruist I would now be saying how glad I am that you have taken Schreber under your wing and shown psychiatry what treasures are heaped up there. But, as it is, I must content myself with the invidious role of wishing I had got in first, though that's not much of a consolation. It couldn't be helped, I was plagued with other things that were more important to me than psychiatry proper. I shall probably be led back to psychiatry by a circuitous route. For more than a year now, amid unspeakable difficulties, I have been analysing a Dem. praec. case, which has yielded very strange fruits; I am trying to make them comprehensible to myself by a parallel investigation of incestuous fantasy in relation to "creative" fantasy. Once my thoughts have matured I must seek your advice. I am still brooding on it.

I too have received the Australian invitation. What will you write? I really don't know what to do.[5]

The definition of symbol fits if regarded from the purely intellectual standpoint. But what if a symbol is put in the place of a clear concept in order to repress it? To take an example: in answer to the question, How was the first man created? an American Indian myth says: from the *hilt of a sword* and a *shuttle*.[6] Here symbol for-

---

[4] Alfred Busch (1876–1938+), psychiatrist at Tübingen, later professor at Cologne.
[5] See below, 254 J n. 2.
[6] Cited in *Symbols of Transformation*, CW 5, par. 201, n. 29 (also in 1911/12 version). See addenda.

mation seems to be aiming at something quite different from concept-formation. Symbol formation, it seems to me, is the necessary bridge to the *rethinking* of long familiar concepts from which the libidinal cathexis is partly withdrawn by canalizing it into a series of intellectual parallels (mythological theories). This is precisely one of the problems I am brooding on now. As you see, I approach the problem from a rather different angle. This is one reason why Silberer's view, which I had to reject earlier,[7] does not satisfy me entirely.

I have taken your "pleasure and reality principle" to heart and have had to adopt your terminology for the time being. "Pleasure and reality principle" is indeed an excellent term with a wide range of application. My only regret is that I was not in possession of this point of view earlier.

Coming now to the question of the Congress, Vienna would be too much of a jump from Lugano. Rather than that I would suggest Nuremberg again, where we were accommodated very nicely last time. For us Swiss, Vienna really is a far cry, also for the Americans and even for the Berliners. For me personally Vienna would be very pleasant, since I like Vienna and don't mind the long journey. But Nuremberg, with its central position, requires roughly the same sacrifices from everybody, so I would like to suggest it to your local group. Reduced fares on Swiss railways are out of the question, I'd say. (The Gotthard line, for instance, is a private company!) Would you please inform your group that (exercising my authority) I should like them to put it to the vote at their next meeting whether Nuremberg is accepted or whether they propose some other city. Please let me know the result of the vote soon. I shall also get the other local groups to vote on this point.

On April 5th I'm going on a 16-day motoring trip with my wife to the south of France. I am looking forward to the holiday as I've been working very hard.

I hope all is well with you and I am glad for your health's sake that you don't have too much to do.

Many kind regards, JUNG

[7] See above, 213 J par. 3.

244 F

Dear friend,   25 March 1911, Vienna, IX. Berggasse 19

Rank has sent you the results of the vote on the location of the Congress. The Viennese are over-determined by their wish to see something new. Not a single vote for Nuremberg. In choosing Munich, they have doubtless forgotten how overcrowded it is in the autumn. A Swiss city would certainly have attracted many of them if not for the great distance. Conclusion: exert your authority! I am aware that the situation in America has also been on your mind.

Criticism in our own camp will be very necessary. Stekel is having Adler review his book for the *Zentralblatt*;[1] I can't prevent this because they are the editors. But we still have the *Jahrbuch*. I should be glad to review it myself, but I find it hard to take a moderate tone and perhaps I am too authoritarian. Maybe you can find a serious and well-informed critic. I could suggest one nearby. And we inside our circle really ought to come to a decision about Adler, before he is held up to us by outsiders. His things strike me as more and more stupid as time goes on.

I can see no reason to give up my plan to visit you before the Congress. The only uncertainty has to do with the date; our summer plans are very complicated and are not yet fully settled. I shall be spending the first three weeks at Karlsbad, where I shall have leisure for working. In the first half of September I should like (for anonymous reasons)[2] to take a little trip with my wife.

What to do about Australia? I have been wondering if we couldn't write a short programmatic article for their programme; a few pages extracted from our Worcester Lectures—and if we mightn't do it together. I could write something and send it to you to complete or modify; then we could sign it together. Write to me about it after your little trip, for which I wish you and your wife the best of weather and spirits.

Very cordially yours, FREUD

[1] The review was not published.
[2] See below, 270 F n. 1.

245 J

Dear Professor Freud,

1003 Seestrasse, Küsnach-Zürich,
28 March 1911

A brief reply to your letter received today. Before anything else happens I will write to Seif and ask what the chances are for the Congress in Munich. The final decision of the local groups will depend on that.

Silberer's manuscript, which I find lacking in clarity, has so antagonized Bleuler that he started yelling even before he was hit, as you see from the enclosed. Have you read the manuscript? If not, I will send it to you at once. In any case Silberer will have to wait until the second number of the *Jahrbuch*. I have written to Bleuler that it is all right with me if he exerts an influence on the publications in the *Jahrbuch*, and it is up to him to express his wishes. Do you agree?

I would very much like you or one of your people to review Stekel's book, and should also be grateful if you would state our position regarding Adler. In Zürich the interest in Adler is so slight that I haven't even been able to find anyone to speak about his things at the Society.

As regards Australia I too am thinking of something along the American lines. An extract from the association experiment, theory of complexes, and Dem. praec., so I won't be poaching on your preserves!

I go south on April 5th, and tomorrow to Berlin. Kraus is on holiday (not my fault!), instead Prof. von Bergmann[1] awaits me (the name sounds authentic). Dr. Busch of Tübingen is here and tells me that except for the chief the whole clinic has been smitten with ΨA. Things are on the move!

Kindest regards, JUNG

246 F

Dear friend,   30 March 1911, Vienna, IX. Berggasse 19

I hope you are not annoyed at receiving this letter devoted to business matters before your trip. You must tell me some time who Bergmann is (the old man[1] has long been dead), and what he wanted of you.

---

[1] Gustav von Bergmann (1878–1955), pupil of Friedrich Kraus at the Charité, later professor of internal medicine in Munich and Berlin. See next letter, n. 1.

---

[1] Ernst von Bergmann (1836–1907), eminent surgeon, co-discoverer of asepsis.

410

Bleuler is *a nuisance!*[2] But we have to put up with it. My recent tender remarks have produced no adequate reaction. I have not read Silberer's manuscript, I don't know what is in it, it is probably not as bad as his (Bleuler's) prudishness imagines. I am prepared to read it as well as the questionable Pfister you speak of, as soon as I receive them. What you have written to Bleuler is perfectly all right with me. I am now reading the second proofs of my article for the *Jahrbuch*.[3] I am also doing something for the second number in collaboration with *our* Oppenheim, a serious classical philologist and a very decent fellow,—a short paper that is to be my first foray into folklore: "On a Certain Variety of Indecent Comic Dream."[1] I only hope that my totally amoral co-director will have no objection. For Australia I had in mind a closer cooperation, but have it your way; I will send you my extract in any case. We are suddenly having lovely spring weather and I am feeling rather lazy. — I see that the promised preface to *The Interpretation of Dreams* is only being set at the very end. Bergmann wants to publish a second edition of "Dreams" in the *Grenzfragen* series.[5]

You have been very kind to the Viennese in your handling of the Congress question. Unfortunately they are a lot of rabble and I shall feel neither horror nor regret if the whole show here collapses one of these days. Nor will I proclaim with Horace: *fractus si illabatur orbis,* etc.[6]

Have I blundered for reasons of diplomacy with my aggressive footnote to Putnam's lecture?[7] It looks like it. Very well, I shall review

[2] English in original.

[3] "Formulierungen über die zwei Prinzipien des psychischen Geschehens," *Jahrbuch*, III:1 (1911) = "Formulations on the Two Principles of Mental Functioning," SE XII.

[4] The ms. of the jointly written paper disappeared—evidently Oppenheim retained it when he resigned from the Vienna Society in Oct. 1911 (see above, 160 F n. 4, and below, 273 F n. 1)—and came to light in 1956, in Australia, where Oppenheim's widow had emigrated. It was published in 1958; see "Dreams in Folklore," SE XII, and editor's note. / Oppenheim had spoken to the Vienna Society the evening before (29 Mar.) on, among other subjects, the phallic significance of the name Oedipus.

[5] *Über den Traum* (a condensed version of *Traumdeutung*), first pub. in *Grenzfragen des Nerven- und Seelenlebens*, ed. Leopold Löwenfeld and H. Kurella (Wiesbaden: Bergmann, 1901; 2nd edn., 1911) = "On Dreams," SE V.

[6] I.e., "si fractus illabatur orbis, / impavidum ferient ruinae" (should the heavens crack and tumble down, as the ruins crushed him he would not fear)—Horace, Ode III, iii, 7–8 (tr. J. P. Clancy, 1960).

[7] Referring to a footnote Freud appended to his translation of Putnam's lecture

411

Stekel's book. It will increase the tensions though. But let it go its way. Once more I wish you a fine trip.

Very cordially yours, FREUD

247 J

Dear Professor Freud, Central Hotel,[1] Berlin, 31 March 1911

A few words in haste! Just before leaving Zürich I had a telephone call saying that Honegger had committed suicide with morphine.[2] He was to have reported for military duty the next day. The sole motive was to avoid a psychosis, for he did not under any circumstances want to give up living in accordance with the pleasure principle.

I have been well received here and though I haven't seen Kraus I found his whole clinic infected with ΨA. I think things in Berlin are off to a good start. I have had three consultations at the Charité.

Kindest regards,

Most sincerely yours, JUNG

---

in the *Zentralblatt*, I:4 (Jan. 1911): "Putnam is not only one of the most eminent neurologists in America but also a man everywhere greatly respected for his unimpeachable character and high moral standards. Although he has left his youth far behind him, he took his open stand last year in the front rank of the champions of psycho-analysis" (SE XVII, p. 272). Freud apologized to Putnam for adding "a note about your qualifications to the translations of your lectures, little knowing that the German version would be distributed in America. It must have seemed very odd that someone as unknown as myself should vouch for you over there" (letter of 14 May 11, *Putnam and Psychoanalysis*, p. 121). See also below, 253 F n. 9, and Jones, II, pp. 82f./75.

---

[1] "am Central Bahnhof, Friedrichstrasse"; printed letterhead.
[2] On 28 March, of an injection of a concentrated morphine solution, at the cantonal clinic at Rheinau (Cant. Zürich), where he had gone to work as assistant physician on 1 Feb. (See Walser, op. cit. in 148 J n. 3.) / *Minutes*, III, report no reference to Honegger's death at the Vienna Society. It was, however, mentioned in the *Bulletin*, no. 5 (Apr. 1911), p. 5.

248 F

Dear friend,   2 April 1911, Vienna, IX. Berggasse 19

Fate wills it that I must write to you again before your Easter flight. I am sorry to hear about Honegger. He was a fine man, intelligent, gifted, and devoted. I had been counting on him to become an invaluable help to you; I know that his loss must be a severe blow to you. Something in his makeup seems to have rebelled against adapting to the necessities of life. Do you know, I think we wear out quite a few men. Your impressions of Berlin, on the other hand, are most gratifying. I have always held that loud abuse has the least lasting effect.

I could have taken the patient you wired me about from Berlin, because I was just in the process of throwing out the Dutch woman (G——'s sister-in-law) who had become unbearable. Yesterday I received another wire: H——[1] is not coming.

I am sorry to hear that Jones is planning to leave Toronto.[2] We should be at a great loss without him in America. In Zürich we shall have to make a personal effort with the Americans.

And now for the last time I wish you and your dear wife luck on your little trip.

Yours cordially, FREUD

249 J

                          1003 Seestrasse, Küsnach-Zürich,
Dear Professor Freud,   3 April 1911[1]

A short communication to the Praesidium. The Berlin group has come up with the cogent suggestion that Weimar be chosen as the place for the Congress. There were weighty objections to Munich because of the crush of tourists in September. If Weimar should be

---

[1] Apparently a prospective patient.

[2] Jones remained on the faculty of the University of Toronto until 13 Nov. 1913, when he resigned (Hale, in *Putnam and Psychoanalysis*, p. 206), though he actually had left Toronto for England in June 1912 (Greenland, "Ernest Jones in Toronto, II," *Canadian Psychiatric Association Journal*, XI:6, Dec. 1966). In early 1911, however, Jones had difficulties with the University over charges of malpractice by a hysterical patient; these were cleared up, but he found Toronto "an unpleasant atmosphere for a free thinker" (Jones to Putnam, 13 and 23 Jan. and 7 Apr. 11, in *Putnam and Psychoanalysis*).

[1] Typewritten letter, signed; complimentary closing and postscript handwritten.

chosen, the Berlin group will take over the arrangements for the Congress. The central office requests your group to give decisive backing to the Berlin proposal so that the question of location can be settled soon. As Weimar is easily accessible from all sides, no valid objections can be made.

Many thanks for your news. Kind regards,

Yours sincerely, JUNG

Many thanks for your letter, just received.
Jones's intentions are news to me. H——
is a scoundrel, as I have already told the
people at the Charité.

250 F

Dear friend,   7 April 1911, Vienna, IX. Berggasse 19

A bit of news that will be no more distasteful to you en route than later in case your post should be forwarded. Otto Gross has turned up. He has written me a most respectful letter from Steinhof sanatorium near Vienna, with an *urgent* request that I publish an enclosed communication *as soon as possible*. It is scribbled in pencil and entitled: "In Self-Defense. Concerning the so-called Bleuler-Jung school." It makes two accusations: that Bleuler stole the term Dementia sejunctiva from him and used it as a designation for schizophrenia, and that your article "The Significance of the Father, etc." was derived from statements he made to you in the course of his analysis. Nothing more.

I have answered, declining to publish his piece. I told him that I have always disliked disputes over priority (complexive symptom![1]), that the first item was a trifling matter of terminology, while the second involved a discovery that everyone can make for himself; that I myself never laid claim to ideas I had dropped in conversation; and that he had no need of such recriminations because his originality was recognized by all, including the two of you.

I have heard nothing further. Weimar is an excellent suggestion. What would your little great-grandfather say of our doings?

Kind regards. I wish you and your wife better weather than we are having.

Yours, FREUD

[1] Written sidewise in the margin, with an arrow.

414

251 F

Dear friend,   11 April 1911, Vienna, IX. Berggasse 19

I have now read Silberer's paper. I can't see why Bleuler should be up in arms. It is a sensitive piece of psychological miniature painting, in the manner known to us from his earlier work, as modest and thoughtful as a paper on such a subject could be. I believe that the functional phenomenon has now for the first time been demonstrated with certainty, and from now on I shall take it into account in interpreting dreams. Essentially it is pretty much the same thing as my "endopsychic perception."[1] I definitely urge you to accept the paper. — What shall I do with the manuscript?

Gross has written me a furious letter demanding that I return his article "In Self-Defense." Which I have done.

I am meeting Ferenczi in Bozen during the Easter holidays.[2]

With kind regards,

Yours, FREUD

252 J

                                      1003 Seestrasse, Küsnach-Zürich,
Dear Professor Freud,   19 April 1911

I got home yesterday evening in order to leave tomorrow for the Congress in Stuttgart.[1] Since we roared (not rode) through the countryside, I was unable to write you in a sensible way, for I would have had to write to you sensibly and that is not possible on picture postcards. You can easily imagine that the shades of Honegger accompanied me on my journey. This blow struck home. How wasteful children are, even with their own, precious, irreplaceable lives! Not to speak of friendship and the distress of other people! When I contemplate his fate I cannot but admit that suicide is a thousand times better than sacrificing the most brilliant gifts of the mind in all their abundance to the Moloch of neurosis and psychosis. If only he had left off quarrelling with the order of the world and instead quietly

---

[1] Quoted by Jones, II, pp. 499/450 (misdated 4 Apr.). / Freud added discussions of Silberer's concepts to *The Interpretation of Dreams*; see SE V, index.
[2] Bozen is now the Italian Bolzano. / Easter was 16 Apr.

---

[1] Annual meeting of the German Society for Psychiatry, 21–22 Apr.

submitted to its necessities! It was his first act of self-sacrifice, and alas it had to be suicide. He did it well, without fuss, no sentimentalities like letters, etc. He prepared a strong injection of morphine without betraying his intentions in any way. There is a touch of grandeur about the manner of his going. I am trying to get hold of any manuscripts he may have left behind (?) so as to save for science anything that can be saved.[2] It is an evil thing that such people, marked by the gods, should be so rare and, when they exist, should be the victims of madness or an early death.

Gross is a complete nut, for whom Steinhof is a fitting sinecure. He would be better employed on something productive instead of writing polemics. Infringement of priority is out of the question, since the passage in my paper mentioning Gross[3] was the formula we agreed on. Furthermore he was perfectly free to use his ideas himself and if he didn't that's his affair. He battens like a parasite wherever he can.

Brill and Jones cannot come to an agreement; according to Jones's letters Brill has some resistances. In all likelihood the two of them are squabbling about supremacy. I think a big success would do Jones good too. The trouble is he is always getting in his own way; even his marriage was utter nonsense.[4]

Today I have written Bleuler that in your opinion we should print Silberer. Accordingly, I have invited Bleuler to give free rein to his divergent opinion in the *Jahrbuch* in the form of a critique[5] (otherwise his resistance might choke him). Joining the Society has done him no good at all. He brushes aside my little civilities with disdain. I have written a critique of his theory of negativism[6] and concentrated

---

[2] The question mark is Jung's. / "His researches are in my possession and their publication is in preparation," Jung stated in "Wandlungen und Symbole der Libido," Part II, *Jahrbuch*, IV:1 (1912), 184, n. 1 = Hinkle tr., pt. II, ch. 2, n. 33. However, no publication or surviving papers have been traced. Jung credited Honegger with certain case material that he cited, e.g., the hallucination of a "solar phallus" (*Jahrbuch*, III:1, 211; without attribution in 1952 revision: CW 5, par. 151). According to Herman Nunberg (*Memoirs*, New York, 1969, p. 116), who had been on the staff of the Burghölzli at the time, Honegger himself had developed this delusional idea.

[3] "The Significance of the Father in the Destiny of the Individual," CW 4, par. 695, n. 8.

[4] In his memoir *Free Associations* (pp. 139–40, 197), Jones told of his relationship with "Loe" (Kann) in 1905–1912: though they never married, Jones wrote that "she took my name." In his letters to Putnam he always refers to her as "my wife" (*Putnam and Psychoanalysis*, pp. 220, 249, etc.).

[5] Bleuler did not publish such a critique.

[6] "Kritik über E. Bleuler: *Zur Theorie des schizophrenen Negativismus*," *Jahr-*

mainly on the complex theory, which he has relentlessly shunned in his paper. I think it is high time to start putting our house in order now that he is in the Society. As a director of the *Jahrbuch* he should, in all conscience, not write psychological papers in which the psycho-analytical point of view is simply killed with silence. Our opponents can do that too.

Please would you send Silberer's paper back to me. I would like to go through it again with a more critical eye. It can't be included in this issue anyway as there's no more room.

Dr. G—— is bearing up bravely and his wife is furious with you and with me. Frau Prof. I —— is coming to me for treatment very shortly.

The Munich group has been founded, with Seif as president.[7] Riklin is giving up his lunatics and starting to practise on his own. He has plenty to do. Busch of Tübingen sped home poisoned with ΨA.

Binswanger had already told me the delicious story (Putnam) before you wrote me about it. I myself noticed nothing, of course; it needed Binswanger's beady eye sharpened by an outsize father complex to spot the joke. The remark went down well with me, so I let it pass in silence.

When I get back from Stuttgart I will write again and tell you what the people are up to there.

Many kind regards,

Most sincerely yours, J U N G

253 F

Dear friend,   27 April 1911, Vienna, IX. Berggasse 19

I am awaiting your report on Stuttgart, but I shall write to you to-day so as not to leave you for too long without news. My chief tor-mentor—la C—— —is off on a holiday and I am feeling delightfully lazy.

I have already returned Silberer to you. I haven't had much luck with Bleuler myself; it's like embracing a piece of linoleum. But we must bear it. With his usual caricature of politeness he has sent me his

---

buch, III:1 (1911) = "A Criticism of Bleuler's Theory of Schizophrenic Nega-tivism," CW 3.

[7] Officially on 1 May, with six members. (*Bulletin*, no. 6, Aug. 1911, p. 1.)

critique of Stekel for the *Münchener*[1] to "improve on," and at my request he has written a very commendable reply to Oppenheim that will be published in the *Zentralblatt* (No. 9).[2] In my answer I took Silberer under my protection. To return the compliment I sent him *my* review[3] of Stekel's book for the *Jahrbuch* and asked him to keep it until you ask him for it. But he has sent it back, which gives me a chance to tone it down a little! Because in the meantime Stekel has moved close to us again, and I should like to treat him more gently. First because all in all he is a good-natured fellow and devoted to me, secondly because I am bound to put up with him as one does with an elderly cook who has been with the family for years, and thirdly and mainly because we have no way of knowing what he may discover and misrepresent if we rebuff him. He is absolutely incorrigible, an offense to all good taste, a true child of the ucs., a "strange son of chaos,"[4] but what he says about the ucs., with which he is on much better terms than we are, is usually right. Yesterday we had a discussion about his book. I read the review in question aloud; he reacted as if he didn't feel spat upon but had only felt a few drops of rain. So it passed off quite well. As an editor he is conscientious and self-sacrificing, which makes him irreplaceable.

With Adler it is different; his behaviour is simply puerile. I should like to throw him out on the next occasion; but Stekel wants to keep him and promises to make him see the light.

Yesterday little Rank returned from the university tour of Greece in a state of bliss. I had given him the money for it in return for the work he had done on the third edition of *The Interpretation of Dreams*. It was hard-earned money, but that didn't prevent the poor boy from bringing me two—and not cheap at all—Greek vases in token of his gratitude. He is a fine man. He has just given me a splendid paper on the Lohengrin theme for the *Applied Psychology*.[5]

I have already drafted the piece for Australia; it is so bad that I don't like to bother you with it. Of course you will receive the preface

[1] Bleuler's review of Stekel, *Die Sprache des Traumes*, in *Münchener medizinische Wochenschrift*, LVIII:21 (23 May 11), 1142f.

[2] "Freud'sche Theorien in der IV. Jahresversammlung der Gesellschaft deutscher Nervenärzte, Berlin, 6.–8. Okt. 1910," *Zentralblatt*, I:9 (June 1911), 424–27.

[3] See below, 262 F n. 3 and 284 F.

[4] Holograph: "*des Chaos wunderlicher Sohn*"; cf. "des Chaos vielgeliebter Sohn," *Faust II*, Act II, Classical Walpurgis-Night, Again on the Upper Peneus, line 7 from end.

[5] See below, 279 J n. 2.

to *The Interpretation of Dreams*. A new edition of the Worcester Lectures[6] is being published next winter. A Frenchman with a Russian name (Jankelevitch)[7] in Bourges has applied for authorization to translate the Worcester Lectures, the *Theory of Sexuality* and the *Everyday Life*—which he wishes to set before the *grande nation* as a sampling of psychoanalysis.

I don't know if I have told you or anyone else the *core* of the Putnam story, which is really delicious. If I have, you must forgive me, I never know any more whether I have written something or not. My supposed piece of diplomacy was simply an act of vengeance against Putnam. The accent is on the inserted remark "although he has left his youth far behind him"—because in his article in the *Journal of Abnormal Psychology*, he had written "Freud is no longer a young man."[8] You see, it's my "old-age complex," whose erotic basis is known to you. It is also the source of a fine example of name-forgetting, which will appear in the *Zentralblatt*.[9]

I didn't want to write about G—— while the thing was still in progress. It was a splendid analysis; he is an able fellow. These Dutchmen have a kind of rugged vitality, something like the Swiss.

For the summer we have rented rooms on the Rittenplateau in Oberbozen.[10] I shall be going to Karlsbad on 9 July. But I don't know yet whether I shall visit you the week before or the week after the Congress. The last week in September seems more likely, because of my wife who is not planning to come along. But you yourself might have a word to say on the subject, if only because of your military service.

Kind regards to you, your wife and family.

Very cordially yours, FREUD

[6] *Über Psychoanalyse*, 2nd edn., 1912.

[7] S. Jankélévitch (1869–1951), otolaryngologist, born in Odessa; he translated at least eight works of Freud's.

[8] English in original.

[9] "Ein Beitrag zum Vergessen von Eigennamen," *Zentralblatt*, I:9 (June 1911), 407, added to the 4th German edn. (1912) of *The Psychopathology of Everyday Life* (SE VI, p. 31): "I know I don't much like to think about growing old, and I have strange reactions when I'm reminded of it. For instance, I recently charged a very dear friend of mine in the strangest terms with having 'left his youth far behind him', for the reason that once before, in the middle of the most flattering remarks about me, he had added that I was 'no longer a young man'." Also see below, 266 F n. 1.

[10] Now Soprabolzano, Italy.

254 J

1003 Seestrasse, Küsnach-Zürich,
Dear Professor Freud, 8 May 1911

It is bad of me to have kept you waiting again so long. The reason is that I came down last week with an atrocious attack of influenza, caught from my children, so that I could do only the most urgent work with a fearful effort. I hadn't the strength for anything else. To-day I am sufficiently recovered to give you at least a sign of life.

First I must tell you about Stuttgart. It wasn't all that important. Still, it was interesting to observe how psychiatry is beginning to cast sidelong glances at causation—the physical side, of course. Bonhoeffer[1] (Dresden) reported on psychogenic disturbances. Naturally he didn't say a word about ΨA, but in an unguarded moment he dropped a remark about wish-fulfilment, and in conversation afterwards I took the greatest pleasure in rubbing his nose in it. Kraepelin's lecture was utterly sterile and dull and antiquated. His appearance is incredibly plebian. In the evening he gave a very waggish address which started off with "complexes," etc. He toasted the speakers, with the exception of himself, of course, for which he deserves the diagnosis "autoerotic megalomania." I almost called out "Hear, hear." I mention as a curiosity a privatdocent of psychiatry from Giessen who has *never* set eyes on anything from the Freudian school. All unsuspecting he fell into my hands, and this provided some fun for a couple of hours. I was no longer annoyed by anything but simply had to laugh an awful lot. I was in good company—Seif, Binswanger, Stockmayer.

The New York group has now come into being, and Seif has successfully founded one in Munich. Pleasant news!

My Australian article is finished too. It's about "The Doctrine of Complexes,"[2] a stupid thing you had better not see.

It will interest you to hear that Stockmayer is taking up a post in Binswanger's sanatorium. I think I have already told you that Frau Prof. I—— is coming to me for treatment.

As to my intellectual activities, I am at the moment working up some popular small talk on ΨA which a literary magazine, the *Zürcher*

---

[1] Karl Bonhoeffer (1868–1948), professor of psychiatry, later at Berlin University. Father of Dietrich Bonhoeffer, anti-Nazi Protestant pastor, killed by the S.S. in 1945.

[2] "On the Doctrine of Complexes," *Transactions of the Ninth Session, Australasian Medical Congress* (Sydney), II (1913). In CW 2. / The Congress was in Sept. 1911. Havelock Ellis also submitted a paper.

Jahrbuch, has wrung out of me.[3] I am trying to be popular again—not to my advantage, as you will see. Then I am plagued by all those poor devils who have "pissed out" excruciating dissertations on me (to speak in the basic language[4]). Besides the psychology of religion and mythology, the "manifest forms of unconscious fantasies" are eating me alive. I have made remarkable discoveries some of which I am thinking of using at the Meeting of Swiss Psychiatrists on June 16,[5] and also at Weimar. (Concerning the date of the Congress, or suggestions for it, see the forthcoming *Bulletin.*)

The meeting in Munich is still very much on my mind. Occultism is another field we shall have to conquer[6]—with the aid of the libido theory, it seems to me. At the moment I am looking into astrology, which seems indispensable for a proper understanding of mythology. There are strange and wondrous things in these lands of darkness. Please don't worry about my wanderings in these infinitudes. I shall return laden with rich booty for our knowledge of the human psyche. For a while longer I must intoxicate myself on magic perfumes in order to fathom the secrets that lie hidden in the abysses of the unconscious.

Finally and in confidence: Pfister is now in analysis with Riklin. He has obviously had enough of being roasted over a slow fire by his complexes.

Kindest regards,

Most sincerely yours, JUNG

255 F

Dear friend,   12 May 1911, Vienna, IX. Berggasse 19

This time I have really missed your letters, even more than the news they contain. I am very glad there was nothing worse behind your

[3] See below, 290 F n. 1.

[4] I.e., Schreber's jargon.

[5] But held at Lausanne before 12 June, according to 259 J below.

[6] While in Munich, Freud and Jung had discussed Ferenczi's experiences (see above, 158 F n. 8). After he got this letter, Freud wrote to Ferenczi: "Jung writes to me that we must conquer the field of occultism and asks for my agreeing to his leading a crusade. . . . I can see that you two are not to be held back. At least go forward in collaboration with each other; it is a dangerous expedition and I cannot accompany you." (11 May 11; see Jones, III, p. 415/387.) See also below, 293 F n. 6.

silence. I haven't been feeling very well myself and I can say without exaggeration that I am intellectually drained. My business prospectus is going off to Australia[1] tomorrow and is evading your inspection for the same reasons of shame and delicacy that have led your article to evade mine. But you will be receiving the preface to *The Interpretation of Dreams* in the next few days. It will have to be changed, Deuticke says it might make an unfavourable impression. And I must admit that the rabble who read these things don't deserve a shred of honesty.

Because of the long interruption I don't know what I have already told you and what I haven't. Not much has been happening. It may be news to you that Stekel has been trying to make up. I have changed my mind and decided to put up with him. But I am becoming steadily more impatient of Adler's paranoia and longing for an occasion to throw him out. Especially since seeing a performance of *Oedipus Rex* here[2]—the tragedy of the "arranged libido."

I am aware that you are driven by innermost inclination to the study of the occult and I am sure you will return home richly laden. I cannot argue with that, it is always right to go where your impulses lead. You will be accused of mysticism, but the reputation you won with the *Dementia* will hold up for quite some time against that. Just don't stay in the tropical colonies too long; you must reign at home.[2a]

I have heard of Frau Professor I——. In a few days I am expecting the visit of a splendid colleague, Dr. van Emden, whom I met at Debruine's in Leiden. Another Dutchman, Dr. van Römer[3] (see Hirschfeld's *Jahrbücher*), has written to me from a warship in Padang,[4] assuring me of his support of ΨA and his desire to come to Vienna in the autumn. *Perhaps* I have already written to you that French translations of my immortal works are being undertaken in two places (one of them being Maeder's[5]).

I am very curious about the *Jahrbuch*. I am also awaiting the

[1] "On Psycho-Analysis," *Transactions of the Ninth Session, Australasian Medical Congress* (Sydney), II (1913). In SE XII. / See also 254 J n. 2.

[2] By the Berliner Deutsche Theater, under the direction of Max Reinhardt, 5–10 May, in the Zirkusbusch; King Oedipus was played by Alexander Moissi (see above, 230 J n. 1a). (*Neue Freie Presse*, 3 May 11; information through the courtesy of K. R. Eissler.)

[2a] This paragraph published in Jung, *Memories*, Appendix I.

[3] L.S.A.M. van Römer, a neurologist of Amsterdam, who contributed many articles to Hirschfeld's *Jahrbuch*, chiefly on homosexuality in the Netherlands.

[4] In Sumatra, Netherlands East Indies.

[5] Apparently unpublished: not listed in Grinstein.

Bulletin with impatience because of the Congress and the new groups. Things are going fairly well with the *Zentralblatt*, Stekel is taking great pains. Of course perfection is still a long way off.

At home we are worried about Ernst, my third boy, who has a duodenal ulcer or fistula. They say there is no danger. He is being allowed to take his final examinations, but then he will have to spend quite some time in a sanatorium. My wife is in Karlsbad and I shall be going there with my brother on 9 July.

At last I have heard from Jones that he is to receive the *professorship*[6] in a month. That makes his departure from America an honourable one, but for us it is still a loss, because he has made himself irreplaceable. Brill's wife[7] was very ill after giving birth to a little girl but she is home again now and doing well.

With la C—— I have at last accomplished something through ΨA: her symptoms have grown much worse. Of course this is part of the process, but there is no certainty that I can get her any farther. I have come very close to her central conflict, as her reaction shows. She is a grave case, perhaps incurable. But we must be consistent with ourselves, these are the very cases from which we have most to learn.

My kind regards. I hope you won't wait quite so long before your next letter.

Yours ever, FREUD

256 J

1003 Seestrasse, Küsnach-Zürich,
18 May 1911

Dear Professor Freud,

This time I won't spare you my letter as long as I did last time.

The change in Stekel's behaviour is gratifying. The symbolism he has unearthed in his book is considerable, and it would be a pity if we lost his olfactory organ.

I too have had news of Dr. Römer in Padang. He is big chief of homosexuals, the Dutch Hirschfeld, personally known to me from Amsterdam. He is, like all homosexuals, no delicacy.

I congratulate you on your French successes most heartily, though

---

[6] English in original. Jones apparently did not get the professorship; see below, 267 J par. 3.
[7] K. Rose Owen Brill (1877–1963), a physician; upon marrying she gave up her practice. The daughter is Gioia, now Mrs. Philip G. Bernheim.

I myself expect nothing of the French; no pith. As you rightly say, the Dutch are far better. Van Emden is a good fellow. Frau I—— is a let-down. Since she has been here she has lost no time in firing off a few more salvoes at Dr. G——, so the poor man must be quite out of his mind about me. She identifies completely with her unconscious, putting on the look of an innocent, injured child. She deserves all Moebius's remarks about the female sex.[1] Dr. G—— took her *much* too seriously. When she thinks she is getting me on her side with her thousand and one artful dodges, she is on top of the world; but if at the next turning she sees that this goal is still a long way off, there is another explosion of wrath over Dr. G——. All very boring and useless. She plays the saint, the repentant and unrepentant sinner, the baby, the great wit, just as suits her—a veritable quagmire. Luckily for Dr. G—— she is incapable of anything really villainous, although in her mock-innocent way she is unaware of the mischief she might cause.

I was very interested in your news about Frau C——. It seems to me there is an incredible amount of defiance in obstinate cases like this. I have a case that has deliberately concealed a lie for a whole year and caused me no end of difficulties. Naturally the lie formed part of a system, a definite pose that had to be saved at all costs, since it had proved its value in successfully bringing off all sorts of cochonneries in the past. The transference must be something very precious to the neurotic; he preserves all possible ways to it, even those long abandoned, as though they were inviolable sanctuaries.

I am still engaged in writing down my popular fantasies on ΨA for the *Zürcher Jahrbuch 1911*. But my heart is not in it. *Odi profanum vulgus.*[2]

I am extremely sorry to hear of your son's illness. Where the dickens did he get such an ailment?

All is well with us, except for the worry (another false alarm, fortunately) about the blessing of too many children. One tries every conceivable trick to stem the tide of these little blessings, but without much confidence. One scrapes along, one might say, from one

---

[1] Paul Möbius (1854–1907), neurologist in Leipzig, student of the pathology of genius; author of *Über den physiologischen Schwachsinn des Weibes* (1900; = "On the Physiological Feeble-mindedness of Women"), which Freud cited in "'Civilized' Sexual Morality and Modern Nervous Illness" (orig. 1908), SE IX, p. 199.
[2] = "I scorn the profane crowd."—Horace, Ode III, i, 1.

menstruation to the next. The life of civilized man certainly does have its quaint side.

As for your preface to *The Interpretation of Dreams*, I can well understand Deuticke's agonizings. Honesty carried to those lengths is too much; it is rewarded only in heaven and not on earth. The latter consideration might seem the more pertinent to you, too.

Kind regards,

Ever sincerely yours, JUNG

257 J

1003 Seestrasse, Küsnach-Zürich,

Dear Professor Freud,   24 May 1911[1]

A few words in haste! I enclose a letter from Jones from which you can see the present situation in America.[2] There's probably nothing for it but to try to get Brill to affiliate the New York Society with this more central organization. There will have to be sacrifices on both sides. This time I think Brill has put his foot in it with his intransigent behaviour. I'd be very grateful for good advice and also for information about the date of the Congress. Berlin votes for Sept. 21/22. So do I and I will see that Zürich does the same. Then the date you prefer will be a certainty.

With many kind regards.

Most sincerely yours, JUNG

[1] "In May 1911," Jones states (II, p. 162/143), "Jung told Freud he regarded the term libido merely as a designation of *general* tension." But such a statement is not to be found in Jung's letters during this month. Jones probably intended to cite Jung's letters of May 1912, q.v.

[2] On the initiative chiefly of Jones, the American Psychoanalytic Association was founded 9 May 11 in Baltimore, prior to the annual meetings of the American Psychopathological Association and the American Neurological Association. The eight founding members included Putnam (who was elected president), Burrow, Jones (secretary), and Young (see above, 173 J n. 3). See Hale, *Freud and the Americans*, pp. 317f.; "The American Psycho-Analytical Association," *Journal of Abnormal Psychology*, VI (Oct.–Nov. 1911); and Jones, II, p. 98/87. For Brill's founding of the separate New York Society, see above, 238 F.

258 F

Dear friend,   27 May 1911, Vienna, IX. Berggasse 19

I congratulate you on your new unit. I am returning Jones's letter herewith. I had already written to Brill some weeks ago—a touching letter in which I struck my most patriarchal note in an attempt to make him give in. I think we shall have to leave the matter for Weimar, where it will be easy for you to straighten everything out by your personal influence.

Apart from this nothing but hard work.

Very cordially yours, FREUD

259 J

                      1003 Seestrasse, Küsnach-Zürich,

Dear Professor Freud,   12 June 1911[1]

Since last writing to you (too long ago, alas!) I have made good use of my time. I was at the Meeting of Swiss Psychiatrists in Lausanne and spoke on "forms of unconscious fantasy." These things are contributions to, and elaborations of, my paper in the current *Jahrbuch*, which, incidentally, is taking shape terribly slowly (because of the wealth of material). Everything I am doing now revolves round the contents and forms of unconscious fantasies. I think I've already got some really fine results. You will see that this investigation is the necessary preliminary work for the psychology of Dem. praec. Spielrein's case[2] is proof of that (it's in the *Jahrbuch*). Often I longed for you to be here so that I could discuss an extremely difficult case: Dem. praec. with, one can well say, a tremendous unconscious fantasy system which I have to drag into the light of day with unspeakable effort and patience. On top of that, constant danger of suicide. A really devilish case, but extraordinarily interesting and instructive. The case is particularly painful because I am now beginning to see what I did not see with Honegger. It seems that in Dem. praec. you have at all costs to bring to light the inner world produced by the

---

[1] Published in *Letters*, ed. Adler, vol. 1.

[2] Sabina Spielrein, "Über den psychologischen Inhalt eines Falls von Schizophrenie," *Jahrbuch*, III:1 (1911); cited frequently in "Wandlungen und Symbole," part II (cf. CW 5, pars. 200ff.). It was her M.D. thesis.

introversion of libido, which in paranoiacs suddenly appears in distorted form as a delusional system (Schreber), as I have apparently succeeded in doing in the present case but failed to do with Honegger because I had no inkling of it. I tell myself that this lack of knowledge of mine led to his death. What if this view should be confirmed? I have the feeling that I am practising vivisection on human beings with intense inner resistance. It seems that introversion leads not only, as in hysteria, to a recrudescence of infantile memories but also to a loosening up of the historical layers of the unconscious, thus giving rise to perilous formations which come to light only in exceptional cases.

My evenings are taken up very largely with astrology. I make horoscopic calculations in order to find a clue to the core of psychological truth. Some remarkable things have turned up which will certainly appear incredible to you. In the case of one lady, the calculation of the position of the stars at her nativity produced a quite definite character picture, with several biographical details which did not pertain to her but to her mother—and the characteristics fitted the mother to a T. The lady suffers from an extraordinary mother complex. I dare say that we shall one day discover in astrology a good deal of knowledge that has been intuitively projected into the heavens. For instance, it appears that the signs of the zodiac are character pictures, in other words libido symbols which depict the typical qualities of the libido at a given moment.

I still haven't finished my popular exposition for the *Zürich Jahrbuch*. This week I must start work on my Brussels lecture.

Bleuler has declined the presidency, so Maeder is now president of the Zürich group. Unanimous decision for Sept. 21/22 as date of the Congress. Please let me know, if you can, whether you will be coming to us before the Congress or afterwards. Frankly, before would suit me better, as I have to go on military service on Sept. 27. Ferenczi, it appears, is also planning to come to Switzerland about that time.

I hope all is as well with you as with us.

Many thanks for your advice.[3] The worry was real enough—but has proved to be psychogenic, since, as we know, women love to wheedle emotions out of a man.

With kindest regards,

Most sincerely yours, JUNG

[3] In a missing letter from Freud?

260 F

Dear friend,   15 June 1911, Vienna, IX. Berggasse 19

I cannot like you report interesting work and startling findings; I am tired and count the days. That is why I have not taken the trouble to write letters and have made no claims on you.

I shall first answer the easier points in your letter and dispose of the rubbish before going into the mysterious matters you mention.

The enclosure[1] will give you an idea of the style and content of "Viennese criticism." Without wishing to put myself forward, I believe the remarks on *Leonardo da Vinci* are the most striking. No need to return this material.

I have finally[2] got rid of Adler. After I had pressed Bergmann to dismiss him from the *Zentralblatt*, he twisted and turned and finally came up with a strangely worded statement which can only be taken as his resignation. At least, this interpretation is supported by his announcement that he is leaving the ΨA Society. And then he came out with what he had been holding back: "Despite its unprecedented resolution at one time to that effect, the Society has not had sufficient moral influence on you to make you desist from your old personal fight (!!) against me. Since I have no desire to carry on such a personal fight with my former teacher, I hereby announce my resignation." The damage is not very great. Paranoid intelligences are not rare and are more dangerous than useful. As a paranoiac of course he is right about many things, though wrong about everything. A few rather useless members will probably follow his example.[3]

---

[1] Missing.

[2] Holograph: *endlos* ("endlessly," for *endlich*, "finally") *los geworden*. / Adler had attended the Vienna Society meeting for what proved to be the last time on 24 May, when he spoke out to reiterate that the Society in plenary session had declared that his scientific viewpoint was not in any way in contradiction to the findings of other authors, especially Freud; and he participated normally in the discussion, on the subject of the castration complex. It was the last meeting before the summer recess. (*Minutes*, III.) Adler was apparently absent from the 31 May meeting, last of the season (*Bulletin*, no. 6, p. 4).

[3] Adler, along with D. J. Bach, Stefan von Madáy, and Franz Baron von Hye, resigned at this time; Freud announced the resignations at the first autumn meeting of the Society, 11 Oct. (see below, 273 F). On 20 June, a declaration or manifesto was signed by Josef K. Friedjung, Carl Furtmüller (see below, 335 J n. 2), Franz Grüner, Gustav Grüner, Margarete Hilferding (see below, 270 F n. 4), Paul Klemperer, and Ernst Oppenheim (see above, 160 F n. 4), stating that they were partial to Adler but wished to remain members of the Society. For

Stekel, who is now supporting me faithfully, wants to celebrate the Congress with a special number of the *Zentralblatt*, and is asking everyone for a short contribution. It would make a bad impression if the president were not to send in some little note or observation.

Naturally I don't want to descend on you at a bad time, but for me the week after the Congress would be far more convenient than the week preceding it. If I return with you from Weimar to Zürich, we shall be together from the 22nd to the 27th, which is not bad. The period from 14 to 21 September is only seemingly longer, because I shall not be able to leave on the 14th or 15th. Another consideration is that I *might* have to set aside that week for the anniversary lady,[4] and that if it does not turn out that way and I come early, I shall be left without anything to do in the last week of September. In view of the complicated health situation in the family and her obligations during the latter half of September, my wife will certainly not go to Zürich with me. But I expect you to tell me the unvarnished truth about your own possibilities and desires.

The *Jahrbuch* is really dragging its heels. My *Interpretation of Dreams* is also taking its time. I gather that you have great surprises in store for me in the *Jahrbuch*. I shall read it attentively in Karlsbad.

In matters of occultism I have grown humble since the great lesson Ferenczi's experiences gave me.[5] I promise to believe anything that can be made to look reasonable. I shall not do so gladly, that you know. But my ὕβρις[6] has been shattered. I should be glad to know that you are in harmony with F. when one of you decides to take the dangerous step into publication. I believe that is compatible with perfect independence during the work process.[7]

I am very much interested in what you tell me about the system of ucs. fantasies in a case of D. pr. These constructions are known to me from hysteria and obsessional neurosis; they are nothing other than carefully cultivated daydreams. I took them into account by saying that the symptoms spring not directly from the memories but from the fantasies built on them. But there must be cases in

---

the eventual resignation of the six (excluding Friedjung, who remained in the Society) at the 11 Oct. meeting, see below, 273 F n. 1. / The original typescript of the declaration with its seven signatures was recently found in Freud's papers by Miss Anna Freud.

[4] Concerning the Freuds' 25th wedding anniversary, see below, 270 F n. 1.

[5] See above, 254 J n. 6.

[6] = hubris.

[7] This paragraph is quoted in Jung, *Memories*, Appendix I.

429

which the process is simpler and these interpolations are not so abundant. Probably—just as some people have more poetic fantasy than others. In any case, these fantasies provide the closest link between hysteria and the paranoids. They are hard to capture; in the last few years I have not run across a single good example. But I don't think you could have saved Honegger by revealing this system— if he had one. Where I have found one, its production was no more important than were the aetiology and the motives and the rewards held out by real life. These in any case dominated the symptom-formation, so that until they were unmasked the symptoms could persist, even when there was general improvement. On the role of fantasies—your introversion of the libido—I am mulling over a few fundamental ideas. Here's to better days.

Kind regards to you and your beautiful house.

Yours ever, FREUD

261 J

1003 Seestrasse, Küsnach-Zürich,

Dear Professor Freud, 23 June 1911

Naturally the time after the Congress would suit me just as well, I only thought that if you came before you could stay here a bit longer. I gather from your letter that you could come before the Congress, minus your wife, but we were so looking forward to having you both under our roof that I wish you would persuade your wife to come along after all if she possibly can. *Whether after or before the Congress is all the same to me.* So please decide just as suits you best.

Have you seen Havelock Ellis's book on dreams?[1] Won't you do a critical review for the *Jahrbuch*? What a watery brew Ellis has concocted! Just what is needed to make everything unclear.

You are probably right about Honegger. Although it may be true that the fantasy systems in D. pr. exhibit parallels with the daydreams of hysterical patients, it is certain from the start that by no means all cases possess such a system, or at least they do not have it *at their disposal*. That it is *not* of great therapeutic importance to get patients to produce their latent fantasies seems to me a very dubious proposition. The unconscious fantasies contain a whole lot of relevant mate-

---

[1] *The World of Dreams* (London, 1911).

430

rial, and bring the inside to the outside as nothing else can, so that I see a faint hope of getting at even the "inaccessible" cases by this means. These days my interest turns more and more to ucs. fantasy, and it is quite possible that I'm attaching too great hopes to these excavations. Ucs. fantasy is an amazing witches' cauldron:

"Formation, transformation,
Eternal Mind's eternal recreation.
Thronged round with images of things to be,
They see you not, shadows are all they see."[2]

This is the matrix of the mind, as the little great-grandfather correctly saw. I hope something good comes out of it.

Kindest regards, JUNG

Many thanks for the critique! He must be an
ugly customer.[3]

262 F

Dear friend,   27 June 1911, Vienna, IX. Berggasse 19

My wife is touched by the repetition of your kind invitation and promises to reconsider. Since I know all the factors, I think she will stick to her earlier decision and that I shall come *before* the Congress.

I enclose the draft of the invitation to the Congress, without comment. It is agreed, I presume, that you are to chair the Congress. I also think you ought to use the mornings for papers as you did last year, which raises the spirits, and leave business matters for the afternoon. One afternoon will probably not be enough, because time will be needed for the members to make practical suggestions regarding the organization of the International Association. Whether it is necessary on this occasion to hold elections as provided for in our statutes, I do not know. I believe you will have to sift the papers to make sure that nothing of inferior quality is served up.

In respect to ucs. fantasies, I share your assumptions as well as your expectations. Incidentally, if the old gentleman was not referring to these things in his verses, I should be glad to know what they do apply to.

[2] *Faust II*, Act I, A Gloomy Gallery (tr. Philip Wayne, Penguin Classics, p. 77).
[3] Written at the top of the first page.

I trust that we are now rid of Adler. He has resigned from the Society and, after a "declaration,"[1] from the *Zentralblatt* as well. But the battle had its nasty and embarrassing episodes.

In the next few days the librarian of our Society, Dr. jur. Hanns Sachs,[2] will call on you. A charming and highly intelligent fellow, who wants to start a new *non*-medical journal in collaboration with Rank. It is to be called *Eros und Psyche* and to be related to the *Papers on Applied Psychology* as the *Zentralblatt* is to the *Jahrbuch*. I commend him to your benevolence.

I shall review Stekel and Havelock Ellis for the *Jahrbuch*.[3]

With kind regards to you all

Yours, FREUD

Seif has sent in an excellent report on Brussels.[4]

263 J

1003 Seestrasse, Küsnach-Zürich,

Dear Professor Freud,   11 July [1911][1]

I'm sick of work myself and longing for the holidays. Lately I have made the mistake of letting myself be swamped by my practice, my scientific work has fallen badly in arrears, and this is not at all good

---

[1] Adler's name as editor disappears from the masthead in *Zentralblatt*, I:10/11 (July/Aug. 1911), which opens with this "Declaration":

> "I hereby notify the readers of this journal that as of today I am resigning as editor. The director of the journal, Prof. Freud, was of the opinion that there exist such strong scientific disagreements between him and myself which [sic] make further collaboration in editing the journal seem inopportune. I therefore decided to resign as editor of the journal of my own free will.
>
> Dr. Alfred Adler"

[2] Hanns Sachs (1881–1947), Viennese lawyer, joined the Vienna Society in Oct. 1910 (*Minutes*, III); in 1912, he and Rank became co-editors of *Imago* (here called *Eros und Psyche*). He was an original member of the "Committee"; see below, editorial comment following 321 J. Began psychoanalytic practice in 1920, in Berlin; after 1932, in Boston.

[3] Not published.

[4] "Verhandlungen der Internationalen Gesellschaft für medizinische Psychologie und Psychotherapie, 7.–8. August 1910, in Brüssel," *Zentralblatt*, I:12 (Sept. 1911), 605–9.

---

[1] Holograph: 11.VII.10. But the original page numeration of the letters (by an unknown hand) placed this letter here, and its contents accords.

for me. My libido protests vigorously against any kind of one-sided occupation.

Dr. Sachs was here and has left me with a good impression. In all probability we can expect great things of the new journal.

Bleuler has sent in a detailed, rather too favourable report on Forel's views of ΨA for the *Jahrbuch*.[2] One of these days I must check up on Bleuler in a discussion at the Society. In many ways he is incredibly backward for lack of practical experience.

I received the enclosed letter from Adler. He seems to be extending his delusional ideas to me, since he refers to a rumour allegedly circulating in Vienna to the effect that *I have demanded his removal from the Society*. Of course I wrote immediately saying that this was quite out of the question, that on the contrary I would find his loss most regrettable, etc. Who is it starts this kind of rumour?

Dr. Poul Bjerre has sent in a paper for the *Jahrbuch*.[3] We have no lack of material. This year's volume will be a hefty one.

Little Frl. D——[4] from the dim past has come to me for treatment after all and is behaving very nicely.

That's the end of my news. I see from your card[5] that you have made a successful start with your holidays. I envy you. Mine start only in August, unfortunately with this trip to Brussels for the lecture. I wish you the best of luck for your recovery. I hope I can soon send you the *Jahrbuch* as a travelling companion—I am working on the last sheets.

Many kind regards,

Most sincerely yours, JUNG

264 F

Dear friend,   13 July 1911, Karlsbad, Haus Columbus

Yes, I am on holiday now, torturing myself "in obedience to the laws"[1] in the hope of recovering my so-called health. If my irritation

---

[2] "Forels Stellungnahme zur Psychanalyse," *Jahrbuch*, IV:2 (1912).

[3] "Zur Radikalbehandlung der chronischen Paranoia," *Jahrbuch*, III:2 (1911).

[4] See above, 115 J and 116 F.

[5] Missing.

---

[1] Holograph: "*den Gesetzen gehorchend*," an allusion to a classical epigram made popular by Schiller in his "Der Spaziergang" ("wie das Gesetz es befahl"). The

in the following seems excessive, do please consider my abnormal body chemistry.

I know who manufactures these rumours. It's not hard to guess. Adler in person, and I also know why. In writing you things which he knew you could easily refute, he was counting on the automatism of good manners. He knew you would say: no, on the contrary, sorry to hear it. And you let yourself be taken in, which puts me in a difficult situation.

Adler concocted his "rumour" from two private though not confidential remarks of mine: 1): that the journal suffered from the fact that he as editor had no personal contact with you and the other foreign contributors; and 2): that I ought to have taken steps long ago, at the time when he penned his inadmissible observation to the effect that the "Little Anna" material was "consistently slanted"[2] and therefore its mythologies were inconclusive. His rumour has no other basis. And now he hears from you that you regret his resignation, regard it as a loss, etc. From this he will now draw capital; he has obtained a statement of your disapproval of my treatment of him, he has brought us into conflict with one another, etc. Now that the harm is done, I can only request that in future you handle Adler, who undoubtedly has more tricks up his sleeve, with psychiatric caution.

His saying that the better element is resigning from the Society[3] with him is of course nonsense, as you will see for yourself.

I enclose his letter.[4]

I have seen Bjerre's paper; it is very interesting, though not quite clear. You must really rake Bleuler over the coals, Forel deserves no bouquets for what he says about ΨA in his book. You have aroused my curiosity about the *Jahrbuch*.

Dr. van Emden is continuing his course in ΨA with me, so I have company half the day. The other half is spent in the most unworthy of occupations, official concern for my poor Konrad. Karlsbad, I must

---

epigram is by Simonides, 5 cent. B.C., on the monument of the Spartans who fell at Thermopylae: "Stranger, bear this message to the Spartans, that we lie here obedient to their laws."—*Greek Anthology*, Sepulchral Epigrams, no. 249 (Loeb edn. II, 1917).

[2] See above, 227 J.

[3] See below, 273 F n. 1.

[4] The remainder of 264 F came to light under the same circumstances as 199a F, above; see its n. 1. / Adler's letter to Jung has not been recovered.

agree with my doctor here, is just the place to cure the pleasure-seeking habit, since every pleasure becomes a duty.

I wish you all enjoyment of your well-deserved holiday and am delighted with your decision not to let yourself be enslaved by your practice in the future. If I do so, I must be forgiven because of my age, my complexes, and the numerous offspring I have to provide for.

If it is agreeable to you, I shall come on September 16th—alone.

With kind regards to you, your wife, and children,

Yours ever, FREUD

265 J

1003 Seestrasse, Küsnach-Zürich,

Dear Professor Freud, 19 July 1911

I am very annoyed that I have been taken in by Adler. Later he will find that I am much farther away from him than he now thinks. I did, in fact, act to some extent on the psychiatric principle of never arguing with a paranoiac, and simply issued soothing official denials. Bleuler is very much of the same kidney and there is only a few degrees' difference between them (though it's an important one) in practice. He has all but severed personal relations with me; I attribute this solely to the alcohol question.

I have a terrible lot to do and must make heroic efforts to hold my practice at arm's length. Now I have got to the point where I can set aside one day for myself each week, in addition to Sunday, so that I can at last get down to some scientific work. All the hours that used to be free are now completely taken up with lecture courses, seminars, and correspondence (at present also with the perennial visitors). Things are so bad that to my consternation I can no longer enjoy my Sundays since I have to spend all of them resting. This deplorable state of affairs will cease on August 1st. On the 9th I go to Brussels for a week and then, on the 19th, to the mountains with my wife. At the beginning of September I'll be back in Zürich and shall look forward to seeing you on the 15th and harbouring you under my roof as a most welcome guest. My address during this time remains the same.

With many kind regards and best wishes for the success of your pleasure cure,

Most sincerely yours, JUNG

435

266 F

Dear friend,   Karlsbad, 21 July 1911

Your letter has appeased my irritation but at the same time aroused my anxiety. You must not take me as a model; on the contrary, you must arm yourself, before it is too late, against the dragon Practice. Give your charming, clever, and ambitious wife the pleasure of saving you from losing yourself in the business of money-making. My wife often says she would be only too proud if she were able to do the same for me. As it is, I am forced by circumstances, there isn't much left to be saved. In No. 9 of the *Zentralblatt* you will find an example of name-forgetting that occurred in a conversation between Ferenczi and me;[1] to you, I am sure, the explanation will reveal an additional meaning that would not be apparent to others.[2] (*Giovane–Veterano*). It is the old mythological motif: The old god wants to be sacrificed and rise again rejuvenated in the new one. I hope that you will fare better than I have and not just copy me. Your taste for money-making already worried me in connection with your American dealings. On the whole, it will prove to be good business if you forgo ordinary pursuits. Then, I am sure, extraordinary rewards will come your way.

Thank you for communicating your programme; the only item you seem to have omitted is your military service. I shall use your Zürich address as you wish, but please make a note of the fact that after the 31st of this month I shall be (not at Oberbozen but) at:

Klobenstein am Ritten/Tyrol[3]
Hotel Klobenstein

It is half an hour further on the same plateau.

I have received the invitations to the Congress. My cure in Karlsbad is not an unmingled pleasure. I have decided to endow a votive tablet if only I get rid of all the ailments I have acquired here. However, it looks as if I were going to come off with some benefit.

With kind regards to you and your family,

Yours ever, FREUD

---

[1] Freud and Ferenczi were trying to recall a place-name in Sicily. Freud could at first remember only Castrogiovanni, then he recalled the missing name, Castelvetrano. He observed that *-giovanni* sounds like *giovane*, "young," and *-vetrano* like *veterano*, "old." Then followed his comment about Putnam quoted above, 253 F n. 9.
[2] The allusion is to the name Jung.
[3] Since 1918, this region has been Italian; Klobenstein = Collalbo.

267 J

1003 Seestrasse, Küsnach-Zürich,

Dear Professor Freud, 26 July 1911

It's not all that bad with my money-making; nevertheless I grant you are right. The feeling of inferiority that often overcomes me when I measure myself against you has always to be compensated by increased emulation. I need a large practice in order to gain experience, for I do not imagine that I know too much. Also, I have had to demonstrate to myself that I am able to make money in order to rid myself of the thought that I am non-viable. These are all frightful stupidities which can only be overcome by acting them out. I think I am now over the mountain so far as my practice is concerned. During the winter semester I shall be merciless with myself. This stage has to be overcome too. It is, as you know, no light matter to suffer financial success. I have never thrived on it. Scientific work does me far more good.

I have now finished my Brussels lecture. It contains a short, very nice child analysis. It's a shame to throw it away on a congress.

I hear Jones is going back to London. He didn't get his professorship in Toronto because of intrigues. In any event he is coming to Weimar.

In Zürich we are forging ahead with Dem. praecox, as will become apparent in this and the following *Jahrbuch*. Mythological parallels are of immense importance for Dem. pr.; I see more and more how useful my wanderings on the highways and byways of history have been. I am so looking forward to the time we shall have together. There are all sorts of things I want to show you. I hope, too, that you won't find it a bore to be present at the seminars along with Putnam, etc. We could have a very pleasant colloquy of considerable importance for the future of psychoanalysis.

Meanwhile with many kind regards,

Most sincerely yours, J U N G

268 F

Klobenstein am Ritten/Tyrol,
Dear friend,   Hotel Post, 20 August 1911

Today at last I received the *Jahrbuch*.[1] Of course I haven't had time to read it yet, only to cut the pages and glance at a few of them. I take this occasion to tell you how proud I was to see that you placed me at the head of such significant things and to thank you for the way in which you are championing the cause, holding the flag high, and meting out mighty blows to our opponents (with the flagpole, to stick to the metaphor). I am greatly looking forward to our meeting. This place has a very special kind of beauty. I am planning to stay here until 14 September and then go directly to Zürich.

Since my mental powers revived, I have been working in a field where you will be surprised to meet me.[2] I have unearthed strange and uncanny things and will almost feel obliged *not* to discuss them with you. But you are too shrewd not to guess what I am up to when I add that I am dying to read your "Transformations and Symb. of the Lib."[3]

It goes without saying that I should be glad to hear from you, how you all are, how it went in Brussels, and what further plans you have for the holidays.

I am expecting Ferenczi today for a prolonged visit.

With kind regards in friendship from a happy heart,

Yours, FREUD

269 J

1003 Seestrasse, Küsnach-Zürich,
Dear Professor Freud,   29 August 1911

I was overjoyed by your letter, being, as you know, very receptive to any recognition the father sees fit to bestow. It is more pleasing

---

[1] Vol. III:1, which opened with Freud's "Formulations on the Two Principles of Mental Functioning" and the Schreber case, "Psychoanalytic Notes on an Autobiographical Account of a Case of Paranoia" (both in SE XII), and included a major work of Jung's (see n. 3 below). For the full contents of the issue, see appendix 2.

[2] The allusion is to the work that would become *Totem and Taboo*. See below, 293 F n. 2.

[3] I.e., Part I.

than the loud recognition conferred on us by the unremitting malev-
olence of our opponents. At the same time, your letter has got me on
tenterhooks because, for all my "shrewdness," I can't quite make out
what is going on so enigmatically behind the scenes. Together with
my wife I have tried to unriddle your words, and we have reached
surmises which, for the time being at any rate, I would rather keep
to myself. I can only hope that your embargo on discussion will be
lifted during your stay here. I, too, have the feeling that this is a
time full of marvels, and, if the auguries do not deceive us, it may very
well be that, thanks to your discoveries, we are on the threshold of
something really sensational, which I scarcely know how to describe
except with the Gnostic concept of σοφία,[1] an Alexandrian term particularly suited to the reincarnation of ancient wisdom in the shape
of ΨA. I daren't say too much, but would only counsel you (very im-
modestly) to let my "Transf. and Symb. of the Lib." unleash your
associations and/or fantasies: I am sure you will hit upon strange
things if you do. (Provided, of course, that the mysterious hint in
your letter has not already done so in anagrammatic form. With that
letter anything seems possible.)

Well then—I was in Brussels from 11–16 August. The Congress
and its proceedings were so idiotic that I played truant most of the
time. I was present, so to speak, only at my own lecture.[2] It was a
colossal piece of cheek. I knew that after all those longueurs the
public would fall like rabbits. The speaking time was limited to 20
minutes. I took almost an hour, one can't do a decent report on
ΨA in 20 minutes. I felt sure the chairman (van Schuyten,[3] who has
his knife into ΨA anyway) was going to cut me short. And he did.
I told him I would willingly stop at once but would like to leave the
decision to the Congress (ca. 200 people). The Congress granted me
further time by acclamation. The same thing happened a *second
time*. The chairman was hopping mad but had to swallow his rage.
My lecture had the effect of a bombshell. Afterwards one heard
mutterings like "Vous avez déchaîné un orage," "oh, c'est un homme
odieux," etc. A few people left the hall in mute protest. One Danish
doctor flew into a rage with me; I didn't deign to answer him and
that made him more furious than ever, for the rabble likes to be an-

[1] "Sophia," wisdom.
[2] "Über Psychoanalyse beim Kinde," Ier *Congrès international de Pédagogie* [*Proceedings*] (Brussels, 1912), II, 332–43. It was incorporated in *The Theory of
Psychoanalysis*, pars. 458ff.; see below, editorial comment following 321 J.
[3] M. C. van Schuyten, director of an institute for pedology at Antwerp.

swered in kind. But a few of the brighter heads and a few good ones had noticed something and from now on can be counted among our silent collaborators.

After Belgium I went on a mountain tour in the Bernese Oberland with my wife. I have been back in Zürich since yesterday.

Now comes a protest at your not wishing to leave until the 15th when you should already be here on the 15th. Can it be done?

So far I have only four announcements of lectures for Weimar[4] (Sadger, Abraham, Körber,[5] Jung). I have asked Bleuler, Sachs, and Rank, and will also try Pfister. I am counting on you absolutely; would you please let me know the title of your lecture *as soon as possible*. Abraham wrote me that applicants are dragging their heels (at least in Zürich). These are only symptoms of laziness, of course; people will come all right. This time the feminine element will have conspicuous representatives from Zürich: Sister Moltzer,[6] Dr. Hinkle-Eastwick (an American charmer),[7] Frl. Dr. Spielrein (!), then a new discovery of mine, Frl. Antonia Wolff,[8] a remarkable intellect with an excellent feeling for religion and philosophy, and last but not least[9] my wife. I am told that a Dr. van Renterghem[10] of Amsterdam wants to come. In Munich we have won over a privatdocent of psychology, Dr. Fischer[11] (former pupil of Lipps[12] and Wundt).

Perhaps you can round up a few decent lecturers in Vienna; in any case do please get Ferenczi to present something.

[4] For a list of the papers read at the Weimar Congress, see appendix 4.

[5] Heinrich Körber (d. 1927), physician, member of the Board of Health of Berlin; charter member of the Berlin Society.

[6] See above, 211 J n. 2. / The child whose case was the subject of Jung's Brussels lecture (above, n. 2) was Sister Moltzer's patient.

[7] Beatrice Moses Hinkle (1872–1953), American psychiatrist and analytical psychologist, originally from California, student of both Freud and Jung. (At this time married to an Eastwick.) She translated Jung's *Psychology of the Unconscious* (1916). For many years she was a leader of the Jungian group in New York and director of a sanatorium at Washington, Connecticut.

[8] Toni Wolff (1888–1953)—the name she used throughout her later career as an analytical psychologist in Zürich—was Jung's close friend and collaborator for more than 40 years.

[9] Holograph: *last not least* (English).

[10] A. W. van Renterghem (1845–1939), Dutch hypnotist.

[11] Aloys Fischer (1880–1937), professor of philosophy from 1914.

[12] Theodor Lipps (1851–1914), professor of philosophy in Munich; he adopted a psychological approach to philosophy.

I look forward very much to seeing you here again in the near future. I'm expecting Putnam next week.

Many kind regards,

Most sincerely yours, JUNG

270 F

Dear friend,   Klobenstein, 1 September 1911

I am glad to release you as well as your dear wife, well known to me as a solver of riddles, from the darkness by informing you that my work in these last few weeks has dealt with the same theme as yours, to wit, the origin of religion. I wasn't going to speak of it for fear of confusing you. But since I can see from a first reading of your article in the *Jahrbuch* (I shall have to reread it; for the moment Ferenczi has made off with the volume) that my conclusions are known to you, I find, much to my relief, that there is no need for secrecy. So you too are aware that the Oedipus complex is at the root of religious feeling. Bravo! What evidence I have to contribute can be told in five minutes.

Your letter came on a beautiful happy day and has further raised my spirits. Your Brussels experiences are very amusing. It seems to me that we have had enough congresses for a while. Your kind wish that I should arrive at your place on the 15th is unfulfillable, and has been for twenty-five years.[1]

The papers (for the Congress) should be no great problem. I have prodded Ferenczi, who will present something about homosexuality. Rank has just written to me for encouragement to speak on his "Motif of Nudity in Antiquity."[2] He has received it. You might easily persuade Putnam, whom you will be seeing before you see me, to tell us something about his philosophical postulates and misgivings, which he has spoken of in a memorandum to me.[3] To be sure, I don't

[1] Sigmund and Martha Freud's 25th wedding anniversary fell on 14 Sept. 11. Jones states (I, p. 165/150) that the civil ceremony took place on 13 Sept. 1886 in the Town Hall at Wandsbek (Hamburg) and the religious wedding on 14 Sept. in the house of Martha Bernays' mother.

[2] = "Über das Motiv der Nacktheit in Dichtung und Sage," *Imago*, II (1913). For the local reception in Weimar, see Jones, II, p. 96/85.

[3] See Putnam to Freud, late March 1911, in *Putnam and Psychoanalysis*, pp. 116–19. The paper, "Über die Bedeutung philosophischer Anschauungen und

441

think very much of it, but it will make a nice ornament. I myself, since you won't dispense with me, am planning a short supplement to the Schreber analysis, which I am sure will appeal to *you*. Besides, for anyone with sharp ears, it announces things to come. But please don't put me in the lead with this trifle, which really can't be dragged out for more than fifteen minutes. Maybe Putnam will let himself be pushed into that position, or you could take it yourself.

Actually the papers are not the essential part of this congress, which does not require a scientific clou. The accent will be on the organizational deliberations. Now that we have flourishing journals, the situation has changed.

We Viennese have nothing to compare with the charming ladies you are bringing from Zürich. Our only lady doctor is participating like a true masochist in the Adler revolt and is unlikely to be present.[4] We are indeed disintegrating. As you know, this shift to the West is not entirely contrary to my wishes. Under the circumstances my wife is especially sorry not to be coming, but the demands of the season and the household plus the fact that she is not a good traveller have made her decide against it. Moreover, as you know, she is not personally involved in psychoanalysis and regrets Zürich more than Weimar.

Here on the Ritten it is divinely beautiful and comfortable. I have discovered in myself an inexhaustible desire to do nothing, except for the hour or two that I spend reading new things, and I hate to think that the beginning of next month will bring me back to hard labour. But twenty-five years of practice[5] are not yet servitude enough. Maybe forty, or perhaps all in all it is better "to die in harness."[6]

I shall surely write you again before leaving. For now I send my kindest regards to you all. Auf Wiedersehen!

Yours ever, FREUD

Ausbildung für die weitere Entwicklung der psychoanalytischen Bewegung," appeared in *Imago*, I (May 1912); an English version, "A Plea for the Study of Philosophic Methods in Preparation for Psychoanalytic Work," is in Putnam, *Addresses on Psycho-Analysis* (London and New York, 1921). Freud's high regard for Putnam's psychological and psychiatric work did not extend—as he indicates here—to his Hegelian philosophical ideas; see also Jones, II, p. 96/85f.

[4] Margarete Hilferding (1871–?1943); had been voted into the Vienna Society 27 Apr. 10, its first woman member, on Federn's nomination. Married to Rudolf Hilferding, German Social Democrat leader in the 1920's. She was well known as a doctor to the Viennese working class; killed by the Nazis at Auschwitz.

[5] See above, 134 F n. 2.

[6] English in original.

The Weimar Congress

As Jones relates (II, pp. 101f./89f.), Freud travelled alone from his vacation spot near Bozen (Bolzano) to Zürich, where Jung met him upon his arrival early in the morning of 16 September. He stayed in the Jungs' house at Küsnacht for four days, of which we have only Jones's brief account: "There were of course seminars, visitors, and receptions, so it was by no means a pure holiday. Putnam, who was in Zürich, not Küsnacht, participated in all these activities." Putnam, furthermore, spent six hours in analysis with Freud (Hale, in *Putnam and Psychoanalysis*, p. 39). We may suppose that Freud travelled up to Weimar (a day's journey by railroad) with Carl and Emma Jung, probably on the 19th; Putnam may have been of the party also. Bleuler and eight or ten others went from Zürich.

The Third Psychoanalytic Congress was held at the best hotel of Weimar, the Erbprinz, beginning at 8 a.m. on 21 September and continuing on the next day. Karl Abraham was in charge of arrangements. The official report names 55 in attendance, of whom 46 posed for a group photograph (see plate VI). Twelve papers were read—"of a high order," writes Jones (pp. 95f./85f.), including "several classics of psychoanalytic literature." They were abstracted by Otto Rank in the *Zentralblatt*, II:2 (Nov. 1911), 100–105. See appendix 4.

Freud's contribution, a brief postscript to the Schreber case (*Jahrbuch*, III:2), contained this reference to Jung's current work: "[These remarks] may serve to show that Jung had excellent grounds for his assertion that the mythopoeic forces of mankind are not extinct, but that to this very day they give rise in the neuroses to the same psychical products as in the remotest past ages" (SE XII, pp. 81f.). Jung's paper, on contributions to symbolism, has disappeared except in the form of Rank's abstract; it apparently contained material Jung had collected for "Transformations and Symbols of the Libido." (See addenda.)

By acclamation, Jung and Riklin were re-elected president and secretary, respectively, of the International Association. But it was decided that the *Correspondenzblatt*, or *Bulletin*, of which six issues of from 4 to 8 pages each had been published at Zürich since July 1910, would now be incorporated into the *Zentralblatt*; it appeared in three numbers of vol. II (1912): 4, 8, and 9, as the final content of each.

271 J

[Barracks, St. Gallen],[1]

Dear Professor Freud,   4 October 1911

At last I can settle down to write to you. I have now been in barracks for a week doing my duty as a medical jack-of-all-trades, anointing feet, cutting out corns, treating diarrhoea, and am beginning to feel squat and ugly again. Luckily I have some time for myself, so I am not entirely pulverized by the constant spectacle of odious corporeality. Besides, something can be gained even from its most indelicate aspect, to wit, from what is known as the "short-arm inspection."[1a] At this phallic parade of 500 soldiers 14% had phimosis. Here we have the biological incentive to circumcision. The commonest abnormality seems to be a tendency to hypospadias.[2] It looks positively female.

It was all very turbulent at home after Weimar, and the first days of duty were equally hectic. Also I have a foul cold at the moment. However, I am doing everything I can to push on with the printing of the second half of the *Jahrbuch*. Right now I am working on Silberer. The printing started a month ago. Please send the manuscript[3] you were unable to give me in Weimar *direct to Deuticke*.

The Congress in Munich[4] must have been a frightfully stupid affair. I have heard reports of it from various quarters. Frank perpetrated the following pronouncement: "It is enormously important in ΨA that not only the lady patient should repose comfortably on the couch but the doctor as well." Jones and Seif stood up for us. With what result I don't know.

Do you know anything about the outcome of the negotiations between Stekel and Bergmann?

For our interpretation of the Utnapishtim episode in Gilgamesh I have found some rather weird parallels which shed light on Utnap-

---

[1] This and the next letter are on Jung's usual letterhead stationery but clearly were written at the barracks in St. Gallen, like 275 J.

[1a] Holograph: *der sog. "Schwanzvisite."*

[2] Opening of urethra on underside of penis.

[3] "Nachtrag zu dem autobiographisch beschriebenen Fall von Paranoia (Dementia paranoides)," *Jahrbuch*, III:2 (1911) = "Postscript" to the Schreber case, SE XII (Freud's brief Weimar lecture).

[4] International Congress for Medical Psychology and Psychotherapy, 25–26 Sept.; see Jones, II, p. 133/118, for Jones's and Seif's argument with its president, Vogt.

ishtim's gnomic utterances.⁵ I won't reveal anything yet, but must mull them over first.

Two boring things⁶ will be included in the next *Jahrbuch*, but because of their scientific veneer they will impress the kind of public that likes indirect statements. We must do a bit more infiltrating in scientific circles.

I hope you got back to Vienna safe and sound and took home with you many good impressions of Switzerland so that you will wish to come again another year.

With kindest regards and my compliments to your wife,

Yours very sincerely, J U N G

272 J

[Barracks, St. Gallen],
6 October 1911

Dear Professor Freud,

Our letters, as you will have observed, crossed.¹ Like you, I have been afflicted with a frightful cold but thank goodness am over the worst of it now.

I return Specht's² letter herewith. What the underlying sentiments are can be seen from the simple fact that in spite of his gushing enthusiasm for ΨA he has not yet brought himself to invite a single one of its spokesmen to contribute. This tells us much more, it seems to me, than all the pretty words that may be found in private letters. That he prefers people like Münsterberg or Sommer³ to you (or even "Ach"⁴ in Königsberg, Lord have mercy on us, Ach!) is a scandal

---

⁵ The parallels include Longfellow's Hiawatha and the Wandering Jew. See CW 5, pars. 293, 513 (also in 1911/12 version).
⁶ Presumably the papers by Pfenninger and Aptekmann; see below, 279 J n. 6.

---

¹ Freud's letter is missing.
² Wilhelm Specht, editor of the *Zeitschrift für Pathopsychologie* (Leipzig), the first number of which (Aug. 1911) was reviewed in the *Zentralblatt*, II:7 (Apr. 1912).
³ Robert Sommer (1864–1937), professor of psychiatry at Giessen University. In the *Association Studies* Jung was indebted to Sommer's earlier researches; see CW 2, index, s.v. Sommer was first president (1928–30) of the General Medical Society for Psychotherapy. See Jung's tribute to him in his presidential address to the 1937 Copenhagen Congress, CW 10, par. 1066.
⁴ Narziss Kaspar Ach (1871–1946), psychologist and professor of philosophy at Königsberg, later Göttingen.

which he can make good only by conspicuous action. Benevolent neutrality is the better part in this case, as in the Turkish-Italian war.[5] Even so, the document is of historical importance. Don't forget that Specht is seeking contact with the left out of hatred for Kraepelin. Personally no doubt he is gifted, but unbearably conceited. Incidentally, it occurs to me that he asked me for contributions in 1905, but before he knew I was infected with ΨA. He hasn't been heard from since.

I am very glad to know that you have no desire to boost rival enterprises of this kind by any contributions of yours.

I admire the way you put up with Bleuler. His lecture was pretty awful, don't you think?[6] Have you received his big book?[7] He has done some really bad things in it that are sure to muddy our clear conception of Dementia praecox.

As a curiosity, I must tell you that the tidings you send forth have penetrated further than one would ever have believed. One of our officers knew your name and has a dim notion that it is connected with something important and worthy of note. You will be able to use the motto of *The Interpretation of Dreams* in a new and unexpected sense: "Flectere si nequeo superos, Acheronta movebo."[8]

So far my military service has afforded me ample leisure for reading and for going through manuscripts. I am also enjoying a pleasant respite, all the more welcome after our exertions in Weimar. I wish you every success with your campaign against the Adler gang (*lucus a non lucendo*).[9]

Many kind regards,

Most sincerely yours, JUNG

[5] The Tripolitan War between Italy and Turkey had broken out on 28 Sept. Italy invaded and eventually annexed Tripoli (N. Africa); the European powers, though disapproving, remained neutral.

[6] "Zur Theorie des Autismus," presumably = "Das autistische Denken," *Jahrbuch*, IV:1 (1912).

[7] *Dementia Praecox, oder die Gruppe der Schizophrenien*, a 420-page volume in *Handbuch der Psychiatrie*, ed. G. Aschaffenburg (Leipzig and Vienna, 1911) = *Dementia Praecox, or The Group of Schizophrenias*, tr. J. Zinkin (New York, 1950).

[8] = "If I cannot bend the gods, I will stir up Acheron."—Vergil, *Aeneid*, VII, 312.

[9] See above, 162 J n. 5.

273 F

Dear friend,   12 October 1911, Vienna, IX. Berggasse 19

Rather tired after battle and victory, I hereby inform you that yesterday I forced the whole Adler gang (six of them)[1] to resign from the Society. I was harsh but I don't think unfair. They have founded a new society for "free" ΨA[2] as opposed to our unfree variety, and are planning to put out a journal of their own,[3] etc.; nevertheless they insisted on their right to stay with us, naturally in order to provide themselves parasitically with ideas and with material to misrepresent. I have rendered such a symbiosis impossible. The same evening we enrolled three new members, Stärcke and Emden in Holland and Fräulein Dr. Spielrein who turned up unexpectedly.[4] She said I didn't look malicious, as she had imagined I would.

My practice is not quite complete, only seven patients so far. Consequently I have not yet mobilized intellectually; for instance, I have not yet resumed my studies on religion. Besides, there have been all sorts of chores connected with the Society and individual members. My letter to Specht was simply a sharp restatement of the famous question: "Why didn't you say it *scil.* aloud?"[5] If he doesn't apply to you now as I have suggested, it will prove that the whole thing is a fraud.

Eder in London has just sent me the first ΨA paper to have been read before the British Medical Association (*British Medical Journal*, 30 Sept. 1911).[6]

[1] At the 11 Oct. meeting of the Society (first of the new season) Freud announced the resignations of Adler, Bach, Madáy, and Hye (see above, 260 F n. 3). After debate, a resolution was passed to the effect that "membership in the 'Society for Free Psychoanalytic Investigation' is incompatible with membership in the Psychoanalytic Association"; it was followed by the resignations (or expulsions?) of Furtmüller, the Grüners, Hilferding, Klemperer, and Oppenheim (*Minutes*, III: cf. Jones, II, p. 150/133). Freidjung remained; he is listed as a member on 1 Jan. 12 (*Zentralblatt*, II:8, May 1912, p. 475).

[2] The Society for Free Psychoanalysis; see "On the History of the Psycho-analytic Movement," SE XIV, p. 51.

[3] *Zeitschrift für Individual-Psychologie*, founded Apr. 1914 in Vienna but suspended upon the outbreak of the war; resumed 1923 under the editorship of Adler and Ladislaus Zilahi, with *Internationale* prefixed to its title.

[4] August Stärcke (1880–1954), of Huister Heide, and Jan van Emden (see above, 209 F n. 7). Dr. Spielrein now resided in Vienna (*Zentralblatt*, II, 1912, 237).

[5] Schreberism.

[6] M. D. Eder, "A Case of Obsession and Hysteria Treated by the Freud Psycho-

I have just had a letter from Pfister announcing his intention of divorcing his wife. Prosit. High time, I think, if he doesn't want to waste his life. I have strongly urged him to go through with it.

Bleuler is a genius at misunderstanding, rather like a prickly eel, if there is such a thing.

The days in Zürich and Weimar seem even more splendid in retrospect. Toothache and strain sink into oblivion, the exchange of ideas, the hopes and satisfactions that were the substance of those days stand out in all their purity.

I wish you full enjoyment of your military rest, which I hope will not be disturbed by the war in the Mediterranean, and send you, your wife and children my kind regards.

Yours ever, FREUD

274 F

Dear friend,   13 October 1911,[1] Vienna, IX. Berggasse 19

To you in your military solitude I send the following contribution to our conversations on the Gilgamesh material.

Though I do not contest the interpretation of Gilgamesh and Eabani[2] as man and crude sensuality, it nevertheless occurs to me that such pairs consisting of a noble and a base part (usually brothers) are a motif running through all legend and literature. The last great offshoot of the type is Don Quijote with his Sancho Panza (literally: paunch). Of mythological figures, the first that come to mind are the Dioskuroi (one mortal, the other immortal) and various pairs of brothers or twins of the Romulus and Remus type. One is always weaker than the other and dies sooner. In Gilgamesh this age-old

---

analytic Method," *British Medical Journal*, II (1911). Eder (1866–1936) was a charter member of the London Psycho-Analytical Society (1913). His interest was divided between the Zürich and Vienna schools; with his wife and Mary Moltzer he translated Jung's *The Theory of Psychoanalysis* (see below, comment following 321 J) and alone he made a remarkable translation and adaptation of the *Studies in Word-Association*, edited by Jung. In 1920, after an analysis with Ferenczi, Eder resumed his Freudian allegiance. He was a prominent worker in England for the Zionist cause.

---

[1] Quoted in Jones, II, pp. 500f./451f.
[2] Usually called Enkidu by present-day scholars.

motif of the unequal pair of brothers served to represent the relationship between a man and his libido.

These ancient motifs are always being reinterpreted (even, I concede, in terms of astronomy); but what is their original source?

In regard to the motif under discussion it is not hard to say. The weaker twin, who dies first, is the placenta, or afterbirth, simply because it is regularly born along with the child by the same mother. We found this interpretation some months ago in the work of a modern mythologist[3] totally ignorant of ΨA, who for once forgot his science and consequently had a good idea. But in Frazer's *Golden Bough*, Vol. I, one can read that among many primitive peoples the afterbirth is called *brother* (sister) or *twin*, and treated accordingly, that is, fed and taken care of, which of course cannot go on for very long. If there is such a thing as a phylogenetic memory in the individual, which unfortunately will soon be undeniable, this is also the source of the *uncanny* aspect of the "doppelgänger."

I just wanted to surprise you with the news that basically Eabani is Gilgamesh's "afterbirth." All sorts of ideas and connections still remain to be unearthed in this material. It's a pity we can only work together in such technical matters.

Very cordially yours, FREUD

275 J

Barracks, St. Gallen (until Oct. 31),
17 October 1911

Dear Professor Freud,

Many thanks for your two letters and all their news. I was interested in the goings-on in Vienna. May we know the names of the dissidents soon? In my view this purge is a blessing.

Pfister—I saw it coming. He could no more have lifted his marriage out of the rut than Archimedes could have moved the world unless a solid point had suddenly materialized in empty space. It so happens that "a bird loaded with corpse poison"[1] has been miracled

---

[3] Paul Ehrenreich (1855–1914), ethnologist at Berlin University. The interpretation occurs in his *Die allgemeine Mythologie und ihre ethnologischen Grundlagen* (Mythologische Bibliothek, IV, 1, Leipzig, 1910), pp. 239f. See below, 275 J n. 2.

[1] See Schreber, *Memoirs*, pp. 166ff., and Freud's interpretation in "Psycho-Analytic Notes on a Case of Paranoia," ch. II (SE XII, pp. 35f.), where the "miracled birds" are related to young girls.

into existence, which as the rules require bears a girl's name and is gently luring him into the ways of the ungodly. I know this charming little bird. But it seems that she only wants to lure him out of his cage, not to marry him. Still, the main thing is to lure him out. If she succeeds, Pfister can count himself happy.

Your contribution to the symbolism of the brothers, which you hinted at in Zürich, is extraordinarily interesting and very valuable. As I have discovered since then, symbolism is widely disseminated and age-old. I am most grateful for this contribution[2] since it fits in very well with certain other observations which have forced me to conclude that the so-called "early memories of childhood" are not individual memories at all but phylogenetic ones. I mean of course the *very early* memories like birth, sucking, etc. There are things whose only explanation is *intrauterine*: much of the water symbolism, then the enwrappings and encoilings which seem to be accompanied by strange skin sensations (umbilical cord and amnion). Just now my Agathli is having dreams like this; they are closely related to certain Negro birth-myths, where these envelopments in slimy stuff also occur. I think we shall find that infinitely many more things than we now suppose are phylogenetic memories.

Up here I am pretty much cut off from the worldly bustle, I hear and see little. The evenings are perforce dedicated to conviviality. Even in St. Gallen I have visitations from people who are otherwise total strangers.

I hope your cold has long since disappeared. Many kind regards,

Most sincerely yours, J U N G

276 F

Dear friend,　　　　　　　20 October 1911, Vienna, IX. Berggasse 19

Unlike you, I already feel rather tired after only a month of this worldly bustle, especially as not all of it is lucrative. Two-thirds of my time is accounted for, but I still have nothing for my hungry chicks

---

[2] In "Wandlungen und Symbole der Libido," Part II, ch. V, n. 56 (*Jahrbuch,* IV: 1, 1912) Jung wrote: "Professor Freud has expressed in a personal discussion the idea that a further determinant for the motif of the dissimilar brothers is to be found in the elementary observance towards birth and the after-birth. It is an exotic custom to treat the placenta as a child!" In the 1952 revision (CW 5, par. 356) this was worked into the text, without the allusion to Freud.

in the ΨAtical nest. I am writing to you chiefly as a precaution; I hear you are corresponding with Stekel, and I want to assure you in advance that the difficulties and messes he may be making for you are none of my doing, though perhaps you know me well enough and are familiar enough with the circumstances to realize this without my telling you. I merely wanted you to begin your presidential statements in the first number.[1] Further, I shall give you my full support if you don't want to accept the smallest print for the *Bulletin*.[2] You see how petty one becomes when one is reduced to such company as I am here in the Vienna Society. Last Wednesday it was again brought home to me how much of the most elementary educational work remains to be done.[3]

I have run into unexpected difficulties with the new journal. Deuticke, who at first seemed enthusiastic, has brusquely withdrawn. Now I am humbly and gloomily awaiting an answer from two other publishers; one of them is Joh. Amb. Barth. The psychology of religion is getting ahead very slowly. I find it hard to read after the day's demands on my receptivity, and Frazer is so long-winded, so full of details that one must immediately forget.

Did a Professor Schrader[4] from Vienna call on you during the summer (spring)?

I was very much interested in the news about Pfister. ΨA is beginning to shape destinies.

I presume you are eagerly looking forward to your return to civilian life. With kind regards,

Yours ever, FREUD

---

[1] I.e., the first number (II:1, Oct. 1912) of the *Zentralblatt* as the official organ of the International Association, incorporating the *Bulletin*. But Jung's only "presidential statement" appeared not in No. 1 (Oct.) but in No. 4 (Jan.), as part of the *Bulletin*, in the back of the issue; see below, 279 J n. 1.

[2] The *Bulletin* was indeed printed in smaller type (8 point) than the main text of the *Zentralblatt*.

[3] In the meeting of 18 Oct., Tausk (see below, 348 F n. 4) read a paper suggesting that the meaning of dreams, as interpreted by Freud, can just as well be arrived at without psychoanalysis; see *Zentralblatt*, II:4 (1912), 237.

[4] Hans Schrader (1869–1948), professor of classical archaeology in the University; after 1912, at Frankfurt.

277 J

Dear Professor Freud,   [Postmark: St. Gallen] 30 October 1911[1]

A few words in haste to apologize for not having answered your last letter. The last 10 days of duty have completely worn me out. Suddenly I was detailed for a mountain exercise at the back of beyond where I was quite out of touch with the rest of humanity. I return to Zürich early tomorrow morning. To my immense surprise I am being replaced by Lieut. Binswanger, S. ΨA.[2] He sends greetings. Once I am out of the brutalities of military life I shall write you a sensible letter. One just can't think here.

Many kind regards, JUNG

From Emma Jung

Dear Professor Freud,   Küsnacht, 30 October [1911][1]

I don't really know how I am summoning the courage to write you this letter, but am certain it is not from presumption; rather I am following the voice of my unconscious, which I have so often found was right and which I hope will not lead me astray this time.

Since your visit I have been tormented by the idea that your relation with my husband is not altogether as it should be, and since it definitely ought not to be like this I want to try to do whatever is in my power. I do not know whether I am deceiving myself when I think you are somehow not quite in agreement with "Transformations of Libido." You didn't speak of it at all and yet I think it would do you both so much good if you got down to a thorough discussion of it. Or is it something else? If so, please tell me what, dear Herr Professor; for I cannot bear to see you so resigned and I even believe that your resignation relates not only to your real children (it made a quite special impression on me when you spoke of it) but also to your spiritual sons; otherwise you would have so little need to be resigned.

Please do not take my action as officiousness and do not count me among the women who, you once told me, always spoil your friendships.

---

[1] Postcard.

[2] = Societas Psychoanalytica; cf. Societas Jesu.

---

[1] While the holograph gives the date 1910, internal evidence (references to "Wandlungen der Libido" and to Freud's visit) determines the 1911 date. The letter paper, headed "EJ," is used for the letters of 14 and 24 Nov. 11, but no others in the present collection. Salutation: *Lieber Herr Professor.*

My husband naturally knows nothing of this letter and I beg you not to hold him responsible for it or to let any kind of unpleasant effects it may have on you glance off on him.

I hope nevertheless that you will not be angry with your very admiring

EMMA JUNG

278 F

Dear friend,   2 November 1911, Vienna, IX. Berggasse 19

I am glad you are home again and no longer playing soldiers, which is after all a silly occupation. Let this letter welcome you home. I feel sure that the sigla you invented in your army camp, S. ΨA, will come into universal use.

There isn't much to say, except that I should like you to appear in the *Zentralblatt* with announcements from the President's office, that Riklin should send the membership lists to Bergmann, who needs them for his mailing, and that I support Stekel's request that we subsidize a paper by Silberer, which is rather long and has been lying about for some time. It is entitled: On Categories of Symbols,[1] and ought, like everything he writes, to be valuable.

Four publishers have now turned down the new journal (Deuticke, Bergmann, J. A. Barth, Urban & Schwarzenberg). I am hoping to make arrangements next week with H. Heller, the art publisher, who is a member of our group. But it's not so good; this and various other things make a pitiful impression that leaves me depressed. In addition, I have not been fully employed this month; the nestlings are opening hungry mouths, the ones outside my house at least; those at home are still getting enough to eat. My psychology of religion is giving me a good deal of trouble; I have little pleasure in working and constant *douleurs d'enfantement*;[2] in short, I feel rather gloomy and I am not quite well physically either. Old age is not an empty delusion.[3] A morose senex deserves to be shot without remorse.

Magnus Hirschfeld has left our ranks in Berlin. No great loss, he is a flabby, unappetizing fellow, absolutely incapable of learning any-

---

[1] "Von den Kategorien der Symbolik," *Zentralblatt*, II:4 (Jan. 1912).

[2] = "labour pains."

[3] Holograph: *Das Alter ist doch kein leerer Wahn.* Cf. "Und die Treue, sie ist doch kein leerer Wahn," in Schiller's poem "Die Bürgschaft."

thing. Of course he takes your remark at the Congress as a pretext; homosexual touchiness. Not worth a tear.

My son Ernst is well. My daughter Sophie is better but nothing has been decided yet. The rest of them are fine. I hope to hear the same of you and your little barnyard.

Very cordially yours, FREUD

279 J

1003 Seestrasse, Küsnach-Zürich,
Dear Professor Freud,   6 November 1911

The first days after my return were crowded with trivia. Now at last I can breathe again. I have discussed the *Zentralblatt* situation with Riklin and issued the necessary orders. (I have the feeling that nothing moves unless one brandishes a whip.) Most people are only too glad to have a ruler or tyrant over them. Man invented rulers out of sheer laziness.

My message to the *Zentralblatt*[1] will go off at the earliest opportunity. The last stretch of military service has made all work impossible. Reports of meetings of the branch societies will appear as heretofore in the *Bulletin*, hence the reports of the meetings in Vienna should also be directed to the central office. I am making up the *Bulletin* together with Riklin and shall send it to Stekel. Since our space in the *Zentralblatt* is limited, we must have reports of meetings from the branch societies every month so that the material doesn't pile up too much. The reports should be drawn up as hitherto.

Aren't you afraid that the publication of longer papers in the *Zentralblatt* will generate unnecessary competition with the *Jahrbuch*? I'd like to see Silberer's papers in the latter. The *Zentralblatt* would be serving a more valuable purpose if it presented elementary didactic articles, suitable shall we say for beginners and patients. I would gladly vote for a subsidy if the *Zentralblatt* printed monographs of an elementary and didactic nature. It is, after all, intended mainly for medical men, and Silberer's paper can hardly be called medical. Anyway I couldn't take Silberer into the *Jahrbuch* until the January number. For this reason I am not putting up any serious opposition but merely wanted to express (most respectfully) my opinion that papers of this kind are not quite in the right place in the *Zentralblatt*. If his paper

---

[1] "An die Ortsgruppen," dated Nov. 1911, *Zentralblatt*, II:4 (Jan. 1912), 230–31 (*Bulletin*); in it Jung makes the same points as in this paragraph.

has already been lying around a long time its early publication would be desirable.

Rank's "Lohengrin" is excellent.[2] The next *Jahrbuch* will include three things of Silberer's,[3] among them the paper Bleuler objected to for some unaccountable reason; I really can't find anything offensive in it. Pfister will bring his next installment;[4] Sadger speaks of mucus eroticism,[5] with ill-concealed moral indignation. Sachs[6] is in it too. Zürich is represented not only by Pfister but by two *very* scientific items[7] which should lend a quite special cachet to the *Jahrbuch* from the standpoint of the official, well-behaved (censored) consciousness.

My second part[8] is not yet finished; I must in any case postpone it till January because of the bulk of the current *Jahrbuch*.

Not a word from Specht—clear proof of the seriousness of his intentions. I am shedding no tears for Hirschfeld.

Otherwise all is well with us. Kindest regards,

Most sincerely yours, DR. JUNG

From Emma Jung

My dear Professor Freud,   Küsnacht, 6 November [1911][1]

Your nice kind letter has relieved me of anxious doubts, for I was afraid that in the end I had done something stupid. Now I am naturally very glad and thank you with all my heart for your friendly reception of my letter, and particularly for the goodwill you show to all of us.

---

[2] *Die Lohengrinsage: ein Beitrage zu ihrer Motivgestaltung und Deutung (Schriften zur angewandten Seelenkunde*, 13; Leipzig).

[3] "Über die Symbolbildung" (see above, 237 J n. 8); also "Über die Behandlung einer Psychose bei Justinus Kerner" and "Symbolik des Erwachens und Schwellensymbolik überhaupt," *Jahrbuch*, III:2 (1911).

[4] See below, 287 J n. 2.

[5] "Haut-, Schleimhaut- und Muskelerotik."

[6] "Traumdeutung und Menschenkenntnis."

[7] Wilhelm Pfenninger, "Untersuchungen über die Konstanz und den Wechsel der psychologischen Konstellation bei Normalen und Frühdementen (Schizophrenen)," and Esther Aptekmann, "Experimentelle Beiträge zur Psychologie des psychogalvanischen Phänomens." Pfenninger (1879–1915) was a physician at the sanatorium at Herisau (Cant. Appenzell) and a member of the Zürich Society. Aptekmann (1881–19—), from Ekaterinoslav (now Dnepropetrovsk), wrote the present work as her M.D. thesis under Bleuler; returned to Russia.

[8] Of "Wandlungen und Symbole der Libido."

---

[1] Holograph lacks year date, but "1911" has been added in another hand. Salutation: *Mein lieber Herr Professor.* / The letter is cited by Jones, II, p. 431/386.

In explanation of my conjecture I would like to tell you, first, that it is not a question at all of things consciously perceived; you didn't even let us sympathize with your toothache, which ordinarily is a perfect justification for even the worst mood. If I talked about "Symbols" it was chiefly because I knew how eagerly Carl was waiting for your opinion; he had often said he was sure you would not approve of it, and for that reason was awaiting your verdict with some trepidation. Of course this was only a residue of the father (or mother) complex which is probably being resolved in this book; for actually Carl, if he holds something to be right, would have no need to worry about anybody else's opinion. So perhaps it is all to the good that you did not react at once so as not to reinforce this father-son relationship.

The second reason was provided by the conversation on the first morning after your arrival, when you told me about your family. You said then that your marriage had long been "amortized," now there was nothing more to do except—die. And the children were growing up and then they become a real worry, and yet this is the only true joy. This made such an impression on me and seemed to me so significant that I had to think of it again and again, and I fancied it was intended just for me because it was meant symbolically at the same time and referred to my husband.

Please don't be angry if I venture to speak again about the "manifest content" of your talk. I wanted to ask then if you are sure that your children would not be helped by analysis. One certainly cannot be the child of a great man with impunity, considering the trouble one has in getting away from ordinary fathers. And when this distinguished father also has a streak of paternalism in him, as you yourself said! Didn't the fracture of your son's leg fit in with this picture? When I asked you about it you said you didn't have time to analyse your children's dreams because you had to earn money so that they could go on dreaming. Do you think this attitude is right? I would prefer to think that one *should not* dream at all, one should live. I have found with Carl also that the imperative "earn money" is only an evasion of something else to which he has resistances. Please forgive me this candour, it may strike you as brazen; but it disturbs my image of you because I somehow cannot bring it into harmony with the other side of your nature, and this matters so much to me. — The thought also occurred to me that it was perhaps on our account that you didn't send your son to study in Zürich; you did speak about it at one time and for us it would naturally have been a great pleasure to see him now and then.

Another thing I must mention is your resignation in science, if one can call it that. You may imagine how overjoyed and honoured I am by the confidence you have in Carl, but it almost seems to me as though you were sometimes giving too much—do you not see in him the follower and fulfiller more than you need? Doesn't one often give much because one wants to keep much?

456

Why are you thinking of giving up already instead of enjoying your well-earned fame and success? Perhaps for fear of letting the right moment for it pass you by? Surely this will never happen *to you*. After all, you are not so old that you could speak now of the "way of regression," what with all these splendid and fruitful ideas you have in your head! Besides, the man who has discovered the living fountain of ps. a. (or don't you believe it is one?) will not grow old so quickly.

No, you should rejoice and drink to the full the happiness of victory after having struggled for so long. And do not think of Carl with a father's feeling: "He will grow, but I must dwindle," but rather as one human being thinks of another, who like you has his own law to fulfill.

Don't be angry with me.

With warm love and veneration, EMMA JUNG

280 F

Dear friend,   12 November 1911, Vienna, IX. Berggasse 19

Thank you for your letter and parcel. I am busy enough again to have been able to put off answering until Sunday.

I have passed on your wishes or orders to Stekel, who ought normally to get his instructions directly from you. I find it quite justified that you should make your influence felt through your budgetary prerogative. I had been wanting to provide you with an official means of pressure on the *Zentralblatt*. This design was frustrated at the Congress by our good but rather obtuse Stegmann; he was punished by having to put forward the proposal himself on the occasion of our farcical elections. I ceded to his objection, because it seemed to me that as long as the Viennese still included the Adler group they could not be made to abandon their local patriotism entirely. But it is still my aim to see the control of all our periodicals concentrated in your hands. I have put in a word for the subsidizing of Silberer's paper—not for Stekel's but for Silberer's sake. We have asked him if he is willing to wait until the paper can be published in the *Jahrbuch*. If so, you will receive it immediately; if not, we shall set something else aside and publish it at once in the *Zentralblatt*. The whole affair, it now dawns on me, was a superfluous sensation, cooked up by Stekel. When he interferes with you, I beg you never to suppose that I have anything to do with it. You can't imagine how he poisons the whole undertaking for me. Every time I think of him the old litany comes to mind:

"Me piget, pudet, poenitet, taedet, atque miseret."[1]

But I have decided to get along with him.

In my opinion the *Jahrbuch* has no reason to fear the competition of the *Zentralblatt*. The two journals are not adequate to our needs. Of course you are right in saying that in the *Zentralblatt* we should in the main pursue didactic aims, but we are short of contributors. Stekel's writing is too superficial, I am unable to be popular and simple, and we have no other writers. However, I am starting a series of technical and educational articles in the third number. The first: The Handling of Dream-Interpretation in ΨA;[2] second: Observations on the Dynamics of Transference,[3] etc. But a textbook in separate chapters will have to be done by someone else.

I have made no headway with the new non-medical journal. Heller won't publish it either. But I still don't want to abandon the plan.

So much for business. Of science I have still less to say. The Society wants to prepare a second volume of the "Wiener Diskussionen": On Onanism.[4] At the last meeting Fräulein Spielrein spoke up for the first time;[5] she was very intelligent and methodical. — Some ucs. daemon has thus far prevented me from asking you whether you know Storfer of Zürich,[6] whose essay on the special importance of parricide[7]

[1] "I feel disgust, shame, regret, weariness, and pity."—Perhaps a classroom formula for remembering these five impersonal Latin verbs, whose logical subject goes into the accusative and object into the genitive case. Source untraced.

[2] "Die Handhabung der Traumdeutung in der Psychoanalyse," *Zentralblatt*, II:3 (Dec. 1911) = SE XII.

[3] "Zur Dynamik der Übertragung," *Zentralblatt*, II:4 (Jan. 1912) = SE XII. This and the preceding were the first of Freud's "Papers on Technique."

[4] The Vienna Society devoted nine sessions to discussions of masturbation, from 22 Nov. 11 to 12 Apr. 12. They were published later that year as a pamphlet by Bergmann: *Die Onanie*, with fourteen contributions (Diskussionen der Wiener Psychoanalytischen Vereinigung, no. 2). Freud gave the epilogue and wrote an introduction (see "Contributions to a Discussion on Masturbation," SE XII). No. 1 of the Diskussionen, *Über den Selbstmord, insbesondere den Schülerselbstmord*, had been published in 1910; the discussions had taken place in the Vienna Society on 20 and 27 Apr. 10. (See Freud, "Contributions to a Discussion on Suicide," SE XI.)

[5] In a discussion, led by Stekel, of the supposed timelessness of the unconscious. See *Zentralblatt*, II:8 (May 1912), 476.

[6] Adolf Josef Storfer (1888–1944), originally from Rumania; after 1920, managing director of the International Psychoanalytischer Verlag, co-editor of the Gesammelte Schriften of Freud and of *Imago*, and editor of *Die Psychoanalytische*

I published in the last number. I might also be indiscreet enough to ask whether our professor of archaeology, who ran out on me after the first session, has been to see you in the past year. I have heard that he went to Zürich. The reading for my psychology of religion is going slowly. One of the nicest works I have read (again), is that of a well-known author on the "Transformations and Symbols of the Libido." In it many things are so well-expressed that they seem to have taken on definitive form and in this form impress themselves on the memory. Sometimes I have a feeling that his horizon has been too narrowed by Christianity. And sometimes he seems to be more above the material than in it. But it is the best thing this promising author has written, up to now, though he will do still better. In the section about the two modes of thought I deplore his wide reading. I should have liked him to say everything in his own words. Every thinker has his own jargon and all these translations are tedious..

Not least, I am delighted by the many points of agreement with things I have already said or would *like* to say. Since you yourself are this author, I shall continue more directly and make an admission: it is a torment to me to think, when I conceive an idea now and then, that I may be taking something away from you or appropriating something that might just as well have been acquired by you. When this happens, I feel at a loss; I have begun several letters offering you various ideas and observations for your own use, but I never finish them because this strikes me as even more indiscreet and undesirable than the contrary procedure. Why in God's name did I allow myself to follow you into this field? You must give me some suggestions. But probably my tunnels will be far more subterranean than your shafts and we shall pass each other by, but every time I rise to the surface I shall be able to greet you. "Greetings" is a good cue on which to end this long letter. I need only add a "heartfelt," addressed also to your wife and children.

Yours ever, FREUD

Bewegung. In 1938, when Hitler took over Austria, Storfer changed his first name to Albert and fled to Shanghai, where he edited an anti-Nazi illustrated paper, *Gelbe Post.* With the Japanese invasion he was evacuated to Hong Kong, then to Manila, and finally to Melbourne, Australia, where he earned a living as a factory labourer until his death.

7 *Zur Sonderstellung des Vatermordes (Schriften zur angewandten Seelenkunde,* 12; 1911).

281 J

1003 Seestrasse, Küsnach-Zürich,

Dear Professor Freud,   13 November 1911

I am writing a few words in haste. Enclosed is a paper by Bleuler,[1] inflammatory abstinence stuff which he wants to put in the *Jahrbuch* in reply to Ferenczi.[2] It also contains some completely false statements quite apart from the usual fanatic bellowings. Do you feel like adding a few words? Or should Ferenczi take up the polemic?[3] It is not to my taste to have such things in the *Jahrbuch*. Perhaps *you* might be able to persuade Bleuler to withdraw certain statements— his criticism really does go too far.

Most sincerely yours, J U N G

282 J

1003 Seestrasse, Küsnach-Zürich,

Dear Professor Freud,   14 November 1911

Many thanks for your very nice letter which I have just received. However, the outlook for me is very gloomy if you too get into the psychology of religion. You are a dangerous rival—if one has to speak of rivalry. Yet I think it has to be this way, for a natural development cannot be halted, nor should one try to halt it. Our personal differences will make our work different. You dig up the precious stones, but I have the "degree of extension."[1] As you know, I always have to proceed from the outside to the inside and from the whole to the part. I would find it too upsetting to let large tracts of human knowledge lie there neglected. And because of the difference in our working methods we shall undoubtedly meet from time to time in unexpected places. Naturally you will be ahead of me in certain respects but this won't matter much since you have anticipated by far the greatest part already. It is difficult only at first to accustom oneself to this thought. Later one comes to accept it. I am diligently at work on my second part but can no longer get it into the next *Jahrbuch*.

[1] "Alkohol und Neurosen," *Jahrbuch*, III:2 (1911).
[2] "Über die Rolle der Homosexualität in der Pathogenese der Paranoia," *Jahrbuch*, III:1 (1911). For the point at issue, see below, 284 F.
[3] He did: "Alkohol und Neurosen: Antwort auf die Kritik von Herrn Prof. Dr. E. Bleuler," *Jahrbuch*, III:2 (1911).

[1] English in original.

Storfer is known to me. At one time he was interned in Burghölzli because of an infantile suicide attempt (diagnosis: schizophrenia). My guess is that he is giving the local representatives of ΨA a wide berth for this reason. Naturally this is a great secret.

The professor of archaeology you write about has *never* been with me. At the moment my practice has dwindled to a trickle too, which is fine with me. Riklin hasn't much to do either, which is *not* so fine.

In my second part I have got down to a fundamental discussion of the libido theory. That passage in your Schreber analysis where you ran into the libido problem (loss of libido = loss of reality) is one of the points where our mental paths cross. In my view the concept of libido as set forth in the *Three Essays* needs to be supplemented by the genetic factor to make it applicable to Dem. praec.

Deuticke is complaining that I print dissertations in the *Jahrbuch*. I myself haven't much use for experimental studies any more, though two of them[2] will appear in the next number. I can cut down on them. But papers like Spielrein's[3] are worth including. Perhaps you will give me your views. Deuticke feels that the sales of the *Jahrbuch* would fall off if dissertations were included. (Vol. I of my *Diagnostic Association Studies* has even gone into a second edition.[4])

I am sorry to hear the new journal is meeting with difficulties. I don't feel too sorry so far as the *Jahrbuch* is concerned, for with Rank I would be losing a good collaborator because of the new journal. The material now coming in, at least from Zürich, is not an adequate substitute. Bleuler's stubborn opposition is doing a lot of harm since he influences none of his large circle of students in our favour. I am hoping to get Pastor Keller[5] to write something soon.

Did you send your review of Stekel's *Language of Dreams* direct to Deuticke? Bleuler's alcohol polemic is, I trust, already in your hands.

All's well here except for the frightful cases that loom ahead: I am supposed to analyse *Pfister's wife*! I shall resist as long and as fiercely as I possibly can. These days I'm getting practically nothing but divorce cases. To hell with them!

On this note of imprecation, to which I can hardly add a "heartfelt," I bid you adieu.

With best regards, JUNG

[2] See above, 279 J n. 7.
[3] See above, 259 J n. 2.
[4] 1911; unrevised.
[5] See above, 133 J n. 4.

From Emma Jung

Dear Professor Freud,   Küsnacht, 14 November [1911][1]

You were really annoyed by my letter, weren't you? I was too, and now I am cured of my megalomania and am wondering why the devil the unconscious had to make you, of all people, the victim of this madness. And here I must confess, very reluctantly, that you are right: my last letter, specially the tone of it, was really directed to the father-imago, which should of course be faced without fear. This thought never entered my head; I thought that, knowing the transference side of my father-attitude towards you, it would all be quite clear and do me no harm. After I had thought so long before writing to you and had, so I believed, fully understood my own motives, the unconscious has now played another trick on me, with particular finesse: for you can imagine how delighted I am to have made a fool of myself in front of you. I can only pray and hope that your judgment will not prove too severe.

There is one thing, however, I must vigorously defend myself against, and that is the way you take my "amiable carpings," as you call them. Firstly I do not mean at all that Carl should set no store by your opinion; it goes without saying that one recognizes an authority, and if one cannot it is only a sign of over-compensated insecurity. So that is not what I mean, it was only the rest of it that made him anxious and uncertain which seemed superfluous to me. Truth to tell, I must confess that I have missed the mark here too, without suspecting it. Lately Carl has been analysing his attitude to his work and has discovered some resistances to it. I had connected these misgivings about Part II with his constant worry over what you would say about it, etc. It seemed out of the question that he could have resistances to his own work; but now it appears that this fear of your opinion was only a pretext for not going on with the self-analysis which this work in fact means. I realize that I have thus projected something from my immediate neighbourhood into distant Vienna and am vexed that it is always the nearest thing that one sees worst.

You have also completely misunderstood my admittedly uncalled-for meddling in your family affairs. Truthfully I didn't mean to cast a shadow on your children. I know they have turned out well and have never doubted it in the least. I hope you don't seriously believe that I wanted to say they were "doomed to be degenerate." I have written nothing that could even remotely mean anything of the sort. I know that with your children it is a matter of physical illnesses, but just wanted to raise the question whether these physical symptoms might not be somehow psychically conditioned, so that there might for instance be a reduced power of resistance. Since I have made some very astonishing discoveries in myself in this respect and

[1] Holograph lacks year date, but "1911" has been added in another hand.

do not consider myself excessively degenerate or markedly hysterical, I thought similar phenomena possible with other people too. I shall be grateful for enlightenment.

That you should think it worthwhile to discuss your most personal affairs with me is something for which I thank you with all my heart. What you tell me sounds so convincing that I simply have to believe it, although much in me struggles against it. But I must admit that you have the experience and I do not, consequently I am unable to make any convincing rejoinders. You are quite right about one thing, though: despite everything and everybody, the whole affair is only a blessing in clumsy disguise which I beg you to forgive.

Please write nothing of this to Carl; things are going badly enough with me as it is.

EMMA JUNG

283 F

Dear friend,   14 November 1911, Vienna, IX. Berggasse 19

It gives me pleasure to inform you that the new ΨA journal[1] was founded yesterday by Sachs and Rank as editors, Heller as publisher, and myself. The first number is to appear in mid March, 1912. I am counting on your benevolence towards the new-born child, and on your support as well. For it is another of the possessions that I hope to pass on to you one day.

Dr. von Köhler[2] from Vevey (Monrepos) called on me today. He, de Montet,[3] who is his chief, and a Dr. Imboden[4] (from some other place) are well informed and regard themselves as staunch supporters. He spoke of still others and told me that Weber[5] in Geneva

---

[1] *Imago.* See below, 293 F n. 1, and 306 F n. 5.

[2] Egon von Köhler (1886–1938), Austrian physician on the staff of the sanatorium Mon Repos, near Vevey, on Lake Geneva. Later privatdocent in psychiatry, Geneva University.

[3] Karl Imboden (1880–1941), psychiatrist at the cantonal hospital, St. Gallen; joined the Zürich Society.

[4] Charles de Montet (1881–1951), privatdocent in psychiatry, Lausanne University; many publications on psychoanalysis. He had delivered the report on the neurosis theory at the Brussels Congress in 1910; see above, 181 J n. 5, and below, 285 J n. 1.

[5] Rodolphe Weber (1866–1937), professor of psychiatry, Geneva University; later, director of the University. His monograph on "Petite Psychologie" (Short Psy-

has been transformed from a Saul into a Paul. I suggested that they join the Zürich organization and in time set up a group in French Switzerland. Geneva would then become our gateway to France.

As you see, the omens are favourable.

With kind regards,

Yours ever, FREUD

284 F

Dear friend,   16 November 1911, Vienna, IX. Berggasse 19

(Strictly business.)

I have not yet written the review of Stekel and would be grateful if you could release me from the task or grant me a delay. I am consumed by the new project.

Deuticke is being petty again. What difference does it make whether a contribution is a dissertation or not? If we—especially you —like it, that should be enough. Spielrein's paper certainly belongs in the *Jahrbuch* and nowhere else.

———

You are losing nothing by Rank's elevation to the post of editor. When he writes something purely Ψanalytical, he will always contribute it to the *Jahrbuch*, and you couldn't have taken his Lohengrin, for instance. Besides, the *Jahrbuch*, the *Zentralblatt* and the newborn child must not be three individuals, but three organs of a single biological unit.

———

Bleuler's article on alcohol is a problem. We can't very well find fault with him for the inaccuracy of Drenkhahn's figures,[1] and apart from that he is consistent from his own point of view. Furthermore, this is certainly his most sensitive spot, and neither you nor I have anything to gain by increasing the tension. Ferenczi, on the other hand, says he doesn't mind the criticism. The most I could do would

chology), *Archives internationales de Neurologie*, Jan. 1912, was dedicated to Freud.

[1] See above, 163 F postscript (in addenda).

be to point out to Bleuler that he is mistaken in the motivation he imputes to Ferenczi, who is no more of a drinker than I am.

The *Zentralblatt* will surely take Bleuler's article if the *Jahrbuch* does not, although Stekel is always complaining of lack of space. I recommend a counter-concession on your part. What should I do with the manuscript? Return it to you or send it to Ferenczi first, so he can publish a short reply at the same time? I am keeping it pending your decision.

As I hear through Stekel, Silberer does not wish to take the "Categories of Symbolism" away from the *Zentralblatt*. It will be published in No. 4.

Your analysing Pfister's wife strikes me as a bad sign. But that is no longer business.

Undismayed by your bad humour, I send you my kindest regards.

Yours, FREUD

285 J

1003 Seestrasse, Küsnach-Zürich,
Dear Professor Freud,   24 November 1911

I very much hope that the symptoms of my late ill humour have not had any bad aftereffects. I was furious because of something that had happened in my working arrangements. But I won't bother you with that, and will only bring you the good news that Pfister's wife *refuses* to be analysed. This will probably start the ball rolling, and, we must hope, save Pfister from the infantilism that is stultifying him. It will be a hard struggle.

I must congratulate you on the birth of the new journal. I'm afraid I must declare myself incapable of making an inaugural contribution. All my time and energy must be devoted to my Part II.

You had best send that accursed paper of Bleuler's to Ferenczi. Let him react to it *without affect*, stressing, perhaps, the *ethically neutral* standpoint of psychoanalysis as contrasted with Bleuler's sorties into practical hygiene.

Thank you for taking care of Silberer's paper.

I don't know anything about Dr. v. Köhler. The staunch support of de Montet strikes me as very suspicious, seeing that a short while ago he expressed himself in a most peremptory manner about interpretations and sexuality. He is a singularly arrogant fellow. (You can get some idea of his tone from the report on the Brussels Congress in the *Journal für Psychologie und Neurologie.*)[1]

I am writing this letter piecemeal. In the meantime there has been the Meeting of Swiss Psychiatrists,[2] at which Riklin, Maeder, and others including myself delivered lectures on ΨA. Bleuler had previously written Riklin a letter warning him about "invitations," as otherwise there might be "demonstrations." The fact that 5 of the 7 lectures were on ΨA has, I have since discovered, incurred the displeasure of Frank and his confrères. They have kicked up a fuss with Bleuler and he has made himself their mouthpiece; he even suspects that we chose a larger hall in order to invite heaven knows what sort of people. As you may imagine, this letter exasperated me, particularly as, while I was in St. Gallen, Bleuler suddenly descended on Pfister requesting him not to do any more analyses. Once again Bleuler has allowed himself to be worked up because of his everlasting opposition to me. He has never attempted to talk with me about it. All my efforts to win him over have been a total failure. He just *doesn't want* to see it my way.

Maeder has now had a friendly private talk with Maier, hoping to persuade him to show his colours. He often attends our meetings, and we would find it appropriate if he eventually joined our Society, seeing that he takes advantage of it anyway. After this talk Maier evidently went to work on Bleuler, and now Bleuler has suddenly announced his resignation. I enclose Maeder's letter. The blue-marked passage refers to my leaving the last meeting of the Psychiatric Society rather early, because I was tired and thought the proceedings were finished except for two lectures. Apparently this was not so, for Frank, quite unexpectedly, came back to his motion (which had been turned down the previous day) that the next meeting be held in the autumn jointly with the International Society for Psychotherapy, which is to meet in Zürich. I don't know how it happened, but incredibly enough the motion was carried. I have no intention of speaking at this joint meeting, for the vulgarity of the International Society disgusts me. President

---

[1] The proceedings of the Congress, published in the *Journal*, XVII (1910/11), supplement, included de Montet's report, "Problèmes théoriques et pratiques de la psychanalyse," 377–401.

[2] The Society of Swiss Psychiatrists held its winter meeting in Zürich 25–26 Nov. Psychoanalytical lectures were given by Jung, on Contributions to Child Psychology; Maeder, on the Dream Function; and Gincburg, on the Analysis of an Abortive Suicide.—From *Zentralblatt*, II:4 (Jan. 1912), *Bulletin* section.

Vogt[3] [. . .] All through the meeting Bleuler stuck by Frank and fell over backwards to avoid anything psychoanalytical. A week ago, before all this happened, I tried to win Bleuler over with every conceivable inveiglement and was snubbed again. There's simply nothing to be done about it. He just won't budge. Pfister was taken as a pretext, and he has indeed been careless with certain remarks he made about a doctor here who has his knife into us anyway. Bleuler would rather fall out with us than with those pipsqueaks. Shame on him!

With kindest regards,

Most sincerely yours, JUNG

From Emma Jung

My dear Professor Freud,   Küsnacht, 24 November 1911

Heartfelt thanks for your letter. Please don't worry, I am not always as despondent as I was in my last letter. I was afraid you were angry with me or had a bad opinion of me; that was what made me so downhearted, especially because my main complex was hit. Usually I am quite at one with my fate and see very well how lucky I am, but from time to time I am tormented by the conflict about how I can hold my own against Carl. I find I have no friends, all the people who associate with us really only want to see Carl, except for a few boring and to me quite uninteresting persons.

Naturally the women are all in love with him, and with the men I am instantly cordoned off as the wife of the father or friend. Yet I have a strong need for people and Carl too says I should stop concentrating on him and the children, but what on earth am I to do? What with my strong tendency to autoerotism it is very difficult, but also objectively it is difficult because I can never compete with Carl. In order to emphasize this I usually have to talk extra stupidly when in company.

I do my best to get transferences and if they don't turn out as I wished I am always very depressed. You will now understand why I felt so bad at the thought that I had lost your favour, and I was also afraid Carl might notice something. At any rate he now knows about the exchange of letters, as he was astonished to see one of your letters addressed to me; but I have revealed only a little of their content. Will you advise me, dear Herr Professor, and if necessary dress me down a bit? I am ever so grateful to you for your sympathy.

With warmest greetings to you and yours,

EMMA JUNG

[3] See above, 181 J n. 5.

467

286 F

Dear friend,   30 November 1911, Vienna, IX. Berggasse 19

Two days ago Bleuler notified me of his resignation and his reasons for it; his letter ends as follows: "I venture to hope that in view of what has happened you will regard this resignation as a self-evident and necessary step, and above all that it will not affect our personal relations in any way." This sentence authorized me to write a critical answer. My answer was already formulated yesterday and was sent off today—uninfluenced by your letter which came this morning.

I do not know whether I have handled the matter for the best, but the "last trouser-button of my patience had snapped."[1] It may have been impolitic, but one cannot put up with abuse for ever. And possibly his masochism was only waiting for a good whipping. Now he has had it; rest assured of that, though I cannot send you the letter as you have sent me Maeder's, whose sincerity must be evident to any reader. What Bleuler will do now I don't know and I refuse to worry about it any longer. ΨA will manage without him and in the end he will not be very happy between two stools. If, as seems possible, he should now direct his resentment against me and try to come to terms with you and Maeder, I know you will do your best to meet him halfway. But Maier in any case must go.

Thank you for entrusting the matter of Bleuler's alcohol article to me. I shall send it off to Ferenczi tomorrow and at the same time pass on your advice. It will then be returned to you or sent directly to Deuticke, depending on your instructions to Ferenczi.

Riklin is taking his time with his secretarial duties. I see there is hope again for Pfister. Half measures never work in the long run.

I don't know if you ought to stay away from the meeting next autumn. It would be a good opportunity to teach the enemy good manners on your own ground, and perhaps to settle accounts with another Vogt.[2]

Here nothing much has happened. The meetings have been going

---

[1] Holograph: *"alle Knöpfe gerissen an der Hose der Geduld."* From Heine, "Jehuda ben Halevy IV," in *Hebräische Melodien*, Book III of the collection *Romanzero* (1851).

[2] The reference is not only to Oskar Vogt, but also to William Tell's adversary, the Austrian bailiff (*Vogt*), Gessler, in Schiller's drama.

quite well; Dr. and Frau Stegmann[3] have been attending. One should honour an old woman, but not marry her; really, love is for the young. Fräulein Spielrein read a chapter from her paper yesterday[4] (I almost wrote the *ihrer* [her] with a capital "i"), and it was followed by an illuminating discussion. I have hit on a few objections to your [*Ihrer*] (this time I mean it) method of dealing with mythology,[4a] and I brought them up in the discussion with the little girl. I must say she is rather nice and I am beginning to understand. What troubles me most is that Fräulein Spielrein wants to subordinate the psychological material to *bio*logical considerations; this dependency is no more acceptable than a dependency on philosophy, physiology, or brain anatomy. ΨA *farà da se*.[5]

In my work on totemism I have run into all sorts of difficulties, rapids, waterfalls, sand-banks, etc.; I don't know yet if I shall be able to float my craft again. In any event it is going very slowly and time alone will prevent us from colliding or clashing. I read between the lines of your last letter that you have no great desire for interim reports on my work, and you are probably right. But I had to make the offer.

I should be very much interested in knowing what you mean by an extension of the concept of the libido to make it applicable to Dem. pr.[6] I am afraid there is a misunderstanding between us, the same sort of thing as when you once said in an article[7] that to my way of thinking libido is identical with any kind of desire, whereas in reality I hold very simply that there are two basic drives and that only the power behind the sexual drive can be termed libido.

[3] Presumably Dr. Margarete Stegmann (d. after 1920), of Dresden, after 1912 a member of the Berlin Society and a frequent contributor to the *Zentralblatt* and *Zeitschrift*. For her husband, see 218 F n. 15.

[4] "Über Transformation," from "Die Destruktion als Ursache des Werdens," *Jahrbuch*, IV:1 (1912); at the meeting of the Vienna Society. See also below, 288 F, and *Zentralblatt*, II:8 (May 1912).

[4a] At the 29 Nov. meeting of the Vienna Society, in the discussion following Spielrein's paper "On Transformation," Freud remarked, "The presentation . . . provides more opportunity for a critique of Jung because, in his recent mythological studies, he also uses any mythological material whatsoever . . . without selection. . . . Mythological material can be used in this way only when it appears in the original form and not in its derivatives." (*Minutes*, III.)

[5] = "goes by itself." / Passage quoted by Jones, II, p. 501/452.

[6] See above, 282 J.

[7] See "The Freudian Theory of Hysteria" (1908), CW 4, par. 49.

469

This letter must yield to the pressure of time, though I could go on chatting with you about a good many things.

Amid all the vexation a cheerful greeting,

Yours cordially, FREUD

P.S. A fourth edition of the *Everyday Life* is to appear this spring.[8]

287 J *Internationale Psychoanalytische Vereinigung*

Dear Professor Freud, Küsnach-Zürich,[1] 11 December 1911

Again I have kept you waiting because I am unable to get the better of my bad habits.

You will see from the letterhead in what manner I have replied to Bleuler's resignation. We won't let it dampen our spirits. We have accepted five new members in Bleuler's place. No one has followed his example. I suppose he said nothing to you about his co-directorship of the *Jahrbuch*. He knows how to keep his resistance to himself and is all affability with me.

I have given Riklin a piece of my mind. Everything seems to be all right now. He is badly organized in the head and will need Lord knows how many more years to mature.

The new *Jahrbuch* has been held up by the bother of making line-cuts of the cryptograms for Pfister's paper.[2] Correcting Bjerre's paper[3] gave me an awful lot of work, but it's a fine thing. I'll gladly take Spielrein's new paper[4] for the first number of *Jahrbuch* 1912. It demands a great deal of revision, but then the little girl has always been very demanding with me. However, she's worth it. I am glad you don't think badly of her.

So far as possible I shall take note of your objections to my method of dealing with mythology. I should be grateful for some detailed remarks so that I can turn your criticism to account in my second part. I know, of course, that Spielrein operates too much with biology. But

---

[8] Holograph: *Herbst*, "autumn," crossed out and *Frühjahr*, "spring," written above it, with exclamation point.

---

[1] Printed letterhead. For its entire text, see facsimile of 330 J.

[2] "Die psychologische Enträtselung der religiösen Glossolalie und der automatischen Kryptographie," *Jahrbuch*, III:1 & 2 (1911).

[3] See above, 263 J n. 3.

[4] See above, 286 F n. 4.

she didn't learn that from me, it is home-grown. If ever I adduce similar arguments I do so *faute de mieux*. I am all in favour of keeping ΨA within its own boundaries, but I think it a good thing to make occasional incursions into other territories and to look at our subject through a different pair of spectacles. Naturally I don't know how far Spielrein has gone in her new paper.

If in my last letter I showed no (apparent) interest in your study of totemism, that is due solely to the Bleuler affair which left me no time to breathe. Naturally I am extremely interested in the progress of your work; it will be of extraordinary importance to me also, even though, unlike you, I am in the habit of proceeding from the outside in.

As for the libido problem, I must confess that your remark in the Schreber analysis, p. 65, 3,[5] has set up booming reverberations. This remark, or rather the doubt expressed therein, has resuscitated all the difficulties that have beset me throughout the years in my attempt to apply the libido theory to Dem. praec. The loss of the reality function in D. pr. cannot be reduced to repression of libido (defined as sexual hunger). Not by me, at any rate. Your doubt shows me that in your eyes as well the problem cannot be solved in this way. I have now put together all the thoughts on the libido concept that have come to me over the years, and devoted a chapter to them in my second part. I have got down to a fundamental discussion of the problem and arrived at a solution which I am afraid I cannot discuss *in extenso* here. The essential point is that I try to replace the descriptive concept of libido by a *genetic* one. Such a concept covers not only the recent-sexual libido but all those forms of it which have long since split off into organized activities. A wee bit of biology was unavoidable here. My motto to the first part will protect me. One must after all take *some* risks. I wanted to make up for my abstention from theory in my "Psychic Conflicts in a Child." You must let my interpretation work on you as a whole to feel its full impact. Mere fragments are barely intelligible.

Congratulations on the new edition of *Everyday Life*!

Mighty rumblings in Zürich over ΨA. The Keplerbund* is sponsoring a public lecture against this abomination. Protest meetings are afoot!

What other news I have from Germany is sickening.

[5] "Notes on a Case of Paranoia," SE XII, p. 75, par. (3). Jung developed the idea expressed here in "Wandlungen und Symbole der Libido," Part II, chap. 2, pars. 1–2 = *Symbols of Transformation*, CW 5, pars. 190–91. Freud replied in "On Narcissism" (1914), SE XIV, pp. 79–80.

No further criticism[6] of the contents of the new *Jahrbuch* has come to my ears.

All is well with us. Kindest regards,

Most sincerely yours, JUNG

* Papists![7]

288 F

Dear friend,   17 December 1911, Vienna, IX. Berggasse 19

I am very much impressed by your stationery. Opposition is strengthening the ties between us. Maybe Bleuler will treat us better than before, now that he has become an outsider. That would be in keeping with his ambivalence, i.e. his compulsive character.

I am all in favour of your attacking the libido question and I myself am expecting much light from your efforts. Often, it seems, I can go for a long while without feeling the need to clarify an obscure point, and then one day I am compelled to by the pressure of facts or by the influence of someone else's ideas.

My study of totemism and other work are not going well. I have very little time, and to draw on books and reports is not at all the same as drawing on the richness of one's own experience. Besides, my interest is diminished by the conviction that I am already in possession of the truths I am trying to prove. Such truths, of course, are of no use to anyone else. I can see from the difficulties I encounter in this work that I was not cut out for inductive investigation, that my whole make-up is intuitive, and that in setting out to establish the purely empirical science of ΨA I subjected myself to an extraordinary discipline.

This and all sorts of random influences have quite prevented me from working this week; all I can do is wait for better days.

For the next *Jahrbuch*—January 1912 (allegedly)—I am planning a short article "On the Universal Tendency to Debasement in the

---

[6] Cf. Deuticke's complaint about dissertations, 282 J. The issue was published in Mar. 1912; see below, 305 J.

[7] Holograph: *ultramontan!* written between the lines. / The Keplerbund was founded in 1907 at Frankfurt a. M. by Eberhard Dennert (1861–1942), German natural philosopher, as an answer to the Monistenbund (see above, 217 J n. 2). Its aim was to reconcile natural science and Christian faith. / For the Keplerbund lecture, see below, 293 F n. 7.

Sphere of Love," No. 2 of my *Contributions to the Psychology of Love*.[1]

You have asked for an example of my objections to the most obvious method of exploiting mythology.[2] I shall give you the example I used in the debate.[3] Fräulein Spielrein had cited the Genesis story of the apple as an instance of woman seducing man. But in all likelihood the myth of Genesis is a wretched, tendentious distortion devised by an apprentice priest, who as we now know stupidly wove two independent sources into a single narrative (as in a dream). It is not impossible that there are two sacred trees because he found *one* tree in each of the two sources. There is something very strange and singular about the creation of Eve. — Rank recently called my attention to the fact that the Bible story may quite well have reversed the original myth. Then everything would be clear; Eve would be Adam's mother, and we should be dealing with the well-known motif of mother-incest, the punishment for which, etc. Equally strange is the motif of the woman giving the man an agent of fruitfulness (pomegranate) to eat. But if the story is reversed, we again have something familiar. The man giving the woman a fruit to eat is an old marriage rite (cf. the story of Proserpina condemned to remain in Hades as Pluto's wife). Consequently I hold that the surface versions of myths cannot be used uncritically for comparison with our ΨAtical findings. We must find our way back to their latent, original forms by a comparative method that eliminates the distortions they have undergone in the course of their history. The little Spielrein girl has a very good head and I can corroborate the fact that she is very demanding.

The stream of patients from all over the world that made me feel so secure last year, because it enabled me to keep all our Vienna analysts supplied, has failed to materialize. I am almost entirely dependent on Vienna and the Austrian provinces; if the wolves go hungry, I'm afraid they will soon begin to howl. Frau C——, whom I hope to straighten out for Pfister, has not been heard from for a fortnight; she left Pfister on the 3rd. Of course she is right, because she

---

[1] "Über die allgemeinste Erniedrigung des Liebeslebens," *Jahrbuch*, IV:1 (1912). No. 1 was "A Special Type of Choice of Object Made by Men" (see above, 209 F n. 6, last item but one); with No. 3, "Das Tabu der Virginität" (= "The Taboo of Virginity"), these essays were published in 1918 under the common title "Beiträge zur Psychologie des Liebeslebens" = "Contributions to the Psychology of Love," SE XI.

[2] This paragraph quoted in Jones, II, pp. 501f./452f.

[3] At the Vienna Society meeting of 29 Nov., after Spielrein's lecture; see above, 286 F n. 4.

is beyond any possibility of therapy, but it is still her duty to sacrifice herself to science. If she gets here, I can turn some other patients over to my young men. It can't be denied that our great cause looks rather pitiful at the moment.

So let us go on toiling. We too have a destiny to fulfil.

I greet you and your whole family most warmly,

Yours ever, FREUD

289 F

Dear friend,   28 December 1911, Vienna, IX. Berggasse 19

I have received a splendid, really illuminating paper about colour audition from an intelligent lady Ph.D.[1] It solves the riddle with the help of our ΨA. It is fifty-two pages long, too much for the *Zentralblatt*, which is at present cramped for space. Can you use it in the *Jahrbuch*? One reason why I think it would be suitable for the *Jahrbuch* is that Bleuler made his debut[2] with a study of this problem.

Frau C—— is back again. Once again I shall have to be tolerant and patient. It is all settled with Pfister; your interpretation[3] was unjustified; they were really at a loss, they had to consult me.

This letter will arrive just in time to bring you and yours my kind regards before the year ends.

Here's to 1912,

Yours, FREUD

[1] Hermine von Hug-Hellmuth (1871–1924), one of the earliest women members of the Vienna Society; teacher and lay analyst distinguished for her work with children. She was murdered by her nephew, a patient. For details, see Helene Deutsch, *Confrontations with Myself: An Epilogue* (New York, 1973), pp. 136f. / The paper was "Über Farbenhören; Ein Versuch, das Phänomen auf Grund der psycho-analytischen Methode zu erklären," *Imago*, I:3 (May 1912).

[2] Bleuler and Karl Lehmann, *Zwangsmässige Lichtempfindungen durch Schall und verwandte Erscheinungen auf dem Gebiete der anderen Sinnesempfindungen* (Leipzig, 1881).

[3] In a missing letter of Jung's?

290 F

Dear friend,   31 December 1911, Vienna, IX. Berggasse 19

I am writing to you once again this year, because I can't always wait for you to answer and prefer to write when I have time and am in the mood.

Your little piece from Rascher's *Jahrbuch*[1] has arrived as a New Year's greeting. It is a powerful, rough-shod thing which, I hope, will make its way with the readers. But who is Rascher?[2] A publisher? And his *Jahrbuch*? Is it something on the order of the old calendars with articles to edify and inspire us for a new year about which we know nothing?

The last weeks of the year have brought me all sorts of vexations. All in all, when I stop to think of it, it has not been a brilliant year for our cause. The Congress in Weimar was good, so were the days preceding it in Zürich; in Klobenstein I had a brief spell of productivity. The rest has been rather on the minus side. But I suppose there must be such periods.

Under separate cover you will receive a first batch of Technique,[3] which you will probably find disappointingly meagre. The next[4] will be no better, merely less clear. The things I write to order, without inner necessity, as has been the case with these articles, never come out right. My second *Contribution to the Psychology of Love* is finished and will go out to you as soon as I have your answer about the *audition colorée*, that is, with it or by itself. It ends on a pessimistic note. Since I wrote it on gloomy days and am not sure of my objectivity, I have appended an attenuating conclusion. The piece was done a year ago, when my ideas had not really matured.

Frau C—— has told me all sorts of things about you and Pfister, if you can call the hints she drops "telling"; I gather that neither of

---

[1] "Neue Bahnen der Psychologie," *Raschers Jahrbuch fur Schweizer Art und Kunst*, III (1912) = "New Paths in Psychology," CW 7, appendix (original version of *Die Psychologie der unbewussten Prozesse* = "On the Psychology of the Unconscious," one of the *Two Essays*).

[2] The old Zürich bookselling firm of Rascher et Cie., since 1901 headed by Max Rascher (1883–1962), became a publishing house in 1908 and Jung's publisher in 1917 with *Die Psychologie der unbewussten Prozesse*; continued to serve as his official and virtually exclusive publisher until the liquidation of the firm in 1970, after which Walter Verlag, of Olten, became the publisher of Jung's writings.

[3] "The Handling of Dream-Interpretation"; see above, 280 F n. 2.

[4] "The Dynamics of Transference"; see above, 280 F n. 3.

you has yet acquired the necessary objectivity in your practice, that
you still get involved, giving a good deal of yourselves and expecting
the patient to give something in return. Permit me, speaking as the
venerable old master,[5] to say that this technique is invariably ill-ad-
vised and that it is best to remain reserved and purely receptive. We
must never let our poor neurotics drive us crazy. I believe an article on
"counter-transference" is sorely needed; of course we could not publish it, we should have to circulate copies among ourselves.

If you really feel any resentment towards me, there is no need to
use Frau C—— as an occasion for venting it. If she asks you to tell me
about your conversation with her, I beg you, don't let her influence
you or browbeat you; just wait for my next misdeed and have it out
with me directly. My last set-to of this sort was with Ferenczi, who
thought me cold and reserved and complained bitterly about my lack
of affection, but has since fully admitted that he was in the wrong
and that my conduct had been well advised. I don't deny that I like
to be right. All in all, that is a sad privilege, since it is conferred by
age. The trouble with you younger men seems to be a lack of understanding in dealing with your father-complexes.

And now my very best wishes for the year 1912 to the house on the
lake and all its inhabitants.

Yours ever, FREUD

291 J

Villa Spelma,
Dear Professor Freud,   St. Moritz,[1] 2 January 1912

First of all, heartiest New Year wishes to you and yours! May the
new year add many a leaf to the laurel crown of your undying fame
and open new fields for our movement.

I have waited a long time for Frau C—— to inform you, as arranged, about this awkward situation. It has been weighing on my
mind. I don't know what she[2] has told you. This is what happened:
she asked me about her sister, and came to see me. Then she put the

---

[5] Holograph: *würdiger alter Meister*. In "Neue Bahnen der Psychologie," Jung
had used these words to describe Freud, when he paraphrased a passage in Freud's
letter of 29 Nov. 08; see above, 116 F n. 4, and CW 7, 2nd edn., par. 411.

---

[1] Printed letterhead.

[2] Holograph: *Sie*, "you," corrected to *sie*, "she."

crucial question. Sensing a trap, I evaded it as long as I could. It seemed to me that she was not in a fit condition to go back to Vienna. To make things easier for her I told her how disagreeable it was for me to find myself involved. I said she had given me the impression that she expected some sign of encouragement from you, and this seemed like a personal sacrifice on your part. I also told her that I did not pretend my view was right, since I didn't know what was going on. As far as I could make out, I said, all she wanted was a little bit of sympathy which you, for very good reasons best known to yourself, may have withheld. Such sympathy would ease things for the moment, but whether it would lead to good results in the end seemed to me doubtful, to say the least. I myself was unable, often very much *malgré moi*, to keep my distance, because sometimes I couldn't withhold my sympathy, and, since it was there anyway, I gladly offered it to the patient, telling myself that as a human being he was entitled to as much esteem and personal concern as the doctor saw fit to grant him. I told her, further, that this was how it *seemed* to me; I might be mistaken, since my experience could in no way be measured against yours. Afterwards I felt very much annoyed at having allowed myself to be dragged into this discussion. I would gladly have avoided it had not my pity for her wretched condition seduced me into giving her the advantage, even at the risk of sending her off with a flea in her ear. I comforted myself with the thought that, once she was with you, she would soon be on the right track again. My chief concern was to do the right thing and get her back to Vienna, which has in fact been done. I only hope the end justifies the means.

Naturally I would like to take Frau Dr. X.'s paper but must put off definite acceptance until I can estimate the size of the next *Jahrbuch*. We already have a stack of material.

Frau Lou Andreas-Salomé,[3] of Weimar fame, wants to send me a

[3] Lou Andreas-Salomé (1861–1937), born in St. Petersburg, daughter of the Russian general Von Salomé (of French extraction); studied theology in Zürich; friend of Nietzsche (1882); married (1887) to F. C. Andreas, professor of archaeology at Göttingen; 1896, friendship with Rilke, with whom she travelled twice in Russia (1899, 1900); an intimate friend of Bjerre (see above, 225 F n. 4) and, in 1912–13, of the psychoanalyst Victor Tausk (see below, 348 J n. 4). "Frau Lou," as she was often called, remained a psychoanalyst and a close friend of Freud to the end. (See *Sigmund Freud and Lou Andreas-Salomé: Letters*, ed. E. Pfeiffer, tr. W. and E. Robson-Scott, 1972.) The paper on sublimation, which she sent Jung in late March (see below, 307 J) but later took back (313 J), was the one published as "Vom frühen Gottesdienst," *Imago*, II (1913), according to an

paper on "sublimation." This, if it amounts to anything, would be a step towards the "secularization" of the *Jahrbuch*, a step to be taken with great caution but one which would widen the readership and mobilize the intellectual forces in Germany, where Frau Lou enjoys a considerable literary reputation because of her relations with Nietzsche. I would like to hear your views.

I am spending a few days in the Engadin to recuperate from hard work.

With many kind regards and wishes,

Most sincerely yours, JUNG

292 J

1003 Seestrasse, Küsnach-Zürich,

Dear Professor Freud,   9 January 1912

I hope you received my last letter from St. Moritz safely. I have been a niggardly correspondent, having spent a few more days travelling rather breathlessly round Germany visiting various art galleries and improving my education. Today I went back to work.

Bleuler wrote to me that you want to read his manuscript.[1] It will go off to you before long. Keep it until the new issue goes to press, then send it direct to Deuticke.

Stekel has announced a paper on "Religious Symbolism in Dreams."[2] I *urgently* request you to read it beforehand. Since going more deeply into his *Language of Dreams* I find that Stekel's ways rather horrify me. I have no wish to cause him any undiplomatic difficulties. He will accept corrections more readily from you than from me. His superficiality in scientific matters causes difficulties enough as it is.

The "venerable old master" need fear no resentment on my part, especially when he happens to be right. I don't feel in the least put out, nor do I complain of lack of affection like Ferenczi. In this respect you would have more right to complain about me. As regards the counter-transference I am merely a little bit "refractory" and indulge in peculiar fantasies by way of experiment. Pfister's standpoint in this

---

editorial note in the *Freud/Abraham Letters*, Freud 2 May 12. For summary, see Binion, *Frau Lou*, p. 390.

[1] "Das autistische Denken," *Jahrbuch*, IV:1 (1912).
[2] Probably "Ein religiöser Traum," *Zentralblatt*, III (1913).

matter is by no means my own. I am fully convinced that the patient must play the passive part, and that the analyst need never extort anything by means of the counter-transference (on the Christian principle: Look what I've done for you, what will you do for me?). *For me* the cardinal rule is that the analyst himself must possess the freedom which the patient has to acquire in his turn, otherwise the analyst will either have to play possum or, as you say, be driven crazy. I think it is far more a question of our different ways of living than of any disagreement in principle. I do not claim any general validity for my views, so there is no reason for "resentment."

With very best regards,

Most sincerely yours, JUNG

Many thanks for the offprint.[3] For the analyst it is a highly informative and corroborative piece of work. I only wish you would write many more of these fine, instructive things. Though they may seem too simple to you, they are of the greatest value to us.

293 F

Dear friend,   10 January 1912, Vienna, IX. Berggasse 19

I had been racking my brains for a fortnight, wondering why I had received no answer from you—Frau C—— could not have been the reason. Then with happy surprise I found the long awaited word from you in an envelope from the Engadin. And today a letter from Pfister, who assumes that I know you were bitten by a dog and have been in great pain. But I didn't know. I can understand your not writing about it; in a similar situation I would behave in the same way; but now that I know of it, I should prefer to have known right away. The wound must have healed by now, since you yourself have written. I trust there is no reason to worry about the dog.

What you write about the Frau C—— incident almost makes me feel sorry. You mustn't feel guilty towards me; if anything, you might modify your technique a little and show more reserve towards the patient. What the poor thing wants most is an intellectual flirtation that would enable her to forget her illness for a while. I keep cruelly reminding her of it.

---

[3] "The Handling of Dream-Interpretation"; see above, 280 F n. 2. / This postscript was written at the top of the letter, over the heading.

479

Very well; I won't send you Frau Dr. Hellmuth's paper on *Audition colorée*; I have given it to *Imago*, the new journal. The name[1] does not seem to find much favour in Zürich, but we need a handy name that doesn't sound too literary; we found nothing better and perhaps *Imago* has the necessary vagueness. Yesterday we established the contents of the first number. I am contributing the first of three short essays dealing with the analogies between the psychology of primitive peoples and that of neurotics. The first is titled "The Horror of Incest." The others will be called "Emotional Ambivalence" and "Magic and the Omnipotence of Thoughts."[2]

I've just handed my *Contribution to the Psychology of Love*[3] to a helpful member of the family to send off to you.

If you want my opinion of Frau Salomé's offer, here it is: We ought not in principle to decline, provided she contents herself with sublimation and leaves sublimates to the chemists.[4] If it turns out to be idealistic chit-chat, we can reject it politely but firmly.

The "secularization" of ΨA is of no great moment now that we are bringing *Imago* into existence, and there is no need for the *Jahrbuch* to be "stiff and proud." Besides, it seems to me that two recent contributions to ΨA—both most significant—your demonstration of unconscious heredity in symbolism, which amounts to a demonstration of the existence of "innate ideas,"[5] and Ferenczi's proofs of thought-transference, lead us far beyond the original limits of ΨA, and that we should follow. Nor do I wish to hold F. back any longer; let him publish early in 1913[6] but first discuss the matter with you.

---

[1] "The title of the new publication gave us some headaches. . . . Finally my suggestion prevailed and it was called *Imago* after Carl Spitteler's novel in which the tricks and masks of the unconscious, its inroads into consciousness, and its stimulation of the creative powers are presented with consummate mastership."—Hanns Sachs, *Freud, Master and Friend* (Cambridge, Mass., 1944), pp. 65f.

[2] The first essay, "Die Inzestscheu" ("Über einige Übereinstimmungen im Seelenleben der Wilden und der Neurotiker," I), appeared in *Imago*, I:1 (Mar. 1912) = "The Horror of Incest" (*Totem and Taboo*, Some Points of Agreement between the Mental Lives of Savages and Neurotics, I), SE XIII. For the remaining three (sic) parts, see below, 329 F n. 6 and 334 F n. 2.

[3] See above, 288 F n. 1.

[4] Psychological sublimation = *Sublimierung*; in 291 J, Jung quoted Frau Lou's usage *Sublimation*, which is properly a chemical term.

[5] Holograph: "*angeborenen Ideen*," the term used in older psychology. The reference ("your demonstration") is to Jung's "Wandlungen und Symbole der Libido."

[6] Concerning Ferenczi's proofs of thought-transference and his general preoccupation with the occult, see Jones, III, pp. 411–17/384–390. In Dec. 1910 Freud

The choice of one's successor is one of the royal prerogatives. Let us allow our royal science the same privilege.

With kind regards, good wishes and a request for news at an early date.

Yours, FREUD

Many thanks to your dear wife for the fine article about the lecture at the Keplerbund.[7]

294 J

1003 Seestrasse, Küsnach-Zürich,

Dear Professor Freud,   10 January 1912

The enclosed manuscript, partly corrected by me, is the 3rd part of Bjerre's paper.[1] Since it contains many inaccuracies, I would be very glad if you would look through it, suggest certain alterations to Dr. Bjerre, and then publish the paper, or rather this 3rd part, by itself as "Epicritical Remarks," etc. in a later issue. The case itself is good, the theory weak if not wobbly, unnecessarily so because the material permits of a respectable theory.

I shall write to Bjerre accordingly.

Rascher's Jahrbuch is an annual literary publication (art, literature, history, politics, philosophy, etc.) of a specifically Swiss character. My article has already created a sensation.

Kindest regards,

Most sincerely yours, JUNG

---

wrote Ferenczi suggesting he delay publication of whatever he might write on telepathy for a couple of years—until 1913, when he would publish it in the *Jahrbuch*. Ferenczi addressed the Vienna Society on the topic 19 Nov. 13, but, Jones says, "he never did write anything on the subject." See also above, 158 F n. 2 and 254 J n. 6.

[7] On 15 Dec. 1911, Dr. Max Kesselring, neurologist of Zürich, under the auspices of the Keplerbund, gave a public lecture attacking psychoanalysis (*Zentralblatt*, II:8, *Bulletin* section). Also see above, 287 J n. 7.

---

[1] See above, 263 J n. 3. The concluding section of the paper is entitled "Diskussion des Falles und der Behandlung"; the entire paper was published in *Jahrbuch*, III:2 (1911, publication delayed till Mar. 1912).

295 J

1003 Seestrasse, Küsnach-Zürich,

Dear Professor Freud,   23 January 1912

This time the reason for my failure to write is more complicated. We have been the victims of "blackmail"[1] by the newspapers and were publicly reviled although no names were named. I have even consulted a good lawyer with a possible view to bringing a libel action. But there is little prospect of success because the attack was indirect. I have therefore confined myself to a public protest by the International ΨA Association, Zürich branch; it will appear shortly in the press.[2] This whole rumpus was precipitated by my article in *Rascher's Jahrbuch*. The time is most inopportune, as I am overwhelmed with work and grappling with the endless proliferation of mythological fantasies. In order to master the overwhelming mass of material I have to work unceasingly and am feeling intellectually drained.

As you will see from the enclosed letter, Bjerre does not agree at all with our lopping off his long-winded epicrisis and publishing it in the next issue. The gentleman seems to be too big for his boots. I have written Deuticke that he should go ahead and set the end, and that the manuscript is obtainable from you. Have you any ministering spirit who knows German and would correct the style and punctuation? I should be very, very grateful. I would like to avoid difficulties with Bjerre, and Deuticke is willing to print the 3rd part anyway. This would unburden the next issue, which has already taken on menacing proportions because of my copious—still unfinished—opus. But I am now working on the last chapter (VI).

Bleuler's "Autism" is very misleading and extremely unclear theoretically. "Shallow" is probably the right word for it.

I'm told Stekel's paper is brief; it can then be tucked away in an inconspicuous place.

Our French professor from Poitiers[3] has now joined the Zürich group, so we have a professor in our midst again. Since Bleuler's departure we have been having very pleasant evenings at the Society.

---

[1] English in original.

[2] Jung's article, dated 28 Jan. 1912, was published in *Wissen und Leben* (Zürich; former title of the *Neue Schweizer Rundschau*), 15 Feb. 1912, 711–14 = "Concerning Psychoanalysis," CW 4. It was an "epilogue" to a series of polemical articles in the *Neue Zürcher Zeitung* during Jan., initialed by, among others, Forel, Jung, and Franz Marti. For a detailed summary of the series, see Ellenberger, *The Discovery of the Unconscious*, pp. 810–14.

[3] Morichau-Beauchant; see above, 223 F n. 7.

Perceptible harmony all round. Is it true that Adler has offered his services to Specht?[4]

With best regards,

Most sincerely yours, JUNG

On Jan. 20th I lectured to 600 teachers. For an hour and a half I had to thunder out ΨA like Roland sounding his horn.

This letter is quite vacuous. At the moment I am not giving out any libido, it's all going into my work.[5]

296 F

Dear friend,   24 January 1912, Vienna, IX. Berggasse 19

I have no desire to intrude on your concentration but merely wish to inform you that I have taken Bjerre's paper straight to Deuticke, and that I myself have corrected it. You see, it is just as well that I hadn't written to him yet.

A vague report of your newspaper storm in Zürich has already reached me through a patient from St. Gallen.

The second edition of *Gradiva* has gone to the printer's. In a short postscript I make use of the hint you gave me when you discovered the two *Übermächte* stories.[1]

Imago is ready for the printers. They are to begin setting on 1 February.

With kind regards to you and family,

Yours, FREUD

297 J

1003 Seestrasse, Küsnacht-Zürich,

Dear Professor Freud,   [ca. 15 February 1912][1]

A quick word to let you know I am still alive. I am having grisly fights with the hydra of mythological fantasy and not all its heads

---

[4] See above, 272 J n. 2.

[5] The postscripts were squeezed into the margins of the first page.

---

[1] See above, 50 J n. 2. In his postscript, Freud credited the hints to "a friend of mine."

---

[1] Holograph: undated; *ca.* 15/2/12 written at top in another hand. / A new

are cut off yet. Sometimes I feel like calling for help when I am too hard pressed by the welter of material. So far I have managed to suppress the urge. I hope to reach dry land in the not too distant future.

Maeder or Pfister will have told you all about Zürich and our public struggles. At the moment there's a lull in the feud. For autumn Forel has saddled us with his confounded Psychotherapeutic Society[2] and is already threatening us with total annihilation. But so far we are not annihilated in the least and the Society flourishes as never before. Now the pedagogues have begun to move in. The director[3] of the teachers' college in Bern was with me recently and wanted to collaborate. Zürich is seething, ΨA the talk of the town. One can see here how worked up people can get. On Feb. 21st I have to lecture on ΨA to the clinicians; even they are eager to taste the poison. I think all this is an earnest of things to come.

I hope all is well with you. With us everything is peaceful and serene and my wife is working conscientiously at etymology.[4]

With many kind regards,

Most sincerely yours, JUNG

298 F

Dear friend,   18 February 1912, Vienna, IX. Berggasse 19

I was very glad to receive a letter from you. I am not fond of breaking habits and find no triumph in it.[1] Wrenched out of the habit, I no longer remember what I have told you, and besides, I still want to be considerate of your work.

I have edited Bjerre's piece of confusion and delivered it to the

---

printed letterhead, using the spelling "Küsnacht"; this varies in the rest of the letters according to which paper Jung happened to use.

[2] See above, 285 J par. 7, and below, editorial comment following 321 J.

[3] Ernst Schneider, a former student of Pfister's; he joined the Zürich Society on 1 Mar. 12. In 1916, according to Jones (II, p. 123/110), he was dismissed from his directorship because of his psychoanalytic principles. See also *Psychoanalytic Pioneers*, ed. F. Alexander, S. Eisenstein, M. Grotjahn (New York, 1966), p. 171; *Zentralblatt*, II:9 (June 1912), 549.

[4] "Wandlungen und Symbole der Libido" contains many excursions into etymology; cf., e.g., *Symbols of Transformation*, CW 5, par. 188, on "libido."

[1] Holograph: *Ihnen*, "you," for *ihnen*, "them," here tr. as "it."

printer. It is not very pleasant to have to publish such muddles. I am enclosing a prospectus of *Imago* (there are still mistakes). I should have been glad to see your name figure prominently in this journal and the *Zentralblatt*, but instead you hide behind your religious-libidinal cloud. It seems to me that you are still giving me too much precedence. In my paper on the Horror of Incest I have stressed, to your satisfaction, I hope, the part played by you and your followers in the development of ΨA.[2] I myself am busy with my study of Taboo. I have not been consistently well, my daily practice has prevented me from doing much good work. I have had to write an article in English on the unconscious for the Society for Psychical Research;[3] of course it contains nothing new.

Stärcke in Amsterdam has sent me the first newspaper article on ΨA to appear in the Dutch language.[4] Van Emden seems to be hesitating and dawdling as usual. Here in the Vienna Society everything is all right. Recently a young Viennese (Dr. Schrötter)[5] provided experimental confirmation of our dream symbolism—more or less against his will. He suggested to his hypnotized patients that they dream of sexual or homosexual intercourse, and they did so in the symbols known to us, of which, I am assured, they had no knowl-

[2] "Die Inzestscheu" (see above, 293 F n. 2), p. 18 (5th par. of the essay): "For all those who have taken part in the development of psychoanalytic research it was a memorable moment when at a private scientific gathering one of C. G. Jung's students read a communication in his behalf to the effect that the fantasy images of certain mental patients (Dementia praecox) presented the most striking parallels to the mythological cosmogonies of ancient peoples, concerning which the uneducated among the patients cannot possibly have had scientific knowledge." Footnote: "At the Nuremberg 1910 Psychoanalytic Congress. The paper was read by the highly gifted C. [sic] Honegger, now deceased. In subsequent writings, Jung himself and his pupils (Nelken, Spielrein) have further developed the ideas then first touched upon. (Cf. Jung, "Wandlungen und Symbole der Libido," *Jahrbuch*, III:1, 1911.)" The passage was omitted in the book publication of *Totem und Tabu*, 1913, but Freud added a preface in which he stated that he received the first stimulus for the essays from Wundt's work and the writings of the Zürich school, and he cited Jung's "Wandlungen und Symbole der Libido" and "The Theory of Psychoanalysis."
[3] "A Note on the Unconscious in Psycho-analysis," *Proceedings of the Society for Psychical Research* (London), XXVI (1912); SE XII.
[4] Johan Stärcke, "De psychologie van het onbewuste; een nieuwe wetenschap" (The Psychology of the Unconscious; a New Science), *De Telegraaf* (Amsterdam), 11 Jan. 12. Reported in *Zentralblatt*, II:7 (1912), 420.
[5] Karl Schrötter, "Experimentelle Träume," *Zentralblatt*, II (1912): pp. 547 (lecture to the Society, 14 Feb.) and 638ff. (paper). Schrötter, a brilliant student of philosophy, committed suicide on 16 May 13 at the age of 26.

edge whatever. This marks the beginning of a new branch of experimental psychology. A provisional report will appear in the *Zentralblatt*. You will hear more about it later on.

For once everything is all right at home. My kind regards to you, your wife and children.

Yours, FREUD

299 J

1003 Seestrasse, Küsnacht-Zürich,

Dear Professor Freud,   19 February 1912

Heartiest thanks for your two excellent articles. "The Dynamics of Transference"[1] is of extraordinary value for the analyst. I have read it with pleasure and profit. So far as the concept of introversion[2] is concerned, I consider it to be a universal phenomenon, though it has a special significance in Dem. praec. I say quite a lot about it in Part II of my work on libido, which by the way has taken on alarming proportions and despite my need to come to an end refuses to stop. Already I can predict the gloomy outcome: I shall see how much better I could have done it.

Our Society is blossoming like a rose since Bleuler left. The only result of the great newspaper feud is that ΨA is being endlessly discussed in public. It even appears in the carnival newspapers.

Excuse this brevity, but I am in a state of war.

Kind regards,

Most sincerely yours, JUNG

[1] See above, 280 F n. 3. The other article cannot be identified, unless it was the brief " 'Gross ist die Diana der Epheser,' " *Zentralblatt*, II:3 (Dec. 1911) = " 'Great is the Diana of the Ephesians,' " SE XII.

[2] In "Dynamics" (SE XII, p. 102) occurs Freud's first use of this "appropriate" term, which Jung had introduced in "Konflikte der kindliche Seele" (1910; cf. CW 17, par. 13). Freud commented, ". . . some of Jung's remarks give the impression that he regards this introversion as something which is characteristic of dementia praecox and does not come into account in the same way in other neuroses." Here Jung replies.

300 J

1003 Seestrasse, Küsnach-Zürich,

Dear Professor Freud, 25 February 1912

Many thanks for your friendly letter. I am *most* interested in the experimental confirmation of dream analysis. Where can one read about it?

Little to report from Zürich, and little of it pleasant. Pfister has no doubt told you how badly things are going with him. It may even cost him his job. I fear he is too optimistic, too trusting, in spite of warnings. Our opponents are wont to pick on the vulnerable spots; and one of the weak points in our armour is Pfister, whom they can hurt by spreading rumours. Those people are vermin that shun the light.

The students are acquitting themselves splendidly. Recently I lectured to about 150 students on ΨA with great success. A more noteworthy news item is the founding of a lay organization for ΨA,[1] It has about 20 members and only analysed persons are accepted. The organization was founded at the request of former patients. The rapport among its members is loudly acclaimed. I myself have not yet attended a meeting. The chairman is a member of the ΨA Society. The experiment seems to me interesting from the standpoint of the social application of ΨA to education.

I think I am not wrong in suspecting that you rather resent my remissness as a correspondent. In this regard my behaviour is indeed a little irresponsible, as I have allowed all my libido to disappear into my work. On the other hand I don't think you need have any apprehensions about my protracted and invisible sojourn in the "religious-libidinal cloud." I would willingly tell you what is going on up there if only I knew how to set it down in a letter. Essentially, it is an elaboration of all the problems that arise out of the mother-incest libido, or rather, the libido-cathected mother-imago. This time I have ventured to tackle the mother. So what is keeping me hidden is the κατάβασις[2] to the realm of the Mothers, where, as we know, Theseus and Peirithoos remained stuck, grown fast to the rocks.[3] But in time I

---

[1] On 13 Feb. 12, with Franz Riklin as chairman; see *Zentralblatt*, II:8 (May 1912), p. 480. A report of its programmes Oct. 1912 to July 1913, under the name Gesellschaft für psychoanalytische Bestrebungen (Society for Psychoanalytic Endeavours), appeared in the *Zeitschrift*, I:6 (1913), 635; cf. below, 351 J n. 1.

[2] *katabasis* = "descent," i.e., to the Underworld.

[3] Cf. *Symbols of Transformation*, CW 5, par. 449, n. 56 (also in 1911/12 edn.).

shall come up again. These last days I have clawed my way considerably nearer to the surface. So please do forbear with me a while longer. I shall bring all sorts of wonderful things with me *ad majorem gloriam* ΨA.

Most sincerely yours, J U N G

301 F

Dear friend,   29 February 1912, Vienna, IX. Berggasse 19

I am surprised to hear that all is not well with Pfister. In his last letter which came shortly before yours, he was overjoyed at having finally found a woman for whose sake it would be worthwhile to put up with the drawbacks of marriage; nothing seemed amiss. I haven't heard from him since. If he is in trouble, we must do everything in our power to help him.

A provisional report on the dream experiments will appear in the *Zentralblatt*, but not in the next few issues. Your news of your student lecture and the new lay organization is most gratifying; I have nothing comparable to offer.

What you say about my resentment of your tendency to neglect our correspondence warrants more thorough ΨA elucidation. There can be no doubt that I was a demanding correspondent, nor can I deny that I awaited your letters with great impatience and answered them promptly. I disregarded your earlier signs of reluctance. This time it struck me as more serious; my suspicion was aroused by your refusal to inform me of the state of your health after the dog bite and by the C—— episode. I took myself in hand and quickly turned off my excess libido. I was sorry to do so, yet glad to see how quickly I managed it. Since then I have become undemanding and not to be feared. As we know, irresponsibility is not a concept compatible with depth psychology.[1]

But it would be a severe blow to all of us if you were to draw the libido you require for your work from the Association. I have the impression that the organization is not functioning properly at present. The groups know nothing of each other, there is no contact between them. The reason is that the organ designed to promote

[1] Holograph: *Tiefenpsychologie*. The earliest use of this term noted heretofore was in Jung's "On the Doctrine of Complexes," written Mar. 1911; see CW 2, par. 1355. Jung attributed it to Bleuler.

such contact—the *Bulletin*—does nothing. It has appeared only once since the Congress[2] and, as the *Zentralblatt* goes to press a month in advance, the next *Bulletin* cannot come out until April at the earliest. Every month it should offer reports on the activity of the local groups and a message from the president; and it should provide information about the destinies of ΨA in the world at large.

I am told here that Riklin has not been answering letters or acknowledging receipt of manuscripts. The bond within the Association has narrowed down to receiving the *Zentralblatt*. Yet we believed the organization to be necessary. We made sacrifices and alienated people in order to set it up. I am unable to withdraw from the day-to-day concerns of ΨA to the extent that I planned when we founded the Association and I proposed Adler as chairman here. But I am less concerned with the present than with the future; I am determined to make all necessary preparations for it, so as to see everything safe in your hands when the time comes.

I should like also to remind you that you undertook at the last Congress to make arrangements for the next one early in the year. I personally shall not mind if it is dropped this year; that would leave me free in September. But of course I shall attend if it is held.

I have been working rather hard on little things, such as the four papers for the *Zentralblatt*, two of which you have not yet received.[3] The paper on Taboo for *Imago*,[4] which I expect to finish soon, is more significant, I think. The journal itself will emerge from the intrauterine stage in little more than a fortnight.

Let me assure you of my keen interest in your libido paper. With kind regards,

Yours ever, FREUD

302 J

1003 Seestrasse, Küsnacht-Zürich,
Dear Professor Freud,   2 March 1912

I take pleasure in recommending the bearer of this letter. Dr. Schrumpf[1] is a neurologist in St. Moritz who, undeterred by the

[2] In *Zentralblatt*, II:4 (Jan. 1912).
[3] "Papers on Technique": for the two already published, see above, 280 F nn. 2 & 3; for the remaining two, see below, 318 J n. 1 and 329 F n. 4.
[4] See below, 329 F n. 6.

[1] Peter Schrumpf (1882–19—), internist; later at the Charité, Berlin.

opposing trends in present-day science, wishes to make personal contact with ΨA.

With best regards,

Yours sincerely, J U N G

303 J

1003 Seestrasse, Küsnach-Zürich,

Dear Professor Freud,   3 March 1912

Your letter has made me very pensive. First of all I would like to tell you, with reference to the *Bulletin*, that Riklin had strict instructions which once again he has simply neglected. For the sake of my work I wanted to dispense with pure formalities for two months. Riklin has failed in a way I cannot permit to carry out my instructions. I have therefore issued an ultimatum: I shall relieve him of his post if he continues to neglect his duties. I shall accept his resignation at the next opportunity. The reports he received from the local groups should have been sent to the *Zentralblatt* every month.

I have by no means forgotten the arrangements to be made for the Congress. On the contrary I have repeatedly requested the military authorities to let me know when my period of service falls due this year. So far I have not succeeded, because the tour of duty for the mountain troops, to which I am detailed, is not yet fixed. This should be known very shortly. It was for *this reason* that I was unable to set a date for the Congress.

So far as my other activities as president are concerned, I don't know of anything I might do at the moment to establish closer communication between the groups. I shall be grateful for hints. I have taken steps to start a group in Lausanne. But the outlook isn't too good at present because of local opposition. I hope to get something going in London with the help of Dr. Eder (I have treated his wife). Nothing to be hoped for in Italy or France. If we were sure of Dr. van Emden something might take shape in Holland. (Van Renterghem wants to visit me!)

If I have not played an active part in the *Zentralblatt* or *Imago* it is simply because I am fully occupied with the *Jahrbuch*, and also with my own work, which permits no fragmentation of my limited resources. It goes against the grain to write short articles in which I could only peddle banalities. Larger interests must be fitted into a larger framework. All my efforts are needed to keep the *Jahrbuch* up to the mark. There is great danger of its drowning in platitudinous case material. This is not to say that I shall not contribute to *Imago* later if I can lay hands on something that lends itself to concise presentation. The work I am now doing has demanded so much time and energy because, when it finally appears in finished form, it will amount to a book of over 300 pages. Such an undertaking seems to me more important for the continued progress of our cause than my dissipating myself in short articles.

As for the other remarks in your letter, I must own that I have never been able to rid myself of the idea that what I have done and still am doing to promote the spread of ΨA must surely be of far greater moment to you than my personal awkwardness and nastiness. If ever anything serious had befallen me that might have imperilled our work, it goes without saying that I would have informed you. I have my work cut out to put up with my own personality without wishing to foist it on you and add to your burdens. Whenever I had anything important to communicate I have always done so. I have not kept up a lively correspondence during these last weeks because I wanted if possible to write *no letters at all*, simply in order to gain time for my work and not in order to give *you* a demonstration of ostentatious neglect. Or can it be that you mistrust me? Experience has shown how groundless this is. Of course I have opinions which are not yours about the ultimate truths of ΨA—though even this is not certain, for one cannot discuss everything under the sun by letter—but you won't, I suppose, take umbrage on that account. I am ready at any time to adapt my opinions to the judgment of someone who knows better, and always have been. I would never have sided with you in the first place had not heresy run in my blood. Since I have no professorial ambitions I can afford to admit mistakes. Let Zarathustra speak for me:

> "One repays a teacher badly if one remains only a pupil.
> And why, then, should you not pluck at my laurels?
> You respect me; but how if one day your respect should tumble?
> Take care that a falling statue does not strike you dead!
> You had not yet sought yourselves when you found me.
> Thus do all believers—.
> Now I bid you lose me and find yourselves;
> and only when you have all denied me will I return to you."[1]

---

[1] Nietzsche, *Also Sprach Zarathustra*, part 1, sec. 3 (tr. R. J. Hollingdale, Penguin Classics, 1961, p. 103). Jung wrote the passage as prose, following Nietzsche.

491

This is what you have taught me through ΨA. As one who is truly your follower, I must be stout-hearted, not least towards you.

With kindest regards,

Most sincerely yours, J U N G

304 F

Dear friend,   5 March 1912, Vienna, IX. Berggasse 19

Why so "pensive" when the situation is so simple? I have pointed out to you that the Association cannot prosper when the president loses interest in it over a period of months, especially when he has so unreliable an assistant as our friend Riklin. You seem to recognize that I am right, which disposes of one point. You make it clear to me that you don't wish to write to me at present, and I reply that I am trying to make the privation easy for myself. Isn't that my right? Isn't it a necessary act of self-defence?

Otherwise we agree about everything. You write that you have always thought your past and prospective contributions to the cause should mean more to me than your "personal nastiness and awkward-ness"—(your friends would put it more mildly and speak of your "moods"). I beg you to go on thinking so. The indestructible founda-tion of our personal relationship is our involvement in ΨA; but on this foundation it seemed tempting to build something finer though more labile, a reciprocal intimate friendship. Shouldn't we go on building?

You speak of the need for intellectual independence and quote Nietzsche in support of your view. I am in full agreement. But if a third party were to read this passage, he would ask me when[1] I had tried to tyrannize you intellectually, and I should have to say: I don't know. I don't believe I ever did. Adler, it is true, made similar com-plaints, but I am convinced that his neurosis was speaking for him. Still, if you think you want greater freedom from me, what can I do but give up my feeling of urgency about our relationship, occupy my unemployed libido elsewhere, and bide my time until you discover that you can tolerate greater intimacy? When that happens, you will

[1] Holograph: *warum*, "why"; but the German context indicates that it is a slip for *wann*, "when."

find me willing. During the transition to this attitude of reserve, I have complained very quietly. You would have thought me insincere if I had not reacted at all.

Why, I repeat, should you be so "pensive"? Do you think I am looking for someone else capable of being at once my friend, my helper and my heir, or that I expect to find another so soon? If not, then we are at one again, and you are right in expending your pensiveness on your study of the libido. My question about the Congress was only remotely connected with the affective theme of this letter. Thank you for your answer. About the new groups, I agree with you: they must spring up in response to a spontaneous need. Rest assured of my affective cathexis and continue to think of me in friendship, even if you do not write often.

With kindest regards,

Yours ever, FREUD

305 J

1003 Seestrasse, Küsnach-Zürich,
Dear Professor Freud,   10 March 1912

Many thanks for your kindly letter. I haven't the slightest intention of imitating Adler. But often I am empty-headed, especially when all my libido is concentrated on a problem. I shall gather my wits together very soon.

About Pfister: I forgot to mention that he is in a bad way because his position is in jeopardy. He has been too incautious. He is happy enough with his girl, but she is much too young and infantile and still hasn't realized what the situation is; she even wanted to call it off a second time. Pfister is a child himself and needs an intelligent woman. First he married a mother, now it's a daughter. I have told him she is thoroughly infantile; I heard he took it as an encouraging sign. The whole enterprise is decidedly dangerous. However, his libido is in it so it might turn out well. I'm not meddling so long as he doesn't ask me to. His position in the parish is precarious. What would he do if he were expelled? He says he would work with some medical man as a ΨA assistant. With whom? There is no room for him here with us. And what would his young wife or fiancée say about that? Now he is terribly in love and imagines he can't live without the girl. I hope it will be all right in the end. We are very worried about him.

493

I hear bad reports of Stegmann. The dragon he married is an unsavoury spirit and has done him no good at all. I also heard he has made a virulent attack on ΨA.

I have finished my work except for the addenda. You will have received the *Jahrbuch* by now. The setting of Volume IV has begun. Please send *Bleuler's manuscript to Deuticke*. This time B. is firing the opening shot. The new issue will be entirely analytical except for Bleuler.[1] Have you read Spielrein's new paper (manuscript)?[2] I'm afraid I shall have to trim it quite a bit. This always takes me an awfully long time. There are two or three Dementia praecox analyses still to come, one of which (Nelken)[3] is extremely important. I hope I can squeeze it in. The volume will be a regular monster as I want to include my paper *in toto*.

On March 31st I shall go on a holiday for 3 weeks. I'm fagged out. Many kind regards,

Most sincerely yours, J U N G

306 F

Dear friend, 21 March 1912, Vienna, IX. Berggasse 19

I was very glad to hear that you have a few weeks of rest ahead of you, now that the libido paper is finished. I myself shall probably go to the Adriatic with Ferenczi for the three days of Easter. As you know, I take a rather generous holiday in the summer.

As for Spielrein's paper, I know only the one chapter that she read at the Society.[1] She is very bright; there is meaning in everything she says; her destructive drive is not much to my liking, because I believe it is personally conditioned. She seems abnormally ambivalent.

I delivered Bleuler's manuscript at once. The present issue of the *Jahrbuch* is most imposing, but there is no real clou. Pfister's piece is a technical tour de force; it is assuredly sound, but many of the details, though interesting from a theological point of view, are lack-

---

[1] See above, 272 J n. 6.
[2] "Die Destruktion als Ursache des Werdens," *Jahrbuch*, IV:1 (1912).
[3] Jan Nelken, psychiatrist at the Burghölzli, charter member of the Zürich Society. His paper was "Analytische Beobachtungen über Phantasien eines Schizophrenen," *Jahrbuch*, IV:1 (1912). Later in Paris.

[1] See above, 286 F n. 4.

ing in general interest. My sense of disappointment probably springs from the postponement of your "Transformations and Symbols."

We are hard at work in the Society and at the *Zentralblatt* and very much regret that Zürich is beginning to withhold its support at a time when foreign developments are so gratifying. In Russia (Odessa) there seems to be a local epidemic of ΨA.[2] The ferment continues, there are further particulars, but they are hardly worth writing[3] about.

Stegmann has punished himself for his misbehaviour in classical style by his choic of mate. First he married, then he came to me, then he told himself that the reverse would have been more rational. I also have the impression that Binswanger, though behaving quite correctly, has been rather inactive.

My paper on Taboo[4] is coming along slowly. The conclusion has long been known to me. The source of taboo and hence also of conscience is ambivalence. When you receive this letter, *Imago* may already have seen the light of day.[5]

Kind regards to you and your family. I am hoping for good news from you.

Yours ever, FREUD

[2] Two members of the Vienna Society were in Odessa. Leonid Drosnés, a psychiatrist who had read Freud, attempted to psychoanalyse the patient known as the "Wolf Man" and, in Jan. 1910, brought him to Vienna; Freud treated the "Wolf Man" until 1914—see "Aus der Geschichte einer infantilen Neurose," *Sammlung kleiner Schriften zur Neurosenlehre*, IV (1918) = "From the History of an Infantile Neurosis," SE XVII. Drosnés joined the Vienna Society (*Bulletin*, no. 4, Feb. 1911); practised psychoanalysis later in St. Petersburg (*Zentralblatt*, I:12, Sept. 1911). He appears as "Dr. D." in *The Wolf-Man, by the Wolf-Man*, ed. Muriel Gardiner (New York, 1971), pp. 79–85. / Moshe Wulff or Woolf (1878–1971) went to Berlin for medical training and studied psychoanalysis with Abraham; after returning to Odessa, he joined the Vienna Society (*Bulletin*, no. 6, Aug. 1911) and reported on "Russian Psychoanalytic Literature until 1911," *Zentralblatt*, I:7/8 (Apr./May 1911). In 1927 he left the U.S.S.R. and resumed work in Berlin; in 1933 settled in Palestine, and was a co-founder of the Palestine Psychoanalytic Society.

[3] Holograph: *sträuben*, "to struggle against," corrected by Freud to *schreiben*, with exclamation point.

[4] See below, 329 F n. 6.

[5] *Imago: Zeitschrift für Anwendung der Psychoanalyse auf die Geistewissenschaften* (Journal for the Application of Psychoanalysis to the Arts), directed by Freud, edited by Rank and Sachs, published by Heller; I:1 (March 1912), published on 28 March (Freud to Putnam, 28 Mar. 12, in *Putnam and Psychoanalysis*, p. 137).

495

307 J *Internationale Psychoanalytische Vereinigung*

Dear Professor Freud,   Küsnach-Zürich, 22 March 1912

The date of my military service has been settled at last: August 22nd–September 6th. Coincidentally I received an invitation from Fordham University, New York, to give a course of lectures[1] from Sept. 10th on. I felt obliged to accept so as to gain yet more ground for ΨA. In these circumstances I suggest switching the Congress to *August 19/20*. It will then be certain to fall in the holiday season. Munich is central, within easy reach even of people spending their vacations further afield. I shall put the same suggestion to each of the local groups and see what they have to say. Please let me know your own views.

Frau Lou Andreas-Salomé's manuscript[2] has arrived. It looks weird. I shall submit it to your judgment. Bleuler wants to withdraw a manuscript from *Jahrbuch* IV/1 because of "unfounded" anxiety-states (a Dem. praec. analysis).[3] Burghölzli gets sillier every day. I was all the more astonished that Binswanger has sent his assistant there for training without giving him an opportunity to make the least contact either with me or with the Society.

We have introduced compulsory speaking in the Zürich Society as in Vienna because it was absolutely necessary. Often people just sit there like deadheads. Also, the lectures have become rather sloppy of late. I had to handle one gentleman very roughly. It has shaken them up.

Kindest regards,

Most sincerely yours, JUNG

308 F

Dear friend,   24 March 1912, Vienna, IX. Berggasse 19

In spite of all my resolutions, I must write to you again.

I congratulate you on your trip to America, of course you were right in accepting. I wired you because before you communicate with the local groups I should like to acquaint you with my misgivings

---

[1] Holograph: *Course of Lecture* (sic).
[2] See above, 291 J n. 3.
[3] Presumably Nelken's; see above, 305 J n. 3.

about holding the Congress on 19–20 August. My objections are of a general and personal nature, some of them no doubt both at once.

To start from the bottom up, with the personal factors: this date would cut my hard-earned and much longed-for holidays in two. I shall be in Karlsbad with my wife until about 10 August; after that I don't know where we shall be, but a week or so later I should have to start travelling again. August in Munich would probably be torture and the heat most unconducive to concentrated mental effort. The same applies to the other participants, even if they are not in Karlsbad at the time; their holidays would be interrupted and they would certainly suffer from the heat.

Besides, I have the impression that there is no need for a congress this year. Too little has happened since the last one. Our meetings thus far have been so splendid that we ought not to run the risk of an anticlimax.

I think your trip provides excellent justification for skipping the Congress; everyone will admit that it serves the interests of ΨA.

I submit these considerations, some of which also apply to the latest possible date, the end of September, to your judgment. I am quite willing to read Frau Lou A. S.'s essay. — I am afraid what you say about Binswanger agrees with my own impressions. — Compulsory speaking was abandoned long ago in the Vienna Society, but the effect is still with us. At present most of the members are glad to speak and carry the others along with them. I recommend it highly as an educational measure.

Today I am sending you the second edition of *Gradiva*. With kind regards,

Yours ever, FREUD

309 J

1003 Seestrasse, Küsnacht-Zürich,
Dear Professor Freud,   27 March 1912

Many thanks for the second edition of *Gradiva*. I quite agree with your proposal. I shall notify the local groups accordingly, i.e., I presume that I have to consult them. Perhaps we can hold the Congress next spring.

Bleuler has demanded the return of one of the manuscripts already with Deuticke, a very fine Dem. praec. analysis, for fear of public opinion in Zürich. He could have done this long ago, so it is

497

just another low trick. Of course it was a paper produced at the Clinic, which I have now wasted a lot of time correcting.

Please excuse the "meagreness" of this "letter." You will be hearing more from me very soon. Best regards,

Most sincerely yours, JUNG

310 J

Hotel Milan-Bahnhof,
Dear Professor Freud,   Lugano,[1] 1 April 1912

At last I have got away from Zürich so as to be alone with myself for a few days before going to Florence with my wife. As you see I am in Lugano, where it is raining miserably. Nevertheless, I am on my own here and unknown, and that is the acme of pleasure.

I hear that Bleuler's plans for the manuscript are not as murderous as I conjectured in my last letter. Even so, strange things must be going on at Burghölzli. There is talk of Bleuler's retirement. They say he wants to seclude himself in his father's place in Zollikon. (All this is only hearsay, of course.)

I was working on Spielrein's paper just before my departure. One must say: *desinat in piscem mulier formosa superne.*[2] After a very promising start the continuation and end trail off dismally. Particularly the "Life and Death in Mythology" chapter needed extensive cutting as it contained gross errors and, worse still, faulty, one-sided interpretations. She has read too little and has fallen flat in this paper because it is not thorough enough. One must say by way of excuse that she has brought her problem to bear on an aspect of mythology that bristles with riddles. Besides that her paper is heavily overweighted with her own complexes. My criticism should be administered to the little authoress in *refracta dosi* only, please, if at all. I shall be writing to her myself before long.

Frau Lou's manuscript will be sent to you only after your holiday. There are "tremendous" things in it.

I am eager to see *Imago*. I cannot, however, quite suppress the fear that it will drain valuable forces away from the *Jahrbuch*. We have in Zürich too scanty a stock of young blood. Perhaps I am being over-pessimistic because the mass of case material now piling up in the

---

[1] Printed letterhead, illustrated with pictures of the hotel, Lake Lugano, etc.
[2] = "What at the top is a lovely woman ends below in a fish."—Horace, *De arte poetica*, 4 (tr. H. R. Fairclough, Loeb edn.).

ΨA literature has begun to sicken me. Of course this is only a subjective feeling, no doubt induced by my patients. All the same, case material is unbelievably monotonous once you have got over the first shock of wonderment.

I hope you will have some fine and peaceful days on the Adriatic together with Ferenczi. I too must gather strength to produce the 8 lectures, which are to be given *in English*. This forces me to take every word literally. A formidable task. This time I shall travel back via the West Indies.

Kind regards,

Most sincerely yours, J U N G

311 F

Dear friend,   21 April 1912, Vienna, IX. Berggasse 19

I hope you are home again, refreshed by a pleasant holiday. Now perhaps you will be interested to hear about the rather uneventful interval.

I spent three days with Ferenczi on a quiet Dalmatian island;[1] the bora was blowing on the way back, but I wasn't seasick. Since then sheer hard work has prevented me from collecting my thoughts. Van Emden has come to stay for a few weeks until his wife has got the house in The Hague ready to which he is moving to practice ΨA. Spielrein, to whom I was glad not to mention your criticism, came to say good-bye[2] a few days ago and discussed certain intimate matters with me. My correspondence with Binswanger has revived; what I had interpreted as flagging interest might better have been explained by illness and an operation.

Your news of Bleuler is of the greatest interest to me. If he receives an appointment elsewhere or resigns, you can imagine how glad I should be for you to exchange your house on the lake for Burghölzli. But I don't think he will leave unless he gets an appointment. His material circumstances would not allow it. On the other hand, I note to my regret that his withdrawal from the Zürich group seems to have done the group more harm than I could foresee, and I would greatly

---

[1] Arbe, Austrian till 1918; now Rab, Yugoslavia.
[2] She attended a Vienna Society meeting on 27 Mar. (*Minutes*, IV). A membership list of the Vienna Society as of 1 Jan. 14 in the *Bulletin* section of the *Zeitschrift*, II:5 (1914), 413, shows her (as Spielrein-Scheftel) residing in Berlin.

welcome the news that he had rejoined. I shall write to him again when I have an offprint of the *Imago* article, naturally making no mention of what I have just said. As you know, peacemakers are not usually very successful.

I attributed it to your *pre*-holiday mood that you regarded *Imago* as a rival of the *Jahrbuch*. Don't forget that it's the same company under three different names, with slight variations in function. I am looking forward with resignation to Lou Salomé's essay. But now I want to bring up a matter that may warrant intervention on your part. As you can see from the enclosure, Morton Prince has made use of ΨA for a personal attack on Roosevelt,[3] which seems to be creating quite a stir over there. In my opinion such a thing is absolutely inadmissible, an infringement on privacy, which to be sure is not greatly respected in America. But I leave it entirely to you whether you regard a statement as expedient, especially since you will be seeing the American Association in September. If you already have the cutting or have no use for it, may I ask you to return it?

I am eagerly looking forward to your second libido paper with its new concept of the libido, because I imagine that the "Declaration of Independence"[4] you announced a while ago is expressed in it and may indeed have related to nothing else. You will see that I am quite capable of listening and accepting, or of waiting until an idea becomes clearer to me.

I am satisfied with the work being done here and with the group; I recently gave Baron Winterstein,[5] one of our members, a letter of recommendation to you and Bleuler; he seems to be an exceptionally fine man. I am less pleased with the general world situation of the cause; but perhaps that is a mood brought on by overwork.

One learns little by little to renounce one's personality.

With kind regards,

Yours ever, FREUD

[3] Prince, "Roosevelt as Analyzed by the New Psychology," *New York Times*, 24 Mar. 1912, (Sunday) Magazine Section, Part VI, 1–2. For a discussion of Prince's "dissection" of former President Theodore Roosevelt, at this time the Progressive Party's candidate for the presidency, see Hale, *Freud and the Americans*, pp. 415f. Prince's article was criticized by Jones: "Psycho-analyse Roosevelts," *Zentralblatt*, II:12 (Sept. 1912), 675ff. See also below, 316 F n. 2.
[4] English in original. See above, 303 J.
[5] Alfred Freiherr von Winterstein, of Leipzig, lay member of the Vienna Society.

312 J

1003 Seestrasse, Küsnach-Zürich,

Dear Professor Freud,   27 April 1912

It was good of you to have your letter waiting for me on my return. I spent some very pleasant days in Florence, Pisa, and Genoa and now feel quite rested.[1]

With regard to Bleuler, even if the story of his appointment is true it is unlikely that he will go to Breslau. This will be a hard dilemma for him, as he had always hoped to get to Germany. I shall be glad if he stays on, because no successor would be any better, except possibly Dr. Ris in Rheinau.[1a] I myself am out of the running, for I have no intention of giving up my scientific work for the sake of a professorship. Professorships here mean the end of one scientific development. You cannot be an official in a madhouse and a scientist at the same time. I shall make my own way without a professorship.

Morton Prince is just a mudslinger. Nothing can be done directly, since one cannot start a fight with American newspapers. All they are interested in is sensationalism, bribery, and corruption. But in my American lectures I can slip in a parenthetical remark that will make our position clear. Anyway Prince has already been out-trumped by Dr. Allen Starr,[2] as you will see from the enclosed cutting. About this there is even less to be done. Our only available weapon is moral annihilation. But these wretches annihilate themselves as soon as they open their mouths. We are therefore left defenceless.

Our ultimate opponents will be the ones who commit the vilest atrocities with ΨA, as they are even now doing with all the means at their disposal. It's a poor lookout for ΨA in the hands of these crooks and fools!

I hope to see Baron Winterstein at my place next Monday.

[1] This trip was apparently also the occasion of Jung's first visit to Ravenna (information from Mr. Franz Jung, correcting the date 1913 in *Memories*, p. 284/265).

[1a] Friedrich Ris (1867–1931), director of the cantonal clinic at Rheinau (Cant. Zürich) from 1898 until his death.

[2] Moses Allen Starr (1854–1932), professor of neurology at Columbia University, had attacked Freud after an address by Putnam before the New York Academy of Medicine, section in neurology, 4 Apr. 12 ("Comments on Sex Issues from the Freudian Standpoint," *Addresses*, pp. 128ff.). See Hale, *Freud and the Americans*, pp. 301f.; also letters between Putnam and Freud in *Putnam and Psychoanalysis*, pp. 140, 143.

I would like to keep the article on Roosevelt a few days longer for further study, and then send it back to you.

Now and then I correspond "amicably" with Bleuler on scientific matters. There seems to be a tacit agreement between us not to tread on one another's corns.

Störring's[3] assistant in Strassburg, young Dr. Erismann,[4] wants to join us. I have *successfully* treated his sister (whom you may remember). Many thanks for your exceedingly interesting article in *Imago*. A pity the bulk of my manuscript is already with Deuticke; I could have made a number of improvements. Like you, I am absorbed in the incest problem and have come to conclusions which show incest primarily as a fantasy problem. Originally, morality was simply a ceremony of atonement, a substitutive prohibition, so that the ethnic prohibition of incest may not mean biological incest at all, but merely the utilization of infantile incest material for the construction of the first prohibitions. (I don't know whether I am expressing myself clearly!) If biological incest were meant, then father-daughter incest would have fallen under the prohibition much more readily than that between son-in-law and mother-in-law. The tremendous role of the mother in mythology has a significance far outweighing the biological incest problem—a significance that amounts to pure fantasy.

Kind regards,

Most sincerely yours, JUNG

313 J

1003 Seestrasse, Küsnach-Zürich,

Dear Professor Freud, 8 May 1912

I very much regret my inability to make myself intelligible at a distance without sending you the voluminous background material.[1] What I mean is that the exclusion of the father-daughter relationship from the incest prohibition, usually explained by the role of the father as (egoistic) law-giver, must originate from the relatively late period of patriarchy, when culture was sufficiently far advanced for the for-

---

[3] Gustav Störring (1860–1946), German psychiatrist, professor at Zürich 1902–11, later at Bonn.
[4] Theodor Erismann (1883–1961), psychologist (Ph.D., Zürich), later in Bonn, and Innsbruck. For his stepmother, Sophie Erismann, see above, 85 J n. 3.

---

[1] A letter from Freud is apparently missing.

mation of family ties. In the family the father was strong enough to keep the son in order with a thrashing, and without laying down the law, if in those tender years the son showed any incestuous inclinations. In riper years, on the other hand, when the son might really be a danger to the father, and laws were therefore needed to restrain him, the son no longer had any real incestuous desires for the mother, with her sagging belly and varicose veins. A far more genuine incest tendency is to be conjectured for the early, cultureless period of matriarchy, i.e., in the matrilineal family. There the father was purely fortuitous and counted for nothing, so he would not have had the slightest interest (considering the general promiscuity) in enacting laws against the son. (In fact, there was no such thing as a father's son!) I therefore think that the incest prohibition (understood as primitive morality) was merely a formula or ceremony of atonement *in re vili*:[2] what was valuable for the child—the mother—and is so worthless for the adult that it is kicked into the bush, acquires an extraordinary value thanks to the incest prohibition, and is declared to be desirable and forbidden. (This is genuine primitive morality: any bit of fun may be prohibited, but it is just as likely to become a fetish.) Evidently the object of the prohibition is not to prevent incest but to consolidate the family (or piety, or the social structure).

With Bleuler I have had an apparently amicable but in reality painful to-do about a dissertation which he had given me on his own initiative for the *Jahrbuch*, but which I rejected as worthless. Maybe you will be called in as a super-expert. In my view the paper is too stupid and too bad. The female patient it deals with is imbecilic and hopelessly sterile, and the authoress is a goose. The whole thing is a complete bore.

Thank heavens Frau Lou Andreas-Salomé has suddenly been enlightened by a kindly spirit and has taken back her paper for an indefinite period. So we are rid of that worry.

Winterstein has turned up, throbbing with the awe of an initiate admitted to the inner sanctum, who knows the mysteries and the hallowed rites of the καταβάσιον. We welcomed him with the benevolent smile of augurs.

With best regards,

Most sincerely yours, JUNG

[2] = "in worthless matters."

314 F

Dear friend,   14 May 1912, Vienna, IX. Berggasse 19

It will surely come as no surprise to you that your conception of incest is still unclear to me. Sometimes I have the impression that it is not far removed from what we have thought up to now, but this can only be clarified by a more detailed discussion. As for your arguments, I have three observations to make; they are not refutations but should be taken merely as expressions of doubt.

1) Many authors regard a primordial state of promiscuity as highly unlikely. I myself, in all modesty, favour a different hypothesis in regard to the primordial period—Darwin's.[1]

2) Mother right[2] should not be confused with gynaecocracy. There is little to be said for the latter. Mother right is perfectly compatible with the polygamous abasement of woman.

3) It seems likely that there have been father's sons at all times. A father is one who possesses a mother sexually (and the children as property). The fact of having been engendered by a father has, after all, no psychological significance for a child.

But I am writing today for another reason. None of the recent critiques has made more impression than Kronfeld's[3] (on me, I am sorry to say, none).

One of our members, Gaston Rosenstein—good mind, mathematician by profession, philosopher, etc.—has now taken the trouble to refute this shamelessly prejudiced paper in detail.[4] A good deal of his counter-critique strikes me as excellent; other things in it are of course no more intelligible to me than Kronfeld's attack, because I do not

---

[1] Freud discusses Charles Darwin's hypothesis about primitive promiscuity (from his *The Descent of Man*, 1871) in *Totem and Taboo*, part IV: "The Return of Totemism in Childhood" (orig. 1913); see SE XIII, p. 125.

[2] Holograph: *Mutterrecht*, sometimes translated "matriarchy," but in the sense used by the Swiss social philosopher J. J. Bachofen (1815–87), as evidently here, "mother right" is usual; it refers to a society in which women, though not necessarily holding political power, dominate through kinship and religion. Freud cites Bachofen's *Das Mutterrecht* (1861) also in *Totem and Taboo*, part IV; SE XIII, p. 144 (where the translation is "matriarchy"). Cf. *Myth, Religion, and Mother Right: Selected Writings of J. J. Bachofen*, tr. R. Manheim (Princeton and London, 1967).

[3] Arthur Kronfeld (1886–19—), psychiatrist of Heidelberg, later in Berlin; "Über die psychologischen Theorien Freuds und verwandte Anschauungen," *Archiv für die gesamte Psychologie*, XXII (Dec. 1911).

[4] "Eine Kritik," *Jahrbuch*, IV:2 (1912), 741–99.

know the jargon. Because of its nature and length this counter-critique can be published only in the *Jahrbuch*, and I am submitting it to you to that end. It seems to me that a reaction to K. is desirable.

Of course I am willing to express an opinion of the paper in dispute between you and Bleuler, but I should not like to make a decision, because his rights as director are not inferior to mine.

I should welcome a postcard with your answer.

Sincerely yours, FREUD

315 J

1003 Seestrasse, Küsnach-Zürich,
Dear Professor Freud,   17 May 1912[1]

Of course I shall be delighted to publish Rosenstein's rejoinder in the Jahrbuch. Kronfeld is an arrogant gasbag who in my view doesn't even deserve refuting. I have written to him personally that I shall not reply to his criticism, since his criticism (as he himself has admitted) turns out to be a joke. He tried to imitate our method and failed. Thereupon he gave up trying and criticized the method (instead of himself). He has admitted to me in a letter that his position is the following: 1. the method is false and leads nowhere; 2. the facts asserted by ΨΛ *do not exist*. He denied that he was talking like a Schoolman. *We* were the Schoolmen *because we would not listen to logic.*

Rosenstein's reply could appear in Part II of the 1912 volume. The deadline is the end of July.

As regards the question of incest, I am afraid of making a very paradoxical impression on you. I only venture to throw a bold conjecture into the discussion: the large amount of free-floating anxiety in primitive man, which led to the creation of taboo ceremonies in the widest sense (totem, etc.), produced among other things the *incest taboo* as well (or rather: the mother and father taboo). The incest taboo does not correspond with the specific value of incest *sensu strictiori* any more than the sacredness of the totem corresponds with its biological value. From this standpoint we must say that incest is forbidden *not because it is desired* but because the free-floating anxiety regressively reactivates infantile material and turns it into a ceremony of atonement (as though incest had been, or might have been, desired). Psychologically, the incest prohibition doesn't have the significance which

---

[1] Published in *Letters*, ed. G. Adler, vol. 1.

one must ascribe to it if one assumes the existence of a particularly strong incest wish. The aetiological significance of the incest prohibition must be compared directly with the so-called sexual trauma, which usually owes its aetiological role only to regressive reactivation. The trauma is *seemingly important* or real, and so is the incest prohibition or incest barrier, which from the psychoanalytical point of view has taken the place of the sexual trauma. Just as *cum grano salis* it doesn't matter whether a sexual trauma really occurred or not, or was a mere fantasy, it is psychologically quite immaterial whether an incest barrier really existed or not, since it is essentially a question of later development whether or not the so-called problem of incest will become of apparent importance. Another comparison: the occasional cases of real incest are of as little importance for the ethnic incest prohibitions as the occasional outbursts of bestiality among primitives are for the ancient animal cults. In my opinion the incest barrier can no more be explained by reduction to the possibility of real incest than the animal cult can be explained by reduction to real bestiality. The animal cult is explained by an infinitely long psychological development which is of paramount importance and not by primitive bestial tendencies—these are nothing but the quarry that provides the material for building a temple. But the temple and its meaning have nothing whatever to do with the quality of the building stones. This applies also to the incest taboo, which as a special psychological institution has a much greater—and different—significance than the prevention of incest, even though it may look the same from outside. (The temple is white, yellow, or red according to the material used.) Like the stones of a temple, the incest taboo is the symbol or vehicle of a far wider and special meaning which has as little to do with real incest as hysteria with the sexual trauma, the animal cult with the bestial tendency and the temple with the stone (or better still, with the primitive dwelling from whose form it is derived).

I hope I have expressed myself a bit more clearly this time.

Bleuler has withdrawn the dissertation. By golly, it was really too stupid. And I won't have any stupidities in the *Jahrbuch*. As director, Bleuler should make better use of his critical faculties. I only hope you won't be bothered with it.

With many kind regards,

Most sincerely yours, JUNG

316 F

Dear friend,   23 May 1912, Vienna, IX. Berggasse 19

Many thanks for your quick answer and explanations. Rosenstein will send you his article directly, he is willing to accept any cuts and changes you may suggest.

In the libido question, I finally see at what point your conception differs from mine. (I am referring of course to incest, but I am thinking of your heralded modifications in the concept of the libido.) What I still fail to understand is why you have abandoned the older view and what other origin and motivation the prohibition of incest can have.[1] Naturally I don't expect you to explain this difficult matter more fully in letters; I shall be patient until you publish your ideas on the subject.

I value your letter for the warning it contains, and the reminder of my first big error, when I mistook fantasies for realities. I shall be careful and keep my eyes open every step of the way.

But if we now set reason aside and attune the machine to pleasure, I own to a strong antipathy towards your innovation. It has two sources. First the regressive character of the innovation. I believe we have held up to now that anxiety originated in the prohibition of incest; now you say on the contrary that the prohibition of incest originated in anxiety, which is very similar to what was said before the days of ΨA.

Secondly, because of a disastrous similarity to a theorem of Adler's, though of course I do not condemn all Adler's inventions. He said:[2] the incest libido is "arranged"; i.e., the neurotic has no desire at all for his mother, but wants to provide himself with a motive for scaring himself away from his libido; he therefore pretends to himself that his libido is so enormous that it does not even spare his mother. Now this still strikes me as fanciful, based on utter incomprehension of the unconscious. In the light of your hints, I have no doubt that your derivation of the incestuous libido will be different. But there is a certain resemblance.

[1] Holograph: the predicate *sein kann*, here translated "can have," inadvertently omitted.

[2] In the papers that Adler read in the Vienna Society in Jan. and Feb. 1911 (see above, 231 F n. 7 and 233 F n. 4); both were later published in *Heilen und Bilden* (with C. Furtmüller and E. Wexberg, Munich, 1914), pp. 94–114. (Professor H. L. Ansbacher kindly supplied this information.)

But I repeat: I recognize that these objections are determined by the pleasure principle.

I shall be closer to you geographically during the Whitsun weekend. On the evening of the 24th I shall be leaving for Constance to see Binswanger. I am planning to be back on the following Tuesday. The time is so short that I shall not be able to do more.

With kind regards to you and your family,

Yours, FREUD

P.S. Jones has sent a short article on Prince's analysis of Roosevelt for the *Zentralblatt*. I should like to append the blame that is not expressed by Jones.[3]

317 J

1003 Seestrasse, Küsnacht-Zürich,
Dear Professor Freud,   25 May 1912

I hope nothing untoward has happened that would account for your delay in answering my last letter.[1] If I have the assurance that there are no weightier reasons behind the delay, I shall naturally go on waiting and not make any exorbitant demands on your time and nervous energy.

With kind regards,

Most sincerely yours, JUNG

318 J

1003 Seestrasse, Küsnach-Zürich,
Dear Professor Freud,   8 June 1912

Many thanks for kindly sending me your offprint, "Recommendations,"[1] so excellent in content and worthy of emulation!

[3] Freud did so, in the following footnote to Jones's article: "We should like to emphasize that we do not at all favour the tendency to exploit psychoanalysis for the invasion of privacy.—The Editors." (*Zentralblatt*, II:12, Sept. 1912.)

[1] At that time, a letter posted in Vienna normally reached Zürich the following day; cf. above, 84 F n. 1.

[1] "Ratschläge für den Arzt bei der psychoanalytischen Behandlung," *Zentralblatt*, II:9 (1912) = "Recommendations to Physicians Practising Psycho-analysis," SE XII.

On the question of incest, I am grieved to see what powerful affects you have mobilized for your counter-offensive against my suggestions. Since I think I have objective reasons on my side, I am forced to stand by my interpretation of the incest concept, and see no way out of the dilemma. It is not for frivolous reasons or from regressive prejudices that I have been led to this formulation, as will, I hope, become clear to you when you read my painstaking and intricate examination of the whole problem in my second part. The parallel with Adler is a bitter pill; I swallow it without a murmur. Evidently this is my fate. There is nothing to be done about it, for my reasons are overwhelming. I set out with the idea of corroborating the old view of incest, but was obliged to see that things are different from what I expected.

Dr. van Renterghem of Amsterdam is with me for instruction in analysis. He is 67 years old, a psychologically compensated regicide. This is what drives him to Canossa[2] in his old age.

I am hard at work on my American lectures. They are about the theory of ΨA (sexual theory, libido theory, etc.).

Until a few days ago I was away in the mountains for another military exercise—all rather hectic. Some of my mail got lost, so I hope you didn't write to me just then. The last thing I had from you was a postcard.[3]

The fact that you felt no need to see me during your visit to Kreuzlingen must, I suppose, be attributed to your displeasure at my development of the libido theory. I hope we shall be able to come to an understanding on controversial points later on. It seems I shall have to go my own way for some time to come. But you know how obstinate we Swiss are.

With kind regards,

Most sincerely yours, JUNG

[2] I.e., to a place of penance. The reference is to Emperor Henry IV's humbling himself before Pope Gregory VII at Canossa in 1077 after having been deposed and excommunicated. The reference to regicide, above, is unclear.

[3] Missing.

319 F

Dear friend,   13 June 1912, Vienna, IX. Berggasse 19

About the libido question, we shall see. The nature of the change you have made is not quite clear to me and I know nothing of its motivation. Once I am better informed, I shall surely be able to switch to objectivity, precisely because I am well aware of my bias. Even if we cannot come to terms immediately, there is no reason to suppose that this scientific difference will detract from our personal relations. I can recall that there were profounder differences between us at the beginning of our relationship. In 1908 it was reported to me from various quarters that a "negative fluctuation" had occurred in Burghölzli, that my views had been superseded. This did not deter me from visiting you in Zürich, in fact it was my reason for doing so, and I found everything quite different from what I had been led to expect. Consequently I cannot agree with you when you say that my failure to go to Zürich from Constance[1] was motivated by my displeasure at your libido theory. A few months earlier you would probably have spared me this interpretation, all the more so because the circumstances do not warrant it. They are as follows: Because of illness in my family my visit to Binswanger was definitely decided on only a few days in advance. When I saw it would be possible, I wrote to you, so that you must have known at the time of my arrival that I would be in Constance. I then spent two nights and one day on the train, so as to be able to spend two nights and two days in one place. After a period of gruelling work that was just about enough travelling. To go to Zürich I should have had to sacrifice one of the two days and so deprive my host of half the time allotted to him. I had a special reason, unknown to you, for wanting to talk with Binswanger at that time.[2] But if you had come and spent half a day in Constance, it would have been a great pleasure for us all. I did not ask you to come, because it is an imposition to ask anyone to spend a holiday in such a way if he has something better to do or wants to rest. But I should have been pleased if you yourself had thought of it. Binswanger would not have taken it amiss, because he phoned Häberlin asking him to come—as it

---

[1] For an account of the "Kreuzlingen episode," see Jones, II, pp. 104/92 and 162f./143f. (On the former page, Freud's 3 June 12 letter to Abraham is cited as a source, but the text in the *Freud/Abraham Letters* omits the part about the Kreuzlingen visit.) Also see L. Binswanger, *Sigmund Freud: Reminiscences of a Friendship*, pp. 42ff., and Schur, *Freud: Living and Dying*, pp. 260–64.

[2] Binswanger underwent surgery for a malignancy (Schur, p. 262).

happened, he was unable to, because his wife was on holiday. Your remark pains me because it shows that you do not feel sure of me.

Here there is little to report. Our Wednesday evenings have stopped. Oberholzer[2] has come to me for analysis, unfortunately a very abbreviated one. Jones is expected any day,[3] perhaps he has already been in Zürich. This year I have worked much more, and, thanks no doubt to Karlsbad, more easily, than in former years, and I am very glad that in little more than four weeks I shall be leaving for Karlsbad with my wife. I may have ΨAtical company there, van Emden.

Imago is thriving and already has 230 subscribers.

Adler's book *On the Nervous Character*[4] appeared a few days ago. I am unlikely to read it but I have been made acquainted with parts of it. Perhaps he will capture the Viennese citadel that has resisted us so stubbornly. He can have it. Viennese interest in *Imago*, for instance, has been conspicuously small, whereas subscribers turn up in the unlikeliest small towns in Germany.

A big book by Rank about the problem of incest in literature[5] is already in galleys.

With kind regards,

Yours, FREUD

P.S. The postcard you mention is the last thing I wrote you.

320 J

1003 Seestrasse, Küsnach-Zürich,

Dear Professor Freud,   18 July 1912

Until now I didn't know what to say to your last letter. Now I can only say: I understand the Kreuzlingen gesture. Whether your policy is the right one will become apparent from the success or failure of my future work. I have always kept my distance, and this will guard against any imitation of Adler's disloyalty.

Yours sincerely, JUNG

[2] Emil Oberholzer (1883–1958), then of Schaffhausen, a member of the Zürich Society. Later he followed Freud and, with his wife Mira Gincburg (see above, 153 J n. 1) and Pfister, founded the Swiss Society for Psychoanalysis in 1919. The Oberholzers came to New York in 1938 and joined the New York Society. Emil Oberholzer was also distinguished as a Rorschach specialist.

[3] See Jones, *Free Associations*, p. 197.

[4] *Über den nervösen Charakter* (Wiesbaden, 1912) = *The Neurotic Constitution*, tr. B. Glueck and J. E. Lind (New York, 1916).

[5] *Das Inzest-Motiv in Dichtung und Sage* (Vienna, 1912).

321 J

1003 Seestrasse, Küsnach-Zürich,

Dear Professor Freud,   2 August 1912

I don't think you will object to my asking Bleuler to take over the editing of the second half of the current *Jahrbuch* while I am in America. It is a purely editorial matter that will not make undue demands on his time. I think he will agree. I should be glad of any contributions from you and your pupils. For the time being the Zürich production has run out. Even so, the second half is well in hand if all the expected contributions come in. But there's nothing in the offing for January 1913. As I shall not be back until November I will hardly be in a position to make the necessary preparations.

Rank's book has arrived. It is a very distinguished piece of work and will make a big impression. But, as you know, I am not in agreement with his theoretical position on the incest problem. The salient fact is simply the regressive movement of libido and not the mother, otherwise people without parents would have no chance to develop an incest complex; whereas I know from experience that the contrary is true. In certain circumstances, indeed as a general rule, the fantasy object is *called* "mother." But it seems to me highly unlikely that primitive man ever passed through an era of incest. Rather, it would appear that the first manifestation of incestuous desire was the prohibition itself. Later I shall review Rank's book for the *Jahrbuch*.[1] It contains some splendid material, and with the above proviso I fully subscribe to Rank's interpretation. I shall also subject Adler's book to critical scrutiny and take the occasion to underline its improprieties.

My American lectures are now finished and will put forward tentative suggestions for modifying certain theoretical formulations. I shall not, however, follow Adler's recipe for overcoming the father, as you seem to imagine. That cap doesn't fit.

I shall table my presidency for discussion at the next congress so as to let the Association decide whether deviations are to be tolerated or not.

With best regards,

Most sincerely yours, JUNG

---

[1] Jung never published a review of Rank's book on the incest motive.

Martha Freud with her daughter Sophie, summer 1912

The Fordham Lectures; the Committee

In company with his wife and Dr. and Mrs. van Emden, Freud was in Karlsbad for treatment for a month beginning 14 July. The Freuds left Karlsbad on 14 August and went with their children to a resort near Bozen (Bolzano) in the Dolomites, then to another at San Cristoforo, on Lago di Caldonazzo, near Trent. (See plate VII.) Meanwhile, the seasonal meeting of Swiss psychiatrists took place in Zürich on 7 September—see above, 285 J—followed immediately by the third annual meeting of the International Society for Medical Psychology and Psychotherapy, 8–9 September, presided over by Bleuler; psychoanalytical papers were read by Bleuler, Maier, Maeder, Seif, Jones, and Adler. See Seif's report in the *Zeitschrift*, I:1 (1913), 95ff. and Riklin's in *Zentralblatt*, III:2 (Nov. 1912). During September, Freud and Ferenczi were in Rome. See *Letters*, ed. E. L. Freud, pp. 287–293, for several family letters written over this time. A fuller account of the summer is given by Jones, II, pp. 104f./92f.

After his Army service, Jung left Zürich for New York on Saturday, 7 September, according to Emma Jung's letter of the 12th, below. Jung's foreword to the lectures states that they were given in the Extension Course at Fordham University, Bronx, New York, in September, at the invitation of Dr. Smith Ely Jelliffe, founder the next year, with William Alanson White,[1] of the *Psychoanalytic Review* (New York). The lectures, entitled *The Theory of Psychoanalysis*, in an English translation by Dr. and Mrs. M. D. Eder and Sister Mary Moltzer, were published in five issues of the *Review*, I–II (1913–15); German version, "Versuch einer Darstellung der psychoanalytischen Theorie," *Jahrbuch*, V:1 (1913). (In CW 4.) They set forth in detail Jung's chief departures from Freudian principles. For Putnam's criticism of one of the lectures, see his letter to Jones, 24 Oct. 12, in *Putnam and Psychoanalysis*, pp. 276f.

While in New York, Jung gave an interview to the *New York Times*, published Sunday, 29 Sept., sec. V, p. 2: a full page, featuring a full-length photograph and headed " 'America Facing Its Most Tragic Moment'—Dr. Carl Jung." (In *C. G. Jung Speaking*, in press.)[2] Subsequently he visited Chicago, Trigant Burrow in Baltimore (see *Letters*, ed. G. Adler, vol. 1, 26 Dec. 12) and William Alanson White in Washington, D.C. (see below, 323 J). Whether, as he intended, he sailed home, by way of the West Indies has not been established.

[1] Jelliffe (1866–1945), clinical professor of mental diseases, Fordham Medical School, and White (1870–1937), superintendent of St. Elizabeths Hospital, Washington, helped foster psychoanalysis in U.S.A. Both had met Jung at the Amsterdam Congress, 1907. Also see Jung to Jelliffe, 24 Feb. 36, in *Letters*, ed. Adler, vol. 1.

[2] That and other photographs of Jung were made by the Campbell Studio in the Waldorf-Astoria Hotel; see pl. VIII; also *Letters*, ed. Adler, vol. 1, frontispiece.

It was also during this summer that Jones, who was in Vienna, conceived the idea of forming "a small group of trustworthy analysts as a sort of 'Old Guard' around Freud." He was distressed, he writes, by the defections of Adler and Stekel, "and it was disturbing to hear from Freud in July, 1912, that now his relations with Jung were beginning to be strained." Ferenczi and Rank concurred with Jones, who on 30 July wrote to Freud about the idea and received an enthusiastic response. Sachs and Abraham were brought into the "Committee," as the secret group was called, and in 1919 Freud proposed Eitingon as the sixth member. (See Jones, II, ch. VI.)

From Emma Jung

Dear Professor Freud,   Küsnacht, 10 September [1912][1]

The offprints of Part II of "Transformations and Symbols"[2] have just come out and you must be the first to receive one. From Jones, whom I met at the Congress here, I heard that Frau Hollitscher is ill again. I was so sorry to hear this and find it especially sad that her and all your hopes have again come to nothing. I share your sorrow and your worry with heartfelt sympathy and I hope, and wish, that everything will soon take a good turn. How are your wife and the other children? We had a dismal summer too; the children had whooping cough and now measles; Carl was away nearly all summer; since Saturday he has been on the trip to America after spending only one day here between military service and departure. I have so much to do now that I can't let too much libido travel after him to America, it might so easily get lost on the way.

Please greet all your dear ones from me and give my best wishes to your daughter.

           With kindest regards, EMMA JUNG

322 J

KUESSNACHT ZRCH

PROFESSOR FREUD   [11 NOVEMBER 1912][1]
BERGGASSE 19 VIENNA

AGREE WITH STEKEL'S REMOVAL AS EDITOR NOT WITH YOUR RESIGNATION AS DIRECTOR REQUEST ORIENTATION PLEASE SUBMIT RESOLUTIONS TO

---

[1] Holograph: year date omitted; 1910 written in another hand. Writing to Jones, 14 Sept. 12, Freud was grateful for this letter (Jones, II, p. 107/94f.).
[2] See below, 324 F n. 2.

---

[1] Headed with code numbers "99 33 11/11 8/30 N = 1."

C. G. Jung, 1912, in New York. See comment following 321 J

INTERNATIONAL ASSOCIATION OTHERWISE FINANCIAL CHAOS = JUNG
RICKLIN

323 J

1003 Seestrasse, Küsnach-Zürich,

Dear Professor Freud,   11 November 1912

I have just got back from America and hasten to give you my news.
Of course I should have done so from America weeks ago but was so
busy that I had neither the inclination nor the leisure to write.

I found the activities of the ΨA Society most satisfactory. There are
some really bright people in it. Brill has gone to a lot of trouble and
is now reaping the reward of his labours. Altogether, the ΨA movement over there has enjoyed a tremendous upswing since we were last
in America. Everywhere I met with great interest and was favourably
received. Thus I had rich soil to work on and was able to do a very
great deal for the spread of the movement. I gave 9 lectures at the
Jesuit (!) University of Fordham, New York—a critical account of
the development of the theory of ΨA. I had an audience of ca. 90
psychiatrists and neurologists. The lectures were in English. Besides
that, I held a 2-hour seminar every day for a fortnight, for ca. 8 pro-
fessors. Naturally I also made room for those of my views which
deviate in places from the hitherto existing conceptions, particularly
in regard to the libido theory. I found that my version of ΨA won
over many people who until now had been put off by the problem of
sexuality in neurosis.[1] As soon as I have an offprint, I shall take pleasure in sending you a copy of my lectures in the hope that you will
gradually come to accept certain innovations already hinted at in my
libido paper. I feel no need to let you down provided you can take
an objective view of our common endeavours. I regret it very much
if you think that the modifications in question have been prompted
solely by resistances to you. Your Kreuzlingen gesture has dealt me a
lasting wound. I prefer a direct confrontation. With me it is not a

[1] This is apparently what Freud refers to in "On the History of the Psycho-
Analytic Movement" (orig. 1914), SE XIV, p. 58: "In 1912 Jung boasted, in a
letter from [sic] America, that his modifications of psycho-analysis had overcome
the resistances of many people who had hitherto refused to have anything to do
with it. I replied [324 F par. 1] that this was nothing to boast of, and that the
more he sacrificed of the hard-won truths of psycho-analysis the more would he
see resistances vanishing."

question of caprice but of fighting for what I hold to be true. In this matter no personal regard for you can restrain me. On the other hand, I hope this letter will make it plain that I feel no need at all to break off personal relations with you. I do not identify you with a point of doctrine. I have always tried to play fair with you and shall continue to do so no matter how our personal relations turn out. Obviously I would prefer to be on friendly terms with you, to whom I owe so much, but I want your objective judgment and no feelings of resentment. I think I deserve this much if only for reasons of expediency: I have done more to promote the ΨA movement than Rank, Stekel, Adler, etc. put together. I can only assure you that there is no resistance on my side, unless it be my refusal to be treated like a fool riddled with complexes. I think I have objective reasons for my views.

I lectured in Chicago, Baltimore, and at the New York Academy of Medicine with apparent success. I also gave two clinical lectures on Dem. praec. in Bellevue Hospital, New York, and another on Ward's Island,[2] and in Washington I analysed 15 Negroes, with demonstrations.[3] On the way back I stopped off in Amsterdam and got van Renterghem, van Emden, and van der Chijs[4] to start a local group.

I hear difficulties have arisen with Stekel.[5] I'd like to know a bit more about this since the *Zentralbatt* is the official organ. I can hardly conceive of your withdrawing as director. This would be a

---

[2] Bellevue Hospital was and is part of the New York City system. Ward's Island was the location of the New York State Psychiatric Institute.

[3] On 22 Nov. 12, Jung lectured to the Zürich Society on "The Psychology of the Negro"; for his abstract, see *Zeitschrift*, I:1 (1913), 115 (*Bulletin* section); CW 18. He first referred to the work at St. Elizabeths Hospital in *Psychologische Typen* (1921); see *Psychological Types*, CW 6, par. 747: "I have . . . been able to demonstrate a whole series of motifs from Greek mythology in the dreams and fantasies of pure-bred Negroes suffering from mental disorders." Also *Symbols of Transformation* (orig. 1952), CW 5, par. 154 and n. 2, but not in "Wandlungen und Symbole der Libido" (1911/12).

[4] A. van der Chijs (1875–1926), Amsterdam psychiatrist. The Dutch Psychoanalytic Society was actually not founded until 1917, in van der Chijs's house; see below, n. 1 to comment following 327 J.

[5] Jones recounts (II, pp. 154f./136f.) Freud's dissatisfaction with Stekel as editor of the *Zentralblatt* earlier in 1912 and Stekel's refusal to accept Freud's proposal that Victor Tausk edit book reviews. Freud wrote to Abraham 3 Nov. 12 that "the occasion for the split was not a scientific one," but Stekel's presumption in excluding another member of the Society from the reviews (*Freud/Abraham Letters*, p. 125). Stekel's resignation from the society was announced at the 6 Nov. meeting. See *Minutes*, IV, and *Zeitschrift*, I (1913), 112. Stekel's account of the break is given in his *Autobiography* (New York, 1950), pp. 142f.

source of endless difficulties, also for the Association, not to mention the loss of face. It is rather Stekel who should quit. Stekel has done enough damage as it is with his mania for indecent confessions bordering on exhibitionism. I am rather surprised that, as president, I have received no direct news.

　With best regards,

Most sincerely, JUNG

324 F

Dear Dr. Jung,[1]　　14 November 1912, Vienna, IX. Berggasse 19

I greet you on your return from America, no longer as affectionately as on the last occasion in Nuremburg—you have successfully broken me of that habit—but still with considerable sympathy, interest, and satisfaction at your personal success. Many thanks for your news of the state of affairs in America. But we know that the battle will not be decided over there. You have reduced a good deal of resistance with your modifications, but I shouldn't advise you to enter this in the credit column because, as you know, the farther you remove yourself from what is new in ΨA, the more certain you will be of applause and the less resistance you will meet.

You can count on my objectivity and hence on the continuance of our relations; I still hold that personal variations are quite justified and I still feel the same need to continue our collaboration. I must remind you that we first made friends at a time when you had gone back to the toxic theory of Dem. pr.

I must own that I find your harping on the "Kreuzlingen gesture" both incomprehensible and insulting, but there are things that cannot be straightened out in writing.

I am eagerly looking forward to an offprint of your lectures, because your long paper on the libido,[2] part of which—not the whole—I liked

---

[1] Holograph: *Lieber Herr Doktor.*

[2] "Wandlungen und Symbole der Libido," Part II, *Jahrbuch*, IV:1 (1912). The two parts together were reprinted the same year in book form (with subtitle: *Beiträge zur Entwicklungsgeschichte des Denkens*) by Deuticke, Vienna. Tr. Beatrice M. Hinkle as *Psychology of the Unconscious: A Study of the Transformations and Symbolisms of the Libido; A Contribution to the History of the Evolution of Thought* (New York, 1916; London, 1917). Nearly 40 years later, Jung comprehensively revised the work as *Symbole der Wandlung: Analyse des*

very much, has not clarified your innovations for me as I might have wished.

My letter to Riklin,[3] written before I could have known you were back, has given you the information you ask for about developments at the *Zentralblatt*. For the sake of completeness I shall tell you a little more. I presume that you now know why I withdrew as director, instead of changing the editor. I saw that I did not have the power, that the publisher sided with Stekel and would find some indirect way of forcing me out, which would have had grave disadvantages. For a whole year I should have had to take the responsibility for a journal which Stekel manipulated at will and on which I could exert no influence. And by next September[4] we should have been left without an organ. That was intolerable. And so I jettisoned the journal along with the editor.

You ask not unreasonably: But what about the official character of the journal? Naturally this was the first point I made in my discussions with Stekel. I suggested that we settle our dispute by letting the local groups (or the Viennese alone) vote on it. I spoke of his obligations, but he was puffed up with possessive pride and my appeals had no effect. His only answer was: It's my journal and none of the Association's business. At this point I should have taken the logical step of submitting the matter to the President for an official decision if—said president had been within reach. But you had left for America without delegating anyone to attend to your presidential business; we had not been informed either officially or privately when you would return, and rumour had it that you would be gone a long time. If I had known you would be back on 12 November, I should have been glad to wait, to leave the decision to you as my superior, and to let you convince yourself that Stekel was not living up to his contract,

---

Vorspiels zu einer Schizophrenie (Zürich, 1952), with 300 illustrations (the original edn. contained 6) = *Symbols of Transformation: An Analysis of the Prelude to a Case of Schizophrenia*, CW 5 (1956). In his foreword to the revised edition, dated Sept. 1950, Jung wrote: "This book was written in 1911, in my thirty-sixth year. The time is a critical one, for it marks the beginning of the second half of life, when a metanoia, a mental transformation, not infrequently occurs. I was acutely conscious, then, of the loss of friendly relations with Freud and of the lost comradeship of our work together. The practical and moral support which my wife gave me at that difficult period is something I shall always hold in grateful remembrance." (CW 5, p. xxvi.)

[3] Unavailable; evidently the telegram (above, 322 J) was in reply to this letter.
[4] The publication year of the *Zentralblatt* ran from October to September.

that nothing could be done with Bergmann, and that we needed a new organ. As it was, I had to attend to it myself. The only other central authority provided for in our statutes,[4a] the council of presidents of the branch societies, did not exist; you had not activated such a council—a point which we ought perhaps to press at the next Congress.

If I had waited indefinitely for your return, precious time would have been lost. With all the negotiations between Vienna, Zürich, and Wiesbaden it would have been impossible to launch the new organ at the beginning of 1913; we should have had to wait until the middle of the year.

Thanks to my prompt action, we shall have an organ of our own again as of 15 January, with a new name and a different publisher, but otherwise, I trust, no worse for being edited by Ferenczi and Rank. I shall soon send you all the details concerning this new journal. But please don't forget that if I am to put your name on the masthead I need a formal statement from you renouncing the *Zentralblatt* and endorsing the new journal.[5]

In this letter and my letter to Riklin I have acquainted you with the state of affairs. I now expect the president to take over all further negotiations with Bergmann. I know there are complications; the worst that can happen is that each member will receive a worthless journal for a whole year and have to pay an additional 15 marks for his usual one. The sacrifice would be bearable I think. If the central organization wishes to spare the members this expense, it can draw on a fund that was set up for the official organ. Of course we should like best for the title of Association organ to be withdrawn as soon as possible from the *Zentralblatt* and transferred to us. But if necessary we can wait for the *Stekelblatt* to die a natural death. We trust that even in an unofficial capacity we can make ourselves indispensable to analysts.

It may interest you to hear about a letter which was shown around at the Vienna Society, in which Adler describes his impressions at the Zürich Congress. He writes that he found the Zürich people in a state of panic flight from sexuality, but is unable to prevent them from

[4a] See appendix 3, Sec. X.
[5] This took the form of an "announcement by the Association President to the local branches" at the beginning of the *Bulletin* in *Zeitschrift*, I:1 (1913); however, Jung's name did not appear on the masthead of the *Zeitschrift* (see facsimile, and below, 326 J).

making use of his ideas. Maybe that will be a lesson to Riklin, who praised him quite unnecessarily in his report on the Congress.[6]

Requesting your prompt attention to the matters here mentioned and wishing you well in your work, I remain

Sincerely,

Your colleague, FREUD

325 J *Internationale Psychoanalytische Vereinigung*

Dear Mr. President,   Küsnach-Zürich, 14 November 1912[1]

In consequence of the latest developments in Vienna a situation has arisen which is in urgent need of discussion. I therefore invite the presidents of the various European branch societies to a conference in Munich on Sunday, November 24th. Kindly inform me *by return* whether you accept this invitation in principle. Further details concerning the place and date of the conference will be communicated later.

Very truly yours,

for C. G. Jung:

F. RIKLIN

326 J

1003 Seestrasse, Küsnach-Zürich,
Dear Professor Freud,   15 November 1912

Your letter, just arrived, has evoked in me a ΨA attitude which seems to be the only right one at the moment. I shall continue to go my own way undaunted. I shall take leave of Stekel's journal because I refuse to go on working with him. I dare not offer you my name for your journal; since you have disavowed me so thoroughly, my collaboration can hardly be acceptable. I should prefer to meet you on the neutral territory of the *Jahrbuch*, which I hope you will enable me to

---

[6] In his report (*Zentralblatt*, III:2, Nov. 1912, 119f.) Riklin wrote that Adler's paper "showed an approach to the neuroses that does justice to a great many important phenomena." Adler's subject was "The Organic Substratum of the Psychoneuroses." Seif's report (*Zeitschrift*, I, 1913, 98) was more comprehensive and more critical.

---

[1] Typewritten circular, signed by Riklin.

go on editing by not imposing too strict a regimen. I propose to let tolerance prevail in the *Jahrbuch* so that everyone can develop in his own way. Only when granted freedom do people give of their best. We should not forget that the history of human truths is also the history of human errors. So let us give the well-meant error its rightful place.

Whether my liberalism is compatible with the further conduct of the Association's affairs is a question to be discussed by the Association itself at the next Congress.

Adler's letter is stupid chatter and can safely be ignored. We aren't children here. If Adler ever says anything sensible or worth listening to I shall take note of it, even though I don't think much of him as a person. As in my work heretofore, so now and in the future I shall keep away from petty complexes and do unflinchingly what I hold to be true and right.

With best regards,

Most sincerely yours, JUNG

327 J   *Internationale Psychoanalytische Vereinigung*

Dear Sir,   Küsnach-Zürich, 19 November 1912[1]

It is unanimously agreed that the conference will be held in Munich. The meeting will take place at 9 a.m., November 24th, at the Park Hotel. I have taken over the necessary arrangements for the meeting, but would request those concerned to see to their own accommodation.

Very truly yours,

President:
DR. JUNG

The Munich Conference

Jung had called the meeting in Munich in order to discuss and settle formally Freud's plan of leaving the *Zentralblatt* to Stekel and founding a new journal, the *Internationale Zeitschrift*, in place of it. The colleagues present were Freud, Jones (who had been in Italy), Abraham, Seif (of Munich), and from Zürich Jung, Riklin, and J. H. W. van Ophuijsen,

---

[1] Typewritten and signed. Presumably a circular letter sent to all participants.

then secretary of the Zürich Society.[1] All agreed with Freud's course of action.

The conference also settled the theme for the next Congress, which would also be in Munich in September 1913: "The Function of Dream." Maeder was to introduce it, and Rank would be his co-speaker.

Then, during a two-hour walk before lunch, Freud and Jung discussed the "gesture of Kreuzlingen"; Jung admitted an oversight and made an apology, and a reconciliation was effected. Towards the end of a high-spirited lunch, Freud began to criticize the Swiss for omitting his name from their psychoanalytic publications. Suddenly, he had a fainting attack. Jung has described and analysed the episode in *Memories* (pp. 157/153) as has Jones at some length (I, pp. 347f./316f. and II, pp. 164ff./145ff.).

Of the conference, Freud wrote to Putnam, 28 Nov. 12: "Everybody was charming to me, including Jung. A talk between us swept away a number of unnecessary personal irritations. I hope for further successful cooperation. Theoretical differences need not interfere. However, I shall hardly be able to accept his modification of the libido theory since all my experience contradicts his position." (*Putnam and Psychoanalysis*, p. 150.)

328 J

1003 Seestrasse, Küsnach-Zürich,
Dear Professor Freud,   26 November 1912

I am glad we were able to meet in Munich, as this was the first time I have really understood you. I realized how different I am from you. This realization will be enough to effect a radical change in my whole attitude. Now you can rest assured that I shall not give up our personal relationship. Please forgive the mistakes which I will not try to excuse or extenuate. I hope the insight I have at last gained will guide my conduct from now on. I am most distressed that I did not gain this insight much earlier. It could have spared you so many disappointments.

I have been very worried about how you got back to Vienna, and whether the night journey may not have been too much of a strain for you. Please let me know how you are, if only a few words on a postcard.

[1] Ophuijsen (1882–1950), Dutch psychiatrist, at the Burghölzli 1909–13. In 1917 he joined in founding the Dutch Psychoanalytic Society and was for seven years its president; in 1920 he organized the sixth International Psychoanalytic Congress, the first to be held after the war. Following 1935, in New York.

INTERNATIONALE ZEITSCHRIFT
FÜR
ÄRZTLICHE PSYCHOANALYSE

OFFIZIELLES ORGAN
DER
INTERNATIONALEN PSYCHOANALYTISCHEN VEREINIGUNG

HERAUSGEGEBEN VON

PROF. DR. SIGM. FREUD

REDIGIERT VON

DR. S. FERENCZI   DR. OTTO RANK
BUDAPEST   WIEN

PROF. DR. ERNEST JONES
LONDON

UNTER STÄNDIGER MITWIRKUNG VON:

DR. KARL ABRAHAM, BERLIN. — DR. LUDWIG BINSWANGER, KREUZLINGEN. —
DR. POUL BJERRE, STOCKHOLM. — DR. A. A. BRILL, NEW-YORK. — DR. TRIGANT
BURROW, BALTIMORE. — DR. M. D. EDER, LONDON. — DR. J. VAN EMDEN, HAAG. —
DR. M. EITINGON, BERLIN. — DR. PAUL FEDERN, WIEN. — DR. EDUARD HITSCHMANN,
WIEN. — DR. L. JEKELS, WIEN. — DR. FRIEDR. S. KRAUSS, WIEN. — DR. ALPHONSE
MAEDER, ZÜRICH. — DR. J. MARCINOWSKI, SIELBECK. — PROF. MORICHAU-BEAUCHANT,
POITIERS. — DR. OSKAR PFISTER, ZÜRICH. — PROF. JAMES J. PUTNAM, BOSTON. —
DR. R. REITLER, WIEN. — DR. FRANZ RIKLIN, ZÜRICH. — DR. HANNS SACHS, WIEN. —
DR. J. SADGER, WIEN. — DR. L. SEIF, MÜNCHEN. — DR. A. STÄRCKE, HUISTER-HEIDE. —
DR. A. STEGMANN, DRESDEN. — DR. M. WULFF, ODESSA.

I. JAHRGANG, 1913

1913
HUGO HELLER & CIE.
LEIPZIG UND WIEN, I. BAUERNMARKT 3

The *Zeitschrift*: title-page of first issue. See 328 J

May I ask you to be so kind as to make room for me among the contributors to your new journal?¹ I shall try to send you something if occasion arises. You know, of course, how limited my resources are, and how I am squeezed dry by the *Jahrbuch* and my teaching activities. However, I am counting on your patience.

I have already asked Bergmann if he can see me at the end of this week.

Regarding the Congress, I would like to ask if you really do agree with the choice of Rank, or whether you would prefer to be the co-speaker yourself? Or leave it to Ferenczi?

I hope Bleuler has informed you about the articles for the *Jahrbuch*.²
I myself don't know yet what will be in the January issue.

I hope all is well with you personally and with your family,
With kind regards,

Yours sincerely, JUNG

329 F

Dear Dr. Jung, 29 November 1912, Vienna, IX. Berggasse 19

Many thanks for your friendly letter,¹ which shows me that you have dispelled various misconceptions about my conduct and encourages me to entertain the best of hopes for our future collaboration. Believe me, it was not easy for me to moderate my demands on you; but once I had succeeded in doing so, the swing in the other direction was not too severe, and for me our relationship will always retain an echo of our past intimacy. I believe we shall have to lay by a fresh store of benevolence towards one another, for it is easy to see that there will be controversies between us and one always finds it

¹ *Internationale Zeitschrift für ärztliche Psychoanalyse*, edited by Ferenczi, Jones, and Rank and published (bimonthly) by Heller, Vienna. It was the official organ of the Association; first issue, January 1913 (see facsimile). The *Zentralblatt*, no longer the official organ, continued under Stekel's editorship until 1914. Also see "On the History of the Psycho-Analytic Movement," SE XIV.
² During Jung's absence in the U.S.A., Bleuler had chosen the contents of *Jahrbuch* V:1 (1913); see above, 321 J opening.

¹ On 3 Dec. 12, Freud wrote to Abraham: "I received a very kind letter from Jung shortly after returning from Munich, but have not had any news about the outcome of his trip to Wiesbaden." (*Freud/Abraham Letters*, p. 128.) Jung went there on 2 Dec. to confer with Bergmann, publisher of the *Zentralblatt*; see below, 330 J and 331 J.

rather irritating when the other party insists on having an opinion of his own.

Now I shall be glad to answer your questions. My attack in Munich was no more serious than the similar one at the Essighaus in Bremen;[2] my condition improved in the evening and I had an excellent night's sleep. According to my private diagnosis, it was migraine (of the M. ophthalm. type), not without a psychic factor which unfortunately I haven't time to track down now. The dining-room of the Park Hotel seems to hold a fatality for me. Six years ago I had a first attack of the same kind there, and four years ago a second.[3] A bit of neurosis that I ought really to look into.

The director and the editors are extremely pleased to hear that you are not withholding your name from the new journal. They will be grateful even for short contributions, examples from your practice, etc. I should be extremely pleased if my technical papers, three of which have been published in the *Zentralblatt* and which are to be continued in every issue,[4] were to call forth critical or approving comments from other analysts in the correspondence column. It is largely up to the Swiss to see to it that the *Zeitschrift* does not look like a Viennese party organ.

In the second number Ferenczi will probably publish a study[5] of your libido paper, which, it is hoped, will do justice both to the author and to his work. I am gradually coming to terms with this paper (yours, I mean) and I now believe that in it you have brought us a great revelation, though not the one you intended. You seem to have solved the riddle of all mysticism, showing it to be based on the symbolic utilization of complexes that have outlived their function.

Rank accepts with thanks the task assigned to him. He is not a good speaker, but he speaks intelligently. Since everyone likes him, he will be forgiven a certain awkwardness.

All I should like to know about the *Jahrbuch* is the titles of the articles in the next number and how much space is still available in

---

[2] At the start of the trip to America, 20 Aug. 09 (see Jones, II, p. 165/146, and Jung, *Memories*, p. 156/152f.). / The Essighaus was an historic building (1618) in which a well-known restaurant was situated.

[3] See Jones, I, p. 348/317.

[4] I.e., of the *Zeitschrift*. For the first three, see above, 280 F nn. 2 & 3, and 318 J n. 1; the fourth, "Zur Einleitung der Behandlung," *Zeitschrift*, I:1 & 2 (Jan. & Mar. 1913) = "On Beginning the Treatment," SE XII. SE XII contains two further "Papers on Technique," published in the *Zeitschrift*, 1914–15, and a list of all Freud's writings on technique and psychotherapeutic theory.

[5] *Zeitschrift*, I:4 (1913), 391–403.

Internationale Psychoanalytische Vereinigung

Dr. C. G. Jung
Präsident

Küsnach-Zürich, 3 XII.12.

Dieser Brief ist ein unverschämter Versuch, Sie an
meinen Styl zu gewöhnen —
Lieber Herr Professor! Also Vorsicht!

Ich danke Ihnen herzlichst für
eine Stelle in Ihrem Brief, wo Sie von einem
„Stück Neurose" sprechen, dessen Sie nicht los sind.
Dieses „Stück" ist meines Erachtens sehr ernst zu
nehmen, denn es geht, wie die Erfahrung lehrt, in „usque
ad instar voluntariae mortis". Ich habe an diesem
Stück bei Ihnen gelitten, obschon Sie das nicht ge-
sehen und nicht richtig eingesehen haben, als ich meine
Einstellung zu Ihnen erklären wollte — Wäre dieser
Fehler weg, so würden Sie auch, dessen bin ich sicher,
ein anderes Verhältnis zu meiner Arbeit gewinnen.
Dass Sie nämlich — verzeihen Sie mir den unehrerbie-
tigen Ausdruck — meine Arbeit nicht um wenig,
sondern sehr viel unterschätzen, geht aus Ihrer
Bemerkung hervor, dass „ich" ohne es zu beabsichti-
gen, das Rätsel aller Mystik gelöst hätte, welche
auf der symbolischen Verwendung der ausser Dienst
gestellten Complexe ruht?
Lieber Herr Professor, verzeihen Sie
mir nochmals, aber dieser Satz zeigt mir,

479

Jung, 3 Dec. 12 (330 J, p. 1)

the number after that, since I am occasionally asked for this information.

As for me, the next two "Points of Agreement" articles[6] for *Imago* have been weighing on my mind. A multitude of tasks has prevented me from working on them in the last few weeks.

In the family all are well and looking forward to the wedding[7] which is to take place at the end of January. My daughter is going to Hamburg.

With kind regards to you and your wife,

Your untransformed[8] F R E U D

330 J *Internationale Psychoanalytische Vereinigung*

Küsnach-Zürich, 3 December 1912

This letter is a brazen attempt to accustom you to my style. So look out![1]

Dear Professor Freud,

My very best thanks for one passage in your letter, where you speak of a "bit of neurosis" you haven't got rid of. This "bit" should, in my opinion, be taken very seriously indeed because, as experience shows, it leads "usque ad instar voluntariae mortis."[2] I have suffered from this bit in my dealings with you, though you haven't seen it and didn't understand me properly when I tried to make my position clear. If these blinkers were removed you would, I am sure, see my work in a very different light. As evidence that you—if I may be permitted so disrespectful an expression—*underestimate* my work by a very wide margin, I would cite your remark that "without intending it, I have

---

[6] Part II, "Das Tabu und die Ambivalenz der Gefühlsregungen" appeared as two articles in *Imago*, I:3 & 4 (1912) = "Taboo and Emotional Ambivalence," ch. II of *Totem and Taboo*, SE XIII.

[7] Sophie Freud and Max Halberstadt, 14 Jan. 1913.

[8] Holograph: *unverwandelter*.

---

[1] See facsimile.

[2] = "to the semblance of a voluntary death."—Apuleius, *Metamorphoses*, XI, 21; cf. tr. Robert Graves, *The Golden Ass* (Penguin Classics), p. 284. The reference in Apuleius is to the rites of initiation into the Isis mysteries. Jung cited the quotation in "Wandlungen und Symbole," Part II, ch. VIII; cf. CW 5, par. 644, n. 35.

solved the riddle of all mysticism, showing it to be based on the symbolic utilization of complexes that have outlived their function."

My dear Professor, forgive me again, but this sentence shows me that you deprive yourself of the possibility of understanding my work by your underestimation of it. You speak of this insight as though it were some kind of pinnacle, whereas actually it is at the very bottom of the mountain. This insight has been self-evident to us for years. Again, please excuse my frankness. It is only occasionally that I am afflicted with the purely human desire to be understood *intellectually* and not be measured by the yardstick of neurosis.

As for this bit of neurosis, may I draw your attention to the fact that you open *The Interpretation of Dreams* with the mournful admission of your own neurosis—the dream of Irma's injection—identification with the neurotic in need of treatment. Very significant.

Our analysis, you may remember, came to a stop with your remark that you "could not submit to analysis *without losing your authority*."³ These words are engraved on my memory as a symbol of everything to come. I haven't eaten *my* words, however.

I am writing to you now as I would write *to a friend*—this is *our* style. I therefore hope you will not be offended by my Helvetic bluntness. One thing I beg of you: take these statements as an *effort to be honest* and do not apply the depreciatory Viennese criterion of egoistic striving for power or heaven knows what other insinuations from the world of the father complex. This is just what I have been hearing on all sides these days, with the result that I am forced to the painful conclusion that the majority of ΨAsts misuse ΨA for the purpose of devaluing others and their progress by insinuations about complexes (as though that explained anything. A wretched theory!). A particularly preposterous bit of nonsense now going the rounds is that my libido theory is the product of anal erotism. When I consider *who* cooked up this "theory" I fear for the future of analysis.

I want no infantile outpourings of libidinal appreciation or admiration from ΨAsts, merely an understanding of my ideas. The pity of it

³ In *Memories* (p. 158/154), Jung writes of an occurrence during the trip to America in 1909, when he and Freud analysed one another's dreams every day. "Freud had a dream—I would not think it right to air the problem it involved. I interpreted it as best I could, but added that a great deal more could be said about it if he would supply me with some additional details from his private life. Freud's response was . . . 'But I cannot risk my authority!' " Jung had recounted this experience previously in his Seminar in Analytical Psychology, Zürich, March–July 1925 (Notes, privately issued, 1926), concluding with "this experience with Freud . . . is the most important factor in my relation to him."

is that ΨAsts are just as supinely dependent on ΨA as our opponents are on their belief in authority. Anything that might make them think is written off as a complex. This protective function of ΨA badly needed unmasking.

Now for Bergmann. He was quite disoriented and we have yet to ascertain whether you have in fact given up the directorship without breach of contract. He told me that he did not relieve you of your post in his letter. Also, the contract stipulates one year's notice. Naturally I was flabbergasted. So was B., because he had never really thought about it until then. The withdrawal of the International Association took him completely by surprise. He is only now beginning to realize the situation. You will hear from him shortly. I don't know what he is planning. For him it is a serious matter—a loss of over 10,000 marks. In these circumstances I have made a *provisional contract*, to be discussed when he is in the clear with you. He has been vilely duped by Stekel, who should have been thrown out ages ago. On one point I had to admit B. was right. The founding of *Imago* has cost him a lot of subscribers. It goes against my feeling for sound business to start a new journal before either of the old ones is properly under way. This affair makes an unpleasant impression. Such is the general view. Bergmann is offering Vol. III[4] at half price, 4.50 M., from No. 3 to the end. Better terms could not be negotiated (sum total: 652.50 M.) This can in part be furnished from our fund.

With kind regards, J U N G

331 J *Internationale Psychoanalytische Vereinigung*

Dear Mr. President,   Küsnach-Zürich, 4 December 1912[1]

On December 2nd a provisional agreement was reached between the publisher I. F. Bergmann and the undersigned concerning the separation of the *Bulletin* from the *Zentralblatt*. The agreement is worded as follows:

The undersigned representative of the International Psychoanalytic Association, Privatdocent Dr. Jung, Zürich, and the publisher I. F. Bergmann, Wiesbaden, have today reached the following agreement

[4] Of the *Zentralblatt*.

[1] Typewritten circular to the presidents of the branch societies, with handwritten signature and postscript.

subject to approval by Messrs. Freud and Stekel, co-signatories of the agreements between the publisher and the International Psychoanalytic Association dated September/October 1911, and by the majority of the said Association:

The agreements of 21/22 September and 5/9 October 1911 are cancelled and are replaced by the following settlement:

For the subscribed 145 copies of the *Zentralblatt für Psychoanalyse* the International Psychoanalytic Association will pay:

1) for Nos. 1–3 of Vol. III: in accordance with the earlier of the agreements referred to above, one fourth of the previously agreed price of 12 marks = 3 marks per copy, or a total of 435 marks.

2) for the remaining 9 Nos. of Vol. III: for the subscribed 145 copies, half the previous price = 4.50 marks per copy, or a total of 652.50 marks.

Starting with No. 4 of the *Zentralblatt für Psychoanalyse*, the designation "Organ of the International Psychoanalytic Association" will no longer appear on the title-page, and the *Bulletin* of the International Psychoanalytical Association will no longer be printed in it.

With respect to this settlement it should be noted: The first 3 numbers must be paid for in full because they had already been printed at the date of this settlement. The purchase of the remaining numbers is contingent upon the following considerations:

On our part: The Association has the *de facto* right to withdraw unconditionally. It makes use of this right inasmuch as it withdraws the title "Official Organ" forthwith.

On the part of the publisher: Under normal conditions it is impossible to waive a contract for delivery in mid-year.

As against this justified objection of the publisher we maintain that the change of circumstances entitles us to this unusual step, although the absence of an explicit agreement between the Association and the publisher leaves our rights in some doubt. In view of this somewhat complicated situation the above settlement may be considered satisfactory to both parties. On the assumption that we shall soon have a new organ for the Association, the additional burden on each member amounts to a mere 4.50 marks. This sum can be further reduced by approximately half through a contribution from our fund.

I would request you, Mr. President, to lay the matter before your local group and to notify me of your approval.

Very truly yours, DR. JUNG

Letter from Bergmann explaining that he has in fact dissociated himself from you *lege artis*. Under these circumstances I wish him the joy of the loss (10–12,000 marks). I hope you weren't offended by my last letter. I wish you the best of everything and I shall not abandon you. You shouldn't be distressed on my account.

Best regards!

332 F

Dear Dr. Jung,   5 [December] 1912[1] Vienna, IX. Berggasse 19

You musn't fear that I take your "new style" amiss. I hold that in relations between analysts as in analysis itself every form of frankness is permissible. I too have been disturbed for some time by the abuse of ΨA to which you refer, that is, in polemics, especially against new ideas. I do not know if there is any way of preventing this entirely; for the present I can only suggest a household remedy: let each of us pay more attention to his own than to his neighbour's neurosis.

Forgive me if I reverse the ratio observed in your letter and devote more space to practical matters, which at least are easier to deal with in a letter. I am referring to the Bergmann matter, in regard to which I cannot conceal a certain dissatisfaction. Your information sounds as if it came from another planet; I cannot fit the pieces together or draw any inference about the situation of the new *Zeitschrift*. Nor can I make a proposal for defraying any loss to the Association wholly or in part, until I know for what I should be making reparation. Finally, it is hard for me to understand or justify your own bias in the matter.

You yourself have no doubt become familiar while in America with the principle that a man who is out for profit must take a good look at the persons and conditions on which his chances of profit depend. And similarly in Europe ignorance is no excuse for a businessman. I have less sympathy than you with Bergmann; if he has been misled by Stekel, that is his affair. I too have suffered enough at his hands.

If Bergmann believes he did not release me from my position in his letter, he has a very low opinion of his own statements. I am enclosing this letter as well as his previous one. He definitely accepts my notice of resignation and promises to announce it in the next issue of the *Zentralblatt*. And now he denies that he has let me out! If he thought I was bound by contract to stay on until the end of the year, that was

[1] Holograph: 5.XI.12.

the time to call it to my attention, instead of agreeing to publish a notice. So you see there is no question of any "breach of contract" on my part. After this answer from B. I had every reason to consider myself free, whether I was before or not.

I really can't see what B. wants of me now. His behaviour towards me, his siding with Stekel, and his letter cannot be ignored; and I have no desire to countermand the first number of the *Zeitschrift* out of consideration for him. (Please return both enclosed letters.)

Now to the *Imago* question, in which to my regret you take sides against me. I cannot help recalling that when *Imago* was founded you reacted not as president of the International Association but as editor of the *Jahrbuch*. I am unable to look at this matter from the standpoint of the publisher or of the editor, I can only respond to your reproaches from the standpoint of the ΨAtical cause. The *Zentralblatt* was unequal to our non-medical tasks, we needed another organ, which I conceived of as an appendage to the *Zentralblatt* and offered first to Bergmann for that reason. He declined, so it had to be published by someone else. As for the risk that the publisher might in one year acquire a certain number of subscribers, I did not take it very seriously. The two journals definitely have a greater appeal than only one, and in the end one helps the other. Stekel has agitated against *Imago* from the start. —

I am sorry not to be able to discuss your remark on the neuroses of analysts at greater length, but this should not be interpreted as a dismissal. In one point, however, I venture to disagree most emphatically: you have not, as you suppose, been injured by my neurosis.

Although you took the trip to see Bergmann in an official capacity, I nevertheless thank you privately for your efforts. Looking forward to further word from you, I send you my regards.

Very cordially yours, FREUD

333 J

1003 Seestrasse, Küsnach-Zürich,

Dear Professor Freud, 7 December 1912

Since you have taken so badly to my "new style," I will tune my lyre a few tones lower, for the present.

Meanwhile, the Bergmann affair has settled itself. He has effectively discharged you, and has been sufficiently punished for it. In view of the fact that *the contract between the I. ΨA A. and Bergmann does*

*not stipulate that your directorship is the indispensable precondition
for our connection with the Zentralblatt,* we are committed by the
wording of the contract to the subscription. I am convinced that we
are not legally in a position to default on our obligations. In these
circumstances our *provisional* contract strikes me as extremely favourable: we can withdraw the *Bulletin* forthwith, and the price for the
remaining issues will be reduced by half. Bergmann could easily have
insisted on more rigorous conditions. As I said, the agreement is provisional and can still be modified on our side. But this would involve
a court of arbitration, and in the end we might get a worse deal for
lack of the above formula. I therefore plead for acceptance.

Further, I would like you to know that I have designs on reviewing
Adler's book.[1] I have succeeded in descending into its depths, where
I found some delightful things that deserve to be hung aloft. The man
really is slightly dotty. "To arrange" = "to miracle,"[2] for instance. The
"junctim"[3] (so far I haven't plumbed its meaning) recalls the
"Tetem" in Fried. Th. Vischer's *A. E.*[4] "Mungo"[5] finds an echo too.
The style is utterly "praecox." The conclusions are significant: in so
far as a man has no masculine protest[6] against women (woman =

---

[1] Jung did not, so far as is known, publish a review of *Über den nervösen Charakter* (see above, 319 F n. 4). Despite the negative tone of the allusions in this
letter, Jung had written the following in his foreword (autumn 1912) to *The
Theory of Psychoanalysis* (CW 4, before par. 203): "Only after the preparation
of these lectures . . . did Adler's book *Über den nervösen Charakter* become
known to me. . . . I recognize that he and I have reached similar conclusions
on various points. . . ." He gave not unfavourable treatment to the book and
to Adler's theories generally in his paper at the Munich Congress, Sept. 1913; see
below, editorial comment following 356 J, and CW 6, pars. 881–82. He further
developed a more positive evaluation of Adler's work in *Psychological Types*
(orig. 1921), CW 6, esp. par. 693.
[2] ". . . through the arrangement of symptoms, the neurotic strives for increased
power," etc.—H. L. and R. R. Ansbacher, eds., *The Individual Psychology of
Alfred Adler* (New York, 1956), p. 112. "To miracle" (hol.: *anwundern*) is a
Schreberism.
[3] *Über den nervösen Charakter*, p. 55. / "A junctim is the purposively slanted association of a thought and a feeling complex, which actually have little or nothing
in common, for the sake of intensifying an affect."—Ansbacher, p. 283. In German,
Junktim is a parliamentary term for two or more unconnected proposals that are
put to a vote as a unit.
[4] Friedrich Theodor Vischer, *Auch Einer: Eine Reisebekanntschaft* (Stuttgart,
1879). "Tetem," the nickname of an absurd character in the novel (1903 edn.,
p. 286), represents a ludicrous combination of heterogeneous elements.
[5] "Mungo" could not be traced (in Adler or Vischer).
[6] *Über den nervösen Charakter*, p. 50. / "The striving to be strong and powerful
in compensation for a feeling of inferiority."—Ansbacher, p. 45.

under = inferior) he is under = inferior = female. Ergo, practically all men are women. Who would have thought of that? This is the kind of insight I would call "junctim." Maybe it's true. At any rate it is a "memento"[7] and a "safeguarding tendency," if one wants to express oneself in pure "organ jargon."[8] The man has wit, by God.

I won't bother you with other things just now. With kind regards,

Yours sincerely, JUNG

334 F

Dear Dr. Jung,   9 December 1912, Vienna, IX. Berggasse 19

I "heard" from Bergmann today. Only a few sentences but I am quite satisfied. He tells me the *Zentralblatt* will no longer bear the official title. We all thank you for your successful handling of the matter. I incline to your argument that we have no proper contract on which to base our demands and will have your circular approved by our Society on Wednesday (11 Dec.). I repeat the offer I made in my telegram[1] to pay half the ransom, so as not to bother our members.

At last I am done with this business and able to get back to work. The third "Points of Agreement"[2] will be my next task. I dare say no more about your libido innovation now that you have made such fun of me for my discovery that it contained the solution to the riddle of mysticism. But I am very eager to read your English lectures. I hope they will meet with vigorous opposition on the part of our fellow analysts; my own opposition, even if it outlives my reading of the lectures, would be too self-evident to make an impression.

Your intention of attacking Adler's book has my entire approval.

---

[7] *Über den nervösen Charakter*, p. 40. / "A memory image, which is a manifestation of the safeguarding tendency [and] can arise from the retention of a childhood experience, or it may be the product of phantasy."—Ansbacher, pp. 288–89.
[8] *Über den nervösen Charakter*, p. 81. / ". . . used broadly to include nonverbal communication."—Ansbacher, p. 221.

---

[1] Missing.
[2] Part III, "Animismus, Magie und Allmacht der Gedanken," *Imago*, II:1 (1913) = "Animism, Magic and the Omnipotence of Thoughts," ch. III of *Totem and Taboo*, SE XIII. Part IV was "Die infantile Wiederkehr des Totemismus," *Imago*, II:4 (1913) = "The Return of Totemism in Childhood," ch. IV, ibid. For the original general title of the four parts, see above, 293 F n. 2. They appeared in one volume as *Totem und Tabu* (Leipzig and Vienna: Heller, 1913).

Apart from the scientific aspect, such a step will also make for political clarity by putting an end to the rumours current here that you are "swinging over" to him. I myself have not read the book; he has not sent me a copy and I am too stingy to spend my good money on such a product. Are you planning to put your criticism on ice (in the *Jahrbuch*) or to serve it hot (in the *Intern. Zeitsch.*)?

I follow you with interest through all the variations of the lyre that you play with such virtuosity.

With kind regards,

Yours sincerely, FREUD

335 J

1003 Seestrasse, Küsnacht-Zürich,

Dear Professor Freud,   [written between 11 and 14 Dec. 1912][1]

I should be glad to make an occasional contribution to the new journal, provided of course that I have anything worthwhile, which is not always the case. The Zürich group proposes the following title:

"Internationale Zeitschrift für *therapeutische* Psychoanalyse."

This suggestion comes from the *theologians*. They don't want to be left out. The pedagogues are also complaining. Perhaps you will lend a willing ear.

I see from Furtmüller's forthcoming critique in the *Zentralblatt*[2] that the Viennese prophets are wrong about a "swing over" to Adler. Even Adler's cronies do not regard me as one of theirs.[3]

It is deplorable that science should still be treated like a profession of faith.

With kind regards,

Most sincerely yours, JUNG

[1] Holograph: undated.

[2] Carl Furtmüller (1880–1951), Viennese educator and socialist, earlier a member of the Society; Adler's closest friend, most prominent co-worker, and eventual biographer (see his biographical essay in H. L. and R. R. Ansbacher, eds., *Alfred Adler: Superiority and Social Interest*, 1964). 1941–47, in the U.S.A. Furtmüller reviewed Jung's Fordham Lectures in the *Zentralblatt*, IV (1913).

[3] Holograph: *Ihrigen* "yours," instead of *ihrigen* "theirs."

336 J *Internationale Psychoanalytische Vereinigung*

Dear Mr. President,   Küsnach-Zürich, 14 December 1912[1]

In answer to your letter I beg to inform you that I have gratefully taken note of your kind offer to defray half the extra expenses for the *Zentralblatt*. We shall first draw on our fund to cover these expenses and then take the liberty of approaching you if a balance remains. I hope I shall soon be able to send you a draft contract for the *Bulletin*.

Very truly yours, DR. C. G. JUNG

337 F

Dear Dr. Jung,   16 December 1912, Vienna, IX. Berggasse 19

I shall submit your suggestion for changing the name of the *Zeitschrift* both to the Society and to the two editors, and report to you on the outcome.

The habit of taking objective statements personally is not only a (regressive) human trait, but also a very specific Viennese failing. I shall be very glad if such claims are not made on you. But are you "objective" enough to consider the following slip without anger?

"Even Adler's cronies do not regard me as one of *yours*."

Yours nevertheless,[1] FREUD

338 J

1003 Seestrasse, Küsnach-Zürich,

Dear Professor Freud,   18 December 1912

May I say a few words to you in earnest? I admit the ambivalence of my feelings towards you, but am inclined to take an honest and absolutely straightforward view of the situation. If you doubt my word, so much the worse for you. I would, however, point out that your technique of treating your pupils like patients is a *blunder*. In that way you produce either slavish sons or impudent puppies (Adler-Stekel and the whole insolent gang now throwing their weight about

---

[1] Typewritten and signed.

[1] Holograph: *Dennoch ganz der Ihrige.*

534

in Vienna). I am objective enough to see through your little trick.[1] You go around sniffing out all the symptomatic actions in your vicinity, thus reducing everyone to the level of sons and daughters who blushingly admit the existence of their faults. Meanwhile you remain on top as the father, sitting pretty. For sheer obsequiousness nobody dares to pluck the prophet by the beard and inquire for once what you would say to a patient with a tendency to analyse the analyst instead of himself. You would certainly ask him: "*Who's* got the neurosis?"

You see, my dear Professor, so long as you hand out this stuff I don't give a damn for my symptomatic actions; they shrink to nothing in comparison with the formidable beam in my brother Freud's eye. I am not in the least neurotic—touch wood! I have submitted *lege artis et tout humblement* to analysis and am much the better for it. You know, of course, how far a patient gets with self-analysis: *not* out of his neurosis—just like you. If ever you should rid yourself entirely of your complexes and stop playing the father to your sons and instead of aiming continually at their weak spots took a good look at your own for a change, then I will mend my ways and at one stroke uproot the vice of being in two minds about you. Do you <u>love neurotics</u> enough to be always at one with yourself? But perhaps you *hate* neurotics. In that case how can you expect your efforts to treat your patients leniently and lovingly *not* to be accompanied by somewhat mixed feelings? Adler and Stekel were taken in by your little tricks[2] and reacted with childish insolence. I shall continue to stand by you publicly while maintaining my own views, but privately shall start telling you in my letters what I really think of you. I consider this procedure only decent.

No doubt you will be outraged by this peculiar token of friendship, but it may do you good all the same.

With best regards,

Most sincerely yours, JUNG

[1] Holograph: *Truc* (French).
[2] As n. 1.

339 J *Internationale Psychoanalytische Vereinigung*

Dear Professor Freud, Küsnach-Zürich, 21 December 1912

Just between ourselves, I am surprised the editors of the new *Zeitschrift* sent your circulars to the presidents of the local groups without informing me. Actually any such proposition should pass through my hands or at least be communicated to me. In the interests of the cause I shall of course say nothing aloud about it, but merely wish to draw the matter to your attention.

By the same post I am sending you a paper by Dr. Trigant Burrow, 707 Saint Paul Street, Baltimore, which I recommend for your new journal.[1] As Dr. Burrow is a very industrious and conscientious worker, I would like to ask you to enter his name on the list of regular contributors.[2] He has asked me to back his request.

Since this letter is being written before the arrival of your answer to my last "secret letter," I make no mention here of that singularly important topic.

With best regards,

Yours sincerely, JUNG[3]

340 F

Dear Dr. Jung, 22 December 1912,[1] Vienna, IX. Berggasse 19

The main reason why the Vienna local branch rejected the proposed change of title was that the announcements, flyers, and so on, had already been printed or mailed, so that consideration for the publisher made it hard to envisage a change. It was really too late.

---

[1] "Die psychologische Analyse der sogennanten Neurasthenie und verwandter Zustände," *Zeitschrift*, I:4 (1913) = "The Psychological Analysis of So-called Neurasthenic and Allied States—a Fragment," *Journal of Abnormal Psychology*, VIII (1913).

[2] Burrow's name was included in the masthead; see facsimile with 330 J.

[3] In *Memories*, Jung recounts the beginning of his "confrontation with the unconscious" with a memorable dream "around Christmas of 1912," and his preoccupation with carving and building in stone began soon afterward (pp. 170–75/165–69).

---

[1] This letter, apparently not sent, was found among Freud's papers. (Some of its contents is repeated in 342 F.) It was published in *Letters*, ed. E. L. Freud, no. 160, in a different translation.

The matter is of no great importance and will cause no trouble, I trust. I do not think "therapeutic" was a good substitution; the pedagogues will soon find that the new journal will be just as receptive to their contributions as the old one was. —

I am sorry my reference to your slip annoyed you so; your reaction seems out of all proportion to the occasion. In regard to your allegation that since I misuse psychoanalysis to keep my students in a state of infantile dependency I myself am responsible for their infantile behaviour, and to the inferences you draw from this contention, I prefer not to judge, because it is hard to judge in matters concerning oneself and such judgments convince no one. I wish merely to provide you with certain facts concerning the foundations of your theory, and leave you to revise it. In Vienna I have become accustomed to the opposite reproach, to wit, that I concern myself too little with the analysis of my "students." And it is quite true that since Stekel, for example, discontinued his treatment with me some ten years ago, I have never said one word to him about the analysis of his own person. In Adler's case I have been even more careful to do nothing of the kind. Whatever analytical remarks I have made about either were made to others and for the most part after our relations had broken off. Consequently I fail to see why you feel so sure of the contrary.

With cordial regards,

Yours, FREUD

341 J *Internationale Psychoanalytische Vereinigung*

Dear Mr. President,   Küsnach-Zürich, 1 January 1913[1]

The separation of the *Zentralblatt* from the I. Psa. A. has made it necessary to find another place for the *Bulletin*.[2] Professor Freud has very obligingly put his newly founded *Internationale Zeitschrift für ärztliche Psychoanalyse* at our disposal on the same conditions as applied to the former *Zentralblatt*. The first issue will be published

---

[1] The letter is handwritten by Riklin. Evidently a circular to the presidents of the branch societies.

[2] The *Bulletin* appeared three times in *Zeitschrift*, I (1913), 110ff., 302ff., 617ff., under the stated editorship of Jung and Riklin. The final issue contained 12 pages abstracting a discussion of Jung's libido theory at the Zürich Society 13 Jan. and 14 Mar. 13.

in January 1913. The disengagement from the former *Zentralblatt* was effected without difficulty, and we are able to defray the relatively small indemnity (625 marks, including the old subscription price) out of the central account so that members will not incur additional expenses because of this change-over. In order to guard against similar disagreeable experiences in the future the central office will draw up a detailed contract with the director, the editors, and the publisher of the new *Zeitschrift*. Your members are requested to arrange for delivery of the new *Zeitschrift* directly with the publisher, Herr Hugo Heller, Bauernmarkt 3, Vienna I.

With best regards, Yours,

for Dr. Jung:

DR. F. RIKLIN

342 F   *Internationale Zeitschrift für Ärztliche Psychoanalyse*[1]

Dear Mr. President,   Vienna, 3 January 1913
Dear Doctor,[2]

I share your opinion that the circulars of the editors of this journal (not *my* circulars as you put it in your letter) ought to have been submitted to the President, and will inform them of your recriminations. There can certainly be no question of ill will.

Burrow's paper arrived today. Your wish that he be included in the masthead of the journal will be respected both by the editors—whom I have not seen in the last few days—and by myself.

Both your suggestions are most welcome as a sign of your interest in the new organ.

———

I can answer only one point in your previous letter in any detail. Your allegation that I treat my followers like patients is demonstrably untrue. In Vienna I am reproached for the exact opposite. I am held responsible for the misconduct of Stekel and Adler; in reality I have not said one word to Stekel about his analysis since it was concluded some ten years ago, nor have I made any use of analysis with Adler, who was never my patient. Any analytical remarks I have

---

[1] For facsimile of the letterhead, see below, 346 F.
[2] Holograph: *Geehrter Herr Praesident. / Lieber Herr Doktor.*

made about them were addressed to others and for the most part at a time when we had ceased to associate with one another. — In building your construction on this foundation you have made matters as easy for yourself as with your famous "Kreuzlingen gesture."

Otherwise your letter cannot be answered. It creates a situation that would be difficult to deal with in a personal talk and totally impossible in correspondence. It is a convention among us analysts that none of us need feel ashamed of his own bit of neurosis. But one who while behaving abnormally keeps shouting that he is normal gives ground for the suspicion that he lacks insight into his illness. Accordingly, I propose that we abandon our personal relations entirely. I shall lose nothing by it, for my only emotional tie with you has long been a thin thread—the lingering effect of past disappointments—and you have everything to gain, in view of the remark you recently made in Munich, to the effect that an intimate relationship with a man inhibited your scientific freedom. I therefore say, take your full freedom and spare me your supposed "tokens of friendship." We are agreed that a man should subordinate his personal feelings to the general interests of his branch of endeavour. You will never have reason to complain of any lack of correctness on my part where our common undertaking and the pursuit of scientific aims are concerned; I may say, no more reason in the future than in the past. On the other hand, I am entitled to expect the same from you.

Regards,

Yours sincerely, FREUD

343 J

1003 Seestrasse, Küsnach-Zürich,

Dear Professor Freud,   3 January 1913

Although you have evidently taken my first secret letter very much to heart or very much amiss, I cannot refrain, while avoiding that topic, from offering you my friendly wishes for the New Year. It is my hope that the ΨAical movement will continue to advance, its vitality unimpaired and indeed heightened by internal conflicts and crosscurrents. Without them there is no life. When everything goes smoothly, petrifaction sets in. "I seek salvation not in rigid forms."[1]

Don't hesitate to tell me if you want no more of my secret letters.

[1] *Faust*, II, Act I, A Gloomy Gallery.

I too can get along without them. Needless to say I have no desire to torment you. But if you profess a friendly attitude towards me, I must insist on my right to reciprocate, and shall treat you with the same analytical consideration which you extend to me from time to time. You surely know that the understanding of ΨA truths is in direct proportion to the progress one has made in oneself. If one has neurotic symptoms there will be a failure of understanding somewhere. Where, past events have already shown. So if I offer you the unvarnished truth it is meant for your good, even though it may hurt.

I think my honourable intentions are perfectly clear, so I need say no more. The rest is up to you.

From the drift of this letter you will be able to guess what my wishes are for the New Year.

With best regards,

Most sincerely yours, JUNG

344 J *Internationale Psychoanalytische Vereinigung*

Dear Professor Freud, Küsnach-Zürich, 6 January 1913

I accede to your wish that we abandon our personal relations, for I never thrust my friendship on anyone. You yourself are the best judge of what this moment means to you. "The rest is silence."[1]

Thank you for accepting Burrow's paper.

Yours sincerely, JUNG

345 J

Dear Professor Freud, Küsnacht, 9 January 1913[1]

I am prepared to accept Dr. Weissfeld's paper[2] for the *Jahrbuch* and hope to find room for it in the next issue. I must express myself with some reserve because Bleuler has held over two papers from the previous volume.

[1] *Hamlet*, V, ii.

[1] Postcard, typewritten and signed.

[2] Moses Weissfeld (1879–19—), of Bern, originally Russian; "Freuds Psychologie als eine Transformationstheorie," *Jahrbuch*, V:2 (1913).

I thank you for your kind attention and commend the *Jahrbuch* to your continuing goodwill.

Sincerely, DR. JUNG

346 F   *Internationale Zeitschrift für Ärztliche Psychoanalyse*

Dear Mr. President,   Vienna, 27 January 1913[1]
Dear Doctor,

I have the first number of our new *Zeitschrift* before me. I avail myself of this opportunity to thank you for the friendly support which you as president have given the undertaking. It has enabled us from the very start to embark on a policy which we hope to pursue to the satisfaction of all.

Both the editors and the director will be thankful to you for any suggestion as to changes and improvements. The review of the *Jahrbuch*[2] will be continued in the next issue, which will also carry a study of your libido paper by one of the editors.[3] The third number will carry contributions by our American colleagues.[4]

It now appears that a secret contract was concluded a year and a half ago between Stekel and the publisher, providing for my dismissal in the event of a conflict between director and editor. A pretty piece of treachery.

[1] Freud's last surviving letter to Jung. See facsimile.
[2] At its 9 Oct. 12 meeting (the first of the new season), the Vienna Society voted on Freud's motion to establish a review board, to which Federn, Hitschmann, Reitler, and Tausk were assigned. Their task was to review new psychoanalytic publications, particularly the *Jahrbuch*, regularly and publish the reviews in the official organ of the Association, the *Zeitschrift*; see *Minutes*, IV, and *Zeitschrift*, I:1, 112–13. Accordingly, the contents of *Jahrbuch* IV:1 (except papers by Freud and Jones) were reviewed as follows: in I:1, Nelken (see above, 305 J n. 3) and Grebelskaya, by Tausk (see below, 348 J n. 4); Rank and Silberer, by Hitschmann; and Spielrein, by Federn. In I:2, Bleuler, by Rudolf Reitler. For Jung, see next n.
[3] Ferenczi's critique of "Wandlungen und Symbole der Libido" did not appear until I:4.
[4] Putnam, "Bemerkungen über einen Krankheitsfall mit Griselda-Phantasien"; Jones (address given as London), "Die Bedeutung des Grossvaters für das Schicksal des Einzelnen." The next issue contained Burrow's article (see above, 339 J n. 1).

I hope that we shall arrive at a satisfactory understanding on the basis of our common undertakings.

Regards,

Yours very sincerely, FREUD

P.S. I am looking forward to your draft contract and to your decision concerning my contribution to the compensation for Bergmann.

347 J *Internationale Psychoanalytische Vereinigung*

Dear Professor Freud,   Küsnach-Zürich, 31 January 1913

Enclosed please find the *drafts of the contracts*. Please let me have your views. Would you also bring the drafts to the attention of the editors and send the contract with the publisher on to Herr Heller.

The financial settlement with Bergmann can be effected only after I have the consent of the Association as a whole. As I think I have told you already, the compensation for Bergmann will be furnished from the Association's fund. I thank you in the name of the Association for your kind offer.

Please would you let me know whether 7/8 *September* (Sunday and Monday) as date of the Congress is convenient to you personally as well as to the Vienna Society. Meeting place: Munich.

Should it be confirmed that Stekel had a secret contract with Bergmann, this would be precisely the sort of villainy I refuse to be identified with.

For Vol. V Part I of the *Jahrbuch* we have the following in preparation: 1. a paper by Pfister on cryptography and glossolalia. 2. Jones on obsessional neurosis, case material. (I withhold comment on this paper.) 3. Itten: Dem. praec. case material. 4. Sadger: On the sadomasochistic complex. 5. My American lectures on the theory of ΨA.[1]

I have no illusions about the forthcoming review of my paper. It has been badly received all round. A beginner's japes, evidently. Understanding is one of the hardest tasks in the transference.

With best regards,

Yours sincerely, JUNG

[1] See appendix 2.

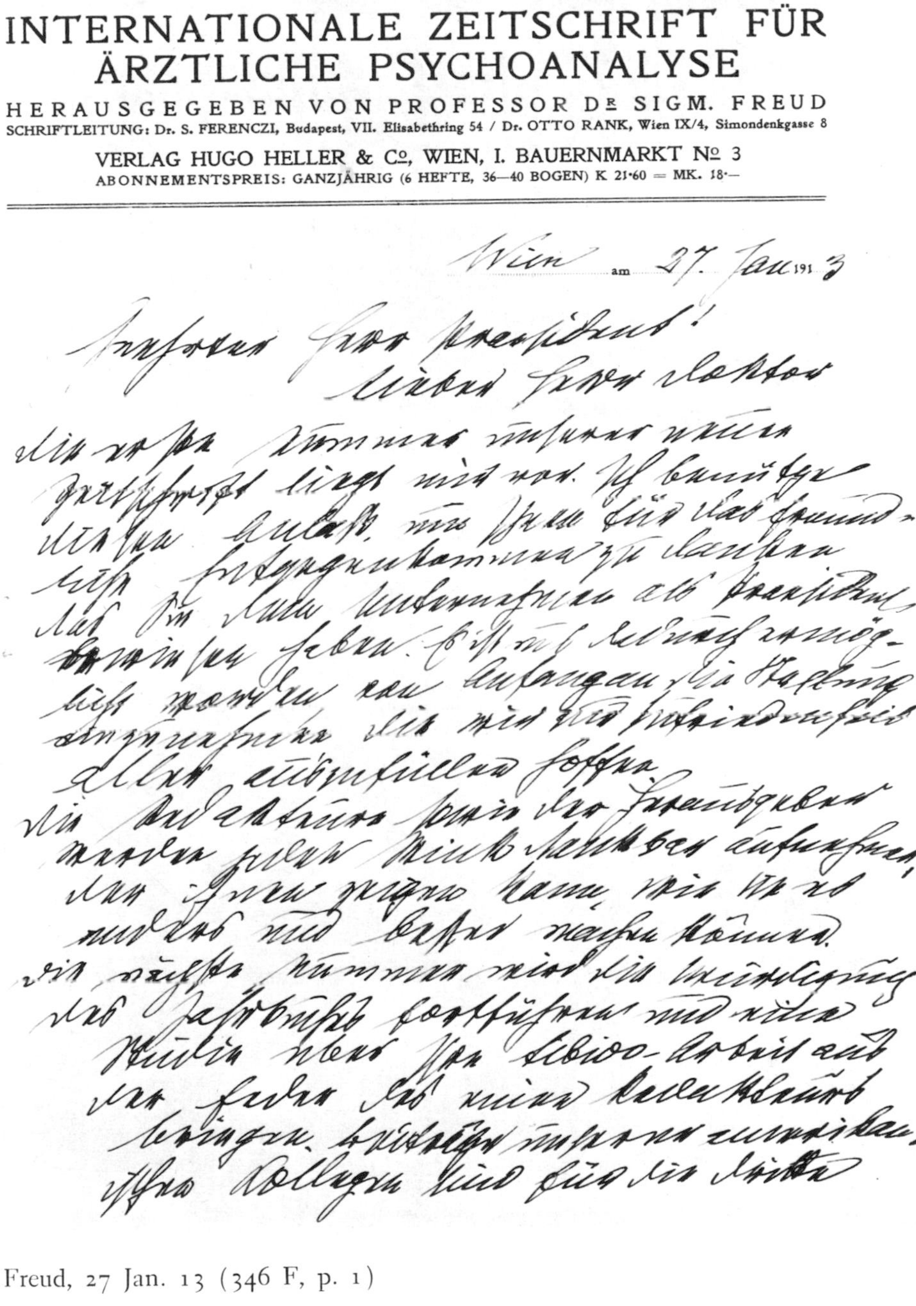

INTERNATIONALE ZEITSCHRIFT FÜR ÄRZTLICHE PSYCHOANALYSE

HERAUSGEGEBEN VON PROFESSOR DR. SIGM. FREUD

SCHRIFTLEITUNG: Dr. S. FERENCZI, Budapest, VII. Elisabethring 54 / Dr. OTTO RANK, Wien IX/4, Simondenkgasse 8

VERLAG HUGO HELLER & Co., WIEN, I. BAUERNMARKT No. 3

ABONNEMENTSPREIS: GANZJÄHRIG (6 HEFTE, 36—40 BOGEN) K 21·60 = MK. 18·—

Wien am 27. Jan 1913

Geehrter Herr Präsident!
Lieber Herr Doktor

Die erste Nummer unserer neuen Zeitschrift liegt mir vor. Ich benütze diesen Anlaß, um Ihnen für das freundliche Entgegenkommen zu danken, das Sie dem Unternehmen als Präsident bewiesen haben. Es ist auch dadurch ermöglicht worden, den Anfang in der Haltung einzunehmen, die wir mit der [illegible] [illegible] auszufüllen hoffen.

Die Redakteure sowie der Herausgeber werden jeden Wink dankbar aufnehmen, der ihnen zeigen kann, wie sie es anders und besser machen können.

Die nächste Nummer wird die Besprechung des Jahrbuchs fortführen und eine Kritik über Ihre Libido-Arbeit aus der Feder des einen Redakteurs bringen. Beiträge unserer amerikanischen Kollegen sind für die [illegible]

Freud, 27 Jan. 13 (346 F, p. 1)

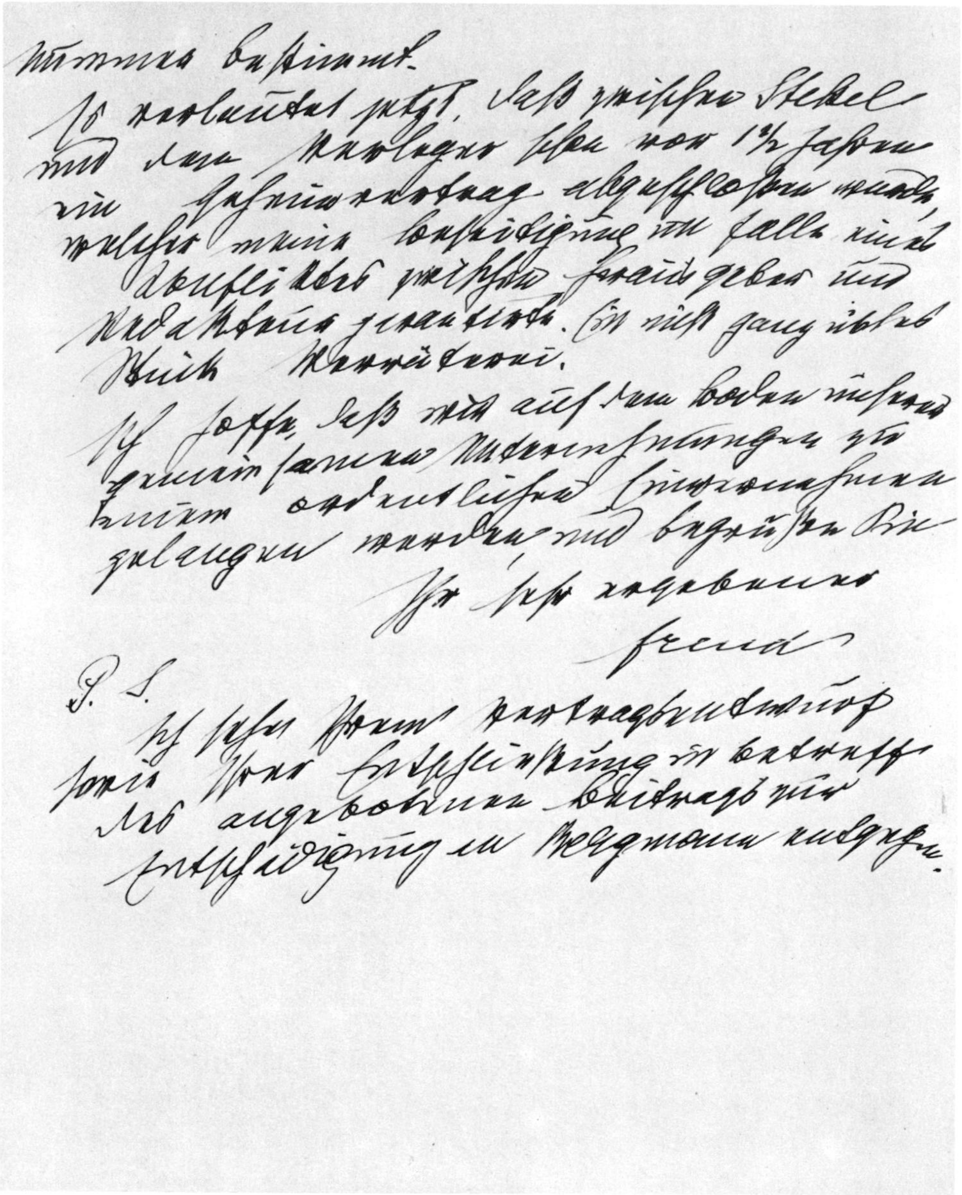

Freud, 27 Jan. 13 (346 F, p. 2)

348 J

1003 Seestrasse, Küsnach-Zürich,
11 February 1913

Dear Professor Freud,

I entirely agree with the changes you have suggested for the contract.[1] Would you please send the copies of the contracts back to me as soon as you have finished with them, as they are my only copies.

I am grateful for your collaboration on the *Jahrbuch* and share your views about the articles chosen by Bleuler. Bleuler *did the editing himself* during my absence.

I have just had a letter from Bleuler asking whether I would be willing to print Kronfeld's reply[2] to Rosenstein's (I must say, *excellent*) critique in the *Jahrbuch*. I think we should do so as a sign of absolute tolerance.

Kraus has treated me scurvily. First he offered me hysteria for his textbook.[3] Then he gave me neurasthenia, which I declined because I know too little about it and don't believe in it anyway. I am extremely glad to be rid of this burden as I have better things to do.

I have written an article for the *Internat. Zeitschrift* in which I have tried to clarify our position with reference to a remark by Tausk in his criticism of Nelken.[4] Basically it is a mere difference of interpretation and not a questioning of the facts.

With best regards,

Most sincerely yours, JUNG

[1] A letter from Freud is apparently missing. For the contract between the Central Office and Freud, see appendix 6.

[2] See above, 314 F n. 1 and 2. Kronfeld's reply did not appear in the *Jahrbuch* nor, it would seem, anywhere else.

[3] Friedrich Kraus and T. Brugsch, *Spezielle Pathologie und Therapie der inneren Krankheiten* (1919–27). Kraus had also invited Freud, in 1912, to write an article on hysteria; this led to a lengthy episode, recounted by Jones, II, 278f./248f. When the Kraus/Brugsch encyclopedia eventually appeared, it contained no articles from the psychoanalytic school.

[4] "Eine Bemerkung zur Tauskschen Kritik der Nelkenschen Arbeit," *Zeitschrift*, I:3 (1913) = "A Comment on Tausk's Criticism of Nelken," CW 18. See above, 305 J n. 3, and 346 F n. 1. / Victor Tausk (1877–1919), of Croatian origin, had been a lawyer and journalist before becoming a psychoanalyst. He joined the Vienna Society in 1909 and completed his medical studies in 1914. His promising career was ended by suicide in 1919. See Paul Roazen, *Brother Animal: The Story of Freud and Tausk* (1969).

349 J *Internationale Psychoanalytische Vereinigung*

Dear Professor Freud,   Küsnach-Zürich, 20 February 1913

I am very sorry that Bergmann's package took you by surprise.[1] I was under the impression that you had been notified in advance. As you know, we still had to pay Bergmann for the subscriptions at a reduced rate and B. insisted on sending his copies to us. I wanted to waive them on behalf of the Association, but then thought that the various local groups could do what they wanted with them.

In my last letter I said nothing about the theme for discussion[2] because I wanted to consult Maeder first. He is not of the same opinion as you. And I must confess that the teleological significance of dreams seems to me an important concept to which far too little attention has been paid in the literature to date. But we are quite willing to meet your counter-proposals, and if necessary drop this theme if something better is found.

In connection with material for the *Internat. Zeitschrift* from our side, I have appealed to Maeder and Riklin. They are about the only productive elements apart from Pfister.

Bleuler has sent in a paper for the *Jahrbuch* entitled "Aversion to Sexuality."[3] It is already in type, and it is "queer." I have also accepted a paper by Stärcke: "On New Dream Experiments."[4] A German version of the Dutch original, and hope you will approve of it. I think Stärcke has already been introduced to you.

It seems to have escaped your attention that in my last letter I asked your opinion about accepting Kronfeld's reply to Rosenstein's critique for the *Jahrbuch*. I don't think you will object to this demonstration of liberalism.

With best regards,

Yours sincerely, JUNG

---

[1] A letter from Freud is apparently missing.
[2] At the Munich Congress; see above, editorial comment following 327 J.
[3] "Der Sexualwiderstand," *Jahrbuch*, V:1 (1913).
[4] Johan Stärcke, "Neue Traumexperimente in Zusammenhang mit älteren und neueren Traumtheorien," ibid.

350 J   *Internationale Psychoanalytische Vereinigung*

Dear Professor Freud,   Küsnach-Zürich, 3 March 1913

This is to let you know that tomorrow I have to go to America for 5 weeks.[1] All the necessary arrangements have been made with Deuticke for the *Jahrbuch*. I have referred him to you should anything out of the ordinary happen. The last manuscripts to be sent to the printer are "New Dream Experiments" by Dr. J. Stärcke, Amsterdam, and my American lectures. These are really quite tame and in no way deserve the hullabaloo they have created. I have expressed in them only a few divergent opinions.

Pfister informs me that Adler has sidled up to him with the proposition that they make common cause against you. This manoeuvre has been rebuffed with indignation here.

I have talked with Maeder again and we have come to the conclusion that we don't want to push ourselves forward in any way. We are quite willing to fall in with another, better suggestion.

Hoche's circular[2] has come into our hands. Maeder is going to send it to you for publication in the *Internat. Zeitschrift*. It is important that this be done as soon as possible, i.e., before the Congress, so that people can see just how Hoche covers up his lack of experience.

I have also received the paper from Graz.[3] It would seem that dawn is gradually breaking in psychiatry.

With best regards,

Most sincerely yours, JUNG

[1] It was on this journey that Jung, on a ship sailing from Genoa to Naples, stood at the railing as the vessel neared the latitude of Rome; but his hope of seeing Rome was never fulfilled. When the ship put in at Naples, Jung went to Pompeii—"I was able to visit Pompeii only after I had acquired, through my studies of 1910 to 1912, some insight into the psychology of classical antiquity" (*Memories*, pp. 287f./268f., where the trip is dated 1912; but Mr. Franz Jung has confirmed that it occurred in 1913.) Of the sojourn in New York only the following details have come to light: "Dr. C. G. Jung lectured on psychoanalysis on 27 Mar. in the Liberal Club in New York (chairman: Rev. Dr. Percy Grant)."—*Zeitschrift*, I:3 (1913), 310 (*Bulletin* section). Percy Stickney Grant (1860–1927) was minister of the Church of the Ascension (Protestant Episcopal) at 5th Ave. and 10th St.; the Liberal Club was on Gramercy Park.

[2] Published in the "Varia" section of *Zeitschrift*, I:2, p. 199. Hoche had circularized colleagues asking for material to use in speaking against Bleuler on "The Value of Psychoanalysis" at the annual meeting of the German Psychiatric Association at Breslau in May. In I:4 there appeared a report of the meeting (by Eitingon) and an outline of Bleuler's and Hoche's remarks (pp. 411–14).

[3] Unidentified; possibly by Dr. Edwin Hollerung, a member of the Vienna Society since 1906—the only one who resided in Graz.

351 J   *Internationale Psychoanalytische Vereinigung*

Dear Professor Freud,   Küsnach-Zürich, 16 April 1913

I would like to commend the enclosed paper by Herr Oczeret[1] to your kind attention for possible inclusion in *Imago*. Those parts of it which I have studied impressed me with their wealth of ideas. I think the predominantly literary interest of the paper renders it suitable for *Imago*.

With best regards,

Most sincerely yours, JUNG

352 J

Dear Professor Freud,   Küsnacht, 28 April 1913[1]

I hereby acknowledge the receipt of Marcinowski's paper.[2]
With best regards,

Yours sincerely, DR. JUNG

353 J   *Internationale Psychoanalytische Vereinigung*

Dear Mr. President,   Küsnach-Zürich, 17 May 1913[1]

With a view to establishing the programme for the Congress in Munich, 7 & 8 September, it would be desirable to have some idea *now* of the kind of lectures that are to be given. I would therefore request you to make inquiries in your group and urge its members to communicate with me at the earliest convenience.

[1] Herbert Oczeret (1884–1939+), from Poland; after 1907 at Zürich University (M.D.). Member of the Zürich Society and of the Society for Psychoanalytic Endeavours, where he gave papers on aesthetic subjects (*Zeitschrift*, I:6, 1913, *Bulletin* section). No paper by Oczeret appeared in *Imago*. Later, psychiatrist in various Swiss sanatoriums.

[1] Postcard, typewritten and signed.
[2] See below, 356 J.

[1] Typewritten and signed. Evidently a circular letter to the presidents of the branch societies.

546

Since the theme for discussion proposed by the Munich meeting, "On the Teleological Function of Dreams," has not met with general approval, I would ask you to inquire whether the proposed theme should stand, or whether better suggestions can be put forward. The Zürich group is of the opinion that the theme is a topical one and well worth discussing. Nevertheless, I think it important that the Association as a whole should express its views on this matter of general concern.

In this respect also, Mr. President, I should appreciate an early reply.

Very truly yours, DR. JUNG

354 J 4th Psychoanalytic Congress in Munich[1]
7th and 8th September 1913

This year's private Psychoanalytic Congress will be held in Munich on the 7th and 8th of September. As on previous occasions of this nature, the first day (the 7th) will be the real day of work, with morning and afternoon sessions. Provision has been made for another morning session on the 8th.

Participants are requested to take an active part in the common work by giving lectures. On the 7th, the theme to be discussed at the morning session is the one proposed at the conference in Munich:

"The Function of Dreams"

The speaker is Dr. A. Maeder, Zürich; co-speaker, Dr. O. Rank, Vienna. Announcements of lectures should be sent to the undersigned by August 1st. Guests are welcome.

President of the International Psychoanalytic Association

DR. C. G. JUNG

Küsnacht-Zürich, June 1913

[1] Printed circular.

547

355 J *Internationale Psychoanalytische Vereinigung*

Dear Professor Freud,   Küsnach-Zürich, 29 July 1913

I am still waiting for the announcement of a lecture from your side. As I would like to have the programme printed soon, I should be grateful for an early reply.

Many thanks for sending me your offprints. I must, however, point out that in your paper "An Evidential Dream,"[1] which in other respects shows the fine qualities I have always admired in your writings, you put forward a conception of our views[2] which rests on a misunderstanding. This misunderstanding turns on the conception of the actual conflict, which for us is *not the petty vexation of the moment* but the problem of adaptation. A second misunderstanding seems to be that you think we deny the wish-fulfilment theory of dreams. We fully admit the soundness of the wish-fulfilment theory, but we maintain that this way of interpreting dreams touches only the surface, that it stops at the symbol, and that further interpretation is possible. When, for instance, a coitus wish appears in a dream, this wish can be analysed further, since this archaic expression with its tiresome monotony of meaning needs retranslating into another medium. We recognize the soundness of the wish-fulfilment theory up to a certain point, but we go beyond it. In our view it does not exhaust the meaning of the dream.

With best regards,

Yours sincerely, JUNG

356 J

1003 Seestrasse, Küsnach-Zürich,
Dear Professor Freud,   18 August 1913[1]

I enclose a manuscript[2] which I would like to submit to you for arbitration as director of the *Jahrbuch*. Professor Bleuler has already expressed his opinion: he rejects it. Since I personally am attacked

---

[1] "Ein Traum als Beweismittel," *Zeitschrift*, I:1 (1913) = SE XII.
[2] In the paper Freud makes no reference to Jung but speaks of "misgivings in the minds of so many psycho-analysts, among them some well-known ones" (SE XII, p. 273).

---

[1] Typewritten and signed.
[2] Unidentified.

in this paper I must, for the sake of objectivity, refrain from expressing my own opinion.

So far three papers have been sent off for the new *Jahrbuch*:

I. Mensendieck.[3] On the Technique of Instruction and Education during Psychoanalytic Treatment.

II. Sadger: The Psychoanalysis of an Autoerotic.[4]

III. Marcinowski: The Cure of a Severe Case of Asthma.[5]

Looking forward to an early reply, I remain, With best regards,

Yours sincerely, DR. JUNG

The Munich Congress

Jung paid a visit to England in early August in order to read papers to two professional bodies. On 5 August he appeared before the Psycho-Medical Society, London, with a paper entitled merely "Psycho-Analysis" (in CW 4, "General Aspects of Psychoanalysis"), in which he applied the name "analytical psychology" to the "new psychological science." On dream theory "I find myself in entire agreement with the views of Adler" (par. 553). At the 17th International Congress of Medicine, London, 6–12 August, his subject was "On Psycho-Analysis" (in CW 4, "Psychoanalysis and Neurosis"), and he set forth his differences with the Freudian theory of neurosis, proposing that "psychoanalytic theory be freed from the purely sexual standpoint. In place of it I should like to introduce an *energic viewpoint* . . ." (par. 566).

Freud had gone to Marienbad in mid July for treatment, with "his three womenfolk," as Jones states (II, p. 112/99): "His daughter tells me it was the only time she ever remembers her father being depressed." In August the Freud family went to a resort in the Dolomites, where Ferenczi joined them. The two men travelled together to Munich, arriving there on 5 September.

The "Fourth Private Psychoanalytic Meeting" took place on 7 and 8 September, with 87 members and guests present. (For the programme, see appendix 4.) Freud, after being induced to contribute by Abraham, read a paper on "The Disposition to Obsessional Neurosis: A Contribution to the Problem of Choice of Neurosis" (SE XII). Jung's subject was "A Contribution to the Study of Psychological Types," published originally in French (*Archives de psychologie*, XII:52, Dec. 1913) (CW 6,

[3] Otto Mensendieck (1871–19—), lay member of the Zürich Society, originally from Hamburg. His paper is "Zur Technik des Unterrichts und der Erziehung während der psychoanalytischen Behandlung," *Jahrbuch*, V:2 (1913). Returned to Germany 1914.

[4] "Die Psychoanalyse eines Autoerotikers," ibid.

[5] "Die Heilung eines schweren Falles von Asthma durch Psychoanalyse," ibid.

App. 1); it was in fact a preliminary study for Jung's major work *Psychological Types* (orig. 1921).

The Congress went on in an atmosphere Jones has described as "disagreeable," and Freud as "fatiguing and unedifying." When Jung stood for re-election as president, 22 out of 52 of the participants abstained from voting, in order that his election should not be unanimous. The story is related in detail by Jones, II, pp. 113ff./101ff. and 168f./148f. See also Freud, "On the History of the Psycho-Analytic Movement," SE XIV, pp. 45, 60; and *The Freud Journal of Lou Andreas-Salomé*, tr. S. A. Leavy (New York, 1964), pp. 168f. The voting figures (incorrect in Jones) are from the report of the Congress in the *Zeitschrift*, II (1914), 407.

357 J

1003 Seestrasse, Küsnach-Zürich,

Dear Professor Freud,[1]   27 October 1913

It has come to my ears through Dr. Maeder that you doubt my *bona fides*. I would have expected you to communicate with me directly on so weighty a matter. Since this is the gravest reproach that can be levelled at anybody, you have made further collaboration impossible. I therefore lay down the editorship of the *Jahrbuch* with which you entrusted me. I have also notified Bleuler and Deuticke of my decision.

Very truly yours, DR. C. G. JUNG[2]

The End of the Jahrbuch

Subsequently, the following announcements appeared in the *Jahrbuch*, V:2 (1913):

Statement by Prof. Bleuler, Director

After the termination of this volume I am resigning as director, but shall of course maintain my interest in the journal as before.

Bleuler

[1] Holograph: *Sehr geehrter Herr Professor.*
[2] In *Memories*, Jung writes: "In October [1913], while I was alone on a journey, I was suddenly seized by an overpowering vision: I saw a monstrous flood covering all the northern and low-lying lands between the North Sea and the Alps. . . . I realized that a frightful catastrophe was in progress. . . . The whole sea turned to blood" (pp. 175/169). Two weeks later the vision recurred, more vividly than before.

Statement by the Editor

I have found myself obliged to resign as editor of the *Jahrbuch*. The reasons for my resignation are of a personal nature, on which account I disdain to discuss them in public.

C. G. Jung

Statement by the Publisher

After the secession of Prof. Dr. Bleuler and Dr. Jung, Prof. Dr. Freud will continue this *Jahrbuch*. The next volume will appear in the middle of 1914 under the title:

Jahrbuch der Psychoanalyse
Edited by Dr. K. Abraham (Berlin)
and Dr. E. Hitschmann (Vienna)

Fr. Deuticke

So reconstituted, the *Jahrbuch* continued publication for one more year. Its first issue (VI:1) contained the two works in which Freud first published an account of the differences between his views and those of Jung and Adler: "On the History of the Psycho-Analytic Movement" and "On Narcissism: An Introduction" (both in SE XIV), written in the early months of 1914.

358 J *Internationale Psychoanalytische Vereinigung*

Dear Mr. President,   Küsnach-Zürich, 20 April 1914[1]

The latest developments have convinced me that my views are in such sharp contrast to the views of the majority of the members of our Association that I can no longer consider myself a suitable personality to be president. I therefore tender my resignation to the council of the presidents of the branch societies, with many thanks for the confidence I have enjoyed hitherto.[2]

Very truly yours, DR. C. G. JUNG[3]

x   x

x

[1] Typewritten and signed, with three x's at the end, written by pen. A circular letter to the presidents of the branch societies. Its text was published subsequently in the *Zeitschrift*, II:3 (1914), 297.

[2] On 30 April, Jung submitted his resignation as privatdocent in the medical faculty of Zürich University. It was accepted by the cantonal education authorities on 3 June. (Extract from the official records, courtesy of Mr. Franz Jung.)

[3] In *Memories*, Jung recounts a thrice-repeated dream in April, May, and June

The Final Break

In a letter of 30 April 1914[1] to the presidents of the six European branch societies—Berlin, Budapest, London, Munich, Vienna, and Zürich—Freud suggested that the presidents' council forgo a meeting and elect a provisional president of the Association by correspondence. He proposed Karl Abraham, since he would be in the most advantageous position to make preparations for the Congress at Dresden in the autumn of 1914.

Accordingly, the branch presidents agreed through correspondence that Abraham serve as provisional president until the next Congress. He edited the *Bulletin* in the next issue of the *Zeitschrift*; Dresden was proposed for the Fifth Congress in September 1914.[2] But Abraham's *Bulletin* in the issue after that (I:5), a mere page in length, contained only three items of information: on 10 July, the Zürich Society had voted to withdraw from the International Psychoanalytic Association; the *Zeitschrift* and *Imago* would continue to publish, but probably not the *Jahrbuch*; and, owing to "events in the great world . . . , our Congress, like many other scientific arrangements, must be postponed for an unspecified time."

At the end of July, Jung was invited by the British Medical Association to lecture at its annual meeting, in Aberdeen, "On the Importance of the Unconscious in Psychopathology" (CW 3). He referred briefly to Freud ("To Freud we owe thanks . . . for having called attention to the importance of dreams") but did not mention the word psychoanalysis.

1914: ". . . in the middle of summer an Arctic cold wave descended and froze the land to ice. . . . All living green things were killed by frost. . . . The third dream, however, had an unexpected end. There stood a leaf-bearing tree, but without fruit (my tree of life, I thought), whose leaves had been transformed by the effects of the frost into sweet grapes full of healing juices. I plucked the grapes and gave them to a large, waiting crowd" (pp. 176/170).

---

[1] Carbon copy of typed letter, found by Miss Anna Freud in the Freud files. It had been typed either by herself or by Otto Rank.

[2] The Fifth International Psychoanalytic Congress, organized by Ferenczi, took place at Budapest, 28–29 September 1918.

359 J

228 Seestrasse, Küsnacht-Zürich

Dear Professor Freud,   [day and month?] 1923[1]

The purpose of this letter is to refer the following case to your medical authority:

Herr J——, who will shortly have the honour of introducing himself to you personally, is suffering from an obsessional neurosis. He has been treated by me for two years, but the illness brought many interruptions the reason for which will become apparent from the report drawn up by the patient himself. In the course of treatment he acquired a more intimate knowledge of his sexual fantasies and also of your scientific writings. The insights they afforded alleviated his symptoms so much that he even began dreaming about you. The wish to be treated by you personally was so unmistakable that I felt it my duty to do everything in my power to support his recuperative efforts and to facilitate his treatment at your hands. The unquestioned help which your views afforded him have prepared him for further progress in this direction.

Herr J—— is by profession a diplomat, very intelligent and very well-to-do. His neurosis is certainly severe, and in addition he is no longer young, but at the same time he is sufficiently flexible for me to refer him to you with a good conscience. Moreover his decision to turn to you for help as a result of the treatment was so logical and convincing that I never doubted its rightness for a moment. For the symptomatology of the case I must refer you to the patient's own report, to which I have nothing to add.[2]

In the sincere hope, dear Professor, that you will favour the patient with your help, I remain,

With respectful regards,

Very truly yours, DR. JUNG

---

[1] Handwritten. Jung wrote only the year date, leaving space for the day and month to be filled in. He was living at the same place, but the houses had been renumbered in the intervening years.

[2] The following information was supplied by Aniela Jaffé: "The case involved a Jew who could not or would not acknowledge his Jewishness. The analysis with Freud did not help him and he turned back to Jung. He then had a dream in which he found himself at an impassable place, beyond which a light shined. At the impasse sat an old woman, who said to him: 'Only he who is a Jew can get through!' This was the beginning of the cure of his neurosis."

APPENDIXES

1

Chronological Table of Letters

	FREUD	JUNG
1906		
Apr. 11 W	1	
Oct. 5 F		2
7 Su	3	
23 Tu		4
27 Sa	5	
Nov. 26 M		6
Dec. 4 Tu		7
6 Th	8	
29 Sa		9
30 Su	10	
1907		
Jan. 1 Tu	11	
8 Tu		12
13 Su	13	
Feb. 20 W		14
21 Th	15	
26 Tu		16
Mar. 3 Su [Jungs in Vienna]		
31 Su [Easter]		17
Apr. 7 Su	18	
11 Th		19
14 Su	20	
17 W		21
17/21 W/Su	22	
21 Su	23	
May 13 M		24
19 [Whitsuntide]		

	FREUD	JUNG
23 Th	25	
24 F		26
26 Su	27	
30 Th		28
Jun. 4 Tu		29
6 Th	30*	
12 W		31
14 F	32	
28 F		33
Jul. 1 M	34	
6 Sa		35
10 W	36	
Aug. 12 M		37
18 Su	38	
19 M		39
27 Tu	40	
29 Th		41
Sept. 2 M	42	
4 W		43
11 W		44
19 Th	45	
25 W		46
Oct. 1 Tu		47
10 Th		48
28 M		49
Nov. 2 Sa		50
8 F		51
15 F	52	
24 Su	53	
30 Sa		54

* With enclosure.

Date			FREUD	JUNG		Date			FREUD	JUNG
Dec.	8	Su	55			Jun.	1	M		97
	16	M		56			7	[Whitsuntide]		
	21	Sa	57				19	F		98
							21	Su	99	
1908							26	F		100
Jan.	1	W	58				30	Tu	101	
	2	Th		59		Jul.	12	Su		102
	5	Su		60			18	Sa	103	
	14	Tu	61	62*		Aug.	5	W	104	
	22	W		63			11	Tu		105
	25	Sa	64	65			13	Th	106	
	27	M	66				21	F		107
	31	F	67			Sept.	1	Tu	[Freud to	
Feb.	14	F	68						England]	
	15	Sa		69			9	W		108
	17	M	70				18	F	[Freud at	
	18	Tu	71						Burghölzli]	
	20	Th		72			23	W	109	
	23	Su		73		Oct.	15	Th	110	
	25	Tu	74				21	W		111
Mar.	3	Tu	76	75		Nov.	8	Su	112	
	5	Th	77				11	W		113
	9	M	78				12	Th	114	
	11	W		79			27	F		115
	13	F	80				29	Su	116	
Apr.	11	Sa		81		Dec.	3	Th		117
	14	Tu	82				11	F	118	
	18	Sa		83			15	Tu		119
	19	Su [Easter] 84					17	Th	120	
	24	F		85			21	M		121
	27	M [Salzburg Congress]					26	Sa	122	
	30	Th		86			30	W	123	
May	3	Su	87							
	4	M	89	88		*1909*				
	6	W	90			Jan.	7	Th		124
	7	Th		91			17	Su	125	
	10	Su	92				19	Tu		126
	14	Th		93			22	F	127	
	19	Tu	94				24	Su		128
	25	M		95			25	M	129	
	29	F	96				26	Tu	130	

* Invitation to Congress.

			FREUD	JUNG
Feb.	21	Su		131
	24	W	132	
Mar.	7	Su		133
	9	Tu	134	
	11/12	Th/F		135
	17	W		136
	21	Su		137
	25	Th [Jungs in Vienna]		
Apr.	2/12	F/M		138
	11	Su [Easter]		
	16	F		139
May	12	W		140
	16	Su	141	
	30	Su [Whitsuntide]		
Jun.	2	W		142
	3	Th	143	
	4	F		144
	7	M	145	
	12	Sa		146
	18	F	147	
	21	M		148
	30	W	149	
Jul.	7	W	150	
	10/13	Sa/Tu		151
	19	M	152	
Aug.	5	Th		153
	9	M	154	
	20	F [To U.S.A. for Clark Conference]		
Sept.	29	W [Arrive Bremen]		
Oct.	1	F		155
	4	M	156	
	14	Th		157
	17	Su	158	
Nov.	8	M		159
	11	Th	160	
	12	F		161
	15	M		162
	21	Su	163	
	22	M		164
	30/Dec. 2	Tu/Th		165
	2	Th	166	
	12	Su	167	

			FREUD	JUNG
	14	Tu		168
	19	Su	169	
	25/31	Sa/F		170
1910				
Jan.	2	Su	171	
	8	Sa		172
	10	M		173
	13	Th	174	
	30	Su		175
	31	M		176
Feb.	2	W	177	
	11	F		178
	13	Su	179	
	20/22	Su/Tu		180
Mar.	2/3	W/Th		181
	6	Su	182	
	8	Tu [Emma Jung]		
	9	W [Jung to America]		183
	16	W [Emma Jung]		
	27	Su [Easter]		
	30–31	W–Th [Nuremberg Congress; visit to Rothenburg]		
Apr.	6	W		184
	12	Tu	185	
	17	Su		186
	22	F	187	
	26	Tu	188	
	30	Sa		189
May	2	M	190	
	5	Th		191
	15	[Whitsuntide]		
	17	Tu	192	
	24	Tu		193
	26	Th	194	
	30	M	195	
Jun.	2	Th		196
	9	Th	197	
	17	F		198
	19	Su	199	

559

			FREUD	JUNG
	22	W (ca.)	199a	
	26	Su		200
Jul.	5	Tu	201	
	10	Su	202	
	24	Su		203
Aug.	6	Sa		204
	10	W	205	
	11	Th		206
	13	Sa		207
	14	Su	208	
	18	Th	209	
	31	W		210
Sept.	8	Th		211
	24/26	Sa/M	212	
	29	Th		213
Oct.	1	Sa	214	
	20	Th		215
	23	Su	216	
	29	Sa		217
	31	M	218	
Nov.	7	M		219
	13	Su		220
	25	W	221	
	29	Tu		222
Dec.	3	Sa	223	
	13	Tu		224
	18	Su	225	
	19	M	226	
	20	Tu		227
	22	Th	228	
	23	Th		229
	26	M [Meetings in Munich]		

1911

			FREUD	JUNG
Jan.	18	W		230
	22	Su	231	
	31	Tu		232
Feb.	9	Th	233	
	12	Su	234	
	14	Tu		235
	17	F	236	
	28	Tu		237
Mar.	1/3	W/F	238	

			FREUD	JUNG
	8	W		239
	13?	M?	240	
	14	Tu	241	
	16	Th	242	
	19	Su		243
	25	Sa	244	
	28	Tu		245
	30	Th	246	
	31	F		247
Apr.	2	Su	248	
	3	M		249
	7	F	250	
	11	Tu	251	
	16	Su [Easter]		
	19	W		252
	27	Th	253	
May	8	M		254
	12	F	255	
	18	Th		256
	24	W		257
	27	Sa	258	
Jun.	4	Su [Whitsuntide]		
	12	M		259
	15	Th	260	
	23	F		261
	27	Tu	262	
Jul.	11	Tu		263
	13	Th	264	
	19	W		265
	21	F	266	
	26	W		267
Aug.	20	Su	268	
	29	Tu		269
Sept.	1	F	270	
	16	Su [Freud to Küsnacht]		
	21–22	F–Sa [Weimar Congress]		
Oct.	4	W		271
	6	F		272
	12	Th	273	
	13	F	274	
	17	Tu		275
	20	F	276	

			FREUD	JUNG
	30	M		277
		[+ Emma Jung]		
Nov.	2	Th	278	
	6	M		279
		[+ Emma Jung]		
	12	Su	280	
	13	M		281
	14	Tu	283	282
		[+ Emma Jung]		
	16	Th	284	
	24	F		285
		[+ Emma Jung]		
	30	Th	286	
Dec.	11	M		287
	17	Su	288	
	28	Th	289	
	31	Su	290	
1912				
Jan.	2	Tu		291
	9	Tu		292
	10	W	293	294
	23	Tu		295
	24	W	296	
Feb.	15	Th (ca.)		297
	18	Su	298	
	19	M		299
	25	Su		300
	29	Th	301	
Mar.	2	Sa		302
	3	Su		303
	5	Tu	304	
	10	Su		305
	21	Th	306	
	22	F		307
	24	M	308	
	27	W		309
Apr.	1	M		310
	7	Su [Easter]		
	21	Su	311	
	27	Sa		312

			FREUD	JUNG
May	8	W		313
	14	Sa	314	
	17	F		315
	23	Th	316	
	25	Sa		317
	26	Su [Whitsuntide; Freud at Kreuzlingen]		
Jun.	8	Sa		318
	13	Th	319	
Jul.	18	Th		320
Aug.	2	F		321
Sept.	7	Sa [Jung to U.S.A. for Fordham U. Lectures]		
	10	Tu [Emma Jung]		
Nov.	11	M		322
				323
	14	Th	324	325
	15	F		326
	19	Tu		327
	24	Su [Munich Conference]		
	26	Tu		328
	29	F	329	
Dec.	3	Tu		330
	4	W		331
	5	Th	332	
	7	Sa		333
	9	M	334	
11/14		W/Sa		335
	14	Sa		336
	16	M	337	
	18	W		338
	21	Sa		339
	22	Su	340*	
1913				
Jan.	1	W		341
	3	F	342	343
	6	M		344
	9	Th		345

* Freud wrote but never mailed this letter.

		FREUD	JUNG
	27	M	346
	31	F	347
Feb.	11	Tu	348
	20	Th	349
Mar.	3	M	350
	23	Su [Easter]	
Apr.	16	W	351
	28	M	352
	11	Su [Whitsuntide]	
	17	Sa	353
Jun.			354*
Jul.	29	Tu	355

		FREUD	JUNG
Aug.	18	M	356
Sept.	7/8	Su/M [Munich Congress]	
Oct.	27	M	357
1914			
Apr.	20	M	358
Jul.	10	F [Zürich resigns from Association]	
1923			
(Date?)			359

* Invitation to Congress.

MISSING ITEMS

Internal evidence at the places here listed indicates a letter or other item definitely or apparently missing. No letter of Freud to Emma Jung survives.

1906

| 7 J n. 1 | 4 Dec. | Freud |
| 9 J n. 1 | 29 Dec. | Freud |

1907

40 F n. 2	27 Aug.	Freud card
49 J n. 1	28 Oct.	Freud (2)
51 J n. 1	8 Nov.	Freud

1908

92 F n. 1	10 May	Jung
110 F n. 1	15 Oct.	Emma Jung
123 F n. 2	30 Dec.	Jung

1909

131 J n. 3	21 Feb.	Freud
133 J n. 1	7 Mar.	Freud telegram
134 F n. 1	9 Mar.	Jung telegram
135 J n. 4	11 Mar.	Jung card
141 F n. 3	16 May	Freud (part)
146 J n. 2	12 June	Jung
161 J n. 2	12 Nov.	Freud card
164 J n. 1	22 Nov.	Jung card
165 J n. 5	2 Dec.	Freud card

1910

175 J n. 5	30 Jan.	Freud
181 J n. 1	2 Mar.	Freud
188 F n. 1	26 Apr.	Jung telegram
211 J n. 1	8 Sept.	Freud cards
215 J n. 3	20 Oct.	Freud card
219 J n. 3	7 Nov.	Freud card

1911

259 J n. 3	12 June	Freud (?)
272 J n. 1	6 Oct.	Freud
289 F n. 3	28 Dec.	Jung (?)

1912

313 J n. 1	8 May	Freud (?)
318 J n. 3	8 June	Freud card
334 F n. 1	9 Dec.	Freud telegram

1913

| 348 J n. 1 | 11 Feb. | Freud (?) |
| 349 J n. 1 | 20 Feb. | Freud (?) |

2

Contents of the *Jahrbuch für psychoanalytische und psychopathologische Forschungen*[1]

I (1909)

[1] For title-page of the first number, see above, 133 J. / The entire contents of the *Jahrbuch* are in German. In general, the titles of the papers by Freud and Jung are translated as in the Standard Edition and the Collected Works; of the papers by others, as in Grinstein. The publication date for each part is conjectured from the letters. The original page numbers are given as an indication of comparative length.

IV (1912)

Part 1 [september]

Part 2 [publication date unconfirmed]

3

Statutes of the International Psychoanalytic Association[1]

I. NAME OF THE ORGANIZATION

"International Psychoanalytic Association."

II. SEAT

The seat (Central Office) of the I.Ps.A. is the residence of the president then in office.[2]

III. PURPOSE OF THE I.Ps.A.

The cultivation and promotion of the psychoanalytic science as inaugurated by Freud, both in its form as pure psychology and in its application to medicine and the humanities; mutual assistance among members in their endeavours to acquire and foster psychoanalytic knowledge.

[1] *Statuten der Internationalen Psychoanalytischen Vereinigung*, a printed four-page leaflet. The copy seen is in the Sigmund Freud Archives (Library of Congress, Washington, D.C.), to which it was contributed by Professor Jung. With it is a printed *Statuten-Entwurf*, "Draft of the Statutes," also contributed by Jung, and bearing pencilled annotations in his hand, which evidently he made while the draft was being discussed at the Nuremberg Congress. (See facsimile.) The more interesting changes from draft to adopted text are mentioned in the following notes. / These Statutes were drafted by Ferenczi and presented to the Congress after he read his paper calling for a permanent international organization. See Rank's abstract, *Jahrbuch*, II:2 (1910), and above, 181 J n. 2. Also see the programme of the Congress, below, appendix 4. / Revised Statutes were adopted at the Hague Congress, Sept. 1920; see *Zeitschrift*, VI (1920), 387ff.
[2] Draft located the seat in Zürich. / The abbreviation *J.Ps.A.V.*, for *Internationalen Psychoanalytischen Vereinigung*, is used throughout the German text.

568

Statuten-Entwurf.

I. Name der Vereinigung:

„Jnternationale Psychoanalytische Vereinigung" *[handwritten]*

II. Sitz:

Der Sitz (Zentrale) der »J. Ps. A. V.« ist in Zürich (Schweiz). *[handwritten]*

III. Zweck der »J. Ps. A. V.«:

Pflege und Förderung der von **Freud** begründeten psychoanalytischen Wissenschaft sowohl als reiner Psychologie, als auch in ihrer Anwendung in der Medizin und den Geisteswissenschaften; gegenseitige Unterstützung der Mitglieder in allen Bestrebungen zum Erwerben und Verbreiten von psychoanalytischen Kenntnissen.

IV. Mitgliedschaft. *[handwritten: der Zweigvereinigung]*

Die Vereinigung besteht nur aus ordentlichen Mitgliedern. Mitglied kann jeder werden, der sich mit der Psychoanalye als reiner Psychologie oder als angewandter Wissenschaft in positivem Sinne beschäftigt. Alle Mitglieder der Zweigvereinigungen sind eo ipso Mitglieder der »J. Ps. A. V.« Bewohner von Orten, in denen keine Zweigvereinigungen existieren, werden von der Zentrale aufgenommen.

V. Pflichten der Mitglieder.

~~Jedes Mitglied entrichtet beim Eintritt in die »J. Ps. A. V.« 10 frcs. (10 Kr., 8 Mark, 2 Dollars) als Eintrittsgebühr.~~ Der jährliche Mitgliedsbeitrag beträgt **10 frcs.** *[handwritten]*

VI. Rechte der Mitglieder.

Die Mitglieder haben das Recht, den Sitzungen aller Zweigvereinigungen beizuwohnen; sie haben Anspruch auf Einladung zum Kongresse; sie sind am Kongresse aktiv und passiv wahlberechtigt. *[handwritten]*

VII. Kongresse.

Die oberste Aufsicht über die »J. Ps. A. V.« fällt dem Kongress zu. Der Kongress wird von der Zentrale mindestens alle ~~vier~~ *zwei* Jahre einmal einberufen und vom Präsidenten der Zentrale geleitet. ~~Der Kongress wählt die Funktionäre der Zentrale.~~

[handwritten: Der Kongress wählt den Präsidenten.]

The draft of the *Statutes*, with Jung's annotations. See appendix 3

VIII. Die Zentrale.

Die ~~zukünftige~~ Zentrale besteht aus einem Präsidenten und zwei Sekretären; sie wird für die Dauer von ~~zwei~~ Jahren gewählt. Sie vertritt die «J. Ps. A. V.» nach außen, ~~──────~~ ~~die Tätigkeit der Zweigvereinigungen~~, redigiert das Korrespondenzblatt, organisiert die Kongresse und hat dem Kongresse über ihre Tätigkeit Bericht zu erstatten.

IX. Das Korrespondenzblatt.

Das Korrespondenzblatt der »J. Ps. A. V.« erscheint einmal im Monat. Es vermittelt den Verkehr zwischen der Zentrale und den Mitgliedern (amtliche Mitteilungen), publiziert die die Psychoanalye betreffenden wissenschaftlichen und persönlichen Nachrichten, registriert die wichtigsten Vorkommnisse in den Zweigvereinigungen und die die Psychoanalyse angehenden literarischen Neuerscheinungen.

X. Der Beirat der Zentrale.

Der Kongress wählt auf Vorschlag des Präsidenten fünf Beiräte aus der Reihe der Mitglieder. Der Präsident wird ersucht den Beirat womöglich einmal im Jahre zusammenzuberufen, um sich über die Lage der Sache in persönlichem Gedankenaustausche zu besprechen.

XI. Die Zweigvereinigungen.

Mitglieder von Zweigniederlassungen, welche bereits Beiträge erheben, werden ohne Bezahlung einer Eintrittsgebühr als Mitglieder der »J. Ps. A. V.« übernommen. Den Jahresbeitrag haben sie wie die anderen Mitglieder zu entrichten. — Die Zweigvereinigungen stehen durch ihren Präsidenten in stetiger Fühlung mit der Zentrale und haben vor wichtigen Entscheidungen sich mit ihr ins Einvernehmen zu ~~setzen~~. ~~Die Zentrale arbeitet eine möglichst~~ ~~einheitliche Geschäftsordnung für die Zweigvereinigungen aus.~~

XII. Änderungen der Statuten.

Die Statuten können nur vom Kongress geändert werden. Zu einer Änderung an den Statuten ist die Zweidrittel-Majorität der anwesenden Mitglieder erforderlich.

The draft of the *Statutes*, with Jung's annotations (*verso*)

IV. MEMBERSHIP

The Association consists of the regular members of the branch societies. Residents of localities where no branch society exists should join one of the branch societies nearest them.[3]

V. DUTIES OF MEMBERS

Every member pays to the Central Office annual membership dues of 10 frs. (10 kronen, 8 marks, 2 dollars).[4]

VI. RIGHTS OF MEMBERS

All members have the right to attend the meetings of all branch societies; they are entitled to receive the *Bulletin* regularly[5] and to be invited to Congresses; at Congresses they are entitled to vote and to stand for election.

VII. CONGRESSES

The over-all supervision over the I.Ps.A. lies in the hands of the Congress. A Congress will be convened by the Central Office at least once every two years[6] and will be presided over by the President then in office. The Congress elects the functionaries of the Central Office.

VIII. THE CENTRAL OFFICE

The Central Office consists of a President and a Secretary, the latter to be elected by the Congress on the motion of the President; its term of office is two years.[7] It represents the I.Ps.A. in external matters and coordinates the activities of the branch societies; it edits the *Bulletin* and must account for its activities to the Congress.

IX. THE BULLETIN

The *Bulletin* of the I.Ps.A. appears once every month. It maintains contact between the Central Office and the members (official com-

---

[3] Draft provided that residents of places where no branch society exists could become members at large.
[4] Draft provided also for an initiation fee of the same amount, from which members of the existing local societies were exempt.
[5] Not in the draft. [6] Draft: every four years.
[7] Draft: two secretaries; term of office, four years.

munications), publishes scientific and personal news relating to psychoanalysis, reports on the most important events in the branch societies and on new literature concerned with psychoanalysis.

X. The Advisory Council to the Central Office

The Advisory Council is made up of the presidents of the branch societies;[8] the President should convene it, if possible, once every year.

XI. The Branch Societies

New branch societies may be formed with the consent of the President; their definitive enrolment is subject to the decision of the next Congress.

XII. Changes in the Statutes

The Statutes may be amended only by the Congress, with a two-thirds majority of the members present required.

Adopted at the Congress in Nuremberg, 31 March 1910
For the I.Ps.A.
The President: Docent Dr. C. G. Jung
The Secretary: Dr. F. Riklin

[8] Draft provided for a council of five, elected by the Congress from the membership on the motion of the President.

4

Programmes of the Congresses[1]

PROGRAMME FOR THE MEETING IN SALZBURG
26–27 APRIL 1908

26 April: Arrival in Salzburg in the evening. Informal gathering in the
Hotel Bristol. Accommodation has been reserved at the Hotel
Bristol for those who have announced their attendance.

27 April: Morning, 8: Session. (The place will be announced on the
evening of the 26th.)

LECTURES

1. Prof. Dr. S. Freud, Vienna: Case Material.
2. Dr. E. Jones, London: Rationalization in Everyday Life.[2]
3. Dr. Sadger, Vienna: On the Aetiology of Psychopathia Sexualis.
4. Dr. Morton Prince, Boston: Experiments Showing Psychogalvanic Reactions from the Subconsciousness in a Case of Multiple Personality.[2]
5. Dr. Abraham, Berlin: Psychosexual Differences between Dementia Praecox and Hysteria.
6. Dr. Stekel, Vienna: On Anxiety Hysteria.
7. Dr. Adler, Vienna: Sadism in Life and Neurosis.
8. Dr. Jung, Zürich: On Dementia Praecox.

---

[1] Two of the invitation circulars are included among the letters, as they were kept
by Freud in his file of Jung's letters: 62 J, for Salzburg, 1908, and 354 J, for
Munich, 1913. The other invitations and programmes given here are translated
from copies in the Sigmund Freud Archives (Library of Congress, Washington,
D.C.), to which they were contributed by Professor Jung (except for the programme of the Munich Congress, 1913; see n. 5).

[2] In English. Prince did not attend, and instead Riklin gave a lecture on "Some
Problems of Myth Interpretation"; see above, 63 J n. 2.

Lecturers are allowed half an hour's speaking-time. The discussion will take place in the evening.

1 p.m. Luncheon at the Hotel Bristol.
Afternoon: Weather permitting, walk.
Evening: Gathering at the Hotel Bristol.
    1. Discussion of the lectures.
    2. Dr. Stein, Budapest: How is the libido freed by analysis to be guided into therapeutically favourable channels?
    3. Dr. Ferenczi, Budapest: What practical hints for child education can be drawn from Freudian experience?
    4. Administrative questions.

[INVITATION]
SECOND PSYCHOANALYTIC MEETING IN NUREMBERG
30 & 31 MARCH 1910

This year, as two years ago in Salzburg, there will be a private meeting of all those who are interested in the progress of Freud's psychology. The proposed agenda will deal with problems of a general nature, including the discussion of a closer organization in the form of a permanent Society. The definitive programme will be sent to participants in March, with further details.

Those wishing to attend the meeting are requested to inform the undersigned by 1 March.

Participants are requested to take an active part, whenever possible, by giving *lectures*. Guests will be welcome.

Announcements of lectures will be accepted by the undersigned until 1 March.

Küsnacht-Zürich
January 1910

DR. C. G. JUNG

Second Psychoanalytic Meeting in Nuremberg
30 and 31 March 1910

REVISED PROGRAMME[3]

30 March:

Morning, 8:30. Lectures by

1. Prof. Freud: The Future Prospects of Psychotherapy.
2. Dr. Abraham: The Psychoanalysis of Fetishism.
3. Dr. Marcinowsky: Sejunctive Processes as the Foundation of Psychoneuroses.
4. Dr. Stegmann: Psychoanalysis and Other Methods of Treatment in Neurological Practice.
5. Dr. Honegger: On Paranoid Delusions.

Afternoon, 5:

1. Lecture by Dr. Löwenfeld. On Hypnotherapy.
2. Report by Dr. Ferenczi: On the Need for Closer Alliance among Adherents of Freud's Teachings, with Suggestions for a Permanent International Organization.

31 March:

Morning, 8:30. Lectures by

1. Dr. Jung: Report on America.
2. Dr. Adler: On Psychic Hermaphroditism.
3. Dr. Maeder: On the Psychology of the Paranoid.
4. Report by Dr. Stekel: Proposals for Group Research in the Field of Symbolism and Typical Dreams.

Afternoon: Informal meeting.

Further details will be announced at the meetings. The proceedings will take place at the Grand Hotel.

[3] The original version of the programme (also in the Sigmund Freud Archives), set in different type, has the following differences: on 30 March afternoon, only Ferenczi's report; Löwenfeld's lecture was scheduled on 31 March morning, and Adler's lecture was not on the programme.

[INVITATION]
THIRD PSYCHOANALYTIC CONGRESS IN WEIMAR
21–22 SEPTEMBER 1911

This year's meeting of the INTERNATIONAL PSYCHOANALYTIC ASSOCIATION will take place on 21 & 22 September in Weimar.

PROVISIONAL PROGRAMME

21 September. Morning, 8: Opening of proceedings. Agenda:
1. Annual Report.
2. The question of the incorporation of the *Bulletin* in the *Zentralblatt für Psychoanalyse*.
3. The organization of the I.Ps.A. in America.

12: Luncheon at the Hotel Erbprinz.

22 September. Morning, 8: Opening of proceedings.

Accommodation will be found chiefly at the Hotel Erbprinz and the Hotel Elefant. For accommodation please communicate in good time with *Dr. K. Abraham*, Rankestrasse 24, Berlin W.

The *announcement of lectures*, which should be limited to 20–30 minutes, is politely requested. Announcements may be submitted to the undersigned until 1 September.

Küsnacht-Zürich

DR. C. G. JUNG
President of the I.Ps.A.

THIRD PSYCHOANALYTIC CONGRESS IN WEIMAR
21–22 SEPTEMBER 1911

PROGRAMME

A. This year's meeting of the INTERNATIONAL PSYCHOANALYTIC ASSOCIATION will take place on 21 & 22 September in Weimar.

B. The majority of the participants will be accommodated at the Hotel Erbprinz. The proceedings will also take place there.

C. PROGRAMME OF THE PROCEEDINGS

I. 21 SEPT., MORNING, 8:

    1. Professor Putnam: On the Significance of Philosophy for the Further Development of Psychoanalysis.[4]

    2. Professor Bleuler: On the Theory of Autism.

    3. Dr. Sadger: On Masturbation.

    4. Dr. Abraham: The Psychosexual Foundation of States of Depression and Exaltation.

[Handwritten insertion: Ferenczi: On Homosexuality.]

    5. Dr. Körber: On Sexual Refusal.

    6. O. Rank (for Dr. Sachs): The Interactions between the Humanities and Psychoanalysis.

II. 12:30: LUNCHEON AT THE HOTEL ERBPRINZ.

III. AFTERNOON:

    1. Dr. C. G. Jung: Annual Report.

    2. Debate on the incorporation of the *Bulletin* in the *Zentralblatt für Psychoanalyse.*

IV. 22 SEPT., MORNING, 8:

    1. Professor Freud: Postscript to the Analysis of Schreber.

    2. Dr. C. G. Jung: Contributions on Symbolism.

    3. C. [sic] Rank: On the Motif of Nakedness in Poetry and Saga.

    4. Dr. Paul [sic] Bjerre: On the Analytical Treatment of Paranoia.*

    5. Dr. Nelken: On Fantasies in Dementia Praecox.

    6. Dr. Juliusburger: On the Analysis of Psychoses.

V. AFTERNOON:

    1. Debate on the organization of the I.Ps.A. in America.

D. An average length of 25 minutes is scheduled for each lecture.

E. Those participants who have not yet applied to Dr. Abraham for accommodation are requested in their own interest to reserve rooms as

---

[4] In German.

* A handwritten notation transposes nos. 4 and 5.

speedily as possible. It is likely that rooms are no longer available at the Hotel Erbprinz. The Hotel Elefant is recommended.

Küsnacht-Zürich
September 1911

DR. C. G. JUNG
President of the I.Ps.A.

FOURTH PRIVATE PSYCHOANALYTIC MEETING IN MUNICH[5]
7 AND 8 SEPTEMBER 1913

7 September, morning, 8:30: Opening of the Session:
1. Report on the Association.
2. Election of President and Secretary.
3. Theme for discussion: *The Function of Dreams.* Speaker, Dr. A. Maeder. Co-speaker, Dr. O. Rank.

12.30: Luncheon at the Hotel Bayrischer Hof.

Afternoon, 3: Resumption of Proceedings:
1. Dr. Tausk: The Psychological and Pathological Significance of Narcissism.
2. Prof. Dr. S. Freud: The Problem of Choice of Neurosis.
3. Dr. L. Seif: On Symbol Formation.
4. Prof. Dr. E. Jones: The Attitude of the Physician towards Current Conflicts.
5. Dr. H. Sachs: The Introduction of Tillage in Myth. A Provisional Statement.
6. Dr. K. Abraham: Neurotic Restrictions of Scopophilia and Analogous Phenomena in Folk-psychology.
7. Dr. Fr. Riklin: The Symbolic Value of Sadism.

After the session, informal gathering with refreshments at the Hotel Bayrischer Hof.

8 September, morning, 8: Lectures by:
1. Dr. J. B. Lang: On the Psychology of Dementia Praecox.
2. Dr. van Emden: On the Analysis of a Case of Ostensible Epilepsy in a Child.
3. Dr. C. G. Jung: On the Question of Psychological Types.
4. Dr. H. Schmid: The Problem of Hamlet.

[5] A copy of this programme is not in the Sigmund Freud Archives; it is translated here from a photocopy of unknown provenance. See n. 6.

5. Dr. P. Bjerre: Consciousness vs. Unconscious.
6. Dr. S. Ferenczi: On the Psychology of Conviction.
7. Prof. Dr. O. Messmer: The Reality Function as an Ontological Problem.
8. Dr. van Ophuijsen: On the Question of Sado-masochism.
9. Dr. Mensendiek: The Prospective Tendency of the Unconscious in Wagner's Early Dramas and in *Parsifal*.
10. Dr. J. v. Hattingberg: On the Anal-erotic Character.

Lecturers are requested to limit their speaking-time to about 20–25 minutes. If time allows, there will be a short discussion after each lecture. Speaking-time for members of the audience can be extended to 5 minutes only.

The proceedings will take place in the Hotel Bayrischer Hof, where participants will also be accommodated. It must nevertheless be pointed out that everyone has to reserve a room for himself and should do so as quickly as possible.

This programme also serves to admit guests introduced by members of the Congress.

The President[6]

[6] The signature is cut off in the photocopy, but the word *Zentralpräsident* is barely legible.

5

Contents (to 1913) of the *Schriften zur angewandten Seelenkunde*, edited by Sigmund Freud[1]

1	1907	Freud: Delusions and Dreams in Jensen's "Gradiva"
2	1908	Riklin: Wishfulfillment and Symbolism in Fairy Tales
3	1908	Jung: The Content of the Psychoses
4	1909	Abraham: Dream and Myth
5	1909	Rank: The Myth of the Birth of the Hero
6	1909	Sadger: From the Love-life of Nicolaus Lenau
7	1910	Freud: Leonardo da Vinci and a Memory of His Childhood
8	1910	Pfister: The Piety of Count Ludwig von Zinzendorf
9	1911	Graf: Richard Wagner in *The Flying Dutchman*
10	1911	Jones: The Problem of *Hamlet* and the Oedipus Complex
11	1911	Abraham: Giovanni Segantini: a Psychoanalytic Inquiry
12	1911	Storfer: On the Exceptional Position of Patricide
13	1911	Rank: The Lohengrin Saga
14	1912	Jones: The Nightmare in Its Relation to Certain Forms of Mediaeval Superstition
15	1913	von Hug-Hellmuth: A Study of the Mental Life of the Child

[1] = Papers on Applied Psychology. The first two numbers were published by Hugo Heller, Vienna; Franz Deuticke, Vienna and Leipzig, took over publication with the third number. The contents of the *Schriften* are in German; Jones's papers were translated. The titles are as in the standard translations, or as in Grinstein.

6

The Contract for the *Zeitschrift*

CONTRACT
between
the International Psychoanalytic Association (abbreviated I.Ps.A.),
represented by its Central Office, currently consisting of Docent
Dr. C. G. Jung and Dr. F. Riklin, both of Küsnacht-Zürich
and
Professor Dr. S. Freud, Berggasse 19, Vienna.[1]

I.

Professor S. Freud is currently director of the *Zeitschrift für ärztliche Psycho-Analyse*, which is edited by a staff under his direction.

II.

The representatives of the I.Ps.A. are empowered to give or to withhold their approval of editors appointed to the *Zeitschrift* by Professor Freud. Professor Freud undertakes, before appointing a new editor, to submit his name to the Central Office of the I.Ps.A., which is under obligation to inform him as soon as possible whether or not it accepts the proposed editor. The I.Ps.A. is empowered to ask Professor Freud to dismiss editors of the *Zeitschrift* whose editorial activity is not in keeping with the requirements of the I.Ps.A.

III.

In the event that Professor Freud and the I.Ps.A. cannot come to an agreement concerning the holders of editorial positions, the Central

[1] Typewritten and signed, with handwritten place and date. The copy seen is a photocopy in the Jung archives in Küsnacht. Neither the original of this or the copy presumably received and signed by Freud has been recovered. / See above, 336 J, 341 J, 346 F, 347 J, and 348 J, for references to the draft of this contract. In the last two letters there are references also to a contract with the publisher Heller, which has not been recovered.

Office is under obligation to ask Professor Freud by registered letter to convene, within fourteen days from the posting of said letter, the Congress of the I.Ps.A. or the Advisory Council to the Central Office, which represents the Congress between sessions, with a view to settling the differences. Professor Freud must convene this body by registered letter to the president of the Central Office, who will make all further arrangements.

If Professor Freud should fail to convene the above-mentioned body within the appointed time, it will be assumed that he accepts the point of view of the Central Office.

IV.

If Professor Freud should fail to submit to the decision of the Congress or of the Advisory Council to the Central Office in accordance with the concluding paragraph of Article III, or if for any reason the editorship of the *Zeitschrift* should fall into other hands than those of Dr. Freud, the I.Ps.A. is empowered to cancel its subscriptions to the *Zeitschrift*, as provided in its contract with Herr Hugo Heller, Vienna.

V.

The I.Ps.A., through its Central Office, undertakes to supply the *Bulletin*, containing a complete report of the activities and proceedings of the I.Ps.A., to the editors at least three times a year and at regular intervals. The Central Office is furthermore prepared to forward complaints over failure to meet this undertaking to the Congress or to the Advisory Council.

Küsnach-Zürich, 2 May 1913

DR. C. G. JUNG
DR. F. RIKLIN

7

The Collected Editions in English

The Standard Edition of the Complete Psychological Works of Sigmund Freud. Translated from the German under the general editorship of James Strachey, in collaboration with Anna Freud, assisted by Alix Strachey, Alan Tyson, and Angela Richards. London: The Hogarth Press and the Institute of Psycho-Analysis. / New York: Macmillan.

I. Pre-Psycho-Analytic Publications and Unpublished Drafts (1886–1899)
II. Studies on Hysteria (1893–1895)
III. Early Psycho-Analytic Publications (1893–1899)
IV. The Interpretation of Dreams (I) (1900)
V. The Interpretation of Dreams (II) and On Dreams (1900–1901)
VI. The Psychopathology of Everyday Life (1901)
VII. A Case of Hysteria, Three Essays on Sexuality and Other Works (1901–1905)
VIII. Jokes and their Relation to the Unconscious (1905)
IX. Jensen's 'Gradiva' and Other Works (1906–1908)
X. The Cases of 'Little Hans' and the 'Rat Man' (1909)
XI. Five Lectures on Psycho-Analysis, Leonardo and Other Works (1910)
XII. Case History of Schreber, Papers on Technique and Other Works (1911–1913)
XIII. Totem and Taboo and Other Works (1913–1914)
XIV. A History of the Psycho-Analytic Movement, Papers on Metapsychology and Other Works (1914–1916)
XV. Introductory Lectures on Psycho-Analysis (Parts I and II) (1915–1916)

XVI. Introductory Lectures on Psycho-Analysis (Part III) (1916–1917)

XVII. An Infantile Neurosis and Other Works (1917–1919)

XVIII. Beyond the Pleasure Principle, Group Psychology and Other Works (1920–1922)

XIX. The Ego and the Id and Other Works (1923–1925)

XX. An Autobiographical Study, Inhibitions, Symptoms and Anxiety, Lay Analysis and Other Works (1925–1926)

XXI. The Future of an Illusion, Civilization and its Discontents and Other Works (1927–1931)

XXII. New Introductory Lectures on Psycho-Analysis and Other Works (1932–1936)

XXIII. Moses and Monotheism, An Outline of Psycho-Analysis and Other Works (1937–1939)

XXIV. Indexes, Bibliography, etc.

The Collected Works of C. G. Jung. Editors: Sir Herbert Read, Michael Fordham, Gerhard Adler; William McGuire, executive editor. Translated from the German by R.F.C. Hull (except Vol. 2). Princeton, N.J.: Princeton University Press (Bollingen Series). / London: Routledge & Kegan Paul.

1. Psychiatric Studies (1902–1906)

2. Experimental Researches (1904–1910) (tr. Leopold Stein in collaboration with Diana Riviere)

3. The Psychogenesis of Mental Disease (1907–1914; 1919–1958)

4. Freud and Psychoanalysis (1906–1914; 1916–1930)

5. Symbols of Transformation (1911–1912; 1952)

6. Psychological Types (1921)

7. Two Essays on Analytical Psychology (1912–1928)

8. The Structure and Dynamics of the Psyche (1916–1952)

9.i. The Archetypes and the Collective Unconscious (1934–1955)

9.ii. Aion: Researches into the Phenomenology of the Self (1951)

10. Civilization in Transition (1918–1959)

11. Psychology and Religion: West and East (1932–1952)

12. Psychology and Alchemy (1936–1944)

13. Alchemical Studies (1929–1945)

14. Mysterium Coniunctionis (1955–1956)

ADDENDA

ADDENDA

18 F n. 10

The Sigmund Freud Memorial Collection at the New York State Psychiatric Institute Library, New York City (see addendum for 194 F n. 3) contains Freud's copy of K. Kahlbaum, *Die Gruppirung der psychischen Krankheiten und die Eintheilung der Seelenstörungen* (Danzig, 1863), copiously annotated by Freud as a young doctor. See Ernest Harms, "A Fragment of Freud's Library," *Psychoanalytic Quarterly*, XL:3 (July 1971).

133 J n. 1

"Little Hans," the five-year-old patient, may now be identified as Herbert Graf (1903–1973), who had a distinguished career as an opera stage director in New York, Philadelphia, and Zürich. His father was the musicologist Max Graf (1875–1958), a founding member of the Vienna Psychoanalytic Society.

143 F n. 2

Hans Olden, "Die Geschichte vom Gläsernen," *Die Zukunft*, vol. 46 (13 Feb. 04), 262ff. A young man of brilliant intellect is obsessed with the idea that his posterior is made of glass; unable to sit or lie down, he suffers a physical decline. His doctor is fascinated by his brilliance and they become close friends, meeting often for conversation. But the youth's parents, in concern over his wasting away, insist that the doctor take drastic action, and he does so: he attaches glass to the underside of the patient's chair and forces him to sit in it, whereupon the glass crashes to the floor. The youth is cured of his obsession and resumes a normal life, but loses his brilliance, falls into bad company, and is brought to trial for a forgery. The doctor, testifying as a witness for the defense, explains that, having been cured, the youth is now sane and not accountable for the crime.

163 F

P.S.[11] Ferenczi calls my attention to an article by Surgeon-Major Drenk-hahn in Detmold in the *Deutsche militärärztliche Zeitschrift* (20 May 1909) showing that, as a result of the anti-alcohol propaganda, cases of illness due to the abuse of alcohol in the Army have dropped from 4.19:10,000 in the year 1886–87 to 0.7:10,000, but that cases of other neuroses and psychoses have risen *in the same proportion.*

The author says literally: "One would almost be justified in asserting that the less men drink, the more prone they are to mental and nervous disorders—but this would seem to be going too far. . . ."

[11] Fragment discovered in the Sigmund Freud Archives at the Library of Congress, after the book had been made up in pages. It is in the form of a photostat of the holograph with an original typed transcript, in the photostat set of Freud letters deposited by the Archives in 1958 and still under restriction. On the transcript, a note in an unknown hand states: "Might be the P.S. to letter 13.1.1910" (174 F); but its connection with 163 F is apparent because of Jung's response in 165 J at n. 4. / Ferenczi cited the statistics from the Drenkhahn article (loc. cit. XXXVIII:10) a year later in his paper on homosexuality (see 281 J n. 2), thus provoking a polemic with Bleuler (ibid. nn. 1, 3, and 284 F).

194 F n. 3

A collection of unpublished letters and postcards written by Freud, in the New York State Psychiatric Institute Library, New York City, includes eight items to Jekels. In a letter of 3 July 10, Freud informs Jekels that he and his wife must regretfully cancel their plans to visit him in Bistrai (the last two weeks of July) because their two younger sons will be with them and Jekels' villa will be too small for the party of four. A letter of 3 Aug. 10, from Noordwijk, indicates that Minna Bernays and two younger Freud daughters had stayed in Bistrai during part of July, and Miss Bernays had then gone to Hamburg to be with her mother, who was gravely ill.

The Institute Library also possesses, in its Sigmund Freud Memorial Room, a collection of about 800 books and other items formerly in Freud's library. The collection was advertised in July 1939 by the Viennese book-dealer Heinrich Hinterberger without mentioning Freud—"books on neurology and psychiatry . . . brought together by a famous Viennese scientific explorer"—and was purchased on the percipient advice of Dr. Jacob Shatzky, the librarian. The catalogue of the collection is printed in Nolan D. C. Lewis and Carney Landis, "Freud's Library," *Psychoanalytic Review*, XLIV:3 (July 1957).

218 F n. 5

It was not the Aztec emperor Montezuma but his nephew and successor Guatemozin who was the subject of this anecdote, and his words were: "And do you think I, then, am taking my pleasure in my bath?"—W. H. Prescott, *The Conquest of Mexico* (1843), Book VII, ch. I. Prescott adds, "The literal version is not so poetical as 'the bed of flowers,' into which this exclamation of Guatemozin is usually rendered."

243 J n. 6

The myth of man's creation from the union of a sword-hilt and a shuttle is not American Indian but from the Kayan of Borneo; it is reported in A. W. Nieuwenhuis, *Quer durch Borneo* (Leiden, 1904), vols. I, p. 129, and II, p. 113. (The information was kindly supplied by Claude Lévi-Strauss and Nicole Belmont, Laboratoire d'Anthropologie Sociale, Paris.)

Comment (par. 3) following 270 F

At Weimar, according to Rank's abstract, Jung spoke of a recent fantasy of a 34-year-old female neurotic "which can be documented and elucidated by historical material." In the fantasy, a man she loves unrequitedly is hung up by the genitals; the same fantasy was found in a 9-year-old boy as a symbolic expression of his unfulfilled libido. Jung cited ethnological and mythological parallels, i.e., the sacrifice of the god of spring by hanging or flaying and, in ancient cults, the sacrifice of the phallus to the Great Mother. The patient's fantasy is not mentioned in "Wandlungen und Symbole," but there are allusions to the parallels. See CW 5, index, s.v. "Attis" and "castration."

589

INDEX

INDEX

Comprising personal names (historical and fictitious), publications, and meetings mentioned in the text and notes. References are by letter number and note number. 252J = reference in text; (252J) = allusion in text; 252J n.1 = reference in note only; 252J+n.1 = reference in text plus information in note. Abbreviations: comm. foll. = editorial comment following the indicated letter. EJ = letter from Emma Jung.

A

A——, Dr. (patient): 53F (also his sister) 54J 55F 58F 65J

Abel, Karl, "Über den Gegensinn der Urworte" (1910?): 217J n.6; *see also* Freud, " 'Antithetical Meaning of Primal Words, The' "; Stekel, review

Abraham, Hedwig Marie: 41J+n.1

Abraham, Hilda C., and Freud, Ernst L., eds., *A Psycho-Analytic Dialogue: The Letters of Sigmund Freud and Karl Abraham* (1965): 35J n.7 37J n.1 48J nn.5,8 84F n.2 87F n.3 91J n.4 comm. foll. 108J 111J n.3 114F n.3 122F n.3 141F n.1 210J n.3 217J n.3 comm. foll. 229J 291J n.3 319F n.1 323J n.5 329F n.1

Abraham, Karl: 53J+n.7 36F 37J+n.1 39J 40F+n.4 41J 44J n.7 48J+nn.5,8 55F 57F 59J 61F 65J 77F 79J 84F+n.2 87F+n.3 91J+n.4 92F 96F 98J 99F 101F 111J+n.3 114F+n.3 115J 117J 122F+n.3 123F 124J 125F 126J 127F 138J+n.7 140J 142J 143F 145F n.4 156F 158F+n.4 160F n.7 168J 180J 186J+n.2 204J 205F 209F 217J n.3 comm. foll. 229J 238F 269J comm. foll. 270F 306F n.2 319F n.1 comm. foll. 321J 323J n.5 comm. foll. 327J 329F n.1 comm. foll. 356J comm. foll. 357J

   Clinical Papers (1955): 36F n.3 84F n.2

   "Dreams and Myths" = *Traum und Mythus* (1909): 27F n.8 84F+n.2

   Dreams and Myths, tr. W. A. White (1913): 84F n.2

   Freud's Writings from 1893 to 1909" = *Freuds Schriften aus den Jahren 1893–1909*" (1909): 91J+n.1 101F (102J) 111J+n.2 (115J) (121J) 122F n.3 123F 142J

   "Hysterical Dream-states" = "Über hysterische Traumzustände" (1910): 209F+n.3

   "On the Significance of Juvenile Sexual Traumas for the Symptomatology of Dementia Praecox" = "Über die Bedeutung sexueller Jugendtraumen für die Symptomatologie der Dementia praecox" (1907): 36F+n.3

   "Place of Marriage Between Relatives in the Psychology of Neuroses, The"

B

Eder, Edith: 303J; tr., see Jung, "Theory of Psychoanalysis, The"
Eder, Montague David: 303J
    "Case of Obsession and Hysteria Treated by the Freud Psycho-analytic
        Method, A" (1911): 272F+n.6
    tr., see Jung, Studies in Word Association; "Theory of Psychoanalysis, The"
Ehrenreich, Paul, Die allgemeine Mythologie und ihre ethnologischen Grund-
    lagen (1910): 274F+n.3
Eisenstein, S., see Alexander, Franz; Eisenstein, S.; and Grotjahn, M.
Eissler, K. R., Goethe; A Psychoanalytic Study 1775–1786 (1963): 231F n.10;
    Talent and Genius (1971): 139F n.1
Eitingon, Max: 45F+nn.1,7 46J 48J 154F 158F 160F 162J 179F comm.
    foll. 321J
    Report on the Annual Meeting of the German Psychiatric Association,
        Breslau, May 1913 (1913): 350J+n.2
Ellenberger, H. F., The Discovery of the Unconscious (1970): 43J n.1 44J n.2
    123F n.5 126J n.2 295J n.2
Ellis, Havelock: 122F+n.4 187F 254J n.2
    "Autoerotism: A Study of the Spontaneous Manifestations of the Sexual
        Impulse," see Studies in the Psychology of Sex, Vol. I
    Studies in the Psychology of Sex, Vol. I (The Evolution of Modesty;
        The Phenomena of Sexual Periodicity; Auto-Erotism; 1899, ²1910):
        122F+n.4 212F+n.11; Vol. VI (Sex in Relation to Society; 1910):
        187F
    World of Dreams, The (1911): 261J+n.1 262F
Ellmann, Richard, James Joyce (1959): 151J n.2
Elvin's Handbook of Mottoes (1860): 11F n.8
Encyclopedia Britannica (1911): 230J n.9
Enkidu, see Eabani
Erasmus: 142J n.1
Erismann, Friedrich: 85J+n.3
Erismann, Sophie: 85J+n.3 193J 312J n.4
Erismann, Theodor: 85J n.3 312J+n.4
Ernst, Paul: 215J+n.9
Eros: 11F 148J
"Eros and Psyche" (early title of Imago, q.v.): 263F
Esdras, see Old Testament
Eulenburg, Count Philipp: 74F n.4
Evangelische Freiheit (Tübingen): 160F+n.6 170J n.4
Eve: 288F

    F

F——, Dr. (patient): 158F 159J
Fairclough, H. R. (tr. of Horace): 310J n.1
Faust: 40F n.4 138J n.5; see also under Goethe
Federn, Ernst, see Nunberg, Hermann, and Federn, Ernst
Federn, Paul: 53F+n.1 128J 130F 231F n.7 270F n.4
    Review (1913) of Spielrein, "Die Destruktion als Ursache des Werdens":
        346F n.2
Ferenczi, Sándor: 33J+n.2 (54J) 67F (77F) (79J) 101F+n.1 106F 107J

FREUD, SIGMUND (6 May 1856, Freiberg, Moravia – 23 September 1939,
London)

Jahrbuch für sexuelle Zwischenstufen (Leipzig): 74F+n.2 255F

James, William: 31J n.3 comm. foll. 154F 166F n.4 174F n. 2

Janet, Pierre: 20F+n.1 31J 33J 43J 44J 123F+n.5 124J 192F n.2 217J
236F n.7

  Obsessions et la psychasthénie, Les (1903): 31J n.4

Jankelévitch, S.: 253F+n.7

Jekels, Ludwig: 79J+n.2 158F 162J 180J 194F+n.3 (addenda)

Jelliffe, Smith Ely: comm. foll. 321J(+n.1)

Jensen, Wilhelm: 26J+n.1 27F+nn.5–6 28J 50J 52F 53F 57F 59J

  From Quiet Times = Aus stiller Zeit (Vol. II): 57F+n.2

  "Gradiva": 24J n.4 (27F) 50J 53F; *see also* Freud, "Delusions and
  Dreams in W. Jensen's 'Gradiva' "

  "In the Gothic House" (in *Superior Powers*) = "Im gothischen Hause"
  (in *Übermächte*): 50J+n.3 (52F) 53F 57F

  "Red Umbrella, The" (in *Superior Powers*) = "Der rote Schirm" (in
  Übermächte): 50J+n.3 (52F) 53F 57F

  Superior Powers = Übermächte (1892): 24J n.4 50J+n.3 (52F) 53F
  (57F) 296F

  "Youthful Dreams" (in *From Quiet Times*, Vol. II) = "Jugendträume"
  (in *Aus stiller Zeit*, Vol. II): 57F

Jeremias, Alfred: *Das Alte Testament im Lichte des alten Orients* (1906):
162J+n.4

Job, *see* Old Testament

Jocasta (in *Oedipus Rex*): 160F n.7

John of the Locusts: 178J

Jones, Ernest: 44J+n.6 (45F) 51J 54J+n.2 55F 63J 65J 72J 77F 79J
85J n.4 87F+n.5 91J 101F 102J 103F 124J 125F 126J 132F+n.2
133J 134F 135J 138J n.4 143F 154F comm. foll. 154F 159J n.5 160F
171F 173J 174F 175J 185F 186J 187F 190F 192F 205F 206J
208F+n.2 213J+n.8 223F+n.4 237J 238F 239J 243J+n.1 248F+n.2
249J 252J 255F+n.6 257J+n.1 258F 267J comm. foll. 270F 271J+n.4
316F 319F comm. foll. 321J EJ 10 Sep. 12 +n.1 comm. foll. 327J 328J n.1
342F n.1 347J comm. foll. 356J

JUNG, C. G. (*cont.*)

    11F nn.1,5–6 18F n.3 24J n.1 27F n.16 29J n.1 41J n.1 48J n.3
    49J 66F+n.1 69J+n.2 75J 77F 80F 86J n.1 101F n.3 110F n.2
    113J n.3 124J 286J n.1 196J n.6; tr. A. A. Brill and F. W. Peterson
    (1909): 69J+n.2 113J n.3 124J+n.3; rev. tr. A. A. Brill (1936): 124J n.3
    "Psychology of the Negro, The" (CW 18) = "Zur Psychologie des Negers"
    (abstract only, 1913): 223F n.6 323J n.3
    "Psychology of Rumour," *see* "Contribution to the . . ."
    *Psychology of the Unconscious: A Study of the Transformations and
    Symbolisms of the Libido; A Contribution to the History of the
    Evolution of Thought*, tr. B. M. Hinkle (1916) = *Wandlungen und
    Symbole der Libido* (1912): 252J n.2 269J n.7 324F n.2; *see also*
    "Transformations and Symbols of the Libido"
    "Reaction-time Ratio in the Association Experiment, The" (CW 2) =
    "Über das Verhalten der Reaktionszeit beim Assoziationsexperiment"
    (1905): 8F n.1
    "Report on America" (abstract in CW 18) = "Bericht über Amerika"
    (Nuremberg paper, 1910): 174F 175J 177F 180J 181J 182F EJ 16
    Mar. 10 comm. foll. EJ 16 Mar. 10 223F n.6
    Report (1907) on applied psychology in German Switzerland (CW 18):
    46J n.1
    Report on Psychoanalysis (for *Rivista di psicologia applicata*, 1908): 59J+n.4
    Review (not published) of Adler, Alfred, *Über den nervösen Charakter*:
    321J 333J+n.1 334F
    Review (1904) of Hellpach, Willy, *Grundlinien einer Psychologie der Hysterie*
    (CW 18): 230J n.7
    Review (1911) of Hitschmann, Eduard, *Freuds Neurosenlehre* (CW 18):
    194F n.3
    Review of Prince, Morton, "The Mechanism and Interpretation of Dreams,"
    see "Morton Prince, M.D., 'The Mechanism . . .' "
    Review (not published) of Rank, *Das Inzest-Motiv in Dichtung und Sage*:
    321J+n.1
    Review (1908) of Stekel, *Nervöse Angstzustände und ihre Behandlung*:
    105J+n.3 106F 107J
    Review (1909) of Waldstein, tr. G. Veraguth, *Das unbewusste Ich und
    sein Verhältnis zu Gesundheit und Erziehung* (CW 18): 115J n.7
    Review of Wittels, *Die sexuelle Not*, *see* "Marginal Notes on . . ."
    "Schizophrenia" (CW 3) = "Die Schizophrenie" (1958): 213J n.4
    Seminar on Analytical Psychology (1926): 330J n.3
    Seminars: 165J 235J 236F 265J 267J
    "Significance of the Father in the Destiny of the Individual, The" (CW 4)
    = "Die Bedeutung des Vaters für das Schicksal des Einzelnen" (1909):
    115J 116F 117J 118F 121J 133J+n.1 138J n.8 163F+n.6 166F
    250F 252J n.3
    "Significance of Freud's Teachings for Neurology and Psychiatry, The"
    (CW 18) = "Über die Bedeutung der Lehre Freud's für Neurologie
    und Psychiatrie" (1908): (51J) 54J+n.1
    Studies in Word Association, tr. M. D. Eder (1918): 1F n.2 34F n.4
    61F n.1 273F n.5; *see also* "Diagnostic Association Studies"

O

641

Index by Wolfgang Sauerlander

Library of Congress Cataloging in Publication Data

Freud, Sigmund, 1856–1939.
  The Freud/Jung letters.

  (Bollingen series, 94)
  "Translated from the unpublished letters in German."
  Bibliography: p. ix.
  1. Freud, Sigmund, 1856–1939. 2. Jung, Carl Gustav, 1875–
1961. 3. Psychoanalysts—Correspondence, reminiscences, etc.
I. Jung, Carl Gustav, 1875–1961. II. McGuire, William, 1917–   ed.
III. Title. IV. Series.
RC506.F69713   616.8′9′00922 [B]   76-166373
ISBN 0-691-09890-5